AUGUSTINE
IN THE PELAGIAN
CONTROVERSY

PATRISTIC THEOLOGY

SERIES EDITORS

John C. Cavadini
University of Notre Dame

Thomas Clemmons
The Catholic University of America

EDITORIAL BOARD

Paul M. Blowers
Milligan University

Ellen Scully
Seton Hall University

Brian Dunkle, SJ
Boston College

J. Warren Smith
Duke University

Andrew Hofer, OP
Dominican House of Studies

Susan Wessel
The Catholic University of America

Joseph T. Lienhard, SJ
Fordham University

Jeffrey Wickes
University of Notre Dame

AUGUSTINE IN THE PELAGIAN CONTROVERSY
DEFENDING CHURCH UNITY

ANDREW C. CHRONISTER

The Catholic University of America Press
Washington, D.C.

Copyright © 2024
The Catholic University of America Press
Certain passages of the book previously appeared in
"Augustine and Patristic Argumentation in His Anti-Pelagian Works:
Change or Continuity?" *Augustiniana* 64 (2014):
187–226, and are used with permission.

All rights reserved
The paper used in this publication meets the minimum requirements
of American National Standards for Information Science—
Permanence of Paper for Printed Library Materials, ANSI Z39.48-1992.

Cataloging-in-Publication Data is available from the Library of Congress

ISBN (paperback): 978-0-8132-3872-2
ISBN (eBook): 978-0-8132-3873-9
ISBN (hardcover): 978-0-8132-3926-2

Interior design by Burt&Burt
The text is set in Minion Pro and Filosofia

For Michele

Contents

Acknowledgments // ix

Abbreviations // xi

Introduction // 1

1 Setting the Stage // 29

2 A Controversy in Carthage // 75

3 The Road to Diospolis // 131

4 From Diospolis to the *Tractoria* // 177

5 A New Opponent: Augustine's Controversy with Julian // 261

Conclusion: Grace and the Church // 299

Appendix: The Chronology of 411 // 303

Bibliography // 325

Index // 363

Acknowledgments

This book is the fruit of a lengthy process of composition: it began as a dissertation at Saint Louis University (defended in December 2015) but then underwent substantial revisions and reorganization in subsequent years until it reached its present form. I am so grateful to all who have supported me in various ways as I worked on this book.

First and foremost, I thank my wife for her unwavering love, support, and no small amount of sacrifice throughout the years as I worked on this project. Thank you, Michele, for everything. As a small token of my gratitude, I dedicate this book to you.

I also thank my daughters for the countless ways they have enriched and brought joy to my life. Therese, Maria, and Zelie, it is an honor to be your father.

I am also grateful to my parents, Joseph Chronister and Laura Weyrauch, for raising me to love Christ and his Church and for fostering in me the intellectual curiosity that eventually led me to this project. Thanks, Mom and Dad.

As I think back over my education, a number of teachers come to mind as significant figures in my formation as a theologian: John Cavadini, Fr. Brian Daley, Harold Ernst, David Fagerberg, Fred Freddoso, Msgr. Michael Heintz, Grant Kaplan, Peter Martens, David Meconi, Fr. Ken Steinhauser, and Joseph Wawrykow. Thank you for all you have taught me.

I would also like to thank the many friends, colleagues, and fellow scholars who have contributed in various ways to this project, whether by providing advice, reading portions of the book, answering questions, or simply offering encouragement along the way: Fr. Don Anstoetter, Fr. Fadi Auro, Packy Brewick, Anthony Dupont, Steve Fahrig, Francis Feingold, Larry and Marsha Feingold, John Finley, John Gresham, Blake Hartung, Fr. Paul Hoesing, Ed Hogan, David Hunter, Jim Keating, Chad Kim, Zach Kostopoulos, Keaton Lambert, Fr. Jim Mason, Adam Messer, Matt Muller, Fr. Ross Romero, Fr. Charles Samson, Fr. Mirco Sosio, and Jeff Wisniewski. A special thank-you is due to Fr. Walter Dunphy and to Giulio Malavasi, who both read the entirety of the manuscript and offered numerous suggestions for improvement. I offer a further special thank-you to the staff of the Kenrick-Glennon Seminary Souvay Memorial Library for all their help: David Morris, Mary Ann Aubin, Franny Behrman, Mary Grosch, and Rose Lawson. My thanks also to all my students at Kenrick throughout the years, who have made my work as a teacher and scholar a true joy.

Final thanks are due to those who have seen this book through the publication process: Tommy Clemmons, John Martino, the anonymous reviewers, and all the rest of the editors at The Catholic University of America Press. You all have helped to make this book much better than it would have been otherwise.

An earlier version of certain passages of this book dealing with Augustine's use of patristic argumentation in the Pelagian controversy appeared in my article, "Augustine and Patristic Argumentation in His Anti-Pelagian Works: Change or Continuity?" *Augustiniana* 64 (2014): 187–226. My thanks to *Augustiniana* for granting permission to reprint these passages.

Abbreviations

Abbreviations of Augustine's writings[1]

b. uid.	*De bono uiduitatis*
bapt.	*De baptismo*
c. ep. Parm.	*Contra epistulam Parmeniani*
c. ep. Pel.	*Contra duas epistulas Pelagianorum*
c. Faust.	*Contra Faustum Manicheum*
c. Iul.	*Contra Iulianum*
c. Iul. imp.	*Contra Iulianum opus imperfectum*
cath. fr.	*Ad catholicos fratres*
ciu.	*De ciuitate dei*
conf.	*Confessiones*
Cresc.	*Ad Cresconium grammaticum partis Donati*
doctr. chr.	*De doctrina christiana*
ep.	*Epistula(e)*
gest. Pel.	*De gestis Pelagii*
gr. et pecc. or.	*De gratia Christi et de peccato originali*
haer.	*De haeresibus*
nat. et gr.	*De natura et gratia*

---

1 The following abbreviations are those employed in the *Augustinus-Lexikon* (Basel: Schwabe, 1986–).

nupt. et conc.	*De nuptiis et concupiscentia*
pecc. mer.	*De peccatorum meritis et remissione et de baptismo paruulorum*
perf. iust.	*De perfectione iustitiae hominis*
perseu.	*De dono perseuerantiae*
retr.	*Retractationes*
s.	*Sermo(nes)*
spir. et litt.	*De spiritu et littera*

Other Abbreviations

ACO	Acta Conciliorum Oecumenicorum (Strasbourg/Berlin, 1914–1984)
A-L	Augustinus-Lexikon (Basel, 1986–)
BA	Oeuvres de Saint Augustin, Bibliothèque augustinienne (Paris, 1936–)
CCL	Corpus Christianorum Series Latina (Turnhout, 1953–)
CPL	Clavis Patrum Latinorum, ed. E. Dekkers (Turnhout, 1995)
CSEL	Corpus Scriptorum Ecclesiasticorum Latinorum (Vienna, 1866–)
FC	The Fathers of the Church (New York/Washington, 1949–)
LCL	Loeb Classical Library (New York/Cambridge, MA, 1912–)
NPNF1	Nicene and Post-Nicene Fathers, First Series (Buffalo: Christian Literature, 1886–1900)
NPNF2	Nicene and Post-Nicene Fathers, Second Series (Buffalo: Christian Literature, 1886–1900)
PL	Patrologiae Cursus Completus, Series Latina (Paris, 1844–65)
PLS	Patrologiae Cursus Completus, Series Latina Supplementa (Paris, 1958–)
SC	Sources Chrétiennes (Paris: Cerf, 1942–)
WSA	The Works of Saint Augustine (Hyde Park, NY: New City Press, 1990–)

AUGUSTINE
IN THE PELAGIAN CONTROVERSY

Introduction

A CONTROVERSY BEGINS

On August 24, 410, Rome was sacked. For three days, Alaric and his army of Visigoths abducted and slew, pillaged and destroyed. That the gates of the Eternal City would yield to enemy forces had seemed impossible—but yielded they had. And so, across the empire, people desperately searched for answers. Some blamed the Christians, suggesting that Rome's abandonment of its traditional devotions to the gods had caused its downfall. In reply, others pointed to the fact that during the sack, Rome's churches had provided sanctuary for her citizens, Christians and non-Christians alike. Christianity, it was argued, had preserved Rome from further destruction.[1] But whoever was to blame, Jerome's words surely conveyed the thoughts of many at that time: "If Rome perishes, what is safe?"[2] In the lead-up to the sack and its aftermath,

---

1 See, e.g., Augustine's discussions in *ciu.* 1.1–8, as well as Peter Brown's comments in *Augustine of Hippo: A Biography*, 2nd ed. (Berkeley: University of California Press, 2000), 297–311.

2 Jerome, *ep.* 123.16 (Latin: CSEL 56:94.5–6; English: my translation). Cited in Brown, *Augustine of Hippo*, 288, and F. G. Maier, *Augustin und das antike Rom* (Stuttgart: W. Kohlhammer, 1955), 43.

many residents of Rome fled the city, some crossing the Mediterranean to Africa.

The following year, Flavius Marcellinus wrote to Augustine, the bishop of Hippo Regius, with an important request. Marcellinus, an imperial tribune recently sent to Carthage to facilitate the reunion of the Catholic and Donatist Churches in Africa, asked Augustine for his response to several questions regarding the teaching of a certain Caelestius. Caelestius, who likely arrived in Africa as a refugee from Rome, had requested ordination in Carthage, but was accused of promoting some questionable teachings on the effects of the sin of Adam and the possibility of human sinlessness, among other topics. Caelestius was associated with an ascetic figure popular in Roman circles named Pelagius, who had also recently arrived in North Africa with the surge of refugees. A single sentence from the opening lines of his reply is enough to indicate Augustine's alarm at Marcellinus's inquiry: "This matter has presently driven all the others from my mind, until I produce something that proves I have been of service, if not sufficiently, at least obediently, to your good desire and that of those who are worried about these matters."[3] Thus began Augustine's overt involvement in the Pelagian controversy, a dispute that would occupy his mind until his death in 430.[4]

To be sure, in the final two decades of his life, the Pelagians were far from being Augustine's sole focus. During this time, he was also, for example, writing against the Donatists, composing *De ciuitate Dei*, *De haeresibus*, his *Enchiridion*, and the *Retractationes*, completing *De Genesi ad litteram*, *De Trinitate*, and *De doctrina christiana*, as well as delivering countless homilies and exchanging numerous letters with acquaintances and friends—not to mention attending to the more mundane demands of his pastoral office. Yet, it is significant that in the midst of all this activity, Augustine allotted so much time to his anti-Pelagian efforts, efforts that included around ten major treatises as well as numerous letters and sermons. As Peter Brown put it, "By

---

3 *pecc. mer.* 1.1.1 (Latin: CSEL 60:3.12–15; English: Teske, WSA I/23, 34).

4 In the past century, scholars have increasingly warned against viewing "Pelagianism" as a monolithic theological system. In this sense, the terms "Pelagian" and "Pelagianism" should be used with some caution, lest it give the impression of more uniformity than actually existed among Pelagius, Caelestius, Julian of Eclanum, and so on. See discussion below.

INTRODUCTION

the time the *causa gratiae* had been won, the Roman world was littered with works of Augustine."[5]

What led Augustine to expend so much time and energy during the final two decades of his life writing treatise after treatise against the Pelagians? An initial hypothesis readily presents itself: Augustine saw in Pelagian doctrine a threat so serious to the orthodox faith that he could not but respond to it—and continue to respond to it until it had been totally defeated. Thus, it might be argued, the Pelagian controversy was sparked and sustained by a violent clash of doctrinal positions. This hypothesis is often supported by scholarly overviews of the controversy, which tend to focus on the diverging theological outlooks of Augustine and Pelagius.[6] Now, my aim is not to diminish the gravity of these doctrinal disagreements or to imply that they did not play a central role in the controversy. Nor do I wish to suggest that scholars have portrayed the controversy *solely* as a "battle of ideas" abstracted from the historical and social realities of the Roman Empire at the beginning of the fifth century.[7] Indeed, previous scholarship has suggested a

---

5 Brown, *Augustine of Hippo*, 356. Serge Lancel similarly comments, "In the remaining twenty years of the bishop's life [Augustine] would spend the best part of his energy and intellectual resources in the debate against Pelagius and his disciples" (Serge Lancel, *Saint Augustine* [London: SCM Press, 2002], 325).

6 See, for example, Eugene TeSelle's comments: "The Pelagian controversy had its origin in two doctrinal questions. One concerned the effect of the sin of Adam and Eve upon their descendants. Did it cause moral weakness, mortality, or perhaps even guilt? Or were they created in the same condition as later humanity? The other concerned the ability of sinners to return to God. Was this within the power of their free will? Or were they able to do it only with divine assistance, and perhaps even because the process was initiated by divine grace?" (TeSelle, "The Background: Augustine and the Pelagian Controversy," in *Grace for Grace: The Debates after Augustine and Pelagius*, ed. Alexander Y. Hwang, Brian J. Matz, and Augustine Casiday [Washington, DC: The Catholic University of America Press, 2014], 1). See also Peter Brown's remark: "What is commonly known to us as the Pelagian Controversy has often been treated as a theological event involving a fundamental clash of ideas between Augustine of Hippo and the followers of Pelagius" (Peter Brown, *Through the Eye of a Needle: Wealth, the Fall of Rome, and the Making of Christianity in the West, 350–550 AD* [Princeton: Princeton University Press, 2012], 291).

7 See, for example, Otto Wermelinger, *Rom und Pelagius: die theologische Position der römischen Bischofe im pelagianischen Streit in den Jahren 411–431* (Stuttgart: A. Hiersemann, 1975), which highlights specific contextual aspects of the controversy that made it as explosive as it was—for instance, the extent to which the final phase of the Donatist controversy may have prompted the initial actions against Caelestius (see p. 8). Stuart Squires's recent introduction to the controversy also does much to highlight the historical context of the controversy, while still focusing on the theological battle(s) between the different participants in the debate (*The Pelagian Controversy: An Introduction to the Enemies of Grace and the Conspiracy of Lost*

variety of contextual factors that contributed to the eruption and growth of the controversy: for example, the similarity of theological themes between Pelagianism and Donatism;[8] the recent arrival of wealthy Roman Christians in Africa;[9] Augustine's rivalry for Pelagius's patrons;[10] Augustine's desire to boost his impact overseas;[11] Augustine's need to defend his reputation in the wake of attacks by Julian of Eclanum.[12] However, it does seem fair to say that, in the final analysis, many who have approached and analyzed the Pelagian controversy have done so with an ultimate interest in or view to the theological battle that raged between so many different agents across the Empire. As an understandable result, there has been a tendency (1) to gloss over the contextual factors that made the controversy as explosive as it was and (2) to misunderstand and mischaracterize the tenor of Augustine's polemic against the Pelagians, especially as it appears in his final works against Julian.[13] Here lies the danger: taken to its extreme, an overview of the Pelagian controversy that ignores or underappreciates the historical and ecclesial contexts in which the controversy unfolded risks portraying the controversy as inevitable, provided that Augustine or his allies and the Pelagians happened to cross paths.

The present study serves, in part, to resist such a portrayal of the controversy by emphasizing the importance of a contextual factor that has often

---

Souls [Eugene, OR: Pickwick Publications, 2019]). Further, Giulio Malavasi, *La controversia pelagiana in Oriente* (Münster: Aschendorff, 2022), offers an excellent contextualized examination of the eastern "theater" of the Pelagian controversy.

8 See, e.g., Walter Dunphy, "A Lost Year: Pelagianism in Carthage, 411 A.D.," *Augustinianum* 45 (2005): 464; Gerald Bonner, "Rufinus of Syria and African Pelagianism," *Augustinian Studies* 1 (1970): 33–34.

9 See Brown, *Eye of a Needle*, 360.

10 See J. J. O'Donnell, *Augustine: A New Biography* (New York: Harper, 2005), 254.

11 See Brent Shaw, *Sacred Violence: African Christians and Sectarian Hatred in the Age of Augustine* (Cambridge: Cambridge University Press, 2011), 313.

12 See, e.g., Brown, *Eye of a Needle*, 382, although this assessment is found elsewhere as well.

13 Augustine's late works against Julian are regularly criticized for their harshness and lack of good manners. For example, John Burnaby writes, "Nearly all that Augustine wrote after his seventieth year is the work of a man whose energy has burnt itself out, whose love has grown cold" (John Burnaby, Amor Dei: *A Study of the Religion of St. Augustine* [London: Hodder & Stoughton, 1938], 231; cited in Brown, *Augustine of Hippo*, 466). Brown himself writes, "[Augustine's] works against Julian have the cold competence of an old, tired man, who knew only too well how to set about the harsh business of ecclesiastical controversy" (Brown, *Augustine of Hippo*, 387). (Although note that Brown emends certain aspects of his portrayal of the old Augustine in the appendices of his 2000 edition: *Augustine of Hippo*, 466.)

INTRODUCTION 5

gone unnoticed or underestimated but that, I argue, was of grave importance for Augustine's entrance into the controversy as well as for his sustained determination to battle Pelagianism for the remainder of his life. This factor was Augustine's sense that the Pelagians represented a major threat to the unity of the Church in his day. For Augustine, the Pelagians embodied a threat to unity for a variety of reasons. One of the most prominent among these was the Pelagians' tendency to claim, with varying degrees of evidence, that their theological opponents were in stark disagreement with the Church's ancient and universal doctrinal tradition.[14] At first glance, this may seem to be a rather banal claim—after all, general accusations of "novelty" or divergence from established Church teaching are commonplace in debates over orthodoxy and heresy. However, what made this claim so serious in this controversy was (1) the bold way in which the Pelagians advanced it and (2) the specific contexts and ways in which it was deployed.

The Pelagian claim that their opponents had diverged from the Church's ancient and universal doctrinal tradition seems to have been first formulated in Rome, where Pelagius and his supporters had been held in suspicion even before the controversy erupted in Carthage in 411. Yves-Marie Duval argues it was at this time, between 406 and 410, that Pelagius composed his *De natura* as a defense of his positions.[15] Pelagius devoted a key section within this work to supporting his views by quoting several renowned Christian authors: Lactantius, Hilary of Poitiers, Ambrose of Milan, John Chrysostom,

---

14 Earlier scholars have, on occasion, noted this or related factors, but in my estimation either have not fully recognized its importance or have only been able to analyze it in a limited way. See, e.g., Brown, *Augustine of Hippo*, 357; Dunphy, "A Lost Year," 465; Robert F. Evans, *Pelagius: Inquiries and Reappraisals* (New York: The Seabury Press, 1968), 85; Wermelinger, *Rom und Pelagius*, 8. See also Gerald Bonner's related comments in "Some Remarks on Letters 4* and 6*," in *Les Lettres de saint Augustin découvertes par Johannes Divjak: communications présentées au colloque des 20 et 21 septembre 1982*, ed. C. Lepelly (Paris: Études augustiniennes, 1983), 158, where he emphasizes the threat that Pelagius's acquittal at Diospolis held for Augustine's understanding of the consistent teaching of the universal Church.

15 Yves-Marie Duval, "La date du 'De natura' de Pélage: les premières étapes de la controverse sur la nature de la grâce," *Revue des études augustiniennes* 36 (1990): 274. Duval's re-dating of Pelagius's *De natura* (which previously was thought to have been written sometime closer to 414) is important as it shows that opposition to Pelagius's views was not simply an African phenomenon. Many scholars have accepted Duval's re-dating; however, for an opposing view, see Johann Tauer, "Neue Orientierungen zur Paulusexegese des Pelagius," *Augustinianum* 34 (1994): esp. 357–58. Michele Cutino also suggests a later dating in, "Il ruolo della Chiesa siciliana nella polemica fra Agostino e i pelagiani," in *Vescovi, Sicilia, Mediterraneo nella tarda Antichità: Atti del I Convegno di Studi (Palermo, 29–30 ottobre 2010)*, ed. Vincenzo Messana, Vincenzo Lombino, and Salvatore Costanza (Rome: Salvatore Sciascia Editore, 2012), 165–92.

Sixtus (thought to be the martyred bishop of Rome), Jerome, and Augustine himself.[16] What is startling about this section of *De natura* is the fact that explicit citation of Christian authors as a means to support one's doctrinal views was a very unusual argumentative tactic at this point in the Church's history.[17] In this sense, Pelagius's explicit "appeal to Tradition"[18] was a calculated and bold move—one that surely would have caught his opponents' attention. It is one thing for an author to claim to be orthodox; it is another for that author to link himself explicitly to revered figures from the past and present. Pelagius had done the latter; now it was up to his opponents to prove him (and, it would seem, Lactantius, Hilary, Ambrose, John, Sixtus, Jerome, and Augustine himself) wrong.

Augustine would not read *De natura* until 414 or early 415. However, it seems that upon their arrival in North Africa around 410, some of those associated with Pelagius began to voice arguments similar to those found in *De natura*.[19] Augustine, writing half a decade later, recalled that as trouble started to brew in 411, a threat was being circulated: "Certain people who held to such [Pelagian] views were trying so hard to persuade some of our brothers of these views that they were threatening that, if they did not support them, they would be condemned by the judgment of the eastern churches."[20]

---

16 See Augustine, *nat. et gr.* 61.71–67.81.

17 Mark Vessey, "The Forging of Orthodoxy in Latin Christian Literature: A Case Study," *Journal of Early Christian Studies* 4 (1996): 499; Éric Rebillard, "A New Style of Argument in Christian Polemic: Augustine and the Use of Patristic Citations," *Journal of Early Christian Studies* 8 (2000): 560. Of course, such citations had occurred earlier in Church history (see, e.g., Basil of Caesarea, *De spiritu sancto* 29), but only rarely. For more discussion, see below.

18 It should be noted that theoretical discussions of the concept of "tradition" do not play a significant role in the controversy. Rather, such theoretical considerations often remain in the background behind the concrete appeals to Christian writers, liturgical practices, et cetera, that both sides of the controversy deploy as one way (among others) to prove the orthodoxy of their own positions.

19 Whether individual Christian authors were being cited is unknown, although Walter Dunphy suggests it is likely that Jerome's opinion was being explicitly invoked (Dunphy, "A Lost Year," 443).

20 *gest. Pel.* 11.25: *haec sunt, quae nonnullis fratribus quidam talia sentientes ita persuadere conabantur, ut de orientalibus comminarentur ecclesiis quod, nisi qui haec tenerent, earum possent iudicio condemnari* (Latin: CSEL 42:79.6–9; English: my translation). A sermon delivered by Augustine in 411 confirms this threat in a more general way: "It's not enough, you see, for these people to hold forth and argue in favor of goodness knows what ungodly novelties; they also try to convict us of saying something new [*aliquid nouum*]" (*s.* 294.19; Latin: PL 38:1347.37–40; English: Hill, WSA III/8, 193).

INTRODUCTION

This threat—while not trivial under any circumstances—would have been particularly explosive in the context of Carthage in 411, for a few reasons. First, the Roman Christian aristocrats and their entourage, who had recently arrived from Italy and among whom Pelagius seems to have had a number of patrons, were known for their familiarity with the East, evidenced, for example, by their affinity for the translations produced by Rufinus, their support for John Chrysostom, and, in some cases, their (or their family members') ascetic connections there.[21] Thus, when they claimed that they knew what passed for orthodox theology in the East, they would have been believed—or, at the very least, their claims would have been recognized as more than just idle speculation. Second, Carthage in early 411 was preparing for a gathering of Catholics and Donatists that had been nearly a century in the making and that Catholics hoped would lead to an end to the schism. New accusations of disunity among the Catholics themselves would not have been welcome. As Walter Dunphy writes,

> "Church Unity" was the slogan in Carthage in early 411. It was not the time for mutual incrimination and charges of heresy within the Catholic fold. Quite apart from the "bad press" it might give to the very concept of Church unity, the Catholics were arguing among themselves about subjects that were not without considerable interest to the Donatists. In particular I mention the question of the holiness of the Church, and above all the understanding of Baptism. Some Catholics were going so far as to claim that the African Catholic Church was out of step with Eastern Christianity on this issue.[22]

In this context, it is easy to imagine how quickly Donatist groups would have used this apparent division within the Catholic community to their own advantage, accusing the African Catholic Church of being just as provincial as they themselves were often labeled.[23] As a result, it is no wonder that the opinions and threats of Caelestius and his allies caught the attention of Marcellinus and Augustine, who were avidly laboring to end the Donatist Schism. Any hint of a *new* fracture within the Catholic Church itself had to be resolved—and quickly. It is within this context that Augustine began to write and preach

---

21 For more on this, see Chapter 1.

22 Dunphy, "A Lost Year," 464–65.

23 More will be said on the Donatist background to the Pelagian controversy in Chapter 1. See also Wermelinger, *Rom und Pelagius*, 268n282.

not just against the various doctrinal views of Caelestius and Pelagius, but also against the claim that the theological views he himself espoused were untraditional or different from those taught elsewhere in the Church.

Dunphy's emphasis on the importance of the theme of "Church unity" for Augustine's early anti-Pelagian efforts has laid the groundwork for the present study. While Dunphy dealt only with the initial year of the controversy, it will become clear here that Augustine's concern about the Pelagians' impact on ecclesial unity continued long after 411, a contextual aspect to the controversy that has, thus far, been little examined by scholars.[24] Indeed, it is in view of this context that Augustine's frequent efforts to demonstrate the antiquity and universality of the doctrinal positions he supported against the Pelagians can be better understood. Again, it is in view of this context that Augustine's interpretation of Pelagius's acquittal at Diospolis becomes more coherent, as he could ill afford to lend support to the Pelagian narrative in which the East was at odds with Africa (or parts of the West in general). Further, it is in view of this context that the intensification of Augustine's argumentation against Julian of Eclanum makes sense, as Julian, himself a bishop (a necessary component for any long-lived schism!), sought among other things to raise support for the Pelagian cause in the East and to prompt discussion of the issues at hand in a public setting. Church unity was, indeed, a theme of Augustine's episcopal ministry more generally. This concern for unity, of course, displays itself throughout the Donatist controversy, and even in Augustine's gradual acceptance of the need for coercion in suppressing the Donatist Church.[25] However, the Pelagians presented Augustine with a threat to Church unity that was potentially far greater in scope than that of Donatism, threatening to divide not just Africa, but the entire Christian world.

THESIS AND PLAN OF THE STUDY

In this study, I argue that Augustine's involvement in the Pelagian controversy was not simply a function of his opposition to certain views on grace, human sinlessness, the moral status of infants, or any of the other doctrinal topics touched on in his numerous anti-Pelagian works. Rather, I contend

---

24 For references to some other scholars who have also noted (typically in passing) the importance of this concern for Church unity, see n. 14 above.

25 Augustine's views on wealth and almsgiving can also be read as linked to his concern for unity. For discussion, see Brown, *Eye of a Needle*, 339–58.

that Augustine's battle against the Pelagians was motivated to a significant degree by his fears that the Pelagians' argumentation and actions over the course of the conflict might lead to significant divisions within the Church. Early in the controversy, Augustine was alerted to this threat by the Pelagians' pointed assertions that their opponents were at variance with the ancient and universal doctrinal tradition of the Church. As the controversy spread, this threat grew more acute when the Pelagians' assertions seemed to have been validated by Pelagius's acquittal at Diospolis. Finally, this threat became critical with the rise of the capable and politically savvy Julian as spokesman for a group of recusant Italian bishops who continued to make such assertions and attempted in various ways to rally a coalition of secular and ecclesial leaders to their cause. In order to avert the possibility of schism (or perhaps less "official" but no less real forms of ecclesial disunity), Augustine sought to undermine (in sometimes novel ways) the Pelagians' claim that they had the Church's doctrinal tradition on their side; he maintained—even in the face of apparent evidence to the contrary at Diospolis—that the East and West were united against Pelagianism; and he (and his allies) endeavored to block Julian's campaign every step of the way.

The first step in proving this thesis will be to examine the pre-history of the controversy. Thus, the initial chapter of this study will address two important contextual aspects of the controversy's outbreak in Carthage in 411: (1) the early development of the Pelagian movement and (2) the North African ecclesial landscape in 411. Our exploration of these two elements will help to show why the Pelagians' claims to speak for the Church's ancient and universal doctrinal tradition prompted such grave concerns for the unity of the Church in Augustine and others in Africa in 411.

Having set the stage in Chapter 1, the remaining four chapters of the study will offer a historical account of the controversy itself and will aim to demonstrate the enduring impact of Augustine's concerns regarding the Pelagians' threat to Church unity as the crisis unfolded. Each of these chapters will treat a particular portion of the controversy. Chapter 2 will focus on the decisive year 411 in which the controversy erupted in Carthage. Chapter 3 will then turn to the years 412 through 415, that is, until the Synod of Diospolis. Chapter 4 will treat 416 through 418, from the time when the African bishops learned of Pelagius's acquittal until the immediate aftermath of Pelagius and Caelestius's condemnation in the summer of 418. Chapter 5 will then treat the years 418 through 430, focusing on the controversy with Julian of Eclanum.

MODE OF ANALYSIS

As Augustine saw it, the Pelagians represented a threat to the unity of the Church in a number of ways as the controversy progressed and especially after Julian became involved. But throughout the controversy, the chief mode in which this threat reared its head, as it were, was in the Pelagians' assertions that their opponents' theology was at variance with the Church's ancient and universal doctrinal tradition. Recognizing the potential for such claims to divide the Church, Augustine, throughout his anti-Pelagian works, consistently sought to refute not only doctrinal stances, but also these claims to ancient and universal tradition. The historical account given in Chapters 2–5 will include significant analysis of Augustine's argumentation in his major anti-Pelagian works in order to indicate just how seriously Augustine took such Pelagian assertions.[26] Of particular note in this argumentation are Augustine's frequent appeals to three types of evidence that he believed bolstered his case that his positions—and not the Pelagians'—were those of the ancient and universal Church: (1) the writings of renowned Christian authors; (2) the Church's liturgical praxis and prayers; and (3) contemporary sources (e.g., recent conciliar decisions, papal statements, reports of popular opinion). By appealing to these types of evidence, Augustine aimed to undermine the Pelagians' claims to speak for the ancient and universal Church and consequently to prevent such claims from spreading and, potentially, leading to ecclesial division in the Church of his day. Let us briefly introduce some key aspects of Augustine's use of such evidence.

The Writings of Renowned Christian Authors

Of the three categories of evidence, Augustine's quotations of renowned Christian authors in the Pelagian controversy has received the most attention from scholars.[27] In general, scholars have argued that Augustine is employing

---

26 It should be noted that this study will not seek to address whether or to what extent Augustine was justified in claiming his theological views—and not the Pelagians'—were simply those of the ancient and universal Church.

27 See, e.g., the following select studies: Andrew Chronister, "Augustine and Patristic Argumentation in His Anti-Pelagian Works: Change or Continuity?" *Augustiniana* 64 (2014): 187–226; Bruno Delaroche, "Note Complémentaire 71: Le recours d'Augustin aux auteurs ecclésiastiques," BA 20/A; Mathijs Lamberigts, "Augustine's Use of Tradition in His Reaction to Julian of Aeclanum's *Ad Turbantium*: *Contra Iulianum I–II*," *Augustinian Studies* 41 (2010): 183–200; Mathijs Lamberigts, "Augustine's Use of Tradition in the Controversy with Julian of

INTRODUCTION

in the Pelagian controversy a form of that type of polemic that would become omnipresent in the medieval period: *patristic argumentation*, the technique of citing the written opinions of ancient Christian authors as evidence for the orthodoxy of particular doctrinal positions.[28] Augustine's use of this form of argumentation is of particular interest because explicit quotation of ecclesiastical authors as authorities was a relatively rare phenomenon prior to the end of the fourth century.[29] Thomas Graumann has traced the use of such appeals to renowned ecclesiastical writers back to Eusebius of Caesarea's circle in their debates with Marcellus of Ancyra.[30] Nevertheless, patristic argumentation remained rare throughout the Trinitarian debates of the fourth century. Yet, only a few decades later, Mark Vessey notes, a significant shift in theological praxis had occurred: "A new generation of theologians... [began] to make a habit of arguing formally from what we should now call 'patristic' texts."[31] This change in argumentative praxis no doubt had many causes—shifts in Christian society due to its increasingly prominent role in the Roman Empire; a growing demand for texts from Christian antiquity; the emergence of certain Christian writers as "heroes" of orthodoxy in the wake of the doctrinal disputes of the fourth century; growing doubts about the effectiveness of other forms of argument in doctrinal debate.[32] Whatever the precise confluence of causes, Vessey remarks that the dawn of this new form of argumentation at the end of the fourth century "amounted to little less than a revolution in Christian literary practice."[33] In this sense, it is significant that Augustine's controversy with the Pelagians was the first debate in the

---

Aeclanum," *Augustiniana* 60 (2010): 11–61; Giorgio Maschio, "L'argomentazione patristica di S. Agostino nella prima fase della controversia pelagiana (412–418)," *Augustinianum* 26 (1986): 459–79; Rebillard, "A New Style of Argument."

28 Admittedly, the use of the term *patristic* argumentation here seems rather anachronistic when used to describe, e.g., Augustine's quotations of Jerome (and even Ambrose).

29 See Vessey, "Forging of Orthodoxy," 499. See also Maschio, "L'argomentazione patristica," 459. For a fuller study of the rise of citations of the Fathers in the East, see Thomas Graumann, *Die Kirche der Väter: Vätertheologie und Väterbeweis in den Kirchen des Ostens bis zum Konzil von Ephesus (431)* (Tübingen: Mohr Siebeck, 2002).

30 See Graumann, *Die Kirche der Väter*.

31 Vessey, "Forging of Orthodoxy," 499.

32 For discussion of this last point, see Julia Dietrich, "Augustine and the Crisis of the 380s in Christian Doctrinal Argumentation," *Journal of Early Christian Studies* 26 (2018): esp. 552–55.

33 Vessey, "Forging of Orthodoxy," 499–500.

West in which citations of renowned ecclesiastical authors took on such an important role.[34]

For his part, Augustine first began using quotations from renowned Christian authors in his writings against the Donatists. There, he cited Cyprian numerous times, especially to undermine the support the Donatists themselves thought they could find in Cyprian's advocacy for rebaptism.[35] His usage of Cyprian within the Donatist controversy was primarily, it seems, a response to what the Donatists themselves were already doing: citing Cyprian as authoritative support for their own views.[36] In this context, Augustine recognized that his only hope to win Donatists over to the Catholic Church was to take up their manner of argumentation and use it against them. The significance of Augustine's use of Cyprian in the Donatist controversy becomes more apparent when compared with his argumentation in other works prior to 411. Indeed, in that period, Augustine hardly ever even referred to, much less quoted, other Christian authors as evidence for the orthodoxy of his own positions.[37] In this sense, it is important to

---

34 See Rebillard, "A New Style of Argument," 560.

35 Augustine seems to have begun using such citations from Cyprian around the year 400, with the works *Contra epistulam Parmeniani* and *De baptismo*, although it remains possible that he had employed such argumentation earlier in one or both of the now lost anti-Donatist works, *Contra epistulam Donati haeretici* of 393/94 or *Contra partem Donati* of 397. For recent discussions of Augustine's use of Cyprian in the Donatist controversy see, e.g., J. Patout Burns, "Appropriating Augustine Appropriating Cyprian," *Augustinian Studies* 36 (2005): 113–30; Anthony Dupont, Matthew Gaumer, and Mathijs Lamberigts, "Cyprian in Augustine: from Criticized Predecessor to Uncontested Authority," in *The Normativity of History: Theological Truth and Tradition in the Tension between Church History and Systematic Theology*, ed. Lieven Boeve, Mathijs Lamberigts, Terrence Merrigan (Leuven: Peeters, 2016), 33–66; Matthew A. Gaumer, *Augustine's Cyprian: Authority in Roman Africa* (Leiden: Brill, 2016).

36 See, e.g., Augustine's comments in *retr.* 2.18: "I wrote seven books on baptism in answer to the Donatists, who were endeavoring to defend themselves by the authority of the most blessed bishop and martyr Cyprian. In them I taught that there is nothing as powerful for refuting the Donatists and for closing their mouths completely, so that they may not defend their schism against the Catholic Church, as the letters and the life of Cyprian" (Latin: CCL 57:104.2–6; English: Ramsey, WSA I/2, 126). See also the literature referenced in the previous footnote.

37 One of the few examples I was able to find is at *ep.* 82.3.24, written to Jerome in 404 or 405, where Augustine refers to Ambrose and Cyprian for support in his interpretation of Gal 2:11–14. Notably, Augustine offers no quotations here and refers to these authors only because Jerome had asked him to list others to support his interpretation (see the relevant section of Jerome's letter, contained in the letters of Augustine at *ep.* 75.3.6). For his part, Augustine appears uncomfortable relying on non-Scriptural authors to support his positions—a discomfort that he will continue to profess in the Pelagian controversy, as we shall

INTRODUCTION   13

recognize that citing other Christian authors as evidence for the orthodoxy
of his positions was not a typical argumentative tactic for Augustine in the
period before 411. Augustine did not feel completely comfortable with it: he
worried that citing other Christian authors for support would make it seem
like he valued their words as much as the words of scripture.[38] Heading into
the Pelagian controversy, Augustine would only resort to such argumentation if the situation demanded it.

As it turned out, Augustine very quickly realized such argumentation
would again be required. Already in 411, it seems likely that he was aware
that such argumentation was being used by the Pelagians, given his report in
De gestis Pelagii about the accusations circulating in 411 in Carthage.[39] As a
result, from the beginning of his anti-Pelagian efforts, Augustine repeatedly
deployed quotations from Christian authors and emphasized the opinions
of those authors in order to demonstrate the antiquity and universality of
the theological positions he held. In doing so, Augustine emphasized that he
was not trying to raise the opinions of mere men above the words of scripture. Rather, these renowned Christian authors functioned for Augustine as
witnesses to the Church's faith from different times and places—their words
and opinions held weight to the extent that they had a reputation for holiness,
learning, defense of the faith, et cetera. It is important to note, however, that
Augustine continued to be apprehensive about citing Christian authors for
support[40] and only rarely used such argumentation even after 411 outside of
an anti-Pelagian or anti-Donatist context.[41] In this sense, his citing renowned
Christian authors to support his own views had not become a habit for him

---

see below. Later, Augustine cites Cyprian in *ep.* 98 while responding to a question about the
effect that participation in pagan sacrifices has on infants. However, the dating of this letter
is uncertain. Traditionally, it has been dated to 408, but recently several scholars have sought
to date it closer to 411–13, that is, to the beginnings of the Pelagian controversy in Carthage.
See discussion and references in Delaroche, "Notes Complémentaires," 466–68.

38 See, e.g., his comments at *ep.* 82.3.24. See also *bapt.* 2.3.4.

39 See *gest. Pel.* 11.25.

40 See *pecc. mer.* 3.7.14, *nat. et gr.* 61.71, and *c. ep. Pel.* 4.8.20. It seems likely his experiences in
the Donatist controversy, where Cyprian's advocacy for rebaptism had proven a difficulty for
the Catholics' anti-Donatist arguments, had made him particularly aware of the fallibility of
renowned Christian authors.

41 One of the exceptions is in a set of letters on seeing God, *epp.* 147 and 148 from 413 or 414.
In *ep.* 147, Augustine discusses Ambrose's views at length; in 148, he cites Ambrose, Athanasius, Gregory of Nazianzus (but actually Gregory of Elvira—see Walter Dunphy, "Rufinus
the Syrian's 'Books,'" *Augustinianum* 23 [1983]: 525–26), and Jerome. It is also important to

after writing against the Donatists; rather, it was a form of argumentation he continued to use sparingly. His decision to employ it against the Pelagians gives some indication of how important he felt it was to rebut their claims.

It should be noted that the frequency with which Augustine deploys such quotations increases over the course of the controversy. However, this was not due to any change in his argumentative principles—as if Augustine originally felt such a style of argumentation was invalid and only later warmed to its usage.[42] Rather, this increased frequency of quotations is merely Augustine's response to the particular and changing demands of the controversy: for example, when Julian of Eclanum and his allies called for competent judges to meet and discuss the relevant theological issues of the Pelagian controversy, Augustine responded in *Contra Iulianum* with citations from a variety of famous (and not so famous) bishops from the Church's history—thus arguing that, in a way, such a meeting had virtually already taken place and judgment had already been passed.

Liturgy and Prayer

Compared with the use of citations of Christian authors, appealing to liturgical practices as evidence for particular doctrinal views was a more established practice in argumentation by the time of Augustine. Such argumentation can be found, for example, in the Trinitarian controversies of the fourth century.[43] Prior to the Pelagian controversy, Augustine also made at least occasional use of such liturgical argumentation.[44] However, this

---

note that here too Augustine is cautious about using quotations from renowned Christian authors; see *ep.* 148.15.

42 Cf. Rebillard, "A New Style of Argument." See Chronister, "Augustine and Patristic Argumentation," for a critique of Rebillard's argument.

43 Of particular prominence were references to doxological and baptismal forms. For discussion, see Maxwell E. Johnson, *Praying and Believing in Early Christianity: The Interplay between Christian Worship and Doctrine* (Collegeville, MN: Liturgical Press, 2013), Chapter 2, esp. 50–65, and Rowan Williams, "Baptism and the Arian Controversy," in *Arianism After Arius: Essays on the Development of the Fourth Century Trinitarian Conflicts*, ed. Michel R. Barnes and Daniel H. Williams (Edinburgh: T&T Clark, 1993), 149–80.

44 For example, as proof that Christians do not worship the martyrs, Augustine writes in *c. Faust.* 20.21 (likely dating from 400–402—see P.-M. Hombert, *Nouvelles recherches de chronologie augustinienne* [Paris: Institut d'Études Augustiniennes, 2000], 25–29): "What bishop, while standing at the altar in the places where [the martyrs'] holy bodies are buried, ever said, 'We offer this to you, Peter or Paul or Cyprian'? Rather what is offered is offered *to* God, who crowned the martyrs, but *at* the memorials of those martyrs he crowned" (Latin:

INTRODUCTION 15

argumentative technique came to be a favorite for Augustine in the course of his battle with the Pelagians, where, assuming such praxis had apostolic origins and was practiced widely in the present-day Church, he employed it to show the universality and antiquity of his positions.[45] While Augustine drew evidence from a variety of liturgical practices and prayers, of particular importance here are Augustine's references to the rite of baptism and the final three petitions of the Lord's Prayer. These pieces of evidence were each consistently employed in different situations. When addressing the Pelagians' rejection of original sin, Augustine frequently referenced the rite of infant baptism, which included exorcism and exsufflation. Again, when attempting to counter the view that sinlessness is possible in this life, Augustine cited the antepenultimate petition of the Lord's Prayer ("Forgive us our debts"). Finally, when refuting the Pelagians' concept of grace, Augustine on numerous occasions employed the final two petitions from the Lord's Prayer ("Lead us not into temptation, but deliver us from evil"). With each of these pieces of evidence, Augustine sought to link his doctrine to the ancient and universal beliefs of the Church. He viewed this evidence as suitable for this purpose precisely because he believed the rite of baptism with which he was familiar was ancient and universal just like the words of the Lord's Prayer.[46] In this sense, the liturgical evidence was not authoritative simply because it was liturgical, but rather because it was thought to be ancient and universal,

---

CSEL 25.1:562.12–16; English: Teske, WSA I/20, 279). This argument is repeated at *ciu.* 8.27. For discussion of Augustine's appeals in the Donatist controversy to the Church's practice of not re-baptizing heretics, see Roland Teske, "Augustine's Appeal to Tradition," in *Tradition & the Rule of Faith in the Early Church: Essays in Honor of Joseph T. Lienhard, SJ*, ed. Ronnie J. Rombs and Alexander Y. Hwang (Washington, DC: The Catholic University of America Press, 2010), 159–62.

45 Some study of Augustine's use of "liturgical argumentation" in the Pelagian controversy has been done. See especially J.-A. Vinel, "L'argument liturgique opposé par saint Augustin aux pélagiens," *Questions liturgiques* 68 (1987): 209–41, which was based on the author's doctoral dissertation, "Le rôle de la liturgie dans la réflexion doctrinale de Saint Augustin contre les pélagiens" (Louvain-la-Neuve, 1986). My own analysis differs from Vinel's, who contends that for Augustine the authoritative value of liturgical praxis was based not on the universality and antiquity of that praxis, but rather on the mere fact of its practice, insofar as that practice enjoyed support from "the authority of the Church" (see, e.g., Vinel, "L'argument liturgique," 235ff.).

46 See, e.g., *pecc. mer.* 3.4.9 for emphasis on the antiquity and universality of the Church's understanding of baptism.

16 INTRODUCTION

practiced by the whole Church from the very beginning.[47] In this sense, Augustine's use of liturgical praxis as evidence complements his citations of renowned Christian authors, who were similarly viewed as witnesses to the ancient and universal teaching of the Church.

Contemporary Sources

In addition to quotations from renowned Christian authors and references to liturgical praxis and prayers, Augustine also employed a third category of evidence to cement his claim that his doctrinal positions were none other than those already taught by the universal Church: evidence drawn from contemporary sources. Three types of evidence drawn from contemporary sources are of particular importance here: (1) the decisions of recent councils and synods; (2) the opinions voiced by Roman pontiffs; and (3) popular belief.

Conciliar Decisions

In his analysis of Augustine's views on doctrinal authority and the sources of doctrine, Robert Eno devotes some space to Augustine's view of councils and synods and of the authority of their decisions.[48] Drawing mainly upon Augustine's anti-Donatist works—which contain the most discussions of councils in Augustine's corpus—Eno attempts to piece together a variety of brief statements made by Augustine to address several questions about Augustine's views on councils that have been raised by scholars. Of greatest interest for our purposes is the question of Augustine's view on the fallibility of councils: Could a council err? A key passage here is *De baptismo* 2.3.4, a

---

47 Maxwell Johnson has recently come to a similar conclusion when discussing Prosper of Aquitaine's famous dictum (*ut legem credendi lex statuat supplicandi*): "[T]he *lex supplicandi* can . . . be said to 'constitute' the *lex credendi*, but not as an isolated norm or principle. Rather, it can function in this way because it conforms to the traditional and biblical *doctrinal* teaching of the church" (Johnson, *Praying and Believing*, 14, italics in original). See Prosper, *Praeteritorum sedis apostolicae episcoporum auctoritates de gratia Dei et libero uoluntatis arbitrio* 8.

48 See Robert Eno, "Doctrinal Authority in St. Augustine," *Augustinian Studies* 12 (1981): 133–72. For more on Augustine and councils, see J. Ernst, "Der heilige Augustin über die Entscheidung der Kerzertauffrage durch ein Plenarkonzil," *Zeitschrift für katholische Theologie* 24 (1900): 282–332; Fritz Hofmann, "Die Bedeutung der Konzilien für die kirchliche Lehrentwicklung nach dem hl. Augustinus," in *Kirche und Überlieferung*, ed. J. Betz and H. Fries (Freiburg: Herder, 1960), 81–89; Fritz Hofmann, *Der Kirchenbegriff des hl. Augustinus in seinen Grundlagen und in seiner Entwicklung* (Münster: Stenderhoff, 1978); Hermann Reuter, *Augustinische Studien* (Gotha, 1887), 231–358; H. J. Sieben, "Konzilien in Leben und Lehre des Augustinus von Hippo," *Theologie und Philosophie* 46 (1971): 496–528.

INTRODUCTION 17

work written against the Donatists in c. 400–401, where Augustine notes that earlier plenary councils are sometimes emended or corrected (*emendari*) by later councils.[49] Augustine's argument here raises an important question: If councils, even plenary councils made up of bishops from the whole world, can be corrected or emended or improved upon in some way, what then is their purpose? Eno addresses this question directly: "The utility of councils lay particularly in their clear and concrete decision-making power concerning disputed questions not immediately soluble by reference to Scripture and Tradition."[50] In this sense, a council was held specifically to arbitrate between different strands of scripture and tradition and to identify the orthodox teaching of the Church. At the same time, Eno notes, a plenary council did not necessarily command total submission: "[A plenary council] was in fact valuable as a court of final appeal when answers were needed quickly, whatever the theoretical problems about its acceptance. Yet there was no guarantee that in the long run a council might not be forgotten or rejected."[51] A council's ultimate authority, it seems, could only be decided in hindsight.

Eno ends his analysis on this rather uncertain note, but what he argues seems to agree with what we find in the Pelagian controversy. At no point in the controversy does Augustine turn to a conciliar decision as definitive proof of the orthodoxy or heterodoxy of a particular position—which is particularly understandable since none of the councils involved were plenary.[52] At the same time, it is clear that the councils that do occur in the course of the controversy are significant for Augustine insofar as they represent, if only in a partial way, the belief of the Church. Thus, Augustine consistently seeks to defend the decisions of these councils and employ them as evidence of the orthodoxy of his own theological positions. In several cases, this defense is

---

49 See *bapt.* 2.3.4 (Latin: CSEL 51:178.11–179.2; English: Tilley and Ramsey, WSA I/21, 423). Augustine is combating here Donatist appeals to a council held in Carthage in 256 that supported the practice of rebaptism.

50 Eno, "Doctrinal Authority," 165.

51 Eno, "Doctrinal Authority," 165.

52 Occasionally, the Council of Carthage of May 1, 418 is referred to as a plenary council (see, e.g., *ep.* 215.2)—but Augustine would want to distinguish between a plenary council of all of Africa (as in *ep.* 215) and a plenary council of bishops drawn from the whole world (as in *De baptismo*). For more on the nomenclature of African synods, see Laurence Dalmon, *Un dossier de l'épistolaire augustinien: la correspondance entre l'Afrique et Rome à propos de l'affaire pélagienne (416–418)* (Leuven: Peeters, 2015), 75, as well as her note on African conciliar activity (pp. 581–92).

unsurprising since the councils held by the African bishops between 416 and 418 all supported Augustine's positions. What is more curious is Augustine's response to the Synod of Diospolis, which—at least ostensibly—seemed to have decided against his views when it acquitted Pelagius of heresy. As we shall see, Augustine makes an impressive effort to reinterpret this apparent defeat at Diospolis. The question must be asked: Why? If this were a mere regional synod, why did Augustine go to such great lengths to defend it? Why did he not simply dismiss it as an incorrect ruling? As we shall see, his defense of Diospolis was part of his broader strategy to safeguard the unity of the Church by proving the antiquity and universality of the theological positions he held in opposition to those of the Pelagians.

Roman Pontiffs

The exact nature of Augustine's view of the authority of the bishop of Rome is a bit unclear. On one hand, Augustine and others in Africa respected the pope as a figure whose authority was in some sense greater than theirs, given the more eminent see he possessed. When writing to Innocent in 416, the bishops of Africa clearly recognized the pope's superior authority and the degree to which they would be aided by his support. However, it is also important to recognize the strategic importance of Rome specifically for the Pelagian controversy. As Robert Eno writes:

> Why did Rome suddenly become involved at this time, when its role had been minor in the Donatist problem? The Africans had condemned Pelagian teachings only to find their work undone by a Palestinian council. The condemnation by one part of the Church was neutralized by the approval of another part. If the prestigious see of Rome with its worldwide respect approved of an African decision, then it would have a more lasting and definitive effect than it would have had otherwise. Another significant aspect was the Roman connection of Pelagius himself. This monk had spent many years in Rome and had acquired a reputation as a serious Christian working for reform. He had circles of friends and disciples in both Roman clergy and laity. It would have been disastrous for their cause if their condemnation had been undone by Roman approval.[53]

Rome was authentically respected by Augustine; it also was a strategic ally in the particular circumstances of the Pelagian controversy. It is with this

---

53 Eno, "Doctrinal Authority," 169.

INTRODUCTION   19

two-part motivation that Augustine and his fellow African bishops appealed to Rome.[54]

However, the reasons why Augustine and his allies appealed to Rome are less important for our purposes than the manner in which Augustine later referenced particular decisions or words of the Roman pontiffs in order to further his polemical aims in his anti-Pelagian works. In many ways, the argumentative tactics Augustine employed in his quotations of and references to the judgments of Innocent and Zosimus mirror those used by Augustine in his citations of renowned Christian authors. Augustine presents the actions taken by these popes as substantiating his own claims to orthodoxy precisely because these figures were recognized by both Augustine and his Pelagian opponents as authoritative in some way[55] and because these actions demonstrated Augustine's and the African Church's unity with the Church of Rome. More broadly, Augustine's references to the Roman pontiffs played into his overall strategy: not only to demonstrate the illogic and heterodoxy of the Pelagian positions, but also to emphasize the universality and antiquity of the positions to which he adhered, as well as the concrete ecclesial unity embraced by the anti-Pelagian side.

Popular Belief

In addition to references to councils and to the words and actions of the Roman pontiffs, Augustine also supplies a third piece of contemporary evidence for the orthodoxy of his positions: popular belief in the doctrines he held as opposed to those promoted by the Pelagians. Among the forms of evidence Augustine supplies in the course of his anti-Pelagian works, the use of evidence drawn from popular belief is relatively infrequent and mainly occurs after 418 as he battles against Julian of Eclanum—although there are early examples of this as well (see, for example, his references to the popular piety of Christian mothers rushing with their infants to the church for

---

54 For more on Augustine and the Roman pontiffs during the Pelagian controversy, see especially Wermelinger, *Rom und Pelagius*, 254–64. See also Dalmon, *Un dossier*, for a close examination of the epistolary exchange between Africa and Rome during this phase of the controversy.

55 Whatever the precise nature of the pope's authority, all parties recognized the de facto importance of the bishop of Rome both as a guide to orthodox theology and as a judge who had the power to excommunicate.

baptism, discussed in Chapter 2).[56] By appealing to the beliefs of the faithful, Augustine attempts to show the universality of the doctrines he upholds. He asserts that these common people have not invented these doctrines by themselves but have simply received them from previous generations of Christians, all the way back to Christ. At the same time, in opposing these popular beliefs, Augustine argues, Julian has distanced himself from the one flock of Christ. In his arrogance, he has succumbed to a deadly poison that has damaged his outlook and has led him to curse and slander all those who hold to the truth and to unity with the Church. In this sense, using popular belief as evidence, Augustine is able (1) to assert that his positions are universal and rooted in the Church's ancient belief and (2) to brand Julian as a prideful heretic, who has rejected the mind of the Church in favor of his own ideas.

SOURCES

While the work of charting the history of the controversy will require reference to a number of primary sources, my analysis of Augustine's argumentation will especially focus on Augustine's major anti-Pelagian treatises.[57] Key sermons and letters as well as certain other treatises immediately relevant to the controversy will also be analyzed.[58] These are the texts which Augustine wrote mainly in response to Pelagian ideas and addressed to persons acquainted with Pelagian teachings. In such writings, I contend, Augustine would feel the most pressure to convince his readers that his positions—rather than those of the Pelagians—find their source in the Church's ancient and universal doctrinal tradition. While other texts from this period also contain discussion relevant to the Pelagian controversy (e.g., *De anima et*

---

56 For two relatively recent examinations of Augustine's appeals to popular belief in the Pelagian controversy, see Jean-Marie Salamito, *Les virtuoses et la multitude. Aspects sociaux de la controverse entre Augustin et les pélagiens* (Grenoble: Millon, 2005), esp. Chapter 8, and Éric Rebillard, "*Dogma Populare*: Popular Belief in the Controversy between Augustine and Julian of Eclanum," *Augustinian Studies* 38 (2007): 175–87.

57 That is, *De peccatorum meritis et remissione et de baptismo paruulorum* (Books 1 and 2 written in 411; Book 3 begun in 411, still incomplete at the beginning of 412); *De spiritu et littera* (412/13); *De natura et gratia* (415); *De perfectione iustitiae hominis* (415); *De gestis Pelagii* (416/17); *De gratia Christi et de peccato originali* (418); *De nuptiis et concupiscentia* (Book 1: 418/19; Book 2: 420/21); *Contra duas epistulas Pelagianorum* (420/421); *Contra Iulianum* (421/22); *Contra Iulianum opus imperfectum* (427–30).

58 For example, *ss.* 293, 294, and 348A; *epp.* 157, 175–77, 179, 186; *De bono uiduitatis.*

INTRODUCTION   21

eius origine), the focus of my project is on those texts written to refute the arguments and accusations of the Pelagians themselves—especially, Pelagius, Caelestius, and Julian of Eclanum. These are the key figures who challenged the orthodoxy of Augustine's positions and accused him and his allies of departing from the Church's traditional teaching. For this reason, I have also decided against addressing in depth the so-called semi-Pelagian controversy and the writings associated with it here, both as a way to focus the scope of this study and because these works were written "against" individuals who Augustine generally recognized were not allies of Pelagius or Julian.[59]

A FEW FINAL NOTES
The Theological Debate

As noted above, the goal of this study is to indicate the importance of Augustine's fear that the Pelagians represented a threat to Church unity. Thus, most of the study will be devoted to (1) highlighting aspects of Augustine's argumentation in his anti-Pelagian writings that reveal this fear and (2) narrating the historical course of the controversy to contextualize this fear. The theological aspects of the controversy, widely discussed elsewhere, will necessarily receive less attention. However, I have attempted at least to signal the main topics of the debate as they shifted over the course of the controversy and to provide summaries of the content of Augustine's major anti-Pelagian writings to give readers a sense of the theological themes of these works. Further, I have devoted some space in Chapters 1 and 2 to the theological aspects of the earliest phase of the Pelagian controversy—in large part because the scholarship on this topic is not as clear as it could be.

The Legitimacy of Augustine's Fears

At some points in the controversy, Augustine's fears about the Pelagians' potential to bring about division within the Church seem quite legitimate— for example, when one considers the actions of Julian of Eclanum and his

---

59 See, for example, Donato Ogliari's comments at *Gratia et Certamen: The Relationship between Grace and Free Will in the Discussion of Augustine with the So-Called Semipelagians* (Leuven: Leuven University Press, 2003), 6. Ogliari's study as a whole offers a solid analysis of the "semi-Pelagian" controversy. See also Rebecca H. Weaver, *Divine Grace and Human Agency: A Study of the Semi-Pelagian Controversy* (Macon, GA: Mercer University Press, 1996).

allies as they mounted a rather significant (if ultimately futile) campaign to secure powerful allies for their cause. At other times, though, one is left wondering if these fears were founded on rather shakier ground. Indeed, Augustine's fears about the Pelagians' potential to foment division often seem rooted in his belief that the Pelagians were rejecting doctrinal positions held by the ancient and universal Church. But how accurate was this belief? For example, was Augustine right to believe that his particular conception of original sin and its effects was simply and obviously that of the universal Church from the time of the apostles? Modern scholars often remain, at the very least, more doubtful than Augustine was on such matters. In this sense, we should note that Augustine sometimes presumes certain things to be true in a historical sense that may, in fact, not be true or, at least, may be rather more complicated than he perceived or acknowledged. Nevertheless, my task in this study is not to evaluate the legitimacy of Augustine's fears. As a result, in the course of the following pages I will present Augustine's fears and concerns as they become evident from his writings and actions without attempting to justify or criticize them.

Types of Unity

When considering Augustine's concerns about "Church unity" as they arise in the Pelagian controversy, it quickly becomes clear that Augustine is anxious about two types of unity.[60] First of all, Augustine is concerned to foster the unity of the Church of his day with the Church of the apostles. This unity is maintained, in Augustine's view, by believing and teaching what scripture and previous generations of Christians believed and taught. But Augustine's concern to maintain this type of unity seems, in his anti-Pelagian works, to be especially at the service of maintaining a second type of unity: unity within the Church of Augustine's day. While Augustine is obviously concerned in principle about Christians abandoning what he views as traditional teachings of the Church, his anti-Pelagian efforts seem aimed more practically at preventing this first type of disunity from leading to division, strife, and even schism in his own day. In the following study, we shall see how Augustine deploys arguments aiming to clarify the Church's traditional teaching precisely in order to stave off the ecclesial division he fears the Pelagians' teachings and actions might incite.

---

60 My thanks to an anonymous reviewer for noting this point.

Terminology

Over the past century, scholars have made a determined effort to nuance traditional heresiological categories and to show the limits of these categories' applicability.[61] The terms "Pelagian" and "Pelagianism" are no exception. In this sense, the reader should note that "Pelagian" and "Pelagianism" are terms to be used with some caution. They can mislead to the extent that they suggest that diverse individuals such as Pelagius, Caelestius, and Julian of Eclanum all shared a defined set of doctrinal views or that they were part of a large, well-organized movement.[62] Indeed, scholars have made strides in recognizing the particular and sometimes differing theological views or emphases of Pelagius, Caelestius, and Julian and in comparing and contrasting their theological views with their opponents' characterizations of those views.[63] Further, scholars have emphasized that the individuals often identified as "Pelagian" did not view themselves as part of a parallel Church

---

61 The limits of the term "Arian" come to mind. Traditionally, anyone who opposed Nicaea has tended to be identified as an "Arian"; however, this practice can obscure significant differences between Arius and later opponents of Nicaea. See, e.g., J. Rebecca Lyman, "Arius and Arians," in *The Oxford Handbook of Early Christian Studies*, ed. Susan Ashbrook Harvey and David G. Hunter (Oxford: Oxford University Press, 2008), 237–57.

62 See, e.g., Mathijs Lamberigts's comments, "Due to intense research over the last 50 years or so, it has become clear that Pelagianism as a well-organized movement never existed. The authors, labelled as 'Pelagians,' took different positions and discussed quite a broad range of topics.... Pelagianism as a consistent doctrine is a construction of its opponents, and Pelagius himself probably did not always recognize his own views in this construction" ("Pelagius and Pelagians," in Harvey and Hunter, *The Oxford Handbook of Early Christian Studies*, 273). See also Bonner, "Rufinus of Syria and African Pelagianism," 31.

63 Lamberigts provides a *status quaestionis* of the diverse views of the various Pelagians: "Pelagius and Pelagians," 263–72. See also the relevant chapters on the theology of Pelagius, Caelestius, and Julian in Squires, *The Pelagian Controversy*. Pelagius himself, for example, while on trial at Palestine in 415, refused to answer for certain propositions drawn from his associate Caelestius's works. Was this a tactical decision that enabled him to avoid explaining his actual views? Or did he actually wish to distance himself from Caelestius? For some discussion, see Guido Honnay, "Caelestius, Discipulus Pelagii," *Augustiniana* 44 (1994): esp. 282–83. However, there are indications that perhaps Pelagius and Caelestius, on certain key issues, were not as different from one another as is sometimes thought: see Andrew Chronister, "Heresiology and Reality: Is Augustine's Portrayal of Pelagius's and Caelestius's Relationship and Views on Grace Accurate?" in *"Sancti uiri, ut audio": Theologies, Rhetorics and Receptions of the Pelagian Controversy Reappraised*, ed. Anthony Dupont, Raúl Villegas Marín, Giulio Malavasi, and Mattia Cosimo Chiriatti (Leuven: Peeters, 2023), 111–32.

or ecclesial structure and that they are best contextualized as a part of the broader ascetic movement of the fourth and fifth centuries.[64]

This deepening understanding of Pelagius, Caelestius, and Julian, of their views, and of the rhetoric of heresiology in general, has prompted important questions: to what extent did these figures' views actually differ from those found in "less controversial" ascetic literature?[65] To what extent did the positions of Augustine diverge from the currents of Christian theology in vogue before the late fourth century?[66] Further, if both sides of the debate were doctrinal innovators at least to some extent, is it really accurate (or fair) to call this conflict the *Pelagian* controversy? Would it not be better to refer to the debate as something like "The Controversy over Theological Anthropology" or "The Controversy over Grace, Free Will, and Nature" or something similar?[67] And more broadly, to what extent are the terms "Pelagian" or "Pelagianism" still appropriate for use?

It is beyond the scope of this study to address in any significant way—much less answer—most of these questions. Doing so would require extensive exploration of the various strands of theological reflection before the late fourth century and a robust analysis of the extent to which Augustine and his interlocutors developed (or corrupted) the theological traditions they inherited. However, I have made the decision to employ the terms "Pelagian" and "Pelagianism" in this study as, properly understood, they seem to remain appropriate for use.[68] Indeed, from a historical perspective, it is worth recalling that there seems to have been a real group of individuals, originally in Rome, who were interested in and, to a greater or lesser degree, supportive of Pelagius's particular "articulation" of Christian asceticism.[69] This group surely included Caelestius, who seems to have circulated his own writings among

---

64 The lack of a clear distinction between what counts as "Pelagian" and what is simply run-of-the-mill ascetic literature has made the identification of certain anonymous texts as "Pelagian" a particularly disputed question among scholars. For some discussion, see Ali Bonner, *The Myth of Pelagianism* (Oxford: Oxford University Press, 2018), 218–59.

65 For example, Bonner, in *The Myth of Pelagianism*, argues for the extreme position that there was nothing new in Pelagius's theology—it was simply that of the ascetic movement.

66 For a concise discussion of this issue, with references to key literature, see, e.g., Ogliari, *Gratia et Certamen*, 262–65.

67 Compare with the preference for referring to the debates of the fourth century as the "Trinitarian controversies" versus the "Arian controversy."

68 Contra Bonner, *Myth of Pelagianism*, esp. 218–59, 305.

69 For more on this historical background, see Chapter 1.

INTRODUCTION

its members. It is with respect to this group that the terms "Pelagian" and "Pelagianism" are especially appropriate, as it is here that we can reasonably speak of a "Pelagian movement"—even if we must necessarily qualify that phraseology by noting that this "movement" was surely loose in its organization and sometimes entertained a variety of theological positions. In any event, the Pelagians seem to have been an identifiable group that participated in the intellectual debates and discussions ongoing in Rome.

However, it seems historically defensible to use the term "Pelagian" at times to refer to individuals who may not have been members of that original group in Rome. Indeed, in the aftermath of the turmoil of 410 and 411—with the sack of Rome, the flight of Pelagius and others from the city, the controversy in Carthage, and the departure of Pelagius and Caelestius for the East—this Roman group likely splintered to some degree: some probably never left Rome, while others traveled to Africa or perhaps Sicily; some then probably departed with Pelagius for Palestine or with Caelestius for Asia Minor, while others remained in Africa or returned to Italy. Nevertheless, one gets a sense from the surviving evidence that at least some of these scattered members of Pelagius's group continued their theological discussions in their new settings, sometimes causing a bit of a stir.[70] As a result, we can easily imagine that the ideas and theological outlook presented by these members of the group would, from time to time, have won over new supporters—and it seems appropriate to call these new supporters "Pelagians" as well.

But what about Julian of Eclanum and the other Italian bishops who had refused to condemn Pelagius, Caelestius, and their alleged views in 418? Is it fair to call these bishops "Pelagians"? So far, I have defended the use of the term "Pelagian" in contexts where we can reasonably connect individuals to Pelagius himself or his group originally found at Rome. But the connection between Pelagius and these Italian bishops is less clear. While it seems probable that Julian was aware of Pelagius during the latter's tenure in Rome given their overlapping social circles, it remains uncertain to what extent Julian actually knew the ascetic himself or had read his writings.[71] Indeed, Julian only mentions Pelagius by name twice in his extant writings.[72]

---

70 See, e.g., *ep.* 156 among the letters of Augustine for a letter from Hilary of Syracuse, notifying Augustine of the spread of problematic (Pelagian-sounding) views in Sicily.

71 Julian does indicate his awareness of Pelagius's *Pro libero arbitrio* in his *Ad Florum* (see *c. Iul. imp.* 4.88), so it seems likely that he had read that work, at least.

72 Lamberigts, "Pelagius and Pelagians," 268.

Notably, however, in both of those instances (found in the *Ad Florum*, written in the early-to-mid-420s) Julian adds a positive descriptor, in one place calling Pelagius *catholicus* and in the other *sanctus*.[73] Of course, the paucity of references to Pelagius could be read as an indication of Julian's relative lack of familiarity with Pelagius. But it seems to me that an equally plausible interpretation is that Julian simply did not wish to focus his campaign on Pelagius himself, but rather on (1) defending the theological principles he and Pelagius seemed to share and (2) attacking the views of Augustine as essentially Manichaean. Nevertheless, it seems significant that when Julian does mention Pelagius, he does so positively. This was surely a conscious decision on Julian's part: one does not praise a condemned figure without good reason, especially when one is trying to have one's own exile overturned![74] In any event, such positive references to Pelagius surely would have caught the attention of Julian's readers and surely would have been read as an affirmation of a link between Julian's cause and Pelagius's—regardless of how close Pelagius and Julian actually were, socially or theologically. It is in this sense that I also feel comfortable referring to Julian, and the other Italian bishops associated with him, as "Pelagians"—although here I am using the term less to suggest that these figures had a direct social connection with Pelagius and more to acknowledge Julian's decision to link himself with a cause that had Pelagius as one of its most prominent leaders.

To summarize: In this study, I will use the term "Pelagian" to refer especially to those individuals who seem to have had some sort of direct connection with Pelagius (or the members of his group in Rome) and were supportive of his theological viewpoint. In a broader sense, I will also use this term to refer to individuals who, in the first three decades of the fifth century, either linked themselves to (or at least found themselves linked with) Pelagius as they strove to resist particular theological positions that to them seemed to devalue the goodness of human nature and/or the reality of human moral responsibility.[75] Similarly, "Pelagianism" will be used to refer

---

73 See Augustine, *c. Iul. imp.* 4.88 and 4.112.

74 A few (non-mutually exclusive) reasons for these positive references come to mind: perhaps Julian viewed Pelagius as something of a kindred spirit; perhaps he felt that Pelagius's condemnation was unjust; perhaps he hoped to gain the favor of Pelagius's networks of support and patronage.

75 It might be argued that figures like John Cassian, on the basis of this last point, could fairly be labeled "Pelagian." While it is true that Cassian sought to push back against certain aspects of Augustine's views, he also clearly saw Pelagius's views as problematic (see, e.g.,

INTRODUCTION

to the general set of views that seem to have been connected to Pelagius or others within his circle.[76]

CONCLUSION

Augustine's involvement in the Pelagian controversy has, in the past, been presented largely as a function of his opposition to the theology of Pelagius and his circle. With this study, I would like to draw attention to another key preoccupation of Augustine's in the controversy: his desire to preserve Church unity. Augustine was, of course, unrelenting in arguing for a particular vision of grace, free will, original sin, and so on. Yet, this quest to defeat the Pelagians was not simply a consequence of a battle of ideas that Augustine was determined to win. Rather, Augustine's involvement in the controversy is better explained by giving due attention to the political and ecclesial situation in which the debate erupted and to the arguments and claims being employed by the Pelagians. With these contexts in view, it becomes possible to understand Augustine's work in the Pelagian controversy as a result of his quest not simply to win a doctrinal battle, but to preserve the unity of the Church and to prevent a schism—a threat that was all too real in Augustine's North Africa.

Squires, *Pelagian Controversy*, 178). This would seem to distinguish him (and other monks in southern Gaul) from figures like Julian of Eclanum who, as I noted above, continued to speak of Pelagius positively.

76 Where possible, I will distinguish the particular positions of Pelagius, Caelestius, and Julian in order to avoid giving the impression of a rigid uniformity of theological views between these figures.

CHAPTER 1

Setting the Stage

In the introduction, we suggested that a decisive factor for Augustine's entrance into, and sustained participation in, the Pelagian controversy was the threat to Church unity he saw in his Pelagian opponents. Although there are several reasons why Augustine perceived the Pelagians as a threat to unity over the course of the controversy, at the beginning of the debate this perception was especially due to Augustine's awareness that the Pelagians were claiming their positions found support in the Church's ancient and universal doctrinal tradition while their opponents' views did not. In this chapter, we will provide some background information to help to explain why Augustine reacted so strongly to such claims made by the Pelagians. We will focus on two topics: (1) the early development of the Pelagian movement and (2) the politico-ecclesial landscape of North Africa in 411. In the course of this twofold investigation, we will seek to answer two questions: (1) How serious was the above-mentioned Pelagian claim from their own perspective—that is, to what extent and for what reasons did the Pelagians actually believe that their positions were traditional while their opponents' were not? (Or, alternatively, was it simply an extemporaneous boast designed to ruffle the feathers of their opponents?) (2) Why did Augustine and his allies take this Pelagian claim so seriously? What we shall discover is that the Pelagian movement, from its inception, was attached to a group of Roman aristocrats intent on cultivating a robust Christian identity—a goal that stoked in them a lively interest in the Christian past and in the affairs and theology of the eastern churches. This interest in the Christian past and in the Christian East was, it seems, adopted by the Pelagians themselves. Augustine himself, who was in touch with many of the same aristocrats, would have been aware of the interests of this circle and, thus, would have recognized that the Pelagian claim was more than a baseless boast. Further, in the context of North Africa in 411—at the very moment when the century-old Donatist schism was, it was hoped, nearing its end—new threats of division would risk endangering that decades-long project of unity.

Let us turn, first, to the early development of the Pelagian movement, as it emerged in the circle of Pelagius and those associated with him. Our aim here is not to give a comprehensive account of the rise of the Pelagian movement and all its many sources and influences, but rather to highlight certain, especially social, aspects of its development that will help to demonstrate the significance of the Pelagians' claim that their doctrinal views were traditional and universally embraced.

PELAGIANISM BEFORE 411
A Historical Sketch

The origins of Pelagianism have been explored by a number of scholars over the past century, with much success, but with certain questions left unresolved. From extant sources, we can glean some bits of information surrounding the background of individuals like Pelagius and Caelestius, but unfortunately much remains unknown. Nevertheless, from these diverse sources, it becomes quite clear that the Pelagian movement did not emerge *ex nihilo* in Carthage in 411, but rather was an import to African soil, especially from aristocratic circles in Rome. It was there that this loosely organized group found its origins in the last decade or so of the fourth century and the first decade of the fifth. Here, the central figure seems to have been Pelagius.[1]

Unfortunately, little is known of Pelagius's life prior to (and after) the main events of the controversy. However, it appears likely he was born in Britain sometime in the mid-fourth century and, at some point, moved to

---

1 Caelestius's importance has at times been underemphasized. Augustine himself calls the Pelagians "Caelestians" and the heresy "Caelestian doctrine" at times (see e.g., *haer.* 88.1 and *c. ep. Pel.* 2.3.5).

SETTING THE STAGE 31

Rome.[2] Although Pelagius is at times identified as a monk (*monachus*), it does not seem he was ever part of a monastery; rather, we should understand this term as a more general reference to the ascetic lifestyle he was known to lead.[3] In any event, it was in Rome that, perhaps from the 390s onward (but at least by the early 400s),[4] he gained a following (at least in part) among the Roman Christian aristocracy. His renown was based on his reputation for personal holiness and his spiritual teaching, which emphasized the need for Christians to embrace the full demands of the Christian faith and moral life.[5] As Augustine himself would later note, "I first heard people mention the name of Pelagius with great praise, when he was far off and residing in Rome."[6] Perhaps around 400, a certain Caelestius became part of Pelagius's circle. From Marius Mercator, an ally of Augustine, we learn that Caelestius was noble by birth and had, perhaps, received legal training.[7] During the controversy he would at times be identified as Pelagius's disciple.[8] Augustine

2 Several ancient authors refer to Pelagius as a Briton: Augustine, *ep.* 186.1 (CSEL 57:45.9–11); Orosius, *Liber apologeticus contra Pelagianos* 12.3 (CSEL 5:620.16); Prosper of Aquitaine, *Chronicon integrum* 740 (PL 51:591.16); Prosper of Aquitaine, *Carmen de ingratis* 1.3 (PL 51:94.5); Marius Mercator, *Commonitorium lectori aduersum haeresim Pelagii et Caelestii uel etiam scripta Iuliani* (ACO 1.5.1., p. 5, ln. 39).

3 See, e.g., Augustine, *gest. Pel.* 14.36; Marius Mercator, *Commonitorium lectori aduersum haeresim Pelagii* (ACO 1.5.1, p. 5, ln. 39).

4 These dates remain conjectures. Nevertheless, given Pelagius's connections by the 410s to the Roman aristocracy, it seems likely that he would have been present in Rome for at least a decade, if not more, to cultivate those relationships. Some attempts have been made to locate Pelagius in Rome at the beginning of the 390s, in the midst of the Jovinianist controversy. However, these efforts have not persuaded all scholars: see below at n. 17.

5 See Brown, *Augustine of Hippo*, 341ff.; Peter Brown, "Pelagius and His Supporters: Aims and Environment," in *Religion and Society in the Age of Saint Augustine* (New York: Harper & Row, 1972), 183–207; and Peter Brown, "The Patrons of Pelagius: The Roman Aristocracy between East and West," in *Religion and Society in the Age of Saint Augustine* (New York: Harper & Row, 1972), 208–26. For a recent *status quaestionis* on Pelagius and related figures, with references to key literature, see Lamberigts, "Pelagius and Pelagians."

6 *gest. Pel.* 22.46 (Latin: CSEL 42:100.7–9; English: Teske, WSA I/23, 354).

7 Marius Mercator, *Commonitorium lectori aduersum haeresim Pelagii* (Latin: ACO 1.5.1, p. 6, ln. 9–10): *nobilis natu quidem et illius temporis auditorialis scholasticus*. Mercator's next comment, that Caelestius was born a eunuch, is perhaps less reliable (*naturae uitio eunuchus matris utero editus* [Latin: ACO 1.5.1, p. 6, ln. 10]).

8 See, e.g., Augustine, *gr. et pecc. or.* 2.8.9. Pelagius seems to have quoted Caelestius in his commentary on Romans—see Pelagius, *Expositio in Romanos* 5.15, in *Pelagius's Expositions of Thirteen Epistles of St. Paul*, vol. 2, ed. Alexander Souter (Cambridge: Cambridge University Press, 1926), 46–47. See also Arnobius Iunior (?), *Praedestinatus* 1.88 (Latin: CCL 25B:52.39–50), where Caelestius is identified as the author of the quotation cited by Pelagius. In this sense,

32 AUGUSTINE IN THE PELAGIAN CONTROVERSY

claims that Caelestius was more forthright than Pelagius in revealing his true beliefs, at least on the topic of original sin[9]—but we need not assume that Pelagius agreed with everything Caelestius himself taught. By 411, both Pelagius and Caelestius were in Carthage, and it was there that the latter provided the spark for the first major Pelagian conflict in North Africa when he was accused of heresy while applying for ordination to the priesthood.

However, it would be a mistake to think that this conflict in 411 was the first controversy the Pelagians had ignited. In fact, several pieces of evidence suggest that even in Rome the Pelagians had needed to defend their views. Augustine reports, for example, that he "began to hear by rumor that [Pelagius] was arguing against the grace of God" even before Pelagius arrived in Africa.[10] Augustine elsewhere mentions Pelagius's apparently fiery reaction to a passage from his own *Confessiones*, in which Augustine famously wrote, "Give what you command, and command what you will [*da quod iubes, et iube quod uis*]."[11] "When these words of mine were cited at Rome by some brother and fellow bishop of mine in Pelagius's presence, he could not tolerate them and, attacking them somewhat emotionally, he almost came to blows with the one who had cited them."[12] Further, we know that Pelagius

---

the relationship between Caelestius and Pelagius was likely more complex than simply that of a student/disciple and his teacher. For discussion of when Caelestius became a disciple of Pelagius, see Walter Dunphy, "Caelestius: A Preliminary Investigation," *Academia* 60 (1994): 33–59, at 40–41. For an overview of Caelestius's life and theology, see Honnay, "Caelestius, Discipulus Pelagii." See also discussion of the relationship between Pelagius and Caelestius in Giulio Malavasi and Anthony Dupont, "When Did Caelestius Become Known as a Disciple of Pelagius? Reassessing the Sources," *Journal of Early Christian Studies* 30 (2022): 343–71 and Chronister, "Heresiology and Reality."

9 See, e.g., *gr. et pecc. or.* 2.12.13.

10 *gest. Pel.* 22.46 (Latin: CSEL 42:100.9–10; English: Teske, WSA I/23, 354).

11 *conf.* 10.29.40, 10.31.45, and 10.37.60. Some have argued that the earliest beginnings of Pelagianism were motivated at least in part by an anti-Augustinianism (although I would caution against emphasizing this aspect too strongly). See, e.g., Henri-Irénée Marrou, "Les attaches orientales du Pélagianisme," *Académie des Inscriptions & Belles-Lettres: Comptes Rendus des Séances* 112 (1968): 459–72; Giovanni Martinetto, "Les premières réactions antiaugustiniennes de Pélage," *Revue d'études augustiniennes* 17 (1971): 83–117; Aimé Solignac, "Autour du *De natura* de Pélage," in *Valeurs dans le stoïcisme: De Portique à nos jours*, ed. M. Soetard (Villeneuve-d'Ascq: Presses universitaires de Lille, 1993), 181–92; Eugene TeSelle, "Rufinus the Syrian, Caelestius, Pelagius: Explorations in the Pre-History of the Pelagian Controversy," *Augustinian Studies* 3 (1972): 61–95.

12 *perseu.* 20.53 (Latin: CSEL 105:260.4–6; English: Teske, WSA I/26, 227). There has been much speculation among scholars over the identity of this bishop. Among the names offered are Paulinus of Nola (see, e.g., Brown, "Patrons of Pelagius," 211); Evodius of Uzalis (see, e.g.,

SETTING THE STAGE 33

had written a letter around 405 (to Paulinus of Nola) seemingly to defend his views on grace.[13] It was likely in this same period that Pelagius composed the *De natura*, which seems to have emerged in a polemical setting.[14] Also during this time, Pelagius composed his *Expositiones* on the Pauline letters.[15]

Duval, "La date du 'De natura' de Pélage: les premières étapes de la controverse sur la nature de la grâce," *Revue des études augustiniennes* 36 [1990]: 283n178, and Solignac, "Autour du *De natura* de Pélage"); and Urbanus of Sicca (Squires, *Pelagian Controversy*, 51n87). Squires's identification is attractive for a few reasons. For example, in *s.* 348A, Augustine informs us of another incident in Rome between an episcopal friend and a Pelagian. Here the bishop is identified as Urbanus and his argument with the Pelagian was about the Lord's Prayer (especially the petition "Lead us not into temptation"). It seems likely that Urbanus's conversation took place before 411 (see my "Heresiology and Reality" for some discussion). As a result, it is possible that this individual could have been Pelagius himself (but it could easily have been Caelestius or some other Pelagian) and that it was also during this conversation that Pelagius had expressed his displeasure at Augustine's prayer in *Confessiones*. It is noteworthy that in *pecc. mer.* 2.2.2–2.5.5, a passage where Augustine quotes this prayer from *Confessiones*, it is used in close conjunction with an appeal to the petition, "Lead us not into temptation." See also *b. uid.* 17.21 and *ep.* 179.3–5, where allusions are made to the prayer from *Confessiones* along with discussion of that petition from the Lord's Prayer. Further, all three of these texts could very well have had Pelagius himself as an indirect target. For a list of other instances where Augustine seems to allude to this line from *Confessiones*, see Pierre-Marie Hombert, *Gloria Gratiae: Se glorifier en Dieu, principe et fin de la théologie augustinienne de la grâce* (Paris: Institut d'Études Augustiniennes, 1996), 593–94. Note that *ep.* 179.5 should be added to that list, as Winrich Löhr points out in *Pélage et le pélagianisme* (Paris: Cerf, 2015), 212n121.

13 See Augustine, *gr. et pecc. or.* 1.35.38. It is possible that Pelagius's lost letter to a bishop named Constantius was also written at this time—see *gr. et pecc. or.* 1.34.37 and 1.36.39.

14 As was mentioned in our introduction, one indication of this polemical setting is Pelagius's unconventional decision to provide quotations from reputed Christian authors as evidence for the orthodoxy of his views (see Augustine, *nat. et gr.* 61.71ff., where the bishop of Hippo responds to Pelagius's quotations). For more on the dating of Pelagius's *De natura* and its context, see Duval, "La date du 'De natura' de Pélage"; Winrich Löhr, "Pelagius' Schrift 'De natura': Rekonstruktion und Analyse," *Recherches augustiniennes* 31 (1999): 235–94; and Solignac, "Autour du *De natura* de Pélage." Pelagius's text is now only extant in the fragments found in Augustine's *De natura et gratia*.

15 See Alexander Souter, *Pelagius's Expositions of Thirteen Epistles of St. Paul*, vol. 2 (Cambridge: Cambridge University Press, 1926). Souter's edition remains in need of some revision, as more recent research has shown. See discussion in Otto Wermelinger, "Neuere Forschungskontroversen um Augustinus und Pelagius," in *Internationales Symposion über den Stand der Augustinus-Forschung vom 12. bis 16 April 1987 im Schloss Rauischholzhausen der Justus-Liebig-Universität Giessen*, ed. C. Mayer, Cassiciacum 39/1 (Würzburg: Augustinus Verlag, 1989), 189–217, esp. 198–201. For a complete English translation of the *Expositiones*, see Thomas P. Scheck, trans., *Pelagius: Commentaries on the Thirteen Epistles of Paul with the* Libellus fidei, Ancient Christian Writers 76 (New York: The Newman Press, 2022). For a helpful study of the theology of the *Expositiones*, especially in comparison with its sources, see Sara Matteoli, *Alle origini della teologia di Pelagio: Tematiche e fonti delle* Expositiones XIII Epistularum Pauli (Pisa: Fabrizio Serra Editore, 2011).

Among other things, Pelagius's comments (at Rom 5:15) contain a list of arguments used by those who oppose the transmission of Adam's sin to his descendants—suggesting that there was ongoing debate over the issue at Rome.[16] In sum, when Pelagius and some of his associates arrived in North Africa around 410, they were already familiar with conflict over their theological opinions.[17] But what were these opinions?

The Controversy Surrounding Pelagius and His Circle in Rome

One of the chief difficulties in identifying the precise views of Pelagius and other figures associated with him is the paucity and poor quality of the evidence available to us.[18] Only three works that are certainly by Pelagius are

16 There is some debate among scholars whether Pelagius agreed with the arguments he cited (allegedly from Caelestius—see n. 8 above). However, given the number of arguments cited, and the fact that the opposing position is given little if any attention, it is hard to believe that Pelagius was not at least sympathetic to the position against the transmission of sin. For more discussion see my "Heresiology and Reality."

17 Some scholars argue that Pelagius and Jerome had butted heads as far back as the early 390s over Jerome's enthusiastic polemic against Jovinian. See, e.g., Georges de Plinval, *Pélage: ses écrits, sa vie et sa réforme* (Lausanne: Payot, 1943), 50–55; Evans, *Pelagius*, esp. 26–42. For an opposing and, I think, more convincing viewpoint, see Y.-M. Duval, "Pélage est-il le censeur inconnu de l'*Adversus Iovinianum* à Rome en 393? ou: du 'portrait-robot' de l'hérétique chez s. Jérôme," *Revue d'histoire ecclésiastique* 75 (1980): 525–57 (see also Duval's "Pélage en son temps"). It has also been suggested that it was Caelestius and not Pelagius who had been at odds with Jerome at that time; see Walter Dunphy, "Jerome against Jovinian, and Other(s): A Note on *Epp.* 50 and 133," *Academia* 64 (1996): 25–53, and Lindsey A. Scholl, "The Pelagian Controversy: A Heresy in Its Intellectual Context" (PhD diss., University of California Santa Barbara, 2011), 87.

18 For a recent catalogue of the works attributed to Pelagius (or to the Pelagians in general), see Volker Henning Drecoll, "Pelagius, Pelagiani," in A-L 4, 645–49. Key studies of Pelagius's theology include Torgny Bohlin, *Die Theologie des Pelagius und ihre Genesis* (Uppsala: Lundequistska bokhandeln, 1957); Gerald Bonner, "Pelagianism and Augustine," *Augustinian Studies* 23 (1992): 33–51; de Plinval, *Pélage*; Drecoll, "Pelagius, Pelagiani"; Yves-Marie Duval, "Pélage en son temps: Données chronologiques nouvelles pour une présentation nouvelle," *Studia Patristica* 38 (2001): 95–118; Evans, *Pelagius*; John Ferguson, *Pelagius: A Historical and Theological Study* (Cambridge: W. Heffer, 1956); G. Greshake, *Gnade als konkrete Freiheit: Eine Untersuchung zur Gnadenlehre des Pelagius* (Mainz: Matthias-Grünewald, 1972); Löhr, *Pélage et le pélagianisme*; Matteoli, *Alle origini della teologia di Pelagio*; Flavio G. Nuvolone and Aimé Solignac, "Pélage et Pélagianisme," in *Dictionnaire de spiritualité, ascétique et mystique, histoire et doctrine*, ed. M. Viller, A. Derville, P. Lamarche, and A. Solignac (Paris: Beauchesne, 1986), XII/2: 2889–2942; B. R. Rees, *Pelagius: A Reluctant Heretic* (Woodbridge: Boydell Press, 1988); Salamito, *Les virtuoses et la multitude*; Squires, *The Pelagian Controversy*.

SETTING THE STAGE

extant in their entirety: the *Expositiones XIII epistularum Pauli* (composed sometime between 406 and 409 while Pelagius was still in Rome), the *Epistula ad Demetriadem* (composed c. 414),[19] and the *Libellus fidei* (composed in 417).[20] Limited fragments from other works that can reliably be attributed to Pelagius are also extant—for example, the *De natura* (composed sometime between 406 and 410)[21] and the *Pro libero arbitrio* (published in late 415 or in 416).[22] A number of other extant works have, at times, been attributed to Pelagius—but the authorship of these remains much debated among scholars.[23] The situation is even worse for Caelestius. None of Caelestius's works remain extant in their entirety, although a variety of fragments from his writings can be found, especially in Augustine's anti-Pelagian writings.[24]

Nevertheless, on the basis of Pelagius's *Expositiones*, the fragments of the *De natura*, and various pieces of information we find in Augustine's works, we can say a few things about some of the controversial opinions the Pelagians seem to have promoted prior to 411.[25] Especially important here are the fragments from Pelagius's *De natura*.[26] Written as a diatribe (i.e., as a debate with a fictive opponent), it seems likely that the *De natura* reflects some of the actual debates Pelagius, his allies, and his opponents were engaged in in Rome.[27] Thus, it is important to note that at the heart of Pelagius's project

---

19 For a recent edition of Pelagius's letter, see Gisbert Greshake, ed., *Pelagius: Epistula ad Demetriadem* (Freiburg: Herder, 2015).

20 For an edition of the *Libellus fidei*, see Peter van Egmond, "*Haec fides est*: Observations on the Textual Tradition of Pelagius's *Libellus fidei*," *Augustiniana* 57 (2007): 345–85.

21 All extant fragments from the *De natura* are found in Augustine's *nat. et gr.* See Löhr, "Pelagius' Schrift," for discussion.

22 Most of the extant fragments of the *Pro libero arbitrio* are found in Augustine's *gr. et pecc. or.* Three additional fragments (one of which is simply a longer version of a fragment found in *gr. et pecc. or.*) are collected at PLS 1:1539–43.

23 See the chart in Drecoll, "Pelagius, Pelagiani."

24 For discussion of Caelestius's *corpus*, see esp. Walter Dunphy, "The Writings of Caelestius," *Academia* 61 (1995): 25–47.

25 Note should also be made of Marius Mercator's account of the origins of Pelagianism in his *Commonitorium lectori aduersum haeresim Pelagii* (ACO 1.5.1, pp. 5–6).

26 It is worth recalling that Augustine sent a copy both of the *De natura* and of his response, *De natura et gratia*, to Pope Innocent (see *ep.* 177.6) and, more significantly, to John of Jerusalem, one of Pelagius's supporters in the East (see *ep.* 179.5). If he had misrepresented Pelagius's thought through selective quotation, Augustine surely would have been reticent to share the entirety of the *De natura* with these key individuals.

27 See Löhr, "Pelagius' Schrift," and Löhr, *Pélage et le pélagianisme*, 200, for more on this point.

in the *De natura* is the contention that it is possible for human beings to live without sin in this life.[28] For Pelagius, God created humanity with the capacity to sin or not sin—to hold anything else would, Pelagius contends, amount to believing in some sort of necessity of sinning, which in turn would put into doubt the reality of human free choice as well as the justice of divine punishment for these apparently unavoidable sins. Given that our free choice cannot be forced to sin, it is, quite simply, possible to live without sinning—and nothing can remove this capacity to avoid sin. It is important to recognize that Pelagius emphasized this point not simply because he enjoyed discussing the finer points of theological anthropology; rather, as a spiritual advisor or guru in Rome, Pelagius's view on the possibility of sinlessness seems to have been connected with a very concrete pastoral aim: he wished to inspire his audience to take their faith seriously and to commit themselves wholeheartedly to the pursuit of holiness.[29]

Pelagius's position on the possibility of sinlessness apparently rubbed some people the wrong way—perhaps because "sinlessness" seemed dangerously close to notions of *apatheia* associated with Stoicism and, more recently, with Origen and his followers. As a result, objections were made to Pelagius's position—some of which can be gleaned from the fragments of his *De natura*. In the fragments of that work, we find two particularly important objections to Pelagius's position: that Pelagius's view (1) does away with the need for grace[30] and (2) ignores the harmful effects of Adam's sin on his descendants.[31] Pelagius's response to these objections is noteworthy. On the one hand, he addresses the accusation that he does not give sufficient attention to the need for grace by asserting that his position on the possibility of living sinlessly does not deny the means (i.e., grace) by which that sort of living is made possible. This response comes off as rather defensive: Pelagius clearly does not want to imply that grace is unnecessary for living sinlessly, although he appears somewhat hesitant—at least in the fragments available

---

28 See, e.g., the first fragments from this work in Augustine, *nat. et gr.* 7.8.

29 Augustine will write later of the impact Pelagius's preaching had had on two of his (Pelagius's) disciples, Timasius and James: "For certain young men, sons of the finest families and well educated in the liberal arts, disciples of Pelagius, abandoned the hopes they had in this world because of his exhortation and devoted themselves to the service of God" (*ep.* 179.2 [Latin: CSEL 44:692.3–6; English: Teske, WSA II/3, 153–54]).

30 See *nat. et gr.* 10.11, 44.52ff.

31 See *nat. et gr.* 19.21.

to us—to clarify what exactly he means by grace.[32] Pelagius also seems to have needed to reassure others on his views of grace more than once: as we already noted, it was during this same period that he wrote a letter to Paulinus of Nola to articulate (and likely defend) his views on the topic.[33]

In contrast, Pelagius's response to the objection about the effects of Adam's sin appears far more confident. Here, Pelagius examines the nature of sin, arguing that sin could in no way do damage to the substance of human nature.[34] Further, he contends that his opponents' view that Adam's sin prompted God to inflict a punishment on humanity that made them more prone to sin is nonsensical: Why would God issue such a counterproductive punishment?[35] Unlike his response to the objection about the necessity of grace—where he essentially agrees that a kind of grace is necessary—Pelagius appears to have no interest in showing here how some sort of damage to human nature as a result of Adam's sin might still be compatible with his position that sinlessness is possible in this life: he seems committed to the view that Adam's sin did no structural damage to human nature. This sense is reinforced when we look at Pelagius's *Expositiones*. Significantly, in her study of that work, Sara Matteoli argues that it is precisely on the issue of Adam's sin and its effects that Pelagius diverges most from the sources he employed to compose the commentary (Origen, Ambrosiaster, the Budapest Anonymous, and Augustine): all of these had acknowledged that Adam's sin had harmed human nature in some way.[36] As we already mentioned above, Pelagius had included a list of arguments against the transmission of Adam's sin in his commentary on Romans.[37] There, Pelagius writes:

32 Eventually he arrives at the position that our ability to avoid sin is itself a grace given to us by God (*nat. et gr.* 51.59).

33 See Augustine, *gr. et pecc. or.* 1.35.38.

34 See *nat. et gr.* 19.21.

35 See *nat. et gr.* 22.24.

36 Matteoli, *Alle origini della teologia di Pelagio*, 188–89. Of course, we should distinguish between (1) the specific position that the guilt of Adam's sin has been transmitted to his descendants (a position most strongly associated with Augustine) and (2) the more generic (and widespread) position that Adam's sin had damaged human nature in some way, resulting, for example, in an increased proclivity to sin. Pelagius's apparent rejection of both these positions thus places him in opposition not simply to Augustine, but also to a much wider swath of early Christian thinkers.

37 It is sometimes noted that it was a common phenomenon of late antique commentaries on scripture to include multiple interpretations of a given scriptural passage to allow the reader to choose the best reading as he or she saw it (see, e.g., Jennifer Ebbeler, *Disciplining Christians:*

These people who are against the transmission of sin try to attack it in this way: "If Adam's sin harmed even those who did not sin, then Christ's righteousness benefits even those who do not believe—because [Paul] says [Rom 5:15] that a person is saved through one man in a way similar to, or rather even more so than people had earlier perished through one man." Next, they say, "If baptism cleanses that ancient sin, those who are born from two baptized parents should not have this sin. For these parents could not transmit to their children what they do not at all have themselves." This is added: "If the soul does not come about from transmission, but only the flesh does, then only the flesh has the transmission of sin and it alone merits punishment." Saying that it is unjust that a soul born today, not from the mass of Adam, should carry so ancient a sin of someone else, they also say that on no account is it granted that God, who forgives a person for his own sins, should impute [to that person] someone else's sins.[38]

Given the presence of these arguments in Pelagius's commentary, it is clear that some sort of debate over the impact of Adam's sin was ongoing at Rome, and that Pelagius, and others in his circle (especially Caelestius, it would seem[39]), had taken a clear stance against any position holding that Adam's sin had damaged human nature.[40] Instead, Pelagius suggested that the impact of

---

Correction and Community in Augustine's Letters [Oxford: Oxford University Press, 2012], 196). While true, it seems significant that Pelagius—contrary to his typically terse comments—devoted so much space to quoting arguments against the transmission of sin (and without, it seems to me, providing any arguments in support of the opposing position). It is difficult not to read the inclusion of these arguments in his commentary as signifying his approval of them, especially when read in concert with his comments in the *De natura*.

38 Pelagius, *Expositio in Romanos* 5:15: *hi autem qui contra traducem peccati sunt, ita illam impugnare nituntur: "si Adae," inquiunt, "peccatum etiam non peccantibus nocuit, ergo et Christi iustitia etiam non credentibus prodest; quia similiter, immo et magis dicit per unum saluari quam per unum ante perierant." deinde aiunt: "si baptismum mundat antiquum illut delictum, qui de duobus baptizatis nati fuerint debent hoc carere peccato: non enim potuerunt ad filios transmittere quod ipsi minime habuerunt. illut quoque accidit quia, si anima non est ex traduce, sed sola caro, ipsa tantum habet traducem peccati et ipsa sola poenam meretur." iniustum esse dicentes ut hodie nata anima, non ex massa Adae, tam antiquum peccatum portet alienum, dicunt etiam nulla ratione concedi ut deus, qui propria homini peccata remittit, imputet aliena* (Latin: Souter, *Pelagius's Expositions*, 2:46–47; English: my translation).

39 As noted above (see n. 8), Pelagius seems to have cited these arguments against the transmission of sin from Caelestius.

40 In this list of arguments, we can also glimpse some aspects of the opposing party's arguments. Note, for instance, the argument about baptism: what we find in Pelagius's commentary is likely a response to an argument that attempted to problematize the Pelagians' position on the transmission of sin on the basis of the practice of infant baptism. This line of argument will be taken up by Augustine again and again in his anti-Pelagian works, as we shall see. It is

SETTING THE STAGE 39

Adam's sin on his posterity essentially amounted to the bad example he gave to them.[41] Pelagius's confidence on this issue is noteworthy—and perhaps echoes of this confidence can be seen in Caelestius's refusal to condemn similar views at his trial in Carthage in 411, as we shall discuss below.

So, to summarize, while still in Rome, Pelagius advocated for the view that it is possible for human beings to be sinless in this life. Presumably due to his support for this view, Pelagius had to defend himself against charges that he denied the need for grace. He also needed to combat another view that would have problematized his position on the possibility of sinlessness—that is, the view that Adam's sin had harmed or weakened human nature. Of course, there was more to Pelagius's theological perspective than simply these issues; but these were the issues that seem to have prompted controversy even before he and some of his associates arrived in Africa around 410.[42] In this sense, we should keep in mind that resistance to Pelagianism was not simply an African phenomenon but had its origins in Rome itself.[43]

Why Follow Pelagius?

We have said that Pelagius had already developed a following when he was in Rome. But what was it that drew people to Pelagius? Without attempting to offer a comprehensive explanation, a few factors can be highlighted. First of all, we might point to the general state of the Church toward the end of the fourth century. In the post-Constantinian era, some of the social dynamics of Christianity had changed quite noticeably. Before Constantine, the choice to become a Christian was—at least at times—not one lightly undertaken. While martyrdom was, of course, not the final end of most Christians of that period, nevertheless, the prospect of it no doubt weighed

---

important to note that it was an argument in play before Pelagius arrived in Africa or Augustine became involved in the controversy: anti-Pelagian sentiment—and concerns about the potential impact of Pelagian views—was not a uniquely African phenomenon.

41 In his comment on Rom 5:12, Pelagius explains that sin entered the world "by example or model" (*exemplo uel forma*) (Latin: Souter, *Pelagius's Expositions*, 2:45).

42 It is possible that some of the other controversial issues that became prominent in Carthage in 411 when Caelestius was accused of heresy had already been debated in Rome. However, we shall delay discussion of these issues until Chapter 2.

43 Of course, it is hard to know whether that anti-Pelagian group in Rome had already been "cross-pollinated" with African (or Augustinian) thought—perhaps via Augustine's *Ad Simplicianum*.

heavily on the Christian and prospective-Christian psyche: to become Christian was to embrace the possibility of persecution and martyrdom at the hands of a hostile world. This awareness no doubt lent itself to a certain fervor among converts to Christianity. However, with Constantine and each passing decade of the fourth century, this primal awareness of the Christian's otherness in the Roman world faded in certain respects. Peter Brown notes that by the late fourth century,

> too many leading families had lapsed into Christianity—by mixed mar-riages, by political conformity. Among such people, no discontinuity existed between the pagan past and the Christian present. The conventional good man of pagan Rome had imperceptibly become the conventional good Christian "believer."[44]

In this sense, to become a Christian, by the end of the fourth century, no longer presupposed a decision to enter a community misunderstood and, in some cases, despised by Roman society. Rather, to become a Christian was, increasingly, to go with the flow, to be an average Roman. In this context, the post-Constantinian societal changes for Christianity had, arguably, allowed a certain laxity to take root in the Church. It was in response to this laxity that a variety of ascetic leaders stepped forward: we may think of the rising tide of monks in Egypt, Palestine, and elsewhere; the dramatic ascetic pursuits of wealthy widows like Marcella, Paula, and Melania in Rome; and the spiritual guidance and writings offered by individuals like Jerome, Rufinus, and, of course, Pelagius himself.

Yet, the simple fact of increasingly widespread Christianization of the Roman world, and the laxity that may have accompanied it, does not com-pletely explain the rise of Pelagius's renown among the Roman Christian aristocracy.[45] What was it about the upper class in Rome that fostered the

---

44 Brown, "Pelagius and His Supporters," 193. More recently, Brown has tempered this por-trait of Roman society at the end of the fourth century by emphasizing that it was really only in the final quarter of that century that leading Roman families had become Christian (see, Brown, *Eye of a Needle*, 31ff.).

45 It should be noted here that the precise social make-up of Pelagius's following remains uncertain. At times, scholars have, as Löhr points out, over-emphasized the ties between Pelagius and certain aristocratic families (see, e.g., Löhr's discussion and critique of this phe-nomenon in *Pélage et le pélagianisme*, esp. 50–61). However, it seems clear from what we shall discuss below that Pelagius had made a name for himself among the rich and powerful in Rome, even if they were not his only, or even most committed, disciples. Pelagius's (and his associates') connection with these aristocrats allowed him access to important social and

SETTING THE STAGE

popularity of someone like Pelagius (or Jerome, for that matter)? Investigating this question, Brown has suggested that Rome's aristocracy was marked, in the late fourth century, by a particular desire to distinguish itself:

> Pelagianism in its hey-day . . . had appealed directly to a powerful centrifugal tendency in the aristocracy of Rome—a tendency to scatter, to form a pattern of little groups, each striving to be an élite, each anxious to rise above their neighbours and rivals—the average upper-class residents in Rome.[46]

Among other things, then, Pelagius's teaching offered such aristocrats a way out of anonymous mediocrity, a path to perfection and to recognition as authentic Christians. Of course, we should not imagine Pelagius's activity simply as that of a late-antique motivational speaker. As Winrich Löhr has pointed out, Pelagius's efforts (as well as that of his close associates) do not seem to have been limited to moral exhortation; rather, the Pelagians were also known as *disputatores*—debaters—who were happy to defend and debate their sometimes controversial views in public settings.[47] Indeed, Löhr notes, "As in ancient philosophy, dialectic and the care of souls were closely linked."[48]

Attracted by his teaching and arguments, Pelagius's aristocratic disciples patronized him and in turn benefited from this teaching and his writings

---

intellectual networks that both contributed to the development of his teaching and spread his fame.

46 Brown, "Pelagius and His Supporters," 189. Brown goes on to suggest that it was precisely this link between Pelagianism and a certain centrifugal movement within Roman aristocracy that was to be the Pelagians' undoing: in the aftermath of the sack of Rome in 410 and the resultant efforts to reunify a dispersed Roman populace, such centrifugal movement reversed into a "centripetal tendency" that undermined the Pelagians' aims to create a small, special sub-Church of authentic Christians (Brown, 190–91).

47 See Löhr, *Pélage et le pélagianisme*, 200.

48 Löhr, *Pélage et le pélagianisme*, 200. Löhr remarks on the same page that Pelagius's *De natura* was likely modeled after a public disputation. Further, it is worth noting that Augustine himself had apparently overheard one such public defense of Pelagian views (see *pecc. mer.* 3.6.12). At the same time, the Pelagians also seem to have been cautious about spreading their writings outside of an inner circle. As a result, Augustine heard about Pelagius's views long before he was able to acquire an actual writing by the ascetic (see *gest. Pel.* 22.46). This "secrecy," too, has some precedent among ancient philosophical schools—see discussion in Anthony Grafton and Megan Williams, *Christianity and the Transformation of the Book: Origen, Eusebius, and the Library of Caesarea* (Cambridge, MA: Belknap Press of Harvard University Press, 2006), 31ff. My thanks to Walter Dunphy for suggesting this connection to me.

in their efforts to cultivate a robust Christian identity. Yet, it is important to recognize that Pelagius's spiritual guidance among the Christian aristocrats of Rome was neither a monopoly nor a one-way street: his popularity with these wealthy Romans enmeshed Pelagius's burgeoning movement within a host of other political, social, and theological alliances that helped to form the group in important ways.[49]

Alliances and Influences

As we noted at the beginning of this chapter, one of the aims of our exploration of the early history of Pelagianism is to discover to what extent and for what reasons the Pelagians believed their own claim that their positions found support in the Church's ancient and universal doctrinal tradition. The answer to this question begins to become clearer when we examine the aristocratic circles in which the Pelagians moved and recognize how these connections likely impacted the nascent movement. In the next section, we will investigate the circles in which the Pelagians found themselves in Rome. This investigation will indicate the extent to which the early Pelagian movement was connected with members of the Roman aristocracy who (1) had a distinct interest in the affairs of the eastern half of the Empire and, more particularly, (2) associated with Rufinus of Aquileia. Having shown Rufinus's proximity to the Pelagian movement, we will then discuss his significance as a major translator of works from the Christian past and the Christian East for a western audience and present the evidence for direct links between the Pelagians and Rufinus. Afterward, we will examine the influence of a figure known as Rufinus the Syrian on the early Pelagian movement. Finally, we will survey other evidence for the Pelagians' familiarity with Christian theological literature as well as the Christian East. In sum, we will show that there are a number of good reasons to think that the Pelagians were very confident in their claim to be familiar with and speak for the Church's doctrinal tradition.

---

49 See Brown, "Patrons of Pelagius." For a slightly different portrait of Pelagius's aims, see Löhr, *Pélage et le pélagianisme*, esp. 116–22. Löhr critiques some aspects of Brown's account and emphasizes the degree to which Pelagius's program was a response to certain proposals of Jovinian.

1. Aristocratic Circles

From surviving evidence, we know that Pelagius himself interacted with individuals in the Roman aristocracy like Paulinus of Nola; Melania the Younger, her husband Pinianus, and her mother Albina; Pinianus's friend Timasius; Juliana and her daughter Demetrias of the *gens Anicia*. As various scholars have noticed, these contacts within the Roman elite are no random group of people, but rather were key actors (or associates/friends/family of key actors) in two contemporary (and not totally distinct) controversies: the Origenist controversy and the outrage sparked by the deposition of John Chrysostom.[50] In these controversies, Pelagius's aristocratic contacts were supporters of both Rufinus of Aquileia and John Chrysostom.[51]

The Origenist Controversy had erupted in the mid-390s in Palestine, when charges of Origenism leveled by Epiphanius, the bishop of Salamis, against John, the bishop of Jerusalem, quickly led to two warring groups: Epiphanius, supported by Jerome, on the one hand, and John, supported by Jerome's now former friend, Rufinus, on the other. After a brief reconciliation between Jerome and Rufinus, the controversy broke out anew around 398, when Rufinus, now in Italy, published a translation of Origen's *De principiis*. Still in Palestine, Jerome relied on his aristocratic contacts in Rome, especially the widow Marcella and the senator Pammachius, to push for a condemnation of Origen by Pope Anastasius (399–401).[52] Theophilus of Alexandria, who like Jerome had previously held Origen in high esteem, soon followed Jerome in switching sides, dedicating himself to ridding the monasteries of the Egyptian desert of Origen's influence. This would lead to the flight of the "Tall Brothers" (a group of monks associated with Origenism) to Constantinople, where they were granted asylum by the bishop, John Chrysostom. This, combined with an earlier failed attempt to win the see of Constantinople for an ally, infuriated Theophilus, who soon secured

---

50 See Brown, "Patrons of Pelagius." See also Elizabeth Clark, *The Origenist Controversy: The Cultural Construction of an Early Christian Debate* (Princeton: Princeton University Press, 1992), esp. Chapters 1 and 5.

51 For more on Rufinus, see Francis X. Murphy, *Rufinus of Aquileia (345–411): His Life and Works* (Washington, DC: The Catholic University of America Press, 1945).

52 Some caution should be exercised in specifying the particular role Pammachius played in the anti-Origenist camp. See Walter Dunphy, "Rufinus the Syrian: Myth and Reality," *Augustiniana* 59 (2009): 79–157, esp. 96–104.

John's exile in 403 at the Synod of the Oak.[53] Eventually the furor would subside—around 405—but Rufinus and Jerome never reconciled before the former's death (c. 410/411).

In the midst of these controversies, both Rufinus and John Chrysostom found support among the same segment of the Roman aristocracy—especially the family and friends of Melania the Elder.[54] Upon the death of her husband when she was twenty-two, Melania controlled a vast fortune, but decided to turn her attention to asceticism.[55] Melania and Rufinus's relationship dated back to the 370s, when they met, traveled together to Egypt, and established monasteries on the Mount of Olives in Palestine. There, they developed a good relationship with John of Jerusalem and welcomed visitors, such as Evagrius Ponticus, who would become a key promoter of Origenism in Egypt, as well as Palladius, who went on to write the *Lausiac History*, an important source for the history of monasticism.[56] In the Origenist controversy, Melania remained an important patron and ally for Rufinus. Around 399 or 400, a few years after Rufinus's return to Italy from Palestine, and at the height of the controversy, Melania too made the trip west and reconnected with friends and family members in part, it would seem, to solidify their support for Rufinus.[57] Among these individuals we can number the following: her granddaughter and this granddaughter's husband, Melania (the Younger) and Pinianus; her cousin's husband, Apronianus, whom Melania converted

53 John was quickly recalled from this first exile, but soon suffered a second, and permanent banishment. For ancient accounts of this complicated episode, see, e.g., Palladius, *Dialogus de vita S. Joannis Chrysostomi*; Socrates, *Historia ecclesiastica* 6.2–21; Sozomen, *Historia ecclesiastica* 8.2–28. See also commentary by Clark, *Origenist Controversy*, esp. Chapter 2; Krastu Banev, *Theophilus of Alexandria and the First Origenist Controversy: Rhetoric and Power*, Oxford Early Christian Studies (Oxford: Oxford University Press, 2015).

54 While the Roman Christian aristocracy seems to have been divided over the Origenist controversy, they were far more unified in their support for John Chrysostom. See Walter Dunphy, "Rufinus the Syrian: Myth and Reality," 102–3. For a more detailed survey of the following, see Clark, *Origenist Controversy*, 20ff.

55 Palladius, *Historia Lausiaca* 46.1.

56 See Clark, *Origenist Controversy*, 21–23.

57 From Palladius, we learn that one of the main reasons for Melania's return to Rome was to prevent her children from falling under "the influence of bad teaching, heresy, or evil living" (Palladius, *The Lausiac History*, trans. John Wortley [Collegeville, MN: Cistercian Publications, 2015], 121). Elizabeth Clark conjectures that this "heresy" was specifically Jerome's polemic against Rufinus and Origen: "Melania wished to prevent her granddaughter from falling into the hands of Jerome's anti-Origenist faction in Rome" (Clark, *Origenist Controversy*, 24).

SETTING THE STAGE

to Christianity and for whom she provided instruction in the faith (via the *Sententiae* of Sixtus translated by Rufinus);[58] as well as Paulinus of Nola, a close friend of the family, who was the first to receive Melania upon her arrival in Italy in 399 or 400. The ties and alliances formed by Melania the Elder would be honored a few years later by her granddaughter, who along with her husband Pinianus hosted Palladius and other supporters of John Chrysostom around 404 or 405 as they appealed to Rome on behalf of the exiled bishop.[59] The leader of the Italian bishops in this appeal was Aemilius, bishop of Beneventum in southern Italy, where, perhaps not coincidentally, Melania the Elder's son, Publicola was *patronus ex origine*.[60]

The specific connections between the supporters of Rufinus and John Chrysostom, on the one hand, and the Pelagians, on the other, are easy to draw. One of the most important links is Paulinus of Nola, who, as we mentioned, was a close friend of Melania the Elder's family. Born around 355 in Aquitaine to a noble family, Paulinus eventually settled at Nola in Campania around 395, where he and his wife pursued a life of asceticism and established a monastery. Sometime between 407 and 413 Paulinus was ordained bishop of Nola.[61] From his ascetic interests, aristocratic status, and annual trips to Rome for the feast of the apostles,[62] it would have been likely enough for Paulinus to cross paths with Pelagius. Sure enough, in a letter addressed to Pope Innocent in 417 as a defense of his views, Pelagius urged the pope to read the letter that he had sent to Paulinus around 405, in which he emphasized the need for grace.[63] However, Pelagius and Paulinus's interaction appears to have run deeper than just a single letter. Indeed, in 417, Augustine and his friend Alypius, the bishop of Thagaste, felt compelled to write to Paulinus to warn him about Pelagius's views, knowing that Paulinus had previously "loved

---

58 Palladius, *Historia Lausiaca* 54.4. See also Brown, "Patrons of Pelagius," 221f.

59 Palladius, *Historia Lausiaca* 61.7.

60 Brown, "Patrons of Pelagius," 214.

61 For more on Paulinus of Nola, see esp. Brown, *Eye of a Needle*, esp. 208–40; Joseph Lienhard, *Paulinus of Nola and Early Western Monasticism: With a Study of the Chronology of His Works and an Annotated Bibliography, 1879–1976* (Köln-Bonn: Peter Hanstein Verlag, 1977); Dennis E. Trout, *Paulinus of Nola: Life, Letters, and Poems* (Berkeley: University of California Press, 1999).

62 Lienhard, *Paulinus of Nola*, 30.

63 See Augustine, *gr. et pecc. or.* 1.35.38, for the relevant quotation from Pelagius's *Epistula ad Innocentium* (CPL 749a), unfortunately preserved only in the fragments found in this work of Augustine's.

Pelagius as a servant of God."[64] Further, Augustine and Alypius report that they have heard rumors that Nola was home to promoters of Pelagianism:

> Some people with you [Paulinus] or rather in your city, at least if what we have heard is true, fight with such stubbornness in defense of this error that they say that it is easier for them to abandon and despise even Pelagius, who condemned the people who hold these views [at the Synod of Diospolis], than to give up the truth, as they see it, of this opinion.[65]

No doubt fearing that Paulinus's warm relationship with Pelagius had continued, Augustine and Alypius thought it necessary to convince the bishop of Nola of the danger of Pelagius's views—likely also hoping to gain Paulinus's support at a pivotal moment in their campaign against the Pelagians.[66]

Beyond these explicit indications of his interaction with Pelagius, a clear link can also be discerned between Paulinus and Julian of Eclanum. Sometime between 400 and 407, Paulinus composed a poem for Julian and his wife, Titia, on the occasion of their wedding.[67] Of note in this connection is the role played by Julian's father-in-law (Aemilius) in organizing support for John Chrysostom among the Italian bishops, mentioned above, which itself indicates a familial link between Julian of Eclanum and the supporters of Rufinus and John Chrysostom.

A couple other suggestive bits of information also surface.

1. Although Augustine had never met Paulinus in person, they had exchanged a number of letters beginning in the mid-390s and, as a result, developed a long-distance friendship.[68] From surviving correspondence,

---

64 *ep.* 186.1 (Latin: CSEL 57:45.11; English: my translation).

65 *ep.* 186.29 (Latin: CSEL 57:68.13–18; English: Teske, WSA II/3, 222).

66 For more on Paulinus's relationship with the Pelagians, see the overview given by Trout, *Paulinus of Nola*, esp. 218–35. We shall discuss *ep.* 186 in more detail in Chapter 4.

67 See Paulinus of Nola, *Carmen* 25. For an argument in favor of a dating closer to the end of this range, see Josef Lössl, *Julian von Aeclanum: Studien zu seinem Leben, seinem Werk, seiner Lehre und ihrer Überlieferung* (Leiden: Brill, 2001), 56–57. For more on the links between Paulinus and Julian, see Lössl, *Julian von Aeclanum*, esp. 44–73, as well as Lienhard, *Paulinus of Nola*, 111ff., and Trout, *Paulinus of Nola*, 232ff.

68 For an overview of the epistolary exchanges between Augustine and Paulinus, see Lienhard, "Paulinus of Nola." See also Trout, *Paulinus of Nola*; Catherine Conybeare, *Paulinus Noster: Self and Symbols in the Letters of Paulinus of Nola* (Oxford: Oxford University Press, 2000); Sigrid Mratschek, *Der Briefwechsel des Paulinus von Nola: Kommunikation und soziale Kontakte zwischen christlichen Intellektuellen* (Göttingen: Vandenhoeck & Ruprecht, 2002). Also see discussion in Ebbeler, *Disciplining Christians*, esp. 81–98.

SETTING THE STAGE

we know that Augustine at times sent his writings to Paulinus, whose library facilitated their spread throughout Italy.[69] Brown has speculated that it may indeed have been Paulinus's library that enabled Pelagius and Julian of Eclanum to read and study Augustine's anti-Manichaean works—for example, *De libero arbitrio*, quoted in Pelagius's *De natura*.[70]

2. As he was nearing his death, Paulinus readmitted to communion those whom he had previously excommunicated.[71] Peter Brown has suggested that the Pelagians in Nola were part of this group.[72]

Another key hinge between the Pelagians and the supporters of Rufinus and Chrysostom is Melania the Younger along with her husband Pinianus.[73] Melania, the namesake of her grandmother Melania (the Elder), was raised in Rome and was the heir of an immense fortune. Determined to lead an ascetical life from an early age, Melania nevertheless was forced into marriage by her parents at the age of fourteen.[74] However, her husband Pinianus reluctantly agreed that after producing two children as heirs, he and his wife would renounce their worldly possessions and follow a path of asceticism. As it happened, two children were born, but both soon died. Nevertheless, Pinianus resolved to hold true to his promise and he and his wife began the process of liquidating their assets—a decision that proved unpopular with their relatives.[75] With the Italian peninsula in upheaval due to Alaric's

---

69 See Brown, "Patrons of Pelagius," 212, and Lienhard, "Paulinus of Nola."

70 See Brown, "Patrons of Pelagius," 212. At *Contra Secundinum* 11 Augustine notes that Paulinus has a copy of *De libero arbitrio*. See also Wermelinger, *Rom und Pelagius*, 227.

71 Uranius, *De obitu sancti Paulini* 2 (PL 53:860).

72 See Brown, "Patrons of Pelagius," 212. Brown's hypothesis is mentioned by Lienhard, *Paulinus of Nola*, 112, and considered plausible by Trout, *Paulinus of Nola*, 235. It is unclear to me, however, on what evidence Brown based his hypothesis.

73 For more on Melania the Younger, see Gerontius, *Vita Melaniae Junioris*, translated with introduction and commentary by Elizabeth A. Clark (Lewiston: The Edwin Mellen Press, 1984). The Greek text of this life has been edited by Denys Gorce, SC 90 (Paris: Cerf, 1962); the Latin text has been edited by Patrick Laurence, *La vie latine de sainte Mélanie* (Jerusalem: Franciscan Printing Press, 2002). See also Elizabeth Clark, *Melania the Younger: From Rome to Jerusalem* (Oxford: Oxford University Press, 2021).

74 Gerontius, *Vita Melaniae Junioris* 1.

75 Gerontius, *Vita Melaniae Junioris* 6–7. Charles Pietri speculates that Melania and Pinianus pursued this path of liquidation "probably under the influence of Pelagius" (Charles Pietri, "Chapitre IV: Les difficultés du nouveau système (395–431): La première hérésie d'Occident: Pélage et le refus rigoriste," in *Histoire du Christianisme des origines à nos jours II: Naissance*

invasion, Melania and Pinianus fled Rome around 408 or 409 with Albina, Melania's mother, and sailed first for Sicily.[76] In Sicily they encountered Rufinus, who notes in the preface to his translation of Origen's *Homilies on Numbers* that Pinianus was encouraging his translation activities.[77] After leaving Sicily, they came to North Africa, where they took up residence at their estate in Thagaste. They remained in North Africa for seven years, where they founded several monasteries; afterward, they journeyed to Palestine, which would become their permanent home.

Several lines can be drawn between Melania the Younger and Pinianus and the Pelagians. First of all, we have direct evidence that in 417 or 418, Melania, Pinianus, and Albina had encountered Pelagius himself in Palestine. Indeed, some scholars have conjectured that their journey to Palestine was motivated at least in part by a desire to restore Pelagius to full communion with the western church after his condemnation by Pope Innocent in January 417.[78] In any event, the trio wrote to Augustine to report to him Pelagius's words, presumably in an attempt to convince the bishop of Hippo that the British ascetic did not actually hold to the heretical views of which he was accused.[79] While it is difficult, of course, to speak with certainty about Pelagius's relationship with Melania, Pinianus, and Albina prior to this meeting in Palestine, it seems unlikely that they would begin to associate with Pelagius only after the orthodoxy of his doctrine was publicly questioned.[80] It is much more likely that they had an existing relationship with the renowned ascetic

---

d'une chrétienté (250–430), ed. Jean-Marie Mayeur, Charles and Luce Pietri, André Vauchez, Marc Venard [Paris: Desclée, 1995], 458). From my point of view, though, it seems just as likely (if not more likely) that close family members and friends in the aristocracy such as Paulinus of Nola would have been the key inspiration for such an act of renunciation. See, e.g., Brown, *Eye of a Needle*, 293.

76 Gerontius, *Vita Melaniae Junioris* 19.

77 See Clark, "Commentary," in *The Life of Melania the Younger*, 109; Rufinus, prologue in W. A. Baehrens, ed., *Origenes Werke: Siebenter Band, Homilien zum Hexateuch in Rufins Über-setzung*, Die Griechischen Christlichen Schriftsteller der ersten drei Jahrhunderte (Leipzig: J. C. Hinrichs, 1921), 2.

78 See, e.g., Pierre-Marie Hombert, "Gratia Christi et de peccato originali (De-)," in A-L 3, 243. See also de Veer, BA 22, 26 for a similar opinion. While possible, it seems more likely to me that their own ascetic pursuits were what drove them to the Holy Land.

79 See *gr. et pecc. or.* 1.1.1.

80 Further, as we shall discuss shortly, a friend of Pinianus (Timasius) was himself a follower of Pelagius.

SETTING THE STAGE

that was rekindled, to some degree, shortly after their arrival in Palestine around 417/18.[81]

A further link between Melania's family and Pelagius can be found in the person of Timasius, who was a friend of Pinianus.[82] Timasius, and his associate James, who were both former disciples of Pelagius, delivered the British ascetic's *De natura* to the bishop of Hippo in late 414 or early 415.[83] This was a watershed moment for Augustine's anti-Pelagian efforts, as it confirmed that the rumors about Pelagius's views were true.[84] From Augustine, we learn that Timasius and James had been persuaded by Pelagius to pursue an ascetical lifestyle and had also followed him in his other teachings.[85] It was Augustine who had challenged them on these Pelagian views, and at that point they delivered Pelagius's treatise to him and asked that it might be corrected. Upon receiving this text, Augustine set to work on his response, *De natura et gratia*, which he sent to Timasius and James when he had completed it.[86]

Outside of the family and friends of Melania the Elder, the Pelagians can also be linked with other wealthy Romans. First of all, some sort of connection might be drawn between the Pelagians and the influential Christian senator Pammachius. Pammachius, who had, along with his wife, decided to pursue an ascetic life, was well-read in Christian literature and was a patron of Jerome in the midst of the Origenist controversy.[87] At his trial in 411, Caelestius "dropped" Pammachius's name in the midst of defending his

---

81 It is often suggested that Pelagius traveled from Rome or Sicily to North Africa with Melania and her family. But we do not have any evidence to confirm this hypothesis.

82 See Augustine, *ep.* 126.6.

83 It should be noted that it remains theoretically possible that the Timasius who was a friend of Pinianus was different from the Timasius who was a disciple of Pelagius: see, e.g., André Mandouze, ed., *Prosopographie chrétienne du bas-empire*, vol. 1, *Prosopographie de l'Afrique chrétienne (303–533)* (Paris: Centre national de la Recherche scientifique, 1982), 1112, who distinguishes the two. Nevertheless, Wermelinger, *Rom und Pelagius*, 39, believes them to be the same person. Augustine's comments at *ep.* 179.2 suggest that Timasius and James were of aristocratic birth, which would certainly support identifying this Timasius with the associate of Pinianus.

84 See *gest. Pel.* 23.47.

85 Augustine, *ep.* 177.6.

86 See *ep.* 168 for Timasius and James's letter of thanks to Augustine.

87 See the entry for Pammachius in Pietri and Pietri, ed., *Prosopographie chrétienne du bas-empire*, vol. 2, *Prosopographie de l'Italie chrétienne*, 2:1576–81. See also Dunphy, "Rufinus the Syrian: Myth and Reality," 96–104, who cautions against overstating the link between Jerome and Pammachius.

views on original sin, noting that he had heard the same views from a priest named Rufinus in the house of Pammachius.[88] It is difficult to know how closely Caelestius might be associated with Pammachius, but, at the very least, he felt his connection to this revered figure was sufficient to offer him support in the midst of his trial.

Another line can be drawn between the Pelagians and one of the wealthiest Roman families (if not *the* wealthiest[89]), the *gens Anicia*.[90] Much like Melania's family, several women of the *Anicii* rose to particular prominence in the late fourth and early fifth centuries due to their turn to asceticism and their correspondence and interactions with the key religious figures of their day. Three women of this family are especially noteworthy: Anicia Faltonia Proba, her daughter-in-law Juliana, and Juliana's daughter Demetrias. Although the *Anicii* seem less closely linked with Rufinus than Melania's family, nevertheless, strong evidence of ties do exist: for example, Gennadius, in his continuation of Jerome's *De uiris illustribus*, singles out Rufinus's letters to Proba as particularly exceptional in the quality of their spiritual exhortation.[91] Further, in 406, John Chrysostom wrote separate letters to Proba and Juliana to thank them for their support of his cause.[92] On the other side of things, we also have clear (if somewhat ambiguous) links between the *Anicii* and Pelagius. First, and most directly, we know that in 413 or 414 Juliana sent out a request to Pelagius (among others) to have him write a letter to her daughter when she took the veil as a consecrated virgin. Pelagius

---

88 See *gr. et pecc. or.* 2.3.3. We will discuss this episode more fully below.

89 Clark, *Origenist Controversy*, 24.

90 For more on this family and their involvement with figures like Rufinus, John Chrysostom, Augustine, and Pelagius, see Patrick Laurence, "Proba, Juliana et Démétrias: Le christianisme des femmes de la gens Anicia dans la première moitié du Ve siècle," *Revue des Études Augustiniennes* 48 (2002): 131–63, and entries in Pietri and Pietri, ed., *Prosopographie chrétienne du bas-empire*, vol. 2, *Prosopographie de l'Italie chrétienne*: Anicia Faltonia Proba (2) 2:1831–33; Anicia Iuliana (3) 1:1169–71; Demetrias Amnia 1:544–47. See also Donato Ogliari, "An Anti-Pelagian *caueat*: Augustine's *Ep.* 188 to Juliana," *Augustiniana* 54 (2004): 203–22; Walter Dunphy, "St. Jerome and the Gens Anicia (Ep. 130 to Demetrias)," *Studia Patristica* 18 (1990): 139–45.

91 See Gennadius, *De scriptoribus ecclesiasticis* 17, and Laurence, "Proba, Juliana et Démétrias," 139n57.

92 See John Chrysostom, *ep.* 168 and 169 (Greek: PG 52:709). For context, see Laurence, "Proba, Juliana et Démétrias," 139–41. Geoffrey Dunn writes, "It is clear from these letters, particularly the one to Juliana, that John was well acquainted with this family" ("The Christian Networks of the Aniciae: The Example of the Letter of Innocent I to Anicia Juliana," *Revue d'études augustiniennes et patristiques* 55 [2009]: 53–72, at 63).

SETTING THE STAGE 51

would respond with his *Epistula ad Demetriadem*.[93] Less directly, in his correspondence with Juliana, we learn that Augustine became increasingly concerned about the proximity of Pelagius to the *Anicii*. First of all, likely in 414, Augustine wrote *De bono uiduitatis* to Juliana in response to her request for his thoughts on widowhood. Although he makes no mention of Pelagius's letter to Demetrias, Augustine nevertheless took care to warn Juliana of the Pelagian heresy—without naming it specifically.[94] We do not know whether Augustine had heard rumors of Anician interaction with Pelagius and his followers, or if he just considered any Roman Christian aristocrats (especially those who had come to North Africa after the sack of Rome) to be in danger of holding Pelagian views. Whatever the case, a few years later in late 417 or early 418, Augustine's fears were confirmed: he had seen Pelagius's *Epistula ad Demetriadem* and had learned from it that it was Juliana herself who had asked Pelagius to write. Despite Juliana's assurances that no one in her family had been tainted by heresy,[95] Augustine now had proof that the *Anicii* had been in contact with Pelagius himself. Augustine and Alypius hastened to write to Juliana to warn her more explicitly about Pelagius and his letter.[96] In addition, other more speculative pieces of evi-

93 See Pelagius, *Epistula ad Demetriadem* (the Latin can be found in Greshake, *Pelagius: Epistula ad Demetriadem*; the English in B. R. Rees, *The Letters of Pelagius and His Followers*, 35–70). At *Epistula ad Demetriadem* 1 (Greshake, *Pelagius: Epistula ad Demetriadem*, 58), Pelagius notes that it was Demetrias's mother who had requested his letter.

94 See *b. uid.* 17.21–18.22 (Latin: CSEL 41:328–32; English: Kearney, WSA I/9, 127–29). It seems possible to me that Augustine had heard of Pelagius's letter, or of Juliana's request for it. As Duval points out ("Pélage en son temps, 99n16), at *b. uid.* 17.21 Augustine alludes to that phrase from the *Confessiones* to which Pelagius had reacted so violently a decade prior (see n. 12 above). The citation of this phrase here inclines me to think that Augustine was aware of Juliana's communication with Pelagius, even if he did not yet have a copy of Pelagius's letter. Walter Dunphy, in a similar vein, suggests that Augustine's awareness of Pelagius's letter to Demetrias had prompted him (around the same time as he was writing *De bono uiduitatis*) to encourage Proba to request Jerome's own letter to Demetrias, to "balance out" Pelagius's (see "St. Jerome and the Gens Anicia," 144–45).

95 Juliana's words are reported in *ep.* 188.2–3 (Latin: CSEL 57:120.25–121.8; English: Teske, WSA II/3, 252–53). Dunn suggests that Juliana's assurance was more of a "statement that she did not consider Pelagius a heretic rather than a claim that she did not have anything to do with Pelagius the heretic" (Dunn, "Christian Networks," 64n67). Donato Ogliari takes Juliana's words here as evidence that the *Anicii* were protecting Pelagius ("An Anti-Pelagian *caueat*," 218).

96 See Augustine, *ep.* 188.

dence for connections between the *Anicii* and Pelagius have been suggested, but they need not detain us here.[97]

These links between the Pelagians and the two powerful families of Melania the Elder and the *Anicii* serve to indicate (1) the close proximity of the Pelagians to the circle of Rufinus of Aquileia and (2) the fact that the Pelagians moved in circles with a distinct interest in the affairs the eastern half of the Empire. Admittedly, some caution is necessary here. The nature of the evidence available to us is such that it does not allow for conclusive proof of the membership of the early Pelagian movement in Rome. We cannot, for example, know for certain that the family and friends of Melania the Elder, or the *Anicii*, were among the most dedicated of Pelagius's supporters—indeed, they probably were not.[98] Nevertheless, the Pelagian links to these groups are clear; and the importance of these links for our purposes readily appears when we recognize that these groups gave the Pelagians a connection to the eastern churches as well as to the theology and translations of Rufinus of Aquileia.

2. Rufinus of Aquileia, the Roman Aristocracy, and Pelagianism

Before discussing Rufinus's influence on the Pelagians, it is important to recall his influence on the Roman Christian aristocracy more broadly. Rufinus, it must be remembered, found himself in the midst of controversy specifically due to his continuing efforts to translate Origen into Latin at the request of these prominent Romans. Why, despite accusations of heresy, did these powerful individuals continue to request further translations of Origen and others? When they voiced support for Rufinus, what was it that motivated that support? What was it that drew them to Rufinus? Peter Brown suggests that at the heart of this support was, in fact, Rufinus's work of translation itself. Brown writes,

---

97 Patrick Laurence, for example, suggests there are veiled references to Anician aid given to Pelagius in Jerome's letter to Ctesiphon (*ep.* 133)—see Laurence, "Proba, Juliana et Démétrias," 155–56. Laurence's account strikes me as overly speculative. It would be an error to over-emphasize the relationship between the *Anicii* and Pelagius; see Peter Brown, who criticizes de Plinval (*Pélage*, 214–16) for just this (Brown, "Patrons of Pelagius," 208n3). See also Dunn, "Christian Networks," who offers a measured review of the evidence for connections between Pelagius and the *Anicii*.

98 If they had been, we might have expected to have seen a much more vocal campaign specifically in his support after his condemnation. Even Julian of Eclanum's campaign seems less about Pelagius himself, and more about the theological principles at stake.

SETTING THE STAGE

In opting for Rufinus [over Jerome], one suspects, members of a newly Christianized aristocracy were opting against a *farouche* expatriate, in favor of a man whose work of translation gave them back their classical past in Christian guise—and introduced their Christian past in classical guise. Apronianus was a typical new convert: his Christian instruction was undertaken by Melania the Elder. He received impeccable Pythagorean maxims, under the name of the martyr—Pope Sixtus. Gaudentius, Bishop of Brescia, got Clement of Rome, "come home at last—as a Roman." The importance of this translating activity should not be underestimated. We are in a world where Seneca writes letters to St. Paul; and where Pope Zosimus may have chosen the *titulus sancti Clementis* as the *venue* for his crucial examination of Pelagius and Caelestius, not only because its ample forecourt would hold a large crowd, but, also, because of the memory of a predecessor recently "made Roman" by Rufinus.[99]

As Brown argues, Rufinus gave the Roman Christian aristocracy exactly what it was looking for: a past to be proud of and, I would add, inspiration for the future.[100]

As Brown has noted elsewhere, at the end of the fourth century, the highest echelon of the Roman aristocracy had only just begun to witness conversions to Christianity from its own ranks.[101] There is a sense in which these very wealthy converts were believers in search of *terra firma*. As part of the highest ranks of Roman society, their pre-Christian days had been marked by their patronage, especially that of their city. Their pride was to be known as lovers and benefactors of their city, and all the history and glory associated with it.[102] But upon conversion to Christianity, and the broadened worldview associated with it, this former bedrock of aristocratic life no longer seemed quite so grand. Unmoored, to a degree, from the traditional life of the aristocrat, a new foundation, a new purpose was needed. For such

---

99 Brown, "Patrons of Pelagius," 221.

100 Further evidence of the Roman Christian aristocracy's search for a "Christian past" might be seen in Jerome's composition of *De uiris illustribus*. See brief comments by J. J. O'Donnell, "The Authority of Augustine," *Augustinian Studies* 22 (1991): 7–35, at 21.

101 See, e.g., Brown, *Eye of a Needle*, 102: "Christianity itself, though rendered prominent, even troublesome, by Constantine, was still, in the Rome of the 370s as in almost every other region of the West, a church of 'mediocre' persons whose opinions barely scratched the granite surface of the high nobility of Rome." I am much indebted to Brown for the following overview of the Christian elite in Roman society.

102 See Brown, *Eye of a Needle*, 64.

aristocrats, their Christian existence was in need of a past that they could celebrate (much as they had celebrated the past of their city) and a future they could work toward (as they had worked toward the future of their home through patronage).

As Brown points out in the passage quoted above, what figures like Rufinus gave to aristocrats like Melania, Paulinus, and others, was a sense that their Christian existence was not some novelty, but part of a tradition already stretching back hundreds of years, linked with the city of Rome itself, and vibrantly alive throughout the Empire. The texts of Clement and Sixtus of Rome connected these noble Romans with figures who had lived two centuries prior. Further, Rufinus's translations of eastern theological texts from figures like Origen, Basil, and Gregory of Nazianzus not only supplied his patrons' faith with intellectual heft but also helped these aristocrats to chart a path forward as Christians by enabling them to understand the new demands and changed worldview their belief would require. It is here that we can see broad overlap between the programs of Rufinus and Pelagius. Just like Rufinus, Pelagius had a vision for moral reform; and just like Rufinus, Pelagius seems to have propagated that vision through writings circulated among the upper class in Rome. Indeed, the literary culture of the Roman Christian aristocracy is crucial for understanding the rise of Pelagianism, for it was within this elite context, fed by the ascetic and theological writings of figures like Ambrose, Origen, Basil, and others, that Pelagius developed and disseminated his thought. And indeed, much of the Pelagian material submitted to this group would not have differed substantially from other texts already in circulation. Walter Dunphy, for example, notes that one of the first translations Rufinus submitted to his patrons upon his return to Rome in 397 was the *Regula* of Basil of Caesarea.[103] Dunphy suggests that, had portions of this translation come down to us anonymously, we might very well have attributed it to a Pelagian, due to its emphasis on the human capacity to follow the divine law and avoid sin.[104]

It is difficult to say with certainty whether there was any direct personal interaction between Rufinus and the Pelagians (although we will consider two pieces of possible evidence below). However, it is clear that at least some of Rufinus's translations made their way into Pelagian hands, and that the

---

103 See Dunphy, "Rufinus the Syrian: Myth and Reality," 125ff. See Basil of Caesarea, *Regula*, ed. K. Zelzer (CSEL 86).

104 See Dunphy, "Rufinus the Syrian: Myth and Reality," 128ff.

SETTING THE STAGE   55

Pelagians found much to like in those translations. As noted already, it was in the course of his time in Rome that Pelagius wrote his *Expositiones* on the Pauline letters as well as the *De natura*. In both texts we see the presence of Rufinus's translations. As we have already mentioned, in his *De natura*, Pelagius cited a number of well-respected Christian authors to support his own doctrinal views.[105] Among these are included several quotations drawn from a book of aphorisms attributed to the martyred bishop of Rome, Sixtus, which Rufinus had recently translated for Apronianus and his wife Avita.[106] More important, however, is Rufinus's translation of Origen's commentary on Romans, which Pelagius used while composing his own *expositio* on Romans.[107] Although this translation was only published after Rufinus's death (c. 410/11), it appears that it was completed by c. 405/6 and that Pelagius gained early access to it (which itself shows yet again the proximity of Pelagius to the circles of Rufinus).[108] While scholars have debated how to interpret the views on original sin presented in the commentary (and whether they might be characterized as Pelagian or anti-Pelagian),[109] all are agreed that Rufinus/ Origen's vision of human nature as well as the commentary's strong emphasis on free will were happily adopted by Pelagius. As Robert Evans writes,

> It is not too much to say that Pelagius owed to Origen-Rufinus both the stimulus of important theological ideas and some of the verbal formulae by

105 See Augustine, *nat. et gr.* 61.71–67.81.

106 See *nat. et gr.* 64.77. For more on Rufinus's translation of this text see F. X. Murphy, *Rufinus*, 119ff., and Henry Chadwick, *The Sentences of Sextus* (Cambridge: Cambridge University Press, 1959), esp. 117ff. See also Evans, *Pelagius*, 43–65.

107 For more on Pelagius's usage of Rufinus's translation, see A. J. Smith, "The Latin Sources of the Commentary of Pelagius on the Epistle of St. Paul to the Romans: The Commentary of Pelagius on 'Romans' Compared with that of Origen-Rufinus," *Journal of Theological Studies* 20 (1919): 127–77; Bohlin, *Theologie des Pelagius*, 87–103; Caroline P. Hammond Bammel, "Rufinus' Translation of Origen's Commentary on Romans and the Pelagian Controversy," *Antichità Altoadriatiche* 39 (1992): 131–42; de Bruyn, *Pelagius' Commentary*.

108 See Caroline P. Hammond Bammel, "The Last Ten Years of Rufinus' Life and the Date of His Move South from Aquileia," *Journal of Theological Studies* 28 (1977): 428; Bammel, "Rufinus' Translation," 131; and Caroline P. Hammond Bammel, "A Product of a Fifth-Century Scriptorium Preserving Conventions Used by Rufinus of Aquileia," *Journal of Theological Studies* 29 (1978): 373. It should be noted that Pelagius, too, circulated his works privately among friends, as Bammel notes ("A Product," 373; see also Mercator, *Commonitorium super nomine Caelestii* [ACO 1.5.1, p. 67]).

109 Bammel declares that "with regard to the doctrine of original sin Rufinus' translation of Origen on Romans was clearly opposed to Pelagian views" ("Rufinus' Translation," 138). Dunphy, however, is not so sure ("Rufinus the Syrian: Myth and Reality," 134–38).

which those ideas came to expression. This far-reaching influence extends from the important conceptions of *lex naturae* and "grace of creation" through the teachings on baptism and faith to the doctrines of freedom, sin as "habit," and the possibility of sinlessness. . . . Pelagius finds a number of ideas and terms in his source which he employs prominently in his own exegesis of particular Pauline passages and which form important parts of what can be called Pelagius' total theological scheme.[110]

There has been much debate among scholars about the extent to which Rufinus's translation is faithful in its theology to Origen's original.[111] These debates are important for assessing the theological origins of Pelagianism. However, regardless of how faithful that translation was or was not, when Pelagius read it, he no doubt believed he was gaining access to the thought and wisdom of Origen, the exegetical master from the East—and he found himself, largely, in agreement with it. And indeed, this is the crucial importance of Rufinus that we have been attempting to draw attention to: for the Pelagians (as for others), Rufinus was a key conduit for ancient and/or eastern works of theology—theology that buttressed, or perhaps even laid the groundwork for, their own theological vision and writings.[112]

110 Evans, *Pelagius*, 19–20. See also de Bruyn's comments: "Pelagius frequently includes an interpretation from Origen as one of two or three alternatives, which he introduces, as is his custom, with a formulaic 'or' (*siue*). More generally, he draws on Origen's—or rather, Origen-Rufinus's—view of the human condition, particularly for his defence of human freedom and his understanding of divine grace" (de Bruyn, *Pelagius' Commentary*, 5). See also Bohlin, *Theologie des Pelagius*, esp. 77–103.

111 See, e.g., Caroline P. Hammond Bammel, *Der Römerbrieftext des Rufin und seine Origenes-Übersetzung* (Freiburg: Herder, 1985), esp. 43–58. See also Dunphy, "Rufinus the Syrian: Myth and Reality," esp. 123ff.

112 One final, if more speculative and less direct, connection between Rufinus and the Pelagians is the role that two episcopal supporters of Rufinus may have played at the Synod of Diospolis in 415 that acquitted Pelagius of heresy. Pier Franco Beatrice has recently argued ("Chromatius and Jovinus at the Synod of Diospolis: A Prosopographical Inquiry," *Journal of Early Christian Studies* 22 [2014]: 437–64) that two of the judges at Diospolis were Chromatius, the bishop of Aquileia, and Jovinus, the bishop of Ascalon (and, perhaps, the former bishop of Padua). As Beatrice notes, both these bishops had substantial contact with Rufinus, and thus their theological outlook as well as their network of friends and allies may have overlapped substantially with that of Pelagius. If Beatrice's identification is correct, that would mean that Pelagius entered into the Synod of Diospolis with key allies on the judicial bench. However, significant questions remain as to whether Beatrice's identification should be accepted. For more, see Chapter 4, n. 83.

SETTING THE STAGE 57

3. Rufinus the Syrian?

Having addressed Rufinus of Aquileia's connection with the Pelagians, let us consider two final pieces of evidence for the influence of an individual named Rufinus on the Pelagians: (1) a statement made by Caelestius before the diocesan *iudicium* in Carthage in 411 and (2) Marius Mercator's account of the early history of the Pelagian heresy in his *Commonitorium aduersum haeresim Pelagii*. Both these texts mention someone named Rufinus who stands at the origin of the Pelagian movement. Who was this Rufinus?

In 411, before a panel of bishops in Carthage, Caelestius was accused of denying that Adam's sin had harmed his posterity.[113] In response, he argued as follows: "I said that I was in doubt about the transmission of the sin, but that I would, nonetheless, agree with one to whom God has given the gift of knowledge, for I have heard differing views from those who have been raised to the priesthood in the Catholic Church." Caelestius was then asked to identify those priests who had rejected the transmission of sin. He replied, "The holy priest, Rufinus, who stayed at Rome with the holy Pammachius. I heard him say that there is no transmission of sin."[114] As Walter Dunphy has noted, until the seventeenth century, it was assumed that Caelestius's Rufinus was, in fact, Rufinus of Aquileia.[115] Indeed, Jerome had indicated his rival had played a role in the early spread of Pelagian ideas, and Jerome's polemics were taken at face value.[116] However, in the seventeenth century, Marius Mercator's *Commonitorium aduersum haeresim Pelagii* was rediscovered and published, which led to the scholarly consensus that it was not Rufinus of Aquileia who introduced the theological principles behind Pelagianism to the West, but rather a shadowy figure identified as Rufinus the Syrian.[117]

---

113 An excerpt from the ecclesiastical proceedings is found at *gr. et pecc. or.* 2.3.3–2.4.3. For more on this episode, see Chapter 2 and the appendix.

114 *gr. et pecc. or.* 2.3.3 (Latin: CSEL 42:168.8–15; English: Teske, WSA I/23, 420, slightly modified).

115 See Dunphy's discussion in "Marius Mercator on Rufinus the Syrian: Was Schwartz Mistaken?" *Augustinianum* 32 (1992): 279–88, esp. 282–85.

116 See, e.g., Jerome, *In Hieremiam prophetam* 4.prologue (Latin: CSEL 59:221; English: Graves, *Jerome: Commentary on Jeremiah*, 112); *Dialogus aduersus Pelagianos*, prologue (Latin: CCL 80:3–5; English: Hritzu, FC 53:230–34); *ep.* 133.1–3 (Latin: CSEL 56:241–47; English: Fremantle et al., NPNF² 6:272–75).

117 For an overview of the "discovery" of Rufinus the Syrian, see Dunphy, "Rufinus the Syrian: Myth and Reality," esp. 87ff. See also pp. 80–81 for further biographical details scholars have tended to attribute to the Syrian. Some important studies that contributed to this scholarly

In this memorandum composed around the time of the Council of Ephesus (431), Mercator writes as follows:

> A thesis contrary to the Catholic faith was raised a long time ago among some of the Syrians and especially in Cilicia by Theodore, the former bishop of the town of Mopsuestia. To this day, it is muttered by a very small number of these people. It is not professed openly, but, for now, is maintained within the churches by these supposed Catholics, who corrupt themselves with it. They maintain that the first parents of the human race, Adam and Eve, were created mortal by God and that they did not wound any of their posterity by their sin of transgression, but harmed themselves alone: they made themselves, and no one else at all, guilty of the commandment before God. Rufinus, a former Syrian by birth [*quondam natione Syrus*],[118] first brought this thesis, which is absurd and also hostile to the correct faith, to Rome at the time of Anastasius, of holy memory, the supreme pontiff of the Church of Rome. Since he was cunning, he did not dare to promote that thesis himself, defending himself from Anastasius's ill-will. He then deceived Pelagius the monk, a Briton by race, and initiated and trained him first of all in this aforementioned impious vanity.[119]

There are a number of intriguing pieces of information in this short history of the origins of Pelagianism, but for now let us focus on the mention made of Rufinus. On the basis of this text, it seems that this Rufinus who rejected the view that Adam's sin was transmitted to his children could not be Rufinus

---

consensus include Berthold Altaner, "Der *Liber de fide*: ein werk des Pelagianers Rufinus des 'Syrers'," *Theologische Quartalschrift* 130 (1950): 432–49; Bonner, "Rufinus of Syria and African Pelagianism"; Marrou, "Les attaches orientales du Pélagianisme"; F. Refoulé, "Datation du premier concile de Carthage contre les Pélagiens et du 'Libellus fidei' de Rufin," *Revue des études augustiniennes* 9 (1963): 41–49; TeSelle, "Rufinus the Syrian, Caelestius, Pelagius."

118 As Dunphy and others have noticed, this is a rather confusing phrase in the Latin, which has led to numerous proposals for emendation. See below.

119 Mercator, *Commonitorium lectori: quaestio contra catholicam fidem apud nonnullos Syrorum et praecipue in Cilicia a Theodoro quondam episcopo oppidi Mampsisteni iamdudum mota, nunc usque penes paucos eorum admodum roditur nec ea palam profertur, sed ab ipsis qui de ea fornicantur uelut catholicis intra ecclesias interim retinetur, progenitores uidelicet humani generis Adam et Euam mortales a deo creatos nec quemquam posterorum sua praeuericatione transgressi laesisse, sed sibi tantum nocuisse; se mandati reos apud deum fecisse, alterum penitus nullum. hanc ineptam et non minus inimicam rectae fidei quaestionem sub sanctae recordationis Anastasio Romanae ecclesiae summo pontifice Rufinus quondam natione Syrus Romam primus inuexit et, ut erat argutus, se quidem ab eius inuidia muniens, per se proferre non ausus, Pelagium gente Brittanum monachum tunc decepit eumque ad praedictam adprime imbuit atque instituit impiam uanitatem* (Latin: ACO 1.5.1, p. 5, ln. 30–40; English: my translation).

of Aquileia, for Mercator describes him as a Syrian by birth. Another text also found and published in the seventeenth century further cements this view: the *Liber de fide*, a text of Pelagian origin (or at least Pelagian influence) with strong anti-Origenist sentiment and a polemic against the transmission of the sin of Adam, concludes with the following colophon: *Explicit Rufini presbyteri prouinciae palestinae liber de fide translatus de graeco in latinum sermonem*—typically understood as "Here ends the Book on Faith of Rufinus, a priest of the province of Palestine, translated from Greek into Latin."[120] This Rufinus, it has been argued, must be Mercator's Rufinus (same name, same polemic against the transmission of sin), who must be Caelestius's Rufinus (same name, same polemic against the transmission of sin)—and who cannot be Rufinus of Aquileia, who was not from Syria and who certainly would not have written a text containing polemic against Origen. Instead, we are left with attributing the origin of Pelagianism in the West to a figure called Rufinus the Syrian, who is often also identified as the priest named Rufinus from Jerome's community in Bethlehem who came through Rome during the papacy of Anastasius.[121]

Recently, however, Walter Dunphy has attempted to turn the tide of this scholarly consensus.[122] In Dunphy's view, Caelestius's Rufinus and Mercator's Rufinus are in fact Rufinus of Aquileia—not the otherwise unknown (and invented, Dunphy would say) figure known as Rufinus the Syrian. Dunphy's argument is multi-pronged and cannot be discussed in full here. However, a few points are worth summarizing:

1. The identification of Caelestius's, Mercator's, and the *Liber de Fide*'s Rufinus as "Rufinus the Syrian" and not as Rufinus of Aquileia rests mainly on the fact that Mercator identifies his Rufinus as a Syrian and on the fact that the *Liber de Fide* contains polemic against Origen.

---

120 The most recent edition of the *Liber de Fide* can be found in *Rufini Presbyteri Liber De Fide*, ed. Mary William Miller (Washington, DC: The Catholic University of America Press, 1964). See Walter Dunphy, "Rufinus the Syrian: Myth and Reality," 85, for the text of the colophon and a discussion of its interpretation. See also Miller, *Rufini Presbyteri Liber de Fide*, 1–7.

121 See Jerome, *ep.* 81.2, and Dunphy, "Rufinus the Syrian: Myth and Reality," 80–81. See also discussion in Miller, *Rufini Presbyteri Liber de Fide*, 3–7. The identification of "Rufinus the Syrian" with the priest Rufinus from Jerome's monastery has not received universal support; see, e.g., Henri-Irénée Marrou, "Les attaches orientales du Pélagianisme," 464–65.

122 Dunphy, "Rufinus the Syrian: Myth and Reality." See also his earlier article, "Marius Mercator on Rufinus the Syrian."

2. Dunphy notes that, other than a few details, Rufinus the Syrian and Rufinus of Aquileia look very similar: "Both . . . came to Rome from the East just before the turn of the century. They were both proficient in Latin and Greek. They both . . . enjoyed the patronage of the Anicii. They both introduced to Rome teachings that would subsequently be condemned as heretical. They both met with the disapproval of Pope Anastasius. They both refrained from publishing their theological opinions under their own names. They both had a formative influence on the Pelagians. . . . They both exited the stage of history at about the same time in 410/11."[123]

3. Rufinus of Aquileia's theology is not far removed from that of Pelagius in many areas, and it would make sense if Rufinus had rejected at least certain aspects of a theology that asserted a transmission of sin from Adam to his progeny.[124]

4. A few things are odd about this Rufinus the Syrian: we hear of him nowhere else, other than in Mercator. Further, it seems very strange that Caelestius, for example, would have appealed to some little-known priest as support for his views while on trial in Carthage.

5. The text of Mercator's account is transmitted by a single manuscript that is riddled with textual errors. The most important line (*Rufinus quondam natione Syrus*) has itself been regarded as problematic by scholars and in need of some sort of emendation.

Given all this, Dunphy suggests that calling into question Mercator's identification of Rufinus as *quondam natione Syrus* is not out of order. Once this is done, Dunphy points out, the case for Rufinus the Syrian quickly begins to dissolve (as long as one posits that the *Liber de Fide* was written by someone other than Rufinus of Aquileia).[125] In my view, Dunphy's argument, while rather speculative at times, is plausible on the whole. Much of the evidence

---

123 Dunphy, "Rufinus the Syrian: Myth and Reality," 82. When Dunphy refers to the *Anicii* here, I suspect he means to refer to the family of Melania the Elder, who were not of the *gens Anicia* (see p. 104 of the same article where a similar misprint occurs). See Clark, *The Life of Melania the Younger*, 83–85, for more on Melania's familial background.

124 Dunphy is careful to point out that he does not intend to suggest that Rufinus did or would have agreed to all the doctrinal views that came to characterize the Pelagian position (see pp. 147–50).

125 Dunphy treats the authorship and history of the *Liber de Fide* briefly in "Rufinus the Syrian: Myth and Reality," esp. 150–56. See also Dunphy's other studies—several of which touch on themes of some relation to this "Rufinus the Syrian"—in the bibliography.

SETTING THE STAGE

for the existence of the Syrian rests on three potentially problematic words within a single problematic manuscript. Nevertheless, more research is needed to test certain aspects of Dunphy's hypothesis.[126]

So where does this leave our investigation of the eastern connections of the early Pelagian movement? While a definitive identification of the Rufinus mentioned by Caelestius and Mercator seems out of reach at the moment, we are nevertheless left with two solid options: (1) Rufinus of Aquileia and (2) the otherwise unknown Rufinus from Syria. If Dunphy is correct, this identification simply adds more weight to what we have said above about the impact of Rufinus of Aquileia on the early Pelagian movement. While above we focused on the role of Rufinus's translations, here we would have evidence for direct interaction between the Aquileian and the Pelagians—and, even more so, evidence that Rufinus played a key role not only in supplying the Pelagians with authoritative quotations with which to defend themselves, but even in inspiring certain aspects of their theology (if Mercator's account is to be trusted). But once again we must recall that Rufinus's authority was founded not on his own theological ingenuity, nor simply on his not-negligible ecclesial status as a priest, but more on his reputation as a conduit for the best of ancient and eastern theology.[127] When Rufinus spoke or wrote, people listened not so much because of who he was, but because of whom he had read and translated.[128] In this sense—if Dunphy is correct that Caelestius and Mercator were referring to Rufinus *of Aquileia*—the early Pelagian movement had, as one of its main inspirations, someone reputed for his knowledge of the Church's theological traditions. It only stands to reason that this fact would embed in the Pelagians a deep conviction that their theology was rooted in the tradition and would find support in the East. But of course, even if Dunphy is wrong, even if Caelestius and Mercator *were* referring to a Rufinus from Syria, about whom we now know little or nothing else, we could arrive at a similar conclusion: a priest from the East, from the very

---

126 For example, more research is needed on Rufinus's view of the effect of the sin of Adam on his progeny. In his article, Dunphy pushes back on earlier discussions of Rufinus-Origen's treatment of Rom 5:12ff. that had labeled Rufinus-Origen as clearly opposed to a Pelagian position (see Dunphy, "Rufinus the Syrian: Myth and Reality," esp. 134ff.).

127 For more on the importance of the fact that Rufinus was a priest, see Dunphy's comments in "Rufinus the Syrian: Myth and Reality," 148–49.

128 A similar dynamic takes place when Jerome, also a priest, is quoted by Augustine and the Pelagians: Jerome's point of view matters precisely because he had read much (and in *both* languages—see *pecc. mer.* 3.6.12—my thanks to Walter Dunphy for his emphasis on this point).

region where Mercator alleges the seeds of Pelagianism first germinated, had transplanted those eastern views to the West, where they grew to full stature in the words and writings of Pelagius and Caelestius.

4. Pelagian Familiarity with the Christian Past and the Christian East

Having considered the Pelagians' connections with Roman aristocrats, Rufinus of Aquileia, and (possibly) Rufinus the Syrian, we will now turn to our final section and briefly highlight several other pieces of evidence for Pelagian familiarity with Christian theological literature as well as evidence for their links with the East. To begin, let us turn to the evidence found in Pelagius's writings.

An examination of Pelagius's extant works reveals his direct awareness of several texts and authors from the Christian tradition. As we already noted above, Pelagius's *De natura*, likely written before his departure for Africa, contains quotations from Lactantius, Hilary of Poitiers, Ambrose of Milan, John Chrysostom, Sixtus (presumed to be the martyred bishop of Rome), Jerome, and Augustine.[129] A decade or so later, Pelagius offers particular praise for Ambrose's theology: "The blessed bishop, Ambrose, in whose books the Roman faith shines forth with special brilliance, stood out like a beautiful flower among the writers in the Latin language; not even an enemy dared to find fault with his faith and utterly flawless interpretation of the scriptures."[130] It remains, of course, difficult to know how familiar Pelagius actually was with Ambrose's body of writing—or that of the other authors whom he cited. But in any event, he (or someone else in his circle) had done enough research to find several proof texts to fit his purposes.[131]

Beyond citations, Pelagius's awareness of other works of Christian literature can be glimpsed especially in his *Expositiones*. A century ago, A. J. Smith published an extensive study of Pelagius's Latin sources in his commentary on Romans.[132] There, Smith identified three important sources: the commentary by the anonymous author known as Ambrosiaster; Augustine's early

---

129 See *nat. et gr.* 61.71–67.80.

130 Pelagius, *Pro libero arbitrio* 3. Quoted in Augustine, *gr. et pecc. or.* 1.43.47 (Latin: CSEL 42:159.25–160.1; English: Teske, WSA I/23, 413).

131 For more on Pelagius's citation of Ambrose, see Giulio Malavasi, "'Erant autem ambo iusti ante Deum' (Lc 1,6): Girolamo e l'accusa di origenismo contro Pelagio," *Adamantius* 23 (2017): 247–54.

132 A. J. Smith, "The Latin Sources of the Commentary of Pelagius on the Epistle of St. Paul to the Romans," *Journal of Theological Studies* 19 (1918): 162–230; 20 (1919): 55–65, 127–77.

SETTING THE STAGE

commentaries on Romans; and Rufinus's translation of Origen's commentary. More recently, connections between Pelagius's commentary and texts by other Latin authors such as Cyprian, Tertullian, and Lactantius have been posited.[133] In addition, Pelagius's *Expositiones* also betray a certain degree of familiarity with eastern sources beyond Rufinus's translations of Origen. In the passage quoted from Marius Mercator in the previous section, the ally of Augustine claims that the heresy later called Pelagianism had its first beginnings in Syria under the watchful eye of Theodore of Mopsuestia. This allegation has led scholars to investigate whether and to what extent Mercator's genealogy is accurate. Initial suspicions might suggest caution, as Mercator was not well-disposed toward Theodore, given Theodore's association with Nestorius. Yet, Mercator's claims do not appear without foundation. Stylistically, for example, Pelagius's commentaries on Paul show similarities with extant Antiochene examples.[134] Theologically, there seems to be some overlap as well, especially regarding the effects of Adam's sin.[135] And further, as we shall mention again below, Theodore would later host Julian of Eclanum in the 420s.[136] But when exactly a direct relationship between the Pelagians and Theodore and other Antiochenes developed, and whether there was such a relationship present prior to 411, is difficult to determine.[137] The best evidence for early links between the Pelagians and Antiochene theology, though, is found in a set of anonymous glosses on the Latin text of Paul's

---

133 See de Bruyn, *Pelagius's Commentary*, 5–7.

134 See de Bruyn, *Pelagius's Commentary*, 3–5.

135 See Marrou's discussion in "Les attaches orientales du Pélagianisme," 469ff. See also Nestor Kavvadas, "An Eastern View: Theodore of Mopsuestia's *Against the Defenders of Original Sin*," in Hwang et al., *Grace for Grace*, 271–93. Kavvadas points out that Theodore's theology cannot easily be described as Pelagian or Augustinian: on some topics (e.g., original sin), Theodore gravitates toward a Pelagian perspective; in other areas (e.g., the relationship between grace and free will), he appears more Augustinian.

136 See Mercator, *Commonitorium aduersum haeresim Pelagii* (ACO 1.5.1, p. 19, ln. 26–27); Mercator, *Epistula lectori* (ACO 1.5.1, p. 23, ln. 23–24). See also discussion in Lössl, *Julian von Aeclanum*, 292–98.

137 For example, parallels to Pelagius's Pauline commentary have been found in John Chrysostom's homilies and Theodore of Mopsuestia's commentaries. However, de Bruyn notes that most scholars believe it unlikely that Pelagius used either of these directly (de Bruyn, *Pelagius's Commentary*, 3). Matteoli agrees, arguing that Greek sources did not have any direct influence on the *Expositiones* (*Alle origini della teologia di Pelagio*, 15). For further discussion of Theodore's relationship with the Pelagians, see Giulio Malavasi, "The Involvement of Theodore of Mopsuestia in the Pelagian Controversy: A Study of Theodore's Treatise *Against those who say that men sin by nature and not by will*," *Augustiniana* 64 (2014): 227–60. See also Malavasi, *La controversia pelagiana in Oriente*, 116–62.

letters witnessed to by a manuscript in Budapest and by interpolations in manuscripts of Pelagius's *Expositiones*.[138] These glosses—drawn, it seems, from a more expansive, but now-lost, commentary or set of glosses—exhibit a clear relationship to Antiochene exegesis (as well as that of Origen) and seem to have been composed by someone who knew Greek.[139] H. J. Frede, in his study of the glosses, noted that Pelagius used the glosses during the composition of his own *Expositiones* on the Pauline letters, thus indicating that Pelagius was, at least, indirectly indebted to Antiochene theology.[140] It seems reasonable to speculate that Pelagius was aware of the dependence of these glosses on Greek sources—but it is, again, difficult to know for sure (the glosses do not, in their current state, identify their sources by name).

More connections between Pelagians and the East can be made when we look at the events of the controversy, as well as the writings of Julian of Eclanum. For example:

1. After leaving North Africa in 411, both Pelagius and Caelestius traveled to the East. Pelagius was in Palestine by early 415 at the latest, while Caelestius was rumored to have been ordained a priest in the province of Asia (perhaps in Ephesus[141]) by 416 and later appeared in Constantinople on a few occasions. While in Palestine, Pelagius seems to have benefited from the favor of John of Jerusalem. Further, it is possible that Pelagius modified his positions (or at least the language he used to describe his positions) to maintain John's support.[142]

---

138 See H. J. Frede, *Ein Neuer Paulustext und Kommentar, I. Untersuchungen; II. Die Text*, Vetus Latina: die Reste der altlateinischen Bibel, Aus der Geschichte der lateinischen Bibel 7–8 (Freiburg: Herder, 1973–1974), esp. I:164–246; Souter, *Pelagius's Expositions of Thirteen Epistles of St. Paul*, vol. 3, *Pseudo-Jerome Interpolations*. For recent discussion of the connection between these glosses and the *Liber de Fide*, see Dunphy, "Glosses on Glosses," Parts 1–3.

139 See Frede, *Ein Neuer Paulustext*, I:205–17; Dunphy, "Glosses on Glosses," esp. Part 1:233–36.

140 Frede, *Ein Neuer Paulustext*, I:196–205.

141 Mercator (*Commonitorum super nomine Caelestii* [ACO 1.5.1, p. 66, ln. 22–24]) mentions that Caelestius sought the *locum presbyterii* at Ephesus but does not confirm whether he was actually ordained there. Mercator seems to suggest in the next line that Caelestius also sought the *locum presbyterii* in Constantinople a few years later. Perhaps having obtained ordination in Ephesus, Caelestius later sought a transfer to the see of Constantinople. In any event, the bishops of Milevis in 416 report the rumor that Caelestius had been ordained in Asia (see *ep.* 176.4).

142 See Giulio Malavasi, "John of Jerusalem's Profession of Faith (CPG 3621) and the Pelagian Controversy," *Studia Patristica* 97 (2017): 399–408.

SETTING THE STAGE 65

2. Following his exile from his diocese in 418, Julian of Eclanum (and the eighteen other deposed bishops) sent a letter to Rufus, bishop of Thessalonica, hoping to gain his support.[143] In his work *Ad Turbantium*, a response to the first book of Augustine's *De nuptiis et concupiscentia*, Julian cited John Chrysostom's homily *Ad neophytos* as well as a work against the Manichees he believed was authored by Basil of Caesarea in support of his own views.[144] Sometime thereafter, Julian traveled to the East himself, where he stayed with Theodore of Mopsuestia.[145] He would at some point, likely during this time period, translate Theodore's commentary on the Psalms into Latin.[146] Later, he appeared in Constantinople and sought Nestorius's aid.[147]

3. Annianus of Celeda,[148] an ally of Pelagius who may have taken part in the Synod of Diospolis and who wrote several books (now lost) in response to Jerome's *ep.* 133 (the letter to Ctesiphon),[149] is best known

143 See *c. ep. Pel.* 1.1.3.

144 See *c. Iul.* 1.6.21 where Augustine quotes Julian's words. Nello Cipriani has argued that this work against the Manichees was actually by Serapion of Thmuis. See Nello Cipriani, "L'autore die testi pseudobasiliani riportati nel *C. Iulianum* (I,16–17) e la polemica agostiniana di Giuliano d'Eclano," in *Congresso internazionale su S. Agostino nel XVI centenario della conversione (Roma, 15–20 settembre 1986). Atti I. Cronaca del Congresso. Sessioni generali. Sezione di studio I* (Rome: Institutum Patristicum Augustinianum, 1987), 439–49. See also Nello Cipriani, "Sulle fonti orientali della teologia di Giuliano d'Eclano," in *Giuliano d'Eclano e l'Hirpinia Christiana*, edited by A. V. Nazzarro (Naples: Arte tipografica, 2004), 162ff.

145 See Marius Mercator, *Epistula* (ACO 1.5.1, p. 23). For more on Julian's interactions with Theodore of Mopsuestia, see Malavasi, "The Involvement of Theodore of Mopsuestia."

146 See Theodore of Mopsuestia, *Expositio in Psalmos Iuliano Aeclanensi interprete*, ed. de Connick, CCL 88A (Turnhout: Brepols, 1977).

147 See Marius Mercator's introduction to his translation of several of Nestorius's sermons (ACO 1.5.1, p. 60, ln. 5–18). While Julian and Caelestius were in Constantinople at the same time, it seems they were part of separate groups and that Nestorius himself may have been, at least initially, unaware of any connection between them: for discussion, see Malavasi, *La controversia pelagiana*, 163–70.

148 For more on Annianus, see "Annianus" in Pietri and Pietri, *Prosopographie chrétienne du bas-empire*, vol. 2, *Prosopographie de l'Italie chrétienne*, 1:141–42 and Nuvolone, "Pélage et Pélagianisme," esp. 2908–2912.

149 See Jerome, *ep.* 143.2, where Jerome seems to indicate that Annianus had been at the Synod of Diospolis. Walter Dunphy, however, has doubts about Jerome's statement and—very plausibly, in my view—wonders whether Jerome was in fact discussing Pelagius's presence at Diospolis, not Annianus's (see Walter Dunphy, "A Prelude to the Synod of Diospolis: The *Liber Apologeticus* of Orosius," *Academia* 62 [1995]: 147n37).

for his translations of some works of John Chrysostom.[150] Annianus undertook this project, he says, to combat the errors of the Manichees and "Traducianus"—presumably Augustine or some other proponent of the doctrine of original sin.[151] It has been speculated that he was also the translator of Chrysostom's homily *Ad neophytos*, which, as mentioned above, would be used by Julian of Eclanum to argue against original sin in *Ad Turbantium.*[152]

What these brief examples show is that, in the midst of controversy and in the face of opposition in the West, several of the most prominent Pelagians often fled eastward for aid and defense. On the one hand, this was an obvious choice: Where else could they turn? In light of the rest of the information we have discussed here, however, the Pelagians' strong eastward orientation seems to have been more than just a matter of practical necessity. From its earliest days, the Pelagian movement associated with individuals interested in the Christian East, who instilled in the movement the confidence that their theology was simply that of the eastern churches. Thus, in times of conflict it was only natural that they would seek aid in the East.

Conclusion

The purpose of this section was both to discuss the origins of the Pelagian movement and to indicate why the Pelagians would feel confident in asserting that their positions were simply those of the Church's ancient and universal doctrinal tradition. On this latter point, as we have shown, it is important to emphasize that the particular segment of the Roman aristocracy in which Pelagius and his followers cut their teeth, as it were, was notably interested in the Christian theological tradition and in the Christian East. They were fed by the translations of Rufinus of Greek figures like Origen, Basil of Caesarea, and Gregory of Nazianzus and of ancient Roman Christians like Clement and Sixtus. They gathered in support of John Chrysostom. One of their chief members, Melania the Elder, had spent much of her adult life in the East.

---

150 See, e.g., Kate Cooper, "An(n)ianus of Celeda and the Latin Readers of John Chrysostom," *Studia Patristica* 27 (1993): 249–55. For more on the importance of Chrysostom for the Pelagians, see Malavasi, *La controversia pelagiana*, 90ff.

151 See Annianus, *Epistula ad Euangelium* (PG 50:472).

152 See Augustine, *c. Iul.* 1.6.21. See Nello Cipriani's brief note on Annianus and *Ad neophytos* in "Sulle fonti orientali," 158.

SETTING THE STAGE

Within that context, the Pelagians had access to the translations of Rufinus and perhaps were directly influenced by him. Further, they came into contact with earlier Latin exegesis and absorbed the traditions of Antiochene interpretation. Given all of this, it only makes sense that the Pelagians would feel their theology to be in very close unity with the Christian past and the East and had little doubt that they were more aware of those theological traditions than other Christians in the West.

When key Pelagians arrived in North Africa around 410, they brought with them that strong presumption of traditional support and promptly, it seems, began asserting it to win over those who opposed their theology. This was a decisive strategic error. Essentially proclaiming that their opponents were not in unity with the Christian past or the Christian East, these proponents of Pelagianism had struck a nerve. For all North Africa was preparing for a conference to be held in June 411 between the Catholics and Donatists, a conference that aimed to put an end to a century-old division. A new accusation of disunity was the last thing bishops like Aurelius of Carthage and Augustine wanted to hear.[153]

Let us turn now to explain a bit more about the state of the Church in North Africa in 411 to indicate how troubling this accusation of disunity would have been.

CHRISTIANITY IN NORTH AFRICA IN 411

On October 14, 410, the western emperor Honorius issued a decree announcing that during the summer of the following year a conference would be held in Carthage between the Catholics and Donatists, with the imperial tribune Flavius Marcellinus sent to function as judge between the two groups.[154]

---

153 See Walter Dunphy's comments in this regard: "A Lost Year," 464–65.

154 For more the history of the Donatist controversy and the Conference of 411, see W. H. C. Frend, *The Donatist Church: A Movement of Protest in Roman North Africa* (Oxford: Clarendon Press, 1952); Jean-Paul Brisson, *Autonomisme et Christianisme dans l'Afrique Romaine de Septime Sévère à l'invasion vandale* (Paris: Editions E. de Boccard, 1958); Lancel, *Saint Augustine*, esp. 271–305; Erika Hermanowicz, *Possidius of Calama: A Study of the North African Episcopate at the Time of Augustine* (Oxford: Oxford University Press, 2008); Shaw, *Sacred Violence*. Shaw's work on the nature of the Donatist movement offers important corrections to Frend's classic. See also the helpful collection of essays in Richard Miles, ed., *The Donatist Schism: Controversy and Contexts*, Translated Texts for Historians, Contexts (Liverpool: Liverpool University Press, 2016), especially John Whitehouse's brief summary of the history of the schism "The Course of the Donatist Schism in Late Roman North Africa," 13–33. I have

This conference, or rather legal hearing, was, from the point of view of the Catholics, long overdue.

The past century had seen many ups and downs for the Catholic party's hopes for an end to (or suppression of) the Donatist schism, a schism that had erupted shortly after the election and consecration of Caecilian as bishop of Carthage in 306.[155] In addition to other complaints against him, Caecilian's consecration came to be called into question due to the fact that at least one of his episcopal consecrators had been accused of being a *traditor* during the persecution of Diocletian. Caecilian's opponents soon elected and consecrated Majorinus, who, upon his death in 313, was succeeded by Donatus—the bishop from whom the schism would take its name.[156] In the first decade or so of the schism, the emperor Constantine would intervene several times in an attempt to reconcile the two sides, and rulings repeatedly favored the Catholics—but to no avail.[157] After Constantine, imperial officials would be pulled into the battle from time to time, but to little lasting effect. In 347 an imperial decree attempted to impose unity on the two parties under the leadership of Gratus, the Catholic successor to Caecilian. This decree and the persecution of Donatists that accompanied it gave Catholics a clear edge for a time. However, the Catholic triumph was short-lived and came to a swift end in 361 when the emperor Julian allowed exiled Donatists to return to their sees and reclaim their property.[158] This return ushered in a Donatist resurgence. Under the strong leadership of Parmenian, Donatus's successor as bishop of Carthage (c. 363–91/92), the Donatists solidified their numbers throughout North Africa, despite a few sporadic persecutions by imperial officials.[159] By the early 390s, the Donatists held a clear majority. But it was upon Parmenian's death that Donatist power began to wane. Parmenian was succeeded by Primian, whose leadership drew opposition from within

---

drawn much from the literature cited here to summarize the course of the Donatist Schism on the following pages.

155 For dating of this initial episode, see Shaw, *Sacred Violence*, 812–19. For discussion of the eruption of the schism, see Frend, *Donatist Church*, 1–24.

156 Of course, it is important to remember that the Donatists believed themselves to be Catholic; the label "Donatist" was imposed upon them by their opponents. See discussion of the difficulties of nomenclature in, e.g., Shaw, *Sacred Violence*, 5–6.

157 For the Constantinian phase of the schism, see Frend, *Donatist Church*, 141–68.

158 See Frend, *Donatist Church*, 182–92.

159 See Frend, *Donatist Church*, 193–207

SETTING THE STAGE

the broader Donatist community and led to the consecration of one of his deacons, Maximian, as a rival bishop. The Maximianists were vigorously opposed by Primian and his supporters, who even sought imperial support to suppress their opponents. However, as the Donatist party found themselves confronted by internal divisions and strife, the Catholics gained new momentum with the rise of Aurelius, consecrated as bishop of Carthage c. 392, and Augustine, consecrated coadjutor bishop of Hippo in 395.

With Aurelius and Augustine, the Catholics gained the strong leadership they had been sorely lacking.[160] Soon, they began to take a new approach to their anti-Donatist efforts, focusing their energies on a three-pronged attack: 1) claiming that the Donatists were not simply schismatics, but also heretics (and thus deserving of legal action under anti-heresy laws); 2) emphasizing that the Donatists were riddled with internal divisions of their own, especially because of the Maximianists; 3) highlighting the violence of certain Donatists, especially the circumcellions.[161] In advancing these arguments, Aurelius and Augustine sought imperial support for the suppression of Donatism, but also confronted Donatists directly. Augustine in particular sought to challenge key Donatists to debates and to host discussions with them, a strategy that the rest of the Catholic episcopate resolved to take up in 401.[162] While this initial effort bore little fruit, it was taken up in a new and more robust way in 403, when the Catholic bishops invited their Donatist counterparts to meet with them and gained support from the secular authorities to require a Donatist response to this invitation before local governmental officials.[163] Unsurprisingly, the Donatists refused to meet, recognizing that the weight of imperial support was clearly on the side of their opponents.

In the midst of this campaign for meetings with the Donatists, several prominent episodes of Donatist violence occurred, including an attack on Possidius, the Catholic bishop of Calama. This violence would prove to be a turning point for the Catholics. After Possidius was attacked by a Donatist priest, it was thought that the Donatist bishop Crispinus would discipline

---

160 See Frend, *Donatist Church*, 227ff.; Whitehouse, "The Course of the Donatist Schism," 28–29.

161 See Shaw, *Sacred Violence*, 141ff.; Whitehouse, "The Course of the Donatist Schism," 29.

162 See Lancel, *Saint Augustine*, 287.

163 See Frend, *Donatist Church*, 258ff., and Lancel, *Saint Augustine*, 286ff.

the priest who had carried out the attack.[164] However, no action was taken. As a result, Possidius changed his tactics and accused Crispinus of heresy. The case was eventually brought before the proconsul of Africa, who decided in favor of the Catholics: Crispinus was declared a heretic and ordered to pay a fine of ten pounds of gold, the penalty indicated by the Theodosian law of 392. This was a momentous victory for the Catholics. As Brent Shaw notes, "[This] was the first time that a formally empowered official of the Roman state had decreed 'a Donatist'—and, by implication, all such persons—to be a heretic and therefore subject to imperial laws on heresy."[165] As a result, clear precedent had been set for imperial action against the Donatist *heretics*. The emperor Honorius would soon confirm this proconsular decision. In early 405 Honorius issued an Edict of Unity and several other anti-Donatist memos, which aimed at bringing Donatism under the force of existing anti-heresy laws, especially those previously targeting the Manichees.[166] The penalties were mainly financial in nature—for example, preventing Donatists from inheriting or bequeathing property—but were clearly designed to make life exceptionally difficult for members of the Donatist Church.[167]

However, despite imperial support for their cause, Catholics continued to find opposition or disinterest at the local level: not all local officials were equally motivated to apply the imperial decrees.[168] Further, in the spring of 410, after several years of sporadic implementation and amid political turbulence at the imperial court and throughout Italy, Honorius seems to have issued an edict that granted religious toleration to the Donatists or at least was exploited by the Donatists to argue for such toleration from local authorities.[169] But this reprieve for the Donatists was short-lived. A delegation of bishops was sent by the Catholics to Ravenna to meet with Honorius and to request a renewal of the initiatives against Donatism. In

---

164 For an account of the events, see Augustine, *Cresc.* 3.46.50ff., and Possidius, *Vita Augustini* 12.

165 Shaw, *Sacred Violence*, 534. See also Hermanowicz, *Possidius of Calama*, esp. Chapter 3.

166 See Hermanowicz, *Possidius of Calama*, 150ff.

167 It should be noted that the Catholics, while continuing to pursue legal action in accord with these laws against the Donatists, also often sought to have the financial penalties reduced—whether out of mercy, or for more practical reasons. See Hermanowicz, *Possidius of Calama*, 155, and Shaw, *Sacred Violence*, 535–36.

168 See Hermanowicz, *Possidius of Calama*, 153ff.; Shaw, *Sacred Violence*, 537–38.

169 See Hermanowicz, *Possidius of Calama*, 188ff.; Shaw, *Sacred Violence*, 539.

SETTING THE STAGE

addition, they asked for the emperor to convene a meeting between the Catholics and Donatists. On August 25, 410, the day after Alaric had invaded Rome, the Catholic delegation received their answer: the edict of toleration was rescinded. Two months later, on October 14, Flavius Marcellinus was commissioned by the emperor to preside over a legal hearing between the two parties—albeit a hearing with a foregone conclusion: the suppression of the Donatist Church.

It is tempting, retrospectively, to write off this conference between the Catholics and Donatists as yet another ineffectual effort to end the Donatist schism.[170] Indeed, Donatism arguably remained present in North Africa in some form at least until the turn of the seventh century, and possibly into the eighth.[171] Yet it is also clear that the conference, and the policies put in place afterward, did have a real effect on the schism between the two Churches, at least in certain geographical areas.[172] But whatever the actual effects afterward, it is hard to overestimate the Catholic hopes for the conference leading up to June 411. Indeed, this meeting would be the culmination of roughly two decades of persistent Catholic ascendancy and persistent imperial support for the Catholics. It would be the first time Catholics and Donatists met together in such numbers and in such a setting. It would be the most powerful initiative fostered by the state to bring an end to the schism. Catholics were so eager for union that they were even prepared to make certain concessions to the Donatists: for example, the Catholic bishops promised (1) to step down should the Donatists prove victorious at the conference and (2) to share governance with the Donatist bishops or to step down to allow a third party to be elected bishop should the ruling favor the Catholic party.[173]

---

170 In his overview of Donatism for *Augustine through the Ages*, Robert Markus tersely describes the conference in the following way: "In 411 a huge conference called by the imperial authorities failed to bring about any solution" (Robert A. Markus, "Donatus, Donatism," in Fitzgerald, *Augustine through the Ages*, 285).

171 See Frend, *Donatist Church*, 300–314. See also the brief discussion in J. Patout Burns and Robin M. Jensen, *Christianity in Roman Africa: The Development of Its Practices and Beliefs* (Grand Rapids, MI: Eerdmans, 2014), 80–82. It should be noted that the existence and identification of Donatism post-411 is a much-debated topic in the literature. See, e.g., David E. Wilhite, *Ancient African Christianity: An Introduction to a Unique Context and Tradition* (Oxford: Routledge, 2017), 210–14, for some discussion.

172 In Calama guidelines were followed to prevent the election of a new Donatist bishop after Possidius's rival Crispinus died. See Hermanowicz, *Possidius of Calama*, 221–22.

173 See Lancel, *Saint Augustine*, 297, and *Gesta collationis Carthaginensis* 1.16 (Latin: CSEL 104.85–86).

It stands to reason that Catholic hopes for an end to the schism were at an all-time high.

It was at this very moment, or shortly before, that Pelagius, Caelestius, and others in their circle arrived in Carthage, bringing with them theological views and arguments that had already stirred controversy in Rome. In Carthage, however, these same views and arguments were like a spark to a powder keg. How can we account for this sudden eruption of controversy in North Africa? Several explanations present themselves. First of all, it may be that theological currents in North Africa were simply far more hostile to Pelagianism that those present in Rome. But even if this were true, one would still need to explain why the controversy would erupt so suddenly in 411, when the Church in North Africa—and in Carthage, in particular—was already intensely focused on the resolution of the Donatist schism.[174] Given how busy the ecclesial authorities would have been in 411, any explanation of the beginnings of the Pelagian controversy should address whether and to what extent the early stages of the Pelagian controversy were connected with the "end" of the Donatist schism.

In an article on the beginnings of the Pelagian controversy in North Africa, Walter Dunphy offers some suggestive comments on this very topic.[175] First of all, Dunphy notes that certain of the Pelagians were focused on theological issues not at all foreign to those of the Donatist schism—for example, personal holiness and baptism and its effects—although there were, of course, differences in positions between the two groups.[176] It is possible that existing antipathy toward the Pelagians—perhaps having arrived in North Africa via certain aristocratic refugees or figures like Paulinus, the deacon from Milan who would accuse Caelestius of heresy—was able to gain ground in a Carthaginian setting in which the Catholic authorities were already focused on the some of the theological issues central to Pelagianism.[177] While this is certainly part of the answer, Dunphy supplements this explanation with

---

174 This explanation also fails to account adequately for the fact that it was the Milanese deacon Paulinus who would accuse Caelestius of heresy and the Italian Marcellinus who had notified Augustine of the controversy.

175 Dunphy, "A Lost Year."

176 Dunphy, "A Lost Year," 464. See also Bonner, "Rufinus of Syria and African Pelagianism," 33–34. However, I remain unconvinced by Bonner's suggestion that there was some sort of alliance between certain Donatists and Pelagians (p. 35).

177 For more on Paulinus's role in the events of 411, see Chapter 2.

SETTING THE STAGE

another that should be emphasized: the Pelagians were seen to be a threat to the very unity of the Church that was so eagerly sought by the Catholic leaders in 411. As Dunphy notes, "'Church Unity' was the slogan in Carthage in early 411."[178] It was in the midst of that campaign for unity that supporters of Pelagius and Caelestius began to accuse other Catholics in Carthage of being in a de facto state of doctrinal schism with the eastern churches.[179] As we have seen above, the Pelagians were immersed in social networks with a strong interest in the Christian past and the Christian East; moreover, they were known to be part of the circle of Rufinus's patrons and thus had access to eastern theological texts in translation. All these facts no doubt stoked the Pelagians' confidence in their own doctrinal views, convincing them that theirs was the theology supported by the Church's doctrinal tradition and by the Church in the East. And so, when they encountered opposition to their views, one of their reactions was to point out the apparent doctrinal disunity between their opponents and the East.[180] In the context of Carthage in 411, few accusations could have been more explosive. At the very moment when Catholic hopes for reunion with the Donatists were about to be realized, newcomers to the area had begun undermining the Catholics' very claims to catholicity by accusing them of holding to theological views that were not traditional, particular to Africa or to the West, and at odds with the great Churches of the East. In addition, those making these claims were funded by some of the wealthy Roman refugees now present in Africa. With the future of Italy uncertain, it was possible that these powerful patrons would be in Africa permanently—thus offering the potential both for a lasting source of funding for the Pelagian movement and for an even more deeply divided Africa.[181] In that context, it is easy to see why Marcellinus, charged with establishing unity in North Africa, would feel the need to intervene and to alert Augustine to the issues at hand.[182] In my view, the presence of such accusations of disunity helps to explain the sudden eruption of the Pelagian controversy, in the midst of intense focus on relations with the Donatists.

178 Dunphy, "A Lost Year," 464.

179 *gest. Pel.* 11.25.

180 The Pelagians may very well have deployed similar accusations while still in Rome; however, the particular situation in Carthage would have made such accusations more incendiary.

181 See Peter Brown's discussion of this contextual factor in *Eye of a Needle*, 360.

182 See Dunphy, "A Lost Year," 442.

CONCLUSION

This chapter has aimed to provide two important elements of background to the present study: first, the early development of the Pelagian movement and second, a survey of the politico-ecclesial landscape of North Africa in 411. My argument here has been that the beginnings of the Pelagian controversy in Carthage in 411 make the most sense when we acknowledge the importance of Pelagian accusations that their opponents' theology was divorced from the Church's doctrinal tradition and at odds with the doctrinal views held in the East. First and foremost, our exploration of the pre-history of Pelagianism has indicated the extent to which the early Pelagian movement developed within a social network interested in the Christian past and in the Christian East, fed, as it were, by Rufinus's translations. Within that setting, it becomes clear that the Pelagian accusation was not an idle or casual one, but one apparently well-researched and deeply engrained within the Pelagian movement's outlook. At the same time, our overview of the battle between the Donatists and the Catholics, and its climax in 411, indicates just how threatening such an accusation would have been to Catholic authorities devoting their full attention to Church unity. Indeed, the fact that Augustine remembers overhearing this accusation over five years later speaks to its importance.[183]

With this pre-history detailed, let us now turn to the heart of this study and analyze the progression of the controversy and Augustine's attempts to assert the universality and antiquity of the doctrinal views he championed against the Pelagians. As we do so, we shall see how the Pelagians' apparent threat to Church unity continued to play a central role in the controversy over the following two decades.

---

183 See *gest. Pel.* 11.25.

CHAPTER 2

A Controversy in Carthage

Having discussed the early development of the Pelagian movement and the political and ecclesial landscape of North Africa in 411, we can now turn in this and the following chapters to the heart of this study. Each chapter will focus on a particular period of the controversy and offer a historical account of that period.[1] In the midst of this historical account, we will analyze Augustine's major anti-Pelagian texts (as well as a few of his sermons and letters) to explore the ways in which he sought to respond to the threat to ecclesial unity he saw in the Pelagians. Doing so will indicate the extent to which this apparent threat to unity motivated and characterized Augustine's response to the Pelagians.

The present chapter is devoted to the beginnings of the Pelagian controversy in Africa in 411. As we shall see, it did not take long for Augustine to grow concerned with the danger the Pelagians posed for the ecclesial unity, especially due to their claims that their

---

1 Several other studies of the history of the controversy have been published, the most important of which remains Wermelinger, *Rom und Pelagius*. See also Stuart Squires's recent overview of the controversy, *The Pelagian Controversy*.

opponents had diverged from the Church's ancient and universal doctrinal tradition.

THE BEGINNINGS: PELAGIUS ARRIVES IN NORTH AFRICA AND CAELESTIUS IS BROUGHT TO COURT

As we mentioned in the introduction, the eruption of the Pelagian controversy in Africa was indirectly sparked by the sack of Rome.[2] Between late 408 and 410, Alaric and his Visigoths besieged Rome three times, with the final, brief siege leading to the sack of the city on August 24, 410. Over the course of these tumultuous years, droves of Romans fled their homes, with some crossing the Mediterranean and arriving at African ports such as Hippo Regius and Carthage. Among the Roman refugees who passed through Hippo was Pelagius, who likely arrived in Africa in the fall of 410.

Unfortunately, Augustine was out of town. He would later receive word, presumably upon his return to Hippo, that Pelagius had been welcomed and apparently had made no mention of anything about grace during his stay.[3] However, one detail of Pelagius's stay did seem odd to Augustine, at least upon later reflection. Pelagius, Augustine notes, "departed from [Hippo] more quickly than one might have expected."[4] Although he perhaps wished to avoid a personal encounter with the bishop of Hippo, Pelagius did leave a letter for Augustine, to which Augustine politely (and briefly) replied.[5] After leaving Hippo, Pelagius traveled to Carthage, where he remained for several months before departing once again around June 411, likely for Palestine. While Augustine saw Pelagius (from afar?) once or twice while he was in

---

2 The chronology of 411 is much debated in the scholarship. In this section, I have presented my own view of the sequence of events, which owes much to Walter Dunphy's proposal in "A Lost Year: Pelagianism in Carthage, 411 A.D.," *Augustinianum* 45 (2005): 389–466. For a more detailed examination (and defense) of the chronology presented here, please see the appendix at the end of this study.

3 See *gest. Pel.* 22.46. Recall that Augustine had already heard of potential issues surrounding Pelagius's view of grace. See Chapter 1.

4 *gest. Pel.* 22.46 (Latin: CSEL 42:100.16–17; English, Teske, WSA I/23, 354). Dunphy suggests that Pelagius may have heard that trouble was brewing in Carthage and departed quickly to attempt to calm the storm, as it were (see Dunphy, "A Lost Year," 463).

5 See Augustine, *ep.* 146. See also n. 31 in the appendix for more on this exchange.

Carthage in 411, they, for better or for worse, never had the opportunity for a serious conversation.[6]

Of course, it should be remembered that, from what we know, Pelagius had no overt role in the eruption of the so-called "Pelagian" controversy in Africa. That honor instead rests with Caelestius, often identified as a disciple of Pelagius.[7] Sometime after arriving in Carthage, Caelestius approached the diocesan authorities requesting ordination to the priesthood, perhaps in late 410 or early 411. At that time, it was typical for the suitability of a candidate for ordination to the priesthood to be examined by the leaders of the local Church, especially in the case of candidates from other dioceses.[8] In the course of this process, Paulinus, a deacon of the Church of Milan who was also present in Carthage,[9] submitted a *libellus* (which, in a juridical context, can refer to a formal legal brief[10]) to the diocesan authorities, accusing Caelestius of serious doctrinal error.

The precise motive behind Paulinus's action against Caelestius in Carthage is uncertain. Paulinus, the former secretary and future biographer of Ambrose, was present in Africa as the administrator of the Church of Milan's properties there,[11] a position that likely enabled him to develop a close working relationship with the authorities in Carthage, both secular and ecclesiastical. Some have suggested that Paulinus's action against Caelestius was undertaken at the request of the African authorities, who were troubled by Caelestius's views but perhaps felt it would be imprudent to present themselves so obviously as opponents of a rather well-connected Italian

---

6 "Later, I saw his face in Carthage once or twice, as I recall, when I was very busy with the preparations for the conference which we were about to hold with the Donatists" (*gest. Pel.* 22.46 [Latin: CSEL 42:100.17–19; English: Teske, WSA I/23, 354]).

7 For literature on Caelestius, see Chapter 1, n. 8.

8 See Dunphy, "A Lost Year," 395–96.

9 For more on Paulinus, see A. Paredi, "Paulinus of Milan," *Sacris Erudiri* 14 (1963): 206–30; É. Lamirande, "La datation de la *Vita Ambrosii* de Paulin de Milan," *Revue des Études Augustiniennes* 27 (1981): 44–55; E. Zocca, "La *Vita Ambrosii* alla luce dei rapporti fra Paolino, Agostino e Ambrogio," in *Nec timeo mori. Atti del Congresso internazionale di studi ambrosiani nel XVI centenario della morte di sant'Ambrogio. Milano, 4–11 aprile 1997*, ed. M. Rizzi and L. F. Pizzolato (Milan: Vita e Pensiero, 1998), 803–26; and Claire Sotinel, "Paulinus diaconus," in A-L 4, 537–40. My thanks to Giulio Malavasi and Anthony Dupont for sharing some insights on the role of Paulinus with me.

10 For more on "*libellus*" as a technical term, see Dunphy, "A Lost Year," 396n19.

11 See Arnobius Iunior, *Praedestinatus* 1.88.

refugee.[12] Alternatively, it could be that Paulinus had already encountered Caelestius and his ideas during his time in Italy (or perhaps more recently in Carthage) and was simply acting on his own initiative in submitting his accusation to Aurelius, the bishop of Carthage.[13] A third possibility is that Paulinus had acted at the behest of some segment of the Roman refugees who were opposed to Caelestius in Carthage. Given the state of the evidence, it is impossible to know for sure. But Paulinus's actions might very well be explained by a combination of all three options. Indeed, it seems appropriate to connect Paulinus's actions with the controversy surrounding Pelagius and his circle in Rome. When Rome was sacked, key participants on both sides of that debate likely ended up in Carthage, where they would no doubt have continued their conversations (perhaps in a more "heated" way than earlier, given the stress of the times!). It is not hard to imagine that the Roman anti-Pelagian party would have sought to torpedo Caelestius's candidacy for the priesthood. Paulinus, a native Italian likely with solid connections to the local ecclesiastical leadership, would have been a well-placed advocate for their cause—especially if he were already aware of and opposed to Pelagius's circle. It is worth noting that in the extant fragment of the acts of Caelestius's trial, Paulinus betrays a certain intensity and perhaps even personal animus in his exchanges with Caelestius, to the point that Aurelius has to intervene calmly to explain one of Paulinus's accusations.[14] This could indicate some "prior history" between Paulinus and Caelestius. Or it could simply be a courtroom performance on Paulinus's part—or even a "good cop/bad cop" routine planned by both Paulinus and Aurelius. In any event, Aurelius and the other African authorities may have welcomed Paulinus's accusations against Caelestius. Once informed of Caelestius's views (and the accusations of heresy and disunity his associates were circulating), the Africans would probably have been opposed to his candidacy for the priesthood anyway— but the fact that it was the Italian Paulinus who had accused Caelestius would have provided the Africans with the plausible deniability that they needed

---

12 See, e.g., Wermelinger, *Rom und Pelagius*, 8.

13 See discussion in Picard-Mawji, "Le passage," 8. It seems likely that Paulinus was still in Italy in 405 (Lamirande, "La datation," 51); thus, he could very well have been aware of the debates surrounding Pelagius's and his circle's views. Mention can be made here of the possible anti-Pelagian context of Paulinus's writing of the *Vita Ambrosii*; however, this possibility depends on the dating of the work, which remains the subject of debate. See Zocca, "La *Vita Ambrosii*," and Lamirande, "La datation."

14 See *gr. et pecc. or.* 2.3.3–2.4.3.

A CONTROVERSY IN CARTHAGE

to avoid the appearance of public opposition to a well-connected Roman.[15] Indeed, as we shall note again below, African authorities like Aurelius and Augustine were distinctly resistant at this stage to being perceived publicly as opponents of Caelestius and Pelagius.[16]

Whatever the story behind Paulinus's actions, his *libellus* had its intended effect: a hearing or trial (*iudicium*)[17] was scheduled, perhaps in February 411, where Caelestius had to defend himself before Aurelius of Carthage and several other bishops for allegedly teaching the following six propositions:

1. Adam was created mortal such that he was going to die whether he sinned or not.

2. The sin of Adam harmed him alone and not the human race.

3. Newborns are in that state in which Adam was before the transgression.

4. The entire race of human beings does not die through the death or transgression of Adam nor does the entire race of human beings rise again through the resurrection of Christ.

5. The Law leads one to the kingdom of heaven just as the Gospel does.

6. Even before the advent of the Lord there were sinless people—i.e., people without sin.[18]

---

15 Paulinus, thanks to his actions in 411, would remain tied to the African anti-Pelagian campaign. We will return to Paulinus when we discuss the events of 417 in Chapter 4.

16 Augustine and Aurelius, for example, agreed not to attack their opponents by name (*gest. Pel.* 22.46). We might also point to Augustine's cautious engagement with Pelagius's *Expositiones* in *pecc. mer.* 3. Of course, it remains possible that the later hesitancy to critique Pelagius and Caelestius by name was the fruit of backlash Aurelius had received after Caelestius's trial.

17 It is probably better to think of this as a hearing or trial rather than a "council" as it is sometimes termed in the literature. See Dunphy, "A Lost Year," 432–33.

18 Marius Mercator, *Commonitorium super nomine Caelestii* 2: *Adam mortalem factum, qui siue peccaret siue non peccaret, moriturus fuisset; quoniam peccatum Adae ipsum solum laesit et non genus humanum; quoniam paruuli qui nascuntur, in eo statu sunt, in quo Adam fuit ante praeuaricationem; quoniam neque per mortem uel praeuaricationem Adae omne genus hominum moriatur neque per resurrectionem Christi omne genus hominum resurgat; quoniam lex sic mittit ad regnum caelorum quomodo et euangelium; quoniam et ante aduentum domini fuerunt homines inpeccabiles, id est sine peccato* (Latin: ACO 1.5.1, p. 66, ln. 9–17; English: my translation). In *gest. Pel.* 11.23, Augustine reproduces a version of the same list as he found it in the proceedings of the Synod of Diospolis (where the accusations against Caelestius were lodged against Pelagius). See also *gr. et pecc. or.* 2.2.2–2.4.4 and 2.11.12. Neither the version in Mercator nor that found at *gest. Pel.* 11.23 offer the original Latin wording of the propositions as the lists found in those texts were translated from the original Latin into Greek and then

Perhaps in preparation for the trial (or at some point in the midst of the process), Caelestius submitted his own *libellus*, albeit a very brief one, in which he sought to defend his orthodoxy by affirming that infants are in need of redemption through baptism.[19] At the trial itself, he refused to condemn any of the propositions. Based on an extant fragment of the trial's minutes,[20] we know that Caelestius insisted that infants needed baptism, but also admitted to having doubts that Adam's sin was transmitted to his descendants. He defended himself by stating that this issue was an open question and that he knew priests who held a variety of positions on the topic. Significantly, after being pressed by Paulinus to name a priest who rejected the transmission of sin, Caelestius referred to "the holy priest Rufinus"—who, as we noted in Chapter 1, could very well have been Rufinus of Aquileia.[21] In the end, Caelestius's attempts at self-defense failed to convince his judges, and, as Augustine would later write, he received a "sentence worthy of his perversity"—although the exact nature of the conclusion of the trial would later be called into question.[22]

At some point in the midst of this controversy over Caelestius's views, Flavius Marcellinus, the imperial official who had been sent to Carthage to adjudicate the reunification efforts between Catholics and Donatists at the Conference of June 411, wrote to Augustine in Hippo requesting his thoughts on the disputed questions.

---

back into Latin again, likely resulting in some verbal changes. The original Latin wording of propositions 2 and 3 is found at *gr. et pecc. or.* 2.2.2–2.3.3, where Augustine includes an excerpt from the *acta* of Caelestius's *iudicium* at Carthage in 411. A slightly different list is offered at *Praedestinatus* 1.88. For discussion of these propositions, see, e.g., Wermelinger, *Rom und Pelagius*, 9ff., and Honnay, "Caelestius, discipulus Pelagii," 274–79. The source of these propositions is a bit unclear, although the *Praedestinatus* indicates that at least some of them were drawn from Caelestius's books. Nevertheless, it seems likely that the propositions as we have them were paraphrases. Indeed at *gr. et pecc. or.* 2.4.3 Aurelius must clarify the meaning of one of the propositions for Caelestius, which would seem to indicate that it was not a direct quotation.

19 See *pecc. mer.* 1.34.63 and *ep.* 175.6.

20 See *gr. et pecc. or.* 2.3.3–2.4.3.

21 See *gr. et pecc. or.* 2.3.3.

22 See *gest. Pel.* 22.46 (Latin: CSEL 42:100.23; English: Teske, WSA I/23, 354) and discussion of Caelestius's appeals in Chapter 4.

THE THEOLOGICAL DEBATE AT CARTHAGE

Before turning to Augustine's entrance into the controversy, it seems worthwhile to pause for a moment to sketch out the contours of the theological debate at Carthage, at least as far as they can be reconstructed from extant sources. A key source of information here is a brief report Augustine includes in the third book of his response to Marcellinus, *De peccatorum meritis et remissione*, where he notes that he had set out to write the first two books in response to the questions Marcellinus had sent him. Augustine writes,

> You had proposed some questions to me so that I would write something to you against those who say that Adam, even if he had not sinned, would have died and that nothing of his sin passed to his descendants via generation (especially in light of the baptism of little ones, which the universal Church celebrates in a most tender and maternal manner), and that there are, have been, and will be children of men who have absolutely no sin in this life.[23]

In this sense, Marcellinus's request seems to have centered on a couple major issues: (1) Adam's sin and its effects (and the implications of these effects for understanding the practice of infant baptism) and (2) the possibility of sinlessness. It is no stretch to infer that these were the issues at the heart of the debate in Carthage. Indeed, we can readily see the connection between Marcellinus's questions and Propositions 1, 2, 3, 4, and 6, listed by Paulinus in his *libellus*. This is further confirmed by what we find in Augustine's earliest anti-Pelagian efforts: *De peccatorum meritis* and *ss.* 293 and 294, as we shall see below. In addition, a brief note at the end of *De peccatorum meritis* 2, in which Augustine addresses the topic of the origin of the soul, suggests that this, too, was a topic of debate in Carthage.[24]

On the whole, there is a clear connection between this debate in Carthage and the earlier Roman phase of the controversy; however, an expansion of the debate to new (albeit adjacent) topical areas also seems to have taken place. Indeed, Propositions 2–4 deal explicitly with the theme of Adam's sin and deny that that sin had been transmitted to the rest of the human race or had damaged human nature in some way—a topic that had already been

---

23 *pecc. mer.* 3.1.1 (Latin: CSEL 60:128.17–21; English: my translation).

24 See *pecc. mer.* 2.36.59, where Augustine essentially admits his uncertainty. Marcellinus wrote to Jerome around this time to request his opinion on the origin of the soul, who in turn referred him back to Augustine (see *ep.* 165 among the letters of Augustine for Jerome's response to Marcellinus). See Dunphy's discussion: "A Lost Year," 440–46.

debated in Rome, as we have seen. Again, Proposition 6, which speaks to the possibility of sinlessness in this life, offers us a topic that, as we noted in Chapter 1, was at the heart of Pelagius's project. In addition, the issue of the origin of the soul seems to have already been connected with the topic of Adam's sin and its transmission in Rome, as the arguments reported in Pelagius's *Expositiones* indicate.[25] On the other hand, Propositions 1 and 5 seem to address topics that were not among the chief points of debate in Rome, at least as far as we can tell. Nevertheless, Proposition 5 is linked to Pelagius: in his *Expositiones*, Pelagius divides salvation history into three stages and suggests that there was a mechanism for salvation proper to each of those three stages (so, in the first stage, the law of nature led people to live good lives; in the second, it was the Mosaic law; in the third, the Gospel).[26] On the other hand, Proposition 1 does not appear to have a direct antecedent in Pelagius—although it is worth noting that when Pelagius speaks about death as a consequence of Adam's sin in the *Expositiones*, he means *spiritual* death rather than physical death.[27] It seems plausible to think that some, objecting to Pelagius's and Caelestius's views on the effects (or lack thereof) of Adam's sin on human nature, had pointed to the universality of physical death as evidence to the contrary. This objection may very well have prompted some in Pelagius's circle (Caelestius?) to hypothesize that physical death was not a punishment for the sin of Adam. Interestingly, writing in 418, Augustine reports that his opponents no longer hold that Adam would have suffered physical death even if he had not sinned.[28] This report reinforces the sense that this position was one originally taken up on the fly, as it were. Thus, what we seem to be uncovering here are some back-and-forth exchanges that

---

25 See Pelagius, *Expositio in Romanos* 5:15 (a translation of the relevant passage is available in Chapter 1, n. 38).

26 See, e.g., Pelagius's comments on Rom 10:5. For more on this theme in the *Expositiones*, see Matteoli, *Alle origini della teologia di Pelagio*, 39–53. See also *nat. et gr.* 2.2, where we find what appears to be an Augustinian summary of Pelagius's thought on the capacity of those who have not heard of Christ to attain eternal life. See also *gr. et pecc. or.* 2.26.30.

27 See, e.g., Pelagius's comments on Rom 5:12: "*And so death passed into all men in that all have sinned.* When they sin in this way, they likewise die in this way: for it did not pass into Abraham, Isaac, and Jacob, about whom the Lord says, 'For to him they all are alive.' But he says 'all' are dead here because among the multitude of sinners mention is not made of the few just people, as in this passage: 'There is not one person who does good, not even one' and 'Every man is a liar.' Or: Death passed into all those people who were living in a human and not a heavenly manner" (Latin: Souter, *Pelagius's Expositions*, 2:45; English: my translation).

28 See *ep.* 193.12.

A CONTROVERSY IN CARTHAGE

were part of the debate in Rome or Carthage: some more "central" Pelagian positions were objected to and responses of varying quality, probably from various parties, were offered to these objections. The fact that this position (rejecting the view that physical death is a punishment for Adam's sin) seems to have been later abandoned suggests that it was not very well thought-through, but likely was conjured up in the heat of a debate—perhaps in Carthage, or perhaps earlier in Rome.[29]

Other fragments of the early debate over Pelagianism can be observed when we turn to another disputed question: the purpose and effects of infant baptism. Although the topic of infant baptism does not appear explicitly in the list of propositions Paulinus included in his *libellus*, it seems clear, based on (1) Marcellinus's questions to Augustine and (2) the content of the *libellus* Caelestius himself had submitted to his episcopal judges, that it was a major focus of the debate in Carthage in 411. Here, too, we see continuity between the debate at Carthage and the debate at Rome. Indeed, in his *Expositiones*, one of the arguments against the transmission of sin that Pelagius reports in his comment on Rom 5:15 deals with baptism: "If baptism cleanses that ancient sin, those who are born from two baptized parents should not have this sin. For these parents could not transmit to their children what they do not at all have themselves."[30] This argument reads as a response to an anti-Pelagian objection. Likely, the Pelagians' opponents in Rome had argued that their denial of the transmission of Adam's sin would render infant baptism unnecessary or pointless. This line of argument seems to have resurfaced in Carthage. In this context, it is worth noting that various Pelagians seem to have responded to this argument in different, and sometimes mutually exclusive, ways.[31] First of all, to account for the necessity of infant baptism, a few different explanations seem to have circulated. Some floated the idea that there was a distinction between the kingdom of heaven and eternal life, such that unbaptized infants would gain eternal life if they died, while only

---

29 Later, in *De haeresibus*, Augustine once again includes this position in his list of key Pelagian views. Did Augustine discover new evidence that (some of) the Pelagians did, in fact, hold this position? Or was he simply summarizing the chief points of the debate in Carthage in 411?

30 Pelagius, *Expositio in Romanos* 5:15 (Latin: Souter, *Pelagius's Expositions*, 2:47; English: my translation).

31 See Augustine's comments on the contradictory positions held by the Pelagians at *pecc. mer.* 1.34.64.

baptized infants would be admitted into the kingdom of heaven.[32] Others, perhaps perceiving that this distinction was problematic, suggested that infants had sins of their own that needed to be forgiven.[33] Still others seem to have suggested that infants received baptism not for the forgiveness of sins but for sanctification in Christ.[34] At the same time, it seems like the Pelagians also went on the offense, critiquing the notion of the transmission of sin from several points of view—for example, as we quoted above, questioning why, if this transmitted sin were the reason for infant baptism, children born of baptized parents would need to be baptized.[35] These varied and sometimes conflicting positions betray a significant amount of back and forth and debate—even before Augustine became involved.

We should draw attention to one final significant detail about the debate in Carthage: the topic of grace does not seem to have played any significant role, as far as we can tell. None of the propositions submitted by Paulinus touch on grace explicitly. We could possibly recognize a certain connection between Proposition 5 (on the Law and Gospel) and the topic of grace—but it is certainly far from explicit.[36] Instead, it seems to have been Augustine who introduced this topic—namely, in a section at the beginning of *De*

32 See, e.g., *pecc. mer.* 1.30.58. F. Refoulé believes that this distinction was not actually proposed by the Pelagians but rather had its source in Augustine's good faith attempt to clarify his opponents' view that infants go neither to the kingdom of heaven nor to hell—see "La distinction 'Royaume de Dieu—Vie éternelle' est-elle pélagienne?" *Recherches de science religieuse* 51 (1963): 247–54. However, Refoulé's argument seems to rely in large part on an attempt to compare Augustine's characterization of this position with a section of the *Liber de fide*, which Refoulé believed to be one of Augustine's key sources in *pecc. mer.* However, this view has fallen out of favor, with more scholars now holding that the *Liber de fide* was not a source for Augustine in *pecc. mer.* Refoulé also seems not to consider as fully as he might have the possibility that Augustine had multiple sources for his information about the debate in Carthage—and that some of his sources may have reported debates on the ground. But this is, in my view, precisely the sense one gets from Augustine's comments on the contradictory views circulating in Carthage (*pecc. mer.* 1.34.64).

33 See *pecc. mer.* 1.34.63. Augustine finds this position rather laughably bad. But it is worth noting that one of Pelagius's sources for his *Expositiones*—the Anonymous Commentary now extant in a Budapest manuscript—seems to have floated a similar notion (see Matteoli, *Alle origini della teologia*, 103–4).

34 See *pecc. mer.* 3.6.12.

35 See also *pecc. mer.* 2.9.11, 2.25.39, 2.25.41, and 2.30.49 for a few more arguments of this sort.

36 It seems more likely that Proposition 5 was found problematic simply because it seemed to equate the Law and the Gospel.

peccatorum meritis 2.[37] Indeed, some evidence in support of this hypothesis is found in the fact that Marcellinus (or others in his circle who read Augustine's work) seems to have been thoroughly confused by Augustine's take on sinlessness—so much so that Augustine needed to write a sequel, *De spiritu et littera*, to clarify his position on grace and the possibility of avoiding sin. Nevertheless, this section at the beginning of *De peccatorum meritis* 2 is particularly significant as it is there that Augustine refers to his prayer from the tenth book of the *Confessiones—da quod iubes et iube quod uis*—a prayer that had apparently provoked Pelagius's anger at Rome.[38] In that same section, Augustine also emphasizes the importance of reading the sixth petition from the Lord's Prayer ("Lead us not into temptation") as evidence of the need for grace to avoid sin. A few years later, Augustine will mention that he had been told by a friend who had debated the Pelagians in Rome that they, the Pelagians, had interpreted this petition in a problematic way (i.e., as though it were just a petition to avoid unfortunate events over which we have no control).[39] All of this suggests that Augustine had, already in 411, made the connection between the controversy in Rome and the recent events at Carthage—and that his emphasis on grace in *De peccatorum meritis* 2 was inspired by the rumors he had heard.[40]

AUGUSTINE ENTERS THE CONTROVERSY

After Augustine received Marcellinus's request, he seems to have set to work gathering information about the debate at Carthage. He acquired a copy of a book by either Caelestius himself or someone in his circle, as well as Caelestius's *libellus* from his trial.[41] At some point in the midst of this information-gathering, Augustine traveled to Carthage for the Conference with the Donatists, perhaps arriving in April or May of 411. Despite being busy with preparations for the Conference, Augustine seems to have found time to read the acts of Caelestius's trial and speak with Aurelius about the situation. By the end of June 411, Augustine had completed an initial response to Marcellinus: the first two books of *De peccatorum meritis et remissione*

---

37 See *pecc. mer.* 2.2.2–2.5.6.

38 See discussion of this episode in Chapter 1.

39 See *s.* 348A.11.

40 For additional discussion of this point, see my "Heresiology and Reality."

41 See the appendix for more.

et de baptismo paruulorum. A few days later, though, Augustine gained access to Pelagius's *Expositiones* in which he discovered a new argument regarding infant baptism that he had not considered in the first two books of *De peccatorum meritis*. As a result, he began composing a supplement to the work for Marcellinus that would eventually become its third book. In these same days at the end of June, Augustine delivered a few sermons in Carthage touching on the controversial issues at the request of the Aurelius, the bishop of Carthage.[42] Augustine likely remained in Carthage for several more months, perhaps departing for Hippo in late September. By early 412, he had still not yet completed the third book of *De peccatorum meritis*, but likely would do so shortly thereafter.[43]

Before turning to Augustine's first responses to the controversy in Carthage, it would be good first and foremost to make a few comments on the significance of certain aspects of Augustine's entrance into the controversy. Indeed—contrary to the assertions of some earlier scholarship[44]—we should recognize that Augustine entered into the controversy with a good deal of preparation and research: his response to Marcellinus was based not only on whatever Marcellinus had reported in his letter (which is now lost, unfortunately), but also on the book (by Caelestius?) he had read; Caelestius's *libellus*; the acts of Caelestius's trial; and, perhaps, other sources. Even more importantly, Augustine crafted his response with a view to the situation on the ground in Carthage in 411. He likely wrote the bulk of the first two books of *De peccatorum meritis* in Carthage and also delivered several sermons there that summer at the request of the bishop Aurelius. In this sense, his initial

---

42 See *ss*. 293 (delivered on June 24), 294 (delivered on June 27), and 299 (delivered on June 29). *Ss*. 293 and 294 are typically dated to 413 (and *s*. 299 either to 413 or 418), but it seems to me that they are better dated to 411. See the appendix for more.

43 For some discussion of this delay in completing the third book, see appendix, n. 73.

44 See, e.g., Peter Brown's comments in *Augustine of Hippo*, 345. See also Walter Dunphy's discussion of the matter at "A Lost Year," 403. Also helpful are Dunphy's comments at "Unexplored Paths," 29: "When Augustine began to preach and write against the Pelagians he was already aware of their views, and this new development in which a leading Pelagian had been accused of (and condemned for?) heresy must be taken into account when we read his first anti-Pelagian sermons and writings. It is not merely a question of adjusting the date of an event by a matter of a few months. At stake is our understanding of Augustine's knowledge of Pelagian teaching when he began to take the Pelagians to task. This vital year in an unfolding crisis in Western Christendom has been glossed over with an account of events that does not stand up to scrutiny, and with that account we have been given an image of Augustine that does him little justice."

A CONTROVERSY IN CARTHAGE

responses to the Pelagians were well-informed not only about his opponents' doctrinal views but also about the particular arguments they were making in Carthage in 411. Notably, in *De gestis Pelagii* (written in late 416 or early 417), after recalling Marcellinus's initial request to write *De peccatorum meritis* as well as his own decision to cite Cyprian in *s.* 294, Augustine reports, "Certain people who held to such [Pelagian] views were trying so hard to persuade some of our brothers of these views that they were threatening that, if they did not support them, they would be condemned by the judgment of the eastern churches."[45] Walter Dunphy has rightly suggested that it was precisely within the context of this alleged disagreement with the eastern churches that Marcellinus called upon Augustine to enter the debate in early 411.[46] Indeed, as Dunphy notes, Marcellinus's role in the events of 411 cannot be explained only by the fact that he was a concerned Catholic layman. Rather, it should also be understood as an element of Marcellinus's broader mission in North Africa: to bring about unity in the African church.[47] At the very time when one schism was about to be healed (that with the Donatists), another threatened to replace it. As a result, it would be plausible to conjecture that Augustine's decision to enter the fray at the request of Marcellinus and Aurelius was likewise motivated in large part by these concerns over unity and the potential for further schism. If this was, in fact, one of Augustine's main motivations, we would expect to see in his earliest responses to the Pelagians a desire not only to combat the Pelagian views, but to ground his own views securely in the Church's ancient and universal doctrinal tradition. Let us turn now to Augustine's earliest anti-Pelagian efforts—*pecc. mer. 1–2, ss.* 293 and 294, and *pecc. mer.* 3—to see whether this hypothesis holds up under scrutiny.

---

45 *gest. Pel.* 11.25 (Latin: CSEL 42:79.6–9; English: my translation). Further, in *s.* 294, Augustine reports that the Pelagians were accusing their opponents of novelty (see *s.* 294.19). It is also worth noting the possibility that even in 411 the views of Ambrose were being cited by the Pelagians as evidence in their favor: see Vittorino Grossi, "Il ricorso ad Ambrogio nell'*Opus imperfectum contra Iulianum* di Agostino d'Ippona," in *Giuliano d'Eclano e l'Hirpinia Christiana: Atti del convegno 4–6 giugno 2003* (Napoli: Arte Tipografica, 2004), 115, for this suggestion. At *pecc. mer.* 2.13.19—2.14.21 Augustine addresses the fact that the Pelagians were citing the case of Elizabeth and Zechariah (who are described as blameless in Luke 1:6) as evidence for the possibility of sinlessness in this life. As we shall see in Chapter 3, Pelagius cites Ambrose's commentary on this passage in the section of his *De natura* that offers patristic testimony in support of his views. Was Ambrose's authority being invoked in 411? If so, it stands to reason that it would have increased Augustine's concern greatly.

46 See Dunphy, "A Lost Year," 442.

47 See Dunphy, "A Lost Year," 440ff.

DE PECCATORUM MERITIS ET REMISSIONE 1–2

Augustine completed the first two books of *De peccatorum meritis*, at the latest, a few days before June 27, 411. Thus, they contain what was likely Augustine's first response to the controversy in Carthage. Broadly speaking, these books are Augustine's reply to the various questions supplied to him by Marcellinus, as well as the various Pelagian documents and information he was able to obtain. Augustine divides this reply into two parts: the first book deals mainly with the topic of the sin of Adam and its effects, especially in relation to infant baptism; the second book then turns to the issue of sinlessness and its possibility in this life.[48]

Book 1

Augustine begins his reply in the first book by addressing a view apparently promoted by Caelestius: that Adam would have died even if he had not sinned.[49] Augustine's reply to this view is, in the main, founded on scriptural bases, which he uses to undermine his opponent's position.[50] However, he soon turns to a set of more concerning issues that will occupy his attention for the remainder of Book 1: (1) the Pelagians' rejection of the notion that Adam's sin is in some way transmitted to his progeny via propagation and (2) the impact of this rejection on the rationale for infant baptism. These views are introduced at *pecc. mer.* 1.9.9, where Augustine considers an interpretation of Rom 5:12 ("Through one man sin entered the world and through sin death and thus it was passed on to all human beings in whom all have sinned") apparently offered by Caelestius or others in his general orbit.[51] They advanced that, in this verse, Paul referred not to the transmission of some sort of hereditary sin, but rather to the transmission of sin via imitation: Adam's sin is passed on to all insofar as all imitate him in sinning. As a result, Augustine relates, "they are even unwilling to believe that, in the case of little ones, original sin is removed through baptism because they

---

48 See Augustine's own summary of his efforts in the first two books at *pecc. mer.* 3.1.1.

49 See *pecc. mer.* 1.2.2. See also Proposition 1 from Paulinus's *libellus* above.

50 A response to this position is also given briefly in *s.* 299, likely delivered on June 29, 411.

51 Note that this interpretation is also found in Pelagius's comment in his *Expositiones* on Rom 5:12.

A CONTROVERSY IN CARTHAGE   89

contend that there is no sin at all in newborns."[52] In this sense, Augustine is
quick to connect the Pelagians' rejection of original sin with their view of
infant baptism. We should pause to consider this point briefly. Given what
Augustine indicates throughout the remainder of Book 1, it seems likely
that Caelestius, Pelagius, and others surrounding them had no established
position on the purpose of infant baptism, although they admitted that
babies should be baptized.[53] As a result, and as we have already noted above,
one gets the sense that their views on this issue were developed somewhat
on the fly in response to their opponents' objections to their dismissal of
original sin—objections that cited the practice of infant baptism as evidence
against the Pelagian viewpoint.[54] In this sense, while Augustine did not invent
this argumentative strategy, he was more than happy to take it up himself.
Indeed, he quickly turns to the practice of infant baptism as evidence when
he begins to problematize the Pelagian opposition to any sort of hereditary
transmission of the sin of Adam.

In the first lines of his response, Augustine notes that if Rom 5:12 had
indicated the transmission of sin via imitation, then Adam certainly would
not have been the person imitated. Indeed, if the transmission of Adam's sin
occurred via imitation, then Paul would not have said "one man" in Rom
5:12, but rather "the devil"—who was the first sinner. Of course, Augustine
does admit that all humans can be said to imitate Adam when they sin, just
as they can be said to imitate Christ when they act righteously. Nevertheless,
Christ gives humanity more than just a good model for imitation: he also
grants grace to human beings, enabling them to work righteously. This grace,
Augustine notes, is clearly revealed in the practice of infant baptism:

---

52 *pecc. mer.* 1.9.9 (Latin: CSEL 60:10.16–18; English: my translation).

53 See, e.g., *pecc. mer.* 1.26.39 and *s.* 294.2. Nevertheless, Augustine certainly suspects that at
least some of them only grant this because to reject it would undeniably make them heretics
(*pecc. mer.* 3.13.22).

54 At *pecc. mer.* 1.17.22, after mentioning that some of the Pelagians had apparently floated
the idea that infants are forgiven of *personal* sins in baptism, Augustine notes, "These people
were themselves driven to say this, unless I am mistaken, as a result of some other position
they previously adopted. That is, they must admit that sins are forgiven in baptism, and they
refuse to admit that there is a sin derived from Adam which they concede that the little ones
are forgiven. Hence, they are forced to accuse infants of sin, as if they are safer in accusing
infants by the very fact that the accused cannot speak in their own defense" (Latin: CSEL
60:22.3–8; English: Teske, WSA I/23, 45).

By this grace he brings into his body even infants who have been baptized—and they are certainly not yet able to imitate anyone. Therefore, just as he in whom all are brought to life—in addition to offering himself as an example for righteousness to those imitating him—gives the most hidden grace of his spirit to the faithful and pours out this grace also on infants, so too he in whom all die—in addition to being an example of imitation for those who transgress by their will the precept of the Lord—corrupts in himself all who are to come from his lineage by the hidden corruption of carnal concupiscence.[55]

Here, then, Augustine artfully problematizes the Pelagian position by referring to the theological principles that undergird the practice of infant baptism. But note how Augustine's argument is structured. Before he offers any extensive exegesis of Rom 5:12 and its surrounding verses (which he will do shortly: *pecc. mer.* 1.10.12–15.20), Augustine addresses what appears to have been the underlying Pelagian concern about original sin: that is, that it would be unjust for Adam's sin to affect the moral status of other human beings who have not (yet) willed to participate in that sin (through imitation). Infant baptism, and the sacramental theology associated with it, offers Augustine evidence for the validity of the theological "mechanics" involved in the transmission of original sin: since in baptism the moral status of infants is affected by someone else's action (Christ's) without any imitation of Christ on the infants' part, so too, in birth, infants' moral status can be affected by someone else's action (Adam's) without any imitation of Adam by these infants. In this way, Augustine grounds his defense of the "mechanics" of the transmission of original sin not simply in a compelling exegetical exposition, but first and foremost in a common practice of the Church, a practice that even his opponents admit is valid and important, and a practice that Augustine believed to be rooted in the ancient and universal tradition of the Church.[56]

After offering an interpretation of Rom 5:12–21 at *pecc. mer.* 1.10.12–15.20, where he argues that Paul teaches the transmission of sin via propagation, Augustine turns back to the topic of baptism. Augustine notes that, given Paul's comments in Romans, Christians must believe that Adam's sin infects his progeny even without their imitation and, thus, that infants are in need of baptism, not due to their own personal sins, but due to original sin. However,

---

55 *pecc. mer.* 1.9.10 (Latin: CSEL 60:11.13–20; English: my translation).

56 Of course, Augustine's assumption that the practice of infant baptism was undeniably apostolic in origin would be questioned by many scholars today.

A CONTROVERSY IN CARTHAGE 91

the Pelagians have put forward another argument: that infants are baptized not for the forgiveness of sins, but so as to enter the kingdom of God.[57] This particular position, and its corollaries, will occupy Augustine's attention for much of the rest of Book 1. Augustine begins his response by pointing out that the advocates of this position find themselves in a bind when they go on to propose that unbaptized infants who have died will attain eternal life. No Christian, Augustine says, would grant this. After the citation of a few passages from Paul that problematize this notion, Augustine turns to his readers, asking them to reflect on a common Christian practice:

> But if infants have not been hurt by any illness of original sin, why are they carried to Christ the physician (that is, to receive the sacrament of eternal salvation) due to the holy fear of those running with them and why is it not said to them in the Church: "Take these innocents away from here! The healthy have no need for a doctor, but the sick! Christ did not come to call the just, but sinners"? Never has such a false statement been said, never is it said, absolutely never will it be said in the Church of Christ.[58]

Here, Augustine appeals to two pieces of evidence: (1) the pious practices of parents who rush with their infants to the Church to have them baptized and

---

57 See *pecc. mer.* 1.18.23. Augustine reports a few years later in 418 that Pelagius was reputed to have said, "I know where little ones who die without baptism do not go; I do not know where they go" (*sine baptismo paruuli morientes, quo non eant, scio; quo eant, nescio*) (*gr. et pecc. or.* 2.21.23 [Latin: CSEL 42:182.13–14; English: Teske, WSA I/23, 430])—which Augustine interprets to mean that Pelagius knew such unbaptized infants could not enter the kingdom of heaven but was unsure where they went instead. One gets the sense that Pelagius and those associated with him did not spend much time reflecting on the purpose of infant baptism until it was raised as evidence against their views in Rome and later in Carthage. It was at that point, presumably, that they needed to provide some sort of account for the practice, and various solutions were offered.

58 *pecc. mer.* 1.18.23: *si nulla originalis peccati aegritudine sauciati sunt, quomodo ad medicum Christum, hoc est ad percipiendum sacramentum salutis aeternae, suorum currentium pio timore portantur et non eis in ecclesia dicitur: auferte hinc innocentes istos. non est opus sanis medicus, sed male habentibus. non uenit Christus uocare iustos, sed peccatores numquam dictum est, numquam dicitur, numquam omnino dicetur in ecclesia Christi tale commentum* (Latin: CSEL 60:23.14–21; English: my translation). Note that I have replaced the CSEL's *curantium* with the reading found in all the manuscripts, *currentium*—a reading the has clear parallels in Augustine's anti-Pelagian works. See Delaroche's comments at "Notes complémentaires," 460–62, where he also suggests this emendation and identifies some of these parallels: *ep. Io. tr.* 4.11; *en. Ps.* 50.10; *ss.* 174.7, 176.2, 293.10, 294.18; *Gn. litt.* 10.11.19; *ep.* 166.7.21; *Io. eu. tr.* 38.6. To these, *s.* 183.12, *nupt. et conc.* 2.2.4, and *c. Iul.* 1.7.31 and 6.7.17 might be added (see Harmless, "Christ the Pediatrician," 23n59). For a rare example of this before the Pelagian controversy, see *c. litt. Pet.* 2.101.232.

(2) the Church's reception of these infants for baptism. In so doing, Augustine highlights the widespread belief among the faithful that even infants need baptism to obtain eternal life—as well as the Church's recognition of and support for that belief. Augustine appeals to this example of popular piety frequently in his anti-Pelagian works.[59] He does so, I suggest, because, once again, he is attempting to ground his theological views not simply in his own exegesis (which could easily be disputed by his opponents), but in a concrete, widespread practice that, he argues, the Church has always supported.

A similar argumentative tactic is deployed shortly thereafter. After asserting that a necessary part of baptism is repentance, Augustine notes that his opponents might dispute this in the case of infants, who appear developmentally incapable of expressing repentance. In response, Augustine again refers to the practice of the Church:

> If [infants] should not be called repentant, because they do not yet have a mind capable of repentance, they should not be called believers, because they likewise do not yet have a mind capable of believing. But if they are correctly called believers, because they in some sense profess the faith by the words of those bearing them, why should we not also first regard them as repentant, since we see that they renounce the devil and this world by the words of these same people bearing them?[60]

Here, Augustine once again counters a Pelagian argument by appealing to the custom of the Church—in this case, the custom of identifying infants as believers despite the fact that they are too young to profess the faith personally. Augustine deploys this custom as evidence to demonstrate that, similarly, infants should be recognized as repentant, given that repentance is expressed on their behalf through their sponsors' renunciation of the devil and this world.

A little later, Augustine again addresses the view that unbaptized infants might obtain eternal life. Noting that John 3:3 ("Unless one has been born again, one will not see the kingdom of God") limits the kingdom of God to the baptized but says nothing about eternal life, Augustine, nevertheless,

---

59 See, e.g., the citations in the previous footnote.

60 *pecc. mer.* 1.19.25 (Latin: CSEL 60:24.23–25.3; English: Teske, WSA I/23, 47, slightly modified). Augustine emphasizes a few sections later that "the rule of the Church . . . includes baptized infants among the faithful" (*pecc. mer.* 1.20.28 [Latin: CSEL 60:27.11–13; English: Teske, WSA I/23, 49]). See also his comments at *pecc. mer.* 1.25.38.

A CONTROVERSY IN CARTHAGE

93

asserts that there is no difference between the kingdom, salvation, and eternal life. To prove this, he first turns to John 6:54 ("Unless you eat my flesh and drink my blood, you will not have life in you"):

> [The Pelagians] do, of course, have a place in which to take refuge and hide, because the Lord did not say, "Unless one has been reborn of water and the Spirit, one will not have life," but said, "one will not enter into the kingdom of heaven." For if he had said the former, no doubt could arise on this point. Let the doubt, then, be removed; let us, I say, listen to the Lord, not to the suspicions and conjectures of mortals. Let us listen to the Lord, I say, as he speaks, not about the sacrament of the holy bath, but of the sacrament of his holy table which no one approaches properly unless he is baptized. The Lord says, "Unless you eat my flesh and drink my blood, you will not have life in you." What more are we looking for? What answer can anyone make to this, unless stubbornness turns its feisty muscles against the firmness of the clear truth?[61]

It is important to note that the strength of Augustine's argument here rests not simply on John 6:54, but on the practice of giving the Eucharist even to baptized infants, which Augustine seems to have assumed to be widespread and ancient.[62] John 6:54 suggests that eternal life is reserved only for those who have received the Eucharist. Augustine thus argues that since only baptized infants have received the Eucharist, only baptized infants who die will see eternal life (Jn 6:54) and enter the kingdom of God (Jn 3:3). His rhetorical question at the end of the passage emphasizes this conclusion: John 6:54, combined with the practice of infant communion, indicates the falsity of the Pelagian view that unbaptized infants will enjoy eternal life.

Augustine further solidifies his rejection of the Pelagian distinction between the kingdom of God and eternal life a few sections later. Here he cites John 3:35–36 ("The Father loves the Son and has placed all things in his hand. One who believes in the Son has eternal life, but one who does not believe in the Son will not have life. Rather the anger of God remains over him."). Augustine notes that the crucial point here is to determine to which category baptized infants belong—to the "believers" or to the "unbelievers." Once again, he turns to the custom of the Church to find his answer:

---

61 *pecc. mer.* 1.20.26 (Latin: CSEL 60:25.22–26.8; English: Teske, WSA I/23, 48).

62 As is the case with the issue of the apostolicity of infant baptism, modern scholarship would tend to find Augustine's historical assumption about the antiquity of infant communion to be controversial.

In which of these classes, then, are we to put infants? Among those who believe in the Son, or among those who do not believe in him? "In neither of them," someone will say, "because they cannot as yet believe, and they should not be counted as unbelievers." That is not what the rule of the Church [*ecclesiastica regula*] indicates, which adds baptized infants to the number of the faithful. Moreover, if those who are baptized are counted among the faithful on account of the power and the celebration of this great sacrament, although they do not in their heart and on their lips do what pertains to believing and confessing, then certainly those who lack the sacrament should be regarded as among those who do not believe in the Son.[63]

Here, then, Augustine appeals to the *ecclesiastica regula*—the practice or rule of the Church—which regards baptized infants as numbered among the believers. Referring also to the fact that the baptismal rite does not expect these infants to believe and confess verbally or even in their hearts but relies totally on "the power and the celebration" of the sacrament, Augustine notes that those who have not encountered the sacrament should be considered unbelievers. The surpassing power of the sacrament is what makes infants believers, not some underlying innocence all infants have.[64]

After briefly turning to address some potential concerns over God's justice, Augustine continues his argument, this time examining Christ's role as savior, a topic that prompts a few important comments. He argues that the heart of Christ's mission was to take away the sins of the world (Jn 1:29)—and that Christ is the savior even of infants. As a result, it seems that even infants have need of forgiveness. Hence, Augustine notes that some Punic names for baptism and the Eucharist are particularly fitting:

> Punic Christians are perfectly correct in calling baptism "salvation" and in calling the sacrament of Christ's body "life." What is their basis for doing this, if it is not, as I believe, the ancient and apostolic tradition? This tradition leads them to regard it as a mark of the Church of Christ that without baptism and participation in the Lord's table no human being can attain either to the kingdom of God or to salvation and eternal life.[65]

---

63 *pecc. mer.* 1.20.28 (Latin: CSEL 60:27.8–17; English: Teske, WSA I/23, 48–49, slightly modified).

64 A similar argument can be found at *pecc. mer.* 1.33.62.

65 *pecc. mer.* 1.24.34 (Latin: CSEL 60:33.17–22; English: Teske, WSA I/23, 53).

A CONTROVERSY IN CARTHAGE

Here Augustine draws evidence from a local tradition to show the equivalence of the kingdom of God, salvation, and eternal life. However, it is important to note that Augustine explains why this Punic tradition should be viewed with authority: because Punic Christians do so on the basis of "the ancient and apostolic tradition." Augustine is quick to ground his evidence in an indisputable authority—in this case, the apostolic tradition. He rhetorically asks his reader why Punic Christians would call baptism and the Eucharist "salvation" and "life"; this question is intended to evoke the obvious answer: that this practice was an ancient and apostolic tradition.[66]

After this brief consideration of the Punic names for baptism and the Eucharist, Augustine returns to his examination of Christ's identity as savior, focusing in particular on the way in which Christ brings light to those in the darkness of sin. Citing John 12:46 ("I came into the world as light so that everyone who believes in me does not remain in darkness"), Augustine notes that some of the Pelagians seem to have interpreted this in light of John 1:9 ("He was the true light that enlightens every human being that comes into this world"), arguing that newborn infants have already received the light of Christ by the very fact of being born.[67] After challenging this interpretation in a variety of ways, Augustine asserts:

> Mother Church has no doubt that this [enlightenment] takes place in little ones by means of the sacrament; she offers them her maternal heart and lips so that they may be initiated in the sacred mysteries, because they cannot yet believe unto righteousness with their own heart or make profession with their own lips unto salvation. And no believer hesitates to call them believers—a name which is, of course, taken from believing. And yet, it was not these little ones themselves, but others who made the responses for them during the sacred rites.[68]

Here, Augustine emphasizes the Church's maternal solicitude for infants—a solicitude displayed in the Church's practice of offering baptism even to those unable to request it for themselves. In keeping with John 12:46, though, it is

---

66 Of course, Augustine offers no argument to back up his claim that this Punic tradition is based on an apostolic tradition. For our purposes, this matters little: what is important for us in this study is simply to show that Augustine attempted to ground his views in apostolic authority.

67 See *pecc. mer.* 1.24.35–1.25.38. Translations of John 12:46 and John 1:9 taken from Teske, WSA I/23, 53–55.

68 *pecc. mer.* 1.25.38 (Latin: CSEL 60:37.4–10; English: Teske, WSA I/23, 55).

of decisive importance for Augustine that his readers recognize the Church's practice in acknowledging baptized infants as believers: for Christ came into the world as light to rescue those who believe in him from darkness. Just as the Church truly recognizes infants as believers, it must be recognized that they have been rescued from darkness. Finally, in an intriguing statement that he does not fully unpack here, Augustine notes that infants become believers through the vicarious action of their godparents (as representatives of Mother Church), who make the responses in the baptismal liturgy on their behalf. Later, in *s.* 294 and in the third book of *De peccatorum meritis*, Augustine will draw out the connections between the way in which infants receive the benefits of baptism and the way in which infants participate in the sin of Adam. But here, Augustine is content to note only the Church's conviction (as indicated by the practice of referring to baptized infants as believers) that infants, too, have need of salvation from the darkness of sin.

Following this reference to the Church's practice, Augustine continues his examination of the soteriological work of Christ by offering a long list of scriptural citations (*pecc. mer.* 1.27.40–1.27.54) aimed at demonstrating that the purpose of the Incarnation was to redeem sinful humanity.[69] After this lengthy section, Augustine briefly articulates his position on concupiscence and the goodness of marriage (*pecc. mer.* 1.29.57) and then offers a close reading of John 3, which he once again uses to problematize the Pelagians' attempts, among other things, to distinguish the kingdom of God from eternal life (*pecc. mer.* 1.30.58–33.62). He then turns to the final section of Book 1, where he addresses the moral status of infants more directly. Augustine introduces this topic by reflecting on the baptismal rite itself, which is one of the only pieces of evidence he produces in this concluding section:

> What shall I say about the very form of the sacrament? I wish that some of those who think differently would bring a little one to me for baptism.

---

69 One comment within this long list of citations bears mentioning. When introducing his citations from Hebrews, Augustine writes, "Some people regard the Letter to the Hebrews as uncertain. I have, nonetheless, read that some who hold views contrary to this position of ours concerning the baptism of little ones have wanted to use it as evidence for certain of their views. I myself am moved more by the authority of the Eastern Churches which includes it among the canonical books" (Latin: CSEL 60:47.20–25; English: Teske, WSA I/23, 61). Could this reference to the view of the eastern churches be intended by Augustine to indicate his awareness of the opinions of those in the East and to associate himself closely with them? (Recall that the Pelagians had accused their opponents of being at odds with the eastern churches.)

A CONTROVERSY IN CARTHAGE 97

> What does my exorcism do for the child, if it is not held in servitude to the devil? These persons would have to make the responses to me on behalf of the same little one whom they present, because the child could not make the responses on its own. How, then, are they going to say that the child renounces the devil, if the devil had no claim on the child? How are they going to say that the child is turning back to God, if the child had not been turned away? How are they going to say that, among other things, the child believes in the forgiveness of sins, if the child receives no forgiveness? If I thought that they held views contrary to these, I would not permit them to approach the sacraments with the little one.[70]

Augustine presents several important pieces of evidence in this passage. First of all, he highlights how baptism, even the baptism of infants, involves an exorcism.[71] This exorcism would have been similar to that which adults underwent in their own process of initiation. The rite likely began with prayers said over the candidate for baptism, ordering any demonic presences to depart. These demands were then followed by the *exsufflatio*. William Harmless describes the rite as follows:

> Besides these verbal pleas, the exorcist would also breathe upon, or more precisely, 'hiss at' the candidate. This gesture, the *exsufflatio*, was a conventional sign of contempt and had become, in Christian circles, a standard exorcistic act. . . . The use of breath was not accidental. For the ancients, one's breath was one's life, one's *spiritus*, the power that animated the flesh. Thus this *exsufflatio* meant spitting out the demonic breath that had invaded the candidates' God-given life-force.[72]

Following the rite of *exsufflatio*, "the *competentes* would give voice to their new-found freedom by formally renouncing Satan."[73] In the case of an infant, this formal renunciation would have been spoken on behalf of the child by

---

70 *pecc. mer.* 1.34.63 (Latin: CSEL 60:63.26–64.7; English: Teske, WSA I/23, 70).

71 Later in the controversy, Augustine will frequently refer to the rites of exorcism and exsufflation as irrefutable proof of original sin. It is a curiosity that he does not deploy references to it more often here. For more on exorcism and exsufflation, see Jane Merdinger, "In League with the Devil? Donatist and Catholic Perspectives on Pre-Baptismal Exsufflation," in *The Uniquely African Controversy: Studies on Donatist Christianity*, ed. Anthony Dupont, Matthew Gaumer, and Mathijs Lamberigts (Leuven: Peeters, 2014), 153–78.

72 William Harmless, *Augustine and the Catechumenate* (Collegeville, MN: The Liturgical Press, 1995), 264.

73 Harmless, *Augustine and the Catechumenate*, 265.

the parents or godparents, as Augustine notes. The actual baptism would have occurred shortly thereafter following the profession of the creed.[74]

What Augustine is pointing out here is that any Pelagian who might bring a child to him for baptism would have to affirm the child's need for exorcism and then, among other things, renounce the devil and profess the creed (including belief in the forgiveness of sins) on behalf of the child. As a result, Augustine notes, the baptismal rite would require the Pelagian either to implicitly confess the infant's need for forgiveness of sins or, in essence, to lie, playacting large portions of the rite, given that certain elements of it would be meaningless for a sinless child. However, Augustine notes that even the Pelagians found the second option unattractive:

> Some of these people recognized that nothing worse and more detestable could be said or thought than this: that a false or deceptive form of baptism is conferred upon little ones—a form of baptism in which the remission of sins seems to be spoken of and to be done and yet does not happen. Just as they grant that baptism is necessary for little ones, they grant that redemption, too, is necessary for them—as is contained in a very brief *libellus* of a certain one of them, who nevertheless was unwilling to speak more clearly in that document about the remission of any sort of sin. And just as you yourself told me in your letter, they now admit, as you say, that the remission of sins takes place also in infants through baptism. No surprise there. Indeed, redemption could not be understood in any other way. Yet, they say, "They began to have sin not from their origin, but already in their own life after they were born."[75]

In this sense, Augustine notes that, in a sort of self-inflicted *reductio ad absurdum*, some of the Pelagians, unwilling to criticize the baptismal rite or to portray it as deceptive, posited that in baptism infants are forgiven of their own personal sins. By highlighting this rather odd position, Augustine is reinforcing the strength of the evidence he drew from the form of the sacrament of baptism. The fact that the Pelagians were so unwilling to contradict the practice of the Church that they (or at least some of them) instead promoted such a laughable position indicates for Augustine and his readers just how strong and unassailable the practice and form of infant baptism is.

---

74 In the case of adults, the exorcism would have taken place earlier in Lent, with baptism only to occur at Easter. See Harmless, *Augustine and the Catechumenate*, 261–62.

75 *pecc. mer.* 1.34.63 (Latin: CSEL 60:64.9–20; English: my translation). The *libellus* referred to here is that of Caelestius, submitted as part of his trial.

A CONTROVERSY IN CARTHAGE

After a brief response to the notion that infants might have committed personal sins and an examination of the condition of infants (which he suggests points toward their fallenness), Augustine brings the first book of *De peccatorum meritis* to a conclusion. Throughout the book, though, we have seen Augustine repeatedly refer to various pieces of evidence (especially associated with the practice of infant baptism) that he deploys to ground his theological views and exegetical explanations in the practice of the Church. Of course, it might be asked: What is it about, say, the practice of infant baptism that leads Augustine to believe that it might serve as persuasive evidence for his position that infants are infected with original sin? Why should the Pelagians accept Augustine's appeals to these practices and rites? In many cases in *De peccatorum meritis*, it appears that Augustine simply assumes that his readers will accept the authority of the evidence he supplies from the baptismal rite. He does so, most likely, because the Pelagians themselves agreed with the practice of infant baptism—and, thus, there was no question over its validity.[76] However, in one passage he provides more explicit support for this evidence and suggests some reasons as to why it should be accepted as authoritative.

This key passage is found at *pecc. mer.* 1.26.39, the section introducing a long series of Scriptural citations that indicate the purpose of the incarnation. Augustine's goal here is to emphasize that Christ came to forgive sins and to rescue all people from the power of darkness, even those merely infected with original sin (i.e., infants). He describes this purpose with a long statement, filled with rhetorical flourishes:

> . . . the Lord Jesus Christ came in the flesh and, after he had taken on the form of a slave, was made obedient unto death on a cross. He did this for no other reason except so that by this dispensation of his most merciful grace he might bring to life, save, free, redeem, and illumine all those who have been constituted as members of his body and have him as their head in order that they might attain the kingdom of heaven. These people earlier had been constituted in the death, feebleness, servitude, captivity, and darkness of sins and had been under the power of the devil, the prince of sins. And so he became the mediator of God and men in order that through him, after the hostilities of our impiety had come to an end by the peace of his grace, we might be reconciled to God for the sake of eternal life,

76 See, e.g., *pecc. mer.* 1.26.39.

having been snatched away from the eternal death that was threatening people such as us.[77]

Augustine then notes that those who do not need to be brought to life, saved, freed, redeemed, and illumined, likewise do not need baptism. However, he points out that even the Pelagians grant that little ones should be baptized. Why? Because they "cannot come against the authority of the universal Church, which was beyond a doubt handed down through the Lord and the apostles."[78] Here, then, Augustine explicitly attempts to ground infant baptism (1) in its universal practice throughout the Church and (2) in the teaching of Christ and the apostles after him. What gives the practice of infant baptism its authority as evidence, Augustine claims, is the fact that it is universal and ancient.[79]

Book 2

In the second book of *De peccatorum meritis*, Augustine's attention shifts to the possibility of human sinlessness. As a result, Augustine's discussion of baptism sharply declines. However, another aspect of the Church's liturgical

---

77 *pecc. mer.* 1.26.39: *appareat dominum Iesum Christum non aliam ob causam in carne uenisse ac forma serui accepta factum oboedientem usque ad mortem crucis nisi ut hac dispensatione misericordissimae gratiae omnes, quibus tamquam membris in suo corpore constitutis caput est ad capessendum regnum caelorum, uiuificaret, saluos faceret, liberaret, redimeret, inluminaret qui prius fuissent in peccatorum morte, languoribus, seruitute, captiuitate, tenebris constituti, sub potestate diaboli principis peccatorum ac sic fieret mediator dei et hominum, per quem post inimicitias impietatis nostrae illius gratiae pace finitas reconciliaremur deo in aeternam uitam ab aeterna morte quae talibus inpendebat erepti* (Latin: CSEL 60:37.13–24; English: my translation). Note, especially, the use of homeoteleuton and asyndeton here, which serves to emphasize both the work of Christ and the state of humanity prior to the incarnation.

78 *pecc. mer.* 1.26.39 (Latin: CSEL 60:38.7–9; English: my translation). It should be noted that the order in which Augustine presents the scriptural quotations seems designed to bolster his case that this teaching comes from the Lord and the apostles: he offers citations from the Gospels, Peter, John, Paul (and Hebrews), Revelation, and Acts, that is, moving from Jesus in the Gospels through the apostles and the early Church in Acts. My thanks to Walter Dunphy for pointing this out to me.

79 In an article in which he examines Augustine's recourse to liturgical praxis in the Pelagian controversy, J.-A. Vinel argues that such liturgical evidence has argumentative power for Augustine merely because it is backed by the authority of the Church and not because the praxis is universal and ancient (Vinel, "L'argument liturgique opposé par saint Augustin aux pélagiens," esp. 235ff.). I would suggest that my analysis offered here indicates that just the opposite was the case for Augustine: liturgical praxis has argumentative value for him precisely because he thinks that praxis can be traced back to the apostles themselves.

A CONTROVERSY IN CARTHAGE

101

praxis comes to the fore: the Church's practice of praying for the forgiveness of sins and for the divine aid to avoid sin in the future. Augustine wastes no time citing this evidence. After summarizing his first book and stating that he will turn to the question of human sinlessness in the second (*pecc. mer.* 2.1.1), Augustine immediately addresses the Church's practice of prayer: "The solution of this question concerning human life free from sin's stealthy attack or unexpected conquest is especially required on account of our daily prayers."[80] Augustine notes that the Pelagians seem to emphasize the power of human free choice so much that no help is needed from God in order to act righteously. On the Pelagian view, then, "we need not pray so that we do not enter into temptation, that is, that we are not overcome by temptation, either when it deceives and takes hold of us in our ignorance or when it pushes and pulls us in our weakness."[81] For Augustine, this undercuts a key aspect of Christian prayer, one that is emphasized especially in the Lord's Prayer. He writes,

> We cannot put into words how harmful and destructive to our salvation which is in Christ, how contrary to the religion by which we have been taught, and how strongly opposed to the piety by which we worship God it is that we do not beg the Lord to receive such a benefit or that we suppose that the words, "And bring us not into temptation," were inserted in the Lord's Prayer without any purpose.[82]

Augustine's words here are forceful, as he emphasizes several times how pernicious the Pelagian teaching is for the Church's life of prayer. His use of the penultimate petition from the Lord's Prayer serves as a final piece of evidence: Pelagian teachings not only undermine the Church's life of prayer in general, but especially that singular prayer that Christ himself had given to the Church. In this way, Augustine connects his own theology with the Church's liturgical praxis and, even more so, with the instructions of Christ himself.[83]

---

80 *pecc. mer.* 2.2.2: *huius autem quaestionis solutio de hominis uita sine ulla subreptione uel praeoccupatione peccati propter cotidianas etiam nostras orationes maxime necessaria est* (Latin: CSEL 60:72.5–7; English: Teske, WSA I/23, 79).

81 *pecc. mer.* 2.2.2 (Latin: CSEL 60:72.11–13; English: Teske, WSA I/23, 79).

82 *pecc. mer.* 2.2.2 (Latin: CSEL 60:72.13–19; English: Teske, WSA I/23, 79, slightly modified).

83 As noted above, it seems that in this section Augustine is addressing the rumors he had heard of the Pelagians' problematic views on grace, despite the fact that grace seems not to have been a major topic of controversy in Carthage. The specific use of the Lord's Prayer

After highlighting in a prefatory way the danger of Pelagian views for the Christian life of prayer, Augustine turns to address in more detail the Pelagian view that morally upright action is possible through the power of the human will alone.[84] In response, Augustine points out, first of all, that God through scripture (1) indicates that all human persons sin and (2) advises humanity on how to seek forgiveness after falling into sin. This Scriptural foundation in turn leads Augustine to discuss the reason why all people sin. Here, he points to concupiscence—that desire or inclination to sin that remains in the human person even after baptism. After this, he notes that this disordered desire, intrinsic to fallen humanity, is countered precisely in the final three petitions of the Lord's Prayer.[85] A few lines later, he explains in detail:

> If, then, we consent to these desires stemming from the concupiscence of the flesh by an illicit turn of the will, we say in order to heal this wound, "Forgive us our debts." And drawing a remedy from the works of mercy, we add, "As we also forgive our debtors." But so that we do not consent to it, we beg for help with the words, "And bring us not into temptation".... Finally, we mention what will be accomplished in the end, when what is mortal will be swallowed up by life: "But deliver us from evil." At that time, after all, there will be no concupiscence of the sort that we are commanded to fight and to which we are commanded not to consent. We can, then, briefly ask for this whole cluster of three benefits as follows: "Forgive us those times in which we have been carried off by concupiscence; help us not to be carried off by concupiscence; take concupiscence away from us."[86]

In this sense, Augustine turns to the final three petitions of the Lord's Prayer as a response to Pelagian claims about the possibility of sinlessness and the power of human free will. In Augustine's view, Christ's words and the tradition of Christian prayer itself indicate that human free will is not strong enough in and of itself to avoid sin—and that it does, at least from time to

---

seems also to be due to these rumors: as we noted above, *s.* 348A reports how the Pelagians had interpreted several key petitions from the Lord's Prayer while they were still in Rome.

84 *pecc. mer.* 2.3.3.

85 "For this reason, when the Lord was teaching us to pray, he advised us to say, among other things, 'Forgive us our debts, as we also forgive our debtors. And bring us not into temptation, but deliver us from evil'" (*pecc. mer.* 2.4.4 [Latin: CSEL 60:74.6–10; English: Teske, WSA I/23, 80]).

86 *pecc. mer.* 2.4.4 (Latin: CSEL 60:74.16–75.8; English: Teske, WSA I/23, 81).

A CONTROVERSY IN CARTHAGE   103

time, succumb to temptation. Thus, grounding his argument in evidence given authority by its origins in scripture and the Church's constant and universal tradition of prayer, Augustine seeks to convince his readership once more of the dangerous novelty of the Pelagian position.[87]

Augustine devotes the remainder of the second book to a set of responses to four questions that might be asked surrounding the issue of sinlessness: (1) Is it possible to be sinless in this life? (*pecc. mer.* 2.6.7); (2) Is anyone actually sinless? (*pecc. mer.* 2.7.8–16.25); (3) Why does no one live a sinless life? (*pecc. mer.* 2.17.26–19.33); (4) Could there ever be anyone who has never sinned and will never sin? (*pecc. mer.* 2.20.34–36.59). Augustine's response to the second question is particularly important for our purposes. Here, Augustine aims to show that there are no human beings who actually live without sin. Most of the evidence Augustine produces comes from scripture itself. For example, Augustine argues that holy individuals such as Noah, Daniel, and Job were all sinners—as can be seen either through their acts recounted in scripture (e.g., Gn 9:21) or through their own confession (e.g., Dn 9:20). However, interspersed among such arguments are repeated references to the Lord's Prayer—and more particularly, its antepenultimate petition: *Forgive us our debts*.[88] The reason why Augustine repeatedly refers to this petition is important to grasp. First and foremost, his use of it seems to be a response to an existing debate over the petition between the Pelagians and their opponents. Indeed, while discussing the case of Daniel, Augustine writes,

> Nor can one say in this case what some people argue in opposition to the Lord's Prayer. They say, "Although the apostles, who were holy and already perfect and who had absolutely no sin, said this prayer, it was on behalf of the imperfect and those still sinners that they said, 'Forgive us our debts, as we also forgive our debtors.' Thus by saying 'our debts,' they showed that there existed in the one body both those who still had sins and they themselves who had absolutely no sin."[89]

---

87 As La Bonnardière writes when discussing Augustine's use of the antepenultimate petition of the Lord's Prayer, "He intends to affirm that, in his defense of the Lord's Prayer, he is faithful to the line traced by the commandment of the Lord, the behavior of the Apostles, the catechesis of the Fathers and the liturgical practice of the Church" ("Les commentaires simultanés," 142).

88 See *pecc. mer.* 2.10.13, 2.13.18, 2.14.21, 2.16.25.

89 *pecc. mer.* 2.10.13 (Latin: CSEL 60:84.11–19; English: Teske, WSA I/23, 87).

104 AUGUSTINE IN THE PELAGIAN CONTROVERSY

From this quotation, we learn that at least some of the Pelagians had sought to explain (perhaps in response to a prior objection by their opponents) in what sense the apostles would have prayed the Lord's Prayer.[90] Augustine rejects their contention that, in effect, the apostles had no need to pray (at least certain of the petitions of) the Lord's Prayer for their own benefit. Given the testimony of scripture regarding individuals like Noah, Daniel, and Job, Augustine argues that the Lord's Prayer should be taken at face value—and, thus, as evidence against the Pelagian claims about the possibility of sinlessness. In this sense, then, Augustine's argument in this section is both an answer to that second question regarding the possibility of sinlessness and an attempt to reclaim the Lord's Prayer as evidence.

For example, observe Augustine's comments at *pecc. mer.* 2.13.18. Here, after addressing the cases of Noah, Daniel, and Job, Augustine notes that there are "persons on earth who are righteous, great, brave, prudent, chaste, patient, pious, merciful, and who endure all temporal evils with equanimity for the sake of righteousness."[91] However, he asserts that even these people, just like Noah and others, are not sinless and that "none of them are so arrogantly insane that they think that they have no need of the Lord's Prayer for some sins of their own."[92] In this passage, Augustine the rhetor is clearly at work: seeking to refute the Pelagians' interpretation of the Lord's Prayer, Augustine associates this position with arrogance and insanity. In this way, Augustine portrays the Pelagian position not just as incorrect but, even more so, as laughably wrong: no one in their right mind—and especially not a saint—would presume that he or she need not pray the Lord's Prayer for himself or herself. Augustine goes on to counter the Pelagian interpretation of the Lord's Prayer again a few sections later:

> We believe, after all, the testimonies of the scriptures concerning the praises of these persons [e.g., Noah, Daniel, Job, Elizabeth, Zechariah, etc.], and by those same testimonies we also believe that no living person is found

---

90 In this sense, Augustine's reliance on the Lord's Prayer as evidence does not seem to be original to Augustine but was taken up by him from earlier anti-Pelagian argumentation. Thus, its usage is similar to the way Augustine deployed the evidence of infant baptism in Book 1. Further evidence for this can be found in *s.* 348A, delivered in 416, where Augustine recounts a discussion that the bishop Urbanus had had with an unidentified Pelagian in Rome (probably before 410) regarding the Lord's Prayer (for more on Urbanus, see Chapter 1 n.12).

91 *pecc. mer.* 2.13.18 (Latin: CSEL 60:90.13–15; English: Teske, WSA I/23, 90).

92 *pecc. mer.* 2.13.18 (Latin: CSEL 60:90.18–20; English: Teske, WSA I/23, 90, slightly modified).

A CONTROVERSY IN CARTHAGE

righteous in the sight of God. For this reason, we pray that he may not enter into judgment with his servants, and we believe that the Lord's Prayer, which he gave to his disciples, is necessary for all the faithful, not only in general, but even for each individual.[93]

And finally, in the last paragraph of this section, Augustine asserts once more: "Each of [the saints] truthfully says of himself, *Forgive us our debts, as we also forgive our debtors*."[94] Thus, after dismissing the Pelagian view, Augustine references the Lord's Prayer several times as evidence for his own view: the Church prays the Lord's Prayer precisely because all are in need of divine aid and forgiveness. In this way, Augustine attempts to ground his view in what he believes to be a universal practice of the Church that stretches back to the apostles.[95]

The remainder of Book 2 offers little in the way of appeals to evidence grounding Augustine's views in the Church's ancient and universal doctrinal tradition.[96] There is, however, a topic brought up at the very end of Book 2 that does have some relevance for our investigation. In the final paragraph of this book (*pecc. mer.* 2.36.59), Augustine briefly discusses the issue of the origin of the soul, as noted above. We know from elsewhere that the Pelagians supported a creationist view (the notion that God directly creates a soul for each new human being) and strongly opposed traducianism (the view that the soul is transmitted along with the body from a child's parents): see, for example, Pelagius, *Expositio in Romanos* 5.15, and the *Liber de fide* 28. Intriguingly, Jerome, when listing the various hypotheses on the soul's origin, associated traducianism with the western church (see Jerome, *ep.* 126.1, where he says the greater part of the West holds to this view). If this was, in fact, the case, the Pelagians' rejection of traducianism would have also been a rejection of a western view and a choice for a view held more prominently elsewhere in the Church (i.e., in the East). As noted above, we know that the

---

93 *pecc. mer.* 2.14.21 (Latin: CSEL 60:93.27–94.4; English: Teske, WSA I/23, 92).

94 *pecc. mer.* 2.16.25 (Latin: CSEL 60:98.10–12; English: Teske, WSA I/23, 95).

95 For more on the use of the Lord's Prayer in liturgy in early Christianity, see W. Rordorf, "The Lord's Prayer in the Light of Its Liturgical Use in the Early Church," *Studia Liturgica* 14 (1981): 1–19. As Rordorf notes, "In all the eucharistic liturgies, eastern and western alike, even in the oldest we possess, the Our Father forms an integral part of the *Missa fidelium*" (5).

96 One possible exception is found at *pecc. mer.* 2.27.43, where Augustine notes that the practice of infant baptism indicates that infants suffer from "the bite of the serpent" and, hence, original sin.

origin of the soul seems to have been a point of dispute in Carthage in 411. Thus, it seems possible, as Walter Dunphy has suggested, that the Pelagians were using Jerome's opinion (or perhaps his sense of the regnant view in the East) to challenge both traducianism and, more importantly, original sin (which they viewed as intrinsically connected with that account of the soul's origin).[97] Augustine's brief response to this issue in *De peccatorum meritis* 2 is largely aimed at separating the two topics (namely, the topic of the soul's origin and that of the transmission of original sin). In this way, he perhaps sought to undermine not only the connection the Pelagians drew between the two topics but also their possible view that an eastern rejection of the doctrinal of original sin could be inferred from an eastern rejection of traducianism.[98]

All told, then, *De peccatorum meritis* 2 continues the first book's attempts to ground anti-Pelagian doctrinal views in the Church's ancient and universal tradition—especially through references to the Lord's Prayer. Indeed, the fact that Augustine began his entire response to the Pelagian view of the possibility of sinlessness by framing it as a threat to the Christian practice of prayer (*pecc. mer.* 2.2.2) indicates how keen he was to ground his own position in the Church's universal practice and belief. Taken together, Book 1 and Book 2 are noteworthy for Augustine's repeated attempts to ground his views in the Church's practice—whether it be baptism and its associated rites or the recitation of the Lord's Prayer. In this sense, Augustine framed the Pelagian issue as a threat not just to a set of ideas or doctrinal positions, but to the concrete life of the Church as experienced by the faithful throughout the Christian world.

SERMONES 293 AND 294

Shortly after completing the first two books of *De peccatorum meritis*, Augustine delivered three homilies in Carthage at the end of June 411—*ss.* 293, 294, and 299—which evince a close relationship with the themes and argumentation of *De peccatorum meritis*. While all three sermons are important for the study of the earliest phase of the Pelagian controversy in Carthage, I will

---

97 See Dunphy, "A Lost Year," 443.

98 My thanks to Walter Dunphy for sharing some insights on this issue with me.

A CONTROVERSY IN CARTHAGE

restrict my analysis to the first two sermons, as they bear most directly on our investigation of Augustine's argumentation.[99]

Sermo 293

Sermo 293 was the first of this series, and was delivered on June 24, the feast of the nativity of St. John the Baptist. Most of Augustine's sermon is concerned with comparing John and Christ and exploring the ways in which John acts as Christ's forerunner. However, the final sections of the sermon take a decidedly anti-Pelagian turn, as Augustine addresses several objections of apparently Pelagian origin.[100] Of particular interest for our purposes is the second objection, which prompts Augustine's most developed response out of the three. After affirming (as part of his rather brief response to the first objection) that all who are "brought to life" (i.e., in salvation) are brought to life through Christ, Augustine faces a second question: "What then—does even an infant need a liberator?"[101] Augustine's response begins as follows:

> Clearly an infant needs a liberator, clearly! A witness to this is the mother who faithfully runs to the church with her little one in need of baptism. A witness to this is a greater mother, the Church herself, who receives the little one to cleanse him and either to send him off freed or to raise him up in piety. Who would dare to give testimony against so great a mother? Finally, there is a witness of that misery also in the little one himself: his tears. As much as it can, weak nature bears witness, understanding very little—or

99 I have decided against analyzing *s.* 299 here, as the anti-Pelagian portion of this sermon is relatively brief and deals mainly with the specific issue of whether physical death is a result of sin or is merely natural—a topic that, throughout Augustine's anti-Pelagian corpus, tends not to prompt "arguments from tradition" (see, e.g., *pecc. mer.* 1.2.2–1.8.8 where this same issue is taken up).

100 See Dolbeau, "Deux Sermons," 411–12. Dolbeau notes that the three objections have affinities with some of the propositions Caelestius was accused of holding and suggests that they may have been shouted out by someone in the congregation. It seems more likely to me that Augustine is posing the objections himself. Given Augustine's comments elsewhere, I doubt that a supporter of Caelestius would publicly question at this stage in the debate—that is, after Caelestius's trial and after Caelestius had already confirmed in his *libellus* that infants are in need of redemption—whether infants need a liberator.

101 *s.* 293.10 (Latin: Dolbeau, "Deux Sermons," 459; English: my translation). This objection seems connected with one of Caelestius's alleged propositions: "Newborns are in that state in which Adam was before the transgression" (Marius Mercator, *Commonitorium super nomine Caelestii* 2 [Latin: ACO 1.5.1, p. 66, ln. 11–12; English: my translation]; see Dolbeau, "Deux Sermons," 411–12).

rather still understanding nothing at all. It begins not with laughter—it begins with tears.[102]

Note how Augustine proceeds here by offering three pieces of evidence to support his view that infants need a liberator.[103] To begin, he highlights not only the fact that Christian mothers believe that their children need to be baptized, but also that they believe it with a strong conviction (which they display by "running" to the church!). Augustine then turns to the point of view of a "greater mother"—that is, the Church. Far from rebuking these ordinary mothers for error or superstition, the Church has confirmed them in their belief by baptizing their little ones. If these ordinary mothers were wrong in their belief, the Church would certainly act differently. As Augustine points out a little later in his response, "If the infant doesn't have anything in it to be healed [*saluetur*], let it be taken away from here [i.e., the church]. Why don't we say to these mothers, 'Take these little ones away from here! This is Jesus, he is the savior [*saluator*]. If they don't have something in them to be healed [*saluetur*], take them away from here!'"[104] A third piece of evidence is found, Augustine notes, in the infants themselves and their crying: their tears reveal their miserable state.

Of these three "witnesses," the first two (and especially the second) weigh particularly heavily for Augustine, as he spends the most time reflecting on them. But all three pieces of evidence are united in their argumentative purpose. First of all, by pointing to the pious practices of Christian mothers, to the Church's custom of baptizing infants, and even to the wailing of newborns, Augustine is attempting to convince his congregation that his view that infants need a liberator is not only *his* view. Rather, it is the view of all Christian mothers who have rushed with, perhaps, a sick child to the Church to have the little one baptized. It is the view of the Church, who receives those little ones for baptism. And it is a view that is suggested, albeit

---

102 *s.* 293.10: *Plane indiget, indiget plane. Testis est mater fideliter currens cum paruulo baptizando ad ecclesiam; testis est ipsa maior mater Ecclesia suscipiens paruulum abluendum, et aut liberatum dimittendum, aut pietate nutriendum. Quis audeat dicere testimonium contra tantam matrem? Postremo et in ipso paruulo miseriae ipsius testis est fletus. Quantum potest, natura testatur infirma, parum intellegens, immo nihil adhuc intellegens; non incipit a risu, incipit a fletu* (Latin: Dolbeau, "Deux Sermons," 459; English: my translation).

103 We have seen a variation of this argument before at *pecc. mer.* 1.18.23, but here the presentation is much more vivid.

104 *s.* 293.11 (Latin: Dolbeau, "Deux Sermons," 462; English: my translation).

A CONTROVERSY IN CARTHAGE

in a more peripheral way, by the weakness and unhappy state of infants.[105] In this way, Augustine attempts to undermine the objection not simply by offering a theological account of, say, original sin—an account that could easily be tarred as simply "Augustinian" or "African" or "western"—but by grounding his view in popular belief, the universal practice of the Church, and the everyday experience of hearing a baby cry. These first two are, of course, particularly important because they implicitly serve to challenge the Pelagian claim that had been circulating in Carthage: that the Pelagians' opponents' views were opposed to those of the eastern churches. Without spelling it out completely, this appeal to what were, in Augustine's view, universal Christian practices grounded his view of original sin in the Church's universal doctrinal tradition.[106]

Sermo 294

A few days later, on June 27, 411, Augustine would deliver another sermon— and this time, Pelagianism takes center stage. In this second sermon, Augustine investigates whether his unnamed opponents have an adequate explanation for the practice of infant baptism, following up on some of the issues raised at the end of *s.* 293. Much of the sermon attempts to challenge the proposed distinction between the kingdom of heaven and eternal life

---

105 Augustine makes a similar, brief, argument about crying infants in *s.* 294.12. See also *pecc. mer.* 1.25.36, and 1.35.65–66, as well as Delaroche, "Notes Complémentaires," 507–9. It should be noted that Cyprian (*ep.* 64.6 [CSEL 3.2:721.7–10]) also references the crying of infants in connection with their need for baptism. Augustine will cite the passage immediately prior to this in *s.* 294 and *pecc. mer.* 3.

106 See also Harmless's discussion of this passage in "Christ the Pediatrician," 26ff. As we noted above already (see n. 58), Augustine repeatedly refers to the popular piety of Christian mothers rushing with their infants to the church for baptism. In addition to being used at *pecc. mer.* 1.18.23, *s.* 293.10, and *s.* 294.18 (although this last usage is far less robust than the first two), we can also see a similar argument deployed in a few other sermons that we may be able to date to early in the controversy (and perhaps even to 411): *en. Ps.* 50, *s.* 174, and *s.* 176. For consideration of the dating of these sermons see Hombert, *Nouvelles recherches de chronologie augustinienne,* 163n332 and p. 393. However, keep in mind that Hombert assumes the traditional chronology of 411 to be correct—that is, he assumes the Pelagian controversy did not erupt in Carthage until the fall of 411 (for more on this traditional chronology, see the appendix)—and so will be forced to date these sermons to after that point). Once Caelestius's trial is moved earlier in 411, it becomes possible (and preferable) to date some of these sermons to 411. The argument found in these sermons also reappears later in the controversy with Julian. See also *s.* 183.12, which dates to sometime after 416.

AUGUSTINE IN THE PELAGIAN CONTROVERSY

(to which much of the first book of *De peccatorum meritis* was devoted).[107] As part of his response to this proposal, Augustine walks his congregation through several verses of John 3 in the middle of the sermon.[108] The details of this argument need not detain us here, but there are a few important elements of it that we should pause to discuss. First of all, while commenting on John 3:14–15 ("And just as Moses lifted up the serpent in the desert, so must the Son of man be lifted up, so that everyone who believes in him may not perish, but may have eternal life"), Augustine highlights a connection between the baptismal liturgy and the theology of original sin:

> You're bringing me babies, and telling them to look on the one who has been lifted up, even though you deny they have received the serpent's poison. Surely, if you are really well disposed to them, if you are moved by their innocence in their own personal lives, don't deny that they have contracted some guilt from the first life, not their own, but that of their first parent. Don't deny it; admit the poison, in order to beg for the medicine; otherwise they aren't cured. Or why do you tell them to believe? Here, you see, the answer is given by those who are carrying the babies. They are healed at someone else's words, because they're wounded at someone else's deed. "Do they believe in Christ?" goes the question; the answer is given, "They do." For infants who can't speak, who remain silent, who cry, and by crying are somehow or other praying to be helped, the answer is given, and is effective. Or does that serpent even try to persuade people of this, that it is not effective? Far be such a thought from the minds of Christians of any sort whatsoever. So the answer is given, and it is effective. The spirit of the babies shares in a kind of common life [*conspiratione quadam communicat spiritus*]; they believe by means of others, because they sinned by means of another.[109]

Here, Augustine is doing a few things. First of all, he is highlighting once again the custom of bringing infants forward for baptism in the Church— something that Christians would not do (and the Church would not encourage) if it were unnecessary or pointless.[110] However, he digs into this practice

---

107 *s.* 294.2. See also *pecc. mer.* 1.18.23ff., where Augustine also deals with this view.

108 A parallel is found in *pecc. mer.* 1.30.59ff.

109 *s.* 294.12 (Latin: PL 38:1342.23–39; English: Hill, WSA III/8, 187–88).

110 As in *s.* 293, he will emphasize a bit later that if infants are without sin, there should be no reason to baptize them: "Now where do you place the babies for me? You are already saying they aren't wounded by any poisonous bite. Then take them away from gazing on the serpent

A CONTROVERSY IN CARTHAGE

a bit more deeply here than we have seen previously. In the present sermon, Augustine cites a key moment of the baptismal liturgy—specifically, the part in which the godparents are asked to profess belief in Christ on behalf of their soon-to-be-baptized godchild.[111] Augustine had previously alluded to this aspect of the rite in *De peccatorum meritis*.[112] But here, instead of focusing on the fact that infants can truly be called believers, Augustine draws attention to the way in which the rite of baptism suggests the reality of the transmission of original sin: just as infants are now confessing the faith through their godparents, so too, previously they had rejected God through Adam, their origin. Indeed, for Augustine, the "mechanics" of the transmission of original sin has an echo of sorts in the way in which the grace of baptism is given to infants: both original sin and this grace enter into an infant through the agency of another.[113] In this way, the baptismal liturgy and the theology surrounding it offer a certain credibility to what would otherwise be a rather odd claim: that infants share in Adam's guilt. As in *s.* 293, Augustine here makes no specific claims about the universality of the evidence he has offered. Yet, he clearly expects his congregation to be familiar with this baptismal dialogue and to consider its usage to be widespread.

Another appeal to the Church's baptismal customs follows shortly thereafter. Noting John 3:18 ("Whoever believes in him is not judged; but whoever does not believe has already been judged"), Augustine explains that "judgment" is elsewhere in John used as a synonym for "condemnation."[114] In this sense, Augustine argues, only believers avoid God's condemnation and, drawing once again on John 3:15, only believers have eternal life. To this, he adds John 3:36: "Whoever lacks faith in the Son does not have life; but the wrath of God abides upon him." Having cited these key passages, Augustine now turns back to the Church's practice of infant baptism to demonstrate that only baptized infants will gain eternal life.

---

that has been lifted up. But if you don't take them away, you are saying that they need healing, you are confessing that they have been poisoned" (*s.* 294.13; Latin: PL 38:1343.17–20; English: Hill, WSA III/8, 188, slightly modified).

111 See also *s.* 174.8, which may also date to the summer of 411, where a similar reference is made to this portion of the rite of baptism.

112 See, e.g., *pecc. mer.* 1.19.25 and 1.25.38.

113 In this sense, the argument given here is somewhat similar to that at *pecc. mer.* 1.9.10.

114 *s.* 294.14 (Latin: PL 38:1343.23–37; English: Hill, WSA III/8, 189).

112 AUGUSTINE IN THE PELAGIAN CONTROVERSY

> Where do you place baptized babies? Surely in the ranks of believers. I mean, that's why even by the ancient, canonical, well-established custom of the Church baptized babies are called "faithful." And that's how we inquire about them: "Is this infant a Christian?" "Yes, a Christian," is the answer. "Catechumen, or one of the faithful?" "One of the faithful." From faith, of course, and faith from believing. So you will count baptized babies among believers; nor will you dare in any way at all to judge otherwise, if you don't want to be a manifest heretic. So that's why they have eternal life; because whoever believes in the Son has eternal life.[115]

In this sense, the fact that it is the custom of the Church to identify baptized infants as "believers" demonstrates that even infants fall under the sentence of John 3:36, which would appear to restrict eternal life to those who believe and, thus, to those have received the sacrament of baptism. It is also important to note here that Augustine emphasizes that this "custom" is ancient, canonical, well-established (*antiqua, canonica, fundatissima*).[116] In this way, Augustine attempts to ground his argument in what he believes to be the Church's universal and ancient practice, even going so far as to threaten his opponents with the label of "heretic."[117]

The remainder of the sermon turns to several Pelagian arguments surrounding the moral status of infants and the transmission of original sin. It is Augustine's final response to such arguments that is the most impactful and, indeed, the most important for our purposes. Toward the end of his long homily, Augustine urges his congregation,

> I beg you, please be quiet for a little while longer. I'm only going to read to you. It's Saint Cyprian whom I have just taken into my hands, an ancient bishop of this see. Listen for a moment to what he thought about the baptism of infants, or rather what he demonstrated that the Church had always thought. It's not enough, you see, for these people to hold forth and argue in favor of goodness knows what ungodly novelties; they also try to convict us of saying something new. So that's why I am reading Saint Cyprian, so that

---

115 *s.* 294.14 (Latin: PL 38:1343.45–55; English: Hill, WSA III/8, 189, slightly modified).

116 Note, too, the use of asyndeton here to emphasize these words.

117 We saw Augustine deploy this custom as evidence previously at *pecc. mer.* 1.19.25, 1.20.28, and 1.33.62, but its usage here is much more forceful.

A CONTROVERSY IN CARTHAGE

you may see the canonical meaning, and the Catholic sense in the words I
have been using just now.[118]

Augustine goes on to offer a lengthy quotation from Cyprian's *ep.* 64, which
was a synodal letter prompted by a question about the timing of infant baptism (i.e., whether it was necessary to wait until the eighth day to baptize
infants in accord with the Mosaic law's requirement in the case of circum-
cision).[119] Here, Cyprian emphasizes infants' freedom from personal sin, but
affirms their need for baptism due to the fact that they have contracted the
"contagion of ancient death" by their birth "in the flesh according to Adam."[120]
Augustine argues that Cyprian's response clearly presupposes the Bishop
of Carthage's belief in original sin: "See how, having no doubts about this
matter [i.e., about original sin], he solves the one there were doubts about
[i.e., the timing of baptism]. He took this from the foundation of the Church,
to secure a stone that was coming loose."[121] In this sense, Augustine artfully
suggests to his congregation what they should draw from this quotation:
that Cyprian believed in original sin and, in fact, took it as a settled point of
doctrine coming from the very *fundamentum* of the Church.

Broadly speaking, the choice to quote Cyprian was clearly strategic and
prepared beforehand, given that Augustine had the text of Cyprian's letter
with him. As a result, we should note the placement of the quotation in the
context of the sermon: it is offered just before the sermon's conclusion as the
final and, arguably, most powerful piece of evidence. Cyprian was Augustine's
last "witness," brought in to close the case, as it were, against Pelagianism.
But why Cyprian? There seem to be a few elements to this choice. In a most
basic sense, Augustine cited Cyprian precisely because he was a holy bishop
who lived long ago (*sanctus Cyprianus . . . antiquus episcopus sedis huius*)

---

118 *s.* 294.19: *rogo uos, ut paululum acquiescatis. lego tantum. sanctus Cyprianus est, quem
in manus sumpsi, antiquus episcopus sedis huius: quid senserit de baptismo paruulorum, imo
quid semper ecclesiam sensisse monstrauerit paululum accipite. parum est enim quia isti disse-
runt, et disputant nescio quas impias nouitates; et nos conantur arguere, quod aliquid nouum
dicamus. ad hoc ergo lego sanctum Cyprianum, ut uideatis quomodo sit intellectus canonicus,
et catholicus sensus in his uerbis quae paulo ante tractaui* (Latin: PL 38:1347.33–42; English:
Hill, WSA III/8, 193, slightly modified).

119 Cyprian, *ep.* 64.5 (Latin: CSEL 3.2:720.8–721.2).

120 Cyprian, *ep.* 64.5 (Latin: CSEL 3.2:720.20–21).

121 *s.* 294.19: *uidete quemadmodum de hac re nihil dubitans, soluit illam unde dubitabatur. Hoc
de fundamento Ecclesiae sumpsit, ad confirmandum lapidem nutantem* (Latin: PL 38:1348.12–
15; English: my translation).

and thus could, in Augustine's view, speak to the antiquity of the theological positions Augustine was defending. But there was more to it than that. First of all, recall that in the Carthaginian context there was no greater ecclesiastical hero than Cyprian: his words were sure to appeal to the locals—both Catholics and, if any were present, Donatists. And this is a factor we should not overlook. Delivering this sermon the day after Marcellinus's ruling in favor of the Catholics was published, Donatist antipathy toward the Catholics was likely at an all-time high. It is not difficult to imagine that, in this context, the Donatists would have been inclined to undermine the Catholic cause in whatever way possible. The growing dispute over Caelestius and his views, which appeared to be dividing the Catholic community in Carthage, provided a perfect opportunity for Donatists to highlight the faults of the African Catholic Church. It seems plausible to read Augustine's use of this quotation from Cyprian in this light. While Cyprian's reception within the African Catholic Church was at times complicated by his advocacy for the practice of re-baptism, the Donatists were able to appeal to him and his views in a more full-throated way. In this sense, we can see Augustine's citation of the revered martyr-bishop as an attempt to head-off any potential Donatist exploitation of the unrest prompted by the trial of Caelestius. Yet, it is equally important to recognize that Cyprian enjoyed a favorable reputation—at least as a martyr, if not as a theologian—throughout the Roman Empire, both East and West, and especially in Rome, where he was closely associated with his sometime correspondent and fellow martyr-bishop Cornelius.[122] As a result, it seems likely that Augustine's appeal to Cyprian was also calculated to draw the sympathy of the Roman refugees in his congregation and to

---

122 As Joseph Jungmann notes, "[Cyprian's] memorial day was celebrated at Rome already in the fourth century, and the oldest sacramentaries present Cornelius and Cyprian together on the fourteenth of September" (*The Mass of the Roman Rite: Its Origins and Development*, 2 vols. [Notre Dame, IN: Christian Classics, 2012], 2:174). Further, Jonathan Yates remarks, "Cyprian's authority was widely respected. It is not insignificant that references to his being valued in both the East and the West occur both near the beginning and at the end of his writings against the Pelagians: Cyprian's 'worldwide' appreciation was a fact consistently exploited by Augustine" ("Augustine's Appropriation of Cyprian the Martyr-Bishop against the Pelagians," in *More than a Memory: The Discourse of Martyrdom and the Construction of Christian Identity in the History of Christianity*, ed. J. Leemans [Leuven: Peeters, 2005], 134). See also discussion of Augustine's use of Cyprian in Han-luen Kantzer Komline, "Grace, Free Will, and the Lord's Prayer: Cyprian's Importance for the 'Augustinian' Doctrine of Grace," *Augustinian Studies* 45 (2014): 247–79. Finally, see Augustine's own later comments on Cyprian's universal renown at *c. ep. Pel.* 4.8.21.

A CONTROVERSY IN CARTHAGE

convince them, along with the native Africans, that the Pelagians were the ones promoting novelties.[123]

Sermo 294 appears to be Augustine's first sermon devoted entirely to the Pelagian issue. Thus, its argumentation and themes can help reveal (1) how Augustine understood and sought to respond to Pelagianism shortly after becoming aware of it and (2) what Augustine's chief concerns were with Pelagianism and with the threat it held for the Church at large. In this sense, Augustine's deployment of several appeals to non-Scriptural pieces of "evidence" to ground his doctrinal positions in the ancient and universal faith of the Church is particularly noteworthy—especially the final piece of evidence, the quotation from Cyprian. In this context, it is important to keep in mind what we discussed in our introduction: prior to the beginning of the Pelagian controversy, Augustine rarely even referred to other early Christian authors outside of his anti-Donatist writings and did so in those writings mainly as a response to the Donatists' own appeals to the former bishop of Carthage. Thus, Augustine's appeals to earlier Christian authors up to 411 was, in the main, reactionary. Given that, I would suggest that here too Augustine's appeal to Cyprian was likely reactionary—perhaps not to a Pelagian appeal to Cyprian, but rather to the Pelagians' claims that seem to have been circulating around Carthage that their opponents' views were untraditional[124] and contrary to those found in the East.[125] Augustine does not directly tackle the specific objection about the "eastern churches" in this sermon—although he motions toward it especially in his references to the practice of infant

---

123 It might seem odd that Augustine does not appeal to Cyprian as an advocate for ecclesial unity in this context, given Cyprian's focus on that issue and given Augustine's concerns about the Pelagian threat to unity. But we should recall that it was not as if the Pelagians considered themselves to be a separate Church. In fact, the Pelagians were the ones accusing their opponents of disunity. Thus, making an explicit appeal to Cyprian's thought on unity would have gained Augustine little in this context. Augustine instead focused on showing that the Pelagians themselves were falling out of unity with the ancient and universal Church due to their positions.

124 *s.* 294.19.

125 *gest. Pel.* 11.25. Further, given the citations of earlier Christian authors Augustine will later discover in Pelagius's *De natura* toward the end of 414 or beginning of 415, it seems plausible that those associated with Pelagius were already aware of Pelagius's claims of traditional support for his views in that writing which was likely composed prior to his arrival in Africa. We should also recall that Caelestius himself had appealed to the view of the priest Rufinus (*gr. et pecc. or.* 2.3.3) during his hearing at Carthage—this itself was an appeal to authority, and a particularly weighty authority if that Rufinus was, in fact, Rufinus of Aquileia, known for his activity in the East. My thanks to Giulio Malavasi for suggesting this point to me.

baptism and the customs associated with it, which he clearly assumes to be universal.[126] Here, he is more focused on the charge of novelty—something, as he points out, he aims to refute by appealing to Cyprian.[127]

All told, *ss.* 293 and 294 show us that Augustine, in what were likely his earliest anti-Pelagian sermonic efforts, was concerned to defend the antiquity and universality of the views opposed by the Pelagians—even if it required him to make use of forms of argumentation that he deployed only rarely (i.e., the citation of earlier Christian authors). Of particular note here have been his references to (1) the popular piety that leads mothers to hasten to have their infants baptized, (2) the Church's own endorsement of that popular piety, (3) the role of godparents in the baptismal rite for infants and its parallels with the transmission of original sin, (4) the Church's custom of referring to infants as believers, and (5) the words of Cyprian, used as evidence for the antiquity of the doctrine of original sin. Of course, Augustine's argumentation is not limited to such evidence. Nevertheless, their prominence is significant—especially the citation of Cyprian.

DE PECCATORUM MERITIS ET REMISSIONE 3

As we have noted above, a few days after completing the first two books of *De peccatorum meritis*, Augustine received a copy of Pelagius's *Expositiones* on the Pauline letters. There, in the *expositio* on Romans, Augustine discovered that Pelagius had quoted an argument used by the opponents of original sin different from those he had previously encountered: "If the sin of Adam did harm even to those who are not sinners, then the righteousness of Christ also benefits even those who are not believers, because [Paul] says that human beings are saved through the one man in a similar way and in fact to a greater extent than they perished through the other."[128] Augustine decided to refute

---

126 Note that this lack of a specific response to the objection about the eastern churches may be one reason why Augustine adds a citation of Jerome in *De peccatorum meritis* 3. See discussion below.

127 Here it is important to recognize that Augustine is not placing the emphasis so much on Cyprian as on Cyprian's witness to the Church's faith. Hence, he instructs his congregation to listen to what Cyprian "demonstrated the Church had always held." See discussion in Chronister, "Augustine and Patristic Argumentation in His Anti-Pelagian Works."

128 *pecc. mer.* 3.2.2 (Latin: CSEL 60:129.19–22; English: Teske, WSA I/23, 117, slightly modified). See Pelagius, *Expositio in Romanos* 5.15, in *Pelagius's Expositions of Thirteen Epistles of St Paul*, 2:46–47. In the *Praedestinatus*, Arnobius Iunior states that Pelagius is quoting Caelestius here (*Praedestinatus* 1.88). As Delaroche points out, this argument is slightly different from,

A CONTROVERSY IN CARTHAGE

this argument in a letter to Marcellinus that would become the third book of *De peccatorum meritis*. While he began its composition in Carthage (around the same time or shortly before he delivered *ss.* 293 and 294 in late June), Augustine would not finish it until much later (likely at some point in 412).[129]

Book 3 is ostensibly aimed at refuting the new argument against the transmission of sin that Augustine had found in Pelagius's *Expositiones*. However, Augustine deals with this argument rather quickly (*pecc. mer.* 3.2.2–3.2.3). In the remainder of the third book, Augustine (1) clarifies for his readers that he is not accusing Pelagius of holding these positions (*pecc. mer.* 3.2.4–3.3.6); (2) grounds his own views in both scripture (*pecc. mer.* 3.4.7–3.4.9) and the ancient and universal faith of the Church (*pecc. mer.* 3.5.10–3.7.14); (3) addresses a few lingering Pelagian objections to the transmission of sin (*pecc. mer.* 3.8.15–3.10.18); and (4) summarizes once more his arguments against the Pelagians (*pecc. mer.* 3.11.19–3.13.23).[130] Overall, the vast majority of Book 3 deals with the same topics as Book 1. As a result, several similar argumentative strategies are deployed—although there are some notable novelties in his argumentation as well. Perhaps even more than in Book 1, though, Augustine here aims to prove that his views are grounded in the ancient and universal belief of the Church.

Indeed, the first lines of the third book indicate Augustine's desire to emphasize the universality of his views:

---

but similar to, other arguments Augustine had already refuted in the first two books (see Delaroche, BA 20/A, 362n8).

129 Dunphy suggests that the Carthaginian portion of the third book ends around *pecc. mer.* 3.5.10, where Augustine quotes a letter from Cyprian and tells Marcellinus that he can find a copy of this letter at Carthage. See "A Lost Year," 449. See n. 73 in the appendix for discussion of some of the possible reasons why its completion was delayed.

130 One point of interest in this section is Augustine's discussion at *pecc. mer.* 3.12.21–3.13.22 of 1 Cor 7:14, where St. Paul notes that unbelieving spouses/children are in some way sanctified by believing spouses/parents. Augustine had previously dealt with this verse at *pecc. mer.* 2.25.41 and *s.* 294.18. A comparison of these three treatments of this verse at the beginning of the controversy may help to reinforce the dating of the texts proposed here. The way Augustine addresses the verse in *pecc. mer.* 2 and *s.* 294 are very similar (e.g., noting the example of food that can be sanctified through prayer, but which, nevertheless, remains subject to the normal digestive processes when eaten). However, the treatment in Book 3 evinces further reflection on Augustine's part (he has investigated Pelagius's own treatment of the verse and has chosen a different, and perhaps better, example than food). In this sense, it is possible that we could read this usage of 1 Cor 7:14 as evidence that *s.* 294 was delivered before the composition (of the end of) Book 3.

> I had already completed two lengthy books about the questions you had proposed to me so that I would write something to you against those who say that Adam, even if he had not sinned, would have died and that nothing of his sin passed to his descendants via generation (especially in light of the baptism of little ones, which the universal Church celebrates in a most tender and maternal manner), and who say that there are, have been, and will be children of men who have absolutely no sin in this life.[131]

While in large part his opening statement is only a summary of what Marcellinus had originally asked of Augustine, it is important to note what seems to be an editorial remark by Augustine: that "the universal Church celebrates [infant baptism] in a most tender and maternal manner [*quem more piissimo atque materno uniuersa frequentat ecclesia*]." Augustine, even in the opening words of this third book is keen to highlight the weight that the practice of infant baptism carries as evidence, a weight premised upon its presumed universal and constant practice within the Church. In this same vein, a few lines later Augustine frames his work in the first two books as follows: "I thought that I had produced a work such that the defenders of the faith which our ancestors have handed down on these matters would not stand utterly defenseless against the innovations of those who hold other ideas."[132] Augustine suggests that what is at stake is the faith that has been handed down by previous generations. His aim is to highlight the antiquity of this faith and link his own position to it, while dismissing the Pelagian views as novel.

Augustine again asserts that his views are simply those of the universal Church shortly thereafter when addressing the new argument (quoted above) against original sin which he had recently discovered in Pelagius's *Expositiones*. The argument proposes that if Adam's sin harms those who had not sinned themselves, then the righteousness of Christ should benefit even those who do not believe. As the latter is certainly false, the Pelagians conclude that, likewise, Adam's sin could not have harmed those who have not yet sinned themselves. In response to this argument, Augustine once again aims to defend his view of original sin by appealing to an element of what he takes to be the universal sacramental praxis of the Church. He does so by challenging his opponents to explain how baptism benefits infants (which they surely must not deny "if they have not forgotten that they are

---

131 *pecc. mer.* 3.1.1 (Latin: CSEL 60:128.15–21; English: my translation).

132 *pecc. mer.* 3.1.1 (Latin: CSEL 60:129.3–5; English: Teske, WSA I/23, 117, slightly modified).

A CONTROVERSY IN CARTHAGE

Christians"[133]). Augustine states that whatever this benefit is, it must be a benefit bestowed on believers for, as the Pelagians say, Christ's righteousness offers no benefit to unbelievers. As a result, Augustine notes,

> They are forced to count baptized little ones among the number of believers and to consent to the authority of the holy Church present everywhere, which does not consider them unworthy of the name of "the faithful." The righteousness of Christ would be able to profit them, even according to these people, only if they were believers. Therefore, just as by the response of those through whom they are reborn the Spirit of righteousness transfers into them a faith that the infants could not yet have by their own will, so the flesh of sin of those through whom they are born transfers into them an injury [*noxam*] that they have not yet contracted by their own life.[134]

As we have seen him do previously,[135] Augustine here begins by highlighting the ecclesial custom of identifying baptized infants as believers—a custom that he emphasizes is followed everywhere (*ubique*). He then makes another move we have seen before.[136] Having established that baptized infants are believers, he draws attention to the process by which they became believers—namely, to their baptism and to the baptismal rite in which their godparents spoke on their behalf. Augustine argues that the process by which these infants became believers is analogous to that by which they became sinners: both were accomplished in a vicarious way, through the action of another person. In this sense, Augustine grounds his theology of original sin not simply in several key Pauline passages but links it to what he believes to be a universal practice of the Church, emphasizing the implications that practice has for the theological mechanics of the transmission both of sin and of faith. In so doing, Augustine accentuates the conflict between Pelagian views and what he takes to be the universal Church's belief as expressed by her sacramental actions.

Following a discussion of Pelagius himself (and whether he holds the views he reports in his *expositio* on Romans), Augustine shifts to the second

---

133 *pecc. mer.* 3.2.2 (Latin: CSEL 60:130.9; English: Teske, WSA I/23, 118).

134 *pecc. mer.* 3.2.2 (Latin: CSEL 60:130.11–18; English: my translation).

135 See, e.g., *pecc. mer.* 1.19.25, 1.20.28, 1.25.38, 1.33.62 and *s.* 294.14.

136 See *s.* 294.12 for a parallel. See also *pecc. mer.* 1.9.10. A semi-parallel is found at *pecc. mer.* 1.25.38, although there Augustine does not make a direct connection with the vicarious nature of infants' association with Adam's sin.

main section of the third book, in which he addresses Rom 5:12 and argues it must refer to the transmission of original sin from Adam. This is a key section because, in it, Augustine goes to great lengths to demonstrate that his interpretation of the verse is simply that of the Church writ large. He begins his argument in a rather standard way: offering several other scriptural citations to support his reading of Rom 5:12 and to reject alternative interpretations. This brief scriptural section is notable, though, for its concluding line. After stating that the only potentially ambiguous part of Romans 5 is Paul's statement that Adam was a "pattern of what is to come" (Rom 5:14), Augustine nevertheless concludes that if one considers the surrounding context, the passage "still could not have another sense than that through which it came about that universal Church from antiquity maintained that believing little ones have received the forgiveness of original sin through Christ's baptism."[137] Here, then, Augustine explicitly asserts that the belief that infants receive the forgiveness of original sin in baptism is ancient and universal. The remainder of this section is devoted to a defense of this claim, provided in large part by quotations from the writings of Cyprian and Jerome.

It seems likely that it was around this point in Book 3, or perhaps slightly before, that Augustine completed the Carthaginian portion of its composition.[138] After his return to Hippo later in 411, Augustine added a small amount to the book, but it remained incomplete when he wrote *ep.* 139 (as late as February 412).[139] Presumably, he completed the book at some point in 412. Regardless of that timeline, though, it is notable that upon resuming his work on the book Augustine seems to have immediately taken up the same letter from Cyprian that he had treated in *s.* 294 to defend the claim that the Church's teaching on the purpose of infant baptism is ancient and universal.[140] "Blessed Cyprian," he says, "has rightly made it quite clear how the Church has from the beginning preserved this [teaching] in her faith and

---

137 *pecc. mer.* 3.4.9: *non tamen poterunt alium sensum habere, nisi per quem factum est, ut antiquitus uniuersa ecclesia retineret fideles paruulos originalis peccati remissionem per Christi baptismum consecutos* (Latin: CSEL 60:135.7–13; English: Teske, WSA I/23, 121, slightly modified).

138 See Dunphy, "A Lost Year," 449.

139 See *ep.* 139.3.

140 See *pecc. mer.* 3.5.10 and *s.* 294.19.

A CONTROVERSY IN CARTHAGE 121

understanding."[141] Further, Augustine notes, "although [Cyprian] furnished [these little ones] with the great protection of a defense, he nevertheless confessed that they were not free from original sin."[142] Augustine then offers two quotations from Cyprian's *ep.* 64. In the first quotation (which was not employed in *s.* 294), Cyprian indicates that he has been asked whether it would be permissible to baptize infants before they are eight days old, when the Law had decreed that male infants should be circumcised. Cyprian replies that a recent council had treated this very issue and determined that infants could certainly be baptized prior to the eighth day, lest they die and their souls be lost.[143] After supplying the quotation from Cyprian, Augustine turns to his reader, emphasizing Cyprian's opinion on the perilous state of unbaptized infants: "Do you see what he says, how he thinks that to depart from this life without that saving sacrament is deadly and lethal, not merely to the flesh, but also to the soul of the infant?"[144] Augustine quickly offers a second quotation from Cyprian—the one he had used in *s.* 294—in which the martyr-bishop indicates that infants have no sins of their own, but have contracted "the contagion of ancient death" from Adam.[145] Indeed, Cyprian argues, the infant receives baptism not for the forgiveness of "its own sins, but for those of another [*non propria, sed aliena peccata*]."[146] Augustine then

---

141 *pecc. mer.* 3.5.10: *unde non inmerito beatus Cyprianus satis ostendit, quam hoc ab initio creditum et intellectum seruet ecclesia* (Latin: CSEL 60:135.14–15; English: Teske, WSA I/23, 121).

142 *pecc. mer.* 3.5.10: *cum magnum eis defensionis patrocinium praestitisset, ab originali tamen peccato eos inmunes non esse confessus est* (Latin: CSEL 60:135.21–22; English: my translation). Teske's translation has a different sense: "[A]lthough he offered them the strong protection of his defense, he did not admit that they were free from original sin" (Teske, WSA I/23, 121). Teske has taken the *non* with *confessus est* rather than *esse*. This translation choice weakens Augustine's statement and makes it seem as if he were merely employing an argument from silence (i.e., since Cyprian does not state that infants are *without* original sin, he must have believed that they do have original sin). In fact, Augustine is making a stronger claim: Cyprian affirms that infants are not free from original sin.

143 Cyprian, *ep.* 64.2 (CCL 3C:419). Augustine had not mentioned this conciliar context in *s.* 294.

144 *pecc. mer.* 3.5.10: *aduertisne quid dicat, quemadmodum sentiat non tantum carni, sed animae quoque infantis exitiabile esse atque mortiferum sine illo salutari sacramento exire de hac uita?* (Latin: CSEL 60:136.16–19; English: Teske, WSA I/23, 122, slightly modified). Augustine references this passage at several other points later in the controversy—see, e.g., *nupt. et conc.* 2.29.51.

145 *pecc. mer.* 3.5.10 (Latin: CSEL 60:137.4; English: Teske, WSA I/23, 122).

146 *pecc. mer.* 3.5.10 (Latin: CSEL 60:137.6–7; English: Teske, WSA I/23, 122). See Cyprian, *ep.* 64.5 (CCL 3C:424–25).

states: "You see with what immense confidence this great man speaks on the basis of the ancient and undoubted rule of faith [*ex antiqua et indubitata fidei regula*]. He offered these most certain proofs so that he might bolster what was uncertain by means of their strength."[147] Augustine emphasizes here that Cyprian's opinion was not simply his own but was drawn from the ancient rule of faith itself. Indeed, Augustine argues that Cyprian and the other bishops gathered in council, deliberating on the question of whether a child could receive baptism before the eighth day, were so certain of the Church's view of the danger faced by unbaptized infants that they were able to resolve the disputed question. In this sense, Augustine tries to show that Cyprian's words not only indicate the support of a renowned and ancient bishop and martyr for Augustine's position, but also make clear that the viewpoint espoused by Cyprian was not in dispute in Cyprian's own day. As a result, Augustine can claim that his view on original sin is at least as old as Cyprian, but no doubt much older, while the Pelagian opinion is utterly novel: "And now, with the presumption of a new argument (I do not know whose argument it is) some people are striving to make something uncertain for us which our forefathers presented as very certain so as to resolve questions some saw as uncertain."[148] In this way, the Pelagians are presented as innovators attempting to overturn long-held beliefs.

Having demonstrated the antiquity of the doctrine of original sin through reference to Cyprian, Augustine next calls forward Jerome, who will help him to emphasize the universality of this doctrine as well as the novelty of the Pelagian position. This choice to quote Jerome requires some explanation as it appears, in fact, to be a very calculated decision. At a most basic level, the appeal to Jerome may possibly be read as a response to an objection by Augustine's opponents that Cyprian's view was idiosyncratic or simply reflective of African or western theology. For this reason, Augustine emphasizes Jerome's knowledge of both Latin and Greek and his familiarity

---

147 *pecc. mer.* 3.5.11 (Latin: CSEL 60:137.8–13; English: Teske, WSA I/23, 122, slightly modified).

148 *pecc. mer.* 3.6.12 (Latin: CSEL 60:138.8–11; English: my translation). Perhaps unexpectedly, in this treatment of the quotation from Cyprian, Augustine does not draw as much attention to the importance of the conciliar decision as he does to Cyprian's own words. He explains the decision of the council but does not emphasize it rhetorically in the same way he does with the quotations from Cyprian (here I disagree with Éric Rebillard's reading of the passage—see Rebillard, "A New Style of Argument," 567). However, this is no doubt due to the fact that an obscure African council would hold less argumentative weight than the position of Cyprian himself (especially among Roman émigrés).

A CONTROVERSY IN CARTHAGE

with a wide variety of ecclesiastical literature.[149] It is also possible that the appeal to Jerome here should be read as a subtle rejoinder to Caelestius's appeal to Rufinus (of Aquileia?) at his trial in Carthage. Indeed, when asked by Paulinus to name a priest that had rejected the transmission of sin, Caelestius mentioned the "holy priest Rufinus."[150] Could Augustine have been intentionally using Jerome's testimony as a counterpoint to that of Jerome's old friend-turned-nemesis, Rufinus?[151] In addition, as Walter Dunphy points out, another possible reason for the appeal to Jerome is that it seems likely that Jerome was being used as an authority by the Pelagians in Carthage in 411.[152] As we noted earlier, at some point around 411, Marcellinus wrote to Jerome requesting his point of view on the origin of the soul (Jerome was a supporter of creationism).[153] This issue is, of course, intimately tied to the doctrine of original sin—and creationism posed a key difficulty for Augustine in his theological account of the transmission of Adam's sin. Indeed, the topic surfaces several times in *De peccatorum meritis* (see especially *pecc. mer.* 2.36.59) and Augustine would later write his own letter to Jerome on this same issue several years later (*ep.* 166).[154] Further, Dunphy calls attention to the fact that Pelagius cites Jerome in his *De natura* (albeit to defend free will, not to promote a particular account of the soul's origin). All told, Dunphy concludes, it seems likely that Jerome's "opinion was being invoked," and Augustine felt the need to respond.[155]

When Augustine appeals to Jerome, he first establishes Jerome's authority on the basis of his knowledge of ecclesiastical writings and his teaching—"a man who is presently engaged in ecclesiastical writings due to his labor and reputation for very excellent teaching."[156] Then Augustine indicates that Jerome, too, provides evidence for the orthodoxy of the doctrine of original

---

149 See below for more on this.

150 See *gr. et pecc. or.* 2.3.3.

151 This, of course, assumes that the Rufinus referred to by Caelestius was, in fact, Rufinus of Aquileia and not some other Rufinus.

152 See Dunphy, "A Lost Year," 443.

153 See Jerome's letter in reply to Marcellinus and Anapsychia found in the letters of Augustine (*ep.* 165).

154 For Augustine's most complete investigation into the problem, see his *De anima et eius origine* (written in several stages, sometime after 419).

155 Dunphy, "A Lost Year," 443.

156 *pecc. mer.* 3.6.12 (Latin: CSEL 60:138.13–14; English: my translation).

sin. When commenting on Jonah 3, Jerome indicates that the reason why all the people in Nineveh—even the smallest among them—fasted after hearing Jonah's words was that no human beings are without sin and that all are "held subject to the sin of Adam the transgressor."[157] Augustine then notes that, given Jerome's learning and familiarity with ecclesiastical authors, he (Jerome) could no doubt list numerous other commentators on scripture who hold to the same doctrine. Augustine emphasizes his point with repetition:

> If we could easily question this highly learned man, how many commentators on the divine scriptures in both languages and how many authors of Christian treatises would he mention who have thought nothing else from the time Christ's Church was founded, received nothing else from their predecessors, handed on nothing else to their successors![158]

Indeed, Augustine himself states that he has never encountered any other doctrine in the books he has read—and, until very recently, had never even heard anyone advance the tenets of the Pelagian doctrine. A striking feature of this passage is that, despite a lack of concrete evidence for the universality of the doctrine of original sin, Augustine has rhetorically emphasized Jerome's learning to such a degree that concrete evidence may seem unnecessary in the mind of the reader: Jerome is so learned that the reader should accept his words merely as a summary of the positions of all other ecclesiastical writers of *both languages*.[159] In this way, Augustine artfully expands Jerome's apparent affirmation of infantile guilt into evidence for a universal belief in original sin. In the context of Augustine's argument, this serves two purposes. First, it reinforces Augustine's point that the doctrine of original sin is deeply rooted in the Church's faith. Second, it indicates just how novel the Pelagian position is: Jerome, much like Cyprian, takes the certitude of the doctrine for granted when he uses it to interpret an aspect of the book of Jonah.

Continuing to press this latter point, Augustine then mentions the case of Jovinian, who had recently caused a controversy in Rome by teaching that

---

157 *pecc. mer.* 3.6.12 (Latin: CSEL 60:138.22–23; English: Teske, WSA I/23, 123). See Jerome, *Commentariorum in Ionam prophetam* 3.5 (Latin: SC 323:268).

158 *pecc. mer.* 3.6.12 (Latin: CSEL 60:138.23–139.3; English: Teske, WSA I/23, 123, slightly modified).

159 For emphasis on this point, see Dunphy, "A Lost Year," 443–44.

virginity was not preferred to marriage in God's eyes.[160] Augustine suggests that a denial of original sin may have helped Jovinian's case—presumably, virgins would be more willing to renounce their vows if they realized they could bear children free from original sin. Yet, Augustine notes, it appears that Jovinian did not employ this tactic. Further, Augustine highlights the fact that, in his *Aduersus Iouinianum*, Jerome argued for the superiority of virginity by appealing to the universality of sin and the subsequent need for an ascetical life to overcome sin—thus presupposing, Augustine argues, that Jovinian would have accepted this principle of the universality of sin and, consequently, the doctrine of original sin.[161]

Augustine's argument here seems to be a bit of a stretch. But putting the issue of whether Jovinian held some version of the doctrine of original sin to the side, it is important to understand why Augustine refers to Jovinian. First of all, we should note the broader context: Jovinian, Pelagius, and Caelestius were possibly all present in Rome at roughly the same time in the early 390s. Thus, Augustine proposes, if the Pelagians had already been spreading their views on original sin at that time, Jovinian would have been familiar with (and receptive to) them. But because (the argument would continue) Jovinian seems not to have been familiar with the Pelagian view, it seems that view had to have been invented even more recently than the time of the Jovinianist Controversy. A second reason for Augustine's reference to Jovinian is that many of Pelagius's allies in Carthage were likely Roman refugees. Thus, it seems plausible that it was with this audience in mind that Augustine

---

160 For more on the Jovinianist controversy, see Y.-M. Duval, *L'affaire Jovinien: d'une crise de la société romaine à une crise de la pensée chrétienne à la fin du IV et au début du Ve siècle* (Rome: Institutum Patristicum Augustinianum, 2003), and David G. Hunter, *Marriage, Celibacy, and Heresy in Ancient Christianity: The Jovinianist Controversy* (Oxford: Oxford University Press, 2009).

161 Jerome writes, "But according to the Letter of James, 'we all sin in many ways' (Jas 3:2), and 'no one is clean from sin, even if one's life lasts only a single day' (Job 14:4–5). 'For who is going to boast of having a chaste heart? Or who is going to presume to be clean from sins' (Prov 20:9)? We are held guilty in the likeness of Adam's transgression. For this reason, David too says, 'See, I was conceived in iniquities and my mother conceived me in transgressions' (Ps 51:7)" (*Aduersus Iouinianum* 2.2 [PL 23:296]; in *pecc. mer.* 3.7.13; Latin: CSEL 60:140.18–25; English: Teske, WSA I/23, 124). It should be noted that in *Aduersus Iouinianum* 2.3, Jerome employs the Lord's Prayer to refute the notion that Christians do not sin after baptism. Could the anti-Pelagians in Rome and/or Augustine himself have drawn inspiration from this approach?

chose to reference Jovinian.[162] But how does Augustine use this discussion of Jovinian to further his polemical aims? Augustine's point is not to use the testimony of a heretic (as if he were just as reliable a witness to orthodox doctrine as Cyprian or Jerome), but rather to try to indicate both the novelty of the Pelagian doctrine and universality of belief in original sin prior to the outbreak of Pelagianism. In this sense, the reference to Jovinian functions as an *a fortiori* argument: if even a heretic who would have benefited from a denial of original sin accepted the doctrine, then even more so have all orthodox Christians assented to this teaching.

As he concludes this section, Augustine offers a clear explanation of his purpose in quoting Cyprian and Jerome:

> I have not quoted these words because we rely upon the views of certain writers as if upon a canonical authority [*canonica auctoritate*], but so that it would be evident that, from the beginning up to the present time when this new opinion arose, this teaching on original sin was preserved in the faith of the Church with such great constancy that, in order to refute other false ideas, the commentators on God's words appealed to it as utterly certain rather than that anyone tried to refute it as false.[163]

Note Augustine's caution here—something that was not displayed in *s.* 294. Augustine is very careful here, and, as we shall see, elsewhere, to emphasize that when he quotes individuals like Cyprian and Jerome, he does not intend to present them as canonical authorities, as if they were equal to scripture. As we already discussed in the introduction, Augustine was writing at a time when so-called patristic argumentation was still in its infancy. Augustine himself was evidently uncomfortable with its usage,[164] although he had previously been forced to employ it to combat the Donatists' appeals to Cyprian. Now in the Pelagian controversy it became necessary once more: desperate times called for desperate measures. Augustine's anxiety over this issue—and his apparent concern that he might be accused of some sort of

---

162 Regarding the rather odd appeal to Jerome's *Aduersus Iouinianum* here, Dunphy writes, "When it came to offering a writing from Jerome to support his case it may seem surprising that Augustine should select Jerome's *Aduersus Iouinianum*, a writing that was highly controversial in Rome when it was published. But at the end of the day in that earlier dispute Jovinian was the condemned heretic and Jerome, his opponents liking it or not, was the voice of orthodoxy" ("A Lost Year," 444).

163 *pecc. mer.* 3.7.14 (Latin: CSEL 60:141.1–7; English: Teske, WSA I/23, 124, slightly modified).

164 See, e.g., Augustine's comments at *ep.* 75.3.6 and *bapt.* 2.3.4.

A CONTROVERSY IN CARTHAGE

impropriety—suggests just how important it was for him to demonstrate the antiquity and universality of the doctrine of original sin. He was willing to risk employing a relatively novel form of argument to defend what he believed to be the universal Church's ancient faith in a context where he felt the threat of schism was all too real.

After briefly refuting a few other arguments reported by Pelagius in his *expositio*, Augustine turns to his conclusion, where he recaps his main arguments. The two final elements of this recap are of particular importance for us. First, he addresses again a Pelagian argument that had surfaced earlier at *pecc. mer.* 2.25.41, that St. Paul's words at 1 Cor 7:14 ("For a husband who does not believe is sanctified in his wife . . . otherwise, your children would be unclean, but now they are holy"[165]) seem to indicate that children of baptized parents do not have original sin.[166] After suggesting a few possible interpretations of the verse so as to reject that Pelagian conclusion, Augustine identifies the true danger in the Pelagian assertion that children of the baptized are born holy:

> That argument—the novelty of which we must labor against by means of the ancient truth—aims at this: that infants seem to be baptized entirely superfluously. But this is not said openly, lest the Church's custom, which has been established so profitably, be unable to bear those who violate it.[167]

In these lines, Augustine indicates, perhaps in the clearest way yet, that the same practice both offers resistance to the Pelagian view and, at the same time, is threatened by that view: the Church's well-established practice of infant baptism. For Augustine, the Pelagians' theology appears to lead them to the brink of questioning the practice of infant baptism—but it is, in fact, that practice's very universality and antiquity that keeps them from following their positions to their logical conclusion.

A few lines later, Augustine then mentions the main topic of his second book: the Pelagian belief that human sinlessness is possible in this life. Here, he makes a brief reference to the Lord's Prayer, and by doing so implicitly hearkens back to his arguments in the second book, where he faulted the

---

165 See *pecc. mer.* 3.12.21 (Latin: CSEL 60:148.19–22; English: Teske, WSA I/23, 129).

166 For more on Augustine's response to this argument see n. 130 above.

167 *pecc. mer.* 3.13.22 (Latin: 60:149.20–23; English: my translation).

Pelagians for basically presenting the view that some Christians may not need to pray the Lord's Prayer given their own holiness and lack of sin:

> These people claim, however, that some human beings, who already have the use of their own reason, will live, have lived, or are now living without any sin. We should hope that this will be the case; we should strive to make it so; we should pray that it will be so. We should not, however, presume that it is already the case. After all, for those who hope for and strive after and pray for this with suitable prayers, whatever is left of their sins is daily removed by the words we truthfully say in the prayer, "Forgive us our debts, as we also forgive our debtors."[168]

In this way, Augustine closes the final book of *De peccatorum meritis* by firmly rooting his argumentation in solid evidence drawn from the Church's liturgical tradition: the practice of infant baptism and the daily recitation of the Lord's Prayer. In so doing, he has attempted to ground his positions in the Church's universal practice, a practice that he claims can be traced back to the apostles themselves. And in this way, he concludes the third book just as he began it: by asserting that the Pelagians run afoul of the Church's ancient and universal doctrine.

CONCLUSION

As I have argued so far, it is important to recognize the broader context of Augustine's entry into the Pelagian controversy in 411. In the aftermath of the sack of Rome, a sizeable contingent of (in some cases, quite wealthy) Italian refugees had arrived in Africa. Some of these new arrivals were not only circulating their own theological positions but were also accusing others of holding novel positions[169] and of diverging from the faith of the eastern churches.[170] All this was happening while the Catholics and Donatists prepared to meet at Carthage in June of 411 to settle their dispute once and for all (or so the Catholics hoped) before the imperial tribune Marcellinus. The last thing that was needed was division within the Catholic community—and yet this is precisely what seemed to be happening.

---

168 *pecc. mer.* 3.13.23 (Latin: CSEL 60:150.1–8; English: Teske, WSA I/23, 130).

169 *s.* 294.19.

170 *gest. Pel.* 11.25.

A CONTROVERSY IN CARTHAGE   129

Augustine initially set out to respond to the Pelagian threat in the three books of *De peccatorum meritis* and in *ss.* 293 and 294.[171] While it is true that one of Augustine's aims in these works was to defend certain doctrinal views (and to attack others), it would be a mistake to attribute his anti-Pelagian activity to this motivation alone. Indeed, as we have seen, when we keep in mind the historical context and pay attention to Augustine's argumentation and to the way in which he attempted to assert the orthodoxy of certain positions, it becomes clear that Augustine was concerned not simply to demonstrate that his opponents' positions were false, but to do so while asserting the universality and antiquity of his own positions. Through our analysis above, we have seen Augustine draw attention to the Church's practice of infant baptism, to certain details of the baptismal rite, to the Church's daily custom of reciting the Lord's Prayer. Augustine attempts to ground his anti-Pelagian arguments in such pieces of evidence precisely because they enable him (1) to argue that the Church's ancient and universal practice militates against the Pelagian positions and thereby (2) to undercut the divisive arguments employed by the Pelagians. Of course, the most important pieces of evidence are those deployed in *s.* 294 and *pecc. mer.* 3—namely, the citations of Cyprian and (in the case of *pecc. mer.* 3) Jerome. As we have already noted, the very fact that Augustine would cite renowned Christian authors demonstrates how seriously Augustine took the growing crisis, and how concerned he was to head-off potential disunity or schism within the Church. While this concern is readily apparent at the beginning of the controversy, it only grows as the first phase of the crisis reaches its crescendo several years later in the aftermath of the Synod of Diospolis.[172] Let us now turn to our next chapter, which will treat the road to this synod and the events of the synod itself.

---

171 Augustine's anti-Pelagian efforts would continue throughout 411. See, for example, *s.* 299, mentioned briefly above. See also his lengthy *ep.* 140 (also known as *De gratia testamenti noui*), which we will mention briefly at the beginning of the next chapter.

172 It might be asked why Augustine did not do more in these initial anti-Pelagian works to emphasize the unity of the Africans and the West with the eastern churches. Part of the answer may simply be Augustine feared to draw more attention to the Pelagian claim by addressing it more directly. Indeed, it is only in 416/17 in *gest. Pel.* that he admits that that claim was circulating—and he brings it up there because (he argues) he has evidence that fourteen eastern bishops were opposed to Pelagianism. The best method Augustine seems to have had at his disposal to prove that his positions were not opposed to those taught in the East was patristic argumentation. But Augustine, as we have said, took time to warm up to this argumentative technique. Further, Augustine may have also had limited access to relevant works of eastern theology.

CHAPTER 3

The Road to Diospolis

Having explored the events and writings of 411 and the beginning of 412, we now turn in this chapter to the period from 412 to the end of 415. The early portion of this period was relatively calm for Augustine, at least as far as concerned the controversy with the Pelagians. However, in 414 and 415, the debate began escalating once again, leading to an important confrontation at the Synod of Diospolis in December of 415. It was also likely in late 414 that Augustine gained access to Pelagius's *De natura* and, for the first time, had proof that the rumors about Pelagius's views on grace were accurate. *De natura* also gave Augustine evidence of Pelagius's use of patristic argumentation—no doubt heightening Augustine's sense of the Pelagian threat to the unity of the Church. As we begin our analysis of this period in this chapter, let us turn to the immediate aftermath of 411 and examine Augustine's continuing anti-Pelagian efforts.

A SEQUEL TO *DE PECCATORUM MERITIS* 2: *DE SPIRITU ET LITTERA*

As we saw in the previous chapter, after drafting the first two books of *De peccatorum meritis* and part of the third in the summer of 411, Augustine seems to have been caught up in other matters for the remainder of the year that delayed the completion of the book.

After returning home to Hippo at some point in the second half of 411, Augustine encountered a great deal of administrative work, having been absent from his diocese for perhaps five months. In *ep.* 139, written likely in late 411 or early 412, Augustine shares with Marcellinus his dismay that such necessities have prevented him from completing the third book of *De peccatorum meritis* as well as from addressing Marcellinus's concerns with the first two books.[1] However, it seems that the questions and concerns of the Pelagian controversy were not far from Augustine's mind. In this letter to Marcellinus, Augustine mentions another work that he had been composing: a response to five diverse questions that a certain Honoratus had sent to him. Augustine would entitle this work written for Honoratus *De gratia noui testamenti* (= *ep.* 140).[2] Here, Augustine takes Honoratus's questions and organizes his response to them via a sixth question of his own making. As Augustine recalls later in his *Retractationes*, "But, considering the new heresy mentioned above that is hostile to the grace of God [i.e., Pelagianism], I proposed for myself a sixth question on the grace of the New Testament."[3] In this way, Augustine uses his response to Honoratus as an opportunity to reflect on grace and to spread his particular understanding of the New Testament's doctrine of grace—as well as to head off any potential influence the Pelagians might have had on Honoratus in Carthage. For this reason, *De gratia noui testamenti* is sometimes classed among Augustine's anti-Pelagian works. Despite his on-going administrative duties and continuing efforts to deal with the aftermath of the Donatist Conference, it is clear that the issues of the Pelagian controversy were not far from Augustine's mind.

The first half of 412 likely saw the completion and publication of *De pec-catorum meritis*, although it is unclear when exactly it was finished. Unfortunately for Augustine, *De peccatorum meritis* did not satisfy all Marcellinus's concerns. As Augustine suggests in *ep.* 139 and explains more clearly at the beginning of *De spiritu et littera*, Marcellinus had difficulty accepting some

---

1 *ep.* 139.3 (Latin: CSEL 44:152.5–153.19). At this point, Augustine states that he has forgotten what Marcellinus's concerns were.

2 For more on *ep.* 140, see Isabelle Bochet, "Une nouvelle lecture du *Liber ad Honoratum* d'Augustin (= *epist.* 140)," *Revue des études augustiniennes* 45 (1999): 335–51; Gerald Bonner, "The Significance of Augustine's *De Gratia Novi Testamenti*," *Augustiniana* 41 (1991): 531–59. See also the helpful introduction available in Pierre Descotes, *La grâce de la nouvelle alliance*, BA 20/B (Paris: Institut d'Études Augustiniennes, 2016).

3 *retr.* 2.36 (Latin: CCL 57.120.17–19; English: my translation). See also Augustine's comments at *ep.* 140.37.83 where he warns his reader about the enemies of grace.

THE ROAD TO DIOSPOLIS

of Augustine's conclusions in *De peccatorum meritis* 2.[4] More specifically, Marcellinus objected to Augustine's assertion that it was possible for humans to be sinless in this life, but that an example of such sinlessness would not be found (aside from Christ). Marcellinus (or others in his circle[5]) did not understand how something could be possible and yet without an example. While Augustine seems to have received this objection from Marcellinus in 411, his response would be delayed until 412 or perhaps even early 413 in the form of *De spiritu et littera*.[6]

De spiritu et littera is rather different from Augustine's other major anti-Pelagian treatises in the sense that its composition was not prompted by a "new development" in the controversy. Every other major anti-Pelagian treatise was written after Augustine acquired or became aware of some new Pelagian text, argument, or statement.[7] While *De spiritu et littera* does target the Pelagians and addresses certain of their views on grace and its role in

---

4 See *ep.* 139.3 (Latin: CSEL 44:152.5–153.19) and *spir. et litt.* 1.1 (Latin: CSEL 60:155.5–10). See also *retr.* 2.37 (Latin: CCL 57:120.3–121.25).

5 See Augustine's comments at *spir. et litt.* 35.61 as he begins to conclude his treatise: "Let us, then, at last bring the book to a close; I do not know whether we have accomplished anything with all its length. I do not mean in your regard, for I know your faith, but with the minds of those on account of whom you wanted me to write" (Latin: CSEL 60:221.5–8; English: Teske, WSA I/23, 185).

6 A precise dating here is impossible to give. It would seem that the book was completed at the latest by September 413, when Marcellinus was executed for allegedly supporting Heraclian's rebellion. But see Volker Henning Drecoll, "Marcellinus, Flauius," in A-L 3, 1162, who suggests that the composition of *De spiritu et littera* could have continued after the execution. However, it seems that Drecoll's chronology of 411–13 (see "Gratia," in A-L 3, 208n189) is a bit off: he assigns *ep.* 139 to December 412–February 413, instead of December 411–February 412, which pushes back his chronology for the completion of *De peccatorum meritis* and commencement of *De spiritu et littera* into 413.

7 *De peccatorum meritis* 1–2 was prompted by Marcellinus's questions, Caelestius's trial, and the anonymous Pelagian book (by Caelestius?) that Augustine had acquired. *De peccatorum meritis* 3 was prompted by (perhaps among other things) Augustine's reading of Pelagius's *Expositiones*. *De natura et gratia* is written to refute Pelagius's *De natura*. *De perfectione iustitiae hominis* refutes the *Definitiones* attributed to Caelestius. *De gestis Pelagii* offers an interpretation of the *acta* of the Synod of Diospolis, including Pelagius's own words as found therein. *De gratia Christi et de peccato originali* responds to a few statements made by Pelagius and also addresses several other Pelagian writings. *De nuptiis et concupiscentia* 1 was written in response to rumors that the Pelagians had accused Augustine of condemning marriage by holding the doctrine of original sin. *De nuptiis et concupiscentia* 2 was written to refute a summarized version of Julian of Eclanum's *Ad Turbantium*. *Contra duas epistulas Pelagianorum* was, obviously, written to refute two Pelagian letters. The *Contra Julianum* is a refutation of Julian's *Ad Turbantium*. The *Opus imperfectum contra Julianum* is a refutation of Julian's *Ad Florum*.

the pursuit of a sinless life, overall the treatise is less a refutation of Pelagian views than a positive presentation and scriptural account of Augustine's own position on the mechanics of grace, free will, and the avoidance of sin. Indeed, specific Pelagian views are only referred to in a handful of places in the treatise (anonymously, of course), and the views that are mentioned are little different from those already reported in *De peccatorum meritis* 2, especially in the section on grace at the beginning of that work (which itself, as we noted previously, seems to have been informed especially by rumors Augustine had heard of the Pelagians' views in Rome).[8] Overall, *De spiritu et littera* is an attempt by Augustine to wade into the issues he had touched on in *De peccatorum meritis* 2 more deeply and thoroughly. But much had likely changed since the writing of the first two books of *De peccatorum meritis*: Pelagius and (almost certainly) Caelestius had left Africa for other shores, and the initial furor that had surrounded them (or at least the latter) in the first half of 411 had probably subsided.[9] Augustine had, it would seem, received no new word on Pelagius's or Caelestius's positions and had not gained access to any new texts. Instead, his main aim in *De spiritu et littera* was to address the concerns of Marcellinus himself (although it remains possible that Marcellinus had asked Augustine to explain himself on behalf of others[10]). As a result, direct polemics against the Pelagians are rather limited in this text.[11]

Given this context, we should expect Augustine's argumentation in this text to be different from that found in, say, *De peccatorum meritis*. And this is what we find. As was already noted above, the majority of Augustine's arguments in *De spiritu et littera* are based in scripture, as the bishop of Hippo attempts to trace out the roles of law and grace in the pursuit of righteousness. Indeed, there are only a few instances in *De spiritu et littera*

---

8 The main passages where Pelagian views are cited are *spir. et litt.* 2.3–4 and 8.13–9.15 (but note that there are a handful of other passages where Augustine briefly alludes to the Pelagians).

9 On occasion, a resurgence of Pelagianism in Carthage is posited for 413 (see, e.g., Drecoll, "Gratia," 205). However, it is important to note that this resurgence is tied directly to the dating of *ss.* 293 and 294 (traditionally dated to the summer of 413). Once these sermons are moved to the summer of 411, there is no concrete evidence that suggests a revival of Pelagianism in Carthage in 413. See Dunphy, "A Lost Year," 459.

10 See n. 5 above.

11 It should be noted that Augustine does deploy at *spir. et litt.* 13.22 the key phrase from Book 10 of *Confessiones* ("*da quod iubes*") that had angered Pelagius (see *perseu.* 20.53).

THE ROAD TO DIOSPOLIS

where Augustine relies on non-Scriptural evidence. The first is at *spir. et lit.* 11.18, where we find a reference to the dialogue prior to the preface of the Eucharistic Prayer.[12] In this passage, Augustine is discussing righteousness and its origin. Having argued that righteousness comes only as a gift by the grace of God, Augustine notes:

> Such thoughts [i.e., that righteousness comes from God] make them pious, because piety is true wisdom. I mean the piety which the Greeks call θεοσέβεια. The words we read in the Book of Job commend it to us, "See piety is wisdom" (Job 28:28). Moreover, if it is translated into Latin according to its etymology, it can be called the worship of God [*dei cultus*], which was principally established so that the soul might not be ungrateful to God. For this reason in the truest and only sacrifice we are admonished to give thanks to the Lord our God.[13]

Augustine's argument here is a bit winding, but it seems to progress as follows:

1. righteousness comes from God;

2. people who recognize that righteousness comes from God are pious;

3. piety is the same as wisdom;

4. the word for piety in Greek can be translated as "worship of God";

5. the purpose of worship (=piety) is to give thanks to God;

6. Evidence: in the liturgy, where we offer true worship to God, we are told to give thanks to the Lord our God.

Diagrammed in this way, the reference to the liturgical prayer of the Church serves as evidence for the intrinsic connection between worship and thanksgiving—and, more broadly, as evidence for the connection between thanksgiving and piety. For Augustine, then, the liturgy voices the fundamental

---

12 Augustine discusses this dialogue elsewhere. See, e.g., *s.* 227, which seems to date to early in the Pelagian controversy: "Therefore, when it is said, 'Lift up your heart,' you respond, 'We lift it up to the Lord.' And lest you attribute the fact that you lift your heart up to the Lord to your own powers, merits, or labors—since it is a gift of God that you lift up your heart—for this reason the bishop or priest who is offering also says (after the people have responded, 'We lift our heart up to the Lord'), 'Let us give thanks to the Lord our God' since we have lifted up our heart. Let us give thanks since if he were not to give it, our hearts would be on the ground [and not lifted up]. And when you say, 'It is right and just,' you all testify that we give thanks to him who brought it about that we lift up our heart to our Head" (Latin: SC 116 [1966]:238.49–240.59; English: my translation).

13 *spir. et litt.* 11.18 (Latin: CSEL 60:170.7–13; English: Teske, WSA I/23, 154).

theological point he is trying to make: righteousness comes from God, and it is right and just for us to give thanks to God for having enabled us to act righteously.

A second reference to the Church's traditions of prayer is found at the end of *De spiritu et littera*. After summarizing his argument, Augustine offers a final discussion of the type of righteousness possible in this life versus the type possible in the next. He begins by noting the extent to which people in this life can be said not to sin: "But if there can be said to be a certain lesser righteousness corresponding to this life, by which the righteous person lives from faith, although he is apart from the Lord and therefore walking by faith, not yet by sight—if this can be said, then, not absurdly is it also said that it pertains to this righteousness that one does not sin."[14] Augustine continues on to note that in this life, walking by faith and not by sight, the righteous have a less-than-perfect love for God—something that will be perfected only in the beatific vision. In practice, this less-than-perfect love results in the fact that even the righteous are confronted with temptations in this life. Furthermore, it seems that even the righteous in this life do, at times, consent to these temptations and sin. To support this claim, Augustine turns to the Lord's Prayer as well as several passages from scripture:

> Do such righteous persons living from faith have no need to say, "Forgive us our debts, as we also forgive our debtors"? Do they prove false the words of scripture, "No living person will be found righteous in your sight" (Ps 143:2)? Or the words, "If we say that we have no sin, we deceive ourselves, and the truth is not in us" (1 John 1:8)? Or the words, "There is not a human being who will not sin" (1 Kgs 8:46)? Or the words, "There is not a righteous person on earth who will do good and will not sin" (Eccl 7:21)?[15]

Although Augustine combines the reference to the Lord's Prayer here with other passages from scripture, it is important to note that he is not simply referring to the petition as just another scriptural passage. Rather, note how he divides the petition from the Lord's Prayer from the scriptural quotes that follow. In this way, Augustine draws the authority of the petition not

---

14 *spir. et litt.* 36.65: *sed si dici potest quaedam iustitia minor huic uitae conpetens, qua iustus ex fide uiuit, quamuis peregrinus a domino et ideo per fidem ambulans, nondum per speciem, non absurde dicitur etiam ad istam pertinere ne peccet* (Latin: CSEL 60:225.16–19; English: my translation).

15 *spir. et litt.* 36.65 (Latin: CSEL 60:227.5–13; English: Teske, WSA I/23, 188).

THE ROAD TO DIOSPOLIS

simply (or even mainly) from its scriptural source, but rather from its use in the Church's prayer. Augustine hopes that the Christian practice of praying the Lord's Prayer provides compelling evidence to support his argument.

All in all, *De spiritu et littera* offers little in the way of evidence designed to counter the Pelagians' claims that their positions are those of the ancient and universal Church. Given the context and aim of the work as outlined above, though, this is to be expected. Nevertheless, the discussion of the dynamics of liturgical prayer and the reference to the Lord's Prayer in the concluding section of the treatise are significant: they show that even in a less polemical context, Augustine was keen to highlight the ways in which Pelagian doctrine ran counter to the universal Church's life of prayer.

A GROWING CONFLICT: 413–15

With the completion of *De spiritu et littera*, we might say that the first phase of the Pelagian controversy came to an end—that is, Augustine's reaction to the initial disturbances caused by Caelestius in Carthage in 411. Our sources have little to say about any anti-Pelagian activities undertaken by Augustine in 413, aside from the completion of *De spiritu et littera* (if that had not already taken place in 412). It is possible that, in the absence of new information, other matters took precedence. However, it does seem from our sources that Augustine was far from disinterested or unconcerned about the spread of Pelagianism. This concern appears very prominently in 414, when news from a variety of sources began to reach Augustine's ears.

The first hint of trouble came in the aftermath of a joyous event in Carthage: the veiling of Demetrias, a young member of the wealthy *gens Anicia*, who had decided to pursue a life of consecrated virginity.[16] Following the sack of Rome in 410, Demetrias, along with her mother Juliana and grandmother Proba, had fled to Africa.[17] It was there that they seem to have met

---

16 For more on this episode and the family of the *Anicii* in relation to the Pelagian controversy, see Geoffrey D. Dunn, "The Christian Networks of the *Aniciae*: The Example of the Letter of Innocent I to Anicia Juliana," *Revue d'études augustiniennes et patristiques* 55 (2009): 53–72; Dunphy, "St. Jerome and the Gens Anicia (Ep. 130 to Demetrias)"; Andrew S. Jacobs, "Writing Demetrias: Ascetic Logic in Ancient Christianity," *Church History* 69 (2000): 719–48; Laurence, "Proba, Juliana et Démétrias"; Ogliari, "An Anti-Pelagian *caueat*."

17 The *Anicii* left Italy and arrived in Africa not without controversy and strife. Proba had been accused of allowing Alaric and his army entry into the city of Rome (see Laurence, "Proba, Juliana et Démétrias," 142ff.). Upon their arrival in Africa, they and many women in their entourage were taken captive by Heraclian, Count of Africa (who would in 413 lead a

Augustine and his friend Alypius, the bishop of Thagaste, who both played some role in Demetrias's decision to cancel her plans to wed and undertake a life of asceticism.[18] The veiling ceremony likely took place in Carthage in late 413 or in 414.[19] Following this event, Demetrias's mother Juliana sent letters to notable Christians, requesting a letter of advice for her daughter as she embarked on a life of asceticism. Perhaps among others, these requests were sent to Pelagius and Jerome.[20] Augustine first mentions Pelagius's *Epistula ad Demetriadem* in 418[21]—however, we do have indications that he was aware years earlier that Juliana had written to Pelagius, and perhaps even that Pelagius had responded to her.

In 414, shortly after Demetrias's veiling, Augustine wrote *De bono uiduitatis* for Juliana, who had apparently been requesting that he write on widowhood for her for some time.[22] Augustine divides this brief work into two

---

short-lived rebellion against Emperor Honorius). The *Anicii* avoided being sold into slavery only by paying a sizeable ransom (see Jerome, *ep.* 130.7, and Laurence, "Proba, Juliana et Démétrias," 146f.).

18 See *ep.* 188.1.1, where Augustine and Alypius allude to their role in Demetrias's decision.

19 We lack specific references for the dating of this ceremony, but it seems to have occurred after Heraclian's revolt in 413. See Dunn, "Christian Networks," 59, and Laurence, "Proba, Juliana et Démétrias," 150. Aurelius, the bishop of Carthage, likely presided over the ceremony (Augustine and Alypius were not present as *ep.* 188.1.1 makes clear).

20 See Jerome, *ep.* 130, and Pelagius, *ep. ad Demetriadem.* For a recent analysis of Pelagius's letter, see Löhr, *Pélage et le pélagianisme,* 80–123.

21 Augustine's first explicit references to the *Ad Demetriadem* are found in *ep.* 188 to Juliana, which dates to the spring of 418 (see Chapter 4, n. 196 for more on its dating). One curiosity is that the Spanish priest Orosius, whom Augustine sent to Palestine in 415 (see below for more), had access to the *Ad Demetriadem* in 415, as it is quoted in his *Liber apologeticus,* likely written that year (see *Liber apologeticus* 29–30 and below for more on its dating). It seems unlikely that Orosius would have failed to have delivered a copy of Pelagius's *Ad Demetriadem* to Augustine upon his return to Africa in 416. But why did Augustine wait nearly two years to reference the letter? Perhaps he feared to make enemies out of the *Anicii.* And perhaps, he also initially felt there was nothing problematic in the letter. Indeed, Augustine reports at *gr. et pecc. or.* 1.37.40 that this letter almost convinced him that Pelagius held an orthodox view on grace—until he read other things (probably the *Pro libero arbitrio*) Pelagius had written later that revealed the ambiguous way Pelagius spoke of grace. In any event, it seems that when Pelagius mentioned the *Ad Demetriadem* explicitly in his letter to Pope Innocent of 417, Augustine decided it was time to write to the *Anicii* directly (albeit cautiously)—see Chapter 4 for more on this episode.

22 See *b. uid.* 1.1. Juliana's husband (Demetrias's father) Olybrius had died in 410 (see discussion in Geoffrey D. Dunn, "Anicius Hermogenianus Olybrius," in *Studies in Latin Literature and Roman History XIV,* ed. Carl Deroux, Collection Latomus 315 [Brussels: Éditions Latomus, 2008], 440–44). It seems likely that *De bono uiduitatis* was written soon after Demetrias's

THE ROAD TO DIOSPOLIS 139

parts, the first offering an instruction on widowhood (*b. uid.* 1.1–15.19) and the second offering encouragement to Juliana as she seeks to live according to this state (*b. uid.* 16.20–23.29). It is at the beginning of this second part (*b. uid.* 16.20–18.22) that there are clear hints of Augustine's awareness of Pelagius's connection with the *Anicii*. There, Augustine encourages Juliana to recognize that her attraction to chaste widowhood is a gift from God[23] and warns her of dangerous views "hostile to the grace of Christ"[24] that suggest that free choice by itself is capable of carrying out God's commandments. Augustine goes on to criticize those who would teach such views: "But far be it from any person of sound mind to think this! So let us ask [God] to give us what he commands us to have [*ut det, quod ut habeamus iubet*]."[25] Here we see what seems to be a reference to Augustine's prayer from Book 10 of *Confessiones*—similar to the references found in *De peccatorum meritis* and in *De spiritu et littera*.[26] Augustine's reference to this prayer here is, in my view, no coincidence. While he does refer to his prayer a number of times (and with varying degrees of fidelity to the formulation found in *Confessiones*),[27] Augustine's usages of it in anti-Pelagian contexts early in the controversy should attract particular attention, given Pelagius's apparently strong reaction to it while still in Rome.[28] Even more attention should be paid to it in situations where Augustine had reason to believe that his reader knew Pelagius or others in his circle—for there, such references can be read as not-so-subtle attempts to criticize Pelagius himself without mentioning his name.[29] It even seems possible that Augustine wanted Juliana to forward *De bono uiduitatis* to Pelagius himself, as at the end of this anti-Pelagian section he expresses the hope that Juliana would send the work to those

---

veiling, as in it Augustine notes that Demetrias "has just now begun (*modo coepit*)" her consecrated life (*b. uid.* 19.24 [Latin: CSEL 41:335.15]).

23 See *b. uid.* 16.20.

24 *b. uid.* 17.21 (Latin: CSEL 41:329.1; English: Kearney, WSA I/9, 127).

25 *b. uid.* 17.21 (Latin: CSEL 41:329.15–16; English: Kearney, WSA I/9, 127).

26 The usage of this line from *Confessiones* is less impactful in *De spiritu et littera* than in *De peccatorum meritis* or here. See n. 11 above, as well as Chapter 1, n. 12.

27 See Hombert, Gloria Gratiae, 593–94. Hombert includes references containing words of a similar valence to *dare* and *iubere*, which lengthens his list quite substantially.

28 See *perseu.* 20.53.

29 Such seems to have been the case in *pecc. mer.* 2 and will be the case later in *ep.* 179, written to John of Jerusalem (see Chapter 4 for discussion of this letter).

who had fallen into the error he has described.[30] In sum, then, it seems very likely that Augustine was aware of Pelagius's connection with the *Anicii* and sought to warn them that they were in danger.[31]

Given the context of this passage, two pieces of evidence deployed by Augustine stand out. First, while exhorting Juliana to be thankful to God for the gifts he has bestowed upon her and her daughter, Augustine turns to the dialogue prior to the preface of the Eucharistic Prayer, which we saw him do previously in *De spiritu et littera*:

> Many people indeed have many gifts from God, and with unholy vanity boast about them, because they do not know from whom they have received them. No one is blessed by having God's gifts, if he or she is ungrateful to the giver. In the course of the sacred mysteries we hear the command, "Lift up your hearts," and we are able to do this with the help of him from whose command this exhortation comes. For this reason, what then follows is not a tribute of praise to ourselves for this great benefit of our hearts being lifted up, as though we did it by our own strength, but "Let us give thanks to the Lord our God." We are immediately further encouraged to do this, because "it is right," and because "it is just." Bear in mind where these words come from and recognize by what law [*sanctione*] and by how much holiness [*sanctitate*] they are commended to us.[32]

Whereas in *De spiritu et littera* Augustine only briefly referred to this dialogue, here he offers a more expansive treatment, emphasizing that the liturgical prayers themselves indicate to us that our ability to lift up our hearts to God is itself a gift from God for which we ought to be thankful. To drive home his point, he reminds Juliana that this insight is drawn from the liturgy itself—a source that Augustine clearly believes should lend authority to the

---

30 See *b. uid.* 18.22. Duval notes that Augustine's references to *Confessiones* here and in *De peccatorum meritis* were susceptible of being read by Pelagius and that he would also have been able to find a justification for that prayer in those places; see "Pélage en son temps," 98–99n16.

31 An additional piece of evidence that is less conclusive, but still worth mentioning, is the fact that Augustine had previously sent his *De sancta uirginitate* to Juliana (see *b. uid.* 23.29). Augustine had composed the majority of this work around 403 or 404, but, it seems, only published it around 411 after adding a brief prologue and, more importantly, a lengthy section at the end that bears the signs of Augustine's anti-Pelagian concerns (for more on the dating of *De sancta uirginitate*, see Hombert, *Nouvelles recherches de chronologie augustinienne*, 109–36). One wonders whether Augustine was already aware of Pelagius's connections with Juliana's family when he sent her *De sancta uiginitate*.

32 *b. uid.* 16.20 (Latin: CSEL 41:328.3–13; English: Kearney, WSA I/9, 126, slightly modified). See also the quotation from *s.* 227 cited above in n. 12.

THE ROAD TO DIOSPOLIS

theology it contains. Shortly thereafter, Augustine explains why he felt it necessary to emphasize the need for gratitude:

> The nonsense that certain people have been saying—something we should avoid and shun—compels me to warn you about these things. This nonsense, which is hostile to the grace of Christ, has begun to creep through many people's ears into their souls—something that must be said with tears. Through it, people are being persuaded that not even prayer to the Lord seems necessary for us so that we might not enter into temptation. For they strive to defend the free choice of man to such a degree that we are able to fulfill what God commands by it alone, even unaided by the grace of God. And from this it follows that the Lord said for no reason, "Keep watch and pray lest you enter into temptation" (Mt 26:41), and that we daily say for no reason in the Lord's Prayer itself, "Lead us not into temptation."[33]

What we find here is the reappearance of an important argumentative tactic: Augustine has once again cited the practice of daily recitation of the Lord's Prayer so as to evidence the heterodoxy of the Pelagian position. The Pelagian view on grace effectively undermines this universal practice, and, Augustine leads us to understand, that very fact reveals the error of the Pelagian view (for how could the practice of reciting this prayer given by Christ himself be wrong?).

While Augustine's anti-Pelagian argument here is not limited to the evidence he draws from the preface of the Eucharistic Prayer and the Lord's Prayer, it is noteworthy that, in such a short passage, these two pieces of evidence occupy such a prominent place. Both are aimed at demonstrating how contrary to the Church's ancient and universal doctrine the Pelagian understanding of grace is. Notably, both pieces of evidence (or variations of them) were used in *De spiritu et littera*. However, there Augustine did not seem particularly interested in emphasizing this sort of evidence—no doubt due to the context of that work. But here, writing to someone aware of Pelagius's views and, potentially, a disciple of his (or at least in danger of becoming one), Augustine devotes a significant portion of this passage to disabusing his reader of the notion that the Pelagians can claim the universal and ancient Church's support for their views. This argumentation seems to indicate just how important it was for Augustine to rebut that Pelagian claim.

---

33 *b. uid.* 17.21 (Latin: CSEL 41:328.20–329.8; English: my translation).

Perhaps around the same time as he was writing *De bono uiduitatis*, other news of Pelagian activity reached Augustine. At some point in 414 Augustine received a short letter from Hilary, an otherwise unknown Catholic layman from Syracuse in Sicily, who requested Augustine's response to a set of teachings circulating in Syracuse:

> They say that human beings can be without sin and easily keep the commandments of God if they will, that an infant who was not baptized because prevented by death cannot deserve to perish because it is born without sin, that a rich man who remains in his riches cannot enter the kingdom of God unless he has sold all his possessions, and that it does not profit him if he has perhaps observed all the commandments by the use of his riches, and that one ought not to swear at all. And with regard to the Church, which church is it about which scripture says that it does not have wrinkle or spot? Is it this one in which we are now gathered, or is it that one which we hope for? But a certain man claimed that it is this church in which we now gather with people and that it can be without sin.[34]

Augustine replied to Hilary in *ep.* 157, which was completed by early 415 at the latest.[35] In his response, Augustine tackles each of the questions brought up by Hilary, but devotes most of the letter to the issues of the possibility of sinlessness (which he subdivides into two topics: the possibility of sinlessness proper [1.2–3] and the necessity of grace [2.4–10]), the moral status of infants (3.11–22), and wealth (4.23–39). Of particular note is the section on sinlessness, for there Augustine employs the Lord's Prayer as evidence twice—and the first instance occurs in the very first paragraph of that section, thus indicating its importance as evidence.[36] The section on the moral status of infants,

---

34 *ep.* 156 (Latin: CSEL 44:448.12–449.1; English: Teske, WSA II/3, 15). The inquiry about wealth—different from other Pelagian material we have encountered thus far—seems related to the text *De diuitiis*, which has often been grouped among other "Pelagian-sounding" ascetic texts of unknown authorship. For a study of *De diuitiis*, see Andreas Kessler, *Reichtumskritik und Pelagianismus: die pelagianische Diatribe de divitiis; Situierung, Lesetext, Übersetzung, Kommentar* (Freiburg Schweiz : Universitätsverlag, 1999). See also Brown, *Eye of a Needle*, 308–21.

35 We know it was completed by this point because Orosius seems to have brought it with him when he left Hippo for Palestine (sometime between December 414 and May 415—see Duval, "La date du 'De natura' de Pélage," 259). See Orosius, *Liber apologeticus* 3. For more on Orosius, see below.

36 See *ep.* 157.1.2 and 157.2.5. After stating that his unnamed opponents should refrain from spreading the view that sinlessness is possible in this life, Augustine writes, "For the Lord's Prayer is necessary for all; the Lord gave it even to the rams of the flock, that is, to his own

THE ROAD TO DIOSPOLIS   143

on the other hand, relies on scriptural arguments, something that is perhaps surprising given its thematic similarity to *De peccatorum meritis* 1. However, I believe Augustine had strategic reasons for not deploying the non-scriptural evidence we saw him use in that book (and which we discussed in Chapter 2). Augustine's treatment of the moral status of infants in *ep.* 157 focuses on the issue of the sin of Adam and its transmission to his descendants. In particular, Augustine is responding to the Pelagians' claim that infants are guilty of no sin. To refute this, Augustine turns, as he did in *pecc. mer.* 1.9.9–1.15.20, to Rom 5:12–21, which he views as proof that Adam's sin does lead all (even infants) to condemnation insofar as this sin is transmitted to his descendants not via imitation but via propagation. The argumentation in *ep.* 157 is very similar to that found in this section of *De peccatorum meritis* (albeit with some re-arrangement and additions). One key omission in *ep.* 157, though, is the evidence Augustine deploys at *pecc. mer.* 1.9.10, where he points out that the Church baptizes infants even though they have not yet sinned. For Augustine, this ecclesial practice offers evidence that Adam's sin is not passed on through imitation (for why would infants need to be baptized if they have not yet imitated Adam in his sin?). But why does he not deploy that argument here in *ep.* 157? In my view, the reason (or *a* reason) is that Augustine is not setting out in *ep.* 157 (unlike in *De peccatorum meritis*) to explain what the effect of infant baptism is. Indeed, recall that much of the rest of *De peccatorum meritis* 1 (after *pecc. mer.* 1.15.20) is devoted to this very topic. There, Augustine must refute the Pelagians' various arguments that infant baptism has some other purpose besides the remission of original sin. Knowing that he will show later in the book that infant baptism is for the forgiveness of original sin, Augustine feels comfortable at *pecc. mer.* 1.9.10 deploying the practice of baptizing infants as evidence. But here, in *ep.* 157, the effect of infant baptism has not been raised as an issue. Augustine, no doubt wishing to avoid (1) entering a discussion of that complex topic and (2) employing evidence that the Pelagians have been known to question (in *De peccatorum meritis* we learn that they sometimes claim that infants are baptized [1] so as to enter into the kingdom of heaven or [2] for the remission

---

apostles, in order that each would say to God, 'Forgive us our debts, as we also forgive our debtors.' After all, one for whom these words in the prayer will not be necessary would have to claim to live here without sin. If the Lord foresaw that some other people of that sort were going to exist, better persons, of course, than his apostles, he would have taught them another prayer by which they would not ask that their sins be forgiven, since all their sins were already forgiven in baptism" (*ep.* 157.1.2; Latin: CSEL 44:450.3–11; English: Teske, WSA II/3, 18).

144 AUGUSTINE IN THE PELAGIAN CONTROVERSY

of personal sin), Augustine opts in *ep.* 157 not to use the baptismal evidence he had used at *pecc. mer.* 1.9.10.

In any event, after responding to the questions on sinlessness and the moral status of infants, Augustine notes his own familiarity with these teachings, summarizing his involvement in the Pelagian controversy thus far.

> We have said much about these questions in our other works and sermons in church, because there were also among us certain persons who sowed these new seeds of their error wherever they could, some of whom the mercy of the Lord healed from that disease through our ministry and that of our brothers. And I suspect that there are still some here, especially in Carthage, but they now whisper in hiding, fearing the most well-founded faith of the Church. For in the church of the same city one of them by the name of Caelestius had already deviously begun to seek the honor of the priesthood, but he was brought by the solid faith and freedom of the brothers straight to an episcopal court on account of these discourses opposed to the grace of Christ.[37]

We find here the first time that Augustine identified one of his Pelagian opponents by name—in this case, Caelestius.[38] Augustine, goes on to defend his decision to reveal the identity of his opponent: "But because he [Caelestius] went off, having been found guilty and detested by the Church rather than corrected and subdued [i.e., at the *iudicium* in Carthage in 411], I was afraid that it was perhaps he himself there who was trying to disturb your faith, and for this reason I thought I should mention his name."[39] Augustine then notes the startling proliferation of Pelagianism: "But it makes no difference whether it is he or others who partake of his error. For there are more than we could hope. And where they are not refuted, they seduce others to their sect and thus they grow so that I do not know where they are going to burst

---

37 *ep.* 157.3.22 (Latin: CSEL 44:470.27–471.11; English: Teske, WSA II/3, 29–30).

38 As Augustine notes in *gest. Pel.* 22.46 and elsewhere, it seems that he and Aurelius (bishop of Carthage) had originally thought it better to refute the Pelagian teachings without identifying the Pelagians themselves: "We thought that one proceeded against them in a better manner, if their errors were refuted and opposed without mentioning anyone's name, while the persons themselves were corrected by fear of an ecclesiastical court rather than punished by the court itself" (Latin: CSEL 42:100.23–101.1; English: Teske, WSA I/23, 354).

39 *ep.* 157.3.22 (Latin: CSEL 44:471.18–22; English: Teske, WSA II/3, 30). It is unclear whether Caelestius traveled to Sicily after his departure from Carthage. In *De perfectione iustitiae hominis*, likely written sometime after *ep.* 157 (perhaps later in 415—for more on the dating of this work, see below), Augustine reports that Caelestius is said not to be in Sicily (*perf. iust.* 1.1).

THE ROAD TO DIOSPOLIS

forth."[40] These comments give a good snapshot of the state of Pelagianism by the beginning of 415: although Caelestius had been condemned in Carthage in 411, it appears his departure from North Africa had not completely suppressed the spread of Pelagian views. Augustine's words suggest that the situation had become rather dire. While he would still prefer that people holding such views be "healed within the framework of the Church rather than cut off from its body like incurable members," he notes the very real possibility that "more should rot while sparing the rotten."[41] In this sense, it seems that for Augustine, "healing within the Church" is becoming a less viable option.

While Augustine's comments in *ep.* 157 about the spread of Pelagianism should, perhaps, be taken with a grain of salt—after all it serves his aims to emphasize rhetorically both the danger of Pelagian views and the speed with which those views were spreading—these statements do suggest that more was going on "behind the scenes" in the years 413 and 414 than we now have access to in extant sources. That is to say: in this period, Augustine was not simply waiting for information about the Pelagians to come to his doorstep—rather, he was actively seeking news out, while continuing to work against the Pelagian views as opportunities arose. One comment in *ep.* 157 is particularly significant in this regard. As we quoted above, Augustine notes at *ep.* 157.3.22 that some Pelagian disciples had been converted through Augustine and his fellow bishops' efforts. While *ep.* 157 does not indicate the identity of these former Pelagians, it stands to reason that they were probably Timasius and James, who gave Pelagius's *De natura* to Augustine.

DE NATURA AND *DE NATURA ET GRATIA*
Context

Augustine likely received a copy of the *De natura* from Timasius and James in late 414 or early 415 and read it at once with much interest, setting aside other work.[42] In the book, which was likely written sometime between 406

---

40 *ep.* 157.3.22 (Latin: CSEL 44:471.22–472.2; English: Teske, WSA II/3, 30, slightly modified).

41 *ep.* 157.3.22 (Latin: CSEL 44:472.2–5; English: Teske, WSA II/3, 30, slightly modified).

42 See *nat. et gr.* 1.1. It is unclear whether Pelagius's work actually bore the title *De natura* (see Duval, "La date du 'De natura' de Pélage," 257n2). We know that Augustine had received the *De natura* by the time Orosius left for Palestine (sometime between December 414 and May 415—see Duval, "La date du 'De natura' de Pélage," 259), as he mentions that Augustine

and 410 (and, thus, prior to his departure from Rome), Pelagius articulated his views on human nature and the human capacity to avoid sin.[43] As Winrich Löhr has noted, based on the fragments available to us, the work seems to have been composed in the style of a diatribe, in which Pelagius battled with a fictionalized opponent who opposed Pelagius's positions on issues related to the topic of sinlessness.[44] Augustine reports that his acquisition of the book was a critical development in the controversy.[45] Indeed, recall that when Pelagius was still in Rome, Augustine had heard rumors that he held views contrary to the grace of God. It was from that time on that Augustine was hoping either to speak with Pelagius in person or to acquire one of his writings on the subject, so as to gain incontestable proof that such rumors were true.[46] While, of course, Augustine had received a copy of Pelagius's *Expositiones* on the Pauline epistles in 411, the short exegetical comments found in that work did not offer the decisive evidence Augustine sought.[47]

---

is writing a refutation of it at *Liber apologeticus* 3. For some references to Timasius and James and their delivery of the *De natura*, see *nat. et gr.* 1.1, *gest. Pel.* 23.47–25.49, *ep.* 177.6, *ep.* 179.2 and 10, *ep.* 19*.3. See also *ep.* 168, which is Timasius and James's letter of thanks to Augustine, extracted from *gest. Pel.* 24.48.

43 All extant fragments of Pelagius's text are found in Augustine's *De natura et gratia*. For more on Pelagius's *De natura* and its dating, see Duval, "La date du 'De natura' de Pélage" and Löhr, "Pelagius' Schrift 'De natura.'" Duval was instrumental in re-dating the *De natura* to Pelagius's Roman period (although a similar dating was provided earlier by TeSelle, "Rufinus the Syrian, Caelestius, Pelagius," 72). While many scholars have accepted Duval's argument, some still register doubts. See, e.g., Cutino, "Il ruolo della Chiesa siciliana nella polemica fra Agostino e i pelagiani"; Drecoll, "Pelagius, Pelagiani"; Tauer, "Neue Orientierungen zur Paulusexegese des Pelagius," esp. 357–58.

44 For more, see Löhr, "Pelagius' Schrift," esp. 271–72. As Löhr notes elsewhere, "The work gives the impression of reproducing debates on the position of Pelagius or of preparing for such debates" (Löhr, "Augustinus und sein Verhältnis zu Pelagius: eine Relecture der Quellen," *Augustiniana* 60 [2010]: 69). Löhr also notes that the work seems to have been intended for internal consumption only among Pelagius's disciples. Thus, when Timasius and James handed the work over to Augustine, it was easily interpreted as a betrayal by Pelagius. Pelagius never claimed the work as his own but did complain of uncorrected works having been stolen from him, which could be a reference to the *De natura* and Timasius and James's actions. See Löhr, "Augustinus und sein Verhältnis," 68. See also Augustine's description of the work at *gest. Pel.* 23.47.

45 See *gest. Pel.* 23.47: "[After receiving the *De natura*] it then became clear to me without any doubt how hostile the venom of that perversity was to Christian salvation" (Latin: CSEL 42:101.10–12; English: my translation).

46 See *gest. Pel.* 22.46.

47 Recall, too, that in that work Pelagius reported a variety of exegetical positions without always clearly defining his own views—see Augustine's comments in *De peccatorum meritis* 3.

THE ROAD TO DIOSPOLIS   147

But the *De natura* handed over by Timasius and James, with its in-depth analysis of the possibility of not sinning and its arguments against opposing views, offered Augustine exactly what he needed. From this point on, Augustine no longer had any doubts that the rumors he had heard were true.[48]

At times, another aspect of the *De natura* has been cited as a key factor in the decisive importance of this work for Augustine. In the book's concluding section, Pelagius seeks to bolster his case by deploying quotations from Lactantius, Hilary of Poitiers, Ambrose, John Chrysostom, Sixtus (believed by Pelagius to be the martyred bishop of Rome), Jerome, and Augustine himself. As Augustine notes, Pelagius quoted these authors to "answer those who said that he was the only one who held these views."[49] In Robert Evans's view, these quotations were crucial for Augustine:

> Augustine's decisive reaction against Pelagius' work *On Nature* cannot be adequately explained by any new teaching which he found there, not having been acquainted with it before as a teaching of Pelagius. We come then to the second and positive answer to our large question: Augustine reacts decisively to the work *On Nature* because he finds there a whole section in which Pelagius has supported his own position by quoting from works of weighty Catholic authors: Lactantius, Hilary of Poitiers, Ambrose, John Chrysostom, Xystus the Martyr bishop of Rome, Jerome, and finally Augustine himself. Pelagius becomes a serious threat at that moment when Augustine sees him marshaling the forces of Catholic orthodoxy behind him.[50]

On the one hand, I think Evans is right to indicate that Pelagius's citations of renowned Christian authors were important for Augustine. As I have been arguing throughout this study, such Pelagian arguments—and their potential to prompt disunity—were critical for Augustine's entry into the controversy. And yet, I am not convinced that Augustine's reading of these citations in the *De natura* was as shocking to Augustine as Evans makes it out to be.[51] In my view, if Evans were right, we might expect to see a significant

---

48 See Augustine's comments to this effect in *ep.* 186.1, from a few years later in 417.

49 *nat. et gr.* 61.71 (Latin: CSEL 60:286.14–15; English: Teske, WSA I/23, 252). It remains possible that others beyond these authors were cited by Pelagius and that Augustine simply did not mention them (see Löhr, "Pelagius' Schrift," 270n97)—although it seems more likely to me that if Pelagius had supplied additional quotations, Augustine would have responded to them.

50 Evans, *Pelagius*, 85.

51 An exception might be Pelagius's citation of Augustine himself. This citation added a new complication for Augustine, as he now had to defend one of his own works and show how it

shift in Augustine's argumentation after his reading of the *De natura*. That is, we might expect to see a much greater reliance on arguments seeking to indicate that Augustine's positions were simply those of the ancient and universal Church. And while we do see a steady increase in these arguments post-*De natura*—including more frequent appeals to renowned Christian authors—Augustine's argumentation in this period is largely in continuity with his initial reaction to the Pelagian threat.[52]

But why is that the case? Why do we not see a substantial shift in argumentation? In my view, it is because Augustine was already aware that his opponents were deploying arguments like those in Pelagius's *De natura*. As we have discussed previously, Augustine already knew in 411 that the Pelagians were accusing their opponents of novelty and of departing from the faith of the eastern churches.[53] Further, his use of citations from Cyprian (in *s.* 294 and *pecc. mer.* 3) and Jerome (in *pecc. mer.* 3) suggests that Augustine was aware that the Pelagians were making arguments similar to those he found in *De natura*. All this makes sense, as *De natura* was likely written prior to Pelagius's arrival in Africa and, thus, would already have been in circulation among Pelagius's disciples (including, likely, Timasius and James) in 411.[54] When Augustine read the *De natura*, then, what he found was not something startlingly new, but confirmation of rumors and reports: rumors and reports that Pelagius denied the need for grace and that the Pelagians claimed their opponents were at odds with the ancient and universal doctrinal teaching of the Church. It also confirmed for Augustine what he seems to have suspected for some time: that Pelagius himself was the leader of the "enemies of grace." With these rumors and reports confirmed, Augustine set out to continue the fight he had begun almost four years prior, albeit with a renewed vigor and sense of focus: to refute Pelagius's problematic doctrinal positions and to

---

was not in line with Pelagius's views.

52 See discussion below of *De natura et gratia* and *De perfectione iustitiae hominis*. Of course, the lack of an immediate increase in citations of other Christian authors could also have been a problem of access—perhaps Augustine did not have access (either in Hippo or in Carthage) to a wide selection of texts from other authors and it took him some time to acquire more. For some discussion of Augustine's familiarity with earlier Christian writers, see Mark Edwards, "Augustine and His Christian Predecessors," in *A Companion to Augustine*, ed. Mark Vessey (Chichester: Wiley-Blackwell, 2012), 215–26. See also O'Donnell, *Augustine*, 120–26.

53 See *s.* 294.19 and *gest. Pel.* 11.25.

54 On this point, it is worth recalling that Augustine had interacted with Timasius in 411 (see *ep.* 126.6).

THE ROAD TO DIOSPOLIS

challenge his (and his associates') claims to speak for the Church's doctrinal tradition. Let us now turn to Augustine's response to Pelagius's work, his *De natura et gratia*—a work he wrote for Timasius and James, but perhaps hoped would be passed on to Pelagius himself.[55]

De natura et gratia

Augustine seems to structure his *De natura et gratia* based on the flow of Pelagius's own work, responding to each of Pelagius's major points and arguments in sequence.[56] As we noted above, the *De natura* especially dealt with the possibility of sinlessness (*possibilitas non peccandi*). It also weaves through several other related topics, including the nature of sin, sin's effect on human nature, and the nature of grace. In his response, Augustine tends to make argumentative moves similar to those found in his previous anti-Pelagian works—for example, emphasizing that sinlessness is theoretically possible, but only through the grace of God. As he has done before, Augustine also refrains from mentioning Pelagius's name, still hoping to preserve his friendship with the man so as to more easily bring him to conversion.[57] The most important section of *De natura et gratia* for our purposes is that in which Augustine deals with Pelagius's citations of renowned Christian authors, for here Augustine is forced to address Pelagius's claims to speak for the Church's doctrinal tradition directly. However, earlier in the work, Augustine also addresses the effect of Pelagian views on the Church's liturgical praxis and life of prayer in several passages drawing on evidence such as the Lord's Prayer, the practice of infant baptism, and the introductory dialogue to the Eucharistic Prayer.[58] The arguments Augustine deploys in these passages are, by now, very familiar, as we have already seen them in previous anti-Pelagian works. As a result, there is no need for an extensive

---

55 See Löhr, "Augustinus und sein Verhältnis," 79.

56 For a reconstruction of the *De natura*'s (possible) structure, see Löhr, "Pelagius' Schrift," 276–78.

57 Duval also notes the relatively courteous tone Augustine employs through his *De natura et gratia*, which no doubt reflects a conscious decision to attempt to maintain friendly ties with Pelagius and his allies so as to more easily secure their conversions (see Yves-Marie Duval, "La correspondance entre Augustin et Pélage," *Revue des* études *augustiniennes* 45 [1999]: 366–67).

58 See *nat. et gr.* 18.20 (Lord's Prayer), 21.23 (infant baptism), 34.39 (Lord's Prayer), 35.41 (Lord's Prayer and dialogue prior to the Eucharistic Prayer), 53.62 (Lord's Prayer), 58.68 (Lord's Prayer), 60.70 (Lord's Prayer), 67.80 (Lord's Prayer).

discussion of them here; nevertheless, it will be helpful to highlight a few to indicate Augustine's continuing efforts to demonstrate to his readers the way in which Pelagian views undercut key aspects of what he takes to be the Church's ancient and universal beliefs.

First of all, we can turn to Augustine's comments at *De natura et gratia* 18.20, which occur as Augustine is concluding the first section of his response to Pelagius. This section focuses on the possibility of sinlessness in general. As Augustine brings it to a close, he addresses Pelagius's views on prayer. Augustine notes that Pelagius acknowledges the need for individuals to pray for pardon after they have sinned. However, Augustine draws attention to the fact that Pelagius seems not to admit the need for prayer to avoid sin in the first place. Augustine emphasizes how worrying this omission is: "His silence on this point is utterly astounding, since the Lord's Prayer teaches that we should ask for both of these: both that our debts be forgiven and that we not be led into temptation, the former so that past sins be wiped away, the latter so that future sins be avoided."[59] The way in which Augustine expresses shock and wonder at Pelagius's apparent omission of the need to pray for the grace to avoid sin is intended to prompt the same sentiment in his readers. Indeed, Augustine's reference to the Lord's Prayer here aims to increase this shock all the more: Pelagius seems to have forgotten about a key petition in the prayer which Christ himself gave to the Church and which the Church has prayed daily from the very beginning.

A similar argument is deployed albeit with more force near the end of *De natura et gratia* (only a few paragraphs before Augustine begins discussing the quotations from renowned Christian authors employed by Pelagius). There, while discussing James 4:17 ("Resist the devil and he will flee you") Augustine observes how far removed the Pelagian views are from orthodox Christian piety.

> But there is this difference between these people and us. We not only do not deny but even proclaim that we should demand God's help, even when we resist the devil. These people, however, attribute such power to the will that they remove prayer from a life of piety. For, precisely in order that we may resist the devil and that he may flee from us, we say in prayer, "Bring us not into temptation." Precisely for this reason we have been warned, like

---

59 *nat. et gr.* 18.20 (Latin: CSEL 60:245.26–246.2; English: Teske, WSA I/23, 225).

THE ROAD TO DIOSPOLIS 151

soldiers, by our commander who exhorts us with the words, "Watch and pray so that you do not enter into temptation" (Mark 14:38).[60]

Here, Augustine pointedly warns that the Pelagian views essentially destroy the purpose of Christian prayer, contradicting Christ's instructions on prayer found in the Gospels. Writing this passage, Augustine intends for his reader to be shocked by the implications of Pelagius's position. He employs the device of *correctio* to emphasize the difference between Pelagius's position and his own: not only do Catholics not deny the need for God's help (that is, as he claims the Pelagians seem to do), but they even proclaim this need.[61] He then points to the consequence of a denial of a need for God's help—the Pelagians take prayer away from piety—and reinforces the reader's shock at this consequence by highlighting a key element of the Christian life of prayer, the Lord's Prayer. By using this piece of evidence in this way, Augustine not only disparages the Pelagian viewpoint but also grounds his own assertion of the need for grace in the Church's tradition of prayer and in Christ's very instruction on prayer. This two-pronged attack leaves the reader with the sense that Augustine's position is clearly traditional while the Pelagian position is obviously novel.[62]

Of course, as we mentioned above, the most important element of *De natura et gratia* for our purposes is the lengthy section at the end of the work where Augustine grapples with the quotations that Pelagius had provided in his *De natura* from Lactantius, Hilary of Poitiers, Ambrose, John Chrysostom, Sixtus, Jerome, and Augustine himself. At *De natura et gratia* 61.71, Augustine reports that Pelagius offered these citations from Christian authors in order to "answer those who said that he was the only one who held these views [on the possibility of human sinlessness]."[63] Over the course of the next ten or so paragraphs, Augustine addresses these quotations one by one, generally responding to them by offering an alternative interpretation of the passage quoted (and thus arguing that the quotation does not, in

---

60 *nat. et gr.* 58.68 (Latin: CSEL 60:284.26–285.4; English: Teske, WSA I/23, 251, slightly modified).

61 For more on the device of *correctio* see Heinrich Lausberg, *Handbook of Literary Rhetoric: A Foundation for Literary Study*, trans. Matthew T. Bliss et al., ed. David E. Orton and R. Dean Anderson (Leiden: Brill, 1998), §§784–86.

62 Similar uses of the Lord's Prayer are found at *nat. et gr.* 34.39, 35.41, 53.62, 58.68, 60.70, and 67.80.

63 *nat. et gr.* 61.71 (Latin: CSEL 60:286.12–15; English: Teske, WSA I/23, 252).

fact, support Pelagius's views[64]). On two occasions, however, he also offers additional citations from the same author in which that author appears to support Augustine's own position. Let us now consider several of these responses.

The first response is atypical—but Augustine's prefatory remarks here are important. Replying to the first two quotations Pelagius provides, Augustine notes he cannot find the name of the author whom Pelagius is citing—either because Pelagius did not offer it, or because the manuscript's copyist omitted it.[65] Due to this issue, Augustine immediately asks why he needs to discuss the quotations at all "especially since I am not bound by the writings of any people of this sort [*huiusmodi*], for I owe assent without any refusal only to canonical [writings]."[66] While some have taken Augustine's statement here to indicate that he granted no authority to non-scriptural writings, it seems to me that Augustine is actually rejecting the authority of opinions put forward by anonymous authors.[67] In this context, it is worth recalling that Augustine was aware that the Pelagians circulated their texts anonymously. As a result, it seems possible that this statement was something of a jab at his opponents' publication habits. But in any event, and more to our point, Augustine also seems to be specifying here some parameters for the use of opinions from non-scriptural authors. First and foremost, since anonymous authors carry no authority, we can surmise that the strength of a particular opinion is intrinsically tied to its author. But second, since only scriptural texts require unconditional assent, we should understand that all non-scriptural authors

---

64 Indeed, at the beginning of this passage, Augustine notes that the quotations Pelagius provides are "neutral [*media*]" (*nat. et gr.* 61.71).

65 These two quotes are actually from Lactantius's *Diuinae Institutiones* 4.24 and 4.25 (CSEL 19:373 and 377).

66 *nat. et gr.* 61.71: *maxime quoniam me in huiusmodi quorumlibet hominum scriptis liberum—quia solis canonicis debeo sine ulla recusatione consensum* (Latin: CSEL 60:286.22–24; English: my translation). Note that Teske translates *huiusmodi* differently in his version: "especially since I am not bound by the writings of any mere human beings" (WSA I/23, 252). Teske seems to have mistranslated *huiusmodi* here and as a result has given the passage a sense it did not originally have. Éric Rebillard follows Teske's translation and argues that Augustine, in this passage, is rejecting the authority of all non-scriptural writings and, thus, the authority of all the citations Pelagius provides (Éric Rebillard, "A New Style of Argument in Christian Polemic: Augustine and the Use of Patristic Citations," *Journal of Early Christian Studies* 8 (2000): 569). For a critique of Rebillard's position, see Chronister, "Augustine and Patristic Argumentation in His Anti-Pelagian Works."

67 See the previous footnote.

THE ROAD TO DIOSPOLIS

are liable to err, at least from time to time. Augustine's comments here echo those we had already seen in the previous chapter when we were discussing *De peccatorum meritis* 3. There, he noted that he was quoting Cyprian and Jerome not because their words had the same authority as scripture, but because their opinions witnessed to the antiquity and universality of the doctrinal views Augustine was attempting to defend.[68] While Augustine's task in *De natura et gratia* is ostensibly more "defensive" than in *De peccatorum meritis* as he is combating specific quotations offered by Pelagius,[69] it is important to recognize that he is not simply attempting to "neutralize" the quotes Pelagius offers (despite his initial statement that the passages are "neutral [*media*], neither against our view nor against his"[70]). More than that, in several cases he aims to "reclaim" the authors of these quotes from Pelagius and, as a result, to undergird his own claim to be on the side of the ancient and universal Church.

We can see this aim on display when Augustine turns to Pelagius's citations of Hilary of Poitiers (which he addresses after a brief critique of the two anonymous quotations). Both citations are deployed by Pelagius to suggest that Hilary thought sinlessness was possible in this life.[71] In response to the first, Augustine notes that avoiding sin requires the grace of God, which the quotation does not deny. To the second, in which Hilary states that Job "refrained from evil," Augustine responds that refraining from evil is not quite the same thing as being without sin and that, in any event, God's grace is required for both (which, again, the quotation does not deny). In this way, Augustine rejects Pelagius's attempt to claim Hilary as an ally by showing that his words can be understood to agree with Augustine's own theology. After doing so, Augustine provides his own citation from Hilary, in which the bishop of Poitiers announces that no one is without sin.[72] After

---

68 See *pecc. mer.* 3.7.14.

69 However, recall that even in *De peccatorum meritis* Augustine was responding to people in Pelagius's circle who were likely already aware of his *De natura* and the authorities cited by Pelagius there. As we have said, Augustine also seems to have been aware of the general contours (if not the specifics) of such arguments "from tradition." In this sense, Augustine's citations in *De peccatorum meritis* were also "defensive."

70 See *nat. et gr.* 61.71 (Latin: CSEL 60:286.15–16; English: Teske, WSA I/23, 252).

71 See *nat. et gr.* 62.72. The first is from Hilary's *In Matthaeum commentarius* 4.7 (SC 254:126); the second, *Tractatus in Iob*, frag. 2 (CSEL 65:230).

72 Hilary, *Tractatus super Psalmos* 118.15.10: *si enim peccatores deus sperneret, omnes utique sperneret, quia sine peccato nemo est. sed spernit discedentes a se, quos apostatas uocat* (CCL

154 AUGUSTINE IN THE PELAGIAN CONTROVERSY

the citation Augustine writes, "You see how he did not say that there *was* no one without sin, as if he were speaking about the past, but said that there *is* no one without sin."[73] In this sense, Augustine takes care to emphasize for his readers that Hilary believes the very same thing that Augustine had been asserting earlier in the treatise: the universality of human sinfulness. Augustine then strengthens Hilary's opinion by linking it to the words of John: "As I said, I am not arguing about this point; after all, if one does not yield to the apostle John who said, 'If we say that we have no sin' (1 John 1:8)—not that we had no sin—how is the person going to yield to bishop Hilary?"[74] Of course, Augustine's claim that he is "not arguing" is purely rhetorical—that is exactly what he is doing.[75] In the course of this passage then, Augustine has (1) diffused the impact of the quotations offered by Pelagius, (2) provided a different quotation from Hilary that supports his own view, and (3) further established Hilary's authority by linking his view directly with the apostle John. In this way, Augustine has not simply neutralized Pelagius's use of Hilary, but has actually reclaimed the bishop for his own side and, in addition, strengthened Hilary's authority by closely associating him with the apostle John. Thus, Augustine has traced the genealogy of his own positions to Hilary and, through Hilary, to John and the apostolic age.

Augustine next turns to Pelagius's use of a passage from Ambrose's commentary on Luke.[76] In this passage, Ambrose comments on Luke 1:6's affirmation of the "blamelessness [*sine querella*]" of Elizabeth and Zechariah, arguing that sinlessness is possible.[77] Notably, Augustine does not reproduce the quotation from Ambrose but merely refers to it. This failure to provide

---

61A:146.6–8).

73 *nat. et gr.* 62.73 (Latin: CSEL 60:288.24–289.2; English: Teske, WSA I/23, 254, italics added).

74 *nat. et gr.* 62.73 (Latin: CSEL 60:289.2–5; English: Teske, WSA I/23, 254).

75 This is a usage of *paralipsis/praeteritio* (see Lausberg, *Handbook*, §§882–86, 902).

76 The crucial section of the quotation is as follows: *quid ad hoc referunt qui peccatis suis solacia praeferentes sine peccatis frequentibus hominem putant esse non posse et utuntur uersiculo quia scriptum est in Iob: nemo mundus a sorde nec si una die uita eius est; in terra numerosi menses eius ab ipso? quibus respondendum est prius ut quid sit hominem sine peccato esse definiant, utrum numquam omnino peccasse an desisse peccare. si enim hoc putant sine peccato esse, desisse peccare, et ipse consentio* (Ambrose, *Expositio euangelii secundum Lucam* 1.17 [CCL 14:14.261–15.269]).

77 Augustine first responded to a Pelagian argument for the possibility of sinlessness based on the case of Elizabeth and Zechariah in 411 (see *pecc. mer.* 2.13.19–2.14.21). Is it possible that Ambrose's authority was being invoked at that time as well? See Grossi, "Il ricorso ad Ambrogio nell'*Opus imperfectum contra Iulianum* di Agostino d'Ippona," 115, for this suggestion.

THE ROAD TO DIOSPOLIS

the quotation is no doubt a strategic decision given the fact that Ambrose's explicit affirmation that sinlessness is possible poses a difficulty for Augustine. In response, Augustine initially asserts that Ambrose surely believed that this sinlessness would come about by the grace of God rather than by human effort alone.[78] After this attempt to distance Ambrose from Pelagius's theological positions, Augustine goes on the offensive and cites several other passages from Ambrose that would suggest to readers the agreement between Augustine and the Bishop of Milan about grace. The first passage cited is from Ambrose's third hymn, in which he affirms the need to pray for the gift of the Holy Spirit.[79] Augustine comments, "The aforementioned bishop even advises that this Spirit must be obtained by prayers—and so the will, without divine aid, does not suffice for that."[80] Augustine then cites another passage from Ambrose, in which the Bishop of Milan employs Proverbs 8:35 LXX (*a deo praeparatur uoluntas hominum*).[81] Ambrose's use of this scriptural verse, one which Augustine himself frequently deploys in his anti-Pelagian works, is a clear signal to the bishop of Hippo that Ambrose fully grasped the importance of divine grace in human good action.[82] Finally, Augustine provides a quotation from Ambrose that appears to affirm the universality of human sinfulness as well as the necessity of grace, emphasizing that the Church was "from the beginning not spotless" but that through God's grace it is being

---

78 *nat. et gr.* 63.74: *numquid tamen negat gratia dei fieri per Iesum Christum dominum nostrum?* (Latin: CSEL 60:289.13–14).

79 *uotisque praestat sedulis sanctum mereri spiritum* (Ambrose, *hymnus* 3.7–8; Latin: PL 16:1473). For a detailed examination of Augustine's use of this verse from Ambrose's hymn in *nat. et gr.* see Brian Dunkle, "'Made Worthy of the Holy Spirit': A Hymn of Ambrose in Augustine's *Nature and Grace*," *Augustinian Studies* 50 (2019): 1–12.

80 *nat. et gr.* 63.74 (Latin: CSEL 60:289.17–19; English: my translation).

81 *uisum est, inquit, mihi. potest non soli uisum esse, quod uisum sibi esse declarat. non enim uoluntate tantum humana uisum est, sed sicut placuit ei, qui in me, inquit, loquitur Christus, qui ut id quod bonum est nobis quoque bonum uideri possit operatur; quem enim miseratur et uocat. et ideo qui Christum sequitur potest interrogatus cur esse uoluerit christianus respondere: uisum est mihi. quod cum dicit, non negat deo uisum; a deo enim praeparatur uoluntas hominum. ut enim deus honorificetur a sancto, dei gratia est* (Ambrose, *Expositio euangelii secundum Lucam* 1.10 [CCL 14:11.169–12.177]).

82 For more on Augustine's use of Proverbs, including the key verse 8:35, see A.-M. La Bonnardière, *Biblia Augustiniana: Le livre des Proverbs* (Paris: Études augustiniennes, 1975), esp. 66ff., and Athanase Sage, "Praeparatur voluntas a Domino," *Revue des études augustiniennes* 10 (1964): 1–20.

transformed.[83] After providing this quotation, Augustine exclaims, "Who can fail to see why [Pelagius] does not add these words [to his own quotation from Ambrose]?"[84] Augustine goes on to clarify an aspect of Ambrose's statement: this "beginning" referred to by Ambrose is, in fact, a reference to humanity's origin in Adam. As a result, Ambrose declares that "in those who are by nature children of wrath, drawing from Adam what was corrupted in him, it is impossible for human nature that they be spotless from the beginning."[85] In this sense, through supplemental citations from Ambrose, Augustine has offered evidence that the bishop of Milan preached both the necessity of grace and the reality of original sin. In this sense, Augustine's treatment of Pelagius's citations of Ambrose are much like those of Hilary. Augustine has not only neutralized the quotations offered by Pelagius but has supplied his own quotations so as to reclaim Ambrose for his side.

Following the section on Ambrose, Augustine replies to quotations from several more authors (John Chrysostom, Sixtus, and Jerome). Here, Augustine focuses his efforts on rejecting Pelagius's attempt to claim these authors as his supporters by reinterpreting the quotes provided. Interestingly, the last of Pelagius's quotations is one from Augustine himself.[86] Similar to his responses to quotations from Hilary and Ambrose, Augustine begins here by explaining the quotation in a way that makes clear its distance from Pelagius's theology and then offers several additional quotations from the same work to emphasize more fully the divergence between his own theology and that of Pelagius.

Overall, then, while Augustine's *De natura et gratia* does not evince any radically new forms of argumentation by Augustine, it does offer a steady supply of those types of evidence (references to the Lord's Prayer, quotations from renowned Christian authors, etc.) Augustine has deployed

---

83 *nec ab initio inmaculata—humanae enim hoc inpossibile naturae—sed per dei gratiam et qualitatem sui, quia iam non peccat, fit ut inmaculata uideatur* (Ambrose, *Expositio euangelii secundum Lucam* 1.17 [CCL 14:15.280–282]). Brian Dunkle notes the significance of the fact that this statement occurs shortly after the passage from Ambrose's commentary on Luke cited by Pelagius (see Dunkle, "Made Worthy," 7). In this way, Augustine not only "neutralizes" Ambrose as a supporter for Pelagius, but also neutralizes Ambrose's commentary on Luke, as if that text were particularly pro-Pelagian.

84 *nat. et gr.* 63.75: *haec uerba iste cur non addiderit quis non intellegat?* (Latin: CSEL 60:290.25; English: Teske, WSA I/23, 255). Note the use of *interrogatio* here.

85 *nat. et gr.* 63.75 (Latin: CSEL 60:291.4–8; English: Teske, WSA I/23, 255, slightly modified).

86 Pelagius cites Augustine's *De libero arbitrio* 3.18.50 (Latin: CSEL 74:131.10–16).

THE ROAD TO DIOSPOLIS

throughout his anti-Pelagian works to combat the Pelagian claim to speak for the Church's ancient and universal doctrinal tradition. As we noted above, the continuity of Augustine's argumentation from *De peccatorum meritis* to *De natura et gratia* seems to suggest that the particularities of the arguments Augustine found in Pelagius's *De natura*—especially with regard to his citations of other Christian authors—was not startlingly new to Augustine. While he may not have known the specific appeals the Pelagians were making to renowned Christian writers before reading the *De natura*, it seems very likely that Augustine knew of the general contours of such appeals and that this knowledge motivated (in part) his anti-Pelagian response from the beginning, as I have been arguing. On the other hand, the *De natura* did, as we noted above, offer Augustine proof that these sorts of arguments were being used and that the rumors surrounding Pelagius were accurate. This proof seems to have led Augustine to attempt to confront Pelagius himself more directly, as we shall see.

* * * * *

As Augustine began his work on *De natura et gratia* (which he would complete sometime later in 415[87]), he also commissioned a young Spanish priest named Orosius to carry out a sensitive mission.[88] Orosius had arrived in Hippo at some point relatively recently, having journeyed to Hippo at least in part to seek Augustine's support in his efforts against Origenist and

---

87 The book was complete by the time he sent *ep.* 169 to Evodius sometime later in 415, where he mentions that he has written "a large book against the heresy of Pelagius at the urging of some brothers whom he had convinced of a destructive opinion opposed to the grace of Christ" (*ep.* 169.13; Latin: CSEL 44:621.20–23; English: Teske, WSA II/3, 113). Of note here is that this is the first time Augustine has mentioned Pelagius by name and identified his error as a heresy. This is a bit curious, as Augustine's prohibition on naming names was still in effect in *De natura et gratia*. Perhaps Augustine felt comfortable being more forthright in this letter to Evodius, who was a friend and could be trusted not to spread Augustine's letter (and full opinion) around. For a similar assessment, see Duval, "La correspondance," 375n70. Duval elsewhere takes Augustine's forthrightness here as an indication that Evodius was already fully aware of Augustine's thoughts on Pelagius and was, in fact, the bishop who had informed Augustine of Pelagius's violent reaction against his *Confessiones*—see Duval, "Pélage en son temps," 98–99n16. However, I am more inclined to identify that bishop as Urbanus of Sicca—see discussion in Chronister, "Heresiology and Reality."

88 See Squires, *The Pelagian Controversy*, 97–101, for more on Orosius. Orosius is most famous for his *Historiae aduersum Paganos* (CSEL 5:1–600), composed a few years later.

Priscillianist factions in his homeland.[89] To aid his petition, the Spaniard had written a memorandum for Augustine on the issues, *Commonitorium de errore Priscillianistarum et Origenistarum.*[90] Upon meeting Orosius, Augustine was quite impressed—so much so that he decided to enlist the young Spaniard's help.[91] At some point between January and May of 415,[92] Orosius left for Palestine on Augustine's orders. Orosius's journey seems to have had several aims—one of which was to meet with Jerome and possibly learn more about Origenism and how to combat it.[93] However, more importantly, it seems that this trip to Palestine was also motivated by Augustine's concerns about Pelagianism. When he left for Palestine, Orosius brought with him a set of documents relevant to the controversy. Two of these were letters for Jerome (*epp.* 166 and 167). In them, Augustine asked for Jerome's thoughts on the origin of the soul as well as on James 2:10 ("Whoever observes the whole law, but offends on one point, has become guilty of all")—two topics with obvious connections to Augustine's anti-Pelagian concerns. Of particular interest is *ep.* 166. There, Augustine asks Jerome how the creationist viewpoint might be reconciled with the transmission of original sin. In the course of the letter, he employs some arguments familiar to us from his anti-Pelagian works of 411 in order to defend the Church's teaching on original sin:

> Who would tolerate it if those who run to baptism with their infants believe that they run on account of their flesh, not on account of their souls? Blessed Cyprian was not creating some new decree but preserving the most solid faith of the Church. In order to correct those who thought

---

89 He was likely also fleeing the Germanic invasion of Spain (see Craig Hanson, introduction to FC 99, 98ff.).

90 See CSEL 18:149–57. Augustine would accept the task set for him by Orosius and compose his *Contra Priscillianistas* for Orosius later in 415.

91 See Augustine's comments on Orosius in *ep.* 166.2 (Latin: CSEL 44:547.5ff.) and *ep.* 169.13 (Latin: CSEL 44:621.12ff.).

92 For dating, see Duval, "La date du 'De natura' de Pélage," 259. Duval indicates that Orosius could have left as early as December. However, in 416 Augustine will state, "*priore anno, cum filius meus presbyter Orosius, qui nobiscum est ex Hispania seruus dei, isset ad orientem*" (*s.* 348A.6 [Latin: Dolbeau, "Le sermon 348A," 56.82–83]). (Duval did not have access to this sermon when he published his article.) As a result, it seems that Orosius departed at some point after the start of the new year in 415 (although it remains possible that Augustine had forgotten the exact date of departure if it was in December and close to the new year!).

93 For a survey of some of the different possible reasons for Orosius's journey to the east, see Squires, *Pelagian Controversy*, 125–26—although I think Squires underestimates the significance of Pelagianism in Orosius's journey.

THE ROAD TO DIOSPOLIS   159

that an infant should not be baptized before the eighth day, he said not
that the flesh but that the soul would be lost, and along with certain of his
fellow bishops he declared that an infant can rightly be baptized as soon as
it is born. . . . Let no one hold another opinion contrary to the most well-
founded practice of the Church where, if the faithful ran to the Church for
baptism for the sake of infant bodies, even the dead would be presented
for baptism.[94]

In addition to this reappearance of Cyprian, it is also worth noting that earlier in the letter (§6) Augustine refers to the two passages that he cited from
Jerome's commentary on Jonah and work against Jovinian in *De peccatorum
meritis* 3. In this sense, Augustine clearly had the debates of 411 on his mind
when he wrote to Jerome.

There is further evidence for the significance of Pelagianism as a motivation for Orosius's trip. Indeed, along with these two letters for Jerome,
Orosius also appears to have brought copies of several other items eastward:
Augustine's *ep.* 157,[95] *De peccatorum meritis*,[96] as well as a list of the propositions Caelestius was accused of holding at Carthage in 411.[97] Further, Orosius

---

94 *ep.* 166.23–24 (Latin: CSEL 44:579.6–580.4; English: Teske, WSA II/3, 91).

95 See Orosius, *Liber apologeticus* 3, where he indicates that he read the letter aloud at a
diocesan meeting held in Jerusalem in July 415.

96 Jerome, in *Dialogus aduersus Pelagianos* 3.19, written by the end of 415, mentions three
books of Augustine addressed to Marcellinus, two on baptizing little ones and the third on
those who say that one can be without sin without the help of God—it seems likely that these
refer to the three books of *De peccatorum meritis* (the first and the third concern baptism, the
second deals with sinlessness) and that Orosius had delivered these to Jerome. In any event, it
seems likely Jerome had read *pecc. mer.* 3, as immediately before his reference to Augustine's
anti-Pelagian efforts, he provides one of the same quotations from Cyprian's *ep.* 64 (albeit a
slightly longer version) that Augustine offers at *pecc. mer.* 3.5.10—see *Dialogus aduersus Pelagianos* 3.18. Augustine also references this passage in Cyprian in his *ep.* 166.8.23 for Jerome,
although without a direct quotation this time.

97 The propositions Caelestius was accused of holding at the trial in 411 were known in Palestine in 415, given their inclusion in the slate of positions leveled against Pelagius at the Synod
of Diospolis. Robert Dodaro suggests that Orosius had brought a list of these six propositions
from the Carthaginian *iudicium* of 411 with him to the east after he received them from
Augustine—see "Note on the Carthaginian Debate over Sinlessness, A.D. 411–412 (Augustine,
pecc. mer. 2.7.8–16.25)," *Augustinianum* 40 (2000): 190. However, in 416/17 Augustine seems
not to have had a list of these propositions in his possession as he reported that he could not
even remember with certainty the exact list that was condemned in 411 (*gest. Pel.* 11.23). It does
seem correct to me to identify Orosius as the one who brought the list to the east, especially
since he was seen as capable of reporting on the process relating to Caelestius's condemnation
in Carthage to those gathered at the *conuentum* in Jerusalem in July 415. It seems likely that
Orosius stopped in Carthage in order to retrieve a copy of Paulinus's *libellus* (or the acts of

was tasked with delivering a letter to Pelagius himself. In a sermon offered in the second half of May or early June of 416, Augustine describes Orosius's mission:

> I have been in the habit of writing to [Pelagius] in a friendly way as a servant of God, as he has done to me, and so last year, when my son the priest Orosius, who is a servant of God with us from Spain, had gone to the East with letters of mine, I wrote by him to the same Pelagius, not branding him in my letter as a heretic, but urging him to hear from the priest what I had commissioned him to say.[98]

As we noted above, reading the *De natura* did not seem to present any new information to Augustine, but it did offer confirmation that the rumors that had circulated about Pelagius's role and arguments were true. As a result, in the aftermath of reading the *De natura*, Augustine seems to have attempted to reach out to Pelagius to correct him directly in the spirit of friendship.[99] Orosius was a key part of that outreach, as he was tasked not simply with delivering Augustine's letter, but also, it seems, with explaining its import to Pelagius.[100]

While Orosius's journey to the East may have begun with the hopes of putting an end to Pelagianism via the fraternal correction of Pelagius, it in fact contributed to setting off a series of events that would cause serious trouble for Augustine and his allies. We will discuss these events shortly, but before turning to Palestine, we must address one further anti-Pelagian work composed by Augustine in 415 or thereabouts: *De perfectione iustitiae hominis*.

---

the *iudicium*) before departing for Palestine. If Orosius did in fact stop at Carthage to retrieve a copy of the *libellus/acta*, it would seem to provide additional evidence that combatting Pelagianism was one of the key reasons for his trip to the East.

98 *s.* 348A.6 (Latin: Dolbeau, "Le sermon 348A," 56.81–85; English: Hill, WSA III/11, 312–13). We shall discuss this sermon in more detail in the next chapter. In the meantime, for the dating of the sermon, see Dolbeau, "Le sermon 348A," 50. For more on Augustine's correspondence with Pelagius, see Duval, "La correspondance." See also Duval's discussion in "Pélage en son temps," esp. 113ff.

99 For more on this point, see Löhr, "Augustinus und sein Verhältnis zu Pelagius," 79.

100 In this context, it is important to recall that messengers in the ancient world could be far more than mere "mailmen"—they were often tasked, especially in official contexts, with explaining the contents of a letter and acting on behalf of the letter's author before its recipient. For discussion of the function of messengers especially in the later stages of the Pelagian controversy, see Dalmon, *Un dossier*, 159–68.

DE PERFECTIONE IUSTITIAE HOMINIS

Perhaps sometime after Orosius left for Palestine, Augustine received a document entitled *Definitiones, ut dicitur, Caelestii* from two bishops, Eutropius and Paul, who had asked him for a refutation of it. Eutropius and Paul, who may have originally been from Spain,[101] had apparently received the work from others who had come from Sicily. As a result, it seems that the document originated from the same milieu as Hilary's request in *ep.* 156 that we discussed above. This document, which may not have been written by Caelestius himself,[102] contained several syllogistic arguments intended to prove that human beings have the capacity to avoid sin. Two banks of scriptural quotations apparently followed these arguments, the first offering passages in support of the author's position, and the second containing those passages commonly cited against the document's thesis juxtaposed with still more passages allegedly in support of the Pelagian viewpoint. In *De perfectione iustitiae hominis*, Augustine may have reproduced the majority or perhaps even the entirety of the document, critiquing his opponent's arguments point-by-point.

As we have come to expect, given the *Definitiones'* aim to prove the possibility of sinlessness, Augustine focuses on arguing in support of the necessity of grace without categorically denying the possibility of living sinlessly. At the same time, though, he also emphasizes that it seems very unlikely that anyone has actually lived sinlessly. As we noted above, Augustine's reading of Pelagius's *De natura* (and its appeals to renowned Christian authors) did not change the substance of Augustine's anti-Pelagian argumentation.[103] However, what we do see after his reading of *De natura* is a steady increase

---

101 Orosius refers to two bishops named Eutropius and Paul at *Commonitorium* 1 (Latin: CSEL 18:151.7ff.) as *mei domini*, possibly indicating that he knew them well and that they were also from Spain (see, e.g., Teske, WSA I/23, 269). However, Volker Henning Drecoll prefers to identify Eutropius and Paul as North African bishops (although he does not seem to consider the possibility that they were Spanish)—see Volker Henning Drecoll, "Perfectione iustitiae hominis (De-)," in A-L 4, 678.

102 Augustine notes that the content and style is similar to what he knows of Caelestius's writing, but he does not take a firm position on the authorship itself (see *perf. iust.* 1.1). Walter Dunphy writes, "[The *Definitiones*] may, indeed, have been a reference manual of arguments and biblical texts that [Caelestius] prepared for his followers. Alternatively, it may be the work of an admiring disciple who collected these from his writings and lectures" ("The Writings of Caelestius," 34). See also Honnay's comments in "Caelestius, discipulus Pelagii," 281.

103 As I suggested above, this was because Augustine was already largely familiar with such Pelagian arguments.

162 AUGUSTINE IN THE PELAGIAN CONTROVERSY

in arguments aiming to demonstrate the ancient and universal Church's opposition to Pelagian views. This steady increase is evidenced in *De perfectione iustitiae hominis*, where Augustine references the Lord's Prayer in no less than sixteen different passages.[104] While not all of these references are explicitly designed to demonstrate the opposition of the universal Church to Pelagianism, the frequent appeals to this central prayer of Christianity function as a constant refrain of sorts throughout the work, repeatedly reminding the reader of Pelagianism's apparent incongruity with that prayer. Further clarity on this point can be obtained via a few significant examples.

One such example is found at *perf. iust.* 10.21, where Augustine responds to a list of scriptural citations provided by Caelestius that suggest following God's commandments is neither burdensome nor difficult to accomplish. To explain in what sense the commandments can be called "not burdensome [*non . . . grauia*]," Augustine first recalls the primary commandment of God: to love. Love, Augustine agrees, enables one to fulfill the commandments with ease: love "makes the burden of the commandment light, not merely not pressing one down by its heavy load, but raising one up as if upon wings."[105] However, Augustine asks, from where does the human person receive this power to love? For Augustine, this power comes from God—and the prayers prayed by Christians indicate this source:

> Scripture mentions that God's commandments are not burdensome precisely so that the soul that finds them burdensome may understand that it has not yet received the strength that makes the Lord's commandments what he taught us they are, namely, light and sweet. Thus such a soul might pray with a groaning of the will to obtain the gift that makes them easy. After all, we pray, "May my heart become spotless" (Ps 119:80), and, "Guide my journeys according to your word, and let not sinfulness lord it over me" (Ps 119:133), and, "May your will be done on earth as it is in heaven," and "Bring us not into temptation," and other prayers of this sort, which it would take a long time to mention. By these, we pray for precisely this: that we might carry out God's commandments.[106]

---

104 See *perf. iust.* 6.14, 6.15, 7.16, 8.18, 8.19, 9.20, 10.21, 11.24, 11.28, 12.30, 13.31, 15.34, 15.36, 19.40, 20.43, and 21.44.

105 *perf. iust.* 10.21 (Latin: CSEL 42:21.7–9; English: Teske, WSA I/23, 289).

106 *perf. iust.* 10.21 (Latin: CSEL 42:21.15–25; English: Teske, WSA I/23. 289).

THE ROAD TO DIOSPOLIS   163

Augustine's argument here hinges on this list of petitions drawn from the psalms and from the Lord's Prayer, all of which would have been said (at one time or another) during the liturgy. While he does not directly attack the Pelagian view here, the implication is clear: the Pelagians undermine the very prayer of the Church, as it begs God for aid in the pursuit of righteousness.

Another key passage comes at *perf. iust.* 19.40. In this part of his treatise, Augustine is responding to Caelestius's attempts to counter specific biblical passages that were frequently cited against the Pelagians. Caelestius's basic method seems to have been to quote an apparently anti-Pelagian scriptural verse and then to juxtapose this verse with several other verses that seemed to support the Pelagian position. Augustine complained that this method would cause harm and confusion among the faithful, making it seem as if scripture were self-contradictory.[107] In the present case, Caelestius notes that Rom 9:16 ("It does not depend upon the one who wills or runs, but upon God who shows mercy") is often employed against the Pelagians. Caelestius argues that in response to this verse, one should quote 1 Cor 7:36 ("Let him do what he wills") along with several verses from Philemon, Deuteronomy, Sirach, and Isaiah, all of which emphasize human action and free will. Augustine responds to this apparent contradiction in scripture, saying:

> However much these people try to hide, here they are exposed. For they reveal that they are arguing against the grace and mercy of God for which we pray when we say, "May your will be done on earth as it is in heaven" or "Bring us not into temptation, but deliver us from evil." After all, why do we make these petitions in prayer with such groans, if it depends upon the one who wills and runs, not "upon God who shows mercy" (Rom 9:16)? It is not that this is done without our will, but that our will does not accomplish what it does unless it is helped by God. This is the sound faith that leads us to pray: to seek in order that we may find, to beg in order that we may receive, to knock in order that the door may be opened for us. One who argues against this faith closes in his own face the door of God's mercy.[108]

Here, Augustine once again indicates how contrary the Pelagian positions are to the Church's tradition of prayer. Augustine asserts that this tradition of

---

107 "[Caelestius] does not offer an explanation of [these testimonies]; rather, by mentioning others apparently opposed to these, he compounded the difficulties" (*perf. iust.* 11.23 [Latin: CSEL 42:23.25–24.1; English: Teske, WSA I/23, 290]).

108 *perf. iust.* 19.40 (Latin: CSEL 42:42.20–43.7; English: Teske, WSA I/23, 301).

prayer emerges from the Church's faith—it is that ancient and universal faith that grounds Christian prayer and teaches Christians how to pray. Augustine concludes with a rhetorical flourish: "I do not intend to say anything more on a matter of such importance, because I am better off to entrust it to the prayerful groans of the faithful than to my writings."[109] The Church's life of prayer is better testimony to faith and to true doctrine than anything Augustine himself could write.[110]

Another significant passage is found in the conclusion of *De perfectione iustitiae hominis*. Here, Augustine summarizes his argument against his opponent's advocacy for the possibility of sinlessness. Citing 1 John 1:8 ("If we say that we have no sin, we deceive ourselves, and the truth is not in us"), Augustine notes that some might interpret this passage to refer simply to concupiscence—the disordered desire that leads to sin. In this sense, such an objector could argue that John did not really intend to say that all people have actually consented to this sin. To challenge this interpretation, Augustine turns to the Lord's Prayer.

> Such persons draw these subtle distinctions [between sin and concupiscence], but they should bear in mind what we are praying in the Lord's Prayer when we say, *Forgive us our debts*. Unless I am mistaken, there would be no need to say this, if we never consented at all to the desires of this same sin by a failing of words or by taking pleasure in some thought; rather we would only have to say, *Bring us not into temptation but deliver us from evil*.[111]

In this sense, the Lord's Prayer suggests a key problem with a possible interpretation of 1 John 1:8. As we have seen time and time again, Augustine employs the Lord's Prayer as chief evidence against various facets of the Pelagian view. Against their optimism regarding the possibility of living sinlessly, Augustine often recalls the line, *Forgive us our debts*. Against the Pelagians' apparent denial of the need for grace, he cites, *Bring us not into temptation but deliver us from evil*. Of course, it is important to recognize here that the Lord's Prayer does not seem to gain its argumentative strength simply from its scriptural context. Rather, I would suggest that even more

109 *perf. iust.* 19.40 (Latin: CSEL 42:43.7–9; English: Teske, WSA I/23, 301).

110 Of course, the rhetorical nature of this statement is underlined when in the next line Augustine decides to talk more about this topic anyway (see *perf. iust.* 19.41).

111 *perf. iust.* 21.44 (Latin: CSEL 42:47.24–48.2; English: Teske, WSA I/23, 304).

THE ROAD TO DIOSPOLIS

powerful than that scriptural context was the fact that Christians universally prayed this prayer from the beginning until Augustine's day. In that sense, any view that seemed to do away with the need for such a prayer attacked the heart of the life of the Church. Augustine indicates how high the stakes are in the final lines of his work:

> In any case, I do not believe that one should resist this idea too much [i.e., that there have been some righteous people without any sin]. For I know that such is the view of some whose position on this matter I dare not reprehend, though I cannot defend it either. But clearly, if someone denies that we ought to pray so that we do not enter into temptation—and one denies this who maintains that the help of God's grace is not needed for a human being to avoid sin, but that the human will is sufficient, once the law has been received—I have no doubt that such a person should be banished from everyone's hearing and should be condemned by everyone's lips.[112]

While Augustine is willing to "agree to disagree" with the Pelagians and others who think it possible to avoid sin in this life,[113] he does not find such a détente possible when it comes to God's grace. On that topic, Augustine makes clear that the Pelagian threat is of dire consequence for the Church's life of prayer and thus should be completely expelled from the fold.

One element of Augustine's argument in *De perfectione iustitiae hominis* that is slightly new is Augustine's emphasis on the importance of fasting (*ieiunium*) and almsgiving (*elemosynae*).[114] For Augustine, prayer, fasting, and almsgiving represent the heart of the Christian life and the pursuit of righteousness. In a lengthy but important passage, he writes:

> The Lord said in the gospel, *Do not display your righteousness before men in order that they might see you* (Matt 6:1), so that we would not measure our life by the goal of human glory. In his explanation of this righteousness, he included but three elements: fasting, almsgiving, and prayer. By fasting he meant, of course, the whole chastisement of the body. By almsgiving he meant every instance of good will and every good deed, whether in giving or in forgiving, and by prayer he suggested all the forms of holy desire. The

---

112 *perf. iust.* 21.44 (Latin: CSEL 42:48.13–20; English: Teske, WSA I/23, 304).

113 Here Augustine likely has Ambrose in mind. See *nat. et gr.* 63.74.

114 See, e.g., *perf. iust.* 8.18, 8.19, 9.20, 11.24, 11.28, 15.34. Augustine had mentioned the works of mercy and almsgiving briefly in *ep.* 157.1.3, but his reflections on it are much more developed here. See also *s.* 351 for some similar themes.

166 AUGUSTINE IN THE PELAGIAN CONTROVERSY

chastisement of the body holds in check that concupiscence which ought to be not merely held in check, but ought not to exist at all and will not exist in that perfection of righteousness in which there will be no sin whatsoever. Now in the use of things which are permitted and licit, it often introduces its lack of moderation. In the very beneficence by which the righteous show concern for their neighbor, there occur some things which are harmful, though they were thought to be helpful. At times through weakness when one's efforts at doing good and in labor fail to meet the needs of others or benefit them little, there creeps in a weariness that dulls the cheerfulness that God loves in a giver. It creeps in more if one is making less progress, and it creeps in less if one is making more progress. For these and similar reasons we do right to say in prayer, *Forgive us our debts, as we also forgive our debtors* (Matt 6:12), provided that we do what we say. Then, either we would love even our enemies or if, being still little ones in Christ, we do not yet do this, we would pardon from the depths of our heart one who repents over having sinned against us and asks forgiveness, if we want our heavenly Father to hear our prayer. If we do not want to be argumentative, we have in that prayer a glass held before us in which we can see the life of the righteous who live from faith and run perfectly, though they are not without sin. Hence, they say, *Forgive us*, since they have not yet arrived at the end of their race.[115]

There are several important elements to this passage. First of all, note how Augustine describes the Christian life: it is a life of fasting, almsgiving, and prayer. For Augustine these crucial facets of the Christian life are aimed at both overcoming sin and receiving forgiveness when one inevitably fails to overcome it.[116] Although he is not as explicit in this passage as he sometimes is when highlighting the danger that the Pelagian views have for the Lord's Prayer (or Christian prayer in general), Augustine seems to be aiming to show how different the Pelagian view of the Christian life is from his own (and—the reader is to understand—that of Christians everywhere): whereas the righteous recognize that this life of pilgrimage centers on these three things and the constant need for forgiveness, even in the midst of growth in holiness, the Pelagians seem to think it possible to move beyond such things in this life to a state of perfect righteousness. This runs counter, in Augustine's view, to the Christian life as a lived reality. It also runs counter, Augustine

---

115 *perf. iust.* 8.18–19 (Latin: CSEL 42:16.3–17.10; English: Teske, WSA I/23, 286–87).

116 Elsewhere, Augustine will emphasize that one receives pardon for sin through almsgiving (e.g., *perf. iust.* 11.24).

notes, to the Lord's Prayer, which he turns back to at the end of the passage. Indeed, Augustine argues that the Lord's Prayer perfectly encapsulates the vision of the Christian life he has been describing: it is a life of real progress in righteousness, albeit an imperfect righteousness still liable to stumbles and sins along the way.

All told, Augustine's efforts in *De perfectione iustitiae hominis* are marked by an abiding concern to indicate how opposed the Pelagian vision of the Christian life is to that held by the vast majority of other Christians. Although Augustine never states it quite so blatantly, his repeated references to the Lord's Prayer, as well as to fasting and almsgiving, reveal his desire to prove that the Pelagian view undercuts the central aspects of what it means to be a Christian. In this sense, Augustine has not simply attempted to refute his opponent's views; rather, he has framed this refutation at least in part as a defense of the Christian way of life handed down by the ancient and universal Church to her children. In that sense, it offers us yet more evidence for Augustine's constant desire to undercut the Pelagians' claims to speak for the Church's ancient and universal doctrinal tradition.

PALESTINE IN 415

While Augustine worked on *De natura et gratia* (and, possibly, *De perfectione iustitiae hominis*, depending on its dating), Orosius made his journey eastward. Upon his arrival in Palestine at some point in the first half of 415, Orosius found hostilities already inflamed between the two parties.[117] Indeed, Jerome seems to have been aware of the spread of Pelagian views as early as 412, but his efforts against these new opponents came to a head in 415 when he composed an important letter against the Pelagians to a certain Ctesiphon (by July) as well as his *Dialogus aduersus Pelagianos* (a draft of which was probably complete by December).[118] For Jerome, Pelagianism represented a

---

117 In *s.* 348A.6, Augustine states, "[Orosius], however, found the place where Pelagius was to be greatly disturbed by Pelagius's preaching and by the disagreements of the brothers" (Latin: Dolbeau, "Le sermon 348A," 56.85–86; English: my translation).

118 See Jerome, *Commentarii in Hiezechielem* 6.pref, likely written in 412, which seems to contain a veiled allusion to the Pelagians, characterizing them as disciples of his now deceased opponent Rufinus of Aquileia. For discussion of Jerome's anti-Pelagian activity, see, e.g., Squires, *Pelagian Controversy*, 107–20, and Wermelinger, *Rom und Pelagius*, 46–56. Regarding the letter to Ctesiphon, several scholars have suggested that "Ctesiphon" may have been a pseudonym, although there is no agreement over the real identity of the addressee— see, e.g., Dunphy, "A Prelude to the Synod of Diospolis," 143–44n21. See also Carole Burnett,

resurgence of Origenism, and he linked the Pelagians with his old opponent, Rufinus. For their part, some among the Pelagians, perhaps Pelagius himself, had prompted (or reinforced) this opinion by repeating several accusations against Jerome drawn from other sources, at least one of which came from Rufinus himself.[119] In this agitated environment, Orosius's mission to bring Pelagius to correct his views was, in many ways, a failure from the start, as the situation had no doubt already become too tense for reasoned discussion.

However, the situation had devolved further by the summer of 415, when a diocesan meeting (*conuentum*) was held in Jerusalem on July 28 to discuss the matter of Pelagius and his teachings. The identity of the attendees at this meeting is a bit unclear, but it seems to have been largely populated by Latin clergy present in and around Jerusalem, although it was presided over by John, the bishop of Jerusalem.[120] Orosius himself was called to participate in the meeting, and recounts the details of the meeting in his *Liber apologeticus*, written later in 415.[121] There, the Spanish priest notes that his presence was requested especially in order to narrate the events related to Pelagius and

---

"Dysfunction at Diospolis: A Comparative Study of Augustine's *De Gestis Pelagii* and Jerome's *Dialogus Adversus Pelagianos*," *Augustinian Studies* 34 (2003): 153–73, which offers an analysis of the reliance of the indictment of Pelagius at Diospolis on Jerome's *Dialogus*, thus indicating that at least a draft was complete by the end of 415. Further, at *ep.* 19*.2, likely written at some point in late May or early June of 416, Augustine reports the news of the *Dialogus's* favorable reception at Ravenna. It seems likely that it had been delivered there by Firmus, whom Jerome had sent to Ravenna in 415 (see Jerome's *ep.* 172.2 among the letters of Augustine). See also Duval, "Note Complémentaire: Lettre 19*," BA 46B, 509. It should be noted, too, that the *Dialogus's* original title was likely either *Dialogus Attici et Critobuli* or *Altercatio Attici et Critobuli*. See A. Canellis, "La composition du *Dialogue contre les Lucifériens* et du *Dialogue contre les Pélagiens* de saint Jérôme: À la recherche d'un canon de l'*altercatio*," *Revue des études augustiniennes* 43 (1997): 247–88, and Benoît Jeanjean, "Le *Dialogus Attici et Critobuli* de Jérôme et la Prédication Pélagienne en Palestine entre 411 et 415," in *Jerome of Stridon: His Life, Writings, and Legacy*, ed. Andrew Cain and Josef Lössl (Farnham: Ashgate, 2009), 59–71.

119 For more, see Squires, *Pelagian Controversy*, 117–20; G. Caruso, "Le accuse di Pelagio nel Commentarium in Hieremiam di Girolamo," *Augustinianum* 57 (2017): 107–21; and Wermelinger, *Rom und Pelagius*, 48ff.

120 For discussion, see Wermelinger, *Rom und Pelagius*, 57–60. Dunphy suggests that the meeting was not called by John himself and that the main membership of the meeting could have been a standing group of Latin clerics tasked with overseeing Latin affairs in the Holy Land ("A Prelude," 128). See also Orosius's comments at *Liber apologeticus* 3 (CSEL 5:606.21–23).

121 Orosius, *Liber apologeticus* (CSEL 5:603–64). Orosius wrote this work to defend himself after John of Jerusalem accused him of holding that one cannot be without sin even with the help of God (*Liber apologeticus* 7). It should be noted that Orosius's account is not complete: he omits (perhaps among other things) a conversation between John and Pelagius on the need

THE ROAD TO DIOSPOLIS

Caelestius that had transpired in Africa.[122] In response, Orosius reported several things. First, he informed John that Caelestius had requested ordination in Carthage but was then condemned there. Second, he mentioned Augustine's efforts to refute Pelagius's *De natura* which had been handed over to him by the latter's former disciples. Finally, at John's request, he produced and read aloud a letter that Augustine had recently sent to Sicily (i.e., *ep.* 157 to Hilary).

Following this, Orosius notes that Pelagius was admitted to the room at the request of John in order that he might defend himself.[123] Pelagius was asked if he had, in fact, taught the things that Augustine had mentioned in *ep.* 157. To this, Pelagius responded, "And who is Augustine to me?"[124] Orosius reports that, amid an uproar at Pelagius's apparent lack of respect for Augustine, John ordered Pelagius to sit in their midst and stated, "I am Augustine."[125] At this, Orosius (or others with him) said, "If you are taking the role of Augustine, follow the thought of Augustine."[126] John then turned to all who were gathered and noted that the specific words of Augustine that had been read aloud were directed against someone else. He requested that further evidence be furnished to prove that Pelagius himself was guilty of the same beliefs as those which Augustine had written against. Orosius then spoke up, "Pelagius told me that he teaches that a human being can be without sin and easily keep the commandments of God if he wishes."[127] According to Orosius, Pelagius then admitted that this was the case. However, after Pelagius agreed that sinlessness would only be possible with the help of God, John seems to have turned on Orosius and his allies, questioning whether they believed that sinlessness would be possible *with* the help of God. In the end, Orosius and his allies salvaged the situation as best they could by arguing that the

---

for grace, which is referenced in the acts of Diospolis—see *gest. Pel.* 14.37 and Wermelinger, *Rom und Pelagius*, 59.

122 Orosius, *Liber apologeticus* 3.

123 Orosius expresses his displeasure at the fact that a layman like Pelagius was welcomed into a meeting of clerics (*Liber apologeticus* 4).

124 *Liber apologeticus* 4 (Latin: CSEL 5:607.18; English: my translation).

125 *Liber apologeticus* 4 (Latin: CSEL 5:608.2–3; English: my translation). Orosius explains that by saying this, John meant to take on the role of Augustine vis-à-vis Pelagius in the proceedings.

126 *Liber apologeticus* 4 (Latin: CSEL 5:608.3–4; English: my translation).

127 *Liber apologeticus* 4 (Latin: CSEL 5:608.6–8; English: my translation).

evidence should be sent to Rome, as the matter was a western and Latin controversy that should not be decided in the East. John agreed with this proposal, imposing silence on Pelagius until Rome should decide the case.[128]

However, this *conuentum* at Jerusalem did little to calm the debate. Forty-seven days later (September 13, 415), Orosius presented himself before John of Jerusalem on the occasion of a feast day in the city and was met with a charge of heresy.[129] John believed that Orosius had said that sinlessness was not possible even with the help of God. In response, Orosius wrote his *Liber apologeticus*, mentioned above, which served both as a defense of his own views and an attack on those of the Pelagians.[130] While we will not discuss Orosius's text in detail here, a few points should be mentioned. First, Orosius's presentation of John of Jerusalem's role at the meeting is noteworthy. While attributing much of the failure of the meeting to an ill-equipped (or even malicious) interpreter,[131] Orosius does little to disguise his displeasure at John of Jerusalem's handling of the proceedings. Aside from his efforts to indicate John's partiality toward Pelagius, he also draws attention at one point to the fact that John had apparently quoted Origen, thus reminding his readers of John's association with Rufinus in the midst of the Origenist controversy and no doubt hoping to reignite old animosities.[132] Orosius's efforts to blame

---

128 There is not any evidence that the case was, in fact, forwarded to Innocent in Rome. See Dunphy, "A Prelude," 139–40.

129 See Orosius, *Liber apologeticus* 7.

130 The work also seems to have been a defense presented to Orosius's own allies, who appear to have blamed him at least partially for the failure of the meeting in July—see Wermelinger, *Rom und Pelagius*, 60. We do not know exactly when the *Liber apologeticus* was composed, but it is commonly dated to the fall of 415 before the Synod of Diospolis in December (see, e.g., Hanson, FC 104; Wermelinger, *Rom und Pelagius*, 60). Stuart Squires has suggested that it dates to the period after the Synod of Diospolis and before Orosius's departure from Palestine in the first half of 416, due to a reference at *Liber apologeticus* 8 to the blood of St. Stephen (the relics of St. Stephen were discovered while the Synod of Diospolis was in session)—see Squires, *Pelagian Controversy*, 130–31. However, the absence of any reference to Pelagius's acquittal at Diospolis seems to argue against such a dating in my view.

131 See *Liber apologeticus* 6. Apparently, John's Latin was not good enough to understand Orosius and the letter from Augustine without the aid of a translator. The language barrier will continue to be a problem at the Synod of Diospolis, which we will discuss shortly.

132 See *Liber apologeticus* 5: "And indeed, it was known by many of us that the pronouncements cited by Bishop John had been made by Origen" (Latin: CSEL 5:609.15–16; English: Hanson, FC 99, 120). Attention could also be drawn to Orosius's displeasure at John's request for Pelagius to be admitted to the meeting and at John's attempt to claim the role of Augustine for himself (*Liber apologeticus* 4).

THE ROAD TO DIOSPOLIS 171

John are noteworthy when contrasted with Augustine's interpretation of the Synod of Diospolis in *De gestis Pelagii*, which we shall discuss in the next chapter.[133] A second point of note in Orosius's *Liber apologeticus* is a comment the Spanish priest makes in the opening paragraph of his work. There, after explaining that he has been the victim of calumny and that he aims to defend his own views while unveiling the dangers of the Pelagian positions, Orosius indicates that others more well-known than he have already written against this heresy, albeit without mentioning the heresy's founders by name:

> For the Fathers—both those who have already found eternal rest as martyrs and confessors, Cyprian, Hilary, and Ambrose, as well as those for whom it is still necessary to remain in the flesh and who are the pillars and foundations of the Catholic Church, Aurelius, Augustine, and Jerome— have already published much in their most admirable writings against this wicked heresy without specifying the names of the heretics.[134]

This statement by Orosius seems to indicate his awareness of Augustine's polemical strategy. First, the fact that Orosius knows that Augustine has not mentioned the heresy by name makes it appear likely that Augustine had told Orosius of this strategic decision (although Jerome seems to have taken up this approach independently[135]). Second, and more importantly, the list of earlier Christian authors mentioned by Orosius here suggests that Augustine had made a point to share the quotations he gathered from Cyprian, Hilary, and Ambrose with Orosius to show that they, too, would have opposed the Pelagians' views if they were still alive. Indeed, the authors mentioned here

---

133 There are a number of contrasts between Orosius's and Augustine's anti-Pelagian efforts, in terms of both style and content, although the stylistic differences appear more significant to me. For example, Orosius takes it upon himself to depart from Augustine's practice and name his opponents—see *Liber apologeticus* 1. He also has no qualms about *ad hominem* attacks on Pelagius (see, e.g., *Liber apologeticus* 31, where Orosius mocks Pelagius's physical appearance—something that perhaps indicates Jerome's influence, given similar comments found at, e.g., *Dialogus aduersus Pelagianos* 3.16). While all of this might speak to Orosius's lack of self-restraint and youthful rashness, it could also indicate just how tense the situation was in Palestine in 415. At the same time, the influence of Jerome on Orosius should not be underestimated. For an analysis of the similarities between Orosius's and Jerome's approaches when dealing with the Pelagians, see Giulio Malavasi, "Orosio discepolo di Agostino? L'influenza di Girolamo nel *Liber Apologeticus*," *Augustinianum* 55 (2015): 113–36.

134 Orosius, *Liber apologeticus* 1 (Latin: CSEL 5:604.7–13; English: Hanson, FC 99, 115–16).

135 For example, neither his *ep.* 133 to Ctesiphon nor the *Dialogus* mention the names of Pelagius and Caelestius (and the original title of the *Dialogus*—see n. 118 above—did not have *Pelagianos* in it).

by Orosius represent the complete canon of the writers Augustine has cited against the Pelagians so far.[136] If we are correct to hypothesize that Augustine had shared this list with Orosius, it is significant, as it (yet again) suggests how important it was for Augustine to demonstrate the antiquity of his anti-Pelagian positions and how crucial citations from renowned Christian authors were becoming as evidence for that demonstration.

All told, Orosius's *Liber apologeticus* (as well as Jerome's continuing efforts) likely fanned the flames of controversy all the more. By December the anti-Pelagian forces (or some segment of them[137]) in Palestine had decided to launch a fresh attack on Pelagius, apparently ignoring the resolution from the July meeting to forward the case on to Innocent in Rome. At some point toward the end of the year, two exiled bishops from Gaul, Heros of Arles and Lazarus of Aix, submitted a document indicting Pelagius for heresy to Eulogius of Caesarea, the primate of Palestine.[138] It is unclear to what extent the two exiled bishops were actually responsible for the contents of the document; it has been suggested that Orosius himself may have been the main author.[139] The indictment itself was made up of roughly twenty-nine

136 Commenting on the authors mentioned by Orosius, Wermelinger (see *Rom und Pelagius*, 67) notes the similarity between Orosius's list and that found in Pelagius's *De natura* (the only three missing are Lactantius, Sixtus, and John Chrysostom), and suggests that this list indicates Orosius's awareness of the *De natura*. However, it seems to me that the more important similarity is between Orosius and Augustine, given the inclusion of Cyprian (whom Augustine cited elsewhere, but not in *De natura et gratia*). Nevertheless, Wermelinger is right to point out that Orosius would have been unlikely to reference any of the other three authors: Lactantius, because Pelagius had not mentioned his name; Sixtus, because Jerome was doubtful about the authorship of that text; John Chrysostom, because of his role opposite Jerome's party in the Origenist controversy. A further complicating factor, though, is that Jerome quotes Cyprian against Pelagius twice in his *Dialogus aduersus Pelagianos*, at 1.32 (a citation from Cyprian's *Testimonia ad Quirinum* 3.54) and 3.18 (a citation from Cyprian's *ep.* 64.5). The latter appears dependent upon Augustine's *De peccatorum meritis* (which is referred to in the next paragraph), while the former seems independent (although Augustine will later refer to the same passage at *c. ep. Pel.* 4.10.27). It remains possible that Orosius mentions Cyprian here at Jerome's behest, rather than because of anything Augustine has told him—but when viewed in conjunction with the mentions of Ambrose and Hilary, the link with Augustine's own "citation history" seems too strong to dismiss.

137 We should not assume that all anti-Pelagians in Palestine were united in the decision to pursue further legal action against Pelagius at that time. For example, several scholars have emphasized Orosius's role in the lead up to Diospolis—see, e.g., Burnett, "Dysfunction at Diospolis," 171, and Malavasi, *La controversia pelagiana in Oriente*, 265.

138 For more on Heros and Lazarus, see Wermelinger, *Rom und Pelagius*, 68–70.

139 For discussion, see Wermelinger, *Rom und Pelagius*, 69; Carole Burnett, "Dysfunction at Diospolis"; Malavasi, *La controversia pelagiana*, 265.

THE ROAD TO DIOSPOLIS

propositions: (1) some drawn from alleged writings of Pelagius and Caelestius, (2) the six propositions from Caelestius's trial at Carthage, as well as (3) three propositions based on those that Hilary of Syracuse had reported to Augustine, and to which Augustine had responded in *ep.* 157. Some of the propositions (especially those attributed to Pelagius) had already been cited in the works of Jerome and Orosius,[140] while others (especially those attributed to an unknown work by Caelestius) are not found elsewhere.[141] A local synod was called and held at Diospolis in mid-to-late December,[142] and fourteen bishops gathered together to determine whether Pelagius was guilty of any heresy.[143] Unfortunately, at least from Augustine's perspective, neither Heros, Lazarus, Orosius, nor Jerome were present at the synod and the fourteen bishops were forced to rely on the written indictment of Heros and Lazarus to question Pelagius.[144] Pelagius's defense was convincing to the bishops gathered at Diospolis: he denied that some of the books from which statements were drawn were his, refused to answer to those propositions

140 See Burnett, "Dysfunction at Diospolis," who identifies Jerome's *Dialogus* as a key source for the quotations from Pelagius's works. Of course, Augustine's *ep.* 157 as well as the list of propositions attributed to Caelestius in 411 (two of the documents Orosius seems to have brought to the East) were two other sources.

141 For more on this lost work by Caelestius, see Anthony Dupont and Giulio Malavasi, "The *Liber Caelestii*: A Historical and Theological Analysis of Its Fragments." *Revue d'histoire des textes* 17 (2022): 171–211.

142 A date of December 20 is sometimes given (see, e.g., Wermelinger, *Rom und Pelagius*, 60, who refers to Adolar Zumkeller's discussion in *Sankt Augustinus Lehrer der Gnade: Schriften gegen die Pelagianer* [Würzburg: Augustinus-Verlag, 1964], vol. 2, 47n155). Dunphy says the date cannot be specified precisely beyond late December ("Concerning the Synod of Diospolis and Its Acts," *Academia* 63 [1996]: 104).

143 Dunphy notes that we cannot say with certainty that the synod was called specifically for the purpose of examining Pelagius; there may have been other business of which we are now ignorant (Dunphy, "Concerning the Synod," 104).

144 Heros and Lazarus's absence was apparently due to an illness that afflicted one of them (see Augustine, *gest. Pel.* 1.2). As Dunphy notes, "Augustine lamely explains away [their absence] by saying that one of them was ill, which, of course, does not explain why both should be absent. Augustine's words also betray his disquiet with this fact, and even suggest that he is offering an acceptable reason, but without any basis in fact. He writes: *sicut postea probabilius comperimus*" ("Concerning the Synod," 105). Burnett views their absence as merely the final element in a series of half-hearted and rushed attempts to have Pelagius tried and convicted. She notes, among other things, the apparent lack of care taken in the drafting of the indictment, which failed to rely on the original Pelagian sources, omitted key words, garbled some quotations, and was submitted in Latin without a Greek translation (Burnett, "Dysfunction at Diospolis," 170–71). All in all, Burnett suggests a key motivation for the whole rushed affair was to "vindicate Orosius as soon as possible after his public humiliation in September" (171).

attributed to Caelestius, and explained those statements that were his in a manner acceptable to the episcopal judges.[145] With none of Pelagius's opponents present to challenge his responses, Pelagius was easily acquitted.[146]

CONCLUSION

During the period covered in this chapter, Augustine received worrying news about the spread of Pelagianism from a variety of sources. As he responded to the various questions and information he had received, he consistently sought to refute not only the theological positions of his opponents but also their claims to speak for the Church's doctrinal tradition. Augustine's arguments that aim to establish, on the contrary, that his anti-Pelagian positions were simply those of the ancient and universal Church see a steady increase over this period, but are in continuity with what we have observed since 411—namely, they largely rely on evidence drawn from the Church's traditions of prayer (and especially the Lord's Prayer), as well as, occasionally, the testimony of renowned Christian authors. The main differences between 412–15 and 411 with regard to the kinds of evidence employed are due to the shifting topics of debate—for example, the discourse in 411 focused much more on the issue of original sin, and hence evidence related to the practice of infant baptism was deployed frequently. At times, Augustine's reading of Pelagius's *De natura* is cited as a turning point in the controversy. This is understandable in certain respects, especially in the sense that it confirmed for Augustine the rumors he had heard of Pelagius's role in spreading certain views and the reports he had likely received about the style of arguments

---

145 An analysis of the proceedings of the synod can be found in Augustine's *De gestis Pelagii*, which we shall discuss in the next chapter. For more detailed analyses of the synod itself, see Wermelinger, *Rom und Pelagius*, 78–87, and Squires, *Pelagian Controversy*, 130–36. For an analysis of the charges against Pelagius and an evaluation of the degree to which they corresponded to his true views, see Andrew Chronister, "What Did Pelagius Really Teach? Evaluating the Charges Lodged against Pelagius at the Synod of Diospolis," *Augustiniana* 74 (2024): 51–123.

146 Of note here is Pier Franco Beatrice's recent article: "Chromatius and Jovinus at the Synod of Diospolis: A Prosopographical Inquiry," *Journal of Early Christian Studies* 22 (2014): 437–64. Beatrice identifies two of the bishops at Diospolis as Chromatius of Aquileia and Jovinus of Ascalon (formerly of Padua?), who in turn had connections with Rufinus of Aquileia. If Beatrice is correct, not only were these two bishops native Latin-speakers, they were also part of Rufinus's network, a network with close ties to the Pelagians (as we indicated in Chapter 1). However, there are some reasons to doubt whether Beatrice's hypothesis is correct. For some more discussion of this point, see Chapter 4, n. 83.

the Pelagians were using. However, it is important not to overemphasize this literary encounter, as we have said above. What the reading of the *De natura* did prompt, however, was a new focus on Augustine's part to address Pelagius and his role directly—through his *De natura et gratia*, of course, but also, and perhaps more importantly, through the letter he sent to Pelagius via Orosius. The decision to send Orosius to the East, at least in part, to deliver this letter and to spread warnings about Pelagius and his views backfired and, it would seem, precipitated (or at least contributed to) a series of defeats for the anti-Pelagian cause culminating in Pelagius's acquittal at Diospolis. There is no doubt that this acquittal was a huge blow to Augustine and his allies. Recall that, as we have argued, one of the main reasons for Augustine's entrance into the controversy was to counter the threat to unity posed by the Pelagians when they claimed that their opponents' positions were novel and not in conformity with those of the eastern churches. The Synod of Diospolis, when it acquitted Pelagius and found him to be a Catholic, seemed to validate those claims.[147] As a result, when news of Diospolis reached the ears of Augustine and the African bishops, they took swift and decisive action, as we shall see in the next chapter.

---

147 As Gerald Bonner writes, "Pelagius's acquittal seemed to challenge the principle which Augustine had repeatedly urged against the Donatists: the universality of Catholic belief" (Gerald Bonner, "A Last Apology for Pelagianism?" in *Studia Patristica 49*, ed. J. Baun, A. Cameron, M. Edwards, and M. Vinzent [Leuven: Peeters, 2010], 326).

CHAPTER 4

From Diospolis to the *Tractoria*

The present chapter will analyze the most active phase of the Pelagian controversy—namely, the years 416 through 418.[1] This period witnessed the mobilization of anti-Pelagian forces in the wake of Pelagius's acquittal at Diospolis, the initial condemnation of Pelagianism by Pope Innocent, the "reopening" of the case by Innocent's successor, Zosimus, and the more decisive condemnation of Pelagius and Caelestius by Emperor Honorius, the Council of Carthage, and Pope Zosimus himself in 418. Augustine's efforts in these years include two major anti-Pelagian treatises—*De gestis Pelagii* of late 416 or early 417 and *De gratia Christi et de peccato originali* of the summer of 418—but also numerous letters dispatched to key figures around the empire aiming to rally their support in the fight against Pelagius and his allies. Throughout Augustine's works in this period, we see the same aims that have characterized his anti-Pelagian efforts from

---

1 For in-depth analyses of this period of the controversy (and especially of the interactions between Rome and Africa), see Wermelinger, *Rom und Pelagius*, and Dalmon, *Un dossier*. See also Charles Pietri, *Roma christiana: recherches sur l'Église de Rome, son organisation, sa politique, son idéologie de Miltiade à Sixte III (311–440)* (Rome: École française de Rome, 1976).

the beginning: a desire not only to combat Pelagian doctrinal positions, but also to preserve the unity of the Church by undermining the Pelagians' claim to speak for the Church's doctrinal tradition. However, the latter aim took on renewed importance in the wake of Diospolis, which seemed to confirm that the eastern church was, in fact, on the side of the Pelagians. Augustine's response to Diospolis's judgment is telling, as it helps to reveal how important it was for him to claim universality and antiquity for the anti-Pelagian side. With that in mind, let us now examine the Africans' earliest responses to Diospolis, as news of Pelagius's acquittal spread westward and eventually reached Carthage and Hippo.

THE AFRICAN RESPONSE TO DIOSPOLIS: 416–17

The first report of Pelagius's acquittal arrived in Africa in the spring of 416 with the return of the young priest Orosius from his year-long journey to the East and back.[2] Upon his arrival, Orosius delivered news from the East both to Augustine in Hippo and to a council of bishops gathered at Carthage. Perhaps traveling to Hippo first and arriving there in April or early May, Orosius informed Augustine of Pelagius's acquittal and delivered to him a letter from Jerome and, likely, Jerome's *Dialogus aduersus Pelagianos*.[3] Augustine then likely tasked Orosius with traveling to Carthage to offer a report to the bishops attending a previously-scheduled council for the bishops of the province of Africa Proconsularis, notifying them of the events in the East

---

2 For more on the chronology of 416, see François Dolbeau's excellent examination in "Le sermon 348A de saint Augustin contre Pélage: Édition du text intégral," *Recherches augustiniennes* 28 (1995): 37–63, on which I base much of my summary here. See also discussion in Duval, "La correspondance entre Augustin et Pélage"; Duval, "Pélage en son temps"; Lancel, *Saint Augustine*, 336ff.; and Löhr, "Pelagius' Schrift 'De natura,'" esp. 292–94. Our knowledge of the sequence of events in 416 was substantially expanded with the discovery and publication of a complete version of *s.* 348A by Dolbeau in 1995 as well as the discovery and publication of *ep.* 19* by Johannes Divjak in 1981. For more on the latter, see especially the commentary offered by Y.-M. Duval, "Note Complémentaire: Lettre 19*," BA 46B, 507–16.

3 The letter was likely *ep.* 172 among the letters of Augustine. In *s.* 348A.6, Augustine also reports that he received an anti-Pelagian work by Jerome, which should probably be identified as Jerome's *Dialogus aduersus Pelagianos* (*Altercatio/Dialogus Attici et Critobuli*). Dolbeau suggests that Orosius was the one who brought Jerome's *Dialogus* to Augustine (Dolbeau, "Le sermon 348A," 46).

and delivering to them a letter from Heros and Lazarus.[4] The bishops in turn reviewed the proceedings against Caelestius from 411 and resolved to recognize him and Pelagius as "the authors of an error that is utterly wicked and that ought to be condemned by us all."[5] The bishops then decided to draft a letter to Pope Innocent, notifying him of their action and requesting his confirmation of it.[6]

At times this sequence of events is presented slightly differently—as though Orosius had fortuitously arrived at Carthage on his way back from the East at the very moment when the bishops of Africa Proconsularis were gathered for their council. On this view, Orosius would only arrive in Hippo after the council had taken place (or at least started).[7] But a key piece of evidence seems to militate against this account: indeed, if the Council of Carthage had taken place before Orosius arrived in Hippo, it would be odd that Augustine makes no mention of the council in several key works from May and June (*s.* 348A, *epp.* 179 and 19*).[8] In my view, it is far more likely that Orosius had had a chance to meet with Augustine before attending the council. Indeed, as we shall see, there are good reasons to suspect that the key movers among the African episcopacy had been in communication about a plan of action shortly after Orosius's arrival in Africa—and before any official conciliar decisions were made.[9]

In any event, sometime after Orosius's return, a series of other messengers began arriving in Hippo. First, it seems, was a priest named Innocent, who arrived bearing more letters: one from Jerome and others from some

---

4 See *ep.* 175.1. Mercator indicates that the books of Pelagius used at Diospolis were sent to Africa along with a letter and were read at the African councils (*Commonitorium super nomine Caelestii* [ACO 1.5.1, p. 68, ln. 37–38]). Perhaps it was the letter from Heros and Lazarus to which Mercator was referring. See also Dunphy, "The Acts of the Synod," 213n30, where he briefly discusses this report from Mercator.

5 *ep.* 175.1 (Latin: CSEL 44:654.3–4; English: my translation).

6 We will return to this letter below. For more on the careful composition and argumentation of the letters sent by the Councils of Carthage and Milevis, as well as the letter sent by the five key African bishops (to be discussed below), see Wermelinger, *Rom und Pelagius*, 94–101, as well as Dalmon, *Un dossier*, Chapters 2–4.

7 See, e.g., Dolbeau, "Le sermon 348A," 48.

8 For this reason, Winrich Löhr suggests that the Council of Carthage took place after the writing of *epp.* 179 and 19*: Löhr, "Pelagius' Schrift," 293.

9 For example, the conciliar letters to Innocent betray a coordinated effort. For more discussion, see below—and also Wermelinger, *Rom und Pelagius*, 94–101, as well as Dalmon, *Un dossier*, Chapters 2–4.

(unnamed) individuals.[10] Innocent seems to have departed for a return trip to Palestine shortly after his arrival, bearing Augustine's replies to Jerome and to various other individuals, as well as copies of these letters for Jerome.[11] After Innocent, a deacon named Palatinus and, possibly, the bishop Lazarus of Aix arrived with two additional letters from Jerome.[12] Palatinus also delivered to Augustine a brief document (*chartula*) from Pelagius, in which the ascetic defended himself against the objections brought against him at Diospolis.[13] However, the document lacked any cover letter addressed to Augustine and, as a result, the bishop of Hippo was hesitant to discuss the contents of it, in case Pelagius were to deny that the document was his or that he had sent it to Augustine.[14] One of these many messengers (perhaps Innocent[15]) or the letters they carried also informed Augustine of a shocking event allegedly perpetrated by Pelagius's supporters: an attack on Jerome's monasteries in Bethlehem, in which a deacon was killed, the buildings were burned, and Jerome himself only barely escaped injury.[16]

---

10 See *ep.* 19*.1, written to Jerome. For more on Innocent, see "Innocentius 9," in Mandouze, *Prosopographie*, 604–5; Duval, "Note Complémentaire: Lettre 6*," BA 46B, 445.

11 See *ep.* 19*.1.

12 See *ep.* 19*.1 and *s.* 348A.7. Palatinus was a native of Hippo but seems to have been a deacon in Palestine (see *gest. Pel.* 32.57, but note that the "Charus" mentioned there should read "Palatinus"—see the next footnote below). It is unclear whether both Palatinus and Lazarus came to Hippo, or if Palatinus delivered, in addition to his own letter from Jerome, a letter that Jerome had originally sent through Lazarus (see Dolbeau, "Le sermon 348A," 49). Dolbeau notes that some of these letters from Jerome may be identified with Jerome's *epp.* 123 and 195 (among the letters of Augustine)—see Dolbeau, "Le sermon 348A," 46.

13 See *s.* 348A.7, *ep.* 19*.2, *ep.* 179.7, and *gest. Pel.* 1. At *gest. Pel.* 32.57, Augustine identifies a certain "Charus" as the individual who had delivered Pelagius's *chartula defensionis* to him. However, it seems that this identification was likely due to a lapse in memory on Augustine's part (see Dolbeau, "Le sermon 348A," 47).

14 See *s.* 348A.7 and *gest. Pel.* 1.

15 According to the opinion of Dolbeau, "Le sermon 348A," 47.

16 See *s.* 348A.7 and *gest. Pel.* 35.65. As Dolbeau notes, this attack on Jerome's monasteries, which likely took place by March or April of 416, may have prompted the sudden flurry of letters that seem to have arrived in Hippo within the span of a few weeks (Dolbeau, "Le sermon 348A," 46ff.). See also discussion of the attack in Geoffrey D. Dunn, "Innocent I and the Attacks on the Bethlehem Monasteries," *Journal of the Australian Early Medieval Association* 2 (2006): 69–83; Josef Lössl, "Who Attacked the Monasteries of Jerome and Paula in 416 A.D.?" *Augustinianum* 44 (2004): 91–112; and M.-Y. Perrin, "'The blast of the ecclesiastical trumpet': Prédication et controverse dans la crise pélagienne. Quelques observations," in *Prédication et controverses religieuses des origines du christianisme au XVIIe siècle: Actes de la journée*

FROM DIOSPOLIS TO THE *TRACTORIA* 181

This deluge of news led to swift action by Augustine and the African episcopacy. In the months that followed Orosius's arrival, several important letters were drafted and sent to key figures throughout the empire, warning them of the threat of Pelagianism. In the following pages, we will survey the more important of these efforts in the late spring through early fall of 416, noting Augustine's ever-present desire to convince his audience of the dangers of Pelagianism and the falsity of the Pelagians' claim to speak for the universal Church's doctrinal tradition.

The Responses of Spring through Fall of 416

One of Augustine's first reactions to the onslaught of news from the East appears to be recorded in a sermon discovered and published by François Dolbeau in 1995.[17] In this sermon (*s.* 348A), delivered a few days after Palatinus's arrival in late May or very early June of 416,[18] Augustine was forced to address the issues of the controversy due to the rumors that had apparently been spreading in Hippo about the events in the East and, in particular, about the attack on Jerome's monasteries.[19] The sermon is of importance for our purposes because it showcases some key features of Augustine's strategy against the Pelagians in this period of response to Diospolis.[20]

---

d'étude du 8 février 2007, ed. P. Nagy and M.-Y. Perrin (Mont-Saint-Aignan: Publications de Universités de Rouen et du Havre, 2011), 17–31.

17 A complete version of *s.* 348A was published by François Dolbeau in 1995 (Dolbeau, "Le sermon 348A"). A second manuscript containing a complete version of the sermon was unexpectedly discovered a year later. In light of this second manuscript (which is older and, generally speaking, more textually reliable than that used by Dolbeau in his edition), Dolbeau published in 1999 a revised *apparatus criticus* for *s.* 348A incorporating the variants found in the new manuscript and suggesting some revisions to the published text: François Dolbeau, "Un second manuscrit complet du *Sermo contra Pelagium* (S. 348A augmenté)," *Revue des études augustiniennes* 45 (1999): 353–61. See also Gert Partoens, "Quelques remarques de critique textuelle sur le sermon 348A augmenté de Saint Augustin (Dolbeau 30*)," *Augustiniana* 50 (2000): 175–95. For further discussion of the theology of *s.* 348A, see Anthony Dupont, *Gratia in Augustine's Sermones ad populum during the Pelagian Controversy: Do Different Contexts Furnish Different Insights?* (Leiden: Brill, 2013), 318–30.

18 See Dolbeau, "Le sermon 348A," 50.

19 See *s.* 348A.7.

20 It should also be noted that this sermon contains Augustine's first reference to Pelagius by name and identification as a heretic in a sermon (he had done so in 415 in *ep.* 169 to Evodius of Uzalis).

The sermon itself has a very clear and classic structure: §1, the *exordium*, introduces the topic of the sermon (i.e., the salvific purpose of the Incarnation of the Son of God, who came to save us from our sins and bestow on us the grace needed to bring us to life); §§2–7, the *narratio*, detail the facts of the case (including an examination of the purpose and effects of the Incarnation in §§2–4 and a summary of the events of the Pelagian controversy thus far in §§5–7); §§8–13, the *probatio*, contain Augustine's summary of the Pelagians' views as well as his refutation of these views; and finally §§14–15, the *peroratio*, offer Augustine's conclusion, where he urges his congregation to pray for the grace to live righteously, to strive with their wills, and to reject the counterarguments of the Pelagians (and, as a final addendum, to reject the reports that Pelagius's views were found to be orthodox at Diospolis). Augustine's argumentation here has much in common with what we have seen before in his anti-Pelagian works but is noteworthy for its focus on the consequences that the Pelagian views on grace have for the Church's life of prayer. With this approach, Augustine stresses that the Pelagian positions undercut key aspects of the Church's ancient and universal doctrinal tradition. Indeed, Augustine signals that this will be a key argument in his sermon by claiming in his introduction that the whole Church from the times of the Old Testament through the present has proclaimed the saving grace of God.[21] However, the most significant passage for our purposes occurs in the *probatio*. Here, Augustine's focus is almost entirely on the threat that Pelagianism's denial of grace has for prayer. Indeed, after stating that the Pelagians believe human beings have the capacity to make themselves just, Augustine identifies a critical consequence of this view:

> By these malignant arguments even our prayers are attacked. For they act and argue in such a way that we seem to pray for no reason. The Lord taught us how to pray lest, perhaps, in our prayers we should ask for carnal and temporal things, such as asking not to have a headache, not to die, not to bury a son, not to suffer a loss, not to be put into prison after being captured

---

21 "Today, when the apostle was read, you heard, those of you who were paying attention: *So God*, he says, *commends his charity among us, in that while we were still sinners Christ died for us; much more, being justified now by his blood, shall we be saved from the wrath through him* (Rom 5:8–9). This is *the grace of God through Jesus Christ our Lord* (Rom 7:25), which first of all the prophets, then he himself by his own mouth, next the apostles after he was no longer present in the flesh, and finally the whole Church holds, acknowledges, preaches and commends, cultivates, and reveres" (*s.* 348A.1 [Latin: Dolbeau, "Le sermon 348A," 53.9–16; English: Hill, WSA III/11, 310]).

FROM DIOSPOLIS TO THE *TRACTORIA*

by someone, and other similar things. These are all temporal and worldly things. They grant we pray for these sorts of things, but they do away with what the Lord taught us—not because they dare to deny it, but because they make the sort of arguments whereby it is taken away.[22]

Augustine argues here that, to the extent that the Pelagians deny the necessity of grace for upright action, they by consequence severely restrict the object of petitionary prayer: instead of praying for God's assistance in living righteously, we only pray to receive (or avoid) temporal goods (or evils). In this sense, Augustine argues that the Pelagian view—even if not admitted by the Pelagians themselves—seem to undermine key aspects of the Lord's Prayer that aim at the reception of an eternal good (i.e., salvation). A little later, Augustine turns to this prayer itself, noting the ways in which the Pelagian position seems to undermine its purpose:

> It was on account of this grace that the Lord recommended to us what we should pray for: *Hallowed be*—well, what?—*thy name*. Is God's name not holy then? How can it be hallowed, except in us? Now you there, if it's from your free will, if it's from the powers of your own nature that you can hallow God's name in yourself, what are you praying for, why are you begging from the supreme majesty what you have in your own power?[23]

Augustine then turns to two other petitions of the Lord's Prayer, highlighting an interpretation offered by at least one Pelagian:

> What else? These two petitions: *Forgive us our debts, as we too forgive our debtors*, and *Do not bring us into temptation*. When they are leveled as objections to these people, how do you think they answer? I was shocked, my brothers and sisters, when I heard. I didn't, indeed, hear it with my own ears, but my holy brother and fellow bishop, our Urbanus, who was a priest here and is now bishop of Sicca, when he got back from Rome and there crossed swords with someone holding such opinions—or rather when he mentioned that he had crossed swords with him—he told me what that person had said, when he was being pressed hard by the weight of the Lord's Prayer. For he was pressing him and saying, "If it's in our power not to sin,

---

22 *s.* 348A.9 (Latin: Dolbeau, "Le sermon 348A," 58.123–30 and Dolbeau, "Un second manuscrit," 356; English: my translation).

23 *s.* 348A.11 (Latin: Dolbeau, "Le sermon 348A," 59.162–66; English: Hill, WSA III/11, 315). This is the first time, by my count, that Augustine has employed the first petition of the Lord's Prayer as part of his anti-Pelagian polemic.

and in our power to overcome all temptations to sin by our wills alone, why do we tell God not to bring us into temptation?" What do you think he replied? "We ask God," he said, "not to bring us into temptation lest we should suffer some evil over which we have no control—lest I should fall from my horse and break my leg, and a highwayman should kill me, and that sort of thing. These are things, after all, which I do not have," he said, "any control over. Because my temptations to sin I can overcome if I wish to, and it's without God's help that I can do so."[24]

Augustine goes on to challenge this interpretation of the petition by referring his congregation to Jesus's words at Luke 22:32, where he tells Peter that he has prayed for him that his faith may not fail.

> *I have prayed for you*, that your what may not fail? Your what? Your hand, your leg, your eye, your tongue, by any paralysis, that is, by any enfeeblement of your limbs? No; but *that your faith may not fail*. According to these people we have it entirely under our own control that our faith should not fail.[25]

In this sense, Augustine suggests, Christ himself challenges the Pelagians' understanding of prayer and confirms Augustine's own interpretation of the petitions of the Lord's Prayer. Augustine then notes that the Pelagians' views of grace also impact other aspects of the Church's life of prayer—for example, blessings offered in the liturgy:

> Why is God asked on our behalf to grant us what these people say we ought not to ask for from his eternal majesty, but which we have under our own control? Take the blessings, my brothers and sisters, the blessings we call down upon you; they empty them of meaning. You have heard me, I believe, my brothers and sisters, when I say, "Turning to the Lord, let us bless his name; may he grant us to persevere in his commandments, to walk in the right way of his instruction, to please him with every good work," and other such things. "All this," they say, "is placed absolutely under our own control." So we, then, are quite vainly desiring these things for you.[26]

---

24 *s.* 348A.11 (Latin: Dolbeau, "Le sermon 348A," 59.166–60.181; English: Hill, WSA III/11, 315).

25 *s.* 348A.12 (Latin: Dolbeau, "Le sermon 348A," 60.192–95; English: Hill, WSA III/11, 316).

26 *s.* 348A.13 (Latin: Dolbeau, "Le sermon 348A," 61.196–203; English: Hill, WSA III/11, 316, slightly modified). For more on the use of *conuersi ad dominum* prayers, which Augustine often employed at the end of homilies, see François Dolbeau, "L'oraison 'conuersi ad dominum...': un bilan provisoire des recensions existantes," *Archiv für Liturgiewissenschaft* 41 (1999): 295–322, and M. Klöckener, "Conuersi ad dominum," in A-L 1, 1280–82.

FROM DIOSPOLIS TO THE *TRACTORIA*   185

However, Augustine notes, Paul prayed in a similar way for the Corinthians: "We pray to God that you may do nothing evil" (2 Cor 13:7).[27] In this way, Augustine grounds his liturgical blessings in the practice of the apostle Paul.

While many of Augustine's arguments here recall those used in his earlier anti-Pelagian works, it is noteworthy how much Augustine focuses on the issue of prayer in this sermon—indeed, his refutation of the Pelagians here is founded almost solely on evidence related to that topic. On the one hand, this focus can be explained by his desire to make the stakes of the debate perfectly clear to an audience not entirely aware of the nuances of the controversy: by appealing to the Lord's Prayer and to liturgical blessings, Augustine indicates concretely and experientially the damage that Pelagianism can inflict upon the lives of ordinary believers. At the same time, based on what we have seen so far in Augustine's anti-Pelagian efforts, this focus on prayer here should not be read simply as a tactic designed to score easy points against his opponents. Rather, it is also part and parcel of his strategy to combat the Pelagians' claims to speak for the universal Church's doctrinal tradition. He does so here, in a particular way, by linking contemporary experiences of prayer and blessings to the example given by Christ and by Paul in the New Testament. In so doing, he implies that these contemporary liturgical practices are rooted in dominical and apostolic teaching. As a result, Augustine hopes, the Pelagians' claims are shown to be baseless, and their own novelty is proved.

Perhaps a few days after delivering *s.* 348A,[28] Augustine sent several letters eastward. One of them was to Jerome (*ep.* 19*), which was Augustine's reply to the letter delivered by Palatinus.[29] In the letter Augustine shares a few details about his recent efforts, noting that he has found a courier named Luke to bear the letter to Jerome along with several other items: 1) a letter to Pelagius that "he will receive with bitterness"[30]; 2) a letter to

---

27 *s.* 348A.13 (Latin: Dolbeau, "Le sermon 348A," 61.213–14; English: Hill, WSA III/11, 317).

28 See Dolbeau, "Le sermon 348A," 48.

29 For more on this letter, see M.-F. Berrouard, "Les lettres 6* et 19* de saint Augustin. Leur date et les renseignements qu'elles apportent sur l'évolution de la crise 'pélagienne,'" *Revue d'études augustiniennes* 27 [1981]: 264–77, and Yves-Marie Duval, "Note Complémentaire; Lettre 19*," BA 46B, 507–16.

30 *ep.* 19*.4: *acerbe accepturus est* (Latin: CSEL 88:93.6; English: Teske, WSA II/4, 298). For more on Augustine's correspondence with Pelagius, including this lost letter, see Duval, "La correspondance."

John of Jerusalem and Eulogius of Caesarea (*ep.* 179);[31] 3) a letter to a priest named Passerio (now lost[32]). In addition, Augustine sent copies of Pelagius's *De natura* and Augustine's *De natura et gratia* to Jerome and John (and, probably, Eulogius).[33]

The letter to John and Eulogius seems to have been prompted by a few things. Among them was Augustine's desire to acquire a copy of the *gesta* of the Synod of Diospolis.[34] Indeed, this desire took on a particular urgency after Augustine received a copy of Pelagius's *chartula defensionis*, which, as we noted above, contained a response to the charges raised against him by Heros and Lazarus at Diospolis. However, Augustine's letter does not begin (or end) with that basic request, but rather aims to warn the recipients that Pelagius may have deceived them at Diospolis, lying about his true views. Indeed, the bulk of Augustine's letter seeks to offer an overview and critique of Pelagius's views based on the *De natura*, in the hopes of convincing John to reexamine Pelagius.[35] More importantly for our purposes, a significant portion of the letter (§§3–6) focuses on themes closely related to those found in *s.* 348A, with much of the same evidence supplied: for example, a reference to the Lord's Prayer, Jesus's words reported at Luke 22:32, blessings said over the people, and Paul's prayer for the Corinthians (2 Cor 13:17). Unlike in *s.* 348A, Augustine also brings up the issue of the moral status of infants here (§6), questioning whether Pelagius believes that infants are set free by the

---

31 Some have wondered whether the letter to John and Eulogius referred to in *ep.* 19* is a lost letter different from *ep.* 179. See discussion in Geoffrey Dunn, "Augustine, Cyril of Alexandria, and the Pelagian Controversy," *Augustinian Studies* 37 (2006): 71–72; see also A. Fürst's comments: *Augustins Briefwechsel mit Hieronymus* (Münster: Aschendorffsche Verlagsbuchhandlung, 1999), 211–12. However, the fact that Luke is mentioned as the courier in both *ep.* 179.1 and *ep.* 19*.3 seems to preclude that possibility.

32 Passerio is mentioned in Orosius's *Liber apologeticus* 6–7 and was present at the hearing in Jerusalem in July 415.

33 See *ep.* 19*.3 and *ep.* 179.5. Wermelinger suggests that Augustine also sent Pelagius's *chartula defensionis* to John, given that Augustine cites it at *ep.* 179.7.

34 See *ep.* 179.7. It should be noted that *ep.* 179 makes no mention of Eulogius—but we can infer that a copy of the same letter was sent to him due to Augustine's comments at *ep.* 19*.4.

35 It should be noted, too, that at *ep.* 179.5 Augustine appears to allude to the prayer from Book 10 of *Confessiones* that had so rankled Pelagius when he was still in Rome (*perseu.* 20.53)—although the wording is not exactly the same. It seems likely that Augustine alluded to the prayer here intentionally (as he had done previously in *pecc. mer.*, *spir. et litt.*, and *b. uid.*) perhaps in the hopes of inciting Pelagius to speak more openly about his views (if John happened to show him the letter).

FROM DIOSPOLIS TO THE *TRACTORIA*

grace of Christ.[36] In this way, Augustine focuses much of his argument in this letter, as he did in *s*. 348A, on the threat that Pelagian views hold for the daily life of the universal Church that, he argues, rests on dominical and apostolic teaching.[37]

Given the content of *ep*. 179, we should be hesitant to reduce its purpose to a mere request for the *gesta* of Diospolis. Rather, it must be situated as part of a broader strategy taken up by Augustine in 416—namely, to secure allies from both East and West in a unified campaign against Pelagius and, more importantly, his views.[38] Augustine and the African bishops' efforts to raise support for their campaign in the West is well-known (and we shall discuss this further below). But less discussed are the appeals made to figures in the East, likely because this correspondence has, by and large, not survived. However, as *ep*. 19* makes clear, Augustine sent numerous letters to the East in the late spring of 416: some in response to correspondence he had received, but others to people who had not contacted him.[39] No doubt many of these letters were directed to westerners living in Palestine. But, as *ep*. 179 shows, at least some of that correspondence was addressed to natives of the East. Further evidence of appeals to the East can be gleaned from the fact to be discussed further below that at some point later in 416, Augustine received the *gesta* of Diospolis from Cyril of Alexandria—thus suggesting that Augustine had written to him as well (although it remains possible that Cyril wrote to Augustine unprompted).[40] Further, one wonders whether a letter was sent from Augustine or the African bishops to Constantinople during the summer of 416 to inquire after Caelestius. Marius Mercator reports[41] that Atticus, the bishop of Constantinople, had driven Caelestius out of the city sometime in 416 or very early 417 (before the death of Pope

36 No explicit discussion of infant baptism is offered, though.

37 Löhr comments similarly—see "Pelagius' Schrift," 241.

38 Brown suggests (*Augustine of Hippo*, 359) that Augustine's tone in *ep*. 179 "bordered on insolence." I am not convinced that this is an accurate description. While Augustine does begin his letter by lamenting that John had not written to him, he clearly aims throughout the rest of the letter to win John over to his side and nowhere faults him for his actions in 415 (even though he surely would have heard from Orosius about John's bias in favor of Pelagius).

39 See *ep*. 19*.1 and 4, which mention the letters sent via Innocent as well as those to be delivered by Luke. For a helpful overview of Augustine's efforts to form alliances against Pelagius in the East—especially through the agency of Jerome—see Fürst, *Augustins Briefwechsel*, 210–20.

40 For more on the correspondence between Cyril and Augustine see n. 72 below.

41 See *Commonitorium super nomine Caelestii* (ACO 1.5.1, p. 66, ln. 23–30) and n. 140 below.

Innocent it would seem[42]) and had sent a letter to Carthage (among a few other places) to notify them that this action had been taken. It seems unlikely that Atticus would have taken this action against Caelestius unprompted.[43] All told, in the aftermath of Diospolis Augustine had a distinct desire not to pit West against East in his efforts to overcome Pelagianism—as shall become abundantly clear when we consider *epp.* 175–77 as well as *De gestis Pelagii* below. In my view, that desire emerges not simply out of strategic concerns (e.g., to win over Pelagius's most powerful allies), but also out of his desire to safeguard the unity of the Church, something that I have argued has been a crucial motivation for his anti-Pelagian efforts from the beginning.

While Augustine was hard at work on these various letters, or perhaps shortly after he finished them, the Council of Carthage likely took place, perhaps meeting in early June.[44] Several weeks later, Augustine himself was in Milevis, where a similar council was being held by the bishops of Numidia.[45] Both of these provincial councils produced letters to be sent to Pope Innocent, requesting his support for their efforts against Pelagianism.[46] As

---

42 See Pietri, *Roma christiana*, 1185n2.

43 See Dalmon, *Un dossier*, 605–6, and Pietri, *Roma christiana*, 1185n2, for some discussion. See also Malavasi, *La controversia pelagiana in Oriente*, 85–97, for more on Atticus's anti-Pelagian activity.

44 As Perler points out, regularly scheduled provincial councils in Carthage (of which this was one), normally took place in June or after mid-August (Perler, *Les voyages*, 332). Given other constraints rightly identified by Perler and by Dolbeau ("Le sermon 348A," 50), a date before July is to be preferred.

45 As *ep.* 176 (drafted by the Council of Milevis) mentions the Council of Carthage and its letter to Innocent (see §5), it is clear that Milevis postdates Carthage. See also Dolbeau, "Le sermon 348A," 50.

46 See *epp.* 175 and 176. Wermelinger (*Rom und Pelagius*, 94) oddly states that the councils decided to write to Innocent independently of each other, citing *ep.* 178.2 (a letter from Augustine to a certain Hilary, probably the bishop of Narbonne) as reporting that the Council of Milevis had already taken place when news of the council in Carthage arrived. I suspect a mistranslation is at fault. The key sentence in *ep.* 178.2 reads: "For when we were writing this letter [to Hilary], (1) we had already learned that in the Church of Carthage a decree of the episcopal council had been composed against them and was to be sent by letter to the holy and venerable Pope Innocent and (2) we ourselves from the council of Numidia had already likewise written to the same Apostolic See" (*iam enim cum ista scriberemus, cognoueramus in ecclesia Carthaginensi aduersus eos episcopalis concilii conditum fuisse decretum per epistulam sancto et uenerabili papae Innocentio dirigendum et nos de concilio Numidiae ad eandem apostolicam sedem iam similiter scripseramus*) (Latin: CSEL 44:690.12–16; English: my translation). It should also be noted that the Council of Carthage sent additional documentation on to Innocent, including (1) the letter from Heros and Lazarus that was read before the assembled bishops and (2) the acts of Caelestius's *iudicium* in 411 (see *ep.* 175.1).

FROM DIOSPOLIS TO THE *TRACTORIA*　　　189

Peter Brown remarks, "The discipline learnt during the campaign against the Donatists had borne fruit: only in Africa could three hundred Catholic bishops come together, and agree unanimously to decrees drafted by unquestioned experts."[47] Indeed, in these letters—and especially in that from Milevis—we see a number of arguments that are clearly Augustinian in their provenance.[48] The letters are both brief and to the point, focusing on the chief points of the debate with the Pelagians. In this sense, it is important to note the extent to which these letters rely on the key arguments we have seen Augustine use in *s.* 348A and *ep.* 179. As in that sermon and letter, here too in *ep.* 175 (from Carthage) and *ep.* 176 (from Milevis), great emphasis is placed upon the effect that Pelagianism has upon common features of the Christian life: prayer (*ep.* 175.4; *ep.* 176.2), blessings (*ep.* 175.5), and baptism (*ep.* 175.6; *ep.* 176.2). The bishops at Milevis are particularly emphatic in this regard:

> To omit, therefore, the many other things that they utter against the holy scripture, we for the present single out the two points by which they strive completely to overthrow the whole Christian faith and which are the support of faithful hearts: (1) that God should not be asked to be our helper against the evil of sin and in acting with righteousness and (2) that the sacrament of Christian grace does not help little ones in obtaining eternal life. Making these things known to your apostolic heart, we have no need

47 Brown, *Augustine of Hippo*, 358. Brown's numbers here are rather inflated: in the CSEL edition, 68 bishops are listed as signatories of the letter from Carthage and 59, including Augustine, of that from Milevis. We should also note that these councils were likely previously scheduled and that their anti-Pelagian elements would have been late additions to the agenda.

48 If Augustine was not involved in the drafting of *ep.* 175 (which is unknown: he was not at the Council of Carthage but could have been consulted by the committee that drafted the letter to Innocent), it at least seems likely that Augustine had sent a document with key arguments to Aurelius to help with the drafting of *ep.* 175. Given *ep.* 175's similarities with *ep.* 179 in particular, it is even possible that this document sent to Aurelius was a copy of that letter to John (and Eulogius). Overall, though, I would suggest that the tone of *ep.* 176 is more clearly Augustinian. Among other things, we might point to its expression of hope that Pelagius and Caelestius might be healed within the Church rather than banished from it (§4)—a sentiment frequently present in Augustine's efforts from this period (see, e.g., *ep.* 19*.3 and 177.3). See also Dalmon's comments at *Un dossier*, 287. My suspicion is that Augustine was not directly involved in the composition of *ep.* 175, but merely supplied an outline of arguments and evidence for its drafter(s). (For a different opinion, see, e.g., Johannes Divjak, "Epistulae," in A-L 2, 983, who suggests that *epp.* 175–77 may all have been composed by Augustine.) See also discussion in Mathijs Lamberigts, "Was Innocent Familiar with the Content of the Pelagian Controversy? A Study of His Answers to the Letters Sent by the African Episcopacy," in Scrinium Augustini: *The World of Augustine's Letters*, ed. P. Nehring, M. Strozynski, and R. Toczko (Turnhout: Brepols, 2017), 207–8.

to say many things and to exaggerate so great an impiety by words, since they undoubtedly disturb you so that you cannot at all turn a blind eye to them and hold back from correcting them for fear that they may spread more widely and infect many or, rather, slay many in completely separating them from the grace of Christ in the name of Christ.[49]

Combined with this emphasis on the danger of Pelagianism for concrete aspects of Christian life, the bishops at Carthage and Milevis both carefully avoid criticizing the Synod of Diospolis—an approach also seen in Augustine's efforts thus far.[50]

A third letter (*ep.* 177) was sent to Innocent by a group of five "heavy-weights" among the African episcopacy: Aurelius of Carthage, Alypius of Thagaste, Augustine, Evodius of Uzalis, and Possidius of Calama.[51] Much lengthier and more detailed than the two conciliar letters, this missive aimed to offer Innocent a deeper and more theologically robust analysis of some key themes relating to Pelagius's views on grace. Unlike in the other two letters, Pelagius's *De natura* is directly addressed and critiqued here.[52] Nevertheless, familiar arguments reappear. The petition "Bring us not into temptation" from the Lord's Prayer continues to be cited as evidence against the Pelagians' apparent denial of the need to pray for the grace to avoid sin.[53] Diospolis is also dealt with as before, albeit in more detail: the bishops gathered at the synod are explicitly defended for their understandable decision to acquit Pelagius. They, Augustine suggests, believed that when Pelagius confessed the need for grace he was simply confessing that grace "which they [the bishops] have frequently been accustomed to read in the books of God and to preach to the people of God."[54]

---

49 *ep.* 176.3 (Latin: CSEL 44:666.9–667.2; English: Teske, WSA II/3, 139, with some modification).

50 See, e.g., *ep.* 175.4. The letter from Milevis makes no mention of Diospolis.

51 Dolbeau argues that this letter was likely composed around September 416 (Dolbeau, "Le sermon 348A," 50). Along with this letter, the bishops sent Pelagius's *De natura* and Augustine's *De natura et gratia* (*ep.* 177.6) as well as a letter from Augustine for Pelagius, which Innocent was asked to forward to the British ascetic (*ep.* 177.15).

52 See §§6–15.

53 See §§4 and 19 (§5 is also of importance for the topic of prayer). The citation in §19 is especially important, as it is employed in the final lines of the letter.

54 *ep.* 177.2 (Latin: CSEL 44:670.17–671.1; English: Teske, WSA II/3, 142).

FROM DIOSPOLIS TO THE *TRACTORIA* 191

A noteworthy passage of *ep.* 177 is found at §§16–18 and addresses the topic of the possibility of sinlessness (and its relation to the petition "Forgive us our debts"). What initially makes this section stand out is the fact that this topic was not discussed at all in *ep.* 175 and received only the briefest of mentions in *ep.* 176 (in §2). Here, however, discussion of this topic is significantly more expansive, addressing the fact that certain Catholic authors had posited that some (e.g., Elizabeth and Zechariah) lived sinless lives. Although he does not identify these authors, Augustine clearly has in mind here Ambrose and the passage from his commentary on Luke, quoted by Pelagius in his *De natura*.[55] Why does Augustine feel the need to address Ambrose's view here? We might suggest a few possible explanations. First of all, given the letter's discussion of Pelagius's *De natura* (and the fact that Augustine has sent a copy of it, as well as *De natura et gratia*, along with the letter to Innocent), Augustine likely felt it important to address the one quotation provided by Pelagius in his *De natura* that clearly supported the position he was trying to advance.[56] Further, in *De natura et gratia*, Augustine focused his response to Pelagius's appeal to Ambrose on showing that the former bishop of Milan affirmed the necessity of grace and the reality of original sin, thus sidestepping, to a certain degree, the question of sinlessness. Here, then, Augustine probably felt the need to supplement that earlier argument by addressing the issue of sinlessness itself. Finally, and perhaps most importantly, it seems likely that Augustine chose to address Ambrose's position here because he feared that, especially in an Italian context, the apparent agreement in opinion between Ambrose and Pelagius would lend significant support to Pelagius's case, making it seem as though Pelagius had the backing of a renowned defender of Nicene orthodoxy.[57] As a result, Augustine had to address the issue head-on and attempt to undermine that

---

55 See *nat. et gr.* 63.74. This appeal to Ambrose will be repeated later in Pelagius's *Pro libero arbitrio*. For discussion, see below in our section on *De gratia Christi*.

56 At *nat. et gr.* 63.74, Augustine openly admits that the passage Pelagius has cited does support the view that sinlessness is possible in this life.

57 This could help to explain (at least in part) why Augustine did not feel it necessary to address (even anonymously) Ambrose's position in his letter to John of Jerusalem when he briefly discussed the issue of sinlessness (*ep.* 179.8–9): in the East, Ambrose's reputation likely was less weighty, if only due to geographical distance. It is also possible that Augustine had learned from Orosius that John had cited the same verse from Luke (1:6) as Ambrose and Pelagius to support sinlessness. My thanks to Giulio Malavasi for this point: see his "'Erant autem ambo iusti ante Deum' (Lc 1,6)."

support without denigrating the reputation of Ambrose. The way Augustine does this is revealing. At the end of this section in *ep.* 177 (as previously in *De perfectione iustitiae hominis*[58]), Augustine gently critiques Ambrose's position without mentioning his name before pivoting to cite a petition from the Lord's Prayer:

> But however this question may stand, since, even if no human being is found to be without sin in this life, it is still said to be possible by the help of grace and of the Spirit of God, and one must strive and pray that it may come about, it is more tolerable that a person is mistaken on this point. Nor is it diabolical impiety but human error to affirm that we must work for this and long for this, even if one cannot prove what one claims. For such a person believes that to be possible which it is certainly praiseworthy to want. For us, however, it is enough that there is no one among the faithful in the Church of God, in any state of progress toward or excellence of righteousness, who is of the sort to dare to say that the petition of the Lord's Prayer, *Forgive us our debts*, is unnecessary for him and to say that he has no sin—lest he deceive himself and the truth not be in him, even if he now lives without reproach.[59]

What we find here is that Augustine subtly disposes of one piece of evidence drawn from the Church's past (namely, Ambrose's position) by shifting the focus to another more ancient piece of evidence (the Lord's Prayer).[60] As a result, Augustine essentially reclaims the support of the ancient and universal Church from Pelagius by trumping his evidence. Augustine's careful handling of Ambrose's position—not "diabolical impiety" but "human error"—and his emphasis on the Lord's Prayer reveal how conscious Augustine was of the need to undermine both the specific support Pelagius had claimed to find in the late bishop of Milan, a renowned exponent of orthodox doctrine,

---

58 See *perf. iust.* 21.44.

59 *ep.* 177.18 (Latin: CSEL 44:687.10–20; English: Teske, WSA II/3, 150, slightly modified). Augustine also pivots to the Lord's Prayer at *perf. iust.* 21.44 (albeit to a different petition). In *ep.* 177, Augustine seems more confident in his treatment of this topic than he was in *nat. et gr.* or *perf. iust.* Here, he indicates that it is an error (albeit a tolerable one) to believe that some attain sinlessness in this life (*ep.* 177.18), whereas previously he had left the question slightly more open.

60 Of course, the reference to the Lord's Prayer is supplemented by an allusion to 1 John 1:8. For more discussion of this passage, see Laurence Dalmon, "La lettre 177,16–18 de saint Augustin, écho atténué à un conflit d'exégèse patristique au temps de la controverse pélagienne?" *Zeitschrift für Antikes Christentum* 12 (2008): 544–61.

FROM DIOSPOLIS TO THE *TRACTORIA* 193

and the broader Pelagian claims to have the Church's doctrinal tradition on their side.

All told, these three letters are highly rhetorically charged: their tone, crafted in the manner of appeals from subordinates to a higher and more authoritative see, aims at winning over Innocent's goodwill.[61] Further, the emphasis on tangible elements of the faith seen especially in the two conciliar letters is no doubt designed to shock Innocent into action: this focus on issues like the Lord's Prayer, blessings, and infant baptism aims to make readily apparent the danger of Pelagianism for the ancient and universal doctrinal tradition of the Church—the *fundamenta christianae fidei.*[62] *Ep.* 177 adds to these conciliar efforts by offering a more expansive theological analysis of the issues at play, while at the same time attempting to remove a key support from Pelagius—namely, Ambrose. Recognizing Pelagianism's origins in Rome and having heard rumors of its continued presence there— and, possibly, rumors that members of the Roman clergy might have fallen under its sway[63]—the African bishops knew that they had to emphasize the

---

61 See, e.g., the concluding paragraph to the letter (*ep.* 177.19). For extensive discussion of the African bishops' attempts to both retain their autonomy and position themselves favorably vis-à-vis Rome (i.e., as subordinates), see Dalmon, *Un dossier*, esp. 78–107, as well as her Chapters 3 and 4.

62 See *ep.* 175.6 (CSEL 44:661.11–12). Note, too, *ep.* 178.2, where the same phrase is used.

63 See *ep.* 177.2: "For we have heard that in the city of Rome, where [Pelagius] lived for a long time, there are some who support him for various reasons. Of course, certain of these do so because such things are said to have persuaded you [*quidam scilicet, quia uos talia persuasisse perhibentur*]. But more of them do so who do not believe that [Pelagius] thinks such things, especially since in the East, where he now dwells, ecclesiastical proceedings are said to have happened by which he is thought to have been cleared" (Latin: CSEL 44:670.7–12; English: my translation). Note that there are several variant readings for "*quia uos*" in the CSEL apparatus (including the Maurists' emendation to *quia eis*, which had no support in the manuscripts) but all of them retain some form of *uos.* However, it is a bit unclear to whom this "*uos*" refers. Dalmon argues that we should by no means take it as a reference to Innocent himself, preferring to understand it as a reference to the people of Rome in general (Dalmon, *Un dossier*, 554n148). Dalmon offers the following translation: "à savoir certains d'entre vous parce qu'ils auraient, dit la rumeur, été convaincus par de telles idées" (305). Teske offers a similar translation, clearly following the Maurists: "[Pelagius] is said to have convinced some of them of such ideas" (WSA II/3, 142). I prefer a translation that remains faithful to the CSEL text for a few reasons—first of all, because I think that a faithful translation actually makes a good deal of sense (more below). But secondly, because the translations offered by Dalmon and Teske imply that Augustine was stating quite openly that certain Romans had actually been convinced by Pelagius's arguments. One wonders whether this rather blunt accusation (even if reported as a rumor) fits with the deferential tone of the rest of the letter. Instead, I would suggest that Augustine was reporting that some people supported Pelagius because they

threat of Pelagianism, and counter any claims made by those in Pelagius's circle that *their own* positions were traditional and held by the universal Church, especially in light of Pelagius's recent acquittal before a synod of eastern bishops. This context helps to explain the narrow and precise focus of these somewhat desperate letters to Innocent that aimed to salvage what was increasingly appearing to be an unmitigated disaster.

After all three letters had been written, a bishop named Julius was tasked with delivering them to Innocent, likely in the autumn of 416.[64] With the departure of Julius, the first chapter of the African response to Diospolis closed. As we noted above, throughout this period Augustine wrote to a variety of individuals in both the West and the East, attempting to build a coalition against the spread of Pelagianism in the wake of the acquittal of its alleged author.[65] Part of his strategy to accomplish this was to refrain from criticizing the bishops at Diospolis in these communications. Doing so would only confirm the presence of a de facto rift between the African and Palestinian Churches (or worse, western and eastern churches). Another aspect of this effort is found in Augustine's deliberate focus on the threat that Pelagianism held for concrete aspects of the faith like prayer, blessings,

---

(mistakenly?) believed Pelagius's ideas had found favor among *another* group of people in the Roman Church. This report seems to fit the tone of the letter a bit better than that suggested by Teske's and Dalmon's translations—in large part, I suggest, because the accusation is much less direct. What we have here is not a direct rumor of convinced Pelagians, but rather rumors of rumors: rumors of people supporting Pelagius because they themselves have heard rumors of *other people* supporting Pelagius. But the reason why this is all expressed so carefully, in my view, is because those "other people" were in fact members of the Roman clergy—that is, the "*uos*" Augustine mentions is a somewhat vague reference to the Roman clergy. We know that rumors arrived in Africa at some point (could it have been as early as 416?) that Pelagius had support among certain members of the Roman clergy (see, e.g., *ep.* 194.1). As a result, it seems plausible to me that the African bishops are alluding to those rumors here in *ep.* 177—but only in the most oblique way possible, so as to avoid offending the pope. See also Pietri, *Roma christiana*, 1185–86. My thanks to Walter Dunphy for being a "sounding board" and sharing key insights as I worked through this issue.

64 For Julius as messenger, see *epp.* 181.2, 182.1, 183.1. As Wermelinger notes, the fact that the bearer of the letters was a bishop indicated the importance of the matter at hand (*Rom und Pelagius*, 94). See "Julius 1" in Mandouze, *Prosopographie*, 617–18.

65 A final letter we might add to this category is *ep.* 178, dispatched sometime after the Council of Milevis to Hilary, probably the bishop of Narbonne in Gaul (see Wermelinger, *Rom und Pelagius*, 91n14). The letter is very brief, serving mainly to introduce a certain Palladius who was traveling across the Mediterranean for some unstated reason. However, Augustine uses the letter as an opportunity to warn his fellow bishop about the dangers of Pelagianism, emphasizing especially its threat to Christian prayer (§3). The threat to infant baptism is also mentioned (§1).

and infant baptism—a focus, as we have said, that sought to indicate the Pelagians' distance from the Church's authentic teaching. However, it is also important to note the ancillary role played by the additional documentation that was attached to some of these letters—in particular, Pelagius's *De natura* and Augustine's response to it, *De natura et gratia*. Augustine sent copies of these works to several of his correspondents, including John of Jerusalem (and Eulogius of Caesarea, likely) (*ep.* 179.5), as well as Innocent (*ep.* 177.6).[66] In addition to substantiating his claims about Pelagius's true views, the inclusion of these two works could also have been intended to bolster Augustine's argument that the Pelagians' views separated them from the doctrinal tradition of the universal Church.[67] Indeed, reading his *De natura et gratia*, John and Innocent would gain a refutation not only of Pelagius's doctrinal views, but also of his claims to have the support of key authors like Hilary of Poitiers and Ambrose. All told, in this period we see a keen focus on the part of Augustine (and, likely through his advocacy, the African bishops in general) to emphasize the contrast between Pelagianism and the beliefs and practices of the universal Church, no doubt aiming to squelch or, at least, head-off Pelagian claims to the contrary—claims that certainly appeared to have been confirmed by the acquittal of Pelagius at Diospolis.

The Acts of Diospolis Arrive: *De gestis Pelagii*

At the time when Julius departed for Rome with *epp.* 175–77 and other associated documents, the official acts of Diospolis still had not arrived in Africa.[68] As we have already mentioned, Augustine had learned about the events at Diospolis through a variety of sources and had also received a document (the *chartula defensionis*) presumably composed by Pelagius that contained the British ascetic's defense against the charges brought against him at the synod. However, Augustine remained hesitant to comment at length on these reports, no doubt fearing that the official acts might differ from the reports he had received or that Pelagius might deny authorship of the *chartula*.[69] In the meantime, word of Pelagius's acquittal spread far and

---

66 Augustine also sent copies to Jerome (*ep.* 19*.3).

67 My thanks to Giulio Malavasi for suggesting this point to me.

68 See *ep.* 186.2.

69 See *gest. Pel.* 1. Here, as elsewhere throughout the controversy, we see Augustine's concern to rely on evidence that could be documented and verified.

wide, hastened at least in part by Pelagius and his allies' efforts. In addition to his *chartula defensionis*, a letter that Pelagius had sent to a friend who was a priest appears to have been circulated in which the British ascetic claimed that he had been vindicated by the fourteen bishops at Diospolis and that the bishops had approved of his view that one could be without sin and easily keep the commandments, if one wanted to do so.[70] Augustine likely received a copy of this letter at some point in the fall or early winter of 416, probably after Julius's departure (as it is not mentioned in any of the letters carried by Julius). Writing later, Augustine paints a grim picture of the situation.

> A letter of carnal boastfulness and pride flies about and, leading the way with a swiftness bought by the delay of the Acts [of the synod], it flies first into the hands of men so that it may be said that it pleased fourteen eastern bishops not only that "man can be without sin and keep the commandments of God," but even that man might keep them "easily," and without any mention of God helping, but only "if he wants."[71]

Given all this, Augustine was no doubt increasingly desperate to acquire the *gesta* of Diospolis, as time passed and his request to John and Eulogius continued to go unanswered. As it turned out, the *gesta* did finally arrive sometime after Julius's departure, sent by Cyril of Alexandria.[72]

We do not know precisely why Cyril sent the *gesta* to Augustine. Had Augustine sent a letter to Cyril requesting them?[73] Had Cyril forwarded them

---

70 Augustine reports on this letter at *gest. Pel.* 30.54–31.56.

71 *gest. Pel.* 30.55 (Latin: CSEL 42:109.8–13; English: my translation). The rather calculating motives Augustine imputes to Pelagius and his allies here are a fruit of his reading of the acts of Diospolis and his conviction, by late 416, that Pelagius lied to the episcopal judges.

72 We learn this from a later letter Augustine sent to Cyril (*ep. 4**). We also know that Augustine had written at least one other letter to Cyril—this one pertaining to Jerome's *Dialogus aduersus Pelagianos* (see Augustine, *c. Iul. imp.* 4.88)—although the dating of this letter is uncertain (see discussion in Duval, "Note Complémentaire: Lettre 4*," BA 46B, 434). Augustine's *ep. 4** is often dated to 417 (see, e.g., Bouhot, "Une lettre d'Augustin d'Hippone à Cyrille d'Alexandrie (Ep. 4*)," 150–51; Henry Chadwick, "New Letters of St. Augustine," *Journal of Theological Studies* 34 [1983]: 428; Dalmon, *Un dossier*, 607; Duval, "Note Complémentaire: Lettre 4*," 436; Dunn, "Augustine, Cyril of Alexandria," 72n66). However, it seems to me that the letter should be dated later because of its use of the adjective *Pelagianus* (see §§4 and 5)—a term that Augustine only begins to use in the fall of 419. See Berrouard, "Les lettres 6* et 19*," 272–74, who argues similarly, and Bonner, "Some Remarks on Letters 4* and 6*," 164.

73 See, e.g., Dunn, "Augustine, Cyril of Alexandria," 72, and Bonner, "Some Remarks on Letters 4* and 6*," 157.

FROM DIOSPOLIS TO THE *TRACTORIA*

on to Augustine unbidden?[74] It is impossible to know for sure. However, upon receipt of the *gesta*, Augustine likely set to work immediately, composing an analysis of the proceedings that he would address and send to Aurelius in Carthage sometime in late 416 or early 417.[75] This treatise, *De gestis Pelagii*, is the first of Augustine's major anti-Pelagian works to counter Pelagius by name, reflecting the changed circumstances that the news of Diospolis had brought about in 416. In it, Augustine aims to show that far from approving of Pelagius's doctrines, the fourteen eastern bishops (and Pelagius along with them) had condemned those views. In this sense, Augustine's argument in *De gestis Pelagii* mirrors in many ways the approach to Diospolis we have already observed in his efforts from earlier in 416. However, this text is significant as it was Augustine's first "public" writing on Pelagius's acquittal and was likely intended for mass distribution.[76] In that light, it is particularly important to observe Augustine's argumentation in this text and recognize the ways in which his desire to reject the Pelagians' claim to speak for the universal Church's doctrinal tradition manifests itself. Let us now turn to a close examination of the treatise.[77]

De gestis Pelagii has four main sections: 1. Introduction (§§1–1.2); 2. Commentary on the proceedings of the Synod of Diospolis (§§1.2–21.45); 3. Background on Augustine's awareness of Pelagius and his views, as well as the reasons for his doubts about Pelagius's honesty and orthodoxy (§§22.46–33.58); 4. Summary and conclusion, with a postscript on the attack on Jerome's monasteries (§§34.59–35.66). Several of these sections are of interest to us as we attempt to identify the ways in which Augustine sought to turn the events of the Synod of Diospolis to his favor.

---

74 See Walter Dunphy, "Concerning the Synod of Diospolis and Its Acts," *Academia* 63 (1996): 101–17. See also Duval, "Note Complémentaire: Lettre 4*," BA 46B, 432ff., for discussion of some possibilities for Cyril's sending of the *gesta*.

75 For some discussion of the dating of *De gestis*, see Y.-M. Duval, "Note Complémentaire: Lettre 4*," BA 46B, 431ff.

76 See, e.g., *gest. Pel.* 34.59 and 35.66. We might also say that *De gestis Pelagii* was Augustine's first anti-Pelagian writing intended for broad distribution—see Winrich Löhr's comments to this effect at *Pélage et le pélagianisme*, 34. See also Löhr's comments at p. 31n38.

77 See also my analysis of *gest. Pel.* elsewhere: "Augustine, *Inuentio*, and *De gestis Pelagii*," in *Augustine and Rhetoric: Argumentative Strategies in Early Christianity*, ed. Adam Ployd and Rafał Toczko (Leiden: Brill, 2023), 15–37, and "Taking Augustine at His Word: Re-evaluating the Testimony of *De gestis Pelagii*," *Augustinian Studies* 53 (2022): 153–84.

In the first section of *De gestis Pelagii*, Augustine introduces his topic and argument. His initial paragraph alerts Aurelius, bishop of Carthage, to the fact that the proceedings of the synod have finally come into his hands and expresses his hopes that the present work will enable Aurelius and others to evaluate Pelagius's acquittal at Diospolis in the correct light. Following this introductory paragraph, Augustine the rhetor steps forward:

> And so, first of all, I give unspeakable thanks to the Lord God, our ruler and guard, that my opinion did not deceive me concerning our holy brothers and fellow bishops who sat as judges in this case. For not undeservedly did they approve of his [Pelagius's] responses, not concerning themselves with how he put those things which he was accused of in his writings, but rather with what he had said about them in the present examination. For a case of unsound faith is one thing, but of incautious speech is something else.[78]

With these initial lines Augustine sketches out the thrust of the whole treatise: the bishops gathered at Diospolis judged correctly. The effort Augustine exerts here to signal his agreement with the episcopal judges is palpable[79] and, admittedly, rather jarring—and no doubt it would have been jarring to those of Augustine's readers who were already aware of Pelagius's acquittal and of Augustine's opposition to the views allegedly spread by him. But that seems by design: Augustine, in this introductory section, is attempting to grab his audience's attention and lay the groundwork for a reappraisal of Pelagius's acquittal at Diospolis. What better way to do so than to ally himself with the bishops who had supposedly approved of Pelagius and his views?

Following this introductory section, Augustine turns to the proceedings of the synod and examines the accusations leveled against Pelagius, his responses, and the words of his episcopal judges. The first of these accusations, and Augustine's discussion of it, is particularly significant for us. This objection claimed that Pelagius had written in one of his books that "only one

---

78 *gest. Pel.* 1.2 (Latin: CSEL 42:52.8–14; English: my translation): *primum itaque domino deo, rectori custodique nostro, ineffabiles ago gratias, quod me de sanctis fratribus et coepiscopis nostris, qui in ea causa iudices consederunt, opinio non fefellit. responsiones enim eius non immerito approbauerunt non curantes quomodo ea quae obiciebantur in opusculis suis posuerit, sed quid de his in praesenti examinatione responderit. alia est enim causa fidei non sanae, alia locutionis incautae.*

79 We might note the rhetorical flourishes Augustine employs to emphasize his point: e.g., (1) the hyperbolic way in which he gives thanks to God and (2) the use of litotes (*non immerito*) to cushion his admission that the bishops had approved of Pelagius's answers.

who has knowledge of the law can be without sin."[80] Upon being asked by the bishops whether he taught this view or not, Pelagius replied, "I certainly said it, but not as they understand it. I did not say that one who has knowledge of the law cannot sin, but that one is helped by the knowledge of the law in order that he might not sin, as it is written, 'He gave them the law as a help.'"[81] In turn, the synod fathers agreed that what Pelagius said was not contrary to the Church's doctrine. Augustine's analysis of this outcome is important:

> Clearly, the things he answered are not foreign to the Church, but what was drawn from his book sounds like something else. But the bishops, who were Greek and were hearing these words through an interpreter, did not take care to examine this, only considering what that man who was being interrogated said that he thought, not the words by which, it was said, the same thought was written in his book.[82]

Here Augustine lays out two reasons why the bishops did not find Pelagius guilty of holding a position contrary to the Church's belief: (1) the Greek bishops were not reading Pelagius's book itself but were listening to an interpreter translating the quotation in question,[83] and (2) the bishops were

80 *gest. Pel.* 1.2 (Latin: CSEL 42:52.20–21; English: Teske, WSA I/23, 326).

81 *gest. Pel.* 1.2 (Latin: CSEL 42:52.22–53.1; English: my translation).

82 *gest. Pel.* 1.2 (Latin: CSEL 42:53.3–8; English: my translation).

83 Pier Franco Beatrice ("Chromatius and Jovinus at the Synod of Diospolis: A Prosopological Inquiry," *Journal of Early Christian Studies* 22 [2014]: 437–64) has argued that two of the judges at Diospolis were, in fact, originally from the West and had close ties to Rufinus of Aquileia. As a result, these two Latin-speaking bishops would have been connected with the broader circle of some of Pelagius's supporters. If this were the case, it would seem to undermine the aspects of Augustine's defense of the bishops at Diospolis based on their lack of facility with Latin. Beatrice's article is thought-provoking—and offers a number of intriguing proposals. However, while possible, I remain rather doubtful about Beatrice's hypothesis. First, it is hard to believe that Orosius (or Jerome, in one of his letters to Augustine in the spring of 416) would not have reported to Augustine the presence of western bishops at Diospolis—especially a Latin bishop as well-known as Chromatius of Aquileia. Further, if Augustine knew there had been western bishops at Diospolis, it seems unlikely that he would have identified them, as a group, as bishops of the eastern church or of the Province of Palestine (see *gest. Pel.* 1; *gest. Pel.* 11.25; *c. Iul.* 1.4.19)—it would have been all too easy for his opponents to correct him on this point and undermine his defense of them on the basis of the language barrier. That said, it is possible (if unlikely) that Augustine simply remained ignorant of the western origins of Chromatius and Jovinus. Or perhaps Augustine's defense of the bishops due to their lack of Latin fluency was simply intended to apply to the majority of bishops at Diospolis and not to each and every one individually—indeed, even if Beatrice is correct, twelve of the fourteen bishops would still have been Greek-speaking and possibly reliant upon an interpreter. On another note, Beatrice offers an intriguing suggestion for an identification of the interpreter

only concerned with Pelagius's oral defense, not with the contents of a book attributed to him. In this way, Augustine clarifies what exactly the bishops approved and did not approve and offers some justification for their failure to attend to Pelagius's written words.

Having thus explained the judges' action, Augustine turns to evaluate Pelagius's oral response. He begins by positing that there are two kinds of help that knowledge of the law might give to a person: (1) a help that is necessary for the avoidance of sin and (2) a help that is useful but not necessary for the avoidance of sin. Augustine continues,

> We must, then, investigate to which of these two kinds of helps knowledge of the law belongs, that is, how it helps one not to sin. If it helps in such a way that without it one cannot be without sin [i.e., if it is a "necessary" help], Pelagius not only answered correctly in court, but he also stated the truth in his book. But if it helps in such a way that, if it is present, it is a help, but even if it is absent, one can accomplish that for which it is helpful in some other way [i.e., if it is a help that is useful but not necessary], he answered correctly in court that a person is helped by knowledge of the law not to sin. In this case the bishops were right to be satisfied with this answer, but then he did not state the truth in his book, when he said that only one who has knowledge of the law can be without sin.[84]

After thus explaining the crux of the problem in Pelagius's oral defense, Augustine once more seeks to absolve the judges.

> His judges, unfamiliar with the Latin language and content with the deposition of the man who was pleading his case, left this point unexamined. They did so, especially since there was no one on the opposite side to force the interpreter clearly to explain the words of his book and to show that our brethren were not groundlessly troubled by it.[85]

---

at Diospolis: the lesser-known supporter of Pelagius, Annianus of Celeda (Beatrice, "Chromatius and Jovinus," 457). If correct, it would seem that Augustine was rather justified in complaining about the challenges with using an interpreter at Diospolis, given Annianus's theological leanings. However, it remains doubtful whether Annianus was actually present at Diospolis—see Chapter 1, n. 149. Further, Augustine's comments at *gest. Pel.* 16.39 seem to suggest that the interpreter himself was not a native Latin speaker.

84 *gest. Pel.* 1.3 (Latin: CSEL 42:54.2–12; English: Teske, WSA I/23, 327).

85 *gest. Pel.* 1.3 (Latin: CSEL 42:54.12–16; English: Teske, WSA I/23, 328).

FROM DIOSPOLIS TO THE *TRACTORIA* 201

Here Augustine reiterates one point of his explanation that we have already seen above (i.e., that the judges did not know Latin and thus had to rely on the interpreter) and adds a new one: that the difference between Pelagius's oral defense and his written words was left unexamined since none of Pelagius's opponents were able to attend the synod.[86]

Following this second defense of the judges, Augustine returns to the issue of knowledge of the law and its relationship to the avoidance of sin. Having concluded that Pelagius's written words and oral statement could be reconciled only if "knowledge of the law" were judged necessary (and not simply useful) to avoid sin, Augustine then attempts to discern what Pelagius might mean by "knowledge of the law." He first examines whether Pelagius might mean the sort of knowledge that a legal expert would have. However, Augustine points out a serious problem with this explanation.

> Of course, very few are experts in the law. However, the multitude of the members of Christ spread everywhere and lacking expertise in the law, which is so profound and complex, are commended by their piety of simple faith, firmest hope in God, and sincere charity. This multitude, provided with these gifts by the grace of God, trust that they can be cleansed from their sins through Jesus Christ our Lord.[87]

Augustine is doing a few important things in these lines. First, he is suggesting that there is potentially a certain elitism present within Pelagianism. If Pelagius intends to suggest that legal expertise is necessary to avoid sin, he has essentially condemned average Christians, who lack extensive knowledge of the law, to a life of sin. Second, Augustine is emphasizing the simple faith of average believers. Far from relying on their own knowledge and know-how, average believers trust in the grace of God to cleanse them from sin. They are saved by their trust in God, not by their own knowledge. Augustine's argument here is reminiscent of one he had used earlier in the controversy, when he had appealed to the pious customs of mothers who rush with their babies to the church for baptism.[88] There and here, Augustine contrasts the consequences of Pelagian views with what he characterizes as the simple faith of average believers, aiming to show how that simple faith "spread

---

86 Augustine had previously explained the absence of Heros and Lazarus at *gest. Pel.* 1.2.

87 *gest. Pel.* 1.3 (Latin: CSEL 42:54.16–22; English: my translation).

88 These arguments were discussed in Chapter 2.

everywhere" contradicts the exclusivist tendency of Pelagius's views.[89] In this way, Augustine quickly grounds his own anti-Pelagian critique in the simple faith of the universal Church.

Augustine then turns to another possible definition of "knowledge of the law," making use of a similar sort of argument. Perhaps, Augustine suggests, by "knowledge of the law" Pelagius meant not the sort of knowledge a legal expert has, but rather the knowledge of the faith, handed on to those about to be baptized so as to be able to profess the Creed. But here, too, Pelagius would find opposition.

> Even if that were what he meant, a countless multitude of baptized infants would surround him. They would not argue, but cry out; they would not shout with words, but with the truth of their innocence. They would ask, "What do you mean by having written, 'Only one who has knowledge of the law can be without sin'? Look, we are a huge flock of lambs without sin, and we do not have knowledge of the law!'"[90]

The Church's recognition of the innocence of these baptized infants proves, Augustine argues, that Pelagius's written words do not stand up to scrutiny. In this sense, Augustine once more appeals to a large group of Christians as testimony against Pelagius's view, thus suggesting again that the universal Church is united in its opposition to Pelagianism. He continues,

> Surely, without saying anything, [these baptized infants] would at least force [Pelagius] to be silent. Perhaps they would even force him to admit that he has now been corrected from this perverse view. Or they might at least make him admit that he had earlier held the view which he just stated in the ecclesiastical inquest, but that he had not expressed this idea with sufficient care.[91]

Either what Pelagius had written was wrong, or he had expressed it without sufficient clarity. In either case, Augustine argues, Pelagius's writings need correction. Furthermore, Augustine notes, who would condemn Pelagius for admitting his error? "After all, he would not be defending the view which those words contain, but would be claiming as his own the view which the

---

89 Such arguments will appear with even more regularity in Augustine's works against Julian of Eclanum, as we shall see in Chapter 5.

90 *gest. Pel.* 2.4 (Latin: CSEL 42:55.11–16; English: Teske, WSA I/23, 328).

91 *gest. Pel.* 2.4 (Latin: CSEL 42:55.17–20; English: Teske, WSA I/23, 328).

FROM DIOSPOLIS TO THE *TRACTORIA* 203

truth approves."[92] Augustine then concludes with another defense of the judges:

> It must be believed that the pious judges thought this [i.e., that Pelagius was "claiming as his own the view which the truth approves"]. Nevertheless, if what was in his Latin book was translated diligently, they could have understood it well enough, just as they understood his response produced with Greek eloquence, and, on account of this, easily judged that it was understood to be not foreign to the Church.[93]

Augustine's defense of the bishops gathered at Diospolis is once again emphatic—he urges his readers that they must believe (*credendum est*) that those judges thought that Pelagius was not dissembling but was merely clarifying his written words in his oral response. Of course, to support this, Augustine once again highlights the lack of a suitable translation—the bishops were victims of poor circumstances, nothing more.[94]

With this analysis of the first series of exchanges between Pelagius and his episcopal judges, Augustine displays many of the tactics he employs throughout the work: a forceful and repeated defense of the episcopal judgment coupled with a careful analysis of Pelagius's words. In this way, Augustine aligns himself with the bishops at Diospolis, while at the same time offering a more incisive critique of Pelagius than circumstances allowed the synod fathers to make. The appeals to average Christians and baptized infants offered here are particularly important. While such appeals are not found elsewhere in *De gestis Pelagii*, the use of them here, at the very beginning of his analysis of the proceedings, suggests their importance for Augustine. In this work, he aims to set the tone early: he agrees with the judges; and all Christians agree in their opposition to the views attributed to Pelagius (whether he admits to holding those views or not).

Throughout the subsequent pages of the second section of *De gestis Pelagii*, Augustine continues his close analysis of the proceedings and defense of the episcopal judges. However, at *gest. Pel.* 11.23–24, Augustine advances his argument in a new way. In this passage, Augustine recounts Pelagius's

---

92 *gest. Pel.* 2.4 (Latin: CSEL 42:55.25–56.2; English: Teske, WSA I/23, 328).

93 *gest. Pel.* 2.4 (Latin: CSEL 42:56.2–6; English: my translation). This indicates that Pelagius responded to the judges' questions in Greek.

94 One does wonder if there is a bit of an edge to Augustine's absolution of the bishops here: perhaps they were not as diligent as they should have been in examining Pelagius's books?

204 AUGUSTINE IN THE PELAGIAN CONTROVERSY

and the bishops' responses to a series of propositions attributed to Caelestius (and condemned previously at the *iudicium* in Carthage in 411) as well as some that had been forwarded to Augustine by Hilary from Syracuse.[95] After a brief response to two of these propositions, Pelagius refused to answer to the rest, as he was not their author. He concluded his response by stating, "But to satisfy the holy synod I declare anathema those who hold those views or have at some time held them."[96] To this the synod replied, "Pelagius, who is present here, has given a sufficient and correct account with regard to the previously mentioned propositions, for he has condemned the propositions that were not his."[97] At this point, Augustine goes on the offensive.

> We see, therefore, and we maintain that not only Pelagius, but also the holy bishops, who presided over that court, condemned the following highly destructive evils of this heresy: "That Adam was created mortal." To explain more fully its sense, there was added: "So that he would die, whether he sinned or did not sin." "That his sin harmed him alone and not the human race." "That the law leads to the kingdom just as the gospel does." "That newly born infants are in that state in which Adam was before his transgression." "That the whole human race does not die through the death or transgression of Adam, and the whole human race does not rise through the resurrection of Christ." "That infants have eternal life, even if they are not baptized." "That if wealthy persons who have been baptized do not renounce all their possessions, they have no merit, even if they seem to do something good, and they cannot possess the kingdom of heaven." It is clear that all these propositions were condemned by that ecclesiastical court, with Pelagius himself condemning them along with the participating bishops.[98]

In a deft move, Augustine highlights the fact that when the bishops recognized Pelagius's own condemnation of these propositions, they themselves

---

95 See discussion of *ep.* 157 in Chapter 3.

96 *gest. Pel.* 11.24 (Latin: CSEL 42:77.24–25; English: Teske, WSA I/23, 341).

97 *gest. Pel.* 11.24 (Latin: CSEL 42:78.1–3; English: Teske, WSA I/23, 341).

98 *gest. Pel.* 11.24 (Latin: CSEL 42:78.3–20; English: Teske, WSA I/23, 341). Augustine later suggests that he had initially read Pelagius's condemnation of these Caelestian points as a clear confession of the presence of original sin in infants (*gr. et pecc. or.* 2.14.15). At least momentarily, he may have believed that Pelagius had either corrected his former views or had truthfully denied ever having held such views. However, Pelagius's failure to mention his condemnation of these propositions in his *chartula defensionis* (see *gest. Pel.* 33.57–58) seems to have prompted some doubts about Pelagius's earnestness. These doubts were confirmed for Augustine when he read Pelagius's *Pro libero arbitrio* (see *gr. et pecc. or.* 2.14.15).

FROM DIOSPOLIS TO THE *TRACTORIA* 205

(at least implicitly) condemned those propositions, too. In this passage, then, Augustine goes beyond his prior attempts to emphasize his agreement with the bishops' judgment of Pelagius's oral defense. Here, he can argue that the synod itself condemned key propositions of the Pelagian heresy. This was, needless to say, an important turn of events. Augustine's follow-up to this conclusion is equally important. Immediately after highlighting this condemnation offered by the bishops and Pelagius, Augustine recounts the beginnings of the Pelagian controversy in Carthage (see *gest. Pel.* 11.25). He relates that many in Carthage were disturbed by such propositions—so much so that Marcellinus requested his response to the views promoted by the proponents of such propositions, and Aurelius asked him to preach on the issues in Carthage.[99] Augustine continues:

> [While preaching,] I held in my hands a letter of the glorious martyr, Cyprian; I quoted his words on this subject and commented on them in order to remove this wicked error from the hearts of some people who had been convinced of those propositions which we see were condemned in these proceedings. Certain people who held to such [Pelagian] views were trying so hard to persuade some of our brothers of these views that they were threatening that, if they did not support them, they would be condemned by the judgment of the Eastern Churches. Look, fourteen bishops of the Eastern Church in the very land in which our Lord revealed the presence of his Incarnation acquitted Pelagius only on the condition that he condemned these propositions as opposed to the Catholic faith. Hence, if he was acquitted because he condemned such propositions, they were certainly condemned, as will be seen at greater length and more clearly in what follows.[100]

We have quoted parts of this passage several times before, but now it is important to grasp the whole context. Here, as Augustine gives some background to the debate in Carthage in 411, he reveals for the first time one of the claims the Pelagians had been circulating at the time[101]—namely, that the Pelagians were simply teaching what the eastern churches had always taught. As I have been arguing, this accusation appears to have been of fundamental

---

99 See *pecc. mer.* and *s.* 294, and discussion of these events in Chapter 2 and in the appendix.

100 *gest. Pel.* 11.25 (Latin: CSEL 42:79.1–15; English: Teske, WSA I/23, 341–42, with some modifications).

101 It might be argued that this Pelagian claim was being employed at some point later than 411. However, the context of the passage (which focuses on events in 411 and the earliest period of controversy) suggests otherwise.

importance for Augustine: this accusation, and others like it,[102] help to explain Augustine's mode of argumentation in the Pelagian controversy from its earliest beginnings. But this is the first time Augustine actually mentions this particular accusation. That, in itself, is noteworthy. First and foremost, the fact that he still remembers the accusation over five years later indicates its importance. Second, the reason he mentions it here seems directly tied to a new piece of evidence he is attempting to claim in *De gestis Pelagi*—namely, the support of the eastern churches. Now, in late 416 or early 417 Augustine finally has concrete evidence he can deploy against the Pelagians' claims to have the eastern churches on their side. Previously, he had attempted to counter that Pelagian claim in rather oblique ways—for example, by appealing to Jerome and his knowledge of Christian writers of both languages in *De peccatorum meritis* or through references to the rite of baptism, pious customs, or the Lord's Prayer. But in *De gestis Pelagii*, Augustine attempts to claim the support of fourteen episcopal judges of the Palestinian Church who had, he argues, condemned key propositions of Pelagianism that had been up for debate in Carthage in 411. These fourteen bishops offered Augustine the most robust evidence he had yet encountered to suggest that Pelagianism was universally opposed by the Church—provided, of course, that he could convince his readers that these bishops' acquittal of Pelagius did not mean that they supported his alleged views.[103]

Later in the proceedings, Augustine is faced with a decision rendered by the judges that is more difficult for him to accept—thus threatening his contention that the episcopal judges were opposed to Pelagianism. At *gest. Pel.* 14.32, Augustine is in the course of recounting Pelagius's response to a series of propositions attributed to Caelestius that were raised at the Synod of Diospolis. One is particularly troubling for Augustine: Caelestius was alleged to have taught that "everyone can have all the virtues"—which would "destroy the diversity of graces which the apostle teaches."[104] To this objection Pelagius

---

102 See, for example, Augustine's statement at *s.* 294.19, where he notes that the Pelagians have accused their opponents of teaching "something new" (*aliquid nouum*) (PL 38:1347.39)—that is, heresy.

103 Augustine's reference to Cyprian (and his quotation of the martyred bishop of Carthage in *s.* 294) in this passage should also be noted. Although no quotation is offered here, Augustine nevertheless indicates Cyprian's support for his positions, thus suggesting once again the antiquity of the positions the Pelagians were opposing while at the same time indicating their universality by claiming the fourteen bishops at Diospolis as allies.

104 *gest. Pel.* 14.32 (Latin: CSEL 42:86.14–16; English: Teske, WSA I/23, 346).

FROM DIOSPOLIS TO THE *TRACTORIA* 207

responded: "We said this, but they have found fault with it out of ill will and ignorance. We do not, after all, destroy the diversity of graces; rather, we say that God gives all the graces to one who is worthy to receive them, as he gave them to the apostle Paul."[105] The synod accepted this response, declaring, "Your views on the gift of the graces found in the holy apostle are reasonable and in accord with the mind of the Church."[106] The fact that the synod approved of Pelagius's answer troubled Augustine quite a bit. Augustine notes that he does not disagree that Paul had received all the graces mentioned at 1 Corinthians 12:28; rather, he worries that Pelagius's statement suggests that he believes God's grace is given on the basis of merit. Due to this, Augustine devotes several paragraphs to examining various statements found in Paul that indicate the gratuity of grace. To support his interpretation of Paul, Augustine notes that John of Jerusalem himself had appealed to several of the same Scriptural texts to emphasize the gratuity of grace at the diocesan examination of Pelagius held at Jerusalem earlier in 415:

> As the records show, John, the holy bishop of the church of Jerusalem rightly appealed to this testimony [1 Cor 15:10]. When asked about the proceedings that had been held in his presence before the trial, he gave an account to our fellow bishops who presided together with him at the trial. He said that some people were then murmuring and claiming that Pelagius said, "This can be attained without the grace of God," that is, what he previously claimed, namely, that "human beings can be without sin." John said, "I found him in error on this point and brought out the fact that even the apostle Paul, who labored much, not by his own strength, but by the grace of God, said, 'I have labored more than all of them. Not I, but the grace of God that was with me' (1 Cor 15:10). Again Paul said, 'It does not depend on the one who wills or runs, but on God who shows mercy' (Rom 9:16). There is also the text, 'Unless the Lord has built the house, the builders have labored in vain' (Ps 127:1), and many similar passages from the holy scriptures. But Pelagius said to those who did not accept the passages which we quoted from the holy scriptures, but continued to murmur, 'That is what I believe as well. Let him be anathema who says that human beings can develop in all the virtues without the grace of God.'"[107]

---

105 *gest. Pel.* 14.32 (Latin: CSEL 42:86.16–19; English: Teske, WSA I/23, 346).

106 *gest. Pel.* 14.32 (Latin: CSEL 42:86.20–21; English: Teske, WSA I/23, 346).

107 *gest. Pel.* 14.37 (Latin: CSEL 42:93.18–94.12; English: Teske, WSA I/23, 350, slightly modified).

By recounting John's testimony, Augustine supports his argument in two ways. First, he enlists John of Jerusalem as his ally against Pelagius. Second, he indicates that Pelagius himself affirmed in John's presence the necessity of grace. However, Augustine then goes on to note that in the *Expositio* on Romans attributed to Pelagius, the opposite viewpoint is supported when Pelagius argues that the words in Romans 9:16 ("It does not depend on the one who wills or runs, but on God who shows mercy") were not stated by Paul but by Paul's fictive interlocutor.[108] In this sense, Augustine concludes, "[Pelagius] must either deny that this perverse interpretation is his own, or he must not hesitate to change and correct it."[109] Augustine then addresses the fact that John had apparently criticized Pelagius's opponents at Diospolis:

> Whatever Bishop John said about our absent brothers—whether our fellow-bishops, namely Heros and Lazarus, or the priest Orosius, or others (whose names were not identified in the *gesta*)—I believe that he does not mean this to be to their disadvantage.[110] For if they had been present—far be it from me to say that they could perhaps have caught [John] in a lie—but perhaps they could have mentioned what he perhaps forgot or how the Latin interpreter misled him (even if not due to a desire to trick him, then certainly due to some difficulty with a foreign language that was not well understood). [I believe John did not mean his comments to be to their disadvantage] especially since [John's statement about our absent brothers] was not recorded in the *gesta*,[111] which have been profitably established lest the dishonest deceive and lest the good forget something.[112]

108 Pelagius, *Expositio in Romanos*, in A. Souter, *Pelagius' Expositions of Thirteen Epistles of St. Paul* (Cambridge: Cambridge University Press, 1926), vol. 2, p. 76.

109 *gest. Pel.* 16.39 (Latin: CSEL 42:95.3–6; English: Teske, WSA I/23, 351).

110 It seems that the *gesta* omitted some comments made by John in criticism of Heros, Lazarus, and Orosius or others of Pelagius's opponents.

111 Wermelinger (*Rom und Pelagius*, 111) incorrectly, I think, reads this line as indicating that no minutes were kept for the Jerusalem meeting in July 415. Instead, I take it to refer to the omission of John's critical comments about Heros, Lazarus, and Orosius from the *gesta* of Diospolis. Admittedly, however, Augustine's Latin is a bit confusing on this point.

112 *gest. Pel.* 16.39: *nam quicquid dixit episcopus Iohannes de absentibus fratribus nostris siue coepiscopis Herote scilicet ac Lazaro siue de presbytero Orosio siue de aliis, quorum ibi non sunt nomina expressa, credo quod intellegat ad eorum praeiudicium non ualere. si enim praesentes essent, possent eum fortasse, absit ut dicam, conuincere de mendacio, sed forte commemorare, quid forte fuisset oblitus aut in quo eum fefellerit Latinus interpres, etsi non studio mentiendi, certe alienae linguae minus intellectae nonnulla difficultate, praesertim quia non gestis agebatur, quae improbi ne mentiantur, boni autem ne aliquid obliuiscantur utiliter instituta sunt* (Latin: CSEL 42:95.6–17; English: my translation).

FROM DIOSPOLIS TO THE *TRACTORIA* 209

Augustine's suggestion here that the presence of Heros, Lazarus, or Orosius at the synod would have helped the episcopal judges to assess Pelagius's views more accurately is, at this point, a familiar one. However, what is noteworthy is the way in which Augustine attempts to put a positive spin even on John's apparently hostile comments about Pelagius's accusers. Augustine admits that John seems to have made these hostile comments but argues that John did not really mean for these words to be entered into the record as a judgment against them because the comments in question were not included in the *gesta*. In this sense, even here, when Augustine finds the judges (or at least one of the judges) most opposed to his allies, he tries to lessen that apparent opposition. Further, it is worth noting how Augustine tries *cautiously* to suggest that "perhaps" Heros and Lazarus's presence would have helped remind John what he had "perhaps" forgotten about his conversations with Pelagius in July 415. The repeated use of *fortasse* and *forte* in this passage (along with the phrase *absit ut dicam*) lightens what might otherwise be read as criticism of John. In this way, Augustine registers some subtle complaints against John while, at the same time, maintaining his position of agreement with the episcopal decision at Diospolis.

Shortly thereafter, Augustine returns to his original question: Why did the judges approve of Pelagius's response when he had indicated that grace was given to Paul insofar as he was worthy to receive it? Augustine devotes several lines to an explanation.

> Why, then, someone will say, did the judges give their approval? I admit I am myself still puzzled. But without a doubt something spoken briefly easily evaded their hearing or attention. Or thinking that this could be taken correctly in some way, they thought that they ought not to stir up a controversy over what is almost a single word with him whose clear confessions about this matter they seemed to possess—something that perhaps could have also happened to us if we had sat with them in that courtroom.[113]

Augustine handles this apparent approval of Pelagius's views of grace with care. Note the way that he begins his analysis by admitting his own

---

113 *gest. Pel.* 17.41: *cur ergo, ait aliquis, hoc iudices approbarunt? fateor. ideo iam ipse ambigo. sed nimirum aut breue dictum eorum audientiam et intentionem facile subterfugit aut aliquo modo id recte posse accipi existimantes, cuius de hac re confessiones liquidas sibi habere uidebantur, paene de uno uerbo nihil ei controuersiae mouendum putarunt, quod et nobis forsitan contigisset, si cum eis in illo iudicio sedissemus* (Latin: CSEL 42:96.26–97.4; English: Teske, WSA I/23, 352, slightly modified).

confusion over the judges' decision. In a certain sense, this may seem to be an odd choice. Augustine has devoted the entirety of his analysis so far to aligning himself with the bishops' judgment. Why change tactics here? Why emphasize the bishops' inexplicable approval for Pelagius? It seems to me that Augustine does this precisely to show that the bishops' approval is not inexplicable. In his analysis of this portion of the proceedings of Diospolis, Augustine has labored to explain why Pelagius's statement should have been troubling to the judges: (1) he has offered an examination of key scriptural passages (§§14.32–36); (2) he recounted John of Jerusalem's report at Diospolis (§§14.37); (3) he pointed to Pelagius's words in another text that expressed his view of grace in a clearer fashion (§16.39); (4) he lamented the absence of Heros and Lazarus, who could have pressed Pelagius for more clarity (§16.39); (5) he noted that Pelagius's condemnation of a key Caelestian proposition ("God's grace is given in accord with our merits") earlier at Diospolis appears to conflict with his claim now that Paul received grace because he was worthy (§17.40). Augustine's discussion of this particular statement of Pelagius occupies ten full paragraphs of *De gestis Pelagii*—a sizeable quantity. Indeed, for a sense of scale, *De gestis Pelagii* has sixty-six paragraphs in total, with forty-four of those devoted to an analysis of the proceedings. Thus, Augustine's discussion of this single statement occupies just under twenty-five percent of the analysis of the entire proceedings. After working through this lengthy analysis, the reader is left with a firm sense that Pelagius's words and the judges' approval of those words were deeply troubling to Augustine. Thus, at the conclusion of this analysis, when Augustine addresses the judges' approval and admits his confusion, he is not announcing anything new. Indeed, any intelligent reader would recognize that Augustine dwelt for so long on this particular topic precisely because the judges' approval was so troubling. By announcing this fact, Augustine, in a strategic fashion, faces the worst-case scenario head-on: that the judges did, in fact, side with Pelagius and Pelagius's theological viewpoint. This tactic is brought to its conclusion, though, by Augustine's next words, in which he calmly explains that "without a doubt" (*nimirum*) there are several plausible explanations for the judges' approval of Pelagius's words. In providing this explanation, Augustine eases the minds of his readers, inclining them to accept his analysis.

Having resolved this difficult matter, Augustine is able to continue his analysis, lasting only a few paragraphs more before he quotes the synod's statement of acquittal. Following this quotation, he summarizes his analysis.

FROM DIOSPOLIS TO THE *TRACTORIA*

He begins by cautioning against reading the proceedings as an indication of Pelagius's innocence:

> If these are the proceedings due to which the friends of Pelagius rejoice that he has been found innocent, we certainly hope for and desire his salvation in Christ, for he also took great care to prove our friendship with him, having even produced and read our private letters [*familiaribus epistolis nostris*] at the trial—which have been inserted into the proceedings. But, regarding his being found innocent—which is more believed than clearly demonstrated—we ought not rejoice too quickly.[114]

He continues, adding yet another defense of the episcopal judges:

> In saying this, I do not accuse the court of either negligence or connivance or—what is certainly far from the case—of assenting to godless teachings. But by their trial—deservedly approved and praised—Pelagius nevertheless does not seem to me to have been found innocent among those who know him more fully and more certainly. After all, especially in the absence of those who had lodged the charge against him, the judges were hearing the case of someone who was all but unknown, and they could hardly subject the man to a more rigorous examination.[115]

In this defense, we see the repetition of several arguments Augustine has made previously: (1) that the judges did not approve of Pelagius's heresy (but only his spoken words, which could be understood in an orthodox way); (2) that the absence of Heros and Lazarus made it difficult for the judges to recognize the troubling elements in Pelagius's words as well as the views one finds in his writings. With this defense accomplished, Augustine once again goes on the offensive: "Nevertheless they completely destroyed the heresy itself, provided that the proponents of his error only follow their

---

114 *gest. Pel.* 21.45 (Latin: CSEL 42:99.9–15; English: my translation). The use of the plural of *epistola* can indicate a single letter (see the entry for "epistula" in Lewis and Short), which could be the case here. However, it seems more likely to me, given the use of the first-person plural in this passage (which contrasts with the first-person singular used in subsequent passages), that Augustine is indicating here that at Diospolis Pelagius produced in his defense not only a private letter from Augustine (i.e., *ep.* 146 discussed later in *gest. Pel.*) but also one from Aurelius. If, as seems likely, *ep.* 146 was Augustine's reply to a brief letter of greetings Pelagius had delivered while passing through Hippo in 410, it would make sense for a similar exchange with Aurelius to follow upon the British ascetic's arrival in Carthage. For more discussion of *ep.* 146 see n. 118 below.

115 *gest. Pel.* 21.45 (Latin: CSEL 42:99.16–23; English: Teske, WSA I/23, 354, slightly modified).

judgment."[116] In this sense, Augustine argues, the judges, while approving of Pelagius's oral defense, nevertheless condemned the heresy of which he was accused. Augustine thus suggests, if Pelagius's supporters are so enamored of the judgment at Diospolis, they should follow that judgment and condemn the heresy itself—if they wish to be honest. However, Augustine suspects that Pelagius and his followers are not being honest:

> But how can those who know well what Pelagius usually taught, whether people who opposed his arguments or those who are grateful that they have been set free from this error, fail to hold him suspect, when they read not a simple confession condemning his past errors, but a defense in which he as much as claims that he never held other views than those which this court approved in his answers?[117]

With this, Augustine concludes his analysis of the proceedings and turns next to the third section of his work (§§22.46–33.58), which deals with his growing awareness of Pelagius and his views, as well as some documents written by Pelagius that he had received after Diospolis. This section aims to indicate why doubts remain about Pelagius's honesty and orthodoxy. Augustine details how he came to know about Pelagius and his teachings, explains the contents of a letter he had sent to Pelagius,[118] and analyzes two documents Pelagius had supposedly sent out after his acquittal at Diospolis—namely, a letter Pelagius had sent to a friend and the *chartula defensionis*. Both these documents described the events of Diospolis in a way that, on Augustine's reading at least, diverged in key respects from the official proceedings. At the

---

116 *gest. Pel.* 21.45 (Latin: CSEL 42:99.23–25; English: Teske, WSA I/23, 354, slightly modified).

117 *gest. Pel.* 21.45 (Latin: CSEL 42:99.25–100.6; English: Teske, WSA I/23, 354, slightly modified).

118 That is, Augustine's *ep.* 146, sent to Pelagius probably in 410. For more on Augustine's correspondence with Pelagius see Duval, "La correspondance entre Augustin et Pélage," *Revue d'études augustiniennes* 45 (1999): 363–84, and "Augustin et les règles épistolaires: Sur quelques lettres embarrassées de saint Augustin (Ep. 23, 28, 146)," in *Epistulae antiquae II: Actes du IIe colloque international 'Le genre épistolaire antique et les prolongements européens' (Université François-Rabelais, Tours, 28-30 september 2000)*, ed. L. Nadjo and E. Gavoille (Louvain: Peeters, 2002), 361–65. Contrary to the common reading (repeated, e.g., in Ebbeler, *Disciplining Christians*, 218–21), Duval in the latter piece argues that Augustine's interpretation of *ep.* 146 found in *gest. Pel.* was not an invention of 416 (manufactured in a desire to defend himself for his prior praise of Pelagius), but accurately reflects the nuances of his writing to Pelagius in 410.

FROM DIOSPOLIS TO THE *TRACTORIA*

conclusion of this section, Augustine articulates his reasons for composing *De gestis Pelagii*:

> I wished to write this book . . . in order that, if it does not displease you [Aurelius], by your greater authority . . . it might be made known to those who you think need it, so as to destroy the foolishness and arguments of those who think that, because Pelagius was acquitted, the eastern bishop-judges accepted those teachings. The Christian truth always condemns these teachings, spreading far and wide in all their destructiveness, as contrary to the Christian faith and the grace of God by which we are called and justified. And it has condemned them also by the authority of these fourteen bishops. It would have condemned Pelagius at the same time, if he had not declared those teachings anathema.[119]

Augustine identifies here a central motivation for writing *De gestis Pelagii*: to disprove the rumors suggesting that fourteen eastern bishops had approved of Pelagius's views. Instead, Augustine argues, the facts of the case indicate that those views have been condemned by these fourteen bishops. Far from offering support to the Pelagian claim that the eastern churches would approve of their teachings, the verdict of Diospolis shows just the opposite: that the whole Church is united in its opposition to Pelagianism.

Augustine then turns to the final section of the work (§§34.59–35.66), in which he summarizes the doctrinal conclusions of the synod. He begins by discussing the propositions approved by the bishops (§§35.62–64), noting the sense in which they were approved, distinguishing between the apparent meaning in the written source of the proposition and the interpretation given to the proposition by Pelagius in his oral response. Following this, he offers a list of the propositions that were condemned both by the bishops and by Pelagius (§35.65). Augustine's concluding statement at the end of this section emphasizes his argument:

> The judges gave their approval to Pelagius because he disowned and declared anathema all these propositions, along with any arguments included to support them. Thus they declared that, in rejecting and declaring them anathema, he condemned propositions opposed to the faith of the Church. Accordingly, regardless of the sense in which Caelestius may or may not have published them, regardless of the sense in which Pelagius

---

119 *gest. Pel.* 34.59 (Latin: CSEL 42:114.15–26; English: Teske, WSA I/23, 362–63, with some modifications).

may or may not have held them, let us rejoice and give thanks and praise to God that these evil statements of this newest heresy have been condemned by an ecclesiastical court.[120]

What Augustine is doing in this passage at the end of *De gestis Pelagii* is strategically putting to the side the question of Pelagius's (and Caelestius's) own views in order to show that the views attributed to them have been condemned by fourteen eastern bishops. Indeed, this seems to be Augustine's overarching argument throughout the work. Bringing this argument to its conclusion, Augustine rests his case: the Pelagian heresy, if not Caelestius and Pelagius themselves, has been defeated.[121]

Augustine's approach to Diospolis in *De gestis Pelagii* is largely in continuity with what we observed in his (and the African bishops') responses earlier in 416, especially in the sense that he attempts to distinguish between the acquittal of Pelagius and the "acquittal" of Pelagianism.[122] For Augustine, Pelagius's acquittal was brought about by a number of factors: for example, the absence of Heros and Lazarus, the judges' lack of familiarity with Latin and reliance on a translator,[123] and Pelagius's own (deceptive?) re-interpretations of his written words. Augustine emphasizes these factors while at the same time largely avoiding criticism of the episcopal judges at Diospolis.[124] However, he also goes beyond the arguments found earlier in 416 in a few respects. First, he emphasizes his own agreement with the episcopal judges and their choice to acquit Pelagius based on his oral responses. Second, he argues that the synod itself condemned key propositions of the Pelagian heresy. We should recognize Augustine's approach here as a deliberate tactic. Indeed, its deliberateness becomes all the more evident when we compare his account of Diospolis with Orosius's account of the July 415 Jerusalem meeting in his *Liber apologeticus*. Orosius, for example, clearly blamed John of Jerusalem for the failure of that meeting, going so far as to accuse him

---

120 *gest. Pel.* 35.65 (Latin: CSEL 42:121.13–20; English: Teske, WSA I/23, 366–67).

121 Augustine does add one final paragraph to his text—a postscript of sorts relating news of the attack on Jerome's monasteries apparently carried out by supporters of Pelagius. This report is clearly intended to offer one final piece of evidence for Pelagius's questionable character.

122 See, e.g., *s.* 348A.15 and *epp.* 175.4, 177.2, 179.5.

123 For more on the language barrier, see n. 83 above.

124 Although he does subtly offer criticism from time to time. See, e.g., *gest. Pel.* 16.39 (and possibly 2.4) as well as our comments above.

FROM DIOSPOLIS TO THE *TRACTORIA* 215

(not-so-subtly) of Origenism at one point.[125] So too, as Laurence Dalmon has pointed out, we might compare Augustine's account of Diospolis with that of Jerome, who in 419 would characterize it as a "wretched synod" (*miseribilis synodus*).[126] It is, therefore, significant that Augustine makes no attempt to question the decision of the episcopal judges at Diospolis or even to detract from their competence. Rather, in his presentation of the events at Diospolis, Augustine's central goal seems to be both to align himself as much as possible with those episcopal judges (insofar as he agrees with their decision), and to align those judges with himself (insofar as they have apparently condemned key Pelagian propositions). In this way, far from supporting the Pelagians' claim that their views were simply those of the eastern churches, the decision at Diospolis is interpreted by Augustine to assert the exact opposite: the East, too, has condemned the teachings attributed to Pelagius and Caelestius.[127] This interpretation, of course, fits with the broader pattern of Augustine's anti-Pelagian argumentation, which time and time again employs arguments designed to indicate the opposition of the universal Church's ancient doctrinal tradition to Pelagianism. In *De gestis Pelagii*, though, Augustine makes his case before a broader public, knowing that this text would be distributed widely as part of the Africans' post-Diospolis campaign.[128] It is telling, I suggest, that in such a text Augustine focuses so much of his efforts on proving the unity between East and West in their opposition to Pelagian views—even going so far as to recount for the first time a specific Pelagian claim to the contrary. In that sense, *De gestis Pelagii* indicates once again just how important it was for Augustine to rebut such claims and, I suggest, how

---

125 See *Liber apologeticus* 5.

126 See *ep.* 202.2 (CSEL 57:300.18) among the letters of Augustine, and Dalmon, *Un dossier*, 63–64.

127 At this point, I should note that by emphasizing the tactical and rhetorical dimensions of Augustine's interpretation of the *gesta*, I do not mean to imply that this interpretation is, by that fact, disingenuous or strained beyond all reasonable limits. It is clear that Augustine interprets the evidence in a way that favors his own perspective. However, it also seems to me that his interpretation is plausible—at least in several key respects. For more, see my "Taking Augustine at His Word."

128 See *gest. Pel.* 34.59 and 35.66. In this context, it is worth noting that *De gestis Pelagii* appears to have been Augustine's only work to have been translated into Greek in antiquity (although when this/these translation(s) were produced remains an open question). For discussion and references to key literature, see Giulio Malavasi, "The Greek Version(s) of Augustine's *De gestis Pelagii*," *Zeitschrift für Antikes Christentum* 21 (2017): 559–72.

416

much these claims—and the threat to Church unity that they embodied—motivated his anti-Pelagian efforts in general.

417: A YEAR OF UPHEAVAL
Pope Innocent's Response

We do not know exactly when Augustine completed *De gestis Pelagii*, but it was likely prior to the arrival in Africa of several letters from Pope Innocent in early 417.[129] These letters, which date to January 27, 417, contained Innocent's replies to the African letters of the previous year.[130] In his responses, Innocent largely answered the Africans' letters favorably: he condemned the notion that God's daily help is not necessary for pursuing righteousness and excommunicated Pelagius and Caelestius as well as any who shared their

---

129 The letters in question are *epp.* 181–83 among the letters of Augustine and *ep.* 32 among the letters of Innocent (PL 20:597–98). It stands to reason that Augustine would have mentioned Innocent's letters in *De gestis Pelagii* had they arrived prior to his completion of the work.

130 *ep.* 182 has the date January 27, 417 (*ep.* 182.7), *ep.* 183 and *ep.* 32 only have January 27 (*ep.* 183.5; *ep.* 32 [PL 20:598.1–2]), and *ep.* 181 is undated. However, in *ep.* 32 (a private letter to Aurelius), Innocent notes that he is sending Bishop Julius back with the Apostolic See's judgments on the two synods: *supradictum igitur fratrem nostrum [i.e., Iulium] tuae dilectioni restituo cum apostolicae sedis ad relationem duplicis synodi iudicatis* (PL 20:597). Thus, it seems likely that *ep.* 181 also dates to January 27. We might also date three other relevant letters by Innocent to the period of 416/early 417: *epp.* 33–35 among the letters of Innocent. These three letters were prompted by the rumors of an attack on Jerome's monasteries (which probably occurred at some point in the first few months of 416): *ep.* 33 (CSEL 35.1:98) to Aurelius, requesting that he forward *ep.* 34 (CSEL 35.1:96–97) to Jerome; *ep.* 35 (CSEL 35.1:97–98) is addressed to John of Jerusalem. In *ep.* 35, Innocent notes that he has learned of the attack from Paula and Eustochium. It is unclear when these letters were written. It seems unlikely that they would have been written in the period after the African bishops' letters had arrived at Rome and before Innocent replied (so, between October 416 and January 417), as it would have been odd for Innocent to send a letter to Aurelius related to Palestine before responding to *epp.* 175–77. In some ways, it is attractive to date *epp.* 33–35 before the sending of *epp.* 175–77, as this would help to explain the absence of a reference to the attack on Jerome's monastery in those letters. It would have also given Augustine more confirmation (1) of the fact that the attack had taken place and, perhaps, (2) of its perpetrator (if Innocent's messenger was aware—see discussion in Lössl, "Who Attacked," 98, who suggests that Innocent appears to have been more aware of the details of the attack than he lets on in his letters). Such confirmation would have increased his confidence in assigning blame to the supporters of Pelagius in *De gestis Pelagii* (something he had avoided doing explicitly in *s.* 348A). For more on letters from Innocent to Aurelius (excluding those directly relevant to the Pelagian controversy) see Wermelinger, *Rom und Pelagius*, 123n208.

FROM DIOSPOLIS TO THE *TRACTORIA*

views.[131] We note in particular that the Africans' focus on the concrete aspects of the faith put into jeopardy by Pelagian views seem to have found their mark: for example, in his letter to the Council of Milevis, Innocent noted his shock both at the effect the Pelagians' views would have on daily prayer as well as at their alleged contention that infants can obtain eternal life without baptism.[132] Innocent also praised the Africans for requesting his aid, seizing on the opportunity to frame their letters as an appeal to a higher authority. For example, to the Council of Milevis, he wrote:

> Therefore, following the procedure of the ancient rule, which you know has always been kept by the whole world along with me, you are diligently and fittingly asking what judgment of the apostolic office should be held to—that mystical office, I say, which is looked to by the concern of all the churches in the midst of troubling affairs (aside from those things which are outside its purview).[133]

Innocent also seems to have followed the Africans' lead with regard to Diospolis, in the sense that he declined to take any concrete position on the validity of the decision rendered there, simply reporting he had received a copy of the acts, but that they came into his hands through some of the lay faithful (and thus were of questionable accuracy).[134] However, Innocent also hesitated in some respects to go as far as the Africans had hoped he would.[135] For example, although he had excommunicated Pelagius, Innocent refused

---

131 At *ep.* 181.8 Innocent states somewhat vaguely that anyone who denies the need for the help of God is not worthy of "our communion." However, at *ep.* 182.6 an explicit excommunication is issued: "Hence we declare that Pelagius and Caelestius, that is, the inventors of these new ideas which, as the apostle said, have contributed to no edification but have generated utterly empty questions, are excommunicated from the Church by the authority of our apostolic power" (Latin: CSEL 44:721.3–7; English: Teske, WSA II/3, 168). However, as Dalmon notes (*Un dossier*, 603), there is no evidence that Innocent took actions to publicize this excommunication broadly among the eastern churches. Dalmon suggests (p. 604) that Innocent's caution throughout the whole affair could be due to the enduring fragility of the relations between East and West following the Chrysostom affair.

132 See *ep.* 182.3 and 182.5. Interestingly, Innocent appeals in the latter passage to the practice of infant communion and Christ's words at John 6:54, something that Augustine likewise has done on occasion (see, e.g., *pecc. mer.* 1.20.26).

133 *ep.* 182.2 (Latin: CSEL 44:716.13–717.5; English: my translation). For an in-depth discussion of Innocent's replies and their context, see Wermelinger, *Rom und Pelagius*, 116–33.

134 See *ep.* 183.3.

135 See *ep.* 183 and Wermelinger, *Rom und Pelagius*, 131–33, as well as Pietri, *Roma christiana*, 2:1196–1212. See also Dalmon, *Un dossier*, 602ff., who helpfully explains Innocent's actions

to summon him to Rome, preferring to allow the local bishop in Palestine to deal with him if need be.[136] Further, Innocent also failed to offer an explicit condemnation of Pelagius's *De natura*, even though he reported that it was full of errors.[137] Nevertheless, the African campaign appears to have been largely successful: Pelagius and Caelestius had been condemned and would remain so until they condemned their errors. Unfortunately for Augustine and his allies, Pope Innocent did not live much longer, passing away March 12, 417.[138] Six days later, his successor, Zosimus, was elected. With Zosimus, Pelagius's and Caelestius's fortunes changed when, toward the end of the summer in 417, the new pope decided to reevaluate the cases against the two men.

Pope Zosimus and a New Hope for the Pelagians

Presumably after learning of his condemnation by Innocent, Caelestius resolved to travel to Rome to plead his case in person. Up to this point, Caelestius seems to have been based in Asia Minor, where he had recently been banished from Constantinople.[139] Marius Mercator reports the following on his whereabouts:

> [At Ephesus], Caelestius dared to seek the office of the presbyterate through stealth. Then, after some years he sought it in Constantinople at the time of the bishop Atticus, of holy memory. When he was detected in a similar fashion there, he was expelled from that aforementioned fair city thanks to the great zeal of that holy man. A letter concerning him was sent to the bishops in Asia, Thessalonica, and Carthage. We have copies of this letter

within the context of the complex ecclesial politics of the time, as well as Lamberigts, "Was Innocent Familiar," who examines the theological content of Innocent's response.

136 *ep*. 183.4. See also Wermelinger's discussion, *Rom und Pelagius*, 132.

137 *ep*. 183.5. Löhr notes that Innocent appears hesitant to discuss the book without Pelagius present, perhaps due to uncertainties about its authorship (Löhr, *Pélage et le pélagianisme*, 32).

138 See Wermelinger, *Rom und Pelagius*, 134.

139 Initially, it might seem rather odd that—assuming Mercator's report is reliable—Caelestius's banishment from Constantinople does not appear to have come into play during his trial at Rome (at least as far as we know). However, it is helpful to keep in mind that relations between Rome and Constantinople remained fragile at this point following the Chrysostom affair a decade prior (although ecclesiastical communion between the two sees seems to have been reestablished toward the end of Innocent's papacy: Pietri, *Roma christiana*, 1185n2). For more on this, see Dalmon, *Un dossier*, 602ff. See also discussion in Malavasi, *La controversia pelagiana in Oriente*, 85–86.

FROM DIOSPOLIS TO THE *TRACTORIA* 219

and are ready to provide it. Nevertheless, the aforementioned Caelestius, also banished from here [i.e., Constantinople], proceeded with all haste to the city of Rome at the time of the bishop Zosimus, of holy memory.[140]

In defense of himself and his views, Caelestius composed a *Libellus fidei* for Zosimus, presenting himself as a speculative thinker who had not desired to lead others astray. He wrote to Zosimus, "If I have fallen into some error due to ignorance, as is only human, may it be corrected by your decision."[141] The Africans appear to have learned of Caelestius's journey to Rome and wrote to Zosimus—perhaps a month or two after Zosimus's election in March 417[142]—no doubt hoping to ensure that the pope would continue the policy of his predecessor. However, a reply from Zosimus seems to have been long delayed.[143] At some point, likely late in the summer of 417, Zosimus convened a hearing for Caelestius in the basilica of St. Clement and, after the

---

140 *Commonitorium super nomine Caelestii* (Latin: ACO 1.5.1, p. 66, ln. 23–30; English: my translation). Augustine would later write *ep.* 6* to Atticus, which was a response to a letter Atticus had sent to Aurelius notifying him of actions he had taken in Constantinople against the Pelagians. However, it seems that this was different from the letter referred to by Mercator, as *ep.* 6* seems to date to 420 or later (see especially Berrouard, "Les lettres 6* et 19*," 269–77, and Duval, "Note complémentaire: Lettre 6*," BA 46B, 444–56). For more discussion of Atticus's role in the Pelagian controversy, see Malavasi, *La controversia pelagiana*, 85–97.

141 *gr. et pecc. or.* 2.23.26 (Latin: CSEL 42:185.16–17; English: Teske, WSA I/23, 432 slightly modified). (See also *gr. et pecc. or.* 2.6.7 and 2.12.13.) Caelestius's *libellus* is extant only in fragments: see *gr. et pecc. or.* 2.5.5, 2.6.6, 2.23.26 (see also Augustine's paraphrases of the *libellus*'s contents and/or repetition of elements from these fragments: *gr. et pecc. or.* 1.33.36, 2.2.2, 2.6.7, 2.12.13, 2.23.26; *c. ep. Pel.* 2.3.5, 2.4.6). Based on Augustine's comments on Caelestius's *libellus* at *gr. et pecc. or.* 2.23.26 (when compared with the content of Pelagius's *Libellus fidei*) and Zosimus's *Posteaquam a nobis* 3, it appears that Caelestius's *libellus* was similar in content to Pelagius's. At PL 48:498–505, Garnier took this presumed similarity quite literally in an attempt to reconstruct Caelestius's *libellus* based on a version of that of Pelagius. For a convincing critique of Garnier's reconstruction, see Peter van Egmond, "The Confession of Faith Ascribed to Caelestius," *Sacris Erudiri* 50 (2011): 317–39. Given the problems with Garnier's attempt that van Egmond highlights, we should hesitate to speculate too much about the degree to which Pelagius and Caelestius coordinated their appeals. As a result, there is no need to hypothesize that Caelestius traveled to Palestine to meet with Pelagius before returning to Rome (see, e.g., Squires, *The Pelagian Controversy*, 140n347).

142 See Wermelinger, *Rom und Pelagius*, 151–52, for a helpful chart detailing the (hypothesized) epistolary exchanges between Zosimus and Africa (many of these letters are no longer extant).

143 See Zosimus's comments in *Magnum pondus* 2: "Although many distractions diverted our care and attention away from the greater bonds of ecclesiastical matters, nevertheless, so that the expectation (*expectatio*) of Your Fraternity concerning the coming and examination of that aforementioned person [i.e., Caelestius] would not be drawn out longer, we set everything else aside and sat on the day of the inquiry in the basilica of St. Clement. . ." (Latin: CSEL

details of the case were reviewed, Caelestius was brought in, his *libellus* was read aloud, and he was asked to condemn the charges originally leveled against him by Paulinus, the deacon from Milan, in 411, as well as those condemned in Innocent's letters sent to the African bishops in January of 417.[144] Caelestius apparently refused to condemn the propositions brought forward by Paulinus, but "promised that he would condemn everything which [the Roman] See would condemn."[145] Caelestius also attempted to turn the tables on his opponents, suggesting that Paulinus himself was a heretic[146] and drawing attention both to the rather irregular conclusion (or lack thereof) of his trial in 411 and to the role played by Heros and Lazarus in the affair.[147] Caelestius noted that no final verdict was delivered in 411, but that it was only in 416 that the Africans issued a condemnation, prompted by the letter from Heros and Lazarus reporting what had taken place at Diospolis.[148] Caelestius further claimed that he had had no interactions with these two exiled bishops prior to the composition of their letter in 416 and that later, after he had met Heros, the bishop had apologized for misjudging someone who had not been present and who was unknown to him.[149] Some

---

35.1:99.18–23; English: my translation). This African *expectatio* is also mentioned in Zosimus, *Posteaquam a nobis* 15. See Wermelinger, *Rom und Pelagius*, 153.

144 The proceedings of this examination have not survived, but the contents can be reconstructed to some degree from Paulinus of Milan, *Libellus aduersus Caelestium* (CSEL 35.1:108–111), Augustine's *gr. et pecc. or.* 2.5.5–2.7.8 and *c. ep. Pel.* 2.3.5–2.4.8, Zosimus's *Magnum pondus* (CSEL 35.1:99–103), as well as Marius Mercator's *Commonitorium super nomine Caelestii* (ACO 1.5.1, p. 66 ln. 29–43). See also Wermelinger's detailed narration and discussion of Caelestius's hearing and the subsequent events: *Rom und Pelagius*, 141ff.

145 *gr. et pecc. or.* 2.7.8: *immo se omnia, quae sedes illa damnaret, damnaturum esse promisit* (Latin: CSEL 42:171.12–13; English: Teske, WSA I/23, 422). See also *c. ep. Pel.* 2.3.5, 2.4.8, and *c. Iul.* 6.12.37. Augustine suggests that it was this promise by Caelestius that led Zosimus to show generous leniency to him (Caelestius), despite his apparent rejection of the doctrine of original sin in his *libellus* (see *gr. et pecc.* 2.6.6–7). For more discussion of this passage, see below when we consider *De gratia Christi*.

146 See Paulinus, *Libellus aduersus Caelestium* 5 (CSEL 35.1:109.7–8). Zosimus seems to have been unwilling to entertain accusations against Paulinus. It should be noted, though, that Paulinus was orally requested to travel to Rome later in the fall of 417, as we shall see. So perhaps Caelestius's accusation did produce some uncertainty in Zosimus's mind.

147 See Zosimus, *Magnum pondus* 4 (CSEL 35.1:100.13ff).

148 See Augustine, *ep.* 175.1, as well as Zosimus, *Magnum pondus* 4. This letter from Heros and Lazarus was, in turn, submitted to Innocent along with *ep.* 175.

149 Zosimus, *Magnum pondus* 4 (CSEL 35.1:100.17–22). It is unclear when or where Caelestius met Heros.

FROM DIOSPOLIS TO THE *TRACTORIA* 221

background information on Heros and Lazarus seems to have then been provided: they had illicitly obtained the episcopacy in Gaul, then abdicated it, and finally were excommunicated by Zosimus himself.[150] This profile of Heros and Lazarus revealed that the case against Caelestius rested on a very shaky foundation—namely, the testimony of two less-than-reputable, excommunicated, former bishops with a history of questionable conduct. Given (1) that Caelestius had expressed a willingness to change his views if required, promising to condemn what the Apostolic See would condemn,[151] (2) that he had submitted two *libelli* (one at Carthage in 411 and another to Zosimus in 417) that seemed orthodox to Zosimus, and (3) that his accusers were unreliable witnesses,[152] the case against Caelestius seems to have fallen to pieces in Zosimus's mind.

Shortly after Caelestius's hearing, Zosimus received another appeal, this one from Pelagius, which was supported by a letter from Praylus, John's successor as bishop of Jerusalem.[153] Although he had opted not to travel to Rome, Pelagius's appeal was otherwise much like Caelestius's, offering the pope a profession of faith (his *Libellus fidei*) as part of his letter.[154] In that profession of faith, as seems to have been the case with Caelestius's,[155] Pelagius mainly focused on announcing his (uncontroversial) positions on Christological, Trinitarian, and other creedal topics—although a few statements toward the

150 Zosimus, *Magnum pondus* 5 (CSEL 35.1:100.28–101.4).

151 Augustine and Marius Mercator both emphasize this point as a reason for Zosimus's decision. See, e.g., Augustine, *gr. et pecc. or.* 2.6.7–2.7.8, and Mercator, *Commonitorium super nomine Caelestii* (ACO 1.5.1, p. 66, ln. 31ff.). (It should be noted that Mercator's account is slightly different from Augustine's: Mercator claims that Caelestius promised to condemn the propositions from Carthage.)

152 Pietri emphasizes the negative effect that Heros and Lazarus had on Zosimus's view of the case (*Roma christiana*, 1224–25).

153 See Zosimus, *Posteaquam a nobis* 1–2 (CSEL 35.1:103.7–17). John of Jerusalem had died on January 17, 417.

154 Pelagius had apparently sent his letter before word of Innocent's death (March 12) reached Palestine as it was addressed to him and not Zosimus. An edition of Pelagius's profession of faith (*Libellus fidei*) is found at van Egmond, "Haec fides est," 377–82. Pelagius's letter to Innocent is now extant only in fragments found in Augustine's *gr. et pecc. or.* See *gr. et pecc. or.* 1.30.32, 1.31.33, 1.31.34, 1.35.38, 1.36.39, 1.37.40, 1.41.45, 2.17.19, 2.18.20, 2.19.21, and 2.20.22. It seems possible that Pelagius had also sent along to Rome several of his works to which he had referred in his letter: a letter to Paulinus of Nola, a letter to a bishop named Constantius, the letter to Demetrias, as well as the four books of *Pro libero arbitrio* (see *gr. et pecc. or.* 1.35.38, 1.36.39, 1.37.40, 1.41.45).

155 See Augustine's comments on Caelestius's *libellus* at *gr. et pecc. or.* 2.23.26.

end of the *libellus* were of more relevance for the controversy at hand.[156] He concluded his profession by writing,

> This is the faith, most blessed Pope, which we learned in the Catholic Church and which we have always held, and which we now hold. In this, if something has perhaps been posited less skillfully or not cautiously enough, we wish to be corrected by you, who hold both the faith and the see of Peter. But if our confession is approved by the judgment of your apostleship, whoever wanted to dishonor me will prove himself ignorant, or spiteful, or even not a Catholic—but he will not prove me a heretic.[157]

Zosimus had Pelagius's appeal read out publicly, and, apparently, upon hearing it, all present were convinced of Pelagius's orthodoxy.[158] For Zosimus, the untrustworthy figures of Heros and Lazarus again loomed large in the case against Pelagius: with their credibility shot, and with Pelagius's *libellus* apparently containing nothing problematic, Zosimus determined that the case against Pelagius had been a sham and recognized him as orthodox.

It is sometimes suggested that Zosimus was of Greek origin (given his name) and, as a result, may have been more open to Pelagian ideas.[159] But, as Mathijs Lamberigts helpfully points out in response to such arguments, Pelagius and Caelestius appear to have had the support of a number of influential people in and around Rome.[160] In my view, a more important factor for the events is Zosimus's seeming lack of interest in the nuances of the theological debate—a factor Laurence Dalmon has noted.[161] Note, for example, Zosimus's apparent approval of Caelestius's *libelli*. In *Magnum pondus*, Zosimus writes,

---

156 For example, at *Libellus fidei* 17 Pelagius writes, "We hold one baptism, which we say must be celebrated with the same words of the sacrament in infants as in older people" (Latin: van Egmond, "Haec fides est," 381; English: my translation). And a bit later, at *Libellus fidei* 25: "We confess free choice in such a way that we say that we always need the help of God" (Latin: van Egmond, "Haec fides est," 381; English: my translation). Pelagius in this context also takes care to distinguish his position from that of the Manichees as well as that of Jovinian.

157 Pelagius, *Libellus fidei* 26 (Latin: van Egmond, "Haec fides est," 382; English: my translation). Much like Caelestius, Pelagius emphasized his willingness to accept the pope's correction.

158 See Zosimus, *Posteaquam a nobis* 3 (CSEL 35.1:103.17–28).

159 See, e.g., Gerald Bonner, *St. Augustine of Hippo: Life and Controversies* (Norfolk: Canterbury Press, 1963), 341.

160 See Lamberigts, "Co-operation of Church and State," 364n4.

161 See Dalmon, *Un dossier*, 212 for more on this point. She notes, for instance, that Zosimus's letters to the Africans are focused almost entirely on administrative and juridic matters, with little consideration of the theological issues.

FROM DIOSPOLIS TO THE *TRACTORIA*

The earlier *libellus* given by [Caelestius] in your presence in Africa also should have been considered testimony to his faith; nor should one so easily believe unexamined accusations and matters circulated by rumor. Therefore, within two months either let them come who can prove that the man in question [i.e., Caelestius] thinks differently than how he presented it in his *libelli* and profession of faith. Or, let Your Holiness recognize that no doubts remain after these things, so clear and manifest, which he has produced.[162]

These comments are, in a certain sense, rather odd—there are a few pieces to the puzzle that do not quite fit. As Augustine will note later, in the *libellus* delivered to Zosimus, Caelestius clearly rejected the notion that sin is passed on *ex traduce*.[163] Given that fact, it seems that Zosimus's approval of the *libelli* would indicate that he shared Caelestius's view. But, if that were the case, why had Zosimus earlier in the proceedings attempted to have Caelestius condemn the propositions brought against him by Paulinus in 411 when several of these focused on the effects of Adam's sin?[164] It seems more likely to me that Zosimus simply did not have a good grasp of the theological issues at stake—and had little interest in digging more deeply into the details. First, Caelestius's denial of the transmission of sin was sufficiently vague enough (he did not specifically mention Adam or explain how or whether his sin impacted his descendants) that it may not have seemed to conflict with Paulinus's accusations in Zosimus's mind (as most of these accusations focused specifically on Adam and the effects of his sin). Second, in both *libelli* Caelestius seems to have attempted to refocus the accusations against him by affirming that he believed that infants should be baptized

---

162 *Magnum pondus* 8 (Latin: CSEL 35.1:101.25–102.6; English: my translation).

163 "We said that infants ought to be baptized for the forgiveness of sins not so that we would seem to support [the notion of] a sin arising from transmission [*ex traduce*]. This is far removed from the Catholic understanding since sin is not born with a human being but is later committed by a human being—because it is not a fault of nature but belongs to the will. It is necessary to confess the former to be appropriate [i.e., infant baptism for the forgiveness of sins] lest we seem to create different kinds of baptism; and it is necessary to defend against the latter [i.e., the notion of a sin arising from transmission], lest, on account of the sacrament (and with an injustice done to the Creator), an evil is said to be transmitted to a human being through nature before it is committed by the human being" (*gr. et pecc. or.* 2.6.6 [Latin: CSEL 42:170.13–22; English: my translation]).

164 See Paulinus, *Libellus aduersus Caelestium* 4, and *c. ep. Pel.* 2.4.6. Wermelinger also draws attention to the apparent contradictions of Zosimus' handling of Caelestius's case: "Das Pelagiusdossier in der Tractoria des Zosimus," *Freiburger Zeitschrift für Philosophie und Theologie* 26 (1979): 355.

for the forgiveness of sins—a statement of clear orthodoxy that Zosimus, seemingly uninterested in investigating exactly to what "sins" Caelestius was referring, could readily accept as proof of the falsity of the accusations against him.[165] In his own appeal, Pelagius would do the same and would go a bit further by claiming that his opponents accused him of teaching that infants do not need to be baptized and that some could enter the kingdom of heaven without baptism.[166] Given all of this, Zosimus clearly felt Caelestius's *libelli* were sufficient to disprove the accusations against him and hoped that the Africans, upon further reflection, would agree—or, more accurately, he thought that the Africans *should* agree.[167] In any event, Zosimus seems to have had little patience for theological intricacies: as he concludes his letter *Magnum pondus*, he characterizes the whole affair as a foolish dispute and urges the African bishops to stick to what is taught in scripture.[168] As Dalmon writes, commenting on Zosimus's view of Caelestius's *libellus fidei*, "The naïve remark qualifying the *libellus fidei* of Caelestius ('is there a single passage which does not mention grace or divine aid?') would betray less the pope's Pelagian sensibility than his pure and simple lack of theological sensibility."[169]

Having examined the cases of Caelestius and Pelagius, Zosimus wrote two letters to the African bishops in September of 417 to inform them of his actions.[170] In both letters, Zosimus focused on the misdeeds of Heros and Lazarus, clearly portraying the ex-bishops as the root cause of the deceitful

---

165 It is worth noting what Zosimus writes in *Magnum pondus* when he recalls Caelestius's *libellus* being read aloud in his presence: "When Caelestius was let in, we had the *libellus* that he had submitted read. And not satisfied with this, we examined repeatedly whether he spoke in his heart or on his lips these things which he had written" (Latin: CSEL 35.1:100.7–9; English: my translation). With this, Zosimus seems to assume that Caelesitus's *libellus* was itself perfectly orthodox and that the more serious question was whether Caelestius actually believed what he had professed to believe in the *libellus*.

166 See *gr. et pecc. or.* 2.17.19ff. for Augustine's discussion. Augustine notes that he had never accused Pelagius of holding such positions and suspected that Pelagius was attempting to sidestep the real accusations against him so as to defend himself more easily.

167 On this, Wermelinger suggests that Zosimus's "hopes" for African agreement with his decision are more strategic than earnest: by suggesting that the Africans would surely agree with his decision, Zosimus attempted to make his verdict more palatable—see *Rom und Pelagius*, 153.

168 See *Magnum pondus* 9 (CSEL 35.1:102.6–16).

169 Dalmon, *Un dossier*, 212. See also pp. 213–14 for more, and Pietri, *Roma christiana*, 1222ff, which Dalmon cites in support.

170 See Zosimus, *Magnum pondus* (regarding Caelestius) and *Posteaquam a nobis* (regarding Pelagius). *Magnum pondus* is undated, but was likely composed shortly before *Posteaquam a nobis*, which bears the date of September 21.

FROM DIOSPOLIS TO THE *TRACTORIA*

cases—although he did not shy away from critiquing the Africans for being unduly hasty and for believing rumors and the lies of untrustworthy witnesses.[171] Zosimus made no reference to Innocent or his letters.[172] It seems that in Zosimus's view, as Geoffrey Dunn has convincingly argued, given the faulty premises of the cases against Pelagius and Caelestius, there was no need to give attention to Innocent's decisions, as he had not sufficiently investigated the source of the accusations.[173] The letters also offered very little in the way of theological analysis—Zosimus seems to have found the whole dispute rather foolish, as we noted above. In the end, since the testimony of Heros and Lazarus was at the heart of the case against Pelagius, Zosimus offered him a full exoneration, declaring to the Africans that Pelagius had never departed from the faith.[174] He also forwarded to Africa copies of the letter and *libellus fidei* Pelagius had sent to him, suggesting that they would offer ample proof of Pelagius's innocence.[175]

With Caelestius, though, things were slightly different.[176] Although Caelestius's case was also tied to Heros and Lazarus in important ways—and

171 See, e.g., *Magnum pondus* 4, and *Posteaquam a nobis* 7.

172 The closest he comes to mentioning Innocent and his requirements for Pelagius's and Caelestius's readmission to the Church is at *Posteaquam a nobis* 15, where he suggests to the African bishops that his examination of the cases is sufficient for satisfying the Africans' *expectatio* that Pelagius and Caelestius "condemn the things that should be condemned and follow the things that should be followed" (Latin: CSEL 35.1:107.23–24; English: my translation).

173 See Geoffrey Dunn, "Did Zosimus Pardon Caelestius?" in Lex et religio: *XL Incontro di Studiosi dell'Antichità Cristiana* (Roma, 10-12 *maggio 2012)* (Rome: Institutum Patristicum Augustinianum, 2013), 654–55. No doubt Zosimus also wished to avoid explicitly critiquing his predecessor's handling of the cases. A different perspective is offered by Josef Lössl, who argues that Zosimus saw himself as simply continuing Innocent's policy (*Julian von Aeclanum*, 262ff.). However, if that were the case, why did Zosimus not mention Innocent and his decision explicitly?

174 See Zosimus, *Posteaquam a nobis* 15–16.

175 See Zosimus, *Posteaquam a nobis* 17.

176 Augustine's various accounts of the events of 417 suggest a difference between the cases of Caelestius and Pelagius. With Pelagius, Augustine only states that the British ascetic had temporarily succeeded in deceiving the Apostolic See (*gr. et pecc. or.* 2.21.24). However, his discussions of Caelestius's case are much more detailed and suggest some hesitancy on Zosimus's part to exonerate Caelestius fully (see *gr. et pecc. or.* 2.6.7–2.7.8 and *c. ep. Pel.* 2.3.5–2.4.8). My analysis of Caelestius's case differs from Wermelinger's (*Rom und Pelagius*, 145 and 262), who argues that Zosimus required the Africans to scrap all charges against both Pelagius and Caelestius (see also Lamberigts, "Augustine and Julian of Eclanum on Zosimus," 318). It also differs from Dunn's ("Did Zosimus Pardon Caelestius?," 655), who argues that Zosimus overturned Caelestius's condemnations from 417 (Innocent), 416 (Carthage), and 411 (Carthage). I would agree with Dunn in regard to the condemnations from 416 and 417, but it

226   AUGUSTINE IN THE PELAGIAN CONTROVERSY

although Zosimus appears to have been persuaded of Caelestius's orthodoxy by the *libelli* he had presented in 411 and 417 as well as by his in-person explanations—the pope seems to have recognized that, unlike the case against Pelagius, the one against Caelestius found its legal origins not with the two exiled bishops but with the Africans in 411. Perhaps as a result, Zosimus decided to offer the Africans two months to send any of Caelestius's accusers to Rome so as to supply evidence that Caelestius was lying or thought differently than his *libelli* and verbal declarations at his hearing seemed to suggest.[177] A subdeacon named Basiliscus delivered Zosimus's letters to Africa, likely sometime in mid-to-late October and, on November 2, shortly before his departure, orally informed Paulinus of Milan that he should travel to Rome to appear before Pope Zosimus.[178] Contrary to Zosimus's hopes,

---

seems that the situation was different with the trial in 411: unlike the other two, it had solid legal footing, even if there were irregularities in its conclusion that needed to be addressed. These irregularities are what prompted Zosimus to grant the Africans a two-month window to re-submit evidence for the case.

177 See Zosimus, *Magnum pondus* 8, quoted above. Zosimus sent the *gesta* of Caelestius's hearing along with this letter (see *Magnum pondus* 3). It seems likely that Zosimus recognized he did not have sufficient legal basis to dismiss the case against Caelestius completely and allowed the Africans this brief period to reargue their case on valid grounds, hoping, given the new information offered by Caelestius's *libellus* and the *gesta*, that they would decline and that, thus, the final loose end in the case would be tied up. Zosimus, however, failed to grasp just how strong African opposition to Caelestius was. (I suspect that this misjudgment stemmed, at least in part, from Zosimus's failure to understand the real theological disagreement— see discussion above.) Despite Zosimus's apparent sense that Caelestius had been wrongly accused of holding to heretical positions, he seems to have postponed revoking Caelestius's excommunication (as Augustine reports at *gr. et pecc. or.* 2.7.8), perhaps planning to wait until after Africa responded to exonerate him fully. For some discussion of Zosimus's legal views, see Laurence Dalmon, "Le pape Zosime et la tradition juridique romaine," *Eruditio Antiqua* 1 (2009): 141–54.

178 See Paulinus of Milan, *Libellus aduersus Caelestium* 10: "I have sent this *libellus* since Basiliscus the subdeacon, who was sent by Your Beatitude with the acts of the Apostolic See, gave me a summons (albeit orally) at Carthage on November 2 to come to the Apostolic See for the judgment of Your Holiness (to whom it was suggested that I had had recourse). I would promise not to be absent if the decision delivered had been against me and not for me." (*quem idcirco direxi, quia me, licet sermone, Basiliscus subdiaconus a tua beatitudine cum gestis sedis apostolicae directus Carthagine conuenit quarto Nonas Nouembris die, ut adessem ad apostolicam sedem et tuae iudicio sanctitatis, ad quam me fugisse suggestum est, nec defuturum fore promitterem, si aduersum me et non pro me fuisset lata sententia*) (Latin: CSEL 35.1:110.22–28; English: my translation). The Latin of Paulinus's *libellus* is not always straightforward, but I think Lamberigts has misinterpreted this passage when he says that Zosimus "even lets the deacon Paulinus know in quite clear language that he should not be thinking of coming to Rome" ("Augustine and Julian of Eclanum on Zosimus," 320). Paulinus seems to have decided he had no reason to go to Rome since it was Caelestius who was appealing a decision, not

FROM DIOSPOLIS TO THE *TRACTORIA* 227

the communications from Rome were not met with humble acceptance in Africa, to say the least.

Africa's Response to Zosimus

As we have already noted above, the African bishops seem to have written to Zosimus at least once in the early months of his papacy to confirm that Innocent's policies vis-à-vis Pelagius and Caelestius would be maintained. No doubt when they failed to receive an immediate reply, Augustine and his allies began to worry. Perhaps some of that worry can be glimpsed in Augustine's *s.* 131, delivered in Carthage on Sunday, September 23, 417 (and thus shortly before the arrival of Basiliscus with the letters from Zosimus).[179] Having offered a homily revolving around the theme of grace and warning of the dangers of those who oppose this gift of God, Augustine concludes with the following:

> My brothers, share in my concern. When you find such people, do not hide them. Let there be no perverse mercy in you. By all means, when you find such people, do not hide them. Argue against them when they oppose you, and when they resist take them to us. For already about this matter [the reports of] two councils have been sent to the Apostolic See. From there, too, rescripts have come. The case is over. If only the error would be over at some point, too. Therefore, let us warn them that they may pay attention, let us teach them that they may be instructed, let us pray for them that they may be converted.[180]

Paulinus himself. In the literature there also seems to be some confusion about the date on which Basiliscus arrived in Africa and delivered Zosimus's letters. Many, basing themselves on Paulinus's *libellus* suggest that Basiliscus arrived on November 2 (see, e.g., Dalmon, *Un dossier*, 74; Squires, *Pelagian Controversy*, 140; Teske, WSA I/23, 376). However, it seems more likely that Basiliscus had arrived earlier, and that November 2 was instead the day when he met with Paulinus (see, e.g., Lancel, *Saint Augustine*, 338; Wermelinger, *Rom und Pelagius*, 153–54). Basiliscus seems to have departed within a few days after November 2, because by the time Paulinus sent his reply to Zosimus on November 8 a new messenger was required—the Carthaginian subdeacon Marcellinus (see Paulinus, *Libellus aduersus Caelestium* 13). This flurry of activity at the beginning of November may have been prompted by a desire to avoid dangerous travel during the *mare clausum* period that lasted from November 11 through March 10 (see Wermelinger, *Rom und Pelagius*, 154n92).

179 For more on *s.* 131 see Gert Partoens, "Le Sermon 131 de saint Augustin. Introduction et édition," *Augustiniana* 54 (2004): 35–77.

180 *s.* 131.10: *Fratres mei, compatimini mecum. Vbi tales inueneritis, occultare nolite, non sit in uobis peruersa misericordia; prorsus, ubi tales inueneritis, occultare nolite. Redarguite*

Augustine's statement here has at times been interpreted as evidence that he believed the Roman pontiff held a special authority to put an end to doctrinal debate.[181] That thorny question aside, it seems to me that we can identify a few of Augustine's aims with these words given the broader historical context. First, by pointing out that the Africans had submitted their conciliar decisions to Rome and that Rome had confirmed them, Augustine is indicating, once again, that "anti-Pelagianism" is not simply something supported by him and his immediate allies in Africa: it has garnered the support of the Apostolic See itself. Second, and perhaps more importantly, in citing this fact Augustine seems to be pushing back against rumors of Zosimus's about-face that had likely already begun circulating in Africa.[182] Innocent, Augustine argues, had already issued his decision on the matter and, despite the rumors, Zosimus would surely follow the policy of his predecessor. As it turned out, Augustine was wrong.

Basiliscus's arrival prompted swift action by the African episcopacy. No doubt following a flurry of messages amongst key bishops, the Africans sent an initial response to Zosimus with Basiliscus upon his departure on or

---

contradicentes et resistentes ad nos perducite. Iam enim de hac causa duo concilia missa sunt ad Sedem apostolicam; inde etiam rescripta uenerunt. Causa finita est: error utinam aliquando finiatur! Ergo ut aduertant, monemus; ut instruantur, docemus; ut mutentur, oremus (Latin: Partoens, "Le sermon 131," 77.161–66; English: my translation).

181 Hence the popular reformulation of Augustine's words: *Roma locuta, causa finita est*. See, e.g., Wermelinger, *Rom und Pelagius*, 153–54, for some discussion. Wermelinger suggests that Augustine's emphasis is not so much on Roman supremacy, but on the shared action between Africa and Rome against the Pelagians. Now is not the place to launch into a full discussion of this difficult and much-debated topic; however, I would like to suggest that Augustine's emphasis in the passage quoted above seems to me to be on the Africans' submission of their decision to Rome and the Roman confirmation of the African decision. As a result, the role of Rome looms large here. Contrast this with Hill's translation, which (incorrectly, I think) treats the passage in a way that suggests more of a balance between Africa and Rome by making the first clause into two independent clauses: "You see, there have already been two councils about this matter, and their decisions sent to the Apostolic See; from there rescripts have been sent back here" (Hill, WSA III/4, 322).

182 See, e.g., Bonner, *Augustine: Life and Controversies*, 342–43, and Wermelinger, *Rom und Pelagius*, 153–54. It is worth noting that Augustine seems to have delivered a number of other sermons with anti-Pelagian in Carthage during September and October of 417: see *s*. 163 (September 24); *s*. 26 (September 25 or October 18?); *ss*. 165, 30, and 151 (late September or early October); *s*. 152 (one day after *s*. 151); *s*. 153 (October 13); *s*. 154 (October 14); *s*. 155 (October 15); *ss*. 150 and 156 (October 17). It is possible *ss*. 157–59 were delivered sometime shortly after *s*. 156. For these dates and discussion, see Josef Lössl, "Dating Augustine's Sermons 151–156: Internal Evidence," in *Sancti Aurelii Augustini: Sermones in Epistolas Apostolicas I*, CCSL 41Ba, ed. G. Partoens (Turnhout: Brepols, 2008), xxiii–lv.

FROM DIOSPOLIS TO THE *TRACTORIA*

shortly after November 2. This *obtestatio* seems to have requested a "freeze" of sorts for the case against Caelestius: Zosimus was asked to delay moving forward with a decision and, for the time being, to keep everything in the state it had been.[183] A few days later, a second messenger, Marcellinus, a Carthaginian subdeacon, left from Africa bearing a more extensive bundle of correspondence, including Paulinus of Milan's reply to Zosimus's request that he travel to Rome and an apparently large packet of documentation (*uolumen*) put together by a speedily-organized African council that seems to have been held at the end of October or beginning of November.[184] The contents of this *uolumen* have been lost; however, its main themes can be gleaned from references elsewhere.[185] For example, a few years later, Augustine writes that, in the letter sent to Rome, the African bishops had argued,

183 See Zosimus, *Quamuis patrum* 5 and, especially, 6, where he refers to the African *obtestatio*. It appears that Zosimus had sent an initial response to the *obtestatio* before he received the *uolumen* given his comments *Quamuis patrum* 5 (see Dalmon, *Un dossier*, 500, who proposes this; Wermelinger seems to have missed this document in his list of the exchanges between Rome and Africa: *Rom und Pelagius*, 151–52).

184 See Paulinus of Milan, *Libellus aduersus Caelestium*, as well as Zosimus, *Quamuis patrum* 5. Pietri argues that the Africans chose to send this dossier with the African Marcellinus for political reasons and not because Basiliscus had already departed (Pietri, *Roma christiana*, 2:1227n5). Although it does seem likely to me that Basiliscus had already left with the *obtestatio*, I suspect that Pietri is on the right track here: the Africans delayed and sent the *uolumen* and Paulinus's *libellus* with an African messenger, preferring to trust one of their own with this more critical packet of documents.

185 See Wermelinger, *Rom und Pelagius*, 155ff. From most of the references to the contents of the *uolumen* available to us (see especially Augustine, *c. ep. Pel.* 2.3.5; Paulinus of Milan, *Libellus aduersus Caelestium* 8; Zosimus, *Quamuis patrum*; Marius Mercator, *Commonitorium super nomine Caelestii* [ACO 1.5.1, p. 66, ln. 37ff]), it appears as though the document(s) focused on the case of Caelestius, which was, admittedly, the only case Zosimus had left open to African input. However, several scholars have suggested that the *uolumen* also contained information relevant to Pelagius's case: see, e.g., Wermelinger, *Rom und Pelagius*, 155n94; Dalmon, *Un dossier*, 75. Augustine does note at *gr. et pecc. or.* 2.8.9 that the African synod had mentioned Innocent's opinion of Pelagius's behavior at Diospolis in their response to Zosimus. The African council's response to Zosimus is also mentioned in the context of a discussion of Pelagius is at *gr. et pecc. or.* 2.21.24. But there, Augustine tells us nothing about the contents of these *rescripta*. It would be exceedingly odd if the Africans made no attempt to change Zosimus's mind on the case of Pelagius—and yet the evidence (which, admittedly, is quite fragmentary) suggests the *uolumen* had little to do with him. Perhaps the Africans focused on the case of Caelestius and then said something to the effect of "these same arguments can be applied equally to Pelagius." Or better, perhaps they simply relied on the activity of third parties to change Zosimus's opinion of Pelagius (such seems to be suggested by *gr. et pecc. or.* 2.21.24).

It was not enough for slower and more cautious minds that Caelestius stated that he gave his global assent to the letters of Bishop Innocent but that he ought to openly anathematize those incorrect statements which he put in his *libellus*, lest, if he did not do this, many of the less intelligent would believe that the Apostolic See had approved rather than corrected those poisons to the faith which were found in his *libellus*. That See had, after all, declared the *libellus* Catholic, because Caelestius had answered that he agreed with the letters of Pope Innocent.[186]

Paulinus's reply to Zosimus—his *Libellus aduersus Caelestium*—also likely reflects some of the main arguments of the African council.[187] Indeed, due to its argumentation, it seems probable that Paulinus's letter was drafted under the close supervision of Augustine.[188] At the beginning of this letter, Paulinus emphasizes the fact that Innocent had condemned Pelagius and Caelestius, and that Zosimus had followed Innocent's judgment when he ordered Caelestius to condemn the propositions of which he had been accused.[189] In this way, Paulinus attempts to depict Zosimus as his ally. He then goes on to note that Zosimus and Innocent do not stand alone in their opposition to Pelagianism.

> Already now Caelestius has a case not with me but with the whole Church of God (as the documents of the African bishops given to your Beatitude testify[190]), when he strives to come against the judgment of the Apostle by denying original sin. This sin passed into all men and, until the end of the world, contains the inheritance of that Adam who first sinned. In the case of infants, unless this sin is forgiven through the sacrament of baptism, they cannot possess eternal life and the kingdom of heaven. Against him even his teacher Pelagius litigates, since in an eastern trial Pelagius condemned those very things that Caelestius tries to affirm in his meeting with the Apostolic See. He has against himself also very many ancient Catholic teachers of the Churches—both eastern and western, southern

---

186 *c. ep. Pel.* 2.3.5 (Latin: CSEL 60:464.21–465.2; English: Teske, WSA I/24, 144 with some modifications).

187 So argues Wermelinger, *Rom und Pelagius*, 155.

188 See Wermelinger, *Rom und Pelagius*, 156. See also Paredi's comments: "The *libellus Paulini* is very skillful: perhaps the wording of the refusal sent to the pope was composed by the bishops [Aurelius and Augustine] themselves" ("Paulinus of Milan," 211).

189 See Paulinus, *Libellus aduersus Caelestium* 3–4.

190 This appears to be a reference to the *uolumen*.

FROM DIOSPOLIS TO THE *TRACTORIA* 231

and northern—who in their books would be able to teach that man about original sin, if he wants to be healed. He has the blessed martyr Cyprian, blessed Ambrose the confessor, Gregory Nazianzen, blessed Pope Innocent. He has those people who are even now present in the body who would struggle against him, if, at least, he judges himself fit for so great a contest. Or certainly he has those whom he ought to follow, if he wishes to learn right things rather than teach wicked things. He has, first of all, your Beatitude, whose judgment he had needed to obey when he heard, "Condemn!" He has, finally, those nurslings on whom he ought to have mercy—if he doesn't want to have it on himself—for whom, if I may use the words of the Martyr,[191] "not their own, but sins of another are forgiven."[192]

In a very Augustinian fashion, Paulinus notes that Caelestius finds opponents throughout the whole Church: St. Paul, Cyprian, Ambrose, Gregory, Innocent, Zosimus, and infants in need of baptism.[193] Even Pelagius, his own teacher, had condemned at Diospolis the propositions that Caelestius now refuses to condemn. The use of Cyprian's *ep.* 64 is also familiar, having been used by Augustine already in 411 in *s.* 294 (and shortly thereafter in *De peccatorum meritis* 3). All told, the core of Paulinus's letter relies on the types of arguments that Augustine has deployed throughout many of his anti-Pelagian works, aiming to show the antiquity and universality of the views defended against the Pelagians.

While the Africans engaged Zosimus directly, they also sought to raise support for their cause in and around Rome.[194] As part of this effort,

---

191 Cyprian, *ep.* 64.6 (CSEL 3.2:721.1–2).

192 Paulinus, *Libellus aduersus Caelestium* 8–9 (Latin: CSEL 35.1:109.27–110.19; English: my translation). Regarding the emphasis on original sin here (and, apparently, in the *uolumen*), Wermelinger writes, "For the first time in an African letter to the Roman Church the teaching on 'peccatum originale' is openly presented as the apostolic Faith and justified by Scripture and Tradition" (*Rom und Pelagius*, 156). Original sin was not the primary focus of the letters to Innocent.

193 The inclusion of Gregory of Nazianzus here is an interesting one, as Augustine had not yet quoted anything from Gregory in his anti-Pelagian works. He will do so later, though, in his efforts against Julian. It seems likely that Augustine had begun to search out quotations from other well-known ecclesial figures to bolster his argumentation. Wermelinger suggests that the African *uolumen* included relevant quotations from the authors Paulinus mentions (*Rom und Pelagius*, 276).

194 See Augustine's suggestive comments at *gr. et pecc. or.* 2.21.24: "After the written responses from the council of Africa, into which province that deadly doctrine had wended its way, though it was not very widely spread or very deeply rooted, other teachings of his [i.e., Pelagius's] were made known in the city of Rome through the concern of some believing brothers"

232 AUGUSTINE IN THE PELAGIAN CONTROVERSY

Augustine and Alypius composed a lengthy letter to Paulinus of Nola (*ep.* 186).[195] Another letter (no longer extant[196]) seems to have been sent by them to Juliana of the *gens Anicia*, who, I suspect, was back in Italy by this point.[197] A second letter to Juliana (*ep.* 188) would follow in the spring of 418.[198] These letters are significant as they are addressed to influential and well-connected Christians in and around Rome with a known history of favorable relations

---

(Latin: CSEL 42:183.4–9; English: Teske, WSA I/23, 430 slightly modified). I suspect that these third-party agents were especially focused on changing Zosimus's mind on Pelagius, while the Africans focused on Caelestius (see n. 185 above).

195 The dating of *ep.* 186 is a bit uncertain. An absolute *terminus post quem* is March 417, as Innocent had already died by the time the letter was written (see *ep.* 186.1.2; Teske incorrectly dates the letter to the middle of 416— WSA II/3, 186). A *terminus ante quem* is the summer of 418, before the publication of Zosimus's *Tractoria*: surely the *Tractoria* would have been mentioned if it had already been published. Given Pelagius's appeal to his letter to Paulinus as proof of his orthodoxy in his letter to Innocent, it seems likely that Augustine and Alypius wrote to Paulinus only after receiving Pelagius's letter to Innocent. For more, see Wermelinger's analysis of the letter in connection with the accusations of Zosimus (*Rom und Pelagius*, 160ff.), as well as Pierre Descotes's analysis ("Saint Augustin et la crise pélagienne: Le témoignage de la correspondance," *Revue d'études augustiniennes et patristiques* 56 [2010]: 199–208). See also Trout's discussion of Paulinus's relations with Pelagius (and Julian): *Paulinus of Nola*, 227–34.

196 This (lost) letter should be distinguished from Augustine and Alypius's *ep.* 188 to Juliana (see, e.g., Wermelinger, *Rom und Pelagius*, 205n353). From comments in *ep.* 188, which should probably be dated to the spring of 418 (see Hombert, *Nouvelles recherches*, 227n55, who prefers a date in early 418 rather than late 417 given the letter's close relationship with *s.* 284, dated to May 8, 418), it seems to me that Augustine and Alypius had sent an initial letter to Juliana (obliquely?) warning her of the Pelagian heresy in late 417 (around, I would suggest, the same time as *ep.* 186 to Paulinus), likely after receiving Pelagius's letter to Innocent from Zosimus, where the British ascetic mentioned his letter to Demetrias (see *gr. et pecc. or.* 1.37.40 for the relevant fragment and *ep.* 188.14 where Pelagius's letter to Innocent seems to be mentioned again). In any event, perhaps in March or April of 418 (after the conclusion of the *mare clausum* period?), they received Juliana's reply, in which she professed her family's freedom from any taint of heresy or association with heretics (see *ep.* 188.1.3). Augustine and Alypius then responded with *ep.* 188, making their warnings against Pelagius more explicit by citing and refuting a key passage from Pelagius's *ep. ad Demetriadem* and requesting confirmation (1) that this passage was, in fact, from the letter to Demetrias and (2) that the *Anicii* had received Pelagius's letter. For more on *ep.* 188, see Ogliari, "An Anti-Pelagian *caueat*."

197 We do not know for sure when or even if Juliana had returned to Italy (see Dunn, "Christian Networks of the Aniciae," 60–61, but also Ogliari, "An Anti-Pelagian *caueat*," 206), but the correspondence between Augustine and Alypius and Juliana strikes me as something carried out over a long distance.

198 See n. 196 above.

FROM DIOSPOLIS TO THE *TRACTORIA* 233

with Pelagius.[199] Without denying that Augustine and Alypius were honestly concerned for their acquaintances' orthodoxy and spiritual health,[200] the decision to write to Paulinus and Juliana at this moment also seems to have been motivated by their desire to erode support for the British ascetic at a crucial point in the controversy when all hung in the balance. Given its length, the letter to Paulinus deserves some closer attention.

It is unclear when Augustine learned of Paulinus's interactions with Pelagius.[201] It may have been the arrival of Zosimus's letter and the accompanying documentation from Pelagius (especially the letter to Pope Innocent which included a reference to Pelagius's letter to Paulinus[202]) that spurred him to write to his occasional correspondent. However, another key factor may

---

199 See our discussion of Paulinus and the *Anicii* in Chapter 1, as well as our discussion of *De bono uiduitatis* in Chapter 3. See also Richard Miles's consideration of the letters to Juliana and Paulinus: "'Let's (Not) Talk about It': Augustine and the Control of Epistolary Dialogue," in *The End of Ancient Dialogue*, ed. Simon Goldhill (Oxford: Oxford University Press, 2008), 135–48, esp. 141–48. Some of Miles's chronology is off (for example, he dates *ep.* 188 to 414) and his emphasis on power-politics is a bit heavy-handed, but he offers some important insights on the public nature of letter writing in the ancient world and the impact Augustine's strategic framing of his letters would have had upon this wider audience. It should be noted that around this same time, Augustine also sent a letter (*ep.* 187) to Dardanus, a former praetorian prefect in Gaul, in response to some questions he had submitted to the bishop of Hippo. As Augustine mentions in his *Retractationes*, he tailored his responses with a special concern to refute the Pelagian heresy (*retr.* 2.49). See Brown's brief discussion of Dardanus at *Augustine of Hippo*, 361–62, and *Eye of a Needle*, 378. See also the entry in J. R. Martindale, *Prosopography of the Later Roman Empire*, 2:346–47. (It is also interesting to note that this letter reveals that Dardanus had already read *De peccatorum meritis*, thus indicating its circulation on the continent—*ep.* 187.7.22.) For an analysis of the letter, see Pierre Descotes, "Saint Augustin et la crise pélagienne," 208–17. It might be speculated that Augustine had also sought to contact members of the Roman clergy like the future popes Sixtus and Celestine to gain their support. This would help to explain why both these clergymen wrote to Augustine at some point in the summer of 418 (see *epp.* 191 and 192 for Augustine's brief responses; see also Wermelinger's comments at *Rom und Pelagius*, 205).

200 Against the reading offered by Richard Miles who characterizes much of this correspondence as an exercise in power-politics (see previous note), I want to emphasize with Pierre Descotes ("Saint Augustin et la crise pélagienne," 206–8) that a letter like *ep.* 186 should not be read simply as a piece of a larger political strategy: it was surely also a genuine warning to a friend about whose spiritual health Augustine was concerned.

201 Given that Pelagius's letter to Paulinus dates to c. 405, it is possible that Augustine had learned of it long before Zosimus's letters arrived in Africa in October 417. It has also been speculated (see, e.g., Ebbeler, *Disciplining Christians*, 93) that Pelagius may have included a letter from Paulinus among those testimonial letters he presented in his defense at Diospolis (see *gest. Pel.* 29.53).

202 Assuming *ep.* 186 was written after that letter arrived. See n. 195 above.

have been the arrival in Africa of rumors that Pelagius's ideas had strong support in Nola.[203] Whatever the immediate cause(s) may have been, Alypius and Augustine clearly felt the situation pressing enough to call for a lengthy and detailed examination of several important topics of relevance to the debate.[204] Augustine and Alypius begin their letter by indicating their uncertainty about Paulinus's present disposition toward Pelagius, and then outline Augustine's history of interactions with the British ascetic and his dawning awareness of Pelagius's (heretical) views, which eventually led to the two African councils of 416 and Innocent's reply in 417 (§§1.1–1.2). They assert that Pelagius's error has been condemned by ecclesiastical authority, although some still advocate for these views (§1.3).[205] With that, Augustine and Alypius turn to a lengthy section devoted to analyzing key topics relevant to Pelagius's views: the relationship between free will, grace, and merit; the moral status of infants; and God's justice (§§2.4–7.26). However, the next part of the letter (§§8.27–9.33) is a crucial one for our purposes. Here, Augustine and Alypius target in a particular way those in Nola who are rumored to be supporters of Pelagius's opposition to original sin to such an extent that they are more willing to condemn Pelagius than to affirm that infants are born subject to the sin of Adam.[206] Although there is some theological argumentation in this section,[207] it is also filled with a number of appeals to authority. First, Augustine and Alypius note that Pelagius himself condemned propositions at Diospolis that (1) denied the existence of original sin and (2) asserted that unbaptized infants can obtain eternal life.[208] If anyone attempts to hold that second position, they argue, that person will oppose Jesus, the authority of the Apostolic See, and Pelagius's words before the bishops at Diospolis.

203 See *ep.* 186.8.29. Lancel wonders whether Julian of Eclanum (which was not far from Nola) could have been among those supporters of Pelagius about whom Augustine and Alypius had heard (Lancel, *Saint Augustine*, 414).

204 It seems possible that at least some of the specific topics relate to those discussed in Pelagius's lost letter to Paulinus from c. 405. See Wermelinger, *Rom und Pelagius*, 160.

205 The failure to mention Zosimus's actions does not, in my view, require us to date this letter before October 417. I suspect this is merely a strategic silence.

206 See *ep.* 186.8.29.

207 For example, Augustine argues that if these people reject the existence of original sin, they are forced to assert that God condemns innocent infants to eternal death should they die without baptism, as scripture indicates that one can only obtain eternal life through baptism (see *ep.* 186.8.30).

208 *ep.* 186.8.27.

FROM DIOSPOLIS TO THE *TRACTORIA*

In this way he will argue against the statement of the Lord, who says, *Your fathers ate manna in the desert and died. This is the bread coming down from heaven so that, if anyone eats it, he may not die* (John 6:49–50). . . . And a little later he says, *Truly, truly, I say to you: Unless you eat the flesh of the Son of Man and drink his blood, you will not have life in you* (John 6:54)—that life, of course, which will exist after this death.[209] And he will argue against the authority of the Apostolic See where, when it dealt with this issue, it used this testimony from the gospel lest unbaptized infants be thought capable of having life.[210] And he will argue against the words of Pelagius himself before the bishops who heard his case, the words he expressed when he condemned those who said that unbaptized infants have eternal life.[211]

In this sense, Augustine and Alypius frame these opponents of original sin as opponents of Jesus, Pope Innocent, and the statements that resulted in Pelagius's acquittal before the bishops at Diospolis. In the next paragraph, they reiterate their point, again highlighting the close connection between the teaching of the Apostolic See and that of Christ.

But if [these people in Nola] yield to the Apostolic See or rather to the very teacher and Lord of the apostles, who says that they will not have life in them unless they eat the flesh of the Son of Man and drink his blood—something that only the baptized, of course, can do—they will finally admit that unbaptized infants cannot have life and, for this reason, are still punished by eternal death, though less harshly than all those who have also committed their own sins.[212]

Shortly thereafter (§8.31), Augustine and Alypius emphasize a point that had been at the heart of Augustine's *De gestis Pelagii*: that Pelagius was only acquitted at Diospolis because he condemned certain heretical propositions. They then go on (§9.32) to cite a list of (most of) the propositions that Pelagius and the bishops had condemned at Diospolis, arguing that with this condemnation the Pelagian heresy was itself condemned.[213] All told, Augustine

---

209 Augustine's argument here relies on the practice of infant communion.

210 See *ep.* 182.5.

211 *ep.* 186.8.28 (Latin: CSEL 57:67.20–68.12; English: Teske, WSA II/3, 222).

212 *ep.* 186.8.29 (Latin: CSEL 57:68.18–69.2; English: Teske, WSA II/3, 222–23, slightly modified).

213 This list is very similar (with a few exceptions) to that offered at *gest. Pel.* 35.65.

and Alypius in this section frame those who still support Pelagius's positions as opponents of Christ, the Apostolic See, and the Synod of Diospolis.

In the remainder of their letter, Augustine and Alypius briefly argue that Pelagius's condemnation of heretical propositions at Diospolis was not genuine, given the fact that his recently published *Pro libero arbitrio* seems to contain some of the same views (§§10.34–36).[214] They then conclude their letter (§§11.37–12.41) by noting the need to argue against and pray for the Pelagians and by confessing their own belief that Paulinus surely recognizes the danger they present to the Church.

In sum, *ep.* 186 aims to win over Paulinus not only via theological argumentation but also—in a way reminiscent of *De gestis Pelagii* and *s.* 131—by suggesting that the Pelagian positions have already been condemned: by Diospolis and by Innocent. This latter strategy undergirds the former: by suggesting that Innocent and Diospolis had condemned Pelagianism, Augustine and Alypius lend authoritative credibility to their theological arguments. Further, this approach implicitly claims that opposition to Pelagius is not simply an African position (or worse, an Augustinian and Alypian preoccupation), but something universal and, indeed, grounded in the teachings of Christ himself.

*   *   *   *   *

By the end of 417, the Africans had, it seems, done all they could do to prevent Zosimus from following through on his intended course of action: they had written to the pope directly and had contacted key influencers in and around Rome. At some point they also likely appealed directly to the imperial court, perhaps hoping that secular authority would back them, even if Zosimus did not.[215] The period of *mare clausum* which applied to official trade vessels had begun on November 11—that is, shortly after the likely date of Marcellinus's departure for Rome—and would last until March 10.[216] As a result, the Africans likely suspected that no immediate response would

---

214 See below for more on Pelagius's *Pro libero arbitrio.*

215 See below and Chapter 5 for more on this.

216 See Wermelinger, *Rom und Pelagius*, 154n92. See also Perler, *Les voyages*, 68–74, who surveys various references in Augustine's writings to the times of sea travel. He notes that travel during winter was not impossible but was risky and typically was undertaken only in cases of urgent necessity (73).

FROM DIOSPOLIS TO THE *TRACTORIA* 237

be forthcoming from the Apostolic See. All they could do at this point was wait and see.

418: THE CONDEMNATION OF PELAGIANISM

Our sources for early 418 are few and far between, and we have nothing concrete until the end of April when a flurry of consequential events took place in rapid succession. First, on April 29, Zosimus's letter *Quamuis patrum* arrived in Africa from Rome. Composed on March 18,[217] Zosimus's letter offers his official response to the African *uolumen* of the previous year[218] and focuses solely on the case of Caelestius; Pelagius is not mentioned.[219] After beginning by emphasizing his Petrine authority,[220] Zosimus notes that he had freely decided to consult with the African bishops regarding the case of Caelestius, although given his special authority he had not needed to do so.[221]

217 Or perhaps March 21. The CSEL edition gives XV. Kal. April. (=March 18) but notes in the apparatus that previous editions had preferred XII. Kal. April (=March 21) (see CSEL 35.1:117.2).

218 He had apparently already responded to the African *obtestatio*—see n. 183 above.

219 See n. 185 above where I discuss the *uolumen*'s focus on Caelestius. It could be that Zosimus's decision not to mention Pelagius in his letter simply reflected the Africans' own choice to minimize discussion of Pelagius in the *uolumen* (if in fact that was the case). However, it is hard to believe that the Africans had completely avoided challenging Zosimus's exoneration of Pelagius in *Posteaquam a nobis*, whether in the *uolumen* or in some other communication now lost to us. As a result, I suspect that the silence about Pelagius was also strategic. As I will argue below, the contents of *Quamuis patrum* suggest that Zosimus was beginning to reconsider his judgment regarding Pelagius and Caelestius. However, likely for a variety of reasons, he was not yet ready to acknowledge his reconsideration publicly, perhaps in large part because he felt he first needed to head off any claims that Africa had convinced him he was wrong or had forced his hand—something that would undermine his attempts to bolster Rome's authority. Nevertheless, he likely felt pressure to calm Africa's fears (and anger) to some extent, perhaps (1) knowing that they were planning to hold a plenary council that would be strongly anti-Pelagian in its objectives and (2) wishing to avoid any increase of tensions between the Churches. In this context, he was comfortable addressing the case of Caelestius because he had left that case open to some degree in *Magnum pondus* (in the sense that he had invited the Africans to supply new evidence to substantiate their claims against Caelestius). This was not the situation with Pelagius, whom Zosimus had decisively exonerated in *Posteaquam a nobis*. To bring up Pelagius (or even the Africans' arguments against Pelagius) here in *Quamuis patrum* could suggest that Pelagius's case, too, was still open—something that would indicate that a reconsideration was in progress.

220 See Zosimus, *Quamuis patrum* 1–3.

221 See Zosimus, *Quamuis patrum* 4.

238 AUGUSTINE IN THE PELAGIAN CONTROVERSY

He then states that after reading the *uolumen*, he realized that the Africans seem to have felt that he had not examined Caelestius carefully enough.[222] So as to allow more time for deliberation, he informs the Africans that he has left everything as it was—that is, he has not officially cleared Caelestius of all charges yet.[223] Zosimus's letter is rather difficult to interpret—and has prompted some divergent opinions among scholars[224]—but it seems as

222 See Zosimus, *Quamuis patrum* 5. Zosimus's words here suggest he is rather annoyed by the Africans' apparent nit-picking: "We think and we know that every petition of his [i.e., Caelestius] has been explained in the earlier letter [i.e., *Magnum pondus*] which we sent to you. And we believed that there had been a sufficient response to that writing [i.e., the *obtestatio*] which you had written in response to that letter. But afterward we unrolled the whole *uolumen* of the letter sent through Marcellinus your subdeacon. In this letter, which we at last finished reading, you characterized the whole text of our letter in such a way as though we trusted Caelestius in all things and offered assent to his words, words which had not been scrutinized, if I may say it, down to every last syllable" (Latin: CSEL 35.1:116.14–21; English: my translation).

223 See Zosimus, *Quamuis patrum* 6: "Things which must be discussed for a long time are never finished rashly and what ought to be debated with the greatest judgment should not be decided without great deliberation. Therefore, may Your Fraternity know that after we wrote those things to you and received your letter, we changed nothing. Rather, we left everything in the same state in which it had been previously, since we indicated to Your Holiness by our letter [the initial response to the *obtestatio* mentioned at *Quamuis patrum* 5] that that request [*obtestatio*] which you had sent to us would be observed" (Latin: CSEL 35.1:116.22–117.1; English: my translation). Zosimus had originally given the Africans two months to present new evidence against Caelestius not connected with the testimony of Heros and Lazarus. Presumably, Zosimus's original plan was to clear Caelestius of all charges when those two months expired if the Africans failed to produce compelling evidence. I take his final paragraph in *Quamuis patrum* to mean that Zosimus had decided to hold off on that decision to clear Caelestius, at least for the time being.

224 For example, Wermelinger interprets *Quamuis patrum* as a rejection (or at least dismissal) of the Africans' objection contained in the *obtestatio* and *uolumen*: "Caelestius, as planned, condemned everything which he had been falsely accused of through rumor. This fact was already explained in the first two letters [i.e., *Magnum pondus* and *Posteaquam a nobis*] so that it was not necessary to respond to the *obtestatio*. The detailed letter (*uolumen*) only showed that there is a misunderstanding between the two Churches that needed to be cleared up because Africa believed that he [Zosimus] had trusted Caelestius without close examination. Since this is not the case, there is no reason to depart from the earlier decision, and thus, everything is left in the state in which it was and enough consideration was given to the African objection" (*Rom und Pelagius*, 164). Mathijs Lamberigts seems to follow Wermelinger's assessment: "Zosimus repeated that Caelestius' case was thoroughly examined—even down to the finest details and that, for that reason, no change was required. From his point of view, everything had been sufficiently explained. In other words, up to the middle of March, Zosimus knew of no compelling reasons for questioning the orthodoxy of Caelestius" (Mathijs Lamberigts, "Co-operation of Church and State in the Condemnation of the Pelagians: The Case of Zosimus," in *Religious Polemics in Context*, ed. T. L. Hettema [Leiden: Brill, 2005], 367–68). See also Squires, *The Pelagian Controversy*, 141. However, Wermelinger and Lamberigts's interpretation strikes me as a misreading of the text. At *Quamuis patrum* 6 (see

FROM DIOSPOLIS TO THE *TRACTORIA*

though he was in the process of reconsidering his position from the previous year. Zosimus is careful to emphasize that he is acting on his own initiative—that he has not been forced to any reconsideration by Africa. And yet, in a certain sense, this very ostentatious declaration of independence suggests Zosimus's own growing sense that he will have to reconsider his position publicly. However, it is unclear what precise factors were leading to Zosimus's change of mind: Was he being confronted with imperial pressure? Had the information in the *uolumen* planted seeds of doubt? Had some segment of Roman Christians succeeded in raising sizable opposition to Pelagius and Caelestius in the city? A combination of factors is likely.[225]

The world did not wait for Zosimus to make up his mind, though. The day after Zosimus's letter arrived in Carthage, the emperor Honorius issued an edict from Ravenna condemning Pelagius and Caelestius and their views

---

the previous note) Zosimus appears to indicate that his initial (no longer extant) response to the Africans' *obtestatio* in November (as Dalmon has pointed out, Wermelinger seems to have missed Zosimus's allusion to this lost response to the *obtestatio*—see *Un dossier*, 500) had been to grant a temporary "stay" in the case of Caelestius: that is, he had promised not to proceed further with Caelestius's exoneration. *Quamuis patrum* itself offered the Africans further assurance that their request had been received and honored. While Zosimus did not say anything explicit about reconsidering his judgment, his emphasis on the fact that no one could force him to reconsider any case ironically suggests that he was in fact preparing to reconsider his position: he simply wanted to head off any claims that Africa had forced his hand. Several other scholars have also read *Quamuis patrum* as an indication that Zosimus was beginning to change his mind. See, e.g., Lancel, *Saint Augustine*, 339; Munier, BA 22, 21; Pietri, *Roma christiana*, 1226–30; Teske, WSA I/23, 337. See also some brief discussion in Yves-Marie Duval, "Julien d'Éclane et Rufin d'Aquilée: Du Concile de Rimini à la répression pélagienne. L'intervention impériale en matière religieuse," *Revue d'études augustiniennes* 24 (1978): 245–46.

225 Augustine cites the activity of "believing brothers" in Rome as crucial to Zosimus's change of mind (*gr. et pecc. or.* 2.21.23). He elsewhere states that the Africans' *uolumen* had prompted Zosimus to request a second hearing for Caelestius (*c. ep. Pel.* 2.3.5). Prosper of Aquitaine reports that violence broke out in Rome at some point and that an imperial official named Constantius was attacked by alleged supporters of Pelagius and Caelestius (see *Chronicum Integrum* a. 418 [PL 51:592.10–13]). Wermelinger acknowledges the possibility that imperial pressure played a role in Zosimus's reconsideration but emphasizes the role of the clergy and laity in Rome itself (*Rom und Pelagius*, 164). For Squires, Zosimus was essentially forced to condemn Pelagius and Caelestius after the imperial condemnation and the Africans' council (*The Pelagian Controversy*, 141). See also discussion in Mathijs Lamberigts, "Augustine and Julian of Aeclanum on Zosimus," *Augustiniana* 42 (1992): 320–22, and Lamberigts, "Co-operation of Church and State." Duval remains non-committal but is hesitant to rule out the possibility that the imperial action against the Pelagians was actually enacted with Zosimus's support ("Julien d'Éclane et Rufin d'Aquilée," 245–46).

240   AUGUSTINE IN THE PELAGIAN CONTROVERSY

and banishing them from Rome.[226] And then on the following day, May 1, a plenary council[227] of over two hundred African bishops met at Carthage and issued nine canons against Pelagianism.[228] At some point in the midst of or following these events, Pope Zosimus, finally deciding to reverse course, ordered Caelestius to appear before him in Rome. But Caelestius had already left the city.[229] In the aftermath of Caelestius's failure to appear, Zosimus issued his *Epistula Tractoria*, in which he condemned and excommunicated Pelagius and Caelestius.[230] Zosimus had copies of the letter sent throughout

226 For Honorius's edict, see PL 45:1726–27; 48:379–86; or 56:490–92. Honorius focuses on the issues of Adam's mortality and the transmission of original sin. It is likely that the Africans had sent a delegation to the imperial court at Ravenna at some point (although see Duval's comments: "Julien d'Éclane et Rufin d'Aquilée," 245–46). Perhaps Marcellinus, who delivered the *uolumen* and Paulinus's *libellus* to Zosimus, was also tasked with conveying a message to Ravenna. See Wermelinger, *Rom und Pelagius*, 196n297, and Lamberigts, "Co-operation of Church and State," 368ff. J. Patout Burns argues for an appeal to Ravenna earlier in 417 before news of Zosimus's re-opening of the cases arrived in Africa—see "Augustine's Role in the Imperial Action Against Pelagius," *Journal of Theological Studies* 30, no. 1 (1979): 67–83. Julian of Eclanum will later accuse the Africans of bribing imperial officials to win their support (see, e.g., Julian's words quoted at Augustine, *c. Iul. imp.* 1.42 and 3.35). For further discussion of the Africans' relationship with Ravenna and the imperial action against the Pelagians in 418 and afterward, see Wermelinger, *Rom und Pelagius*, 196–209, and Mar Marcos, "Anti-Pelagian Legislation in Context," in Lex et religio, *XL Incontro di Studiosi dell'Antichità Cristiana (Roma, 10–12 maggio 2012)* (Rome: Institutum Patristicum Augustinianum, 2013), 317–44. See also Brown, *Eye of a Needle*, 371ff., for a helpful contextualization of Africa's appeal to Ravenna.

227 See Dalmon, *Un dossier*, 75, for discussion of the difference between a *concilium plenarium* or *uniuersale* and a *concilium generale*. For more on African councils in general, see Dalmon, *Un dossier*, 581–92.

228 See these canons in CCSL 149:69ff. An English translation is available at Teske, WSA I/23, 378–80. For extensive discussion of the council and canons see Wermelinger, *Rom und Pelagius*, 165–96.

229 See Marius Mercator's account of the events in his *Commonitorium super nomine Caelestii* (ACO 1.5, p. 66, ln. 37–43). See also Augustine, *c. ep. Pel.* 2.3.5. Both Augustine and Mercator suggest that Caelestius had left Rome after being summoned by Zosimus. However, Mathijs Lamberigts argues that Caelestius had likely left in the aftermath of Honorius's edict and not to avoid Zosimus—see "Co-operation of Church and State," 371 (and see also Munier, BA 22, 23).

230 Zosimus's *Tractoria* is extant only in a few scattered fragments: see Augustine, *ep.* 190.23 (CSEL 57:159); Prosper of Aquitaine, *Liber contra collatorem* 5.3 (PL 51:228); Celestine, *Epistola ad Galliarum Episcopos* (PL 50:534). Marius Mercator's *Commonitorium super nomine Caelestii* (ACO 1.5.1, pp. 65–70) also provides important details and some excerpts from the documentation appended to the letter. Wermelinger has gathered these fragments and a list of other materials attached to the *Tractoria* at *Rom und Pelagius*, 307–8. The dating of the *Tractoria* is uncertain, but it was likely released in the early summer of 418 (Plinval dates it to June 29, 418: *Pélage*, 327n1). Given a reference to the *Tractoria* at *gr. et pecc. or.* 2.21.24, which was written in Carthage in the summer of 418, it must have arrived in Africa before Augustine's

FROM DIOSPOLIS TO THE *TRACTORIA* 241

the empire,[231] and required bishops to confirm their agreement with it by their signatures.[232] All told, the arrival of Zosimus's *Tractoria* in Africa, perhaps in early July,[233] must have been a welcome relief. However, it did not by any means spell the end of the controversy or of Augustine's efforts against Pelagianism. Indeed, around the time it arrived Augustine was hard at work responding to a letter sent to him from Palestine by Melania, Pinianus, and Albina. This response, *De gratia Christi et de peccato originali*, would be Augustine's final anti-Pelagian work focused specifically on the views of Pelagius and Caelestius and, in this sense, offers a bookend of sorts to this phase of the controversy. As we shall see, the work also strongly evidences the centrality in Augustine's anti-Pelagian polemic of his efforts to demonstrate that his opponents' views had no support in the Church's ancient and universal doctrinal tradition. Let us now turn to this work before bringing this chapter to a close.

De gratia Christi et de peccato originali

As we discussed in Chapter 1, Melania, Pinianus, and Albina, three elite members of the Roman Christian aristocracy, had come to North Africa likely in the fall of 410, settling on their estate in Thagaste. After roughly seven years in Africa—perhaps in the late spring of 417[234]—they departed to the Holy Land. At some point after their arrival in Palestine,[235] they met with Pelagius

---

departure from Carthage for Caesarea Mauretania around the end of July (see Lancel, *Saint Augustine*, 348, for this date and subsequent pages for more on his journey). Lamberigts convincingly argues that the *Tractoria* must have postdated Honorius's edict and the Council of Carthage: "Co-operation of Church and State," 372–75. For more on the *Tractoria* and its contents, see especially Wermelinger, *Rom und Pelagius*, 209–18, and "Das Pelagiusdossier." See also F. Floeri, "Le pape Zosime et la doctrine augustinienne du péché originel," in *Augustinus Magister*, Congrès International Augustinien (Paris: *Études* augustiniennes, 1954), 2:755–61.

231 Mercator notes that in the East, copies were sent to Egypt, Constantinople, Thessalonica, and Jerusalem (*Commonitorium super nomine Caelestii* 36 [ACO 1.5.1 p. 67, ln. 2–3]).

232 See Mercator, *Commonitorium super nomine Caelestii* 36 (ACO 1.5.1, p. 68, ln. 20–23); Augustine, *c. ep. Pel.* 4.8.20.

233 See Wermelinger, *Rom und Pelagius*, 209n374.

234 See de Veer, BA 22, 25.

235 Löhr suggests this meeting with Pelagius took place in the spring of 417 when Pelagius was attempting to "reactivate" networks of friendship associated with Augustine to defend himself in the wake of Innocent's condemnation ("Augustinus und sein Verhältnis zu Pelagius," 76 and 82). Löhr's contextualization of the conversation is surely correct, but his date seems too early; I would suggest a date toward the end of 417 or even at the beginning of 418.

himself and, as they reported in their subsequent (no longer extant) letter to Augustine, succeeded in having the British ascetic confess that grace is needed at every moment and that infants are baptized for the forgiveness of sins by the same words of the sacrament as adults.[236] Augustine received their letter while he was in Carthage in the late spring or early summer of 418 and promptly set to work dictating a response, clearly unconvinced by Pelagius's statements and perhaps worried that Pelagius's reported confession would lead to a new round of re-evaluations of his case.[237]

Augustine organized his response into two books: the first concerns grace while the second deals with original sin. In both books, Augustine's chief goal is to convince his addressees (and any others who might read the work[238]) that Pelagius's apparently orthodox statements are only a carefully crafted veneer disguising his heretical views. To prove this point, Augustine analyzes a number of key passages from several of the works that Pelagius had recently acknowledged as his own—no doubt restricting himself to these works to avoid accusations that he had based his arguments on works falsely attributed to Pelagius.[239] These passages reveal, Augustine contends, that Pelagius has not changed his positions and still stands firmly outside of the bounds of orthodoxy. Of particular prominence is the *Pro libero arbitrio*, which Pelagius had published in the aftermath of Diospolis as a rebuttal to Jerome's *ep.* 133 to Ctesiphon and *Dialogus aduersus Pelagianos*.[240]

---

236 See *gr. et pecc. or.* 1.2.2, 1.32.35, and 2.1.1. De Veer offers a helpful analysis of the context of this conversation with Pelagius, at least as far as we can grasp it from extant evidence (BA 22, 29–32). Melania and the other addressees were clearly well aware of the debates surrounding Pelagius and his views and perhaps hoped to bring him to recant. See, e.g., Augustine's comments at *gr. et pecc. or.* 2.10.11 and 2.14.15, where he indicates that Melania, Pinianus, and Albina are already familiar with the *gesta* of Diospolis (and perhaps Augustine's *De gestis Pelagii*).

237 See *gr. et pecc. or.* 1.1.1.

238 As Wermelinger points out, the work was intended for broader circulation than just Melania, Pinianus, and Albina: *Rom und Pelagius*, 255. See also Augustine's comments at *gr. et pecc. or.* 2.10.11.

239 See *gr. et pecc. or.* 1.2.2.

240 Pelagius's *Pro libero arbitrio* had four books (*gr. et pecc. or.* 1.41.45) and is now extant in fragments mainly found in Augustine, although three additional fragments from Book 3 (one of which is a longer version of that found at *gr. et pecc. or.* 1.39.43) were discovered a century ago by A. Souter. For fragments from Book 1, see *gr. et pecc. or.* 1.18.19, 1.28.29, 1.29.30, and 2.13.14. For fragments from Book 3, see *gr. et pecc. or.* 1.4.5, 1.39.43, 1.43.47, as well as those collected by Souter at PLS 1:1539–43. It is unclear from which book of *Pro libero arbitrio* the remaining fragments come: *gr. et pecc. or.* 1.7.8, 1.10.11, 1.22.24–1.23.24, 2.15.16. (Note that the list of fragments given by Drecoll ["Pelagius, Pelagiani," 646] omits this final fragment

FROM DIOSPOLIS TO THE *TRACTORIA* 243

However, *Pro libero arbitrio*'s importance is not simply located in the wealth of evidence it provided Augustine; it also seems to have prompted certain key aspects of *De gratia Christi*'s argument. In *Pro libero arbitrio*—as in *De natura*—Pelagius had appealed to Ambrose to prove that Elizabeth and Zechariah were sinless in this life.[241] As a result, Augustine clearly felt the need to demonstrate decisively—and to a degree we have not encountered thus far in the controversy—not only that Ambrose was no Pelagian, but that his writings prove the Pelagian views are nothing but novel heresies. In this sense, another key aim for Augustine in *De gratia Christi* is, once again, to undercut the Pelagians' claims to find support in the Church's ancient and universal doctrinal tradition. As we shall see, this aim reveals itself in several ways throughout the work.

The structure of the first book of *De gratia Christi et de peccato originali* is fairly straight-forward. Augustine begins with a brief introduction (§§1.1.1–1.2.2), in which he thanks Melania, Pinianus, and Albina for writing and acknowledges that Pelagius's confession of the need for grace may appear orthodox at first glance. However, he cautions his readers against trusting Pelagius, as his words have an ambiguity to them that can hide his real views. Indeed, Augustine suggests that Pelagius reveals his true meaning more readily in his written works. So, to prove his case, Augustine devotes much of the remainder of Book 1 to a careful analysis of key passages from Pelagius's acknowledged writings, grouped more or less[242] into discrete sections: *Pro libero arbitrio* (§§1.3.3–1.30.31), his letter to Pope Innocent (§§1.30.32–1.31.34),

---

[2.15.16], which appears to be more of a paraphrase than a direct quote but nevertheless contains important information about the content of *Pro libero arbitrio*.) For evidence that *Pro libero arbitrio* was written as a response to Jerome, see, e.g., *gr. et pecc. or.* 1.39.43 where a quotation from *Pro libero arbitrio* is offered in which Pelagius responds to an argument found in Jerome's *ep.* 133.2 and *Dialogus aduersus Pelagianos* 2.2–3. See also *c. Iul. imp.* 4.88, where Julian indicates that Pelagius has responded to Jerome's *Dialogus*. The fragments discovered by Souter were prefaced by quotations from Jerome's *ep.* 133. Regarding the dating of *Pro libero arbitrio*, it seems that it may have been composed before the Synod of Diospolis (although perhaps only shortly before, given that it seems Jerome's *Dialogus* itself was likely completed toward the end of 415), but was only published afterward (perhaps with a preface of sorts explaining and celebrating Pelagius's acquittal)—see Augustine's comments at *gr. et pecc. or.* 2.14.15 and 2.16.17. For more on *Pro libero arbitrio*, see de Veer's helpful note at BA 22, 682–84.

241 See *gr. et pecc. or.* 1.48.53 and *nat. et gr.* 63.74.

242 Augustine does at times introduce quotations from a work considered in a different section to elucidate the meaning of a passage of the text at hand (see, e.g., *gr. et pecc. or.* 1.22.23, 1.27.28, 1.39.43).

his *Libellus fidei* (§§1.32.35–1.33.36), as well as his other writings mentioned in the letter to Innocent (§§1.34.37–1.41.45).[243]

However, it is the final section of Book 1 (§§1.42.46–1.50.55) that is of particular interest for us. Here, Augustine's argument shifts away from trying to identify Pelagius's real views. Instead, he turns to examine several quotations from Ambrose. What prompted this section is, of course, Pelagius's appeal to Ambrose in *Pro libero arbitrio*, as we noted above. But Augustine's aim here is more than simply to "negate" Pelagius's appeal to Ambrose as a support for his view of sinlessness—although he does do that, too.[244] Rather, in a more positive sense, he is striving to present Ambrose as a model exponent of the Church's view on grace, depicting him as a faithful interpreter of scripture.

Augustine begins by expressing his wish that the Pelagians, if unwilling to listen to scripture, would at least heed the words of faithful interpreters of scripture:

> [The Pelagians] are far from that righteousness that comes to us, not from ourselves, but from God, the righteousness which they ought to have found and acknowledged in the scriptures, especially in the holy and canonical scriptures. But because they read them according to their own ideas, they do not, in fact, see in them even what is obvious. I wish, then, that they would at least pay careful attention to the writings of Catholic authors. They do not doubt that these authors have correctly understood the scriptures, and in them they would find what one should hold regarding the help of divine grace. I wish they would not simply pass it over out of an excessive love of their own opinion.[245]

Augustine then notes Pelagius's own praise for Ambrose:

> Listen to how Pelagius himself simply praises the saintly Ambrose in this recent work of his which he mentions in his own defense, that is, in the third book of *Pro libero arbitrio*: "The blessed bishop, Ambrose," he says, "in whose books the Roman faith shines forth with special brilliance, stood out like a beautiful flower among the writers in the Latin language; not even an enemy dared to find fault with his faith and utterly flawless interpretation of the scriptures." Note the sort and the amount of praise he heaps upon

---

243 The main focus of the final section is Pelagius's *ep. ad Demetriadem* (§§1.37.40–1.40.44).

244 See especially *gr. et pecc. or.* 1.48.53–1.50.55.

245 *gr. et pecc. or.* 1.42.46 (Latin: CSEL 42:159.14–21; English: Teske, WSA I/23, 413).

FROM DIOSPOLIS TO THE *TRACTORIA* 245

a holy and learned man, though he is not comparable to the authority of the canonical scripture.[246]

Augustine's comments here have a few different aims. On the one hand, he wants to suggest that Pelagius's praise for Ambrose is rather excessive, appearing to inflate his authority up to that of scripture. As we have seen previously, Augustine was wary of appealing even to renowned Christian writers to support his own views—no doubt well aware from his disputes with the Donatists that even highly respected saints sometimes got things disastrously wrong—and on occasion cautioned his readers (as we see here) against ascribing too much authority to non-scriptural authors.[247] However, his previous hesitancy to use such arguments has softened by the summer of 418: while he continues to voice the same concerns here, he also actively advocates for the Pelagians to pay attention to the writings and exegesis of figures like Ambrose. Indeed, it appears that Augustine, at this point, more fully embraces the utility and persuasiveness of appeals to renowned Christian writers. In this light, his main critique of Pelagius is not so much his elevation of Ambrose's authority beyond its due, but rather his selective reading of Ambrose's corpus and scriptural interpretation. Indeed, Augustine goes on to argue that Ambrose clearly taught a view of grace opposed to that formulated by Pelagius, offering five quotations from Ambrose's commentary on Luke.[248] The decision to use this commentary is important, as it was a passage from this work that Pelagius himself had used to claim Ambrose's support for his view of the possibility of sinlessness.[249] As a result, by citing *five* passages from that same work that Pelagius had used, Augustine effectively signals that Pelagius's reliance on the bishop of Milan was shallow and selective, even in the context of this single commentary.

After the fifth quotation, Augustine focuses his argument on emphasizing the linkage between Ambrose's views and his scriptural interpretation—clearly attempting to capitalize on the fact that Pelagius had called his understanding of scripture "flawless" (*purissimus*).[250]

---

246 *gr. et pecc. or.* 1.42.46–1.43.47 (Latin: CSEL 42:159.21–160.3; English: Teske, WSA I/23, 413).

247 See, e.g., *pecc. mer.* 3.7.14. See also our discussion in the Introduction.

248 See *gr. et pecc. or.* 1.44.48–1.46.51.

249 Pelagius had cited a passage from Ambrose, *Expositio euangelii secundum Lucam* 1.17. See *nat. et gr.* 63.74 and *gr. et pecc. or.* 1.48.53–1.50.55.

250 *gr. et pecc. or.* 1.43.47 (Latin: CSEL 42:159.27; English: Teske, WSA I/23, 413).

Let him listen to the same bishop of God again in the sixth book of the same work. He says, "The evangelist recalls why they did not welcome him, when he says, 'Because his face was turned toward Jerusalem' (Luke 9:53). His disciples desired to be welcomed in Samaria. But God calls those whom he chooses to call and makes him whom he wishes devout."[251] There you have the thought of a man of God that is a drink drawn from the very fountain of God's grace! "God," he says, "calls those whom he chooses to call and makes him whom he wishes devout." Look and see if this isn't what the prophet said, "I will show pity to those to whom I want to show pity, and I will have mercy on those on whom I want to have mercy" (Ex 33:19; Rom 9:15), and what the apostle said, "Therefore, it does not depend on the one who wills or runs, but on God who shows mercy" (Rom 9:16). It is God, as even this man of God of our own times says, who calls him whom he chooses to call and makes him whom he wishes devout.[252]

Here Augustine argues for a clear and decisive link between Ambrose's opinion and the teaching of scripture itself: Ambrose teaches nothing but what was found in Exodus and in the Apostle Paul. If Pelagius values Ambrose's interpretation so much, why does he fail to follow it?

Having attempted to establish Ambrose's views on grace and to link them with Scriptural teaching, Augustine's final paragraphs in Book 1 seek to undermine Pelagius's appeal to Ambrose as a support for his view of the possibility of sinlessness. Here he begins by acknowledging that there is no need to deny that God could make it possible for a human being to be sinless in this life. However, he goes on to dispute (gently and implicitly) Ambrose's interpretation of Luke's affirmation that Elizabeth and Zechariah were righteous: this affirmation by Luke does not, Augustine suggests (contrary to Ambrose and Pelagius), indicate that they were perfectly sinless. Augustine then adds a quotation from Ambrose's commentary on Isaiah, in which the bishop affirms that no one can be spotless and without sin.[253] Augustine suggests that in his commentary on Luke, Ambrose had either stated that Elizabeth and Zechariah were sinless in an acceptable sense (e.g., beyond reproach, but not totally perfect in every respect) or later changed his

---

251 Ambrose, *Expositio euangelii secundum Lucam* 7.27 (CSEL 32.4:293.17–20).

252 *gr. et pecc. or.* 1.46.51 (Latin: CSEL 42:162.5–17; English: Teske, WSA I/23, 415, with some modifications).

253 See *gr. et pecc. or.* 1.49.54.

FROM DIOSPOLIS TO THE *TRACTORIA*

position.[254] In any event, Augustine notes that, in that passage which Pelagius had quoted, Ambrose also affirms that "it is impossible for human nature to be spotless from the beginning."[255] Augustine then comments:

> There the venerable Ambrose, of course, bears witness to the feebleness and weakness of that very natural ability which Pelagius does not regard faithfully as corrupted by sin—and which he praises arrogantly for that reason. Ambrose certainly contradicts what Pelagius wants, but he does not contradict the apostolic truth where we read, "We too were once by nature children of anger, just as the others" (Eph 2:3).[256]

Just as we saw earlier, here too Augustine emphasizes the linkage between Ambrose's thought and scripture. Pelagius has failed once again to follow the *purissimus sensus* of Ambrose. With that final point made, Augustine brings the first book to a conclusion.

The second book of *De gratia Christi et de peccato originali* turns to the topic of original sin. Here, Augustine does not have quite as much evidence to prove the heterodoxy of Pelagius's position on original sin as he had had in Book 1 with regard to grace. As a result, instead of simply highlighting relevant quotations from Pelagius's writings, he attempts to prove that Pelagius holds the same positions as Caelestius, who had openly denied the reality of original sin. Augustine begins, then, by examining Caelestius's views, as expressed at Carthage in 411 (§§2.2.2–2.4.4) and at Rome in 417 (§§2.5.5–2.6.6). Given how explicit Caelestius's views were in his *libellus* given to Zosimus, Augustine must first explain the pope's apparent failure to condemn the man immediately (§§2.6.7–2.7.8). Afterward, Augustine turns back to Pelagius himself to show that he holds the same views as Caelestius. He first addresses Pelagius's actions at Diospolis and begins by

---

254 Teske (following BA 22, 154n211) notes that this last point suggests that Augustine thought the commentary on Isaiah postdated the commentary on Luke, which is not true, given a reference to the commentary on Isaiah in the commentary on Luke (see Teske, WSA I/23, 419n106). While this interpretation of Augustine's words seems plausible, it remains possible that Augustine was simply suggesting, in a more general sense, that Ambrose surely would have changed his position upon further reflection, as Augustine makes no clear assertion that the commentary on Isaiah was written after that on Luke.

255 *gr. et pecc. or.* 1.50.55 (Latin: CSEL 42:165.16–17; English: Teske, WSA I/23, 416). See Ambrose, *Expositio euangelii secundum Lucam* 1.17 (CSEL 32.4:21.21–22). Augustine had also cited this passage at *nat. et gr.* 63.75.

256 *gr. et pecc. or.* 1.50.55 (Latin: CSEL 42:165.17–22; English: Teske, WSA I/23, 417, slightly modified).

emphasizing that Popes Zosimus and Innocent both judged that Pelagius had obtained his acquittal by deceit (§§2.8.9–2.9.10). Augustine then turns to the proceedings themselves, focusing on Pelagius's condemnation of the propositions Paulinus of Milan had accused Caelestius of holding in 411 (§§2.10.11–2.12.13). To show that Pelagius had deceived the bishops at Diospolis when he condemned these propositions, Augustine cites a few passages from the *Pro libero arbitrio* (§§2.13.14–2.17.18), which appears to have been written shortly before Diospolis but published afterward.[257] In that work, Augustine reports, Pelagius (1) denied that human beings are born subject to any sort of blameworthy evil and (2) attempted to reinterpret the Caelestian propositions he had condemned at Diospolis in a different sense than they had been presented to him at the synod. Augustine then turns to further evidence of Pelagius's deceit: in his letter to Innocent, he had falsely claimed his opponents were accusing him of denying baptism to infants and of promising the kingdom of heaven to some apart from Christ's redemption (§§2.17.19–2.21.23). Finally, Augustine addresses a statement in Pelagius's *Libellus fidei*, where the ascetic indicates that infants should be baptized with the same words as adults and suggests that the problematic opinions reported in Pelagius's *Expositiones* on the Pauline letters were held by the ascetic himself (§2.21.24). Augustine concludes his examination of the evidence by arguing that Pelagius and Caelestius have been justly condemned (§2.22.25).

At this point in Book 2, Augustine shifts his aims. Having brought his argument that Pelagius taught the same positions as Caelestius to a conclusion, he now turns to address a few Pelagian objections to his position. First of all, Augustine argues that, contrary to Caelestius's claims, the topic at stake (original sin) is not an open question: rather, it stands at the heart of the faith. A lengthy discussion follows, in which Augustine addresses the course of salvation history and the ways in which grace and original sin were at the core of the revelation found in both the Old and New Testaments (§§2.23.26–2.32.37). Augustine then turns to another set of objections (§§2.33.38–2.40.46): whether Augustine's views on original sin make marriage something evil and whether, due to original sin, the human beings produced through marriage are no longer God's work.[258] Augustine responds

257 See n. 240 above.

258 The presence of these objections suggests that Augustine had already learned of Julian of Eclanum's resistance to the *Tractoria* and to the condemnation of Pelagius and Caelestius.

FROM DIOSPOLIS TO THE *TRACTORIA*

that marriage remains something good and makes good use of an evil (concupiscence) to produce children who are, admittedly, subject to original sin and the devil, but are not, for that reason, devoid of all goodness. In any event, they can be reclaimed for God through baptism. Having addressed these objections, Augustine brings the second book to a close in a way similar to Book 1—by offering testimony from Ambrose to support his view of the topic at hand, namely, the reality of original sin (§§2.41.47–2.41.48).

There are several ways in which Augustine's argumentation in the second book of *De gratia Christi* reveals his effort to show that his views and opinions are widely held. For example, we might note that Augustine continues to use the argumentative strategy found in *De gestis Pelagii* whereby he sought to portray the judges at Diospolis as perfectly orthodox: they assumed that Pelagius's condemnations of certain propositions were sincere and without deceit.[259] In this way, Augustine aligns himself with these eastern bishops and (implicitly) suggests that the universal Church is opposed to Pelagianism. Further, when Augustine is grappling with the Pelagians' rejection of original sin toward the end of the book, he introduces testimony from the rite of baptism, citing among other things the exorcism that precedes the baptism itself, even in the case of infants.[260] Augustine had previously cited this exorcism as evidence of the presence of original sin in *De peccatorum meritis* 1.34.63. The exorcism and exsufflation that formed part of the rite of baptism will become important testimony for Augustine later in his debates with Julian.

Two additional strategies are of particular importance: (1) his use and characterization of the actions of Pope Innocent and Pope Zosimus against the Pelagians and (2) his appeal to Ambrose at the end of the book. With respect to Innocent and Zosimus, as both pontiffs had (in the end) condemned Pelagius and Caelestius, their testimony offered strong evidence of the validity of Augustine's own arguments. Nevertheless, Zosimus's earlier vacillations were no doubt something of a liability in Augustine's mind: surely his informed readers, aware of Zosimus's actions in 417 (and, possibly, of the early rumblings of Julian and his fellow bishops), would wonder if the *Tractoria* was the final word on the issue. As a result, Augustine had to carefully explain Zosimus's behavior while at the same time emphasizing his

---

For more see Chapter 5.

259 See, e.g., *gr. et pecc. or.* 2.12.13, 2.16.17.

260 See *gr. et pecc. or.* 2.40.45.

final decision and its continuity with Innocent's in 417. The first key passage is at §§2.6.7–2.7.8, where Augustine attempts to explain Zosimus's actions vis-à-vis Caelestius. As we suggested above, Zosimus's decision to re-evaluate the case against Caelestius in 417 seems to have been prompted by a few different factors: his deep concern at the role of Heros and Lazarus in the affair; his general disinterest in the nuances of the theological debate; and his inclination to believe the forthrightness of Caelestius's claims to be open to correction. It would, I suggest, be wrong to characterize the pope as an ally of Caelestius: for example, based on the extant excerpts of Caelestius's hearing it does seem that Zosimus had pushed Caelestius to condemn certain propositions and had, at least to some degree, defended Paulinus of Milan's orthodoxy. Nevertheless, the African bishops no doubt felt after reading *Magnum pondus* and *Posteaquam a nobis* that Zosimus was decidedly on the side of their opponents. As a result, Augustine's depiction of the events is noteworthy. After recounting Caelestius's open denial of original sin in his *Libellus* given to Zosimus, Augustine reports:

> The prelate of that See we just mentioned saw that Caelestius's great presumption was carrying him over the edge, like a madman. In his great mercy he preferred gradually to tie him up with his questions and the answers Caelestius gave, in the hope that he would come to his senses, if that was possible. He did not want to drive him over the edge into the abyss into which he seemed to be headed by striking him with a severe sentence. I did not say, "into which he had clearly fallen," but "into which he seemed to be headed," precisely because he had earlier said in his *libellus* when he was about to deal with such questions, "If, as happens to human beings, some error may have crept in due to ignorance, I want it to be corrected by your decision."[261]

Here Augustine presents Zosimus's initial decision to re-examine Caelestius as motivated by mercy: the pope suspected that Caelestius's thought was problematic but, given Caelestius's willingness to be corrected, he thought it would be better to offer him a hearing to examine his arguments so that he might be corrected more easily. Augustine then continues:

> Having that sort of opening declaration from him, Pope Zosimus tried to bring this man, who was bloated with the wind of false doctrine, to

261 *gr. et pecc. or.* 2.6.7 (Latin: CSEL 42:170.26–171.5; English: Teske, WSA I/23, 422, slightly modified).

FROM DIOSPOLIS TO THE *TRACTORIA*

condemn those points which the deacon Paulinus raised as objections against him and to give his assent to the writings of the Apostolic See which stemmed from his predecessor of holy memory. Caelestius, however, refused to condemn the points which the deacon Paulinus raised as objections; yet, he did not dare to oppose the letters of blessed Pope Innocent. In fact, he promised that he would condemn everything which that See would condemn. Hence, he was treated with gentleness, like someone overwrought, so that he would calm down; on the other hand, no one at that point thought that he should be freed from the bonds of excommunication. Rather, a time of two months was allotted to receive a response from Africa, and he was accorded the chance to come to his senses under a mild sentence aimed at his restoration to health.[262]

The facts Augustine presents here are not false (at least based on the evidence available to us): we know that Zosimus did try to have Caelestius condemn the propositions brought against him by Paulinus[263] and that Zosimus gave the Africans two months to respond before issuing his final judgment. However, what does appear to be a bit "off" here—at least based on the sense we get from, say, *Magnum pondus*—is Augustine's presentation of the motivations behind Zosimus's actions. As Augustine presents it, Zosimus's decision to hear Caelestius's defense was motivated by a desire to prompt him to change his views. Likewise, Augustine suggests that in the aftermath of the hearing, Caelestius was shown leniency so that he might "come to his senses." However, as we noted above, it seems likely that Zosimus had serious doubts about the legitimacy of the case against Caelestius and that, in any event, he thought Caelestius had convincingly demonstrated his own orthodoxy—or at least his willingness to submit to Zosimus's determination of the bounds of orthodoxy.[264] Further, Augustine remains silent about some key facts: For

262 *gr. et pecc. or.* 2.7.8 (Latin: CSEL 42:171.6–18; English: Teske, WSA I/23, 422).

263 See the citations from the *gesta* of Caelestius's hearing found in Paulinus of Milan's *Libellus aduersus Caelestium* 4–5 and *c. ep. Pel.* 2.4.6.

264 On this point, I would like to emphasize that some odd incongruities remain in our understanding of Zosimus's treatment of Caelestius: on the one hand, *Magnum pondus* gives the clear impression that Zosimus found the evidence against Caelestius underwhelming at best and, at times, actually indicative of his orthodoxy. At the same time, unlike with Pelagius, Zosimus did not, it seems to me, immediately clear Caelestius of all charges. I noted above that this was likely due in large part to the legal issues involved (see n. 177): unlike the case against Pelagius, the case against Caelestius did not rest entirely on the testimony of Heros and Lazarus and thus had some legitimate footing that could not simply be dismissed. However, given the fragments of the *gesta* of Caelestius's hearing available to us (and especially

example, although he mentions the two-month waiting period, he offers no explanation of what the purpose of that waiting period was. To do so would have required him to explain the involvement of the now discredited Heros and Lazarus in the affair as well as the irregular conclusion of the trial of 411 and the subsequent need for the Africans to reestablish the basis of their case on firmer ground. He also makes no mention of *Magnum pondus* or its tone. This partial narration of the events of 417 has an important polemical purpose. Indeed, what Augustine is doing here is interpreting Zosimus's actions in the best (and most consistent) light possible given the pope's later condemnation of Caelestius in the *Tractoria*. Augustine wants to emphasize for his readers the final result and to preempt doubts about Zosimus's commitment to his judgment going forward.[265]

From there, Augustine shifts in the next section to discuss Zosimus's and Innocent's views of Pelagius as part of his broader discussion of Pelagius's deceptive responses at Diospolis. Both, Augustine argues, recognized this deception (in the end). He writes:

> But [Pelagius] could not deceive the church of Rome where, as you know, he is well known, although he tried to do so in every way he could. However, as I said, he was utterly unable to do so. After all, the blessed Pope Zosimus recalled the view that his predecessor, a man worthy of imitation, took of those proceedings. He also paid attention to what the faith of the people of Rome, which is praiseworthy in the Lord, held regarding that man. He saw their concerted efforts blaze forth in defense of the Catholic faith, united against his error. Pelagius had lived in their midst for a long time, and they could not fail to be aware of his teachings. They knew quite well that Caelestius was his disciple, and they were able to bear utterly reliable and solid witness on that point.[266]

Zosimus's efforts therein to have Caelestius condemn the propositions brought forward by Paulinus—see Paulinus, *Libellus aduersus Caelestium* 4–5, and *c. ep. Pel.* 2.4.6), I do think it is possible that at least some nagging doubts remained for Zosimus as to whether Caelestius was actually guilty as charged. As a result, the two-month waiting period may not have been *simply* a legal formality but may have actually been prompted (at least to some small degree) by Zosimus's own lingering uncertainties.

265 See also Wermelinger's comments at *Rom und Pelagius*, 259–64. While I depart somewhat from Wermelinger's analysis of the events of 417 (and Augustine's later re-telling of those events), he is surely right to emphasize the importance for Augustine in presenting Zosimus as an ally so as to more easily claim the universality of opposition among orthodox Christians to Pelagianism.

266 *gr. et pecc. or.* 2.8.9 (Latin: CSEL 42:171.28–172.10; English: Teske, WSA I/23, 423).

FROM DIOSPOLIS TO THE *TRACTORIA*

As he had done when discussing Caelestius, Augustine here omits the messy details of Zosimus's about-face with Pelagius. However, the gaps are more noticeable here. Unlike in the case against Caelestius—where there were at least some redeeming aspects to Zosimus's re-examination of the case— Zosimus's reevaluation of Pelagius left no immediate opening for African resistance or "positive spin." Indeed, Zosimus had made it quite clear that Pelagius, at least, was innocent on all counts. As a result, Augustine makes no mention at all here of *Posteaquam a nobis* or Zosimus's actions in the fall of 417, instead opting to fast-forward to the spring or early summer of 418, when Zosimus finally came around. It is important to recognize the way in which Augustine explains how Zosimus eventually came to acknowledge Pelagius's deceit: it was by recalling or honoring (*recolere*) Innocent's opinion and by paying attention to the testimony of the Roman people. In a sense, the way in which Augustine phrases this explanation offers a subtle indication of Zosimus's wavering: the pope had (initially) been deceived by Pelagius but was later set right by others.[267] Nevertheless, the emphasis is once again placed on Zosimus's final (correct) decision, and his agreement with Innocent is highlighted. Indeed, after offering a lengthy quotation from *ep.* 183, which was Innocent's reply in January 417 to the letter of the five African bishops from the prior year, expressing the late pope's opinion of Pelagius's activity at Diospolis,[268] Augustine concludes:

> You see, certainly, in these words how the most blessed Pope Innocent does not seem to speak of him as someone unknown. You see the view he took of his acquittal. You see what his successor, the holy Pope Zosimus, ought to have recalled, as he did recall, so that, with doubt set aside [*remota cunctatione*], he might uphold the judgment of his predecessor on the subject.[269]

---

267 See also Augustine's comments at *gr. et pecc. or.* 2.21.24 where he speaks more explicitly about the fact that Pelagius had initially convinced Zosimus of his orthodoxy. There, too, Augustine cites the importance of the work of some "faithful brothers" in Rome.

268 See *gr. et pecc. or.* 2.9.10 and *ep.* 183.3–4.

269 *gr. et pecc. or.* 2.9.10 (Latin: CSEL 42:173.6–11; English: Teske, WSA I/23, 424, slightly modified). Teske's translation of *remota cunctatione* is "without any hesitation"—which does not seem quite right, given the fact that Zosimus did hesitate quite a bit. I do not think Augustine is denying that there was hesitation on Zosimus's part: he is simply emphasizing that once the truth of the matter was before his eyes, he set aside his doubts and did the right thing, as it were.

For Augustine, this examination of the actions and opinions of Innocent and Zosimus serves, first and foremost, to substantiate the validity of his own interpretation of Pelagius's behavior at Diospolis (to which he will turn in the next section): if neutral third-party judges—judges, it should be added, who have headed the Apostolic See—believe Pelagius obtained his acquittal at Diospolis by deceit, it is clear evidence that Augustine's own position is not simply due to an anti-Pelagian bias. Of course, more broadly, and both here and earlier in his examination of Caelestius's case, Augustine is attempting to show the alignment between himself and the bishops of Rome: they too have found the Pelagians deceitful and their views detestable.[270] In this way, Augustine grounds his anti-Pelagian arguments in the testimony of reputable witnesses to the orthodox faith—witnesses whose testimony would be especially persuasive to the western audience for whom Augustine was writing.[271]

The second key element of Augustine's argumentation in Book 2 is found in its final section, where he considers the views of Ambrose on original sin. This section functions as a *peroratio* of sorts, in which Augustine intends to offer his readers the final and most convincing proof of Pelagius's heresy. With rhetorical effect, Augustine introduces his quotations from Ambrose with a lengthy sentence:

> But now as we are about to conclude this book, we judge it necessary, just as we did with respect to grace, to bring Ambrose, the bishop of God—whose most sound faith Pelagius especially preached among the ecclesiastical writers of the Latin language—to respond to the deceitful chattering of these people about original sin, in the destruction of which grace itself is commended more clearly.[272]

---

270 See *gr. et pecc. or.* 2.21.24 where Augustine notes that in the *Tractoria* Zosimus had called the teachings of Pelagius *execranda*.

271 We should also note the importance of Augustine's reference to the influence of the faith of the Roman people in leading Zosimus to condemn Pelagius. While he does not dwell on this "popular belief" for long here, he will return to the testimony given by the faithful later in his debates with Julian.

272 *gr. et pecc. or.* 2.41.47: *sed iam etiam istum conclusuri librum oportere arbitramur, ut Ambrosium antistitem dei, cuius inter Latinae linguae scriptores ecclesiasticos praecipue Pelagius integerrimam fidem praedicat, sicut de gratia fecimus ita et de peccato originali, in quo delendo ipsa gratia euidentius commendatur, calumniosae istorum loquacitati respondere faciamus* (Latin: CSEL 42:205.3–8; English: my translation).

FROM DIOSPOLIS TO THE *TRACTORIA*

Augustine then immediately turns to four quotations from Ambrose.[273] He does not make any explanatory comments following the individual quotations, but merely quotes one passage after another with only a few words of introduction—allowing the sheer and stark accumulation of evidence to speak for itself. After the quotations, Augustine immediately concludes,

> Pelagius contradicts these words of the man of God, whom he praised so highly, when he says, "As we are begotten without virtue, so we are begotten without vice."[274] What recourse does Pelagius have but to condemn his own error or to repent of his having praised Ambrose so highly? But blessed Ambrose said these things as a Catholic bishop in accord with the Catholic faith. Hence, it follows that Pelagius has strayed from the path of this faith along with his disciple, Caelestius, and has been correctly condemned by the authority of the Catholic Church, unless he should repent, not for having praised Ambrose, but for having held views opposed to his.[275]

This final section of Book 2 is much shorter than its equivalent in Book 1 and does not focus on highlighting the connection between Ambrose's thought and scriptural teaching. However, its blunt brevity seems to have been intentional. Here, at the end of a lengthy consideration of Pelagius's views and a response to several objections, Augustine introduces his star witness to deliver four resounding blows against the opposition. Ambrose, Augustine claims, speaks for the Church and faithfully witnesses to the Church's ancient and universal doctrinal tradition. In that sense, when Pelagius disagrees with Ambrose, he also disagrees with the Church at large and, as a result, has been rightly condemned.

Taking a step back and looking at the final sections of Books 1 and 2 together, there are a few significant aspects to recognize. First and foremost, we should note the obvious: Augustine chose to organize Books 1 and 2 so as to examine Ambrose's views in the *conclusion* of the books—it surely speaks to the importance of these sections that Augustine felt it best to place them at the end of both books, as the final word, as it were, on the topic at hand. Further, reflecting on Augustine's decision to offer quotations from

---

273 Augustine cites Ambrose, *De fide resurrectionis* 2.6 (CSEL 73:254); *De paenitentia* 1.3.13 (CSEL 73:125–26); *Expositio in Isaiam prophetam* (lost); and *Expositio euangelii secundum Lucam* 2.56 (CSEL 32.4:72).

274 A quotation from Pelagius's *Pro libero arbitrio*. See *gr. et pecc. or.* 2.13.14 for the full quotation.

275 *gr. et pecc. or.* 2.41.48 (Latin: CSEL 42:206.9–18; English: Teske, WSA I/23, 445).

Ambrose, we should recognize that, at a most basic level, these appeals to Ambrose were prompted by Pelagius's own words of admiration for the bishop and his scriptural interpretation. Pelagius's rather adulatory praise opens the door for Augustine to trap the British ascetic in a snare of his own making. However, the appeals are more than just an attempt to trap Pelagius. More importantly, the appeals serve to substantiate Augustine's claims that Pelagius's views were at odds with the Church's doctrinal tradition. Pelagius surely expressed the opinion of many Roman Christians with his praise of Ambrose. In that sense, if Augustine could clearly and decisively show Ambrose's opposition to key Pelagian views, it would surely help his cause with Melania, Pinianus, and Albina—as well as his other readers—as he attempted to show the novelty of the Pelagian cause and the antiquity and universality of the views they opposed. As we know, Augustine had already deployed citations from renowned Christian authors at several points in the controversy. However, it is important to recognize that Augustine's efforts here represent a subtle development from these earlier appeals. Previously, we have seen Augustine deploy such quotations in *s. 294*, *De peccatorum meritis*, and *De natura et gratia*. In all of those places, Augustine's use of quotations from figures like Cyprian, Jerome, Ambrose, and others was relatively limited. In *De peccatorum meritis*, Augustine quoted two passages from a letter of Cyprian and two passages from two works of Jerome. A bit earlier, in *s. 294*, Augustine had quoted a slightly lengthier version of one of the passages from Cyprian that he would go on to use again in *De peccatorum meritis*. More quotations were offered in *De natura et gratia*, but as direct responses to quotations Pelagius had provided in his *De natura*. Even in this key section, Augustine only produced four quotations on his own initiative: one from Hilary and three from Ambrose. But in *De gratia Christi*, Augustine offers quotations of a total of eleven different passages in response to what appears to have been a single quotation from Pelagius in his *Pro libero arbitrio*—the same quotation that had been used in *De natura*. Further, only one of these quotations in *De gratia Christi* is a "repeat" from *De natura et gratia*.[276] All of this—both the placement of the quotation sections and the number of quotations offered—suggests just how important it was for

---

276 Namely, the last one in Book 1, found at *gr. et pecc. or.* 1.50.55. In this sense, we should also recognize the amount of research that must have gone on behind the scenes to amass these quotations, whether Augustine did it himself or tasked one of his assistants to do so for him. Hombert suggests Augustine's reading of *Pro libero arbitrio* prompted him to (re-?)read Ambrose's *Expositio euangelii secundum Lucam* in the winter of 417–18 (Hombert, *Nouvelles*

FROM DIOSPOLIS TO THE *TRACTORIA* 257

Augustine when he was writing *De gratia Christi* not just to undermine the support Pelagius attempted to draw from Ambrose but, more importantly, to demonstrate the link between his own anti-Pelagian views and the traditional teaching of the Church. Although he still had some concerns about this form of argumentation,[277] it seems that by 418 Augustine had accepted that the benefits outweighed the potential dangers.

Even though the Pelagians had been condemned, Augustine clearly sensed in *De gratia Christi* that the battle was not over. Indeed, there are indications in this work that Augustine was already aware of the resistance put forward by Julian of Eclanum in the wake of the *Tractoria*. But even aside from that, recent experience had taught him how quickly favor could shift in Rome. Thus, in the summer of 418, it remained crucial for him to demonstrate—in opposition to the claims of the Pelagians—that the positions he supported had powerful backing and clear grounding in the Church's doctrinal tradition.

The Fates of Pelagius and Caelestius

After their condemnations, Pelagius's and Caelestius's importance in the controversy waned. Marius Mercator reports that Pelagius was apparently condemned by a synod under the leadership of Theodotus of Antioch, having been abandoned by his former defender Praylus of Jerusalem.[278] Pelagius left Palestine at that point and thereafter disappears from the record of history. At times it has been proposed that Pelagius spent his final years in Egypt since Cyril of Alexandria had apparently been slow to condemn the Pelagians.[279] However, there is no concrete evidence for Pelagius's presence in Egypt.[280] Further, this hypothesis made more sense before the discovery of *ep.* 4*, where we learn of Cyril's involvement in the Pelagian controversy.[281]

---

recherches, 226–27). Perhaps Paulinus of Milan helped Augustine obtain some of Ambrose's writings (my thanks to Walter Dunphy for this suggestion).

277 See *gr. et pecc. or.* 1.43.47.

278 See Marius Mercator, *Commonitorium super nomine Caelestii* (ACO 1.5.1, p. 68, ln. 41–p. 69, ln. 5). Drecoll, "Pelagius, Pelagiani," 625n3, doubts the reliability of this report, however.

279 See, e.g., Wermelinger, *Rom und Pelagius*, 210, and the letter from a certain Eusebius to Cyril found at CSEL 35.1:113–15.

280 See, e.g., Drecoll, "Pelagius, Pelagiani," 625n3, who emphasizes that this conjecture is unverifiable.

281 See Gerald Bonner's comments in "Some Remarks on Letters 4* and 6*," 156.

In contrast, more is known of Caelestius's life after his condemnation.[282] In 423 or 424 he reappeared in Rome seeking to convince Pope Celestine (422–32) of his orthodoxy. However, his attempts were unsuccessful and he was banished from Italy.[283] In 428 or 429, he was in Constantinople at the same time as Julian of Eclanum and the other bishops who had been deposed from their sees, seeking to gain favor with Nestorius, the bishop of Constantinople.[284] However, perhaps convinced by the anti-Pelagian campaign of Marius Mercator, Emperor Theodosius soon banished the Pelagians from Constantinople.[285] Then, in 431, Caelestius and the rest of the Pelagians were condemned along with Nestorius at the Council of Ephesus.[286] Nothing further is known about Caelestius's life after Ephesus.

CONCLUSION

The years 416 through 418 were a crucial period in the Pelagian controversy, witnessing a series of exchanges between Africa and Rome as the anti-Pelagian forces attempted to respond to Pelagius's acquittal at Diospolis in December 415. Throughout our analysis of this period, we have noted the continuing efforts by Augustine and his allies to convince their interlocutors not simply of the heterodoxy of Pelagius's views, but also of their lack of

---

282 For more on Caelestius after 418, see Honnay, "Caelestius, Discipulus Pelagii," 294–97, and "Caelestius," in Pietri and Pietri, *Prosopographie chrétienne du bas-empire*, vol. 2, *Prosopographie de l'Italie chrétienne*, 1:357–75.

283 Prosper of Aquitaine, *Liber contra collatorem* 21.2 (PL 51:271). See also Honnay, "Caelestius," 295, and Wermelinger, *Rom und Pelagius*, 249–50.

284 For more discussion of Caelestius's activity in Constantinople, see Malavasi, *La controversia pelagiana*, 163–70. Malavasi argues that although Caelestius and Julian were in Constantinople at the same time, they do not appear to have been part of the same group.

285 See Marius Mercator, *Commonitorium super nomine Caelestii* (ACO 1.5.1, p. 65, ln. 35–40) and Honnay, "Caelestius," 295. Nestorius sent Caelestius a supportive letter (for the text of this letter, see ACO 1.5.1 p. 65, ln. 18–33), which Honnay suggests ("Caelestius," 295) should be dated to after Caelestius's banishment from Constantinople.

286 See Marius Mercator, *Commonitorium super nomine Caelestii* (ACO 1.5.1, p. 65, ln. 40–42). See also Honnay, "Caelestius," 296–97. As Honnay notes, it is unclear whether Caelestius was actually present in Ephesus—it seems likely he was not. For some discussion of Ephesus and the Pelagians, see Lössl, *Julian von Aeclanum*, 311–19. For a reference to the condemnation of the Pelagians in the *acta* of Ephesus, see Richard Price, trans., *The Council of Epehesus of 431: Documents and Proceedings*, Translated Texts for Historians 72 (Liverpool: Liverpool University Press, 2020), 409–10. Oddly, this passage indicates that the Pelagians had been condemned on an earlier day of the council, but the minutes for that day contain no references to such an event (see Price, *Council of Ephesus*, 37 and 410n288).

grounding in the Church's ancient and universal doctrinal tradition. Convincing others of this latter point took on particular urgency in the aftermath of Diospolis. Indeed, Pelagius's acquittal in large part seemed to confirm an argument the Pelagians had been making since at least 411, but probably earlier: that the eastern churches shared their views. This context helps to explain the strategic handling of Diospolis employed by Augustine and his allies: nowhere in this period are the bishops at Diospolis criticized to any significant degree for their decision. Instead, as we have seen, Augustine consistently sought to portray these bishops as his allies: even if they had acquitted Pelagius (due to his own deceptiveness, the lack of a reliable interpreter, and the absence of Heros and Lazarus), they had correctly condemned his heresy. This approach to Diospolis was by no means Augustine's only option: indeed, he very well could have emphasized the bishops' failure to analyze Pelagius's statements adequately or highlighted John of Jerusalem's apparent bias, as Orosius had in his *Liber apologeticus*, or tarred the whole affair as a "miserable synod," as Jerome had. However, Augustine chose the path he did at least in part, it would seem, to bolster his claim that the universal Church was opposed to Pelagianism and thereby to defend the unity of the Church.

Other arguments were deployed to make this same point. For example, we also saw Augustine and his allies—especially in their initial responses in 416—highlighting the concrete ways in which Pelagianism conflicted with the Church's belief. Of particular note here was the strong emphasis placed on the Church's life of prayer, which certain aspects of Pelagius's teaching seemed to undermine. The aim of such emphases was to show that Pelagianism attacked some of the basic aspects of daily Christian life since the time of the apostles. In addition to these arguments, we also noticed that Augustine and his allies by 417 and 418 increasingly saw the utility of identifying specific renowned Christian authors who would vouch for their views: Paulinus did it in his letter to Zosimus—a letter, which, I suspect, was written under the close supervision of Augustine—and Augustine himself, as we have just discussed, did it to an exceptional degree in *De gratia Christi*. Finally, we also witnessed Augustine in the aftermath of Innocent's and then Zosimus's condemnation of Pelagius and Caelestius citing the popes' judgments, while attempting to draw attention away from Zosimus's rather embarrassing flip-flopping. Even if he did not phrase it in quite this way, Augustine was trying to emphasize the fact that Rome had spoken (consistently and in agreement with Africa) and that the case was closed. All these strategic arguments indicate the continuing importance for Augustine of the Pelagians' arguments that, in practice, seemed to pit various parts of the Church against each other. During this crucial period of the controversy, Augustine was faced with what appeared to be vindication of these Pelagian claims. As a result, he had to redouble his efforts to prove the contrary—that the Church, ancient and universal, was united against the Pelagians' views.

Although the condemnation of Pelagius and Caelestius in 418 prompted their swift exit from the foreground of the controversy, this condemnation did not by any means mark the end of the debate. Indeed, as we shall see in the next chapter, the rise of Julian of Eclanum and his fellow recusant bishops in many ways presented more serious worries for Augustine. Pelagius and Caelestius, it is true, had patrons in high places (at least at the outset of the controversy)—but they seem to have had little social capital on their own to push back against the condemnations of 418. Julian and his allies, as bishops, had substantially more authority and, it seems, a firmer grasp of political know-how.[287] Their appeals to other bishops and to imperial officials had a de facto weight to them that Pelagius and Caelestius were unable to summon. As a result, Augustine saw in the accusations and arguments of Julian a danger for Church unity that in many ways far exceeded the threat posed by Pelagius and Caelestius, substantial though it was. It is to this final phase of the controversy that we now turn.

---

287 See, e.g., Brown's comments in *Eye of a Needle*, 376.

CHAPTER 5

A New Opponent
Augustine's Controversy with Julian (418–30)

I n this final chapter, we turn to the period 418–30, in which Julian of Eclanum emerged as a key opponent for Augustine—and, indeed, perhaps the most formidable opponent he would ever face. During this period Augustine produced a number a lengthy works to combat the writings and efforts of Julian and his allies—the two books of *De nuptiis et concupiscentia*, the four books of *Contra duas epistulas Pelagianorum*, the six books of *Contra Iulianum*, and the six books of its unfinished sequel, *Contra Iulianum opus imperfectum*. All told, the total length of these books far surpasses Augustine's anti-Pelagian output from the more "action-packed" years of 411 to 418, indicating how seriously Augustine took Julian's efforts.

Augustine's works against Julian are hardly popular today. They are seen by many scholars as repetitive, tiring, and, on the whole, rather unedifying.[1] See, for example, Peter Brown's comments:

---

1 See, e.g., the survey of scholarly views on the controversy with Julian compiled by Stuart Squires in *The Pelagian Controversy*, 144–45.

261

Compared with the sensitive dialogue which Augustine was quite prepared to enter into with pagan Platonists in the *City of God*, before much the same cultivated audience as Julian now addressed, his treatment of the challenge of Julian, a fellow-Christian bishop, was an unintelligent slogging-match. There is an element of tragedy in this encounter. Seldom in the history of ideas has a man as great as Augustine or as very human, ended his life so much at the mercy of his own blind-spots.[2]

Since first publishing those words in 1967, Brown has modified his position a bit, noting that he had deferred too much to existing scholarship in his assessment of the elderly Augustine,[3] and allowed the tone of the final works against Julian to color his total assessment of Augustine's final years.[4] Brown reports that reading the Divjak letters discovered in the early 1980s helped to change his position, revealing, as they do, "a very different, more attractive, because so poignantly painstaking, side of the old man."[5] Despite this re-evaluation of the old Augustine, Brown's original indictment of the works against Julian seems to have remained largely intact. If the old Augustine now appears more sympathetic, it is in spite of his works against Julian, which remain in the eyes of many an exceedingly unfortunate blemish on Augustine's literary efforts.

In addition to contributing to the main aim of this study—that is, of showing how crucial the threat of disunity was for Augustine's anti-Pelagian efforts—this chapter also serves to contextualize these works against Julian better, so that they (and their sometimes acerbic rhetoric) become more intelligible and no longer appear as such an anomaly in Augustine's corpus. The key to this contextualization is found, once again, by recognizing the degree to which Augustine believed Julian and his fellow bishops represented a threat to Church unity. The fervor and tenacity Augustine displays in his writings against Julian should not be understood simply as a function of his certainty about the orthodoxy of his own positions or his desire to exculpate himself in view of Julian's accusations of Manichaeism or his irritation at a young upstart's insults although all of these factors no doubt played a role in shaping Augustine's response. More importantly, Julian was an intelligent,

---

2 Brown, *Augustine of Hippo*, 389.

3 Especially John Burnaby (Brown, *Augustine of Hippo*, 466).

4 See Brown, *Augustine of Hippo*, 466ff.

5 Brown, *Augustine of Hippo*, 466.

A NEW OPPONENT: AUGUSTINE'S CONTROVERSY WITH JULIAN 263

connected, and politically-savvy bishop, supported by almost twenty other bishops. As a bishop, Julian could inspire (and, it would seem, already had begun to inspire) a real schism in the Church—much like Majorinus and his better-known successor, Donatus, had a century before in Africa. Being well-connected and politically-savvy, Julian attempted to draw support from powerful figures in the ecclesial and secular spheres, calling for knowledgeable judges to review the positions condemned in Zosimus's *Tractoria*. As we shall see, the anxiety Augustine felt at these developments is palpable in his writings against Julian.[6]

Our treatment of Augustine's works from this period will differ from that found in earlier chapters. Given the sheer size of the works against Julian—and given that many of Augustine's argumentative tactics are familiar at this point—our analysis will necessarily be more summary in form. With that said, let us return now to the summer of 418, and the aftermath of the condemnations of Pelagius.

RESISTANCE IN ITALY

Following Honorius's edict of April 30, 418, and Zosimus's *Tractoria* later that summer, several attempts were made to resist the prevailing anti-Pelagian winds in Italy. One locus of resistance was in the north, around Aquileia. There, several bishops wrote to their metropolitan (Augustine of Aquileia) to protest Pelagius's and Caelestius's condemnation and Zosimus's requirement that they (the bishops) affirm their agreement with the *Tractoria*.[7] Among other things, these bishops threatened to call for a plenary synod and cited a line from a homily of John Chrysostom to indicate his opposition to the

---

6 Commenting on Augustine's response to Julian's attempts to have the Pelagian issue reviewed by competent judges, Serge Lancel writes, "Augustine acknowledged with disarming frankness that for him there was no question of the enemies of the faith he defended being able to obtain from the powerful of this world 'a time and place to argue about it' (*c. Iul. imp.* 1.10). And the old bishop recalled the grievous experience of the troubles caused by Donatism in his Africa; only too real and sincere was his fear that the public debate desired by Julian would rekindle religious war, and with an even fiercer blaze" (*Saint Augustine*, 419).

7 This *Libellus fidei* is found at PL 48:506–26 and PL 45:1732–1736. See also the edition offered in Peter van Egmond, "A Confession without Pretence: Text and Context of Pelagius' Defence of 417 AD" (PhD diss., Vrije University, 2013), 224–33. Sometimes this *libellus* is attributed to Julian; however, Wermelinger has disputed that attribution (*Rom und Pelagius*, 221). For more discussion of the *libellus* and its context, see *Rom und Pelagius*, 220–26. See also Josef Lössl's brief treatments: *Julian von Aeclanum: Studien zu seinem Leben, seinem Werk, seiner Lehre und ihrer Überlieferung* (Leiden: Brill, 2001), 12–13 and 275–76n142.

doctrine of original sin.[8] While the identities of these bishops remain a mystery, it should not be terribly surprising that support for Pelagius and Caelestius (and their theological outlook) would be found around Aquileia, if we recall the connections between Rufinus of Aquileia and the circles around Pelagius while he was still in Rome.[9] What is more striking, perhaps, is that the bishops' *libellus* evinces a clear dependence on Pelagius's *libellus*, as Wermelinger has noted.[10] It is clear that these bishops had access to at least some of Pelagius's writings—and that their support for him was not simply due to shared views, but was also founded on (at least to some extent) a familiarity with the man and his writings. In that light, the strategy employed by these bishops to link their views to a renowned Christian writer—and, in this case, one from the East—gains some importance for our purposes, indicating once again the tendency of Pelagius and his allies to attempt to link their views with the universal Christian doctrinal tradition in explicit and relatively novel ways.

In addition to these bishops around Aquileia, support for the Pelagian cause also emerged at Rome, where Julian of Eclanum came to the fore as spokesman for a group of seventeen other bishops.[11] Born around 380, perhaps in the Italian region of Apulia, Julian was the son of a bishop named Memor or Memorius.[12] In his youth, Julian received an extensive education,

---

8 See PL 48:524–26. The quote from Chrysostom comes from his homily *Ad neophytos* 5–6 (SC 50:153–54), which would later be cited by Julian in his books written for Turbantius (see *c. Iul.* 1.6.21), albeit via a slightly different translation (see Wermelinger, *Rom und Pelagius*, 221). See also Jean-Paul Bouhot, "Version inédite du sermon 'Ad neophytos' de S. Jean Chrysostome, utilisée par S. Augustin," *Revue des études augustiniennes* 17 (1971): 27–41.

9 See Chapter 1.

10 *Rom und Pelagius*, 222–23.

11 There is, at times, confusion in the literature about how many bishops (including Julian) were members of this group. For example, Teske seems to suggest that there were nineteen bishops total, including Julian (WSA I/24, 13; see also Squires, *The Pelagian Controversy*, 144). Others (e.g., Lancel, *Saint Augustine*, 414) report that there were eighteen total. Augustine's words at *c. ep. Pel.* 1.1.3, appear to support the latter view. It is also unclear whether these eighteen bishops included the ones located near Aquileia or whether they were two separate groups. Lancel, for example, seems to assume that the eighteen included those near Aquileia (*Saint Augustine*, 414).

12 See discussion of the name of Memor/Memorius in Lancel, *Saint Augustine*, 523–24n1. The most important study of Julian's life and theological views is Lössl, *Julian von Aeclanum*. For a helpful overview of Julian of Eclanum's life and efforts against Augustine, see Mathijs Lamberigts, "Iulianus Aeclanensis," in *Augustinus-Lexikon*, 3:836–47. See also Wermelinger, *Rom und Pelagius*, 226–38.

A NEW OPPONENT: AUGUSTINE'S CONTROVERSY WITH JULIAN 265

which he frequently demonstrates in his writings against Augustine by quoting Cicero, Aristotle, as well as various Latin poets.[13] In fact, to supplement his education his father had corresponded with Augustine in 408 or 409, requesting a copy of Augustine's *De musica* for Julian.[14] Julian was married before becoming a bishop, although it is unknown whether he had any children.[15] Perhaps around 416, during Innocent's reign as pope, Julian was consecrated a bishop and given the see of Eclanum in Campania.[16] The precise chronology of Julian's activities following the condemnation of Pelagius and Caelestius is a bit uncertain.[17] Marius Mercator reports that Julian took part in a public debate in Rome over some issues related to Pelagianism, likely in the aftermath of Honorius's edict or Zosimus's *Tractoria*.[18] Julian would also write two letters to Pope Zosimus.[19] One of these has been lost, but parts of the other are extant.[20] In that letter, which was likely his response to the *Tractoria*, Julian refused to condemn Pelagius and Caelestius but was willing to reject some of the propositions attributed to them with some explanatory comments added. Around the same time, Julian and his fellow bishops appear to have appealed to Ravenna, if not to have Honorius's edict reversed, at least to encourage a less-than-enthusiastic implementation of it.[21]

13 See Lamberigts, "Iulianus Aeclanensis," 836. See also Lössl, *Julian von Aeclanum*, 74–146.

14 See *ep.* 101.

15 Lamberigts notes that Julian was living in a state of continence by the time of his controversy with Augustine (Lamberigts, "Iulianus Aeclanensis," 836).

16 See Marius Mercator, *Commonitorium super nomine Caelestii* (ACO 1.5, p. 68, ln. 29–30), where he reports that Julian was consecrated by Innocent. Wermelinger conjectures that Julian's consecration occurred around 416 (*Rom und Pelagius*, 227).

17 See Wermelinger, *Rom und Pelagius*, 229.

18 See Mercator, *Commonitorium lectori aduersum haeresim Pelagii* (ACO 1.5.1, p. 13, ln. 23–39) and CCL 88:336. Wermelinger suggests that this debate likely took place in 418 around the same time Julian wrote his letter to Zosimus as an answer to the *Tractoria* (*Rom und Pelagius*, 229). Lancel places the debate soon after Honorius's edict (*Saint Augustine*, 414). Lössl suggests that the debate may have taken place around June 29 when many people would have been in town for the feast of Saints Peter and Paul. Lössl also wonders whether Julian's adversary may have been Mercator himself (*Julian von Aeclanum*, 278).

19 See the quotation from Julian's *Ad Florum* in Augustine, *c. Iul. imp.* 1.18.

20 For these fragments from Julian's letter, see Mercator, *Commonitorium lectori aduersum haeresim Pelagii* (ACO 1.5.1, p. 12, ln. 7–39), and CCL 88:335–36. See also Wermelinger, *Rom und Pelagius*, 229–31, and Lössl, *Julian von Aeclanum*, 276ff., for discussion. Mercator indicates that this letter to Zosimus circulated widely throughout Italy.

21 So Lössl argues: *Julian von Aeclanum*, 279. As Lössl notes, the general (and husband of Galla Placidia) Constantius had to remind the prefect of Rome, Volusianus, to put the edict of

Julian's efforts included contacting Count Valerius, a high-ranking official at the imperial court.[22] Valerius was also married and apparently theologically literate.[23] No doubt with those details in mind, Julian accused the opponents of Pelagius and Caelestius of promoting ideas that would render marriage evil.[24] He asked Valerius to intervene and assign judges to the case to correct the injustice of Honorius's edict.[25]

All told then, the Pelagian debate was far from settled in Italy in the immediate aftermath of the edict of April 30 and Zosimus's *Tractoria*. From Aquileia to Rome, organized resistance emerged, requesting a review of the case and, if need be, the calling of a synod. It was by no means a foregone conclusion that the condemnations of Pelagius, Caelestius, and their views would remain intact. Indeed, the fact that numerous Italian bishops were willing to take a public stance against Zosimus and Honorius (or at least their decisions) put the longevity of those condemnations very much in question. With that in mind, let us return now to Africa, and examine Augustine's response to these developments.

TROUBLING NEWS FROM ABROAD

As we noted in the previous chapter, it seems that by the time Augustine had finished *De gratia Christi* in Carthage in the summer of 418 rumors had already begun arriving in Africa of resistance to the *Tractoria* and to some of the positions being promoted by the anti-Pelagian forces.[26] As a result, Augustine was under no illusion that Honorius's edict and the *Tractoria* signaled the end of the controversy. Indeed, he seems to have begun the

---

April 30 into effect in a letter sent sometime before December 418 (PL 56:500). This perhaps indicates that Volusianus had been rather slow to implement Honorius's edict.

22 Valerius's exact position at the court is not quite clear (Lössl, *Julian von Aeclanum*, 280). For more on Valerius, see Pietri, *Prosopographie*, 2242–2245.

23 See, e.g., Augustine's words in his *ep.* 200 to Valerius.

24 See Augustine, *nupt. et conc.* 1.1.1.

25 See Julian's comments on this letter to Valerius in his *Ad Florum*, found in Augustine, *c. Iul. imp.* 1.10.

26 See *gr. et pecc. or.* 2.33.38–2.40.46, where Augustine counters an objection that his views render marriage evil, an accusation at the heart of Julian's polemic. It is unclear how exactly this news came to Africa. It is possible that Marius Mercator had made mention of Julian's activities in a letter he sent to Augustine while he was still in Carthage in the summer of 418 (see Augustine's comments in his later reply to Mercator at *ep.* 193.1.1).

A NEW OPPONENT: AUGUSTINE'S CONTROVERSY WITH JULIAN 267

process of following up with various Italian contacts to make certain that there would not be another about-face on the Pelagian issue.[27] However, his anti-Pelagian efforts had to be put on hold when he set out from Carthage (perhaps around the end of July) to travel west with Alypius and Possidius of Calama to Caesarean Mauretania on a special mission from Pope Zosimus.[28] While in the west (indeed, the farthest west he would ever travel), Augustine did have the opportunity for some correspondence. Among other things, he wrote a lengthy letter (*ep.* 190) to Optatus, a bishop in Spain, on the topic of the origin of the soul. Toward the end of the letter, Augustine takes the opportunity to warn Optatus about the views of Pelagius and Caelestius and forwards to him Innocent's letters to the Africans and Zosimus's *Tractoria*. He also provides a quotation from the *Tractoria* (one of the three extant fragments). Afterward, he writes, "These words of the Apostolic See contain the Catholic faith that is so ancient and well-founded, so certain and clear, that it is impious for a Christian to doubt it."[29] The threat of the continuing spread of Pelagian ideas was, evidently, on Augustine's mind.

When he returned to Hippo (probably in October[30]) several letters were waiting for him, many of which concerned Pelagian matters. One was from the Roman priest (and future pope) Sixtus, who had previously been rumored to be a supporter of Pelagius. Sixtus had earlier sent a letter to Aurelius in Carthage to profess his orthodoxy on the issue of grace, but in this letter (addressed to Augustine and Alypius) he spelled out his views in

---

27 For example, Augustine reports at *ep.* 200.1 that he had sent several letters to Valerius in Ravenna (presumably in the spring or early summer of 418). We also learn from Augustine's *ep.* 191 and 194 that the future pope Sixtus (at this time a priest in Rome) had sent a brief letter along with the *Tractoria* to Aurelius to profess his orthodoxy on the issue of grace (he had been reputed to be a supporter of Pelagius and Caelestius). Sixtus would soon address a letter to Augustine and Alypius that arrived sometime later in the summer of 418. It seems likely to me that this letter was prompted by an earlier letter to Sixtus from Augustine and Alypius, perhaps requesting a fuller explanation of his views than was found in the brief letter sent to Aurelius (it is possible, too, that this letter from Augustine and Alypius had been sent prior to the publication of the *Tractoria*, perhaps around the time of *ep.* 188 to Juliana).

28 The mission involved the case of a bishop named Laurentius who had been deprived of his see and had appealed his case to Rome. For more see Lancel, *Saint Augustine*, 348ff.

29 *ep.* 190.23 (Latin: CSEL 57:159.19–160; English: Teske, WSA II/3, 274). The thrust of Augustine's argument is that, although a variety of opinions may be acceptable on the issue of the origin of the soul, there can be no disagreement on the issue of original sin.

30 See Lancel, *Saint Augustine*, 355.

a bit more detail.[31] A letter from Celestine, a Roman deacon (and another future pope), had also arrived during his absence. While the exact contents of Celestine's letter are a bit less certain than Sixtus's, it seems possible that it, too, dealt with Pelagian matters.[32] A letter and book against the Pelagians also awaited him from Marius Mercator, who was an ardent anti-Pelagian based in Rome in 418.[33] Augustine had already received a letter from Mercator earlier in the summer while still at Carthage, but had been unable to draft a response at the time and had forgotten to do so while in Caesarean Mauretania. In the meantime, Mercator had sent a second letter, in which he expressed his disappointment at Augustine's failure to respond, along with a book arguing against the Pelagians via scriptural testimonies.[34] All of these letters merited responses: an initial brief letter to Sixtus (*ep.* 191), which was followed by a lengthier reply (*ep.* 194) later in the year[35]; a short reply to Celestine (*ep.* 192); as well as a slightly longer response to Mercator *(ep.*

---

31 Neither of Sixtus's letters is extant; however, Augustine's replies to Sixtus can be found at *ep.* 191 and 194.

32 See Wermelinger, *Rom und Pelagius*, 205.

33 For more on Mercator, see Robert Dodaro and Edgardo Martín Morales, "Marius Mercator," in *Augustinus-Lexikon*, vol. 3, ed. Cornelius Mayer (Basel: Schwabe, 2004–2010), 1179–1181; Claudia Konoppa, *Die Werke des Marius Mercator: Übersetzung und Kommentierung seiner Schriften* (New York: Lang, 2005); Malavasi, "Marius Mercator's Enemies in Augustine's *Letter* 193"; Pietri and Pietri, *Prosopographie*, 1499–1504; Serafino Prete, *Mario Mercatore polemista antipelagiano* (Torino: Marietti, 1958); Otto Wermelinger, "Marius Mercator," in *Dictionnaire de spiritualité*, vol. 10, ed. Marcel Viller (Paris: G. Beauchesne et ses fils, 1980), 610–15.

34 See *ep.* 193.1. When Augustine refers to this book, he speaks of it as *alium librum* (CSEL 57:168.14–15). Was there an earlier book Mercator had sent to Augustine, or is Augustine simply distinguishing this book from the second letter Mercator had sent? Teske (WSA II/3, 280) seems to think that Mercator had written two anti-Pelagian books but may be confusing these with Mercator's later *Commonitoria* against Caelestius and Julian. Wermelinger, "Marius Mercator" (*Dictionnaire de spiritualité*), 610 speaks of three letters and two books. See also Malavasi, "Mercator's Enemies," 361.

35 *Ep.* 194 was delivered to Rome by Firmus, who had carried Sixtus's original letter to Augustine. (For more on Firmus, see below at n. 38.) *Ep.* 194 is largely filled with discussion of the difficult issue of the justness of God's choice to save some people but not all. Augustine's argumentation is mainly scripturally based, but at the very end of the work he appeals several times to the liturgical rite of baptism (especially the rites of exsufflation and exorcism) as well as the longstanding practice of infant baptism itself—lines of argumentation found previously at *gr. et pecc. or.* 2.40.45 and *pecc. mer.* 1.34.63. Once again, this liturgical argumentation serves to ground Augustine's theological views and interpretation of scripture.

A NEW OPPONENT: AUGUSTINE'S CONTROVERSY WITH JULIAN

193).[36] Augustine seems to have sent them shortly after his return to Hippo, entrusting their delivery to a Roman acolyte named Albinus.[37]

Shortly thereafter, however, a bishop named Vindemialis and a priest named Firmus arrived with additional letters, this time from Count Valerius in Ravenna.[38] Augustine had previously written several letters to Valerius, without receiving any reply—which had no doubt increased his anxiety over the prospect of a reversal of imperial policy in favor of the Pelagians.[39] From the letters—and, perhaps more importantly, from Firmus—Augustine learned of Valerius, his zeal for the faith, as well as the accusations that had been communicated to him by the Pelagians—namely, that their opponents denigrated marriage and human nature with their views on original sin.[40] As Valerius's letters are no longer extant, it is difficult to gauge their tone and attitude toward Augustine. However, Augustine's own responses (*ep.* 200 and *De nuptiis et concupiscentia* 1) suggest that Valerius was, at least to some extent, a supporter of the anti-Pelagian cause but was concerned by the Pelagian accusations he had received.[41]

In the aftermath of this news from Ravenna, Augustine took the somewhat unusual step of composing a book (*De nuptiis et concupiscentia* 1) for

36 Augustine's letter to Mercator contains some familiar arguments, including one founded on the rite of infant baptism. Mercator had reported to Augustine that the Pelagians think that infants "believe" through those who present them for baptism. For Augustine, the mechanics of this "vicarious" believing is analogous to that which undergirds the transmission of original sin. In this sense, since infants can be said to be believers through the agency of others (namely, their parents or godparents), so too they can be said to be guilty through the agency of others (namely, Adam). Augustine had deployed similar arguments previously (see, e.g., *pecc. mer.* 1.9.10 and 3.2.2; *s.* 294.12).

37 For more on Albinus, see "Albinus 1," in Pietri and Pietri, *Prosopographie chrétienne du bas-empire,* vol. 2, *Prosopographie de l'Italie chrétienne,* 1:77–78.

38 Firmus was a trusted messenger in Augustine's circle and seems to have been conversant in matters related to the Pelagian controversy (for example, he had previously delivered Jerome's *Dialogus aduersus Pelagianos* to Ravenna). See "Firmus 2," in Mandouze, *Prosopographie,* 458–59, as well as "Vindemialis 1," in Mandouze, *Prosopographie,* 1215. The letter from Vindemialis was not addressed to Augustine alone but was likely intended for several key bishops in Africa (see *ep.* 200.1)

39 See Augustine's comments at *ep.* 200.1, written later in 418 or early 419 to Valerius.

40 See *ep.* 200, as well as Augustine's comments at *retr.* 2.53.80 and *nupt. et conc.* 1.2.2.

41 It is difficult to gather a completely unbiased portrait of Valerius's views given the rather excessive praise lavished upon him by Augustine in *ep.* 200 and *nupt. et conc.* 1. Dalmon suggests that the letter from Valerius delivered by the bishop Vindemialis was an anti-Pelagian circular (*Un dossier,* 163).

Valerius to rebut the Pelagian accusations. As Augustine notes, he tended to avoid writing books for important individuals unbidden—no doubt fearing that it would look improper.[42] Nevertheless, he clearly felt the present situation was urgent enough to risk such a breach of protocol. And this is an important point to keep in mind: Augustine's efforts against Julian and his allies appear to have been motivated by a real fear on Augustine's part that they would succeed in convincing Valerius or others to re-consider the imperial (and papal) decrees against Pelagianism. For Augustine, the stakes were as high as they had ever been. As a result, Augustine's response to Valerius in the first book of *De nuptiis et concupiscentia* aims to rebut Julian's accusations that Augustine and his allies denigrate marriage, to articulate a proper understanding of concupiscence and its role in the transmission of original sin, and to suggest, yet again, that the Pelagians have abandoned the Church's ancient and universal faith. He makes this final point in a particularly incisive way in the book's conclusion. There, Augustine quotes a passage from Ambrose's *Expositio Isaiae prophetae*, where the bishop of Milan had indicated that sexual union was in some way involved in the transmission of sin.[43] He follows this reference with a citation of Pelagius's praise of Ambrose's faith and then comments, "Pelagius should repent of the views he held in opposition to Ambrose so that he need not repent for having praised Ambrose so highly."[44] As a whole, Augustine's strategy here is the same as that which we observed in *De gratia Christi*, where he concluded each of the two books with quotations of Ambrose. The purpose is clear: to close his book with decisive evidence that Pelagius (and his followers) have abandoned the faith that Ambrose held—a faith whose orthodoxy was beyond dispute, even according to the

---

42 As Augustine writes: "I have never wanted to force an illustrious personage in such a lofty position as you hold, especially someone who is not filling the post at leisure, but is still active in public affairs, and military ones at that to read any of my works, unless he asked me. After all, to do so would be more a sign of impudence than of zeal. If I have done something of the sort in this case, please forgive me on account of those reasons which I have mentioned, and give your kind attention to what follows" (*nupt. et conc.* 1.2.2 [Latin: CSEL 42:213.13–20; English: Teske, WSA I/24, 29]).

43 Ambrose, *Expositio Isaiae prophetae*, frag. 1 (CCL 14:405.1–13), quoted by Augustine at *nupt. et conc.* 1.35.40.

44 *nupt. et conc.* 1.35.40 (Latin: CSEL 41:252.6–7; English: Teske, WSA I/24, 52).

Pelagians themselves.[45] After completing the book, Augustine sent it to Valerius in Ravenna where it likely arrived by the spring of 419.[46]

JULIAN'S CAMPAIGN CONTINUES (419)

Julian's attempts to sway Zosimus and Valerius failed. Sometime before Zosimus's death on December 26, 418, the pope condemned Julian and his episcopal allies.[47] Julian's hope may have been temporarily rekindled by the tumult that ensued after Zosimus's death: the Roman church divided over the election of a successor, with rival parties selecting Eulalius on the one hand and Boniface on the other. Boniface was not recognized as Zosimus's authentic successor until early April 419.[48] In the meantime, it appears that Zosimus's condemnation of Julian remained relatively inconsequential. However, on June 9, 419—no doubt at the request of anti-Pelagian agents— the emperor Honorius issued a second edict condemning the Pelagians and those giving them sanctuary.[49] Julian may have left Rome at this point—but his exact whereabouts for the next few years are uncertain.[50]

However, these defeats did not convince the now deposed bishop of Eclanum to abandon his campaign. First, sometime soon after Augustine's *De nuptiis et concupiscentia* arrived in Italy, Julian obtained a copy and wrote a lengthy four-book response to it for one of his fellow condemned bishops, Turbantius.[51] In the course of these four books, Julian sought to prove that Augustine's positions were essentially Manichaean in origin. He also lamented the fact that the decisions against the Pelagians had been judged by non-experts. Further, he argued that famed eastern bishops like John

---

45 Another passage with similarities to *De gratia Christi* is *nupt. et conc.* 1.20.22, where Augustine appeals to the rite of baptism (and, more specifically, the rite of exorcism) for proof that children are born with original sin. See *gr. et pecc. or.* 2.40.45.

46 See Wermelinger, *Rom und Pelagius*, 232. It seems likely that the messenger was Firmus, who was also tasked with delivering *ep.* 194 to Sixtus in Rome.

47 See *c. Iul.* 1.4.13.

48 For more, see Lössl, *Julian von Aeclanum*, 286n217, and Wermelinger, *Rom und Pelagius*, 239–41.

49 This edict is collected among the letters of Augustine as *ep.* 201. Pope Boniface seems to have taken some action against the Pelagians in 419 as well—see Augustine, *ep.* 16*.3.

50 See Lössl, *Julian von Aeclanum*, 288n227.

51 The extant fragments of this work can be found at CCL 88:340–96.

Chrysostom and Basil of Caesarea would have supported his view.[52] In this sense, Julian's *Ad Turbantium* made use of some of the key argumentative tactics that had prompted Augustine's entry into the controversy back in 411. What is new here, though, is its polemical forcefulness and its accusation of Manichaeism directed at Augustine specifically. As we shall see, the combination of these factors eventually led to Augustine's most impressive attempt to prove the antiquity and universality of his anti-Pelagian positions when he would compose a full rebuttal to Julian a few years later.

During the summer of 419, perhaps shortly after completing *Ad Turbantium*, Julian also composed two important letters.[53] The first was sent to the Roman church. In it, Julian repeated some of his attacks on Augustine from *Ad Turbantium*, accusing him of promoting Manichaean positions, and appealed to the church of Rome to abandon its support for such heretical positions.[54] The second letter was composed in conjunction with the other deposed bishops and was sent to Rufus, the bishop of Thessalonica. This letter focused on many of the same doctrinal issues as the one sent to the Romans; however, it is more important due to its strategic aims. As Josef Lössl has noted, Thessalonica was an important midpoint between Rome and Constantinople, both politically and ecclesially.[55] While both Rome and Constantinople claimed authority over the diocese of Thessalonica, Pope Innocent had earlier offered patriarchal rights to Rufus. In this sense, Thessalonica had gained a certain independence—but an independence highly dependent upon Rome's continuing favor. Lössl comments that, aware of the precariousness of this situation, Julian emphasized in his letter to Rufus the fact that under pressure Zosimus had reversed his decision on the Pelagian issue, supported positions that smacked of Manichaeism, and forced other bishops to agree to it without a synod. Lössl writes,

---

52 See, e.g., Augustine's comments at *c. Iul.* 1.4.14, 1.5.16, 1.6.21, 1.7.30, and 6.22.69. Note, however, that the quotation Julian attributed to Basil seems to have actually been from Serapion of Thmuis. See Cipriani, "L'autore die testi pseudobasiliani riportati nel C. Iulianum," 439–49. Julian will later refer to Theodore (of Mopsuestia, probably) in his *Ad Florum*: *c. Iul. imp.* 3.111.

53 Fragments of these letters survive in Augustine's *Contra duas epistulas Pelagianorum* and have also been gathered at CCL 88:336–40 and 396–98.

54 For more on Julian's authorship of this letter, see Wermelinger, *Rom und Pelagius*, 234–36.

55 Lössl, *Julian von Aeclanum*, 291ff. See also discussion of the relations between Rome and Thessalonica in Geoffrey D. Dunn, "Innocent I and Rufus of Thessalonica," *Jahrbuch der Österreichischen Byzantinistik* 59 (2009): 51–64.

Each of these charges also contained an allusion to Rufus's situation. What would happen to his position if every decision of a Roman bishop could be overturned by his successor? How would his approval of such a teaching be perceived in the East—a teaching like the African position on the transmission of sin that was so foreign to the thought of Eastern theology and seemed so Manichaean? How would the fact that, with the enforcement of this teaching, the principle of synodality had been trampled underfoot in the West be perceived in the region and in the East?[56]

Lössl's commentary is exactly on target here. In this letter, Julian shows himself to be far more than a skilled theological polemicist—he also reveals his skills in ecclesial politics. Julian's appeal to Rufus is highly strategic: as a sort of bridge between East and West, Rufus's support would have given Julian significant leverage in both areas. Of course, as it would turn out, Rufus seems to have done little or nothing to support Julian's cause. But at the time, it was far from decided how Julian's strategy would fare. And this, no doubt, deeply concerned Augustine and his allies.

All told, the fact that by the summer of 419 Julian had suffered several ecclesial and political defeats only seems to have encouraged him to accelerate his campaign by attacking Augustine directly and by making bold and strategic appeals to the Roman church and to Rufus. In this sense, far from dissipating, the Pelagian controversy had, in many ways, only grown more heated in the year after Pelagius and Caelestius's condemnation. In turn, Augustine's responses to Julian reveal just how anxious he was to undermine this campaign.

AUGUSTINE'S RESPONSE (420–22)

Sometime in the second half of 419, Augustine's longtime friend Alypius left Africa for Italy on a mission to Ravenna.[57] While the primary aim of this journey does not appear to have been related to the Pelagian controversy, nevertheless when Alypius returned (likely in the spring of 420), he brought with him copies of Julian's letters to the Romans and to Rufus of Thessalonica

---

56 Lössl, *Julian von Aeclanum*, 292.

57 For discussion of Alypius's travels, see M.-F. Berrouard, "Un tournant dans la vie de l'Église d'Afrique: les deux missions d'Alypius en Italie à la lumière des Lettres 10*, 15*, 16*, 22* et 23*A de saint Augustin," *Revue d'études augustiniennes* 31 (1985): 46–70.

as well as a document with extracts of *Ad Turbantium*.[58] After reading these documents, Augustine set to work crafting a response, writing a second book of *De nuptiis et concupiscentia* for Valerius in Ravenna and the four books of *Contra duas epistulas Pelagianorum* for Pope Boniface. In both works, which were likely sent to Italy in 421, Augustine once again attempted not only to refute Julian's positions but also to demonstrate that the deposed bishop's views ran counter to the Church's ancient and universal faith.

De nuptiis et concupiscentia 2 and *Contra duas epistulas Pelagianorum*

In his supplement to the first book of *De nuptiis et concupiscentia*, Augustine responds to the excerpts of Julian's arguments found in the document brought to him by Alypius. A major theme among these excerpts is Julian's contention that Augustine's positions are ultimately Manichaean in origin and imply that marriage, and its products (i.e., children), are evil. In this context, Augustine's need to characterize his own views as orthodox and held by all Christians was especially urgent. As a result, scattered throughout his rebuttals—which often attempt to undermine Julian's mischaracterizations of Augustine's positions—Augustine uses several arguments we have seen previously that are intended to indicate that his own views are shared by the universal Church. Among these arguments, appeals to the baptismal rite (and related practices) are particularly frequent. For example, early in the book, Augustine notes how many parents rush with their children to the Church for baptism, implying that they would not do so if they did not believe in original sin—an argument that Augustine had used since 411.[59] Later in the book, references to the exsufflation and exorcism that are a part of the baptismal rite recur several times.[60] Augustine notes that such rites would make no sense if infants were not bound by original sin. This argument, too, was first deployed in 411 but would grow increasingly important after 418 as the main focus of the controversy shifted from the mechanics

---

58 Pope Boniface had given the two letters to Alypius when the latter stopped in Rome on his way back to Africa. The summarized version of *Ad Turbantium* was sent by Valerius to Alypius while he was in Rome. It remains unclear who had compiled the summarized version of *Ad Turbantium*.

59 See *nupt. et conc.* 2.2.4. See also, e.g., *pecc. mer.* 1.18.23, *ss.* 293.10, 294.18.

60 See *nupt. et conc.* 2.18.33, 2.29.50, and 2.29.51.

A NEW OPPONENT: AUGUSTINE'S CONTROVERSY WITH JULIAN 275

of grace and free will to the reality and nature of original sin.[61] A few times in this second book Augustine also appeals to the views of Ambrose and Cyprian, noting that if Julian wishes to label him as a Manichee he must treat these two renowned Christians similarly.[62]

One passage toward the end of the book (*nupt. et conc.* 2.29.50–51) draws together a number of these themes. There, Augustine writes, "It is not true, then, as this fellow claims, that 'one who defends original sin is a Manichee through and through,' but it is true that one who does not believe in original sin is a Pelagian through and through."[63] Augustine then appeals to the practice of infant baptism to support this thesis: "For it is not the case that it was after the pestilential doctrine of Mani began to exist that in the Church of God little ones about to be baptized began to be exorcized and undergo exsufflation in order that it might be shown by those rites that they are transferred into the kingdom of God only if they have been rescued from the power of darkness [cf. Col 1:13]."[64] In this sense, Augustine argues that the traditional rites of baptism, including exorcism and exsufflation, existed prior to the time of Mani (d. 276), and thus could not have been drawn from the teaching of that heresiarch.[65] After listing a series of biblical passages that also complicate Julian's accusation that original sin is a doctrine of Manichaean origin, Augustine then turns to the testimony of Catholic commentators on scripture.

> What shall I say about the commentators on divine scriptures who have flourished in the Catholic Church? They have not tried to twist these texts to some other meaning; because they were solidly grounded in the most ancient and solid faith, they were not shaken by the new error. If I wanted to gather them and use their testimonies, it would take too long, and I might perhaps seem to have placed less faith than I ought in the canonical authorities, from which we ought not to be turned aside. Nonetheless—to say nothing of blessed Ambrose, though Pelagius, as I already mentioned, bore such great testimony to the integrity of his faith—Ambrose defended nothing else but original sin in little ones as the reason for their needing

---

61 See *pecc. mer.* 1.34.63, as well as *gr. et pecc. or.* 2.40.45 and *nupt. et conc.* 1.20.22.

62 See *nupt. et conc.* 2.5.15 and 2.29.51.

63 *nupt. et conc.* 2.29.50 (Latin: CSEL 42:305.23–306.1; English: Teske, WSA I/24, 85).

64 *nupt. et conc.* 2.29.50 (Latin: CSEL 42:306.1–5; English: my translation).

65 Here, as elsewhere, Augustine (rightly or wrongly) simply assumes the antiquity of the rites of infant baptism with which he was familiar.

Christ as a physician.[66] Will anyone say that Cyprian, who has received the most glorious of crowns, not only was but even could have been a Manichee, since he suffered martyrdom before that plague appeared in the Roman world? And yet in his book on the baptism of little ones he defended original sin; on its account he said that a little one should be baptized even before the eighth day in case of necessity so that its soul would not perish.[67] . . . Let this fellow dare to call these men Manichees and soil with that wicked charge the most ancient tradition of the Church. In accord with that tradition little ones, as I said, undergo the rites of exorcism and exsufflation so that they may be rescued from the power of darkness, that is, of the devil and his angels, and transferred into the kingdom of Christ.[68]

This passage reveals once again the strategic arguments Augustine deploys to suggest that his views are simply those of the universal Church from the very beginning. After outlining the teaching of scripture, Augustine argues that renowned exegetes like Ambrose and Cyprian have done nothing but teach what they found clearly revealed in scripture. So, too, the Church's liturgical praxis—that is, the rites of exorcism and exsufflation[69]—is founded upon that scriptural teaching. In this sense, Augustine argues that the whole life of the Church even prior to the emergence of Manichaeism speaks to the reality of original sin. Having linked these various pieces of evidence, Augustine concludes his argument with a rhetorical edge: "As for ourselves, we are much more ready to suffer any curses and insults along with these men and with the Church of Christ in the solid antiquity of this faith than to be praised along with the Pelagians with tributes of whatever eloquence."[70] By this, Augustine portrays (1) himself as a simple servant of the Church's traditional doctrine and (2) the Pelagians as eloquent, but heretical, advocates of novelty. All told, the second book of *De nuptiis et concupiscentia* intends to offer Valerius further evidence not only that Julian's attacks are groundless but also that Augustine's views have the support of the universal Church.

---

66 This is yet another reference to Ambrose's *Expositio in Isaiam*, which was quoted earlier at *nupt. et conc.* 1.35.40 and 2.5.15.

67 A reference to Cyprian's *Epistula* 64.2, quoted by Augustine at various earlier points in the Pelagian controversy—see, e.g., *s.* 294.19 and *pecc. mer.* 3.5.10.

68 *nupt. et conc.* 2.29.51 (Latin: CSEL 42:307.15–308.13; English: Teske, WSA I/24, 86–87).

69 For more on exorcism and exsufflation, see Chapter 2, n. 71.

70 *nupt. et conc.* 2.29.51 (Latin: CSEL 42:308.13–16; English: Teske, WSA I/24, 87).

A NEW OPPONENT: AUGUSTINE'S CONTROVERSY WITH JULIAN

In several ways, *Contra duas epistulas Pelagianorum* was, in comparison with *De nuptiis et concupiscentia* 2, a more urgent work for Augustine to write. While Augustine was likely confident by 420 that Valerius was his ally against Julian, Pope Boniface remained something of an unknown quantity. Indeed, the opening lines of *Contra duas epistulas Pelagianorum* reveal the relatively thin ties between Augustine and the bishop of Rome—despite Augustine's emphasis on the connection forged between the two by Alypius during his recent visit.[71] It is worth recalling that after his election, Boniface seems to have done little to enforce Zosimus's condemnation of Julian and his episcopal allies, at least initially.[72] As a result, Augustine may have remained uncertain about Boniface's true leanings. Even Boniface's delivery of Julian's two letters to Alypius was not without some ambiguity. Boniface appears not to have directly asked Augustine to write a response to the letters but shared them to make Augustine aware that Julian was attacking him and his views. As a result, Augustine's composition of *Contra duas epistulas Pelagianorum* for Boniface was—like the first book of *De nuptiis et concupiscentia*—something of a break from his custom, in that he wrote the work for Boniface without any explicit request on the pope's part.[73] The danger of

---

71 "I had come to know you, blessed and venerable Pope Boniface, from the splendid reputation you enjoy, and I had learned from many reliable messengers about the great grace of God with which you are filled. Then my brother, Alypius, was present in person and saw you. You welcomed him with great kindness and sincerity, and he had conversations with you that were inspired by mutual love. Though he stayed with you for only a short time, he became attached to you with a great affection. He made both himself and me known to your heart, and he brought you back to me in his heart. Now my knowledge of Your Holiness is greater to the extent that I am more certain of your friendship. For, though you hold a lofty position, you are not haughty, and you do not refuse to be a friend of the lowly and to return the love which has been shown you. After all, what else is friendship [*amicitia*]? It has received its name from nothing else but from love [*ex amore*] and is faithful nowhere but in Christ, in whom alone it can also be everlasting and blessed" (*c. ep. Pel.* 1.1.1 [Latin: CSEL 60:423.2–15; English: Teske, WSA I/24, 116]). Lössl suggests that the preface of *c. ep. Pel.* betrays a suspicious undertone (*Julian von Aeclanum*, 288). However, these words read to me more like a rather florid *captatio beneuolentiae*.

72 For some discussion of Boniface's attitude with regard to the Pelagians, see Wermelinger, *Rom und Pelagius*, 239–44, and Lössl, *Julian von Aeclanum*, 286–88. Lössl also notes the possibility that, years before, Boniface may have been involved with the group of Romans seeking to protect John Chrysostom in the midst of his troubles in Constantinople—a group that also included Aemilius of Beneventum, Julian's father-in-law (Lössl, *Julian von Aeclanum*, 288n226).

73 Hence Augustine's words in his preface: "Having been made more confident by that brother through whom I have come to know you better, I have ventured to write to Your Beatitude about these matters which at the present arouse by their quite recent provocation a bishop's

Julian's arguments and attempts to win favor in Rome and Thessalonica was simply too great to pass over in silence.

Given the urgent need Augustine seems to have felt to write this work, it is no surprise that *Contra duas epistulas Pelagianorum* contains a significant number of arguments aiming to prove that Augustine's positions are simply those held by the universal Church from the very beginning. As he responds to the two Pelagian letters,[74] Augustine makes use of arguments that, by this point, are very familiar: for example, he appeals to the Lord's Prayer,[75] nods to the rite of baptism itself as evidence for the reality of original sin,[76] recounts the tumultuous events of 417–18 in such a way as to emphasize the eventual agreement between Africa and Rome (and especially Pope Innocent) on the issue of Pelagianism,[77] and attempts to support his interpretation of Rom 5:12 through a citation of a book he believes to have been written by Hilary of Poitiers.[78]

---

concern—if we have any at all—to be vigilant over the Lord's flock" (*c. ep. Pel.* 1.1.1 [Latin: CSEL 60:423.15–18; English: Teske, WSA I/24, 116]).

74 Augustine addresses Julian's letter to the Romans in *c. ep. Pel.* 1 and the letter to Rufus in *c. ep. Pel.* 2–4.

75 Note that Augustine references the Lord's Prayer in several passages: e.g., *c. ep. Pel.* 1.13.27, 1.14.28, 3.3.5, 3.5.14, 3.5.15, 3.6.16, 3.7.17, 3.7.23, 4.2.2, 4.7.17, 4.10.27, and 4.12.37. Discussion of the Lord's Prayer also occurs in the context of Augustine's analysis of some quotations from Cyprian's commentary on this prayer (see *c. ep. Pel.* 4.9.25–10.28). However, not all these passages, in my estimation, constitute liturgical evidence used by Augustine to demonstrate the antiquity and universality of his doctrinal views. For example, in some cases, Augustine simply quotes the Lord's Prayer to identify it as a means of receiving forgiveness of sins (e.g., *c. ep. Pel.* 3.7.17).

76 See *c. ep. Pel.* 3.10.26. While addressing the Pelagians' accusation that the doctrine of original sin is necessarily linked with a traducianist view of the origin of the soul, Augustine explains his own hesitancy to support a particular theory of the soul's origin and his preference to speak on matters that are certain: "In any case this is what I say: (1) original sin is clearly manifest according to the holy scriptures and (2) it has been established by the great antiquity and authority of the Catholic faith and is most well-known by the clear practice of the Church that original sin is forgiven by the bath of rebirth in little ones. As a result, whatever anyone's research or conclusions might be concerning the origin of souls, if it is against this teaching, it cannot be true" (Latin: CSEL 60:519.6–11; English: Teske, WSA I/24, 183, slightly modified). Augustine's reference to the Church's "clear practice" (*clara celebritas*), I believe, points directly to the rites associated with baptism—especially exorcism and exsufflation.

77 See *c. ep. Pel.* 2.3.5–2.4.8. Augustine cites several passages from Innocent's letters to the Africans.

78 *c. ep. Pel.* 4.4.7. The quotation which Augustine believes to be from Hilary is actually from Ambrosiaster. Augustine uses this quotation to validate his own interpretation of Rom 5:12.

A NEW OPPONENT: AUGUSTINE'S CONTROVERSY WITH JULIAN

However, perhaps the most important section of the work occurs at the end of its final book, where Augustine offers over forty citations from the works of Cyprian and Ambrose. Augustine clearly places these citations at the very end of his work to function as final and decisive proof of the Pelagians' doctrinal innovations. Introducing this lengthy section of quotations, Augustine writes:

> The Pelagians say that their "enemies have received our statements in hatred for the truth," and that "the whole West has accepted a doctrine no less foolish than it is wicked." They complain that "for its confirmation the signatures of simple bishops who remained in their own territories without the gathering of a synod were obtained by force," though in reality the Church of Christ both in the West and in the East has been horrified at their "profane and novel language" (1 Tim 6:20). Hence, I think that it is part of our pastoral care not only to use against them as witnesses the holy canonical scriptures as we have already sufficiently done, but also to produce some proofs from the writings of the saints who have commented on them before us with great renown and immense glory. We do this not to equate the authority of any writer to the canonical books, as if it were not at all the case that what is understood by one Catholic may be understood better or more truly than by another who is also a Catholic. Rather, we do this to warn those who attribute some value to the statements of the Pelagians and to show them how Catholic bishops have followed the words of God on these topics before the vain and novel discussions of these people. In that way they may know that we are defending the correct Catholic faith as it was established from the beginning against the recent and destructive presumption of the Pelagian heretics.[79]

Here Augustine explains his intention to provide quotations from other Christian authors who have commented on scripture "with great renown and immense glory"—that is, with a reputation for being reliable witnesses to scriptural truth.[80] While admitting that the authority of such authors is not the same as that of scripture, Augustine nevertheless suggests it would

---

79 *c. ep. Pel.* 4.8.20 (Latin: CSEL 60:542.14–543.4; English: Teske, WSA I/24, 200–201, slightly modified).

80 In the next section, Augustine emphasizes Cyprian's reputation in both East and West and that Pelagius himself had mentioned him "with the honor certainly due him": "Blessed Cyprian, glorious with the crown of martyrdom, is well known, not merely to African and Western churches, but also to the Eastern churches, since his reputation in filled with praise and spreads his writings far and wide. Even the founder of their heresy, Pelagius, mentions

be helpful to keep in mind the way that Catholic bishops who lived before the time of the Pelagian heresy interpreted scripture. Such testimony will make it clear that Augustine is "defending the correct Catholic faith as it was established from the beginning."

After supplying his extensive collection of quotations, Augustine concludes his work, writing,

> It would take too long, if I wanted to cite everything which the saintly Ambrose said and wrote against this heresy of the Pelagians, which was to arise much later. He was not of course, replying to them, but preaching the Catholic faith and building up human beings in that faith. And I neither could cite nor ought I to have cited everything which Cyprian, so glorious in the Lord, put in his letters to show how true and truly Christian and Catholic is this faith we hold. This faith was transmitted through the holy scriptures from antiquity; it was held and preserved by our fathers right down to the present time in which these people have tried to destroy it; it will, by God's mercy, be held and preserved hereafter. For as these and other such testimonies drawn from his letters bore witness that this faith was handed down to Cyprian and handed on by him, so what Ambrose wrote about these matters, before these people began to cause trouble, shows that it was preserved down to our times and that Catholic ears, which are present everywhere, were horrified at their wicked novelties. The condemnation of some of these people and the correction of others has shown in a quite salutary manner that this faith is going to be preserved hereafter. For whatever murmurs they may dare to make against the sound faith of Cyprian and of Ambrose, I do not think that they will break out into such great madness that they will dare to label those memorable men of God we mentioned as Manichees.[81]

Augustine offers here a clear portrait of his view of the process of *traditio*: the true faith is rooted in scripture and has been handed on from generation to generation through Cyprian and Ambrose until the present day. Cyprian's and Ambrose's statements are, Augustine argues, clear proof of the continuity of doctrine and—insofar as they contain the same positions as Augustine— offer evidence that the bishop of Hippo's doctrinal views are simply those of the universal Church from the beginning. Further, since Cyprian and

---

him with the honor certainly due him, when in writing his *Book of Testimonies* he says that he is imitating him" (*c. ep. Pel.* 4.8.21 [Latin: CSEL 60:543.5–10; English: Teske, WSA I/24, 201]).

81 *c. ep. Pel.* 4.12.32 (Latin: CSEL 60:568.12–569.4; English: Teske, WSA I/24, 214–15).

A NEW OPPONENT: AUGUSTINE'S CONTROVERSY WITH JULIAN   281

Ambrose both (on Augustine's account) agree with Augustine's doctrinal views, how could Augustine be a Manichee when Cyprian and Ambrose clearly were not?[82] In this sense, through patristic argumentation Augustine undermines the Pelagians' claims both that the bishop of Hippo and his allies have perverted the Church's doctrinal tradition and that Augustine himself is a Manichee.

This show of force with which Augustine concludes *Contra duas epistulas Pelagianorum* reveals just how seriously he continued to take Julian's efforts to have the Pelagian issue revisited and reconsidered. Indeed, the series of patristic citations in *Contra duas epistulas Pelagianorum* is the most expansive collection found up to this point in the controversy. Augustine is intent on securing Boniface's support and ensuring that the pontiff refuses to bow to the pressure put on him by Julian.[83]

Contra Iulianum

After completing the second book of *De nuptiis et concupiscentia* and the four books of *Contra duas epistulas Pelagianorum* in either late 420 or early 421, Augustine sent them back to Italy.[84] Shortly thereafter, Augustine received a complete copy of Julian's *Ad Turbantium* from a bishop named Claudius.[85] Noticing that the excerpted version he had received from Valerius was deficient in many ways—and fearing that Julian and his allies would accuse him of falsifying Julian's arguments—he took it upon himself to reply

---

82 As Éric Rebillard suggests, "Cyprian represents the Catholic faith before Manicheism, while Ambrose represents it before the arrival of the Pelagians" ("A New Style of Argument," 575).

83 This aim can also be seen in the way Augustine defends Zosimus's condemnation of the Pelagians early in the second book against the Pelagians' complaints (*c. ep. Pel.* 2.4.8). There, Augustine insists on Zosimus's essential agreement with Innocent and argues that Innocent spoke for the traditional faith of the Roman Church when he condemned the view that infants can attain eternal life without the grace of baptism. Indeed, he writes, "whoever deviates from that statement is rather the one who abandons the Roman church" (Latin: CSEL 60:468.14–15; English: Teske, WSA I/24, 146–47). It takes little effort to imagine that Augustine also had Boniface in mind when he wrote those words.

84 It has sometimes been argued that Alypius was the one who delivered these works to Rome and Ravenna due to the accusations of Julian (see *c. Iul. imp.* 1.7 and 1.52.1). However, that perspective has more recently been put into doubt (see, e.g., Berrouard, "Un tournant," 62–63).

85 See *ep.* 207.

to the four books of Julian in their entirety.[86] Augustine's response, *Contra Iulianum*, ended up being six books in length, his longest anti-Pelagian work to date. This work represents the full flourishing of Augustine's many and various attempts to prove that his views are simply those of the universal Church from the beginning. Throughout the work, Augustine uses arguments that have become familiar to us: for example, he appeals to the Lord's Prayer as proof of the Pelagians' false understanding of grace, free will, and the possibility of sinlessness;[87] he cites baptismal practices as evidence for the reality of original sin;[88] he uses the decision of the Synod of Diospolis as evidence of eastern opposition to Pelagianism;[89] he emphasizes the unity of the churches of Rome and Africa against the Pelagians;[90] and he repeatedly cites the words of renowned Christian authors. However, it is the last of these tactics that is especially noteworthy in *Contra Iulianum*, something that can be glimpsed even from the very organization of the work. As mentioned above, there are six books in the work, with the final four functioning as direct refutations of each of Julian's four books of *Ad Turbantium*. However, in the first two books of *Contra Iulianum*, Augustine takes a more novel approach. Here he aims to show that by calling him a Manichee, Julian has also labeled a host of renowned Christian teachers Manichees as well. These teachers are, Augustine argues, no Manichees, but they are also no Pelagians, as their writings reveal. Augustine proves his point by citing an extensive number of Christian authors over the course of the first two books: Irenaeus, Cyprian, Hilary, Ambrose, Gregory of Nazianzus, John Chrysostom, Jerome, et cetera. He makes a point to cite from both the West and the East, from both ancient and more recent authors. In doing so, Augustine seeks to demonstrate the universality of anti-Pelagian theology.[91] However, he also provides these quotations in order to directly undermine Julian's complaint

---

86 See *retr.* 2.62, where Augustine mentions his reasons for responding to *Ad Turbantium* again.

87 See *c. Iul.* 1.8.38, 2.8.23, 2.10.33, 3.1.2, 3.13.27, 3.14.28, 3.21.48, 4.2.6, 4.3.28, 4.3.29, 5.4.15, 5.9.40, 6.14.44.

88 See *c. Iul.* 1.4.14, 1.5.19, 1.7.31, 3.3.8, 3.3.9, 3.5.11, 3.9.18, 6.5.11, 6.7.17.

89 See *c. Iul.* 1.5.19.

90 See *c. Iul.* 1.4.13.

91 Mathijs Lamberigts has argued that Augustine's efforts in *Contra Iulianum* can be seen as a precursor to Vincent of Lerins's *Commonitorium*: "Augustine's Use of Tradition in His Reaction to Julian of Aeclanum's *Ad Turbantium*: *Contra Iulianum* I–II," *Augustinian Studies* 41 (2010): 183–200.

A NEW OPPONENT: AUGUSTINE'S CONTROVERSY WITH JULIAN 283

that the Pelagian issue was settled by incompetent judges. Indeed, at the end of Book 2, Augustine writes:

> Were Irenaeus, Cyprian, Reticius, Olympius, Hilary, Gregory, Basil, Ambrose, and John roused to hatred for you "from the common dregs of workmen," as you joke in Ciceronian language? Were they "soldiers"? Were they "schoolboys"? Were they "sailors, bartenders, fishermen, cooks, and butchers"? Were they "youths dismissed from monasteries"? Finally, were these men "from the ordinary run of clerics," those whom you look down upon as men upset at your refined raillery or rather vanity, "because they cannot judge doctrines by the categories of Aristotle"? . . . These men are bishops, learned, grave, holy men, the staunchest defenders of the truth against wordy vanity. In their reason, learning, and freedom—three qualities you ascribed to a judge—you could not find anything to object to. If a synod of bishops were summoned from all over the world, I wonder whether that many men of their caliber could easily be assembled. . . . If you held the Catholic faith, you would find these judges just as welcome as you now find them terrifying because you attack the Catholic faith. For you attack the Catholic faith which they drank as milk and ate as food; they have served its milk and its food to little ones and to adults and have most clearly and bravely defended it against its enemies, including you who were not born then, though they are now showing you for what you are.[92]

Augustine's repeated use of rhetorical questions at the beginning of this quotation drives home his point: these authors whom Augustine has quoted are competent judges—they are exactly the kind of judges Julian had requested. For Augustine, these authors' opinions individually function as evidence of the heterodoxy of Pelagian doctrine; together, they can be viewed as a virtual synod of the most illustrious teachers the Church has to offer, in that sense indicating the consensus of the entire Church against the heresy.

In Augustine's response to Julian, there is yet another tactic at play. As suggested by the quotation from Augustine offered above, one of the complaints that Julian leveled against Augustine and his allies was that they had incited the mob against their opponents, relying on popular support to see their cause to victory.[93] For Julian, if the debate had been carried out before

---

92 *c. Iul.* 2.10.37 (Latin: PL 44:700.10–46; English: Teske, WSA I/24, 334–35).

93 For more on the dynamic of popular belief in the Pelagian controversy, see Salamito, *Les virtuoses et la multitude*. For a critique of some aspects of Salamito's account, see Rebillard, "*Dogma Populare*."

educated judges, the outcome would have been quite different. As it was, the mob had forced the hand of those in power—whether it be Zosimus or the imperial officials in Ravenna. At various points throughout his works against Julian, Augustine addresses this complaint—but it comes to take on particular significance in *Contra Iulianum*, as Augustine seeks to demonstrate that the entirety of the Church is opposed to Julian, both those who are educated and the common believers. For example, in the first book of *Contra Iulianum*, Augustine writes,

> It is not true, as you falsely claim, that we "set against you only the murmuring of the people." And yet the people themselves do murmur against you precisely because the question is not the sort that can escape the knowledge of the people. Rich and poor, high and low, learned and unlearned, men and women all know what is forgiven at any age in baptism. For this reason every day in the whole world mothers rush with their little ones not merely to Christ, that is, to the anointed one, but to Christ Jesus, that is, to the anointed savior.[94]

Note how Augustine both rejects Julian's accusation and, in a way, acknowledges that an aspect of that complaint is on target. Indeed, Augustine insists that he has not been trying to rile up the crowd against Julian. But, at the same time, Augustine affirms that the Christian faithful are indeed opposed to the Pelagians, precisely because their problematic views run counter to the beliefs of the common people. As he has elsewhere, Augustine then cites the custom of Christian mothers rushing with their infants to the Church for baptism as evidence for widespread belief in original sin. In this way, Augustine turns Julian's complaint into evidence against the Pelagians.

Later in the sixth book of *Contra Iulianum*, Augustine deploys a similar argument:

> If the people are aroused against you by this statement [i.e., an argument Augustine had made in *nupt. et conc.*], should you not rather be warned by this that this Catholic faith is so popular and firmly implanted in all that it cannot even escape the notice of the ordinary folks? It was, of course, necessary for all Christians to know what the faith does in their children in terms of the Christian mysteries. But why do you say that I forget our man-to-man battle and take refuge in the people? Who promised you single combat with me? Where, when, how, with what audience, with what

---

94 *c. Iul.* 1.7.31 (Latin: PL 44:662.9–18; English: Teske, WSA I/24, 289–90).

A NEW OPPONENT: AUGUSTINE'S CONTROVERSY WITH JULIAN   285

referees? Is it best, as you say, "to end the war under the condition offered," so that our struggle may resolve the war for all the rest? Heaven forbid that I should claim for myself the role among the Catholics that you are not ashamed to claim for yourself among the Pelagians. I am only one among many of us who refute your godless novelties as best we can in accord with the measure of faith that God has bestowed on each of us.[95]

In this passage, Augustine artfully counters Julian's complaints by identifying himself not as the champion of the orthodox party, but simply as yet another member of the universal Church deeply formed by the Church's doctrinal tradition and opposed to Pelagian teachings.[96] At the same time, Augustine also emphasizes that Julian wished to present himself as one of the few voices of truth crying out in a Church that had largely apostatized.[97] Augustine makes the same point in another passage in the sixth book of *Contra Iulianum*.

> But extraordinary [*egregius*] man that you are, you do not want to be part of the ordinary flock [*in grege . . . uulgari*]. For once again you spurn the view of the common people after so long a discourse, in which by the reasons given you had aroused them against me more gravely than they had been aroused against you. In considering your discourses, you undoubtedly realized that you neither could nor can accomplish anything by such arguments with people grounded in the truth and antiquity of the Catholic faith. Hence, you again turn your insolent lips to spurning them with scorn, and you run through the levels that make up the people, describing and mocking them individually. Not without reason is the multitude of Christians bitterly opposed to you![98]

With a clever play on words, Augustine begins this passage by linking Julian's view of himself as extraordinary (*egregius*) with his failure to be part of

---

95 *c. Iul.* 6.8.22 (Latin: PL 44:835.50–836.12; English: Teske, WSA I/24, 492).

96 In a similar vein, Salamito notes how Augustine presents himself in his disputes with Julian as not simply being present with the average Christians in their struggle against sin, but as being one among those Christians who are still struggling against sin: "Évêque, Augustine ne se situe pas seulement ici 'avec le peuple' (une attitude que peut admettre sans peine Julien lui-même) mais aussi 'dans le peuple' comme un pécheur parmi d'autres" (Salamito, *Les virtuoses et la multitude*, 228).

97 In this respect, Augustine's anti-Pelagian argumentation sometimes mirrored his anti-Donatist argumentation.

98 *c. Iul.* 6.11.34 (Latin: PL 44:841.22–33; English: Teske, WSA I/24, 498, slightly modified).

the Christian flock (*in grege*). He has isolated himself from the followers of Christ and has spurned them and mocked them. In this way, Augustine turns Julian's complaints about his opponents into an all-too-damning critique of Julian himself.[99]

Augustine completed his *Contra Iulianum* sometime in 421 or 422 and then sent it to the Italian bishop Claudius, who had originally supplied him with the full text of Julian's *Ad Turbantium*.[100] It does not seem that Julian ever received a copy of Augustine's *Contra Iulianum*, perhaps because he had already left Italy at this point. This is unfortunate; it would have been fascinating to see how Julian responded to Augustine's argumentation, especially that found in Books 1 and 2.

FURTHER WARNINGS ABOUT PELAGIANISM

During these early years of controversy with Julian, Augustine was continuing his efforts to enlist others to support the anti-Pelagian cause. Two letters are of particular note in this regard. The first is *ep.* 4*, addressed to Cyril of Alexandria, and likely written sometime in 420 or 421.[101] This letter was prompted by an argument over a passage in *De gestis Pelagii* in which Augustine wrote that not all sinners will be punished eternally.[102] A certain Justus had a copy of *De gestis Pelagii* and was accused of falsifying the passage in question by some people in Alexandria. As a result, Justus traveled to Hippo to determine whether his copy of the work was accurate—which it was. Before he returned to Alexandria, Augustine gave Justus *ep.* 4* to deliver to Cyril. In the letter, Augustine begins by recalling that Cyril had earlier sent him the proceedings from Diospolis. He then notes that he had written *De gestis Pelagii* as a commentary on those proceedings, arguing that, even though Pelagius himself had been acquitted at the synod, his views had been condemned.[103] He then reports the background to Justus's journey. After doing so, he notes that the possibility struck him that those who had accused

---

99 For another such passage, see *c. Iul.* 5.1.4.

100 See *ep.* 207.

101 This letter is sometimes dated as early as 417—but this does not seem likely to me. For discussion, see n. 72 in Chapter 4.

102 See *gest. Pel.* 3.9.

103 See *ep.* 4*.3.

Justus of falsifying *De gestis Pelagii* might have been Pelagian sympathizers themselves. It is possible, Augustine suggests, that they were upset with his view because they believed that sinlessness was possible in this life and that only those who have achieved a sinless state would inherit the kingdom of heaven.[104] Such a view runs afoul, Augustine notes, of that petition of the Lord's Prayer, *Forgive us our debts*. Augustine closes his letter by appealing to Cyril to step in to correct these people, if they do in fact hold Pelagian views. While this letter to Cyril is brief, it contains a few arguments that Augustine had repeatedly deployed to suggest that his fight against the Pelagians was one grounded in the teachings of the universal Church—namely, his emphasis on his agreement with the bishops at Diospolis and his warning that the Pelagian views run counter to the Lord's Prayer. It remains unclear what Cyril's position was vis-à-vis the Pelagian controversy, but Augustine clearly wished to win his support—and used a few of his standard argumentative tactics to attempt to accomplish this goal.[105]

Another letter from these years is *ep.* 6*, addressed to Atticus, the bishop of Constantinople.[106] This letter was prompted by an earlier message that Atticus himself had sent to Africa (to Aurelius of Carthage) reporting some actions he had recently taken against the Pelagians in Constantinople.[107] In his own letter, Augustine takes the opportunity to critique a number of the main argumentative points Julian and his allies tended to advance against Augustine regarding concupiscence, the goodness of marriage, and original sin. The letter is relatively brief, but notable insofar as it is one of the few extant letters that Augustine wrote to a bishop in the East. Like the letter to Cyril, this letter to Atticus reveals Augustine's on-going campaign to secure support in the East for the anti-Pelagian cause, especially in those locales

---

104 It is possible that these people were simply concerned about Origenism, thinking that Augustine was advocating some form of apokatastasis. But it is worth recalling that when the issue was discussed at Diospolis (see *gest. Pel.* 3.9–10), Pelagius had stated that anyone who believes that sinners will not be eternally punished is an Origenist. This is no doubt the reason why Augustine suspected there was some connection between these individuals in Alexandria and Pelagius.

105 For discussion of Cyril of Alexandria's role in the controversy, see Malavasi, *La controversia pelagiana in Oriente*, 97–116.

106 For more on this letter, see Berrouard, "Les lettres 6* et 19*," 269–77, and Duval, "Note Complémentaire: Lettre 6*," BA 46B, 444–56.

107 Though there is some debate in the scholarship, it seems likely to me that this action was later than that taken by Atticus against Caelestius in 416/17 (see n. 140 in Chapter 4).

where he had heard reports of Pelagian activity. Indeed, after their expulsion from Italy, some of Julian's allies took up residence in Constantinople, where they no doubt tried to gather support for their cause.[108] Having heard of the Pelagians' presence in Constantinople, Augustine was quick to offer praise (and instruction) to Atticus, no doubt hoping to reinforce the bishop's resolve to continue his anti-Pelagian policies.

JULIAN'S *AD FLORUM* AND AUGUSTINE'S *OPUS IMPERFECTUM*

While Augustine continued his anti-Pelagian efforts from Hippo, Julian was hard at work in the East. At some point after Augustine finished *De nuptiis et concupiscentia* 2 and *Contra duas epistulas Pelagianorum* and shipped them off to Italy, Julian acquired copies of them. The former bishop of Eclanum was not pleased with what he read. Aside from his theological disagreement with Augustine, Julian also felt deeply wronged by Augustine's reliance on a problematic summary of Julian's *Ad Turbantium* in the composition of *De nuptiis et concupiscentia* 2, accusing the bishop of Hippo of willfully misrepresenting his positions.[109] Likely after he had established a new base of operations in Cilicia with Theodore of Mopsuestia, he began to compose a response to this book, addressing it to his fellow exiled bishop, Florus.[110] *Ad Florum* ended up ballooning into eight books and was completed sometime before 427, when Alypius gained access to a copy while in Rome.[111]

Augustine likely began his response to *Ad Florum*—which would come to be known as *Contra Iulianum opus imperfectum*—in 427 or 428 and by the time of his death two years later had completed his refutation of the first six books. In the eyes of many, this work epitomizes Peter Brown's memorable characterization of the whole of Julian and Augustine's debate as an

---

108 Lössl notes that the bishop Florus, for whom Julian would write his reply to *nupt. et conc.* 2, appears to have built up a network of influential supporters in Constantinople (Lössl, *Julian von Aeclanum*, 296n258).

109 See, e.g., Julian's comments at *c. Iul. imp.* 1.19.

110 For the place of composition, see Mercator, *Commonitorium lectori aduersum haeresim Pelagii* (ACO 1.5.1, p. 19, ln. 27). Julian composed *Ad Florum* mainly in response to Augustine's *nupt. et conc.* 2, however he also mentions *c. ep. Pel.* on occasion.

111 See Marius Mercator, *Epistula lectori* (ACO 1.5.1, p. 23, ln. 17–38). For the dating, see Lössl, *Julian von Aeclanum*, 296n257. See also *ep.* 224.2 and *ep.* 10*.1.

A NEW OPPONENT: AUGUSTINE'S CONTROVERSY WITH JULIAN 289

"unintelligent slogging-match."[112] And, to be fair, the work makes for long and repetitive reading, structured as a paragraph-by-paragraph refutation of *Ad Florum*, which itself was no concise text. The *Opus imperfectum* is filled with a rehashing of topics and arguments we have seen previously—and of no small number of *ad hominem* attacks from both sides.[113] That said, we should resist the temptation to simply reduce Augustine's efforts in this text to a rather reflexive outburst at Julian's attacks. Indeed, with this work, as with his other anti-Pelagian efforts, Augustine was not simply writing to refute Pelagian views. Rather, the *Opus imperfectum* was, I suggest, yet another strategic effort by Augustine to stave off widespread schism in the Church.

To see this, we should recognize a few things. First, Julian's *Ad Florum* was directed to one of his fellow bishops who had taken up residence in Constantinople and had, it seems, been working to attract supporters to the Pelagian cause.[114] While we cannot know with certainty how much Augustine was aware of who Florus was and what he was doing, it is clear from other sources that he was very interested in updates on Julian's allies and their activities.[115] Further, given the indications in *ep. 6** to Atticus of Augustine's concerns over Pelagian activity in the East, it seems likely that Augustine was aware of Julian and his allies' politicking in Constantinople and feared they might eventually succeed in rousing enough support for their cause to pressure Rome or Ravenna to revisit their case, perhaps in a public setting.[116] That, it seems to me, was the real threat Augustine continued to see in Julian.

A few aspects of the *Opus imperfectum* reveal just how seriously Augustine took Julian and his allies' continued efforts. First and foremost, Augustine chose to respond to Julian with a paragraph-by-paragraph refutation

---

112 Brown, *Augustine of Hippo*, 389. See, too, J. J. O'Donnell's comments: "The anti-Julian works . . . resolutely deter affection, fascination, or even respect, and they make wearying and dispiriting reading, even for his most kindly disposed students" (*Augustine: A New Biography*, 283).

113 To be fair, there is some new ground covered from time to time—for example, in the latter half of Book 6, Julian and Augustine "debate" the existence of suffering in unfallen humanity, a topic that does not see as much discussion elsewhere.

114 See Lössl, *Julian von Aeclanum*, 296n258.

115 See, e.g., *ep.* 10* to Alypius, where Augustine mentions (in §1) his surprise that Alypius had not reported to him the bishop Turbantius's renunciation of his Pelagian views.

116 As it turned out, they would partially succeed in this regard after Nestorius's installation as bishop of Constantinople in 428. For some discussion, see Lössl, *Julian von Aeclanum*, 298–302. See also Julian's comments at *c. Iul. imp.* 1.10.

of *Ad Florum*. Ostensibly, a key reason for this structural choice was to address Julian's complaints about Augustine's earlier reliance (in *De nuptiis et concupiscentia* 2) on a defective summary of *Ad Turbantium* and Julian's insinuations that Augustine had misquoted him purposefully. In this context, it was essential for Augustine to demonstrate to his readers that he had nothing to hide: he was not trying to hoodwink his readers by mischaracterizing Julian's arguments. But I think the choice to structure the *Opus imperfectum* as a point-by-point refutation was dictated by more than Augustine's anxieties over Julian's accusations of dishonesty. In this context, it is worth recalling that the *Opus imperfectum* was not Augustine's first use of such an approach to a refutation.[117] Indeed, Augustine had employed a similar methodology on several occasions earlier—for example, when refuting a work by the Manichaean Faustus (*Contra Faustum*),[118] a letter by the Donatist bishop Petilian (*Contra litteras Petiliani* 2), and two letters by the Donatist bishop Gaudentius (*Contra Gaudentium* 1). In the case of *Contra Faustum* (likely written sometime between 400 and 402), Augustine wrote to refute the famous Manichaean bishop's *Capitula*, which addressed the questions of a Manichaean who had converted to Christianity.[119] As Augustine reports in the *Confessiones*, Faustus was well known and widely respected among Manichees.[120] As a result, it seems likely that Faustus's *Capitula* had received a wide distribution in Manichaean circles.[121] Similarly, *Contra litteras Petiliani* 2 (written sometime between 401 and 404) addressed an anti-Catholic letter the Donatist Petilian had circulated among the clergy of his diocese.[122] Augustine himself notes that the letter had gained a wide readership and

---

117 It also has precedent in Christian literature more broadly—e.g., Origen's *Contra Celsum*. My thanks to Walter Dunphy for this suggestion. See also Catherine Conybeare's discussion of Augustine's efforts in the *Opus imperfectum* as marginalia: "Augustine's *Marginalia Contra Julianum*," in *The Late (Wild) Augustine*, ed. Susanna Elm and Christopher M. Blunda (Leiden: Brill, 2021), 83–97.

118 It should be noted that it is unclear whether Augustine cited the entirety of Faustus's *Capitula* or maintained their order—J. Kevin Coyle thinks it is doubtful that Augustine did so ("Faustum, Contra," in Fitzgerald, *Augustine through the Ages*, 356).

119 For the dating of *Contra Faustum*, see Hombert, *Nouvelles recherches de chronologie augustinienne*, 25–29.

120 See *conf.* 5.6.10–5.7.11.

121 Augustine, however, seems to have not obtained the work until after completing *Confessiones* (see *c. Faust.* 1.1).

122 In the first book of *Contra litteras Petiliani*, Augustine had refuted a portion of this letter before he had access to the letter in its entirety.

A NEW OPPONENT: AUGUSTINE'S CONTROVERSY WITH JULIAN   291

that it was so convincing that portions of it were even being memorized by some people.[123] Finally, in *Contra Gaudentium* 1 (probably written in 419), Augustine responded to two letters that the Donatist Gaudentius—who had been one of the spokesmen for the Donatist cause at the conference of 411—had sent to an imperial official named Dulcitius. Gaudentius was the bishop of Thamugadi in Numidia, a lasting stronghold for Donatism well after the supposed end of the schism in 411.[124] In 418 or so, Dulcitius had stepped in with orders to enforce the terms of imperial legislation against the Donatists. This had spurred a tense standoff between himself and Gaudentius—the latter had barricaded himself along with some of the Donatist faithful inside a church and threated to set fire to the building if Dulcitius tried to use force against them. News of the standoff—and perhaps also the letters Gaudentius had sent to Dulcitius accusing him of persecuting the Donatists—had likely spread widely. In this sense, the situation was a crucial make-or-break moment for the dwindling number of major Donatist hold-outs: if Gaudentius's theatrics had been able to stave off imperial action, it might very well have become something of a rallying point for the Donatists in their otherwise losing fight against the Catholic and imperial authorities.

In all three of these cases, it seems as though the chief concerns for Augustine would have been the widespread knowledge of the writings (or situation) he was addressing, as well as the acute threat they posed to the Catholic faithful and to the stability of the Church. These were the factors, I suggest, that led him to respond point-by-point to his opponents' writings. Indeed, in different circumstances, prudence might have argued against reproducing the entirety (or majority) of an opponent's written argument to avoid publicizing it too extensively. But in these three cases, Augustine no doubt felt that the writings in question were already so well known that that concern was not a major inhibiting factor. Indeed, in such a situation, it might instead be advantageous to circulate a version of his opponent's writing with a built-in response—and in doing so, to cause the standalone text to fall out of circulation. Further, such a literary artifice would frame the engagement as a debate of sorts—albeit one in which Augustine always had the final word.

---

123 See *cath. fr.* 1.1.

124 For some discussion of this episode, see Lancel, *Saint Augustine*, 359–60.

While it remains possible that Augustine employed a section-by-section refutation in the *Opus imperfectum* for different reasons than he had elsewhere, the similarities between the three writings just mentioned and the *Opus imperfectum* are rather striking. As a result, the circumstances surrounding these three works can suggest to us a few things about the *Opus imperfectum*: (1) that Julian's accusations of dishonesty against Augustine were not the sole reason for the format of the *Opus imperfectum*; (2) that Augustine was aware (or at least feared) that Julian's arguments had a wide circulation; and (3) that Augustine believed the situation with Julian in 428 was just as serious a threat as that with Gaudentius, Petilian, and Faustus had been (if not more). While none of this evidence is decisive, it should make us hesitant to attribute Augustine's efforts in the *Opus imperfectum* to mere personal motivations—as though he were simply angered by Julian's accusations of Manichaeism and dishonesty or had essentially allowed himself to descend into a grudge match with a young upstart.[125]

Further evidence for Augustine's concerns about the impact Julian's writing had had in Italy can be gathered from Augustine's argumentation in the *Opus imperfectum*. Throughout the work, Augustine continues to argue that his positions are simply those of the ancient and universal Church by making appeals to the types of evidence we have seen him use since 411: for example, the Lord's Prayer,[126] the baptismal rite,[127] popular belief,[128] and the opinions of renowned Christian authors.[129] This last set of evidence is, perhaps, the most important in the *Opus imperfectum*. Indeed, it becomes something of a refrain that when Julian accuses Augustine of Manichaeism, the bishop of Hippo notes that, if that were true, other famous Christians would be just as guilty. When he cites names and passages directly, Ambrose is by far

---

125 See, e.g., Brown: "Augustine's 'teaching' of the terrorized Italians [i.e., in his earlier anti-Julian works] quickly degenerated into a personal duel with Julian" (*Augustine of Hippo*, 386).

126 See *c. Iul. imp.* 1.67, 90, 93, 98, 101, 104, 105, 106, 108; 2.7, 52, 71, 212, 227; 3.109, 110, 116; 4.82, 89, 122; 6.15, 30, 34, 41.

127 See *c. Iul. imp.* 1.50, 56, 57, 60, 117; 2.120, 181; 2.224; 3.82, 144, 146, 164, 182, 199, 208; 3.42; 4.7, 77, 108, 120; 5.9, 64; 6.23

128 See *c. Iul. imp.* 1.19, 33, 41; 2.2–4, 198; 3.216; 6.3.

129 See *c. Iul. imp.* 1.2, 6, 7, 9, 47, 48, 50, 52, 53, 55, 59, 63, 66, 67, 69, 70, 71, 72, 93, 96, 99, 106, 109, 112, 115, 117, 118, 123, 126, 135, 138; 2.1, 2, 8, 9, 14, 15, 21, 31, 33, 36, 37, 73, 113, 163, 164, 176, 178, 202, 208, 214, 228; 3.4, 25, 37, 51, 56, 79, 111, 177, 178, 181, 185, 187, 200, 205, 213; 4.10, 23, 28, 42, 50, 55, 56, 57, 64, 67, 70, 71, 72, 73, 75, 88, 97, 104, 106, 108, 109, 110, 112, 113, 114, 115, 117, 118, 119, 120, 121, 122, 128, 134; 5.5, 20, 25, 30, 41, 43, 60; 6.6, 7, 8, 9, 10, 11, 12, 14, 18, 21, 23, 26, 27, 33, 37, 41.

A NEW OPPONENT: AUGUSTINE'S CONTROVERSY WITH JULIAN

the most common figure identified. Granted, testimony from Ambrose had been important for Augustine since 415 in *De natura et gratia* and had only increased in importance since then. But in the *Opus imperfectum* it reaches new levels. Of the roughly 124 paragraphs that make use of some sort of appeal to one or more renowned Christian authors, 105 include a reference to Ambrose.[130] The second most common is Cyprian, who is referenced in only 28 of these paragraphs.[131] This heavy reliance on Ambrose is notably different from, for example, the first *Contra Iulianum*, where Augustine aimed to provide citations from a broad span of authors, especially in the first and second books.[132] In the *Opus imperfectum*, Augustine does, from time to time, repeat some of the references he had earlier made in *Contra Iulianum* (e.g., to Gregory of Nazianzus, Basil of Caesarea, and John Chrysostom) that serve to show the universality of his views. However, his main focus seems to be to associate himself and his views with Ambrose—and to portray Julian as opposed to the celebrated bishop of Milan. A key reason for this is likely the fact that Julian had criticized Augustine's earlier appeals to Ambrose and Cyprian in *De nuptiis et concupiscentia*.[133] In *Ad Florum*, Julian admitted that Ambrose and Cyprian may have spoken incautiously at times, but professed that these bishops of the Church surely would have agreed with Julian himself if they were still alive.[134] In this context, Augustine no doubt felt as though he needed to reclaim these well-respected bishops from Julian as he replied to *Ad Florum*. However, it is notable that he focuses his efforts mainly to show his alignment with Ambrose. Why might this be?

---

130 See *c. Iul. imp.* 1.2, 6, 9, 47, 48, 52, 59, 66, 67, 70, 71, 72, 93, 99, 109, 112, 115, 117, 118, 123, 126, 135, 138; 2.1, 2, 8, 9, 14, 15, 21, 31, 33, 36, 37, 73, 113, 163, 164, 176, 178, 202, 208, 228; 3.4, 25, 37, 56, 79, 177, 178, 181, 185, 187, 198, 205, 213; 4.10, 23, 28, 42, 50, 55, 56, 57, 64, 67, 70, 71, 72, 73, 75, 88, 97, 104, 106, 108, 109, 110, 112, 113, 114, 115, 117, 118, 119, 120, 121, 122, 128, 134; 5.5, 20, 25, 30, 41, 43, 60; 6.6, 8, 12, 14, 21, 26, 27, 37, 41. In addition to the discussion below, see Grossi, "Il ricorso ad Ambrogio nell'*Opus imperfectum contra Iulianum* di Agostino d'Ippona," 115–56, for discussion of Augustine's use of Ambrose in the *Opus imperfectum*.

131 See *c. Iul. imp.* 1.6, 7, 9, 50, 52, 59, 63, 72, 106, 117; 2.2, 14, 33, 37, 73, 164, 214; 3.51; 4.72, 73, 112, 113; 6.6, 10, 14, 18, 21, 23.

132 Outside of those first two books, Augustine only refers to renowned Christian authors on a few occasions (*c. Iul.* 3.1.2, 3.14.28, 3.17.31, 3.17.32, 3.21.48, 6.22.69, 6.23.70, 6.26.83). Ambrose is referred to in five of these eight paragraphs.

133 Augustine only mentioned Cyprian by name once in *De nuptiis et concupiscentia* (at §2.29.51). It seems to me that Julian may have had Augustine's use of Cyprian in *c. ep. Pel.* in mind as well.

134 See Julian's words at *c. Iul. imp.* 4.106–19.

On the one hand, it may be, in part, a defensive maneuver. It is possible that Augustine does not rely as heavily on Cyprian here as he had done elsewhere because he has become somewhat sensitized to Julian's characterizations of Augustine's views as peculiarly African or "Punic."[135] But surely this cannot be the whole answer; indeed, Augustine on several occasions responds to Julian's attempts to denigrate him for his Punic heritage by appealing explicitly to that other famous Punic Christian, Cyprian.[136] A better explanation, in my view, would be to attribute the emphasis on Ambrose to the fact that Augustine was chiefly concerned with preventing the spread of support for Julian in Italy while refuting *Ad Florum*. By appealing to the famous bishop of Milan so frequently, Augustine was directly targeting any Italian ecclesial leaders who might be wavering in their opposition to Julian and making clear to them that support for Julian was opposition to Ambrose.[137] Augustine would have been hard-pressed to find a more effective means of shoring up Italian support.[138]

Along with these immediate concerns about Julian and his attempts to sway opinion in Italy, Augustine's efforts in the *Opus imperfectum* were likely also influenced by his awareness of opposition to some of his views

---

135 See, e.g., *c. Iul. imp.* 1.7.

136 See *c. Iul. imp.* 1.7, 72, 106; 6.6, 18, 23.

137 It is worth recalling that Ambrose's reputation would likely have been bolstered by the late 420s by the circulation of Paulinus of Milan's *Vita Ambrosii*—written at the request of Augustine himself! The exact dating of this biography is uncertain: options include 412/413 and 422. If 422 is correct, it would be particularly notable, as it would be situated during Augustine's confrontation with Julian. For discussions of the dating, see Paredi, "Paulinus of Milan"; Lamirande, "La datation de la *Vita Ambrosii* de Paulin de Milan"; and Zocca, "La *Vita Ambrosii* alla luce dei rapporti fra Paolino, Agostino e Ambrogio."

138 It might be argued that Augustine would have been better served highlighting the papal actions against the Pelagians or simply emphasizing that support for Julian was opposition to the ancient faith of Rome. However, it seems to me that an appeal to a "third party" witness like Ambrose would work better in this situation. Ambrose provided Augustine with a witness against Pelagianism who was Italian and likely to be considered a hero by Italians—but who was also uninvolved with the case at hand (unlike Innocent and Zosimus, or the church of Rome in general). Plus, appealing to papal opposition to Pelagianism might require Augustine to address the complications of Zosimus's waffling again and again. It is worth noting in this context Otto Wermelinger's view that Augustine felt the *Tractoria* was a rather weak document given its reliance on "old documentation" to provide proof of the heterodoxy of Pelagius's positions. Augustine may very well have feared that Pelagius's allies would claim that the condemnation of Pelagius rested upon faulty evidence from writings Pelagius had not acknowledged as his own in his letter to Pope Innocent. See Wermelinger, "Das Pelagius-dossier in der Tractoria des Zosimus," 360 and 365.

elsewhere.[139] Rumblings of trouble first appeared in Africa around 426,[140] when Augustine learned of a dispute at a monastery in Hadrumetum, south of Carthage. At the monastery, some monks were reportedly confused by Augustine's *ep.* 194 to Sixtus, on the basis of which they had begun holding that human beings do not have free will and that there is no possibility to accrue merit through good works.[141] Amid the growing strife, three monks traveled to Hippo to meet with Augustine personally in the hopes of better understanding his views. After a prolonged stay, the monks returned to the monastery bearing two letters (*epp.* 214 and 215) and a treatise (*De gratia et libero arbitrio*) for the monastery's abbot, Valentine. Augustine soon received a letter from Valentine assuring him that the dispute had ended.[142] However, further conflict seems to have arisen soon thereafter. Reports of this led to Augustine's composition of another treatise for the monastic community—*De correptione et gratia*—in which Augustine sought to explain the function of rebuke in view of his teaching on grace. Although this work may have calmed the tensions in Hadrumetum,[143] it would soon create further trouble overseas. Likely in 427,[144] Augustine received word from two laymen, Prosper of Aquitaine and his friend Hilary, reporting opposition to certain aspects of his views among some monks in and around Marseilles, prompted by their reading of *De correptione et gratia*.[145] These reports would lead Augustine to write the two books of *De praedestinatione sanctorum*.[146] Whereas the turmoil in Hadrumetum had mainly been spurred by some monks who had adopted a more rigorous view of grace than Augustine actually held himself, in Provence, the opposite was true. These monks, while agreeing with certain aspects of Augustine's anti-Pelagian teaching (e.g., the reality of original

---

139 For more on the so-called "semi-pelagian" controversy, see esp. Ogliari, *Gratia et Certamen*, and Rebecca H. Weaver, *Divine Grace and Human Agency: A Study of the Semi-Pelagian Controversy* (Macon, GA: Mercer University Press, 1996).

140 *Ep.* 217, which deals with issues related to grace and free will and which was written for a certain African named Vitalis, may date earlier than the troubles in Hadrumetum. See Ogliari, *Gratia et Certamen*, 26–28.

141 See *ep.* 214.1.

142 See *ep.* 216.

143 As Ogliari notes (*Gratia et Certamen*, 40–41), we have no further evidence of problems at Hadrumetum.

144 See Ogliari, *Gratia et Certamen*, 93.

145 See *epp.* 225 and 226 among the letters of Augustine.

146 The second of the two books is entitled *De dono perseuerantiae*.

sin), felt that Augustine had left insufficient room for human free will in the working out of salvation and was, in fact, "opposed to the opinion of the Fathers and to the mind of the Church."[147] In this sense, unlike in Hadrumetum, the opposition in southern Gaul was far more anti-Augustine—and, in some ways, seemed linked (in spirit if not in reality) with some of Julian's positions.[148] Augustine was happy to emphasize the differences between these monks and the Pelagians[149]—but the spread of opposition to his views no doubt troubled him and would likely have been in the back of his mind when he learned of the circulation of Julian's *Ad Florum* in Italy.

With this context in mind, Augustine's *Opus imperfectum* appears less as a particularly violent volley in his "unintelligent slogging-match" with Julian and more as an impassioned exhortation to allies to stay the course and resist Julian's continuing appeals to powerful authorities in Italy and elsewhere. Indeed, we should not forget that while Augustine was writing the *Opus imperfectum*, Julian was hard at work in Constantinople attempting to secure the favor and support of Nestorius for his cause.[150] It is possible that Augustine learned of these efforts before his death on August 28, 430. In any event, the danger of Pelagianism no doubt frequently occupied Augustine's mind in his final years—a danger that threatened not simply orthodox doctrine, but the unity of the Church itself.

CONCLUSION

From the beginning of the controversy until the end of his life, Augustine was deeply concerned about the threat that the Pelagians spelled for the unity of the Church. With Julian, these concerns only deepened as Augustine was faced with an opponent who was not only a bishop, but also intelligent, well-connected, and politically savvy. Admittedly, it is tempting to allow the eventual outcome of Julian's actions to color our perception of how they would have appeared "in the moment" to Augustine. Indeed, Julian's

---

147 *ep.* 225.2 (Latin: CSEL 57:455.14–15; English: Teske, WSA II/4, 88).

148 Prosper notes at *ep.* 225.3 that these monks have sided with some of the argumentation attributed to Julian in Augustine's *Contra Iulianum*. For some discussion of possible links between the "semipelagians" and Julian, see Lössl, *Julian von Aeclanum*, 321–24.

149 See, e.g., *praed. sanct.* 1.2.

150 Nestorius would end up sending several letters to Pope Celestine inquiring about the status of Julian and some of his fellow exiles in Constantinople. For more, see Lössl, *Julian von Aeclanum*, 298–302, and Malavasi, *La controversia pelagiana*, 162–70.

numerous attempts to have the issues at the core of the controversy revisited all failed.[151] But, as we have said, that failure was hardly a foregone conclusion. Indeed, the pressure Augustine put on his various contacts in Italy and—less frequently, but no less importantly—in the East, may very well have been the decisive factor in Julian's defeat. But why did Augustine go to such lengths to counter Julian? On the one hand, Augustine was certainly convinced that the doctrinal positions he was advocating were orthodox and that those of Julian and his allies were heterodox. Yet we should not separate these doctrinal concerns from their ecclesial context—as if Augustine's many and voluminous writings against Julian were simply motivated by his disagreement with the exiled bishop's views. Rather, as we have argued, Julian's efforts triggered such a significant response from Augustine in large part because of the threat Augustine believed Julian represented for Church unity. Julian, in calling for a review of his case by capable judges, in appealing to Rufus of Thessalonica, in attempting to secure support in Constantinople, had dramatically increased the stakes of the debate. Augustine responded accordingly, arguing time and time again—and in sometimes unprecedented ways[152]—that the Church's ancient and universal doctrinal tradition lay on his side. Augustine's efforts to preserve the unity of the Church were impassioned—and increasingly so, as the years passed and as Julian refused to give up.

All told, this phase of the controversy "ended" somewhat by default with Augustine's death. Julian's attempt to find a powerful patron in Nestorius backfired, and all his later appeals were fruitless. Church unity had been preserved. But, as we know, the issues at the heart of the debate would repeatedly prompt turmoil in succeeding centuries, as the Church sought to reckon with the theological legacies of Augustine and his opponents.

---

151 For more on the Pelagians' fortunes at the Council of Ephesus, and Julian's life post-Ephesus, see Lössl, *Julian von Aeclanum*, 311–29. See also Richard Price, trans., *The Council of Ephesus of 431: Documents and Proceedings*, Translated Texts for Historians 72 (Liverpool: Liverpool University Press, 2020), esp. pp. 36–37, 409–10, 642.

152 E.g., the first two books of *Contra Iulianum*.

Conclusion
Grace and the Church

The Pelagian controversy is often presented as a battle of ideas, of conflicting positions on complicated issues at the heart of the Christian life: for example, grace, free will, original sin, and predestination. While such a characterization is not inaccurate, it at the same time fails to do explanatory justice to some of the controversy's main protagonists and their motivations. As a result, I have attempted in this study to offer a new perspective on Augustine's participation in the controversy by framing the bishop of Hippo's efforts against Pelagius, Caelestius, and Julian of Eclanum less as an increasingly vociferous advocacy for specific doctrinal positions and more as an ardent campaign to contain a growing threat to ecclesial unity, a unity rooted in the Church's doctrinal tradition.

From his earliest foray into the controversy in 411 until his death in 430, Augustine saw in his Pelagian opponents a threat to Church unity. Early on, this threat was raised by certain arguments circulated by supporters of Caelestius and Pelagius in Carthage. These arguments alleged that the African Catholic Church—and likely some segments of the Italian Catholic Church—held positions that were at odds with the Church in the East or with the Church of previous centuries. This was no idle claim, for those making such

299

arguments were known to have come from circles with an affinity for the Church in the East and an abiding interest in the writings of the Christian past. Indeed, Pelagius's *De natura* and the appeals to renowned Christian authors found therein suggest that such claims were not uncommon in Pelagian circles. In the face of this growing threat at Carthage, Augustine used his first anti-Pelagian efforts not only to undermine his opponents' theological positions but also to rebut their claims to speak for the Church's doctrinal tradition—for example, by appealing to Cyprian in a homily given on June 27, 411 in Carthage, by highlighting baptismal practices, and by explaining the purpose of key petitions in the Lord's Prayer. I have argued that, through such evidence, Augustine was attempting to safeguard the unity of the Church from the threat posed to it by Pelagianism.

A few years later, the Pelagian threat to the unity of the Church became more pronounced when Pelagius's acquittal at the Synod of Diospolis in Palestine seemed to confirm the claim that the Pelagian doctrine was that of the eastern churches. Once the news of this shocking turn of events reached Africa, Augustine and his allies launched a campaign to prevent the further spread of not just Pelagianism but also the view that East and West differed on key theological issues. Having appealed to Rome, they initially gained Pope Innocent's support only to see that support waver under his successor, Zosimus. Through a series of ecclesial and political moves, though, the African authorities eventually secured a civil and ecclesiastical condemnation of Pelagius and Caelestius. But again, the aim here was not simply to defeat a theological opponent. Rather, throughout these events and in their aftermath, Augustine sought to convince allies that Pelagian thought represented a serious departure from the Church's doctrinal tradition and that the universal Church was united against Pelagianism. This argument can be clearly recognized in Augustine's approach to the Synod of Diospolis, which the bishop of Hippo claimed had condemned Pelagianism, if not Pelagius himself. In this sense, Augustine emphasized that the Church, both East and West, had condemned the Pelagian heresy.

After the condemnation of Pelagius and Caelestius, Julian of Eclanum came to the fore as the spokesperson for Pelagianism. Julian, a bishop with an excellent education, social ties, and political skill, was soon recognized by Augustine as a far greater threat to Church unity than Pelagius himself had ever been. With Julian, Augustine faced an opponent who not only felt no qualms about directly attacking the bishop of Hippo but who also sought to appeal directly to powerful authorities in both West and East to

CONCLUSION   301

call for a judicial review of the condemnations of those who hesitated to sign Zosimus's *Tractoria*. As a result, Augustine spent a significant portion of the final decade of his life battling with Julian, seeking to undermine the exiled bishop's efforts. As we have seen, a key element to Augustine's strategy was the citation of renowned Christian authors—a tactic that Augustine had used since the beginning of the controversy, but that came to its full flourishing in his writings against Julian. Through such citations, Augustine attempted (1) to convince his readers that the ancient and universal Church was united against Julian and thereby (2) to undermine Julian's campaign that Augustine believed threatened ecclesial unity in the present. Augustine's increasing reliance on this relatively novel form of argumentation indicates just how seriously Augustine was taking the Pelagian threat to unity.

It is the contention of this study that Augustine's anti-Pelagian efforts were fueled to a significant degree by his desire to protect the unity of the Church in his day, a unity rooted in the Church's ancient and universal doctrinal tradition. In a certain sense, we can say that Augustine's efforts in the Pelagian controversy were something of a practical deployment of the ecclesiology he had worked out in theory in his anti-Donatist works.[1] Augustine was deeply committed to Church unity and to the notion that the Church was truly Catholic, truly universal. That commitment, this study argues, drove him to address the threat of Pelagius and his allies—a threat which should not be reduced to the danger of problematic doctrinal views, no matter how significant that danger was in Augustine's eyes. As I have argued, recognizing the centrality of Augustine's ecclesial concerns in his anti-Pelagian efforts helps to make better sense of the controversy's course, from key elements of Augustine's surprisingly well-informed entry into the debate in 411, to his interpretation of the events at the Synod of Diospolis, to his persistent and increasingly vigorous interactions with Julian. Of course, as Augustine's concerns over ecclesial unity pushed him to continue to grapple with the Pelagians, the stress and pressure of these interactions (especially those with Julian) may have contributed to a certain hardening of his positions on grace and the role of human free will in his later years.[2]

---

1 Of course, his and his Catholic allies' efforts against the Donatists were also a practical deployment of those ecclesiological principles.

2 However, there are, of course, other reasons for this "hardening" as well.

* * * * *

Almost ninety years ago, John Burnaby accused the old Augustine of having lost the vital love that had impelled him in his earlier years: "Nearly all that Augustine wrote after his seventieth year is the work of a man whose energy has burnt itself out, whose love has grown cold."[3] It is my sense that Burnaby's assessment will be shared by many who focus their attention on the theological positions promoted in Augustine's final efforts against Julian and against the so-called semi-Pelagians. In those works, Augustine comes to emphasize his more controversial positions: for example, the seeming irresistibility of grace, the narrow scope of God's universal salvific will, fallen humanity's identity as a *massa damnata*, and the inscrutability of the divine plan to save one person but not another. But this study has offered to readers an account of Augustine's efforts that is both more sympathetic and more accurate than that suggested by the quotation from Burnaby above. While Augustine's late works against Julian betray a less compromising side to the elderly bishop, it would, I think, be wrong to portray these works as essentially love-less in their motivation. Indeed, Augustine's love for the Church and commitment to Church unity are, I argue, behind every page of his anti-Pelagian works—especially those written against Julian. This is not to say that a desire to defend Church unity preserved Augustine from erring from time to time in his theological proposals. But focusing solely on those theological missteps—or even on the positive aspects of his anti-Pelagian theology—risks misrepresenting Augustine's anti-Pelagian project as a whole and, indeed, what it meant for him to be involved in the task of theological writing. It is something of an obvious point, but perhaps bears repeating here that Augustine's theological efforts were not the products of periods of dispassionate study and speculation in a university office. Augustine was a bishop whose daily life revolved around liturgy, preaching, teaching, and adjudicating disputes both major and minor. His theological writing was not unconnected to these activities but flowed from them. As a result, when reading Augustine, we do well to keep in view his particular ecclesial orientation—something I have attempted to do in this study. In this way, I hope that readers can recognize in Augustine—and even in the elderly Augustine—a heart that was on fire for Christ and his Church.

---

3 Burnaby, *Amor Dei*, 231; cited in Brown, *Augustine of Hippo*, 466.

Appendix
The Chronology of 411

From the sources available to us, the precise chronology of the early events of the Pelagian controversy in Carthage is not readily apparent. In fact, there seem to be three main ways to construct this chronology—and all three have received support in the scholarship. However, determining the most likely chronology should not be judged a matter of mere historical curiosity. As we will see, assessing when these events unfolded helps to provide important contextual clues for identifying Augustine's own reasons for entering the debate. With that in mind, let us dig a little deeper into the details.

CHRONOLOGICAL DATA

Before we discuss the different chronologies that have been proposed, it will be helpful first to lay out the data points all three options have to incorporate to construct a chronology. These data points are drawn mainly from the writings of Augustine himself, who reflects on the outbreak of the controversy in Carthage in 411 at several points in subsequent years. The most significant passages can be found at *pecc. mer.* 3.1.1 and 3.6.12; *ep.* 139.3; *ep.* 157.3.22; *ep.* 175.1; *gest. Pel.* 11.23, 11.25, 22.46–23.47, and 35.62; *gr. et pecc. or.* 2.2.2–2.3.3;

303

304 APPENDIX

and *retr.* 2.33.60. The challenge in dealing with these passages is that it is not always clear how to arrange the diverse events that Augustine references. However, a few chronological "groups" can be assembled, which must then be combined to construct a complete chronology. Let us now survey these groups. (I have tried to keep the text in the body to a minimum—those wishing to check my math, as it were, should look at the extensive footnotes.[1])

Group 1

The data points in this group can be linked together and arranged due to their connection with Caelestius's trial, Marcellinus's request to Augustine, and Augustine's writing of *De peccatorum meritis*.

Sometime before or during 411

a. Caelestius, and others, begin voicing Pelagian views in Africa.[2]
Caelestius applies for ordination to the priesthood.[3]

---

1 The explanations in these footnotes owe much to Walter Dunphy's work in "A Lost Year: Pelagianism in Carthage, 411 A.D.," *Augustinianum* 45 (2005): 389–466.

2 Robert Dodaro has questioned whether Caelestius was the main agent circulating Pelagian views in Carthage; see "Note on the Carthaginian Debate over Sinlessness, A.D. 411–412 (Augustine, pecc. mer. 2.7.8–16.25)," *Augustinianum* 40 (2000): 187–202. While he is correct to caution against viewing Caelestius as a lone wolf, it seems to me quite plausible that Caelestius was a ringleader of sorts. See below at n. 11 for references to some of Walter Dunphy's work that helps to specify Caelestius's role in 411. See also Dunphy, "Caelestius: A Preliminary Investigation," *Academia* 60 (1994): 33–59, and Dunphy, "The Writings of Caelestius," *Academia* 61 (1995): 25–47.

3 See *ep.* 157.3.22; *gest. Pel.* 11.25, 22.46, and 35.62; Orosius, *Liber apologeticus* 3. There is uncertainty about the date of Caelestius's arrival in Africa. The only indication we have is from Mercator, who writes the following around 429 (see Guido Honnay, "Caelestius, discipulus Pelagii," *Augustiniana* 44 [1994]: 271n3): *Caelestius quidam, eunuchus matris utero editus, ante uiginti plus minus annos discipulus et auditor Pelagii egressus ex urbe Romana Carthaginem Africae totius metropolim venit* (Marius Mercator, *Commonitorium super nomine Caelestii* [CPL 781; Latin: ACO 1.5.1, p. 66, ln. 1–2). There has been some disagreement in the scholarship over the referent of the phrase "*ante uiginti plus minus annos.*" Is this referring to the time Caelestius had spent as a disciple of Pelagius prior to his departure for Africa (see, e.g., Laurence Dalmon, *Un dossier de l'épistolaire augustinien: la correspondance entre l'Afrique et Rome à propos de l'affaire pélagienne (416–418)* [Leuven: Peeters, 2015], 9; Bruno Delaroche, introduction to *Salaire et pardon des péchés, Bibliothèque Augustinienne: Oeuvres de Saint Augustin* 20/A [Paris: Institut d'Études Augustiniennes, 2013], 17; Yves-Marie Duval, "Pélage en son temps: Données chronologiques nouvelles pour une présentation nouvelle," *Studia Patristica* 38 [2001]: 99)? Or is it referring to the timing of Caelestius's departure from Rome for Carthage in relationship to the time of Mercator's writing (see Walter Dunphy, "Caelestius: A Preliminary Investigation," *Academia* 60 [1994]: 40). I am inclined to agree with Dunphy here: it seems the prepositional phrase *ante . . . annos* should be taken as modifying a participle

APPENDIX   305

Sometime during 411

b. After trouble begins to brew as a result of the activity of Caelestius and others, Marcellinus writes to Augustine from Carthage asking him to respond to some of the positions promoted by these people.[4]

c. Probably around the same time as (b) or perhaps slightly before, Paulinus of Milan submits a *libellus* (a formal legal brief) accusing Caelestius of holding several dubious or heretical positions.[5]

d. Probably around the same time as (b) but after (c), Caelestius's trial is held (possibly in multiple sessions[6]), where he is confronted by Paulinus before Aurelius, the Bishop of Carthage, and some number

---

or verb—in this case, *egressus*. If this is the case, it seems Caelestius left Rome around 409, give or take a year or two. See also the discussion in Stuart Squires, *The Pelagian Controversy: An Introduction to the Enemies of Grace and the Conspiracy of Lost Souls* (Eugene, OR: Pickwick Publications, 2019), 55–56, and Zohra Picard-Mawji, "Le passage de Célestius à Carthage: Un moment clé du pélagianisme," *Cahiers Mondes Anciens* 4 (2013): 1–18.

4 See *pecc. mer.* 1.1.1 and 3.1.1; *gest. Pel.* 11.25; *retr.* 2.33.60. An absolute *terminus post quem* here would be the date of Marcellinus's arrival in Africa, which was likely between late October 410 and early January 411. Marcellinus was appointed by the emperor Honorius in the fall of 410 to oversee the conference between the Catholics and Donatists (for the edict issued on October 14, 410 appointing Marcellinus, see Serge Lancel, ed., *Actes de la conférence de Carthage en 411, Tome II* [SC 195:562–69]) and was in Carthage by January 19, 411, when he issued his own edict assigning June 1 as the start-date for the conference (see Lancel, *Saint Augustine*, trans. Antonia Nevill [London: SCM Press, 2002], 296, as well as the text contained in Lancel, *Actes* [SC 195:568ff.]). Dunphy argues Marcellinus probably departed for Africa shortly after the release of the October edict so as to set sail before the commencement of the *mare clausum* period. Upon arrival in Africa, Marcellinus likely would have released his own edict in January only after surveying the situation (Dunphy, "A Lost Year," 435). In any event, it seems unlikely that Marcellinus would have written his letter to Augustine concerning the circulation of Pelagian views prior to the release of this January edict. As for a *terminus ante quem*, the absolute latest date would be sometime before the composition date of *ep.* 139 (January or February 412 at the latest—see below for more on the dating of this letter), in which Augustine notes that he has already completed Books 1–2 of *De peccatorum meritis* some time ago (see *ep.* 139.3). For more on Marcellinus and his correspondence with Augustine, see Madeleine Moreau, *Le dossier Marcellinus dans la correspondance de saint Augustin* (Paris: Études Augustiniennes, 1973). See also Dunphy's considerations of Marcellinus's role ("A Lost Year," 440ff.).

5 See Marius Mercator, *Commonitorium super nomine Caelestii* (ACO 1.5.1, p. 66); Arnobius Iunior, *Praedestinatus* I.88 (CCL 25B:51). Dunphy notes that this *libellus* was likely submitted in response to Caelestius's application for ordination; local church law required candidates for orders to be examined with respect to their suitability (see "A Lost Year," 395–96).

6 See Marius Mercator, *Commonitorium super nomine Caelestii* (ACO 1.5.1, p. 66, ln. 21), Otto Wermelinger, *Rom und Pelagius: die theologische Position der römischen Bischöfe im pelagianischen Streit in den Jahren 411–431* (Stuttgart: A. Hiersemann, 1975), 17, and Walter Dunphy, "Caelestis: A Preliminary Investigation," *Academia* 60 (1994): 42.

of other bishops, but in the absence of Augustine. At some point in the process of the trial, Caelestius submits a brief *libellus*[7] of his own to defend himself. Caelestius is found guilty and, sometime thereafter, leaves Carthage, initially planning to appeal his case to Pope Innocent.[8]

---

7 In this "*libellus breuissimus*," Caelestius affirms that infants are in need of baptism and, hence, redemption (*gr. et pecc. or.* 2.19.21; *ep.* 157.3.22; *pecc. mer.* 1.34.63; *c. Iul.* 3.3.9). Given that Augustine references this *libellus* in *De peccatorum meritis*, we know that Caelestius's trial commenced before Augustine began writing.

8 See *ep.* 157.3.22; *ep.* 175.1; *gest. Pel.* 11.23; *gest. Pel.* 22.46; *gest. Pel.* 35.62; *gr. et pecc. or.* 2.2.2–2.3.3; *retr.* 2.33.60; Mercator, *Commonitorium super nomine Caelestii* (ACO 1.5.1, p. 66, ln. 20–24); Orosius, *Liber apologeticus* 3 (CSEL 5:607). In *ep.* 175.1, the bishops meeting at the Council of Carthage in 416 note that Caelestius's trial took place "roughly five years ago" (*ante ferme quinquennium*) (Latin: CSEL 44:654.5), which is rather vague. Dolbeau suggests that the council of 416 itself likely took place in mid-to-late April of 416 or perhaps very early May (see discussion in "Le sermon 348A de saint Augustin contre Pélage: Édition du text intégral," *Recherches augustiniennes* 28 [1995]: 49). Delaroche's dating of September 416 seems too late (Delaroche, "La datation du *De peccatorum meritis et remissione*," *Revue des* études *augustiniennes* 41 [1995]: 40). Perler suggests the council must have taken place by the end of June (Othmar Perler, *Les voyages de saint Augustin* [Paris: Institut d'études augustiniennes, 1969], 332). In my view, the council likely took place in early June. For more discussion of 416 and this council, see Chapter 4.

The nature of the conclusion of the trial is a bit murky. As Honnay points out ("Caelestius," 277), the "oldest" references to Caelestius's trial do not mention any condemnation or excommunication but only a conviction and rejection (see, e.g., *ep.* 157.3.22, written around 414). It is only later (e.g., in *gest. Pel.* 35.62, from 416/417) that Caelestius is explicitly said to have been condemned by the bishops in 411 (see also discussion in Picard-Mawji, "Le passage," 10–11). Dunphy reads the situation as follows: "In the subsequent debate the Pelagians would insist that since the condemnation was *in absentia* it was not legal. From this it would seem that Caelestius left Carthage before he had given a satisfactory answer to the charges brought against him, and the Africans considered him to be guilty as charged" (Dunphy, "Unexplored Paths Relating to the Outbreak of the Pelagian Debate," *Nanzan Journal of Theological Studies* 30 [2007]: 29n9). Mercator offers the following account, which seems to suggest that some sort of sentence was delivered while Caelestius was still present in Carthage (but as always, it should be mentioned that Mercator's historical account may not be entirely reliable): "Caelestius, in no way accepting, but rather resisting, these same acts [of the *iudicium*], at which he was frequently heard, was deprived of ecclesiastical communion. He committed himself to appealing this sentence to the consideration of the Roman bishop. Soon, he neglected this appeal and set out for Ephesus, the city in Asia. There, he dared to seek the presbyterate through stealth" (*Commonitorium super nomine Caelestii* [CPL 781; Latin: ACO 1.5.1, p. 66, ln. 20–24; English: my translation]). It should be noted that Picard-Mawji ("Le passage," 8) takes Mercator's account to imply that Caelestius left Carthage very quickly after his excommunication, but I am not convinced that that reading is necessitated by what Mercator says here.

APPENDIX 307

e. After receiving Marcellinus's letter (while still absent from Carthage[9]), a significant amount of time passes before Augustine begins his reply.[10]

f. During this time, however, Augustine investigates the situation. He acquires and reads a book (*liber*) by one of the Pelagians (Caelestius?[11]) as well as the *libellus breuissimus* produced by Caelestius during his trial.[12] He possibly seeks and/or receives information from other sources as well.[13] He also (possibly) re-reads, completes, and publishes *De bono coniugali* and *De sancta uirginitate* during this period.[14]

9 Augustine states that Marcellinus sent his letter "from Carthage," which would seem to indicate that Augustine was not in Carthage when he received it. See *retr.* 2.33.60.

10 At *pecc. mer.* 1.1.1, Augustine indicates he has been busy but feels he can no longer be in Marcellinus's debt.

11 See *pecc. mer.* 1.34.64 and Dunphy, "A Lost Year," 410–16. In the past, scholars have tended to think that the book Augustine acquired was the *Liber de Fide* attributed to Rufinus the Syrian (see, e.g., Wermelinger, *Rom und Pelagius*, 19). Others, however, have preferred to identify this *liber* as a now-lost work by Caelestius—see, e.g., Eugene TeSelle, "Rufinus the Syrian, Caelestius, Pelagius: Explorations in the Pre-History of the Pelagian Controversy," *Augustinian Studies* 3 (1972): 76. Dunphy has, in my view, convincingly problematized the identification of this *liber* as the *Liber de fide*, as well as the existence of a "Rufinus the Syrian," as we discussed in Chapter 1. See, e.g., Dunphy, "Marius Mercator on Rufinus the Syrian: Was Schwartz Mistaken?" *Augustinianum* 32 (1992): 279–88; "Rufinus the Syrian: Myth and Reality," *Augustiniana* 59 (2009): 79–157; "Ps-Rufinus (the "Syrian") and the Vulgate: Evidence Wanting!" *Augustinianum* 52 (2012): 219–56. See also Delaroche, "Notes complémentaires," in *Salaire et pardon des péchés, Bibliothèque Augustinienne: Oeuvres de Saint Augustin* 20/A (Paris: Institut d'Études Augustiniennes, 2013), 501–7, who notes the plausibility of the view that the *liber* was by Caelestius.

12 See *pecc. mer.* 1.34.63. For more on the *libellus breuissimus*, see n. 7 above.

13 See, e.g., *pecc. mer.* 1.9.9. For a helpful analysis of the sources used by Augustine in *De peccatorum meritis* see Bruno Delaroche, *Saint Augustin lecteur et interprète de saint Paul dans le De peccatorum meritis et remissione (hiver 411–412)* (Paris: Études augustiniennes, 1996), 357–75.

14 Both of these works are mentioned at *pecc. mer.* 1.29.57 and seem to have been written largely in c. 403–4. However, as Hombert has convincingly argued, both bear clear signs of having been supplemented and published only after Augustine became aware of the Pelagians' views. See discussion in Pierre-Marie Hombert, *Nouvelles recherches de chronologie augustinienne* (Paris: Institut d'Études Augustiniennes, 2000), 109–36, esp. 115–16. Since Augustine refers to these works in *De peccatorum meritis* 1, it seems that they would have been completed before the composition of this book (although it remains possible that Augustine mentioned them in *De peccatorum meritis* without having completely finished them).

308 APPENDIX

g. Possibly before or during the information gathering noted in (f), Augustine comes to Carthage.[15]

h. Upon arrival in Carthage, Augustine reads the acts of Caelestius's trial[16] and, probably, speaks with Aurelius, the bishop of Carthage, about the situation.[17] Augustine and Aurelius decide to avoid

---

15 This is a crucial point and requires some explanation (see discussion in Dunphy, "A Lost Year," 420ff.; what follows is a summary of Dunphy's main points). At *pecc. mer.* 3.1.1 Augustine identifies the circumstances that led him to add a third book to *De peccatorum meritis*: "I had already completed two long books on the questions you presented to me. . . . But only a few days later (*post paucissimos dies*) I read certain writings [i.e., the *Expositiones* on the Pauline letters] of Pelagius, a holy man, as I hear, and a Christian of considerable religious development; they contain brief explanations of the letters of the apostle Paul" (Latin: CSEL 60:128.15–129.8; English: Teske, WSA I/23, 117 [slightly modified]). Augustine goes on to explain that he found a new argument in this writing of Pelagius that he had not addressed in the first two books of *De peccatorum meritis* and thus decided to add a letter (or third book) to address it. The importance of this passage for our present purposes is its indication that the completion of Books 1–2 was in very close proximity with the decision to write Book 3. Now, let us turn to *ep.* 139.3. In this letter, which likely dates to January or February of 412 (I will discuss the dating of this letter below), Augustine speaks more about the writing of Book 3: "You should know that the letter that I also wanted to write to you and to add to [the first two books of *De peccatorum meritis*], which I had already begun to dictate when I was there [*ibi*], is still unfinished, though there has been a small addition to it" (Latin: CSEL 44:152.9–11; English: Teske, WSA II/2, 240). The crucial element of this quotation is Augustine's indication that he had begun the composition of Book 3 when he was "there." Writing *ep.* 139 to Marcellinus in Carthage, it seems very likely that for Augustine "there" would mean "Carthage." In this sense, it would seem that Books 1–2 were, at the very least, completed, if not composed in their entirety, in Carthage (further evidence for the composition of the entirety of these books in Carthage is the strategy Augustine employs in not mentioning Caelestius's name throughout the work—see below for more on this). Of course, it remains possible that there was a significant span of time between Augustine's discovery of Pelagius's *Expositiones* and his commencement of the dictation of Book III. But this seems unlikely for a few reasons. For example, it seems more likely that Augustine would gain access to Pelagius's *Expositiones* in Carthage as opposed to Hippo or some other place (see Dunphy, "A Lost Year," 423). It would also be odd for Augustine to put such a project to the side while it was still fresh in his mind (indeed, the portion of Book 3 that deals with the specific argument cited by Pelagius is very brief and, thus, would not have taken long to compose).

16 At *gest. Pel.* 11.23, Augustine indicates that while he was not present at Caelestius's trial, he read the proceedings of the trial after he came to Carthage.

17 It remains possible that Augustine had already communicated with Aurelius via letter before his arrival in Carthage. But it seems more likely that he would have waited to speak with him in person if he were planning to be in Carthage in the near future—especially given the delicate nature of this situation (see Dunphy, "A Lost Year," 442: "When Paulinus lodged his complaint with Aurelius of Carthage, and that prelate found against Caelestius, the complications were compounded. The decision seemed to pit the 'foreign' Catholics—among whom Marcellinus should be listed, and of whom he was necessarily a representative—against the local African Catholics.").

APPENDIX 309

mentioning any names in connection with the Pelagian ideas they are refuting so as to more easily correct those who have fallen into error. This explains the lack of explicit references to Caelestius and his trial in *De peccatorum meritis*.[18]

i. Augustine completes Books 1 and 2 and, at some point thereafter, submits them to Marcellinus.[19]

j. A few days after completing the first two books, Augustine reads Pelagius's *Expositiones* (or at least the relevant passage from the *expositio* on Romans), which will prompt the writing of Book 3.[20]

---

18 For mention of this strategy, see *gest. Pel.* 22.46; *retr.* 2.33.60; *ep.* 157.3.22; *s.* 348A.5; *ep.* 19*.3; *ep.* 186.1.2. That this was a joint decision made by Aurelius and Augustine can be gathered from a use of the first-person plural in *gest. Pel.* 22.46, as opposed to the use of the first-person singular elsewhere in that same passage: "We thought that one proceeded against them in a better manner if their errors were refuted and opposed without mentioning anyone's name..." (Latin: CSEL 42:100.23–25; English: Teske, WSA I/23, 354). *De gestis Pelagii* was addressed to Aurelius. See Dunphy, "A Lost Year," 430 and 456. The motivation for this silence regarding the names of the Pelagians may have been more complicated than Augustine lets on here. For example, Peter Brown comments that "the existence of influential patrons of Pelagius explains why Augustine showed himself remarkably hesitant before coming to grips with Pelagius by name" ("The Patrons of Pelagius: The Roman Aristocracy between East and West," in *Religion and Society in the Age of Saint Augustine* [New York: Harper & Row, 1972], 217; see also Robert Evans, *Pelagius: Inquiries and Reappraisals* [London: Seabury Press, 1968], 70–80)—although I think Winrich Löhr (*Pélage et le pélagianisme* [Paris: Cerf, 2014], 51 and 56) is quite right to critique this explanation: given that Augustine and the African authorities begin attacking Pelagius and Caelestius by name before Melania, Pinianus, and Albina's departure from Africa in 417, their fear over upsetting powerful patrons cannot be the only reason for this hesitancy to name names. (In this connection, Löhr questions the extent of Pelagius's connection with Melania and various other aristocratic families.)

19 Jennifer Ebbeler suggests that these two books were only initial drafts that were later reworked into the first two books of *De peccatorum meritis et remissione* (*Disciplining Christians: Correction and Community in Augustine's Letters* [Oxford: Oxford University Press, 2012], 192n7, 195). She cites Lancel, *St. Augustine*, 328, but I do not think Lancel meant to imply that Augustine's initial submission to Marcellinus was significantly reworked. In any event, the opening of Book 3 seems to preclude any significant emendations to Books 1–2 after their submission to Marcellinus, for there Augustine justifies the need for a third book by pointing out that he "did not want to add anything to that work which I had brought to a definitive close" (*pecc. mer.* 3.1.1 [Latin: CSEL 60:129.15–16; English: Teske, WSA I/23, 117]).

20 See *ep.* 139.3, *pecc. mer.* 3.1.1, and n. 15 above. Dunphy has made some intriguing conjectures about Augustine's sudden discovery of Pelagius's *Expositiones*. For Dunphy, it seems likely that Augustine received the *Expositiones* from none other than Marcellinus himself, who, as a recent arrival from Italy, could very well have been part of the same circles of acquaintances as Pelagius. After reading the first two books of *De peccatorum meritis*, Marcellinus may have thought (or was concerned others might think) Augustine was tacitly attacking Pelagius— given that other arguments cited by Pelagius were among those refuted by Augustine in Books

310   APPENDIX

k. Augustine begins dictating Book 3.[21]

l. At some point, Marcellinus returns Books 1–2.[22]

m. Augustine returns to Hippo.[23]

January or February 412 (at the latest)

n. Augustine is in Hippo. Book 3 of *De peccatorum meritis* remains incomplete, albeit with a short addition to what was dictated in Carthage.[24] Augustine can no longer remember why Marcellinus returned Books 1–2.[25] It seems he has been back in Hippo for some time, having already written several lengthy letters and works for various individuals, including a few in Carthage.[26]

---

1 and 2—and wanted Augustine to address the issue more directly. This would explain Augustine's cautious praise of Pelagius throughout this book. See Dunphy, "A Lost Year," 423–25.

21 See ep. 139.3.

22 See *ep.* 139.3. It is possible that this occurred before (k) or perhaps even (j), depending on how quickly Marcellinus read the books.

23 See, e.g., *ep.* 139, which Augustine writes from Hippo. It is possible that this occurred before (l). But see below at n. 25.

24 See *ep.* 139.3. We know that this letter could not have been written after the end of February 412, since the purpose of the letter was to appeal to Marcellinus (and through Marcellinus, to his brother Apringius, the proconsul) for clemency on behalf of certain Donatists. Since Apringius's term ended at the close of February, the letter must be dated prior to that. (Although Apringius's name is not mentioned in the letter, the "proconsul" is referred to, and it seems clear that *ep.* 139 is following up on the earlier letters *epp.* 133 and 134 sent, respectively, to Marcellinus and Apringius on this same issue.) For the dating of Apringius's term as proconsul, see A. Clément Pallu de Lessert, *Fastes de provinces africaines: (Proconsulaire, Numidie, Maurétanies) sous la domination romaine,* vol. 2 (Paris: E. Leroux, 1901), 124–26.

25 In *ep.* 139.3, Augustine notes that he cannot remember the reason why he received the books back from Marcellinus, unless it was simply because there was something in need of correction. It is unclear when this return happened, but I think Augustine's forgetfulness suggests that it was significantly before January or February of 412, and perhaps that it occurred in person (and thus in Carthage), as opposed to through a courier, who (likely?) would have carried a letter of explanation for the return (a letter to which Augustine would have been able to refer). On the other hand, Dunphy speculates that Augustine is being somewhat deceptive here and does not want to acknowledge the actual reason for their return ("A Lost Year," 405ff). Bruno Delaroche is unsure how to account for this forgetfulness other than attributing it to the time that has passed since the sending of the work ("Introduction," 34–35).

26 See *ep.* 139.3, where Augustine lists his recent efforts: his summary of the conference with the Donatists (*Breuiculus collationis*), a letter to the Donatist laity (*Ad Donatistas post collationem*), *ep.* 137 (to Volusianus), *ep.* 138 (to Marcellinus), and *ep.* 140 (to Honoratus). In addition, he must have already sent the short letters *ep.* 133 (to Marcellinus) and *ep.* 134 (to Marcellinus's brother Apringius) some time before (as they concern the same matter that, in

APPENDIX   311

Group 2

These data points can be grouped due to passages such as *gest. Pel.* 22.46,
which connect the travels of Pelagius with those of Augustine in 410 and
411. Further insights into Augustine's travels in 411 are gathered from various
sources.[27]

Autumn 410

a. Pelagius arrives[28] in Hippo while Augustine is out of town.[29]

b. Pelagius quickly leaves Hippo, having made no mention of any
   problematic views on grace during his time there.[30]

c. Before departing Hippo, Pelagius leaves a letter for Augustine, to
   which Augustine responds.[31]

---

part, prompted the writing of *ep.* 139—i.e., a request for leniency for a few Donatists who had
confessed to murdering a Catholic priest and maiming another).

27 See Perler, *Les voyages*, 274–304.

28 We are also uncertain if Pelagius traveled with a particular group on his way to Africa.
Various proposals have been made. A popular conjecture is that Pelagius was a companion
of Melania, Pinianus, and Albina, who left Rome before the sack (thus, likely in 408 or 409)
and traveled initially to their estate in Sicily (see, e.g., John Ferguson, *Pelagius: A Historical
and Theological Study* [Cambridge: W. Heffer, 1956], 47–49; Wermelinger, *Rom und Pelagius*,
5–6; Dunphy, "A Lost Year," 392). After the sack of Rome, the group sailed to Africa, perhaps
late in 410, where Melania and her family would take up residence at their estate in Thagaste.
If he were traveling with Melania et al., this could explain why Pelagius had landed in Hippo,
instead of Carthage: Hippo was the port offering the most direct route to Thagaste (see
Dunphy, "A Lost Year," 392). On the other hand, Serge Lancel thinks it more likely that Pelagius
traveled directly from Ostia to Hippo, taking whatever ship was available in the aftermath of
Alaric's sack (see Lancel, *Saint Augustine*, 325n1).

29 See *gest. Pel.* 22.46. From the information available to us, it seems Augustine was away from
Hippo on at least two occasions in the second half of 410. First, it seems likely that Augustine
was in Carthage for the summer, returning to Hippo Regius in October via Utica and Hippo
Diarrhytus (see Perler, *Les voyages*, 274–80). Second, at some point after his return, Augustine
fell ill and left Hippo for a time to recover (see *ep.* 118.5.34 where this illness is mentioned,
as well as *epp.* 122 and 124, where an absence from Hippo in 410 is also noted, although it
seems possible he is referring here to his time in Carthage—see Perler, *Les voyages*, 280–86,
for discussion).

30 See *gest. Pel.* 22.46.

31 See *gest. Pel.* 26.51–28.52; *ep.* 146. It is not explicitly stated by Augustine when this exchange
of letters took place, however this seems to be the most likely point for it to have occurred.
For more on the correspondence between Augustine and Pelagius, see Y.-M. Duval, "La cor-
respondance entre Augustin et Pélage," *Revue des études augustiniennes* 45 (1999): 363–84.
For specific discussion of the dating of this initial letter, see Duval, "La correspondance," 372ff.
See also Löhr, "Augustinus und sein Verhältnis zu Pelagius," 71.

During 411

d. Augustine arrives in Carthage, sometime before May 17 (the date traditionally assigned to *s.* 357, delivered in Carthage; and the day before the Donatists arrived in procession at Carthage).[32]

e. After his arrival in Carthage, Augustine sees Pelagius a few times but has no opportunity to speak with him. Pelagius leaves Carthage (for Palestine?) at some point relatively soon thereafter.[33]

f. June 1–8: The Conference with the Donatists is held in three sessions (June 1, 3, 8), with Augustine in attendance.[34]

g. June 26: Marcellinus publishes his judgment, ruling in favor of the Catholics.[35]

h. At some point before the end of 411, Augustine returns to Hippo. It seems certain that Augustine would have remained in Carthage at least until the publication of Marcellinus's decision at the end of June. But there is good reason to think he stayed in Carthage for several more months, at least until late September.[36] However, it should be noted that we have no definite information on Augustine's travels for the remainder of the year.

---

32 See Perler, *Les voyages*, 287n1. Marcellinus had set May 18 as the arrival date for the Catholic and Donatist bishops attending the conference the following month (see Dunphy, "A Lost Year," 393). See also Lancel, ed., *Gesta Conlationis Carthaginiensis*, CCSL 149A:vii–x for key dates related to the conference with the Donatists.

33 See *gest. Pel.* 22.46. It should be noted that this passage from *De gestis Pelagii* has often been interpreted to suggest that Caelestius's trial occurred after Pelagius's departure from Carthage (e.g., Delaroche, "La datation," 40n10). However, this reading of the passage is not the only possibility. In fact, as Dunphy argues, it seems preferable to read it otherwise (see "A Lost Year," 426ff), as we shall discuss below.

34 See W. H. C. Frend, *The Donatist Church: A Movement of Protest in Roman North Africa* (Oxford: Clarendon Press, 1952), 275ff, for more on the proceedings of the Conference, as well as Lancel, *Gesta Conlationis*.

35 See Flavius Marcellinus, "Sententia Cognitoris," PL 11:1418–20.

36 For example, it is possible that Augustine preached *en. in Ps.* 72 and/or 88 on Sept. 13/14 in Carthage. See Perler, *Les voyages*, 293, 297. (But cf. Dunphy, "A Lost Year," 394n13.) Regarding whether Augustine would remain in Carthage for the summer of 411, Perler writes, "[I]l était très conforme aux habitudes du maître de passer l'été en Proconsulaire, s'il avait dû s'y rendre, et ce n'est pas un séjour de plusieurs mois à Carthage qui a de quoi étonner" (*Les voyages*, 293n2).

APPENDIX

313

January or February 412 (at the latest)
i. Augustine is in Hippo and seems to have been back for some time.[37]

Group 3

The following points are not chronologically ordered but offer additional key events or details important for the chronology of 411.

a. Writing in *pecc. mer.* 3, Augustine pauses to reflect on how rapidly Pelagian views have spread and become a problem. He relates that a short time ago (*ante paruum tempus*) he had overheard a few individuals in Carthage mention that infants are not baptized for the forgiveness of sins but for sanctification in Christ. For several reasons, he did not think it the opportune moment to engage these people on this issue. But now (*iam*), he notes, this view is being zealously defended, it is preserved in writing, he is being asked about it by his brethren, and is being forced to argue and write against it.[38]

b. At *gest. Pel.* 11.25, Augustine indicates that at some point after Marcellinus asked him to write *De peccatorum meritis*, Aurelius in Carthage had Augustine preach a sermon on the Pelagian issue, a sermon that has come down to us as *s.* 294 (delivered on June 27).[39] This sermon must have been delivered after Augustine had completed the first two books of *De peccatorum meritis*.[40]

---

37 See (n) under Group 1 above.

38 See *pecc. mer.* 3.6.12. Here, the key question is when exactly Augustine overheard this conversation in Carthage. Given the rest of the passage, it seems to have taken place before Augustine received the letter from Marcellinus that would prompt his writing of *De peccatorum meritis*.

39 Two other sermons are closely related to *s.* 294: *s.* 293 (delivered on June 24) and *s.* 299 (delivered on June 29). For more on these and for an argument that they should all be dated to the same year, see F. Dolbeau, "Deux Sermons d'Augustin pour les fêtes de Jean-Baptiste et de Pierre et Paul (s. 293 et 299)," *Augustinianum* 57 (2017): 403–92. Note also the connections Dolbeau notices between these sermons and *De peccatorum meritis*. See also Dunphy, "Unexplored Paths." However, for an argument separating *s.* 299 from *ss.* 293 and 294 and supporting its traditional date of 418, see Giulio Malavasi, "Marius Mercator's Enemies in Augustine's Letter 193," in *Studia Patristica*, vol. 75, ed. M. Vinzent and A. Brent (Leuven: Peeters, 2016), 361–70.

40 In *s.* 294.17, Augustine cites the following argument: "'If Adam,' they say, 'harms those who haven't sinned, then Christ ought to benefit even those who haven't believed'" (Latin: PL 38:1345.53–55; English: Hill, WSA III/8, 191). At *pecc. mer.* 3.1.1–3.2.2, Augustine indicates

c. Augustine tells us at *retr.* 2.33.60 that he first (*prius*) responded to the Pelagian heresy "not in books but in sermons and conferences."[41]

THREE CHRONOLOGIES

With our chronological "groups" presented, we can now look at the three main ways that scholars have woven these groups together. We might dub the first of these three views the "traditional account," as it has received consistent support for much of the past half century.[42] According to the traditional account, the quarrel between Caelestius, Paulinus, and the diocesan officials in Carthage erupted in Autumn 411, after Augustine had departed for Hippo (at the end of September?). In this sense, advocates for the traditional account will generally have to insert the data points found in my Group 1 into the gap between Group 2's (h) and (i).[43] Proponents for this view offer several reasons for this chronology. First of all, recognizing that Augustine was not present at Caelestius's trial, they note that this trial must have taken place either before Augustine arrived in Carthage or after he left. As we have said above, Augustine was in Carthage during May and June of 411, when the Donatist Conference was held, and it seems likely that this stay would have extended for several more months, perhaps lasting until late September. Delaroche and Refoulé both argue that the trial must have occurred after Augustine's departure due to Augustine's later account of these events, found

---

that he had discovered this argument a few days after completing the first two books of *De peccatorum meritis.* Thus, *s.* 294 must postdate this discovery.

41 *retr.* 2.33.60 (Latin: CCL 57:117.4–5; English: Ramsey, WSA I/2, 140). See also *pecc. mer.* 3.6.12. A major question is how this sequence of, first, sermons and, then, books relates to the composition of *De peccatorum meritis.* At the same time, note *gest. Pel.* 22.46 where, after mentioning his and Aurelius's decision to avoid naming names, Augustine reports that "we did not cease from speaking against those evils in books and in homilies to the people" (*nec libris igitur aduersus mala illa disserere nec popularibus tractatibus cessabamus* [Latin: CSEL 42:101.1–2; English: Teske, I/23, 354]). Does this report from *gest. Pel.* conflict with the order given in *retr.* and *pecc. mer.?*

42 The most important analyses are those of Refoulé and Delaroche: F. Refoulé, "Datation du premier concile de Carthage contre les Pélagiens et du 'Libellus fidei' de Rufin," *Revue des études augustiniennes* 9 (1963): 41–49; Delaroche, "La datation." See also Perler, *Les voyages,* 299ff and, recently, Picard-Mawji, "Le passage."

43 Along with this, (a) from Group 3 will typically be placed at some point before Group 2's (h); (b) from Group 3 will be pushed to 413, as 413 is the next time when Augustine is in Carthage on June 27.

APPENDIX

in *gest. Pel.* 22.46.[44] In this passage, Augustine details his growing awareness of Pelagius and his teachings, Pelagius's arrival in North Africa, his brief stay in Hippo Regius, and his journey to Carthage. Augustine then mentions his encounter with Pelagius in Carthage: he had seen Pelagius's face once or twice in Carthage "when I was very busy with preparations for the conference which we were about to hold with the Donatists."[45] Immediately after noting Pelagius's hasty departure from Carthage, Augustine writes, "Meanwhile, these teachings were warmly expounded on the lips of those who were reputed to be his disciples to the point that Caelestius was brought before an ecclesiastical court and received a sentence worthy of his perversity."[46] Delaroche argues that Augustine's account here suggests the following two points: (1) Caelestius's condemnation occurred after Pelagius had departed from Carthage, and (2) Pelagius was still present in Carthage when Augustine had already arrived for the Donatist conference.[47] Thus, he concludes, the affair with Caelestius must have occurred after the Donatist conference and after Augustine had departed from Carthage (since he did not attend the *iudicium*). This leaves the fall of 411 as the most plausible date for Caelestius's trial, in Delaroche's view.[48]

However, several problems with this proposal present themselves, as Walter Dunphy has noted.[49] First and foremost is the issue of time. Is there simply enough time between late September 411 and February 412 for Caelestius to apply for ordination, to cause a stir with his views, to be accused of heresy by Paulinus, to undergo multiple examinations before Aurelius and other bishops in Carthage, for Marcellinus to write to Augustine, for Augustine to acquire Caelestius's *libellus* as well as another Pelagian book, to begin to write after some delay, to send Books 1–2 to Marcellinus, to receive them back again, to begin Book 3 but to have a significant delay in continuing work

44 See n. 33 above.

45 *gest. Pel.* 22.46 (Latin: CSEL 42:100.18–19; English: Teske, WSA I/23, 354).

46 *gest. Pel.* 22.46 (Latin: CSEL 42:100.20–23; English: Teske, WSA I/23, 354).

47 See Delaroche, "La datation," 40n10.

48 Delaroche, "La datation," 42. Delaroche's argument contains other details and points which I do not discuss here that allow him to further specify the autumn of 411 and not the winter of 411–12 as the most likely date for the composition of the first two books of *De peccatorum meritis*. Note, however, that more recently Delaroche has argued for a slightly earlier trial date—i.e., during the summer or first part of September (Delaroche, "Introduction," 32). This proposal will be discussed below.

49 See Dunphy, "A Lost Year," for more on the following.

APPENDIX

on it due to numerous other writing tasks, and, finally, to forget why Books 1–2 had been returned?[50] It simply seems impossible to squeeze all of this into roughly four months. But there is more. Advocates for the traditional account have, in general, not noticed the key point highlighted above regarding the composition of Book 3: that it was begun in Carthage and, thus, that Books 1–2 were likely completed (if not composed in their entirety) in Carthage as well.[51] Given that Augustine seems to have written much of *De peccatorum meritis* in Carthage, the traditional dating of Caelestius's trial in the fall of 411 simply does not work.

As a response to Dunphy's critiques, Delaroche has, more recently, modified some of the details of his chronology. Still wishing to keep Caelestius's trial after the conference with the Donatists, Delaroche has suggested that it occurred during the summer of 411 or at the beginning of autumn, at a time when Augustine was away from Carthage.[52] Here Delaroche is indebted to some degree to J. H. Koopmans, who offers a more robust version of this chronology, which we might term our "second" chronology.[53] For Koopmans, Augustine likely left Carthage at the end of June, returning to Hippo—so, shortly after (g) in our Group 2 above. After Augustine's departure, the events found in our Group 1 above would begin to occur. At some point, Augustine would return to Carthage (Koopmans suggests in September), look at the proceedings of the trial against Caelestius, write *De peccatorum meritis* 1–2

---

50 Pierre Descotes, in the context of discussing the dating of *ep.* 140, also acknowledges the problems that the traditional account offers for the final months of 411 and beginning of 412: *La grâce de la nouvelle alliance*, BA 20/B (Paris: Institut d'Études Augustiniennes, 2016), 33.

51 In a more recent piece, Delaroche introduces the possibility that Augustine took a trip to Carthage at the beginning of 412 (see Delaroche, "Introduction," 35n114). A similar proposal is made in brief by Volker Henning Drecoll (see "Gratia" in *Augustinus-Lexikon*, vol. 3, ed. Cornelius Mayer [Basel: Schwabe, 2004–2010], 182–242, at 208n189—although note that Drecoll appears at times to write "412" and "413" where he means "411" and "412"). But a quick trip to Carthage at the beginning of 412 seems very implausible, given the time constraints already in play—not to mention Augustine's dislike of travel.

52 See Delaroche, "Introduction," 32. Unfortunately, Delaroche's chronology here is not entirely consistent and often simply repeats his previous views but with the occasional unexplained alteration. (For example, he still wants to maintain that Marcellinus did not write to Augustine until after Augustine's return to Hippo from Carthage in late September. But then he proposes that Augustine took another trip to Carthage in early 412—see the previous footnote.)

53 J. H. Koopmans, "Augustine's First Contact with Pelagius and the Dating of the Condemnation of Caelestius at Carthage," *Vigiliae Christianae* 8 (1954): 149–53.

APPENDIX

and begin the third book. He would then return back to Hippo by the end of the year.[54]

On the whole, this second chronology is an improvement upon the traditional account. Most importantly, it avoids (or at least lessens) the severity of the "time crunch" at the end of 411 and beginning of 412. But serious questions still remain. Most importantly, is it plausible that Augustine would depart from Carthage only to return roughly two months later? As Perler writes, "One cannot maintain that the bishop, already so busy at Hippo and then at Carthage, although he came from a probably shortened convalescence, undertook, in the same year, two long and difficult trips to Carthage without an extremely serious reason."[55] It could, perhaps, be argued that the Caelestian affair was a serious enough reason to prompt Augustine's return to Carthage. But it is not clear to me that this would have been the case: Why exactly would Augustine need to be in Carthage to respond to the situation? There was no follow-up council or trial for him to participate in—and any records he needed to review or discussions he needed to have (with Aurelius, for example) could, respectively, have been obtained and taken place remotely via letter (even if an in-person consultation would have been preferable).

But again, it could be argued that when Augustine left Carthage at the end of June, he had not gone all the way back to Hippo (as per Koopmans) but had remained relatively close to Carthage. In this case, though, we might wonder why Augustine had not returned to Carthage for Caelestius's trial. While it is true that Caelestius's trial was, at the start, prompted by an application for ordination and, thus, was a matter internal to the Carthaginian church,[56] it is, I think, important to recognize that the case had some unusual qualities from the beginning: the applicant was a Roman refugee, accused of heresy by a Milanese deacon, in a climate where division in the Catholic ranks was absolutely unacceptable.[57] If Augustine had been nearby, it stands to reason that he would have been present—especially given his interest in Pelagius and his views (as manifested by his attention to Pelagius's time in

---

54 Like the first chronology, proponents of this second option will also have to place *s.* 294 (and *ss.* 293 and 299) in 413.

55 Perler, *Les voyages*, 293n2.

56 Delaroche hints that perhaps Aurelius would not have felt it necessary to wait for Augustine (see Delaroche, "Introduction," 32 and n. 99).

57 See Dunphy, "A Lost Year," 464–65.

Hippo as well as his awareness of him in Carthage in May/June 411).[58] But if he did not remain near Carthage, that means Augustine would have had to have made two long trips to Carthage over the course of just a few months.

Given the difficulties with these two chronologies, Walter Dunphy has offered a third.[59] In Dunphy's view, trouble began to brew in Carthage long before Augustine arrived there in April or May of 411. Indeed, Dunphy argues that the trial of Caelestius had already occurred, perhaps in February of 411.[60] Around that time Marcellinus contacted Augustine about the issues raised by Caelestius. Upon his arrival in Carthage, Augustine would have had the opportunity to consult the acts of Caelestius's trial and discuss the matter with Aurelius. Dunphy states that Augustine likely began his response to Marcellinus in June of 411 (perhaps after the conclusion of the conference with the Donatists, and around the time when Pelagius left Carthage). At the end of June, he would preach *ss.* 293, 294, and 299. After finishing the first two books of *De peccatorum meritis*, Augustine would read Pelagius's *Expositiones* and begin a supplemental letter to Marcellinus that would eventually become a third book. On Dunphy's scheme, then, the events (a) through (g) from our Group 1 should be inserted between events (c) and (d) of Group 2; the remainder of the Carthaginian events from Group 1—(h) through (l)—would have occurred during the late spring and summer of 411.

Dunphy's dating avoids the key issues with the first two chronologies: ample time is given for the process of the trial and for the writing of *De peccatorum meritis*, and there is no need to insert a second trip to Carthage. An additional benefit is that this dating allows *s.* 294 (see event [b] in Group 3), as well as the related *ss.* 293 and 299, to be dated to June 411 instead of 413. These sermons are very similar in their content and argument to *De peccatorum meritis* and, thus, would appear to have been delivered around the same time as the composition of this work.[61]

---

58 See *gest. Pel.* 22.46. See also Dunphy, "A Lost Year," 401, 426, and 436.

59 Walter Dunphy, "A Lost Year." See especially the summary of his chronology on pp. 463ff.

60 It remains possible that the trial had occurred even earlier. Dunphy also speculates that Pelagius's hasty departure from Hippo in 410 may have been prompted by his awareness of the tensions in Carthage ("A Lost Year," 436).

61 See Dunphy, "A Lost Year," 458ff, where, among other things, he notes the implausibility of dating these sermons to 413. The summer of 413 was a time of intense upheaval in Carthage due to the revolt of Heraclian. See also Dunphy, "Unexplored Paths," and Dolbeau, "Deux Sermons." With this re-dating, several other sermons related to the Pelagian controversy and delivered in Carthage could also be moved to 411: e.g., *s.* 174 and *en. Ps.* 50.

APPENDIX

Of course, certain difficulties remain for Dunphy's proposal. An issue that proponents of the first two chronologies might point to is that *gest. Pel.* 22.46 seems to indicate that Caelestius's trial occurred after Pelagius's departure from Carthage in May/June 411 (after mentioning Pelagius's departure, Augustine shifts to discuss Caelestius's trial). But this, Dunphy points out, is a misreading of that passage. The temporal word Augustine uses to shift to his discussion of Caelestius is not *postea* (or a similar word), but *interea*.[62] Dunphy notes that, far from indicating a later event, this word suggests that the affair of Caelestius happened while Pelagius was still in Carthage.[63] A second issue is with Group 3's event (a): the conversation on infant baptism overheard by Augustine. For proponents of the first two chronologies this conversation is easily placed in the summer of 411, as it seems to have preceded Augustine's awareness of the situation with Caelestius. Dunphy also wishes to place this event in the summer of 411, but explains that Augustine decided not to engage those discussing the issue because Caelestius's trial was "over and done"; thus, there was no need to set straight individuals of little authority.[64] Delaroche remains unconvinced by this argument.[65] Admittedly, I find Dunphy's interpretation of this passage a bit strained as well: there seems to be a chronological progression in the passage that indicates that the conversation was overheard before Augustine was aware of the particular issues surrounding Caelestius.[66] However, in my view, it is perfectly possible to date this event to 410, when Augustine was in Carthage for the summer.[67]

---

62 *gest. Pel.* 22.46 (Latin: CSEL 42:100.20).

63 See Dunphy, "A Lost Year," 426ff. Note too that Koopmans seems to, in part, recognize this: "Augustine's First Contact," 151.

64 See Dunphy, "A Lost Year," 451ff.

65 See Delaroche, "Introduction," 15n32, and, more fully, "Notes complémentaires," 552–53.

66 Further, I would add that the argument ("little ones are baptized not in order to receive the remission of sins, but to be sanctified in Christ") Augustine overhears and characterizes as "nouitas" (*pecc. mer.* 3.6.12 [Latin: CSEL 60:139.12–13; English: my translation]) is quite similar to another Pelagian argument reported at *pecc. mer.* 1.18.23. As a result, Dunphy's view that this was actually a new form of a Pelagian argument that Augustine had not yet encountered by the summer of 411 does not seem quite right to me (see Dunphy, "A Lost Year," 451n75).

67 See Perler, *Les voyages*, 274ff. It might be objected that 410 was too long ago, for Augustine, writing in *pecc. mer.* 3.6.12 notes that this episode occurred "a short time ago (*ante paruum tempus*)" (CSEL 60:139.10). But note that just a few lines later Augustine says that the Jovinian crisis had occurred "a few years ago (*ante paucos annos*)" (CSEL 60:139.20), even though this was roughly 20 years prior. With these temporal references, Augustine is emphasizing just how

A few other issues remain with Dunphy's chronology. First of all, we might wonder when the first two books of *De peccatorum meritis* were completed. Dunphy is a bit vague on the completion date of these books and at times seems to suggest that their composition would have occurred over the course of the summer.[68] This dating is attractive because it offers Augustine an extended period to research and reflect upon the various facets of the views promoted by Caelestius and others. However, as we noted above, it seems that *s.* 294 had to have been delivered after the completion of the first two books of *De peccatorum meritis*.[69] This means that these books must have been completed, at the latest, a few days before June 27, 411 (and that Augustine began to compose Book 3 around this time as well). As a result, Dunphy's timeline becomes rather compressed, given his view that the composition of Books 1–2 began in June. However, it does not seem overly problematic to me to shift the beginning of the writing process earlier. After Augustine received Marcellinus's questions in, perhaps, February, he likely would have begun to formulate his response and, possibly, acquire information regarding the situation in Carthage from other sources. Thus, he could have arrived in Carthage in April or May already largely prepared to respond to Marcellinus's request. After reading the acts of the trial and meeting with Aurelius, he could have begun writing (drawing, perhaps, on notes he had already made before arriving in Carthage). Given Augustine's capacity to multitask,[70] it does not seem unreasonable to think that he would have already made good headway on Books 1–2 even before the conclusion of the Conference with the Donatists the first week of June. And after the Conference, he would have had much more time to devote to *De peccatorum meritis*, and, I think, would have had no difficulty in finishing these books at least a few days before June 27.

As a result of this minor tweaking of Dunphy's chronology, though, another objection might be raised. At *retr.* 2.33.60 (see Group 3 [c]), Augustine

---

recently the Pelagian heresy has arisen (and so we should recognize that the proximity of the dates is likely, to some degree, exaggerated). See Delaroche, "Notes complémentaires," 552–53.

68 See, e.g., "A Lost Year," 465.

69 See n. 40 above.

70 See, e.g., Augustine's comments in *ep.* 139.3, where he lists a variety of recent projects that he seems to have been composing at roughly the same time. See also *ep.* 224.2, where Augustine mentions his writing habits toward the end of his life as he worked on various projects, some by day and others by night.

APPENDIX   321

indicates that he first responded to the Pelagian heresy in sermons and not in books. But if Books 1–2 were completed before *s.* 294 was delivered, this would seem to contradict that account. Once again, though, this objection can be overturned rather easily: while Augustine had completed these books before the sermons, they nevertheless were not published until much later.[71] As Dunphy points out, Augustine's practice with respect to Marcellinus seems to have been to compose a response, to send it to the imperial official for review, and to publish it only afterward.[72]

While other objections might be raised to Dunphy's proposal,[73] it seems to me that the first two chronologies suffer from serious deficiencies, while Dunphy's, with a few minor tweaks (as just indicated), has much to commend it. In this sense, I would propose the following chronology:

71 As we have said above, even as late as February 412 (with the writing of *ep.* 139), the first two books remained uncorrected and the third book unfinished.

72 Dunphy, "A Lost Year," 404ff. Dunphy points to *ep.* 138.1.1, where Augustine describes this method in a slightly different situation with Marcellinus. An alternative explanation of *retr.* 2.33.60 is offered by Hombert (*Nouvelles Recherches*, ix–xii), who argues that, in this passage, Augustine is not speaking specifically of delivering sermons before the publication of *pecc. mer.* but is describing in a general sense his and his allies' preference early in the controversy to refute Pelagianism via sermons rather than written works.

73 For example, a lingering issue is the apparent hiatus in the composition of Book 3, which likely would have been begun in June 411 but was still incomplete at the time of Augustine's composition of *ep.* 139 (as late as February 412). With Dunphy's chronology, it seems clear that Augustine pushed himself to produce Books 1–2 rather rapidly, and in the midst of busy circumstances in Carthage. Why, then, did he seemingly put the work on the shelf after beginning the third book? Part of Dunphy's reply to this question is to suggest that the chief controversial topic shifted from that of infant baptism to the question of righteousness, sinlessness, and grace over the course of 411 (see Dunphy, "A Lost Year," 436–37). As a result, Augustine would not have felt as much of a push to finish the third book which dealt, in the main, with the issue of baptism and original sin.

To this, it might be added that Pelagius's departure from Carthage could also have removed some of the urgency of Augustine's work. (We do not know when Caelestius left Carthage, but it could very well have been early in the summer of 411 as well.) Indeed, the opening sections of Book 3 can easily be read as a subtle warning for Pelagius to change his views. Given that Augustine was beginning to write Book 3 around the same time as Pelagius's departure—and given that this third book was prompted by a writing of Pelagius himself—it is easy to imagine that Pelagius's departure took some of the wind out of Augustine's sails, as it were.

Finally, it is worth noting that the revised dating of Caelestius's trial may also make it possible to shift some of Augustine's writings typically dated to late 411 or early 412 earlier—so, *ep.* 139 may date to 411, and thus may not be as distant from the commencement of the writing of *pecc. mer.* 3 as Dunphy's chronology would initially suggest.

Summer 410

a. Augustine overhears a few individuals in Carthage mention that infants are not baptized for the forgiveness of sins, but for sanctification in Christ. It seems likely that Caelestius and some other members of Pelagius's circle are already present in Carthage circulating their views.

Autumn 410

b. Pelagius arrives in Hippo while Augustine is out of town.

c. Pelagius quickly leaves Hippo, making no mention of any problematic views on grace during his time there.

d. Before departing Hippo, Pelagius leaves a letter for Augustine, to which Augustine responds.

e. Sometime in late 410 or early 411, Caelestius applies for ordination to the priesthood.

Early 411

f. Marcellinus writes to Augustine from Carthage asking him to respond to some of the positions promoted by Caelestius and his allies.

g. Probably around the same time as (f) or perhaps slightly before, Paulinus of Milan submits his *libellus* accusing Caelestius of holding several dubious or heretical positions.

h. Probably around the same time as (f) but after (g), Caelestius's trial is held. Caelestius submits a brief *libellus* of his own to defend himself. Caelestius is found guilty and, sometime thereafter, leaves Carthage, initially planning to appeal his case to Pope Innocent.

i. After receiving Marcellinus's letter (while still absent from Carthage), a significant amount of time passes before Augustine begins his reply.

j. During this time, however, Augustine investigates the situation. He acquires and reads a book (*liber*) by one of the Pelagians (Caelestius?) as well as the *libellus breuissimus* produced by Caelestius during his trial. He possibly seeks and/or receives information from other sources as well. He also (possibly) re-reads, completes, and publishes *De bono coniugali* and *De sancta uirginitate* during this period.

APPENDIX   323

Spring and Early Summer 411

k. Possibly before or during the information gathering noted in (j), Augustine comes to Carthage, arriving sometime before May 17.

l. After his arrival in Carthage, Augustine sees Pelagius a few times but has no opportunity to speak with him.

m. While in Carthage, Augustine reads the acts of Caelestius's trial and, probably, speaks with Aurelius, the bishop of Carthage, about the situation. Augustine and Aurelius decide to avoid mentioning any names in connection with the Pelagian ideas they are refuting so as to more easily correct those who have fallen into error.

n. June 1–8: The Conference with the Donatists is held in three sessions (June 1, 3, 8), with Augustine in attendance.

o. Augustine completes Books 1 and 2 and submits them to Marcellinus.

p. A few days after completing the first two books, Augustine reads Pelagius's *Expositiones* (or at least the relevant passage from the *expositio* on Romans), and sometime shortly thereafter begins dictating Book 3.

q. June 24: Augustine delivers *s.* 293.

r. June 26: Marcellinus publishes his judgment, ruling in favor of the Catholics.

s. June 27: Augustine delivers *s.* 294.

t. June 29: Augustine delivers *s.* 299.

u. Pelagius leaves Carthage for Palestine at some point around this time.

v. At some point, Marcellinus returns Books 1–2 to Augustine.

Late September 411 (probably)

w. Augustine returns to Hippo.

January or February 412 (at the latest)

x. Augustine is in Hippo. Book 3 of *De peccatorum* meritis remains incomplete, albeit with a short addition to what was dictated in Carthage.

Bibliography

Primary Sources

Ambrose of Milan. *De fide resurrectionis*. CSEL 73. Edited by O. Faller. Vienna: Hoelder-Pichler-Tempsky, 1955.

———. *De paenitentia*. CSEL 73. Edited by O. Faller. Vienna: Hoelder-Pichler-Tempsky, 1955.

———. *Expositio euangelii secundum Lucam*. Edited by M. Adriaen and P. A. Ballerini. CCL 14. Turnhout: Brepols, 1957. See also CSEL 32.4.

———. *Expositio Isaiae prophetae (fragmenta)*. Edited by M. Adriaen and P. A. Ballerini. CCL 14. Turnhout: Brepols, 1957.

———. *Hymni*. PL 16.

Anonymous. *De diuitiis*. PLS 1:1380–1418.

Anonymous Bishops of Aquilaea. *Libellus fidei*. Edited by Peter van Egmond. "'A Confession without Pretence': Text and Context of Pelagius' Defence of 417 AD." PhD diss., Vrije University, 2013. See also PL 48:506–26.

Annianus of Celeda. *Epistula ad Euangelium*. PG 50:472.

Arnobius Iunior [?]. *Praedestinatus*. Edited by F. Gori. CCL 25B. Turnhout: Brepols, 2000.

Augustine of Hippo. *Ad catholicos fratres*. Edited by M. Petschenig. CSEL 52. Vienna: F. Tempsky, 1909. Translated by Maureen Tilly and Boniface Ramsey: WSA I/21. Hyde Park, NY: New City Press, 2019.

———. *Ad Cresconium grammaticum partis Donati libri quattuor*. Edited by M. Petschenig. CSEL 52. Vienna: F. Tempsky, 1909.

———. *Confessiones.* Edited by L. Verheijen. CCL 27. Turnhout: Brepols, 1981. Translated by Maria Boulding: WSA I/1. Hyde Park, NY: New City Press, 1997.

———. *Contra duas epistulas Pelagianorum.* Edited by C. F. Urba and J. Zycha. CSEL 60. Vienna: F. Tempsky, 1913. Translated by Roland Teske: WSA I/24. Hyde Park, NY: New City Press, 1998.

———. *Contra epistulam Parmeniani.* Edited by M. Petschenig. CSEL 51. Vienna: F. Tempsky, 1908. Translated by Maureen Tilly and Boniface Ramsey: WSA I/21. Hyde Park, NY: New City Press, 2019.

———. *Contra Faustum Manicheum.* Edited by J. Zycha. CSEL 25/1. Vienna: F. Tempsky, 1891. Translated by Roland Teske, WSA I/20. Hyde Park, NY: New City Press, 2007.

———. *Contra Gaudentium.* Edited by M. Petschenig. CSEL 53. Vienna: F. Tempsky, 1910.

———. *Contra Iulianum.* PL 44. Paris: J. P. Migne, 1845. Translated by Roland Teske: WSA I/24. Hyde Park, NY: New City Press, 1998.

———. *Contra Iulianum opus imperfectum.* Edited by M. Zelzer. Books 1–3: CSEL 85/1. Vienna: Hoelder-Pichler-Tempsky, 1974. Books 4–6: CSEL 85/2. Vienna: Verlag der Österreichischen Akademie der Wissenschaften, 2004. Translated by Roland Teske: WSA I/25. Hyde Park, NY: New City Press, 1999.

———. *Contra litteras Petiliani.* Edited by M. Petschenig. CSEL 52. Vienna: F. Tempsky, 1909. Translated by Maureen Tilly and Boniface Ramsey: WSA I/21. Hyde Park, NY: New City Press, 2019.

———. *Contra Priscillianistas.* Edited by K. D. Daur. CCL 49. Turnhout: Brepols, 1985. Translated by Roland Teske. WSA I/18. Hyde Park, NY: New City Press, 2001.

———. *Contra Secundinum.* Edited by J. Zycha. CSEL 25.2. Vienna: F. Tempsky, 1892. Translated by Roland Teske. WSA I/19. Hyde Park, NY: New City Press, 2006.

———. *De anima et eius origine.* Edited by C. F. Urba and J. Zycha. CSEL 60. Vienna: F. Tempsky, 1913. Translated by Roland Teske: WSA I/23. Hyde Park, NY: New City Press, 1997.

———. *De baptismo.* Edited by M. Petschenig. CSEL 51. Vienna: F. Tempsky, 1908. Translated by Maureen Tilley and Boniface Ramsey: WSA I/21. Hyde Park, NY: New City Press, 2019.

———. *De bono uiduitatis.* Edited by J. Zycha. CSEL 41. Vienna: F. Tempsky, 1900. Translated by Ray Kearney: WSA I/9. Hyde Park, NY: New City Press, 1999.

———. *De ciuitate Dei.* Edited by B. Dombart and A. Kalb. CCL 47–48. Turnhout: Brepols, 1955. Translated by William Babcock: WSA I/6–7. Hyde Park, NY: New City Press, 2012–13.

———. *De dono perseuerantiae.* Edited by Volker Henning Drecoll and Christoph Scheerer. CSEL 105. Berlin: De Gruyter, 2019. Translated by Roland Teske: WSA I/26. Hyde Park, NY: New City Press, 1999.

———. *De gestis Pelagii.* Edited by C. F. Urba and J. Zycha. CSEL 42. Vienna: F. Tempsky, 1902. Translated by Roland Teske: WSA I/23. Hyde Park, NY: New City Press, 1997.

BIBLIOGRAPHY

———. *De gratia Christi et de peccato originali.* Edited by C. F. Urba and J. Zycha. CSEL 42. Vienna: F. Tempsky, 1902. Translated by Roland Teske: WSA I/23. Hyde Park, NY: New City Press, 1997.

———. *De haeresibus.* Edited by R. Vander Plaetse and C. Beukers. CCL 46. Turnhout: Brepols, 1969. Translated by Roland Teske: WSA I/18. Hyde Park, NY: New City Press, 1995.

———. *De libero arbitrio.* Edited by W. M. Green. CSEL 74. Vienna: Hoelder-Pichler-Tempsky, 1956. Translated by Peter King: *On the Free Choice of the Will, On Grace and Free Choice, and Other Writings.* Cambridge: Cambridge University Press, 2010.

———. *De natura et gratia.* Edited by C. F. Urba and J. Zycha. CSEL 60. Vienna: F. Tempsky, 1913. Translated by Roland Teske: WSA I/23. Hyde Park, NY: New City Press, 1997.

———. *De nuptiis et concupiscentia.* Edited by C. F. Urba and J. Zycha. CSEL 42. Vienna: F. Tempsky, 1902. Translated by Roland Teske: WSA I/24. Hyde Park, NY: New City Press, 1998.

———. *De peccatorum meritis et remissione et de baptismo parvulorum.* Edited by C. F. Urba and J. Zycha. CSEL 60. Vienna: F. Tempsky, 1913. Translated by Roland Teske: WSA I/23. Hyde Park, NY: New City Press, 1997.

———. *De perfectione iustitiae hominis.* Edited by C. F. Urba and J. Zycha. CSEL 42. Vienna: F. Tempsky, 1902. Translated by Roland Teske: WSA I/23. Hyde Park, NY: New City Press, 1997.

———. *De spiritu et littera.* Edited by C. F. Urba and J. Zycha. CSEL 60. Vienna: F. Tempsky, 1913. Translated by Roland Teske: WSA I/23. Hyde Park, NY: New City Press, 1997.

———. *Epistulae.* Epp. 1–55: Edited by K. D. Daur. CCL 31. Turnhout: Brepols, 2004. Epp. 56–100: Edited by K. D. Daur. CCL 31A. Turnhout: Brepols, 2005. Epp. 101–23: Edited by A. Goldbacher. CSEL 34/2. Vienna: Tempsky, 1898. Epp. 124–84A: Edited by A. Goldbacher. CSEL 44. Vienna: Tempsky, 1904. Epp. 185–270: Edited by A. Goldbacher. CSEL 57. Vienna: Tempsky, 1911. Divjak letters: Edited by J. Divjak. CSEL 88. Vienna: Hoelder-Pichler-Tempsky, 1981. Translated by Roland Teske: WSA II/1–4. Hyde Park, NY: New City Press, 2001–2005.

———. *Retractationes.* Edited by A. Mutzenbecher. CCL 57. Turnhout: Brepols, 1984. Translated by B. Ramsey: WSA I/2. Hyde Park, NY: New City Press, 2010.

———. *Sermones ad populum.* Sermons 1–50: Edited by C Lambot. CCL 41. Turnhout: Brepols, 1961. Remaining sermons: PL 38–39. Paris: J. P. Migne, 1845; PLS 3. Paris: Garnier, 1963. Translated by Edmund Hill: WSA III/1–11. Hyde Park, NY: New City Press, 1990–1997.

———. *Sermo 131.* Edited by Gert Partoens. "Le Sermon 131 de saint Augustin. Introduction et édition." *Augustiniana* 54 (2004): 35–77.

———. *Sermo 227.* Edited by Suzanne Poque. SC 116. Paris: Cerf, 1966.

———. *Sermones* 293 and 299. Edited by François Dolbeau. "Deux Sermons d'Augustin pour les fêtes de Jean-Baptiste et de Pierre et Paul (s. 293 et 299)." *Augustinianum* 57 (2017): 403–92.

———. *Sermo* 348A (Dolbeau 30). Edited by F. Dolbeau. "Le sermon 348A de saint Augustin contre Pélage: Édition du text intégral." *Recherches augustiniennes* 28 (1995): 37–63.

Basil of Caesarea. *De spiritu sancto.* PG 32:68–217. Translated by David Anderson, *St. Basil the Great: On the Holy Spirit.* Crestwood, NY: St. Vladimir's Seminary Press, 1980.

———. *Regula.* Edited by K. Zelzer. CSEL 86. Vienna: Hoelder-Pichler-Tempsky, 1986.

Caelestius. *Libellus fidei.* Edited by Peter van Egmond. "The Confession of Faith Ascribed to Caelestius." *Sacris Eruditi* 50 (2011): 317–39.

Celestine. *Epistola ad Galliarum Episcopos.* PL 50: 528–37.

Constantius. *Epistola ad Volusianum.* PL 56: 500.

Cyprian. *Epistulae.* Edited by G. Hartel. CSEL 3.2. Vienna: Apud C. Geroldi filium, 1871.

———. *Testimonia ad Quirinum.* Edited by G. Hartel. CSEL 3.1. Vienna: Apud C. Geroldi filium, 1867.

Gerontius. *Vita Melaniae Junioris* (Greek Text). Edited by Denys Gorce. SC 90. Paris: Cerf, 1962. Translated by Elizabeth A. Clark with introduction and commentary as *The Life of Melania the Younger.* Lewiston: The Edwin Mellen Press, 1984.

———. *Vita Melaniae Junioris* (Latin Text). Edited by Patrick Laurence, *La vie latine de sainte Mélanie.* Jerusalem: Franciscan Printing Press, 2002.

Gesta collationis Carthaginensis. Edited by Clemens Weidmann. CSEL 104. Berlin: de Gruyter, 2018. See also: *Gesta conlationis Carthaginiensis.* Edited by Serge Lancel. CCSL 149A. Turnhout: Brepols, 1974.

Hilary of Poitiers. *In Matthaeum commentarius.* Edited by J. Doignon. SC 254 and 258. Paris: Cerf, 2007.

———. *Tractatus in Iob (fragmenta).* Edited by A. Feder. CSEL 65. Vienna: F. Tempsky, 1916.

———. *Tractatus in Psalmum CXVIII.* Edited by J. Doignon and R. Demeulenaere. CCL 61A. Turnhout: Brepols, 2002.

Jerome. *Aduersus Iovinianum.* PL 23.

———. *Commentariorum in Hiezechielem libri XIV.* Edited by Glorie. CCL 75. Turnhout: Brepols, 1964. Translated by Thomas P. Scheck: Ancient Christian Writers 71. New York: Newman Press, 2017.

———. *Commentarius in Ionam prophetam.* Edited by Yves-Marie Duval. SC 323. Paris: Cerf, 1985.

———. *De uiris illustribus.* Edited by E. Richardson. Texte und Untersuchungen zur Geschichte der altchristlichen Literatur 14. Leipzig: Hinrichs, 1896.

———. *Dialogus aduersus Pelagianos.* Edited by C. Moreschini. CCL 80. Turnhout: Brepols, 1990. Translated by John N. Hritzu: FC 53. Washington, DC: The Catholic University of America Press, 1965.

BIBLIOGRAPHY 329

———. *Epistulae*. Epp. 1–70: Edited by I. Hilberg. CSEL 54. Vienna: F. Tempsky, 1910. Epp. 71–120: Edited by I. Hilberg. CSEL 55. Vienna: F. Tempsky, 1912. Epp. 121–54: Edited by I. Hilberg. CSEL 56. Vienna: F. Tempsky, 1918. A new edition was published in 1996 by M. Kamptnery. Translated by W. H. Fremantle, G. Lewis and W. G. Martley: NPNF[2] 6. Buffalo: Christian Literature, 1893.

———. *In Hieremiam prophetam libri vi*. Edited by S. Reiter. CSEL 59. Vienna: F. Tempsky, 1913. Translated by Michael Graves as *Jerome: Commentary on Jeremiah*. Ancient Christian Texts. Downers Grove, IL: IVP Academic, 2011.

John Chrysostom. *Ad Neophytos*. Edited by A. Wenger. SC 50. Paris: Cerf, 1970.

Julian of Eclanum. *Operum deperditorum fragmenta*. Edited by L. De Coninck. CCL 88. Turnhout: Brepols, 1977.

Lactantius. *Diuinae Institutiones*. Edited by S. Brandt and G. Laubmann. CSEL 19. Vienna: F. Tempsky, 1890.

Marius Mercator. *Commonitorium lectori aduersum haeresim Pelagii et Caelestii uel etiam scripta Iuliani*. Edited by Edward Schwartz. ACO 1.5.1, pp. 5–23. Berlin: de Gruyter, 1924.

———. *Commonitorium super nomine Caelestii*. Edited by Edward Schwartz. ACO 1.5.1, pp. 65–70. Berlin: de Gruyter, 1924.

———. *Epistula lectori*. Edited by Edward Schwartz. ACO 1.5.1, p. 23. Berlin: de Gruyter, 1924.

Origen. *Commentarii in Epistulam ad Romanos*. Edited by Caroline P. Hammond Bammel: *Der Römerbriefkommentar des Origenes: kritische Ausgabe der Übersetzung Rufins*. 3 volumes. Freiburg im Breisgau: Herder, 1990–1998. (Also available in SC 532, 539, 543, 555. Paris: Cerf, 2009–2012.) Translated by Thomas P. Scheck: FC 103 and 104. Washington, DC: The Catholic University of America Press, 2001–2002.

———. *In Numeros Homiliae XXVIII*. Edited by W. A. Baehrens: *Origenes Werke: Siebenter Band, Homilien zum Hexateuch in Rufins Übersetzung*. Die Griechischen Christlichen Schriftsteller der ersten drei Jahrhunderte. Leipzig: J. C. Hinrichs, 1921.

Orosius. *Commonitorium de errore Priscillianistarum et Origenistarum*. Edited by G. Schepss. CSEL 18. Vienna: F. Tempsky, 1889.

———. *Historiae aduersum Paganos*. Edited by Carolus Zangemeister. CSEL 5. Vienna: C. Geroldi Filium Bibliopolam Academiae, 1882.

———. *Liber apologeticus*. Edited by Carolus Zangemeister. CSEL 5. Vienna: C. Geroldi Filium Bibliopolam Academiae, 1882. Translated by Craig L. Hanson: FC 99. Washington, DC: The Catholic University of America Press, 1999.

Palladius. *Dialogus de uita S. Joannis Chrysostomi*. Edited by P. R. Coleman-Norton. Cambridge: Cambridge University Press, 1928.

———. *Historia Lausiaca*. Edited by G. J. M. Bartelink. Milan: Fondazione Lorenzo Valla, 1974. Translated by John Wortley as *The Lausiac History*. Collegeville, MN: Cistercian Publications, 2015.

Paulinus of Milan. *Libellus aduersus Caelestium*. Edited by O. Günther. CSEL 35.1. Vienna: F. Tempsky, 1895.

———. *Vita Ambrosii*. Edited by A. A. R. Bastiaensen. *Vita di Cipriano, Vita di Ambrogio, Vita di Agostino. Testo critico e commento*. Milan: Fondazione Lorenzo Valla – Arnoldo Mondadori Editore, 1975.

Paulinus of Nola. *Carmina*. Edited by W. Hartel. CSEL 30. Vienna: F. Tempsky, 1894.

Pelagius. *Epistula ad Demetriadem*. Edited by Gisbert Greshake. *Pelagius: Epistula ad Demetriadem*. Freiburg: Herder, 2015. Translated by B. R. Rees as *The Letters of Pelagius and His Followers*. Rochester, NY: Boydell Press, 1991.

———. *Expositiones XIII epistularum Pauli*. Edited by Alexander Souter. *Pelagius's Expositions of Thirteen Epistles of St. Paul*, vol. 2. Cambridge: Cambridge University Press, 1926.

———. *Libellus fidei*. Edited by Peter van Egmond. "*Haec fides est*: Observations on the Textual Tradition of Pelagius's *Libellus fidei*." *Augustiniana* 57 (2007): 345–85.

Possidius of Calama. *Vita Augustini*. Edited by Michele Pellegrino: *Vita di S. Agostino. Introduzione, testo critico, versione e note*. Alba: Edizioni Paoline, 1955. Translated by M. M. Muller and R. J. Deferrari: FC 15. Washington, DC: The Catholic University of America Press, 1952.

———. *Indiculus*. Edited by A. Wilmart. *Miscellanea Agostiniana* 2 (1931): 161–208. Translated by Roland Teske: WSA I/2. Hyde Park, NY: New City Press, 2010.

Prosper of Aquitaine. *Praeteritorum sedis apostolicae episcoporum auctoritates de gratia Dei et libero uoluntatis arbitrio*. PL 51. 205–12.

———. *Carmen de ingratis*. PL 51. 91–148.

———. *Chronicum integrum*. PL 51. 535–608.

———. *De gratia Dei et libero arbitrio liber contra collatorem*. PL 51. 213–76.

Rufinus [the Syrian?]. *Rufini Presbyteri Liber de Fide: A Critical Text and Translation with Introduction and Commentary*. Edited by M. W. Miller. Washington, DC: The Catholic University of America Press, 1964.

Socrates Scholasticus. *Historia ecclesiastica*. PG 67:33–841.

Sozomen. *Historia ecclesiastica*. Edited by J. Bidez and G. C. Hansen. Griechischen christlichen Schriftsteller der ersten drei Jahrhunderte 4. Second edition. Berlin: Akademie Verlag, 1995.

Theodore of Mopsuestia, *Expositio in Psalmos Iuliano Aeclanensi interprete*. Edited by L. De Connick, CCL 88A. Turnhout: Brepols, 1977.

Uranius. *De obitu sancti Paulini*. PL 53:859–66.

Zosimus. *Magnum pondus*. Edited by O. Günther. CSEL 35.1. Vienna: F. Tempsky, 1895. See also: Dalmon, *Un dossier de l'épistolaire augustinien*, 504–12.

———. *Posteaquam a nobis*. Edited by O. Günther. CSEL 35.1. Vienna: F. Tempsky, 1895. See also: Dalmon. *Un dossier de l'épistolaire augustinien*, 512–22.

BIBLIOGRAPHY

———. *Quamuis patrum*. Edited by O. Günther. CSEL 35.1. Vienna: F. Tempsky, 1895. See also: Dalmon, *Un dossier de l'épistolaire augustinien*, 524–26.

Secondary Literature

Adam, Karl. "Causa finita est." In *Beiträge zur Geschichte des christlichen Altertums und der byzantinischen Literatur*, edited by Albert Michael Koeniger, 1–23. Bonn: Kurt Schroeder, 1922.

Aka-Brou, Jean Paul. *Naissance d'une tradition patristique: L'autorité d'Ambroise de Milan dans la controverse entre Augustin et les pélagiens (411–430)*. Cerf Patrimoines. Paris: Cerf, 2022.

Aland, K. *Did the Early Church Baptize Infants?* Philadelphia: Westminster, 1963.

Altaner, Berthold. "Augustins Methode der Quellenbenützung. Sein Studium der Väterliteratur." *Sacris Erudiri* 4 (1952): 5–17.

———. "Augustinus und die griechische Patristik." *Revue bénédictine* 62 (1952): 201–15.

———. *Kleine patristische Schriften*. Berlin: Akademie Verlag, 1967.

———. "Der *Liber de fide*: ein werk des Pelagianers Rufinus des 'Syrers.'" *Theologische Quartalschrift* 130 (1950): 432–49.

Annecchino, Marialusia. "La nozione di *impeccantia* negli scritti pelagiani." In *Giuliano d'Eclano e l'Hirpinia christiana: atti del convegno, 4–6 giugno 2003*, edited by Antonio V. Nazzaro, 73–86. Napoli: Arte tipografica, 2004.

Antin, Paul. "Rufin et Pélage dans Jérôme, Prologue 1 *In Hieremiam*." *Latomus* 22, no. 4 (1963): 792–94.

Backus, Irena, and Aza Goudriaan. "'Semipelagianism': The Origins of the Term and Its Passage into the History of Heresy." *Journal of Ecclesiastical History* 65, no. 1 (2014): 25–46.

Bammel, Caroline P. Hammond. "A Product of a Fifth-Century Scriptorium Preserving Conventions Used by Rufinus of Aquileia." *Journal of Theological Studies* 29, no. 2 (1978): 366–91.

———. "Augustine, Origen and the Exegesis of St. Paul." *Augustinianum* 32, no. 2 (1992): 341–68.

———. "The Last Ten Years of Rufinus' Life and the Date of His Move South from Aquileia." *Journal of Theological Studies* 28, no. 2 (1977): 372–429.

———. "Pauline Exegesis, Manichaeism and Philosophy in the Early Augustine." In *Christian Faith and Greek Philosophy in Late Antiquity: Essays in Tribute to George Christopher Stead*, edited by L. R. Wickham and C. P. Bammel et al., Supplements to Vigiliae Christianae XIX, 1–25. Leiden, Netherlands: E. J. Brill, 1993.

———. *Der Römerbrieftext des Rufin und seine Origenes-Übersetzung*. Freiburg: Herder, 1985.

———. "Rufinus' Translation of Origen's Commentary on Romans and the Pelagian Controversy." *Antichità Altoadriatiche* 39 (1992): 131–42.

Banev, Krastu. *Theophilus of Alexandria and the First Origenist Controversy: Rhetoric and Power.* Oxford Early Christian Studies. Oxford: Oxford University Press, 2015.

Bardy, Gustave. "La date du 'De gestis Pelagii.'" In *Les Révisions, Bibliothèque augustinienne: oeuvres de saint Augustin* 12, 588–89. Paris: Desclée, 1950.

———. "Grecs et latins dans les premières controverses Pélagiennes." *Bulletin de littérature ecclésiastique* 49 (1948): 3–20.

Bark, William. "The Doctrinal Interests of Marius Mercator." *Church History* 12, no. 3 (1943): 210–16.

Bartelink, G. "Die Beeinflussung Augustins durch die griechischen Patres." In *Augustiniana Traiectina: communications présentées au Colloque International d'Utrecht 13–14 novembre 1986*, edited by J. den Boeft and J. van Oort, 9–24. Paris: Études augustiniennes, 1987.

Bass, Alden. "An Example of Pelagian Exegesis in the Donatist Vienna Homilies (Ö.N.B. Lat. 4147)." In Dupont et al., *The Uniquely African Controversy*, 197–209.

Bastiaensen, A. A. R. "Augustin et ses prédécesseurs latins chrétiens." In *Augustiniana Traiectina: communications présentées au Colloque International d'Utrecht 13–14 novembre 1986*, edited by J. den Boeft and J. van Oort, 25–57. Paris: Études augustiniennes, 1987.

———. "Augustine's Pauline Exegesis and Ambrosiaster." In *Augustine: Biblical Exegete*, edited by Frederick Van Fleteren and Joseph C. Schnaubelt, 33–54. New York: Peter Lang, 2001.

Batiffol, P. *Le catholicisme de saint Augustin.* Paris: Librairie Victor Lecoffre, 1920.

Beatrice, P. F. "Chromatius and Jovinus at the Synod of Diospolis: A Prosopographical Inquiry." *Journal of Early Christian Studies* 22, no. 3 (2014): 437–64.

———. *Tradux peccati. Alle fonti della dottrina agostiniana del peccato originale.* Studia Patristica Mediolanensia 8. Milan: Vita e Pensiero, 1978.

Beck, John H. "The Pelagian Controversy: An Economic Analysis." *American Journal of Economics and Sociology* 66, no. 4 (2007): 681–96.

Berrouard, M.-F. "L'exégèse augustinienne de Rom. 7, 7–25 entre 396 et 418, avec des remarques sur les deux premières périodes de la crise 'pélagienne.'" *Recherches Augustiniennes* 16 (1981): 101–96.

———. *Introduction aux homélies de saint Augustin sur l'évangile de saint Jean.* Paris: Institut d'Études Augustiniennes, 2004.

———. "Les lettres 6* et 19* de saint Augustin. Leur date et les renseignements qu'elles apportent sur l'évolution de la crise 'pélagienne.'" *Revue d'études augustiniennes* 27, no. 3–4 (1981): 264–77.

———. "Similitudo et la définition du réalisme sacramentel d'après l'Épître 98, 9–10 de saint Augustin." *Revue des Études augustiniennes* 7, no. 4 (1961): 321–37.

———. "Un tournant dans la vie de l'Église d'Afrique: les deux missions d'Alypius en Italie à la lumière des *Lettres* 10*, 15*, 16*, 22* et 23*A de saint Augustin." *Revue d'études augustiniennes* 31, no. 1–2 (1985): 46–70.

Beyenka, B. "The Names of St. Ambrose in the Works of St. Augustine." *Augustinian Studies* 5 (1974): 19–28.

Bochet, Isabelle. '*Le firmament de l'Écriture': l'herméneutique augustinienne*. Paris: Institut d'études augustiniennes, 2004.

———. "Une nouvelle lecture du *Liber ad Honoratum* d'Augustin (= epist. 140)." *Revue des études Augustiniennes* 45, no. 2 (1999): 335–51.

Bohlin, Torgny. *Die Theologie des Pelagius und ihre Genesis*. Uppsala: Lundequistka bokhandeln, 1957.

Bonner, Ali. "The Manuscript Transmission of Pelagius's *Ad Demetriadem*: The Evidence of Some Manuscript Witnesses." *Studia Patristica* 70 (2013): 619–30.

———. "The Manuscript Transmission of Pelagius' Work and Its Implications, with Special Reference to His Letter to Demetrias." *Studia Patristica* 74 (2016): 341–53.

———. *The Myth of Pelagianism*. Oxford: Oxford University Press, 2018.

Bonner, Gerald. "Anti-Pelagian Works." In Fitzgerald, *Augustine through the Ages*, 41–47.

———. *Augustine and Modern Research on Pelagianism*. Saint Augustine Lecture 1970. Villanova: Villanova University Press, 1972.

———. "Augustine and Pelagianism." *Augustinian Studies* 24 (1993): 27–47.

———. "Augustine on Romans 5:12." In *Studia Evangelica Vol. IV-V: papers presented to the Third International Congress of New Testament Studies held at Christ Church*, edited by F. L. Cross, 242–47. Berlin: Akademie-Verlag, 1968.

———. "Caelestius." In *Augustinus-Lexikon*, edited by Cornelius Mayer, 1:693–98. Basil: Schwabe, 1986–1994.

———. *Church and Faith in the Patristic Tradition: Augustine, Pelagianism, and Early Christian Northumbria*. Collected Studies Series 7. Aldershot: Variorum, 1996.

———. *Freedom and Necessity: St. Augustine's Teaching on Divine Power and Human Freedom*. Washington, DC: The Catholic University of America Press, 2007.

———. "Gestis Pelagii, De." In Fitzgerald, *Augustine through the Ages*, 382–83.

———. *God's Decree and Man's Destiny*. London: Variorum Reprints, 1987.

———. "How Pelagian was Pelagius? An Examination of the Contentions of Torgny Bohlin." *Studia Patristica* 9 (1966): 350–58.

———. "The Influence of Origen on Pelagius and Western Monasticism." In *Origeniana Septima: Origenes in den Auseinandersetzungen des 4. Jahrhunders*, edited by W. A. Bienert and U. Kühneweg, 381–96. Leuven: Leuven University Press, 1999.

———. "A Last Apology for Pelagianism?" In *Studia Patristica: Papers presented at the Fifteenth International Conference on Patristic Studies held in Oxford 2007*. Vol. 49, *St. Augustine and His Opponents*, edited by J. Baun, A. Cameron, M. Edwards, and M. Vinzent, 325–28. Leuven: Peeters, 2010.

———. "Les origines africaines de la doctrine augustinienne sur la chute et le peché originel." *Augustinus* 12, no. 45–48 (1967): 97–116.

———. "Pelagianism and Augustine." *Augustinian Studies* 23 (1992): 33–51.

———. "Pelagianism Reconsidered." In *Studia Patristica: Cappadocian Fathers, Greek Authors after Nicaea, Augustine, Donatism, and Pelagianism*, edited by Elizabeth A. Livingston, 237–41. Leuven: Peeters, 1993.

———. "Pelagius/Pelagianischer Streit." In *Theologische Realenzyklopädie*, edited by Gerhard Müller, 26:176–85. Berlin: Walter de Gruyter, 1996.

———. "Rufinus of Syria and African Pelagianism." *Augustinian Studies* 1 (1970): 31–47.

———. "The Significance of Augustine's *De Gratia Novi Testamenti*." *Augustiniana* 41, no. 1–4 (1991): 531–59.

———. "Some Remarks on Letters 4* and 6*." In *Les Lettres de saint Augustin découvertes par Johannes Divjak: communications présentées au colloque des 20 et 21 septembre 1982*, edited by C. Lepelly, 155–64. Paris: Études augustiniennes, 1983.

———. *St. Augustine of Hippo: Life and Controversies*. Norfolk: Canterbury Press, 1963.

Bouhot, Jean-Paul. "Une lettre d'Augustin d'Hippone à Cyrille d'Alexandrie (*Ep.* 4*)." In Lepelly, *Les Lettres de saint Augustin découvertes par Johannes Divjak*, 147–54.

———. "Version inédite du sermon '*Ad neophytos*' de S. Jean Chrysostome, utilisée par S. Augustin." *Revue des études augustiniennes* 17 (1971): 27–41.

Bright, Pamela, ed. and trans. *Augustine and the Bible*. Notre Dame, IN: University of Notre Dame Press, 1999.

Brisson, Jean-Paul. *Autonomisme et Christianisme dans l'Afrique Romaine de Septime Sévère à l'invasion vandale*. Paris: Editions E. de Boccard, 1958.

Brown, Peter. *Augustine of Hippo: A Biography*. 2nd ed. Berkeley: University of California Press, 2000.

———. "The Patrons of Pelagius: The Roman Aristocracy between East and West." *Journal of Theological Studies* 21, no. 1 (1970): 56–72. Reprinted in, *Religion and Society in the Age of Saint Augustine*, 208–26. New York: Harper & Row, 1972.

———. "Pelagius and His Supporters: Aims and Environment." *Journal of Theological Studies* 19, no. 1 (1968): 93–114. Reprinted in, *Religion and Society in the Age of Saint Augustine*, 183–207. New York: Harper & Row, 1972.

———. *Through the Eye of a Needle: Wealth, the Fall of Rome, and the Making of Christianity in the West, 350–550 AD*. Princeton: Princeton University Press, 2012.

Bruckner, A. *Julian von Eclanum, sein Leben und seine Lehre: Ein Beitrag zur Geschichte des Pelagianismus*. Leipzig: J. C. Hinrichs, 1897.

BIBLIOGRAPHY 335

Burnaby, John. Amor Dei: *A Study of the Religion of St. Augustine*. London: Hodder & Stoughton, 1947.

Burnett, Carole C. "Dysfunction at Diospolis: A Comparative Study of Augustine's *De Gestis Pelagii* and Jerome's *Dialogus Adversus Pelagianos*." *Augustinian Studies* 34, no. 2 (2003): 153–73.

Burns, J. Patout. "Appropriating Augustine Appropriating Cyprian." *Augustinian Studies* 36, no. 1 (2005): 113–30.

———. "The Atmosphere of Election: Augustinianism as Common Sense." *Journal of Early Christian Studies* 2, no. 3 (1994): 325–39.

———. "Augustine's Role in the Imperial Action Against Pelagius." *Journal of Theological Studies* 30, no. 1 (1979): 67–83.

———. "A Change in Augustine's Doctrine of Operative Grace in 418." *Studia Patristica* 16 (1985): 491–96.

———. *The Development of Augustine's Doctrine of Operative Grace*. Collection des Études Augustiniennes, Série Antiquité 82. Paris: Études augustiniennes, 1980.

———. "From Persuasion to Predestination: Augustine on Freedom in Rational Creatures." In *In Dominico Eloquio: In Lordly Eloquence – Essays on Patristic Exegesis in Honor of Robert Louis Wilken*, edited by Paul M. Blowers, Angela Russell Christman, David G. Hunter, and Robin Darling Young, 294–316. Grand Rapids, MI: Eerdmans, 2002.

———. "Human Agency in Augustine's Doctrine of Predestination and Perseverance." *Augustinian Studies* 48, no. 1 (2017): 45–71.

———. "The Interpretation of Romans in the Pelagian Controversy." *Augustinian Studies* 10 (1979): 43–54.

———. "Traducianism." In *Encyclopedia of Early Christianity*, edited by E. Ferguson, 2nd ed., 1141. New York: Routledge, 1999.

Burns, J. Patout, and Robin M. Jensen. *Christianity in Roman Africa: The Development of Its Practices and Beliefs*. Grand Rapids, MI: Eerdmans, 2014.

Burns, Thomas. *Barbarians within the Gates of Rome: A Study of Roman Military Policy and the Barbarians, ca.375–425 A.D.* Indianapolis: Indiana University Press, 1995.

Camelot, P.-T. "Autorité de l'Écriture, autorité de l'Eglise: Apropos d'un texte de s. Augustin." In *Mélanges offerts à M.-D. Chenu*, 127–33. Paris: Vrin, 1967.

———. "Le baptême des petits enfants dans l'Église des premiers siècles." *La Maison-Dieu* 88 (1966): 23–42.

Cameron, Averil. *The Later Roman Empire: AD 284–430*. Cambridge, MA: Harvard University Press, 1993.

Canellis, A. "La composition du *Dialogue contre les Lucifériens* et du *Dialogue contre les Pélagiens* de saint Jérôme: A la recherche d'un canon de l'*altercatio*." *Revue des études augustiniennes* 43, no. 2 (1997): 247–88.

Carefoote, Pearce James. "Augustine, the Pelagians and the Papacy: An Examination of the Political and Theological Implications of Papal Involvement in the Pelagian Controversy." PhD diss., Leuven, 1995.

———. "Pope Boniface I, the Pelagian Controversy and the Growth of Papal Authority." *Augustiniana* 46 (1996): 261–89.

Caruso, Giuseppe. "Le accuse di Pelagio nel *Commentarium in Hieremiam* di Girolamo." *Augustinianum* 57 (2017): 107–21.

———. "Ex orientis partibus: Agostino e le fonti greche nel *Contra Iulianum*." In *Transmission and réception des Pères grecs dans l'Occiden, de l'Antiquité tardive à la Renaissance: Entre philologie, herméneutique et théologie*, edited by E. Prinzivalli, F. Vinel, and M. Cutino, 105–20. Paris: Institut d'études augustiniennes, 2016.

———. "Girolamo antipelagiano." *Augustinianum* 49 (2009): 65–118.

———. "'Noua ex ueteri haeresis:' Echi della controversia pelagiana nei prologhi del commentario In Hieremiam di Girolamo." In *Nihil veritas erubescit: Mélanges offerts à Paul Mattei par ses élèves, collègues et amis*, edited by C. Bernard-Valette, J. Delmulle, C. Gerzaguet, 299–311. Turnhout: Brepols, 2017.

———. *Ramusculus Origenis: L'eredità dell'antropologia origeniana nei pelagiani e in Girolamo*. Rome: Institutum Patristicum Augustinianum, 2012.

———. "Il *Testimoniorum liber* di Pelagio tra Girolamo e Agostino." In *Hagiologica: Studi per Réginald Grégorie*, edited by A. Bartolomei Romagnoli, U. Paoli, and P. Piatti, 357–73. Fabriano: Monastero San Silvestro Abate, 2012.

Catapano, Giovanni. "Augustine, Julian, and Dialectics: A Reconsideration of J. Pépin's Lecture." *Augustinian Studies* 41 (2010): 241–53.

Chadwick, Henry. *Augustine of Hippo: A Life*. Oxford: Oxford University Press, 2009.

———. "New Letters of St. Augustine." *Journal of Theological Studies* 34 (1983): 425–52.

———. *The Sentences of Sextus*. Cambridge: Cambridge University Press, 1959.

Chin, Catherine M. and Caroline T. Schroeder, eds. *Melania: Early Christianity through the Life of One Family*. Berkeley: University of California Press, 2017.

Chronister, Andrew. "Augustine and Patristic Argumentation in His Anti-Pelagian Works: Change or Continuity?" *Augustiniana* 64 (2014): 187–226.

———. "Augustine, *Inuentio*, and *De gestis Pelagii*." In *Augustine and Rhetoric: Argumentative Strategies in Early Christianity*, edited by Adam Ployd and Rafał Toczko, 15–37. Leiden: Brill, 2024.

———. "Heresiology and Reality: Is Augustine's Portrayal of Pelagius's and Caelestius's Relationship and Views on Grace Accurate?" In *"Sancti uiri, ut audio": Theologies, Rhetorics and Receptions of the Pelagian Controversy Reappraised*, edited by Anthony Dupont, Raúl Villegas Marín, Giulio Malavasi, and Mattia Cosimo Chiriatti, 111–32. Leuven: Peeters, 2023.

———. "Taking Augustine at His Word: Re-evaluating the Testimony of *De gestis Pelagii*." *Augustinian Studies* 53 (2022): 153–84.

———. "What Did Pelagius Really Teach? Evaluating the Charges Lodged against Pelagius at the Synod of Diospolis." *Augustiniana* 74 (2024): 51–123.

Cipriani, Nello. "Un'altra traccia dell'Ambrosiaster in Agostino." *Augustinianum* 24 (1984): 515–25.

———. "Aspetti letterari dell'Ad Florum di Giuliano d'Eclano." *Augustinianum* 15 (1975): 125–67.

———. "L'autore die testi pseudobasiliani riportati nel C. Iulianum (I,16–17) e la polemica agostiniana di Giuliano d'Eclano." In *Congresso internazionale su S. Agostino nel XVI centenario della conversione (Roma, 15–20 settembre 1986). Atti I. Cronaca del Congresso. Sessioni generali. Sezione di studio I*, 439–49. Rome: Institutum Patristicum Augustinianum, 1987.

———. "La morale pelagiana e la retorica." *Augustinianum* 31 (1991): 309–27.

———. "La polemica antiafricana di Giuliano d'Eclano: artificio letterario o scontro di tradizione teologichi?" In *Cristianesimo e specificità regionali nel Mediterraneo latino (sec. IV-VI)*, 147–80. Rome: Institutum Patristicum Augustinianum, 1994.

———. "La presenza di Teodoro di Mopsuestia nella teologia di Giuliano d'Eclano." In *Cristianesimo Latino e cultura Greco sino al sec. IV. XXI Incontro di studiosi dell'antichità cristiana (Roma, 7–9 maggio 1992)*, 365–78. Rome: Institutum Patristicum Augustinianum, 1994.

———. "Sulle fonti orientali della teologia di Giuliano d'Eclano." In *Giuliano d'Eclano e l'Hirpinia Christiana*, edited by A. V. Nazzaro, 157–70. Naples: Arte tipografica, 2004.

Clark, Elizabeth A. "Melania the Elder." In Fitzgerald, *Augustine through the Ages*, 552.

———. *Melania the Younger: From Rome to Jerusalem*. Oxford: Oxford University Press, 2021.

———. *The Origenist Controversy: The Cultural Construction of an Early Christian Debate*. Princeton, NJ: Princeton University Press, 1992.

———. "Theory and Practice in Late Ancient Asceticism: Jerome, Chrysostom, and Augustine." *Journal of Feminist Studies in Religion* 5 (1989): 25–46.

Coassolo, P. *La preghiera del Signore in S. Agostino*. Fossano: Esperienze, 1962.

Conybeare, Catherine. "Augustine's *Marginalia Contra Julianum*." In *The Late (Wild) Augustine*, edited by Susanna Elm and Christopher M. Blunda, 83–97. Leiden: Brill, 2021.

———. *Paulinus Noster: Self and Symbols in the Letters of Paulinus of Nola*. Oxford Early Christian Studies. Oxford: Oxford University Press, 2000.

Cooper, Kate. "An(n)ianus of Celeda and the Latin Readers of John Chrysostom." *Studia Patristica* 27 (1993): 249–55.

Courcelle, Pierre. *Les Confessions de saint Augustin dans la tradition littéraire: antécédents et postérié*. Paris: Études augustiniennes, 1963.

———. *Histoire littéraire des grandes invasions germaniques*. 3rd edition. Paris: Études augustiniennes, 1964.

———. *Late Latin Writers and Their Greek Sources*. Translated by Harry E. Wedeck. Cambridge, MA: Harvard University Press, 1969.

———. *Les Lettres grecques en Occident. De Macrobe à Casiodore*. Paris: E. de Boccard, 1948.

Coyle, J. Kevin. "Faustum, Contra." In Fitzgerald, *Augustine through the Ages*, 355–56.

Curran, John R. *Pagan City and Christian Capital: Rome in the Fourth Century*. New York: Oxford University Press, 2000.

Cutino, Michele. "Il ruolo della Chiesa siciliana nella polemica fra Agostino e i pelagiani." In *Vescovi, Sicilia, Mediterraneo nella tarda Antichità: Atti del I Convegno di Studi (Palermo, 29–30 ottobre 2010)*, edited by Vincenzo Messana, Vincenzo Lombino, and Salvatore Costanza, 165–92. Rome: Salvatore Sciascia Editore, 2012.

Dalmon, Laurence. *Un dossier de l'épistolaire augustinien: la correspondance entre l'Afrique et Rome à propos de l'affaire pélagienne (416–418)*. Leuven: Peeters, 2015.

———. "La lettre 177,16–18 de saint Augustin, écho atténué à un conflit d'exégèse patristique au temps de la controverse pélagienne?" *Zeitschrift für Antikes Christentum* 12 (2008): 544–61.

———. "Le pape Zosime et la tradition juridique romaine." *Eruditio Antiqua* 1 (2009): 141–54.

———. "Trois pièces de la Collectio Avellana: édition critique, traduction et commentaire." *Recherches Augustiniennes* 36 (2011): 195–246.

Dassmann, Ernst. "Cyprianus." In *Augustinus-Lexikon*, edited by Cornelius Mayer, 2:196–211. Basil: Schwabe, 1996–2002.

———. "'Tam Ambrosius quam Cyprianus' (c. Iul. Imp. 4,112): Augustins Helfer im pelagianischen Streit." In *Oecumenica et patristica. Festschrift für Wilhelm Schneemelcher zum 75. Geburtstag*, edited by D. Papandreaou, W. A. Bienert and K. Schäferdiek, 259–68. Stuttgart: Kohlhammer, 1989.

de Bruyn, Theodore. "Constantius the *Tractator*: Author of an Anonymous Commentary on the Pauline Epistles?" *Journal of Theological Studies* 43 (1992): 38–54.

———. *Pelagius' Commentary on St. Paul's Epistle to the Romans*. Oxford Early Christian Studies. Oxford: Oxford University Press, 1993.

De Clerck, Paul. "'Lex orandi, lex credendi': The Original Sense and Historical Avatars of an Equivocal Adage." *Studia Liturgica* 24 (1994): 178–200.

———. "'Lex orandi, lex credendi': Sens originel et avatars historiques d'un adage équivoque." *Questions Liturgiques* 59 (1978): 193–212.

de Latte, R. "Saint Augustin et le baptême. Étude liturgico-historique du rituel baptismal des enfants chez saint Augustin." *Questions Liturgiques* 57 (1976): 41–55.

de Plinval, Georges. "L'heure est-elle venue de redécouvrir Pélage?" *Revue des études augustiniennes* 19 (1973): 158–62.

———. *Pélage: ses écrits, sa vie et sa réforme*. Lausanne: Payot, 1943.

———. "Recherches sur l'oeuvre littéraire de Pélage." *Revue de Philologie* 60 (1934): 9–42.

Delaroche, Bruno. "La datation du *De peccatorum meritis et remissione*." *Revue des études augustiniennes* 41 (1995): 37–57.

———. "Introduction" and "Notes complémentaires." In *Salaire et pardon des péchés*, translated by Madeleine Moreau and Christiane Ingremeau, BA 20/A. Paris: Institut d'Études Augustiniennes, 2013.

———. "Peccatorum meritis et remissione et de baptismo paruulorum (De-)." In *Augustinus-Lexikon*, edited by Robert Dodaro, Cornelius Mayer, Christof Müller, 4:574–81. Basel: Schwabe, 2012–2018.

———. *Saint Augustin lecteur et interprète de saint Paul dans le De peccatorum meritis et remissione (hiver 411–412)*. Collection des Études Augustiniennes, Serie Antiquite 146. Paris: Études augustiniennes, 1996.

den Boeft, Jan. "Augustine's Letter to Pelagius." In *Augustiniana Traiectina: communications présentées au Colloque International d'Utrecht 13–14 novembre 1986*, edited by J. den Boeft and J. van Oort, 73–84. Paris: Études augustiniennes, 1987.

Descotes, Pierre. *La grâce de la nouvelle alliance*. BA 20/B. Paris: Institut d'Études Augustiniennes, 2016.

———. "Saint Augustin et la crise pélagienne: Le témoignage de la correspondance." *Revue d'études augustiniennes et patristiques* 56 (2010): 197–227.

Didier, J.-C. "Saint Augustin et le baptême des enfants." *Revue des Études augustiniennes* 2 (1956): 109–29.

Dietrich, Julia. "Augustine and the Crisis of the 380s in Christian Doctrinal Argumentation." *Journal of Early Christian Studies* 26 (2018): 547–70.

Divjak, Johannes. "Epistulae." In *Augustinus-Lexikon*, edited by Cornelius Mayer, 2:893–1057. Basel: Schwabe, 1996–2002.

Dodaro, Robert. "'Christus Iustus' and Fear of Death in Augustine's Dispute with Pelagius." In *Signum Pietatis: Festgabe für Cornelius Petrus Mayer osa zum 60. Geburtstag*, edited by Adolar Zumkeller, 341–61. Würzburg: Augustinus-Verlag, 1989.

———. "Language Matters: Augustine's Use of Literary Decorum in Theological Argument." *Augustinian Studies* 45 (2014): 1–28.

———. "Literary Decorum in Scriptural Exegesis: Augustine, *Epistula* 138." In *L'Esegesi dei Padri Latini. Dalle origini a Gregorio Magno. Atti del XXVII Incontro di Studiosi dell'antichità cristiana, 6–8 maggio 1999*, 159–74. Rome: Institutum Patristicum Augustinianum, 2000.

———. "Note on the Carthaginian Debate over Sinlessness, A.D. 411–412 (Augustine, pecc. mer. 2.7.8–16.25)." *Augustinianum* 40 (2000): 187–202.

———. "*Quid deceat videre*: Literary Propriety and Doctrinal Orthodoxy in Augustine of Hippo." In *Orthodoxie, Christianisme, Histoire/Orthodoxy, Christianity, History*, edited by Susanna Elm, Éric Rebillard and Antonella Romano, 57–81. Rome: École française de Rome, 2000.

———. "The Theologian as Grammarian: Literary Decorum in Augustine's Defense of Orthodox Discourse." *Studia Patristica* 38 (2001): 70–83.

Dodaro, Robert, and Edgardo Martín Morales. "Marius Mercator." In *Augustinus-Lexikon*, edited by Cornelius Mayer, 3:1179–1181. Basel: Schwabe, 2004–2010.

Dölger, Franz Joseph. *Der Exorzismus im altchristlichen Taufritual: Eine religionsgeschichtliche Studie*. Paderborn: F. Schöningh, 1909.

Doignon, Jean. "*Testimonia* d'Hilaire de Poitiers dans le 'Contra Iulianum' d'Augustin: Les textes leur groupment, leur lecture." *Revue Bénédictine* 91 (1971): 7–19.

Dolbeau, François. *Augustin et la prédication en Afrique: Recherches sur divers sermons authentiques, apocryphes ou anonymes*. Collection des Études Augustiniennes-Série Antiquité 179. Paris: Études augustiniennes, 2005.

———. "Deux Sermons d'Augustin pour les fêtes de Jean-Baptiste et de Pierre et Paul (s. 293 et 299)." *Augustinianum* 57 (2017): 403–92.

———. "L'oraison 'conuersi ad dominum. . .': un bilan provisoire des recensions existantes." *Archiv für Liturgiewissenschaft* 41 (1999): 295–322.

———. "Un second manuscrit complet du *Sermo contra Pelagium* (S. 348A augmenté)." *Revue des études augustiniennes* 45 (1999): 353–61.

———. "Le sermon 348A de saint Augustin contre Pélage: Édition du text intégral." *Recherches augustiniennes* 28 (1995): 37–63.

Drecoll, Volker Henning. "Gratia." In *Augustinus-Lexikon*, edited by Cornelius Mayer, 3:182–242. Basel: Schwabe, 2004–2010.

———. "Gratia et libero arbitrio (De-)." In *Augustinus-Lexikon*, edited by Cornelius Mayer, 3:253–62. Basel: Schwabe, 2004–2010.

———. "Innerkirchlicher Diskurs und Meinungsführerschaft: Augustins Gnadenlehre in synodalen Texten aus dem Pelagianischen Streit." In *Die christlich-philosophischen Diskurse der Spätantike: Texte, Personen, Institutionen*, edited by Therese Fuhrer, 205–20. Stuttgart: Steiner, 2008.

———. "Kommentar zu Augustin, Epistula 184A." *Revue d'études augustiniennes et patristiques* 62 (2016): 67–93.

———. "Marcellinus, Flauius." In *Augustinus-Lexikon*, edited by Cornelius Mayer, 3:1160–65. Basel: Schwabe, 2004–2010.

———. "Pelagius, Pelagiani." In *Augustinus-Lexikon*, edited by Robert Dodaro, Cornelius Mayer, Christof Müller, 4:624–66. Basel: Schwabe, 2012–2018.

———. "Pelagianismus–eine konstruierte Häresie? Ein Forschungsbericht." *Historische Zeitschrift* 316 (2023): 635–64.

———. "Perfectione iustitiae hominis (De-)." In *Augustinus-Lexikon*, edited by Robert Dodaro, Cornelius Mayer, Christof Müller, 4:678–83. Basel: Schwabe, 2012–2018.

———. "Praedestinatio sanctorum (De-)." In *Augustinus-Lexikon*, edited by Robert Dodaro, Cornelius Mayer, Christof Müller, 4:837–44. Basel: Schwabe, 2012–2018.

Drobner, Hubertus. "The Chronology of St. Augustine's *Sermones ad populum*." *Augustinian Studies* 31 (2000): 211–18.

———. "The Chronology of St. Augustine's *Sermones ad populum* II: Sermons 5 to 8." *Augustinian Studies* 34 (2003): 49–66.

———. "The Chronology of St. Augustine's *Sermones ad populum* III: On Christmas Day." *Augustinian Studies* 35 (2004): 43–53.

Dulaey, Martine. "L'apprentissage de l'exégèse biblique par Augustin (1). Années 386–389." *Revue des études augustiniennes* 48 (2002): 267–95.

———. "L'apprentissage de l'exégèse biblique par Augustin (2). Années 390–392." *Revue des études augustiniennes* 49 (2003): 43–84.

———. "L'apprentissage de l'exégèse biblique par Augustin (3). Années 393–394." *Revue d'études augustiniennes et patristiques* 51 (2005): 21–65.

du Manoir, H. "L'argument patristique dans la controverse nestorienne." *Recherches de science religieuse* 25 (1935): 441–61 and 531–59.

Dunkle, Brian. "'Made Worthy of the Holy Spirit': A Hymn of Ambrose in Augustine's *Nature and Grace*." *Augustinian Studies* 50 (2019): 1–12.

Dunn, Geoffrey D. "Anicius Hermogenianus Olybrius." In *Studies in Latin Literature and Roman History XIV*, edited by Carl Deroux, 429–44. Collection Latomus 315. Brussels: Éditions Latomus, 2008.

———. "Augustine, Cyril of Alexandria, and the Pelagian Controversy." *Augustinian Studies* 37 (2006): 63–88.

———. "The Christian Networks of the *Aniciae*: The Example of the Letter of Innocent I to Anicia Juliana." *Revue d'études augustiniennes et patristiques* 55 (2009): 53–72.

———. "Did Zosimus Pardon Caelestius?" In *Lex et religio: XL Incontro di Studiosi dell'Antichità Cristiana (Roma, 10–12 maggio 2012)*, 647–56. Rome: Institutum Patristicum Augustinianum, 2013.

———. "Innocent I and Rufus of Thessalonica." *Jahrbuch der Österreichischen Byzantinistik* 59 (2009): 51–64.

———. "Innocent I and the Attacks on the Bethlehem Monasteries." *Journal of the Australian Early Medieval Association* 2 (2006): 69–83.

———. "Optatus and Parmenian on the Authority of Cyprian." In Dupont et al., *The Uniquely African Controversy*, 179–96.

———. "The Poverty of Melania the Younger and Pinianus." *Augustinianum* 54 (2014): 93–115.

———. "'...Quid habuerit antiqua consuetudo: Zosimus of Rome and Hilary of Narbonne." *Revue d'histoire ecclésiastique* 110 (2015): 31–55.

———. "Zosimus and Ravenna: Conflict in the Roman Church in the Early Fifth Century." *Revue d'études augustiniennes et patristiques* 62 (2016): 1–20.

Dunphy, Walter. "The Acts of the Synod of Diospolis: Text, Translation, and Notes." *Academia* 67 (1998): 185–228.

———. "Caelestius: A Preliminary Investigation." *Academia* 60 (1994): 33–59.

———. "Concerning the Synod of Diospolis and Its Acts." *Academia* 63 (1996): 101–17.

———. "Glosses on Glosses: On the Budapest Anonymous and Pseudo-Rufinus, A Study on Anonymous Writings in Pelagian Circles (Part 1)." *Augustinian Studies* 44 (2013): 227–47.

———. "Glosses on Glosses: On the Budapest Anonymous and Pseudo-Rufinus, A Study on Anonymous Writings in Pelagian Circles (Part 2)." *Augustinian Studies* 45 (2014): 49–68.

———. "Glosses on Glosses: On the Budapest Anonymous and Pseudo-Rufinus, A Study on Anonymous Writings in Pelagian Circles (Part 3)." *Augustinian Studies* 46 (2015): 43–70.

———. "Jerome against Jovinian, and Other(s): A Note on *Epp.* 50 and 133." *Academia* 64 (1996): 25–53.

———. "The Lost Manuscript of Pseudo-Rufinus: *De fide*." *Augustinianum* 40 (2000): 89–103.

———. "A Lost Year: Pelagianism in Carthage, 411 A.D." *Augustinianum* 45 (2005): 389–466.

———. "Marius Mercator in the *Collectio Palatina*: A Strange Survival." *Augustiniana* 72, no. 2 (2022): 265–88.

———. "Marius Mercator on Rufinus the Syrian: Was Schwartz Mistaken?" *Augustinianum* 32 (1992): 279–88.

———. "The Pelagians and Their Eastern (Antiochene) Sources: Theodore of Mopsuestia on Lk 2.52 in the *Liber de Fide* by Pseudo-Rufinus?" *Revue d'études augustiniennes et patristiques* 58 (2012): 97–111.

———. "A Prelude to the Synod of Diospolis: The *Liber Apologeticus* of Orosius." *Academia* 62 (1995): 123–53.

———. "Ps-Rufinus (the "Syrian") and the Vulgate: Evidence Wanting!" *Augustinianum* 52 (2012): 219–56.

———. "Rufinus of Aquileia in the Middle Ages: The Evidence of Manuscripts." *Nanzan Journal of Theological Studies* 34 (2011): 93–141.

———. "Rufinus the Syrian: Myth and Reality." *Augustiniana* 59 (2009): 79–157.

———. "Rufinus the Syrian's 'Books.'" *Augustinianum* 23 (1983): 523–29.

———. "St. Jerome and the Gens Anicia (Ep. 130 to Demetrias)." *Studia Patristica* 18 (1990): 139–45.

———. "Unexplored Paths Relating to the Outbreak of the Pelagian Debate." *Nanzan Journal of Theological Studies* 30 (2007): 27–54.

———. "An Unlisted Profession of Faith (Pseudo-Rufinus, *De Fide*)." *Sacris Eruditi* 39 (2000): 37–53.

———. "Who was Flavius Marcellinus?" *Academia* 75 (2002): 233–48.

———. "The Writings of Caelestius." *Academia* 61 (1995): 25–47.

Dupont, Anthony. "Augustine's Anti-Pelagian Interpretation of Two Martyr Sermons: Sermones 299 and 335B on the Unnaturalness of Human Death." In *Martyrdom and Persecution in Late Antique Christianity: Festschrift B. Dehandschutter*, edited by J. Leemans, 87–102. Leuven: Peeters, 2010.

———. Gratia *in Augustine's* Sermones ad populum *during the Pelagian Controversy: Do Different Contexts Furnish Different Insights?* Brill's Series in Church History 59. Leiden: Brill, 2013.

———. "Original Sin in Tertullian and Cyprian: Conceptual Presence and Pre-Augustinian Content?" *Revue d'études augustiniennes et patristiques* 63 (2017): 1–29.

———. *Preacher of Grace: A Critical Reappraisal of Augustine's Doctrine of Grace in His* Sermones ad populum *on liturgical feasts and during the Donatist Controversy*. Leiden: Brill, 2014.

Dupont, Anthony, and Giulio Malavasi. "Imitazione o trasmissione dei peccati dei padri nei figli? Dibattiti teologici sul concetto veterotestamentario di peccata patrum nella controversia pelagiana." *Gregorianum* 100 (2019): 487–519.

———. "The *Liber Caelestii*: A Historical and Theological Analysis of Its Fragments." *Revue d'histoire des textes* 17 (2022): 171–211.

———. "Marius Mercator and the Augustinian Concept of Carnal Concupiscence." *Revue d'études augustiniennes et patristiques* 64 (2018): 165–80.

———. "The Question of the Impact of Divine Grace in the Pelagian Controversy: Human *posse, uelle* et *esse* according to Pelagius, Jerome, and Augustine." *Revue d'Histoire Ecclésiastique* 112 (2017): 539–68.

———. "When Did Caelestius Become Known as a Disciple of Pelagius? Reassessing the Sources." *Journal of Early Christian Studies* 30 (2022): 343–71.

Dupont, Anthony, Matthew Alan Gaumer, and Mathijs Lamberigts. "Cyprian in Augustine: from Criticized Predecessor to Uncontested Authority." In *The Normativity of History: Theological Truth and Tradition in the Tension between Church History and Systematic Theology*, edited by Lieven Boeve, Mathijs Lamberigts, Terrence Merrigan, 33–66. Leuven: Peeters, 2016.

Dupont, Anthony, Matthew Alan Gaumer, and Mathijs Lamberigts, eds. *The Uniquely African Controversy: Studies on Donatist Christianity*. Leuven: Peeters, 2015.

Duval, Yves-Marie. *L'affaire Jovinien: d'une crise de la société romaine à une crise de la pensée chrétienne à la fin du IV et au début du Ve siècle*. Rome: Institutum Patristicum Augustinianum, 2003.

———. "Augustin et les règles épistolaires: Sur quelques lettres embarrassées de saint Augustin (Ep. 23, 28, 146)." In *Epistulae antiquae II: Actes du IIe colloque international 'Le genre épistolaire antique et les prolongements européens' (Université François-Rabelais, Tours, 28–30 september 2000)*, edited by L. Nadjo and E. Gavoille, 355–65. Louvain: Peeters, 2002.

———. "La correspondance entre Augustin et Pélage." *Revue des études augustiniennes* 45 (1999): 363–84.

———. "La date du 'De natura' de Pélage: les premières étapes de la controverse sur la nature de la grâce." *Revue des études augustiniennes* 36 (1990): 257–83.

———. "Jérôme ennemi de l'hérésie, non de l'hérétique: De la proclamation d'un principe à son application pratique." In *Les Chrétiens face à leurs adversaires dans l'Occident Latin au IVe siècle*, edited by J.-M. Poinsotte, 211–31. Rouen: Publications de l'Université de Rouen et du Havre, 2001.

———. "Julien d'Éclane et Rufin d'Aquilée: Du Concile de Rimini à la répression pélagienne. L'intervention impériale en matière religieuse." *Revue d'études augustiniennes* 24 (1978): 243–71.

———. "Note Complémentaire: Lettre 4*." In *Lettres 1*–29**, edited by J. Divjak, *Bibliothèque augustinienne* 46B, 430–42. Paris: Brepols, 1987.

———. "Note Complémentaire: Lettre 6*." In *Lettres 1*–29**, edited by J. Divjak, *Bibliothèque augustinienne* 46B, 444–56. Paris: Brepols, 1987.

———. "Note Complémentaire: Lettre 19*." In *Lettres 1*–29**, edited by J. Divjak, *Bibliothèque augustinienne* 46B, 507–16. Paris: Brepols, 1987.

———. "Note sur la lettre d'Evodius à l'abbé Valentin d'Hadrumète." *Revue des études augustiniennes* 49 (2003): 123–30.

———. "Pélage en son temps: Données chronologiques nouvelles pour une présentation nouvelle." *Studia Patristica* 38 (2001): 95–118.

———. "Pélage est-il le censeur inconnu de l'Adversus Iovinianum à Rome en 393? ou: du 'portrait-robot' de l'hérétique chez s. Jérôme." *Revue d'histoire ecclésiastique* 75 (1980): 525–57.

———. "Sur les insinuations de Jérôme contre Jean de Jérusalem: De l'arianisme à l'origenisme." *Revue d'Histoire Ecclésiastique* 65 (1970): 353–74.

———. "Sur quelques manuscrits du *De vita christiana* portant le nom de Pélage." *Latomus* 64 (2005): 132–52.

Ebbeler, Jennifer V. *Disciplining Christians: Correction and Community in Augustine's Letters*. Oxford: Oxford University Press, 2012.

Edwards, Mark. "Augustine and His Christian Predecessors." In *A Companion to Augustine*, edited by Mark Vessey, 215–26. Chichester: Wiley-Blackwell, 2012.

Eno, Robert. "Doctrinal Authority in St. Augustine." *Augustinian Studies* 12 (1981): 133–72.

BIBLIOGRAPHY

Ernst, J. "Der heilige Augustin über die Entscheidung der Kerzertauffrage durch ein Plenarkonzil." *Zeitschrift für katholische Theologie* 24 (1900): 282–32.

Evans, Robert F. *Four Letters of Pelagius*. London: The Seabury Press, 1968.

———. "Pelagius, Fastidius and the Pseudo-Augustinian *De vita christiana*." *Journal of Theological Studies* 13 (1962): 72–98.

———. *Pelagius: Inquiries and Reappraisals*. London: The Seabury Press, 1968.

———. "Pelagius's Veracity at the Synod of Diospolis." In *Studies in Medieval Culture*, edited by John R. Sommerfeldt, 21–30. Kalamazoo, MI: Western Michigan University, 1964.

Fairweather, E. R. "St. Augustine's Interpretation of Infant Baptism." In *Augustinus Magister*, Congrès International Augustinien, 2:897–903. Paris: Études Augustininiennes, 1954.

Ferguson, Everett. *Baptism in the Early Church: History, Theology, and Liturgy in the First Five Centuries*. Grand Rapids, MI: Eerdmans, 2009.

Ferguson, John. *Pelagius: A Historical and Theological Study*. Cambridge: W. Heffer, 1956.

Fitzgerald, Allan D., ed. *Augustine through the Ages: An Encyclopedia*. Grand Rapids, MI: Eerdmans, 2009.

Floeri, F. "Le pape Zosime et la doctrine augustinienne du péché originel." In *Augustinus Magister*, Congrès International Augustinien, 2:755–61. Paris: Études augustiniennes, 1954.

Florovsky, G. "The Authority of the Ancient Councils and the Tradition of the Fathers." In *Glaube, Geist, Geschichte*, edited by G. Müller and W. Zeller, 177–88. Leiden: Brill, 1967.

Frede, H. J. *Ein Neuer Paulustext und Kommentar, I. Untersuchungen; II. Die Text*. Vetus Latina: die Reste der altlateinischen Bibel, Aus der Geschichte der lateinischen Bibel 7–8. Freiburg: Herder, 1973–1974.

Frend, W. H. C. *The Donatist Church: A Movement of Protest in Roman North Africa*. Oxford: Clarendon Press, 1952.

Fürst, Alfons. *Augustins Briefwechsel mit Hieronymus*. Münster: Aschendorffsche Verlagsbuchhandlung, 1999.

———. *Augustinus-Hieronymus Epistulae mutuae*. 2 vols. Turnhout: Brepols, 2002.

Garcia-Allen, C. A. "Was Pelagius Influenced by Chromatius of Aquileia?" In *Studia Patristica*, edited by Elizabeth A Livingston, 17.3, 1251–57. Oxford: Pergamon, 1982.

Garcia-Sanchez, C. *Pelagius and Christian Initiation: A Study in Historical Theology*. Washington, DC: The Catholic University of America Press, 1978.

Gaumer, Matthew A. *Augustine's Cyprian: Authority in Roman Africa*. Leiden: Brill, 2016.

———. "Dealing with the Donatist Church: Augustine of Hippo's Nuanced Claim to the Authority of Cyprian of Carthage." In *Cyprian of Carthage: Studies in His Life, Language and Thought*, edited by H. Bakker, P. Van Geest and H. Van Loon, Late Antiquity History and Religion Series 3, 181–202. Leuven: Peeters, 2010.

Gleede, Benjamin. "Rufinus." In *Augustinus-Lexikon*, edited by Robert Dodaro, Cornelius Mayer, Christof Müller, 4:1232–37. Basel: Schwabe, 2012–2018.

Grafton, Anthony, and Megan Williams. *Christianity and the Transformation of the Book: Origen, Eusebius, and the Library of Caesarea.* Cambridge, MA: Belknap Press of Harvard University Press, 2006.

Graumann, Thomas. *Die Kirche der Väter: Vätertheologie und Väterbeweis in den Kirchen des Ostens bis zum Konzil von Ephesus (431).* Tübingen: Mohr Siebeck, 2002.

Greshake, G. *Gnade als konkrete Freiheit: Eine Untersuchung zur Gnadenlehre des Pelagius.* Mainz: Matthias-Grünewald, 1972.

Gross, Julius. *Entstehungsgeschichte des Erbsündendogmas: Von der Bibel bis Augustinus.* Munich: E. Reinhardt, 1960.

Grossi, Vittorino. "Il battesimo e la polemica pelagiana negli anni 411–413." *Augustinianum* 9 (1969): 30–61.

———. *Leggere la Bibbia con S. Agostino.* Brescia: Queriniana, 1999.

———. "Il peccato originale nella catechesi di S. Agostino prima della polemica pelagiana." *Augustinianum* 10 (1970): 458–92.

———. "Il ricorso ad Ambrogio nell'*Opus imperfectum contra Iulianum* di Agostino d'Ippona." In *Giuliano d'Eclano e l'Hirpinia Christiana: Atti del convegno 4–6 giugno 2003,* 115–56. Napoli: Arte Tipografica, 2004.

———. "Sant'Ambrogio e sant'Agostino: Per una rilettura dei loro rapporti." In *Nec timeo mori: Atti del Congresso internazionale di studi ambrosiani nel XVI centenario della morte di sant'Ambrogio, Milano, 4–11 aprile 1997,* edited by M. Rizzi and L. F. Pizzolato, 405–62. Milan: Vita e Pensiero, 1998.

Gumerlock, Francis X. "Arnobius the Younger against the 'Predestined One': Was Prosper of Aquitaine the Predestinarian Opponent of Arnobius the Younger?" *Augustinian Studies* 44 (2013): 249–63.

Hänggi, A., and I. Pahl. *Prex Eucharistica.* Spicilegium Friburgense 12. Third edition. Freiburg: Universitätsverlag, 1998.

Harmless, William. *Augustine and the Catechumenate.* Collegeville, MN: The Liturgical Press, 1995.

———. "Christ the Pediatrician: Infant Baptism and Christological Imagery in the Pelagian Controversy." *Augustinian Studies* 28 (1997): 7–34.

Hermanowicz, Erika T. *Possidius of Calama: A Study of the North African Episcopate at the Time of Augustine.* Oxford Early Christian Studies. Oxford: Oxford University Press, 2008.

Hofmann, Fritz. "Die Bedeutung der Konzilien für die kirchliche Lehrentwicklung nach dem hl. Augustinus." In *Kirche und Überlieferung,* edited by J. Betz and H. Fries, 81–89. Freiburg: Herder, 1960.

———. *Der Kirchenbegriff des hl. Augustinus in seinen Grundlagen und in seiner Entwicklung.* Münster: Stenderhoff, 1978.

Hohensee, H. *The Augustinian Concept of Authority.* New York: n.p., 1954.

Hombert, Pierre-Marie. Gloria Gratiae: *Se glorifier en Dieu, principe et fin de la théologie augustinienne de la grâce*. Paris: Institut d'Études Augustiniennes, 1996.

———. "Gratia Christi et de peccato originali (De-)." In *Augustinus-Lexikon*, edited by Cornelius Mayer, 3:242–53. Basel: Schwabe, 2004–2010.

———. *Nouvelles recherches de chronologie augustinienne*. Paris: Institut d'Études Augustiniennes, 2000.

Honnay, Guido. "Caelestius, discipulus Pelagii." *Augustiniana* 44 (1994): 271–302.

Hunter, David G. *Marriage, Celibacy, and Heresy in Ancient Christianity: The Jovinianist Controversy*. Oxford: Oxford University Press, 2009.

Hwang, Alexander Y. *Intrepid Lover of Perfect Grace: The Life and Thought of Prosper of Aquitaine*. Washington, DC: The Catholic University of America Press, 2009.

———. "Prosper, Cassian, and Vincent: The Rule of Faith in the Augustinian Controversy." In *Tradition & the Rule of Faith in the Early Church: Essays in Honor of Joseph T. Lienhard, SJ*, edited by Ronnie J. Rombs and Alexander Y. Hwang, 68–85. Washington, DC: The Catholic University of America Press, 2010.

Hwang, Alexander Y., Brian J. Matz, and Augustine Casiday, eds. *Grace for Grace: The Debates after Augustine and Pelagius*. Washington, DC: The Catholic University of America Press, 2014.

Image, Isabella. *The Human Condition in Hilary of Poitiers: The Will and Original Sin Between Origen and Augustine*. Oxford: Oxford University Press, 2017.

Inglebert, Hervé. "Orosius." In *Augustinus-Lexikon*, edited by Robert Dodaro, Cornelius Mayer, Christof Müller, 4:398–403. Basel: Schwabe, 2012–2018.

Jackson, M. G. "The Lord's Prayer in St. Augustine." *Studia Patristica* 27 (1993): 311–21.

Jacobs, Andrew S. "Writing Demetrias: Ascetic Logic in Ancient Christianity." *Church History* 69 (2000): 719–48.

James, N. W. "Who was Arnobius the Younger? Dissimulation, Deception, and Disguise by a Fifth-Century Opponent of Augustine." *Journal of Ecclesiastical History* 69 (2018): 243–61.

Jeanjean, Benoît. "Le *Dialogus Attici et Critobuli* de Jérôme et la Prédication Pélagienne en Palestine entre 411 et 415." In *Jerome of Stridon: His Life, Writings, and Legacy*, edited by Andrew Cain and Josef Lössl, 59–71. Farnham: Ashgate, 2009.

———. *Saint Jérôme et l'hérésie*. Paris: Institut des Études Augustiniennes, 1999.

Jeremias, J. *Infant Baptism in the First Four Centuries*. Philadelphia: Westminster, 1960.

———. *The Origins of Infant Baptism*. London: SCM, 1963.

Johnson, Maxwell E. *Praying and Believing in Early Christianity: The Interplay between Christian Worship and Doctrine*. Collegeville, MN: Liturgical Press, 2013.

———. *The Rites of Christian Initiation: Their Evolution and Interpretation*, 2nd rev. ed. Collegeville, MN: Liturgical Press, 2007.

Jones, A. H. M. *The Prosopography of the Later Roman Empire*. 3 vols. Cambridge: Cambridge University Press, 1971–1992.

Jungmann, Joseph A. *The Mass of the Roman Rite: Its Origins and Development*. 2 vols. Notre Dame, IN: Christian Classics, 2012.

Kantzer Komline, Han-luen. "Always Something New out of Africa: Augustine's Unapologetic Argument from Antiquity." *Augustinian Studies* 51 (2020): 177–96.

———. *Augustine on the Will: A Theological Account*. New York: Oxford University Press, 2020.

———. "From Building Blocks to Blueprints: Augustine's Reception of Ambrose's Commentary on Luke." *Studia Patristica* 85 (2017): 153–65.

———. "Grace, Free Will, and the Lord's Prayer: Cyprian's Importance for the 'Augustinian' Doctrine of Grace." *Augustinian Studies* 45 (2014): 247–79.

Katayanagi, Eiichi. "The Last Congruous Vocation." In *Collectanea Augustiniana. Mélanges T. J. van Bavel*, edited by B. Bruning, 645–57. Louvain: Peeters, 1991.

Kavanaugh, Aidan. *On Liturgical Theology*. New York: Pueblo, 1984.

Kavvadas, Nestor. "An Eastern View: Theodore of Mopsuestia's *Against the Defenders of Original Sin*." In Hwang et al., *Grace for Grace*, 271–93.

Keech, Dominic. *The Anti-Pelagian Christology of Augustine of Hippo*. Oxford Theological Monographs. Oxford: Oxford University Press, 2012.

Kelly, J. N. D. *Jerome: His Life, Writings, and Controversies*. New York: Harper and Row, 1975.

Kessler, Andreas. "Gestis Pelagii, (De-)." In *Augustinus-Lexikon*, edited by Cornelius Mayer, 3:158–67. Basel: Schwabe, 2004–2010.

———. *Reichtumskritik und Pelagianismus: die pelagianische Diatribe de divitiis; Situierung, Lesetext, Übersetzung, Kommentar*. Freiburg: Universitätsverlag, 1999.

Klöckener, M. "Conuersi ad dominum." In *Augustinus-Lexikon*, edited by Cornelius Mayer, 1:1280–82. Basel: Schwabe, 1986–1994.

Konoppa, Claudia. *Die Werke des Marius Mercator: Übersetzung und Kommentierung seiner Schriften*. New York: Lang, 2005.

Koopmans, J. H. "Augustine's First Contact with Pelagius and the Dating of the Condemnation of Caelestius at Carthage." *Vigiliae Christianae* 8 (1954): 149–53.

Kriegbaum, B. *Kirche der Traditoren oder Kirche der Martyrer? Die Vorgeschichte des Donatismus*. Innsbruck: Tyrolia, 1986.

Kurdock, Anne. "*Demetrias ancilla dei*: Anicia Demetrias and the Problem of the Missing Patron." In *Religion, Dynasty, and Patronage in Early Christian Rome, 300–900*, edited by Kate Cooper and Julia Hillner, 190–224. Cambridge: Cambridge University Press, 2007.

La Bonnardière, A.-M. *Biblia Augustiniana: Le livre des Proverbs*. Paris: Études augustiniennes, 1975.

———. "Le canon des Écritures." In *Saint Augustin et la Bible*, edited by A.-M. La Bonnardière, Bible de tous les temps 3, 287–301. Paris: Beauchesne, 1986.

———. "Les commentaires simultanés de Mat. 6,12 et de 1 Jo. 1,8 dans l'oeuvre de saint Augustin." *Revue des études augustiniennes* 1 (1955): 129–48.

Lamberigts, Mathijs. "Augustine and Julian of Aeclanum on Zosimus." *Augustiniana* 42 (1992): 311–30.

———. "Augustine's Use of Tradition in His Reaction to Julian of Aeclanum's *Ad Turbantium*: *Contra Iulianum I–II*." *Augustinian Studies* 41 (2010): 183–200.

———. "Augustine's Use of Tradition in the Controversy with Julian of Aeclanum." *Augustiniana* 60 (2010): 11–61.

———. "Co-operation of Church and State in the Condemnation of the Pelagians: The Case of Zosimus." In *Religious Polemics in Context*, edited by T. L. Hettema, 363–75. Leiden: Brill, 2005.

———. "Les évêques pélagiens déposés, Nestorius et Ephèse." *Augustiniana* 35 (1985): 264–80.

———. "Innocentius episcopus Romanus." In *Augustinus-Lexikon*, edited by Cornelius Mayer, 3:613–19. Basel: Schwabe, 2006.

———. "The Italian Julian of Aeclanum about the African Augustine of Hippo." In *Augustinus Afer: Saint Augustine: africanité et universalité, Actes du colloque international Alger-Annaba, 1–7 avril 2001*, edited by P.-Y. Fux, J.-M. Roessli and O. Wermelinger, 97–111. Fribourg: Éditions universitaires, 2003.

———. "Iulianus Aeclanensis." In *Augustinus-Lexikon*, edited by Cornelius Mayer, 3:836–47. Basel: Schwabe, 2004–2010.

———. "Julian of Aeclanum: A Plea for a Good Creator." *Augustiniana* 38 (1988): 5–24.

———. "Julian of Aeclanum on Natural Virtues and Rom. 2:14." *Augustiniana* 58 (2008): 127–40.

———. "Julien d'Eclane et Augustin d'Hippone: deux conceptions d'Adam." *Augustiniana* 40 (1990): 393–435.

———. "Le mal et le péché: Pélage: La réhabilitation d'un hérétique." *Revue d'Histoire Ecclésiastique* 95, no. 3 (2000): 97–111.

———. "Pelagius and Pelagians." In *Oxford Handbook of Early Christian Studies*, edited by Susan Ashbrook Harvey and David G. Hunter, 258–79. Oxford: Oxford University Press, 2008.

———. "Recent Research into Pelagianism with Particular Emphasis on the Role of Julian of Aeclanum." *Augustiniana* 52 (2002): 175–98.

———. "Reception of Augustine during His Lifetime." In *Augustine in Context*, edited by Tarmo Toom, 230–37. Cambridge: Cambridge University Press, 2017.

———. "Uso agustiniano de la tradición, en la controversia con Juliano de Eclana." *Augustinus* 54 (2009): 409–52.

―――. "Was Innocent Familiar with the Content of the Pelagian Controversy? A Study of His Answers to the Letters Sent by the African Episcopacy." In Scrinium Augustini: *The World of Augustine's Letters*, edited by P. Nehring, M. Strozynski, and R. Toczko, 203–23. Turnhout: Brepols, 2017.

Lamirande, É. "La datation de la *Vita Ambrosii* de Paulin de Milan." *Revue des études augustiniennes* 27 (1981): 44–55.

Lancel, Serge. *Saint Augustin*. Paris: Fayard, 1999. Translated by Antonia Neville as *Saint Augustine*. London: SCM Press, 2002.

Laurence, Patrick. "Marcella, Jérôme et Origène." *Revue des études augustiniennes* 42 (1996): 267–93.

―――. "Proba, Juliana et Démétrias: Le christianisme des femmes de la gens Anicia dans la première moitié du Ve siècle." *Revue des études augustiniennes* 48 (2002): 131–63.

Lausberg, Heinrich. *Handbook of Literary Rhetoric: A Foundation for Literary Study*. Translated by Matthew T. Bliss, Annemiek Jansen, and David E. Orton. Edited by David E. Orton and R. Dean Anderson. Leiden: Brill, 1998.

Leyser, Conrad. *Authority and Asceticism from Augustine to Gregory the Great*. Oxford: Clarendon Press, 2000.

Liebeschutz, W. "Did the Pelagian Movement Have Social Aims?" *Historia* 12 (1963): 227–41.

―――. "Pelagian Evidence on the Last Period of Roman Britain." *Latomus* 26 (1966): 436–47.

Lienhard, Joseph. "Paulinus of Nola." In Fitzgerald, *Augustine through the Ages*, 628–29.

―――. *Paulinus of Nola and Early Western Monasticism: With a Study of the Chronology of His Works and an Annotated Bibliography, 1879–1976*. Köln-Bonn: Peter Hanstein Verlag, 1977.

Löhr, Winrich. "Augustinus und sein Verhältnis zu Pelagius: eine Relecture der Quellen." *Augustiniana* 60 (2010): 63–86.

―――. "Natura et gratia (De-)." In *Augustinus-Lexikon*, edited by Robert Dodaro, Cornelius Mayer, Christof Müller, 4:183–90. Basel: Schwabe, 2012–2018.

―――. *Pélage et le pélagianisme*. Paris: Cerf, 2015.

―――. "Pelagius (Pelagianer)." In *Reallexikon für Antike und Christentum*, edited by Georg Schöllgen et al., 27:1–26. Stuttgart: Anton Hiersemann, 2016.

―――. "Pelagius' Schrift 'De natura': Rekonstruktion und Analyse." *Recherches augustiniennes* 31 (1999): 235–94.

Lössl, Josef. "Augustine, 'Pelagianism,' Julian of Aeclanum, and Modern Scholarship." *Zeitschrift für Antikes Christentum* 11 (2007): 129–50.

―――. "Dating Augustine's Sermons 151–156: Internal Evidence." In *Sancti Aurelii Augustini: Sermones in Epistolas Apostolicas I*, CCSL 41Ba, ed. G. Partoens, xxiii–lv. Turnhout: Brepols, 2008.

———. *Intellectus Gratiae: Die erkenntnistheoretische und hermeneutische Dimension der Gnadenlehre Augustinus von Hippo.* Supplements to Vigiliae Christianae 38. Leiden: Brill, 1997.

———. *Julian von Aeclanum: Studien zu seinem Leben, seinem Werk, seiner Lehre und ihrer Überlieferung.* Supplements to Vigiliae Christianae 60. Leiden: Brill, 2001.

———. "Nuptiis et Concupiscentia (De-)." In *Augustinus-Lexikon*, edited by Robert Dodaro, Cornelius Mayer, Christof Müller, 4:261–68. Basel: Schwabe, 2012–2018.

———. "'Te Apulia Genuit' (*C. Iul. Imp.* 6.18): Some Notes on the Birthplace of Julian of Eclanum." *Revue des études augustiniennes* 44 (1998): 223–37.

———. "Who Attacked the Monasteries of Jerome and Paula in 416 A.D.?" *Augustinianum* 44 (2004): 91–112.

Lupieri, E. "Agostino e Ireneo." *Vetera Christianorum* 15 (1978): 113–15.

Lütcke, K.-H. "Auctoritas." In *Augustinus-Lexikon*, edited by Cornelius Mayer, 1:498–510. Basel: Schwabe, 1986–1994.

———. *"Auctoritas" bei Augustin.* Stuttgart: Kohlhammer, 1968.

Lyman, J. Rebecca. "Arius and Arians." In Harvey and Hunter, *The Oxford Handbook of Early Christian Studies*, 237–57.

Lyonnet, S. "Augustin et Rom. 5,12 avant la controverse pélagienne: À propos d'un texte de saint Augustin sur le baptême des enfants." *Nouvelle revue théologique* 89 (1967): 842–50.

———. "Romains 5,12 chez saint Augustin: Note sur l'élaboration de la doctrine augustinienne du péché originel." In *L'homme devant Dieu: Mélanges Heri de Lubac*, 1:327–39. Aubier: Éditions Montaigne, 1963.

Maier, F. G. *Augustin und das antike Rom.* Stuttgart: W. Kohlhammer, 1955.

Malavasi, Giulio. *La controversia pelagiana in Oriente.* Paradosis 60. Münster: Aschendorff, 2022.

———. "La controversia pelagiana in Oriente." PhD diss., University of Padua, 2017.

———. "'Erant autem ambo iusti ante Deum' (Lc 1,6): Girolamo e l'accusa di origenismo contro Pelagio." *Adamantius* 23 (2017): 247–54.

———. "The Greek Version(s) of Augustine's *De gestis Pelagii*." *Zeitschrift für Antikes Christentum* 21 (2017): 559–72.

———. "The Involvement of Theodore of Mopsuestia in the Pelagian Controversy: A Study of Theodore's Treatise *Against those who say that men sin by nature and not by will*." *Augustiniana* 64 (2014): 227–60.

———. "John of Jerusalem's Profession of Faith (CPG 3621) and the Pelagian Controversy." *Studia Patristica* 97 (2017): 399–408.

———. "Marius Mercator's Enemies in Augustine's Letter 193." In *Studia Patristica*, vol. 75, edited by M. Vinzent and A. Brent, 361–70. Leuven: Peeters, 2016.

———. "Orosio discepolo di Agostino? L'influenza di Girolamo nel *Liber Apologeticus.*" *Augustinianum* 55 (2015): 113–36.

———. "Pelagianism as Novelty in Augustine of Hippo." *Humanitas Hodie* 1 (2018): 55–68.

———. "Pelagians/Pelagianism." In *Brill Encyclopedia of Early Christianity Online*, edited by David G. Hunter, Paul J. J. van Geest, Bert Jan Lietaert Peerbolte. <http://dx.doi.org/10.1163/2589-7993_EECO_SIM_00002649>.

Mandouze, André. *Prosopographie chrétienne du bas-empire.* Vol. 1, *Prosopographie de l'Afrique chrétienne (303-533).* Paris: Centre national de la Recherche scientifique, 1982.

Marcos, Mar. "Anti-Pelagian Legislation in Context." In Lex et religio, *XL Incontro di Studiosi dell'Antichità Cristiana (Roma, 10-12 maggio 2012)*, 317-44. Rome: Institutum Patristicum Augustinianum, 2013.

———. "Papal Authority, Local Autonomy and Imperial Control: Pope Zosimus and the Western Churches (a. 417-418)." In *The Role of the Bishop in Late Antiquity: Conflict and Compromise*, edited by A. Fear, J. Fernández Ubiña, and M. Marcos, 145-66. London: Bloomsbury, 2013.

Marini, A. *La celbrazione eucaristica presieduta da Sant'Agostino: La partecipazione dei fedeli alla Liturgia della Parola e al Sacrificio Eucaristico.* Brescia: Pavoniana, 1989.

Markus, Robert A. "Donatus, Donatism." In Fitzgerald, *Augustine through the Ages*, 284-87.

Marrou, Henri-Irénée. "Les attaches orientales du Pélagianisme." *Académie des Inscriptions & Belles-Lettres: Comptes Rendus des Séances* 112 (1968): 459-72.

———. *A History of Education in Antiquity.* Translated by George Lamb. New York: Sheed and Ward, 1956.

———. *Saint Augustin et la fin de la culture antique.* Paris: E. de Boccard, 1958.

Mártil, G. *La tradición en san Augustin a través de la controversia pelagiana.* Madrid: Talleres Espasa-Calpe, 1943.

Martindale, J. R. *The Prosopography of the Later Roman Empire, Volume 2: A. D. 395-527.* Cambridge: Cambridge University Press, 1980.

Martinetto, Giovanni. "Les premières réactions antiaugustiniennes de Pélage." *Revue d'études augustiniennes* 17 (1971): 83-117.

Maschio, Giorgio. "L'argomentazione patristica di S. Agostino nella prima fase della controversia pelagiana (412-418)." *Augustinianum* 26 (1986): 459-79.

Mathisen, Ralph W. "A New Fragment of Augustine's *De nuptiis et concupiscentia* from the Codex Sangallensis 190." *Zeitschrift für antikes Christentum* 3 (1999): 165-83.

Matteoli, Sara. *Alle origini della teologia di Pelagio: Tematiche e fonti delle* Expositiones XIII Epistularum Pauli. Pisa: Fabrizio Serra Editore, 2011.

Matthews, John. *Western Aristocracies and Imperial Court A.D. 364-425.* Second Edition. Oxford: Clarendon Press, 1990.

Mayer, Cornelius. "Causa finita est." In *Augustinus-Lexikon*, edited by Cornelius Mayer, 1:828. Basel: Schwabe, 1986-1994.

BIBLIOGRAPHY 353

————. "Garenten der Offenbarung: Probleme der Tradition in den antimanichäischen Schriften Augustins." *Augustinianum* 12 (1972): 51–78.

Mayeur, Jean-Marie, Charles Pietri, Luce Pietri, André Vauchez, Marc Venard, eds. *Histoire du Christianisme des origines à nos jours II: Naissance d'une chrétienté (250–430)*. Paris: Desclée, 1995.

McWilliam, Joanne. "Letters to Demetrias: A Sidebar in the Pelagian Controversy *Helenae, amicae meae*." *Toronto Journal of Theology* 16 (2000): 131–39.

Mercati, G. "Some New Fragments of Pelagius I: Two New Fragments of Pelagius." *Journal of Theological Studies* 8 (1907): 526–29.

Merdinger, Jane E. "In League with the Devil? Donatist and Catholic Perspectives on Pre-Baptismal Exsufflation." In Dupont et al., *The Uniquely African Controversy*, 153–78.

Merlin, Nicholas. *Saint Augustin et les dogmes du péché originel et de la grâce; analyses détaillées de ses ouvrages sur ces matières, complétées par d'importantes explications de sa pensée, et suivies de conculsions théologiques*. Paris: Librairie Letouzey et Ané, 1931.

Michel, A. "Traducianisme." In *Dictionnaire de théologie catholique*, edited by A. Vacant, E. Mangenot, E. Amann, et al., 15:1350–65. Paris: Letouzey et Ané, 1950.

Miles, Richard. "'Let's (Not) Talk about It': Augustine and the Control of Epistolary Dialogue." In *The End of Ancient Dialogue*, edited by Simon Goldhill, 135–48. Oxford: Oxford University Press, 2008.

Miles, Richard, ed. *The Donatist Schism: Controversy and Contexts*. Translated Texts for Historians, Contexts. Liverpool: Liverpool University Press, 2016.

Moffatt, J. "Augustine on the Lord's Prayer." *Expositor* 18 (1919): 259–72.

Mommsen, Theodor E. "Orosius and Augustine." In *Medieval and Renaissance Studies*, edited by Eugene F. Rice Jr., 325–48. Ithaca, NY: Cornell University Press, 1959.

Moreau, Madeleine. *Le dossier Marcellinus dans la correspondance de saint Augustin*. Paris: Études augustiniennes, 1973.

Moreschini, Claudio. "Il contributo di Gerolamo alla polemica antipelagiana." *Cristianesimo nella Storia* 3 (1982): 61–71.

————. "Gerolamo tra Pelagio e Origene." *Augustinianum* 26 (1986): 207–16.

Morgenstern, Frank. *Die Briefpartner des Augustinus von Hippo: prosopographische, sozial- und ideologiegeschichtliche Untersuchungen*. Bochum: Universitätsverlag Dr. N. Brockmeyer, 1993.

Mozley, J. B. *A Treatise on the Augustinian Doctrine of Predestination*. 3rd ed. London: J. Murray, 1883.

Mratschek, Sigrid. *Der Briefwechsel des Paulinus von Nola: Kommunikation und soziale Kontakte zwischen christlichen Intellektuellen*. Hypomnemata: Untersuchungen zur Antike und zu ihrem Nachleben. Göttingen: Vandenhoeck & Ruprecht, 2002.

————. "Paulinus Nolanus." In *Augustinus-Lexikon*, edited by Robert Dodaro, Cornelius Mayer, Christof Müller, 4:540–48. Basel: Schwabe, 2012–2018.

Munier, C. and H. Sieben. "Concilium (concilia)." In *Augustinus-Lexikon*, edited by Cornelius Mayer, 1:1085–107. Basel: Schwabe, 1986–1994.

Murphy, Francis X. *Rufinus of Aquileia (345–411): His Life and Works.* Washington, DC: The Catholic University of America Press, 1945.

Mutzenbecher, A. "Einleitung." In Augustine, *De diuersis questionibus ad Simplicianum*, CCL 44. Turnhout: Brepols, 1970.

Nazzaro, Antonio V., editor. *Giuliano d'Eclano e l'Hirpinia Cristiana: atti del Convegno 4–6 giugno 2003.* Napoli: Arte tipografica, 2004.

Nuvolone, Flavio G. "Problèmes d'une nouvelle édition du *De Induratione Cordis Pharaonis* attribué à Pélage." *Revue des études augustiniennes* 26 (1980): 105–17.

Nuvolone, Flavio G. and Aimé Solignac. "Pélage et Pélagianisme." In *Dictionnaire de spiritualité, ascétique et mystique, histoire et doctrine*, edited by M. Viller, A. Derville, P. Lamarche, and A. Solignac, vol. 12, part 2:2889–942. Paris: Beauchesne, 1986.

O'Donnell, J. J. *Augustine: A New Biography.* New York: Harper, 2005.

———. "The Authority of Augustine." *Augustinian Studies* 22 (1991): 7–35.

Ogliari, Donato. "An Anti-Pelagian *caueat*: Augustine's *Ep.* 188 to Juliana." *Augustiniana* 54 (2004): 203–22.

———. *Gratia et Certamen: The Relationship between Grace and Free Will in the Discussion of Augustine with the So-Called Semipelagians.* Leuven: Leuven University Press, 2003.

Pallu de Lessert, A. Clément. *Fastes de provinces africaines: (Proconsulaire, Numidie, Maurétanies) sous la domination romaine.* 2 volumes. Paris: E. Leroux, 1896–1901.

Palanque, J.-R. "La *Vita Ambrosii* de Paulin: Étude critique." *Revue des sciences religieuses* 4 (1924): 26–42, 401–20.

Paredi, A. "Paulinus of Milan." *Sacris Erudiri* 14 (1963): 206–30.

Partoens, Gert. "Augustine on Predestination, Immortal Babies, and Sinning Foetuses: A Rhetorical Analysis of Sermon 165." *Augustinian Studies* 45 (2013): 29–48.

———. "*Contradicit apostolus*: A Particular Use of Rom 9:11 in Augustine's Sermo 165." *Zeitschrift für Antikes Christentum* 13 (2009): 494–512.

———. "Quelques remarques de critique textuelle sur le sermon 348A augmenté de Saint Augustin (Dolbeau 30*)." *Augustiniana* 50 (2000): 175–95.

———. "Le Sermon 131 de saint Augustin. Introduction et édition." *Augustiniana* 54 (2004): 35–77.

Perago, F. "Il valore della tradizione nella polemica tra sant'Agostino e Giuliano di Eclano." *Annali della Facoltà di Lettere e Filosofia di Napoli* 10 (1962–1963): 143–60.

Perler, Othmar. *Les voyages de saint Augustin.* Paris: Institut d'études augustiniennes, 1969.

———. "Les voyages de saint Augustin." *Recherches augustiniennes* 1 (1958): 5–42.

BIBLIOGRAPHY

Perrin, M.-Y. "'The blast of the ecclesiastical trumpet': Prédication et controverse dans la crise pélagienne. Quelques observations." In *Prédication et controverses religieuses des origines du christianisme au XVIIe siècle: Actes de la journée d'étude du 8 février 2007*, edited by P. Nagy and M.-Y. Perrin, 17–31. Mont-Saint-Aignan: Publications de Universités de Rouen et du Havre, 2011.

Picard-Mawji, Zohra. "Le passage de Célestius à Carthage: Un moment clé du pélagianisme." *Cahiers Mondes Anciens* 4 (2013): 1–18.

Pierce, Alexander H. "From Emergency Practice to Christian Polemics? Augustine's Invocation of Infant Baptism in the Pelagian Controversy." *Augustinian Studies* 52 (2021): 19–41.

Pietri, Charles. "Chapitre IV: Les difficultés du nouveau système (395–431): La première hérésie d'Occident: Pélage et le refus rigoriste." In *Histoire du Christianisme des origines à nos jours II: Naissance d'une chrétienté (250–430)*, edited by Jean-Marie Mayeur, Charles and Luce Pietri, André Vauchez, Marc Venard, 453–79. Paris: Desclée, 1995.

———. *Roma christiana: recherches sur l'Église de Rome, son organisation, sa politique, son idéologie de Miltiade à Sixte III (311–440)*. Rome: École française de Rome, 1976.

Pietri, Charles and Luce Pietri, editors. *Prosopographie chrétienne du bas-empire*. Vol. 2, *Prosopographie de l'Italie chrétienne (313–604)*. 2 vols. Rome: École Française du Rome, 1999–2000.

Poque, Suzanne. "L'écho des événements de l'été 413 à Carthage dans la prédication de saint Augustin." In *Homo Spiritalis: Festgabe für Luc Verheijen*, edited by C. Mayer and K. H. Chelius, 391–99. Würzburg: Augustinus-Verlag, 1987.

Prete, Serafino. *Mario Mercatore polemista antipelagiano*. Torino: Marietti, 1958.

———. *Pelagio e il Pelagianesimo*. Brescia: Morcelliana, 1961.

Price, Richard, trans. *The Council of Ephesus of 431: Documents and Proceedings*. Translated Texts for Historians 72. Liverpool: Liverpool University Press, 2020.

Rackett, Michael R. "Sexuality and Sinlessness: The Diversity among Pelagian Theologies of Marriage and Virginity." PhD diss., Duke University, 2002.

———. "What's Wrong with Pelagianism? Augustine and Jerome on the Dangers of Pelagius and His Followers." *Augustinian Studies* 33 (2002): 223–37.

Rebillard, Éric. "Augustin et ses autorités: l'élaboration de l'argument patristique au cours de la controverse pélagienne." *Studia Patristica* 38 (2001): 245–63.

———. *Christians and Their Many Identities in Late Antiquity, North Africa, 200–450 CE*. Ithaca: Cornell University Press, 2012.

———. "*Dogma Populare*: Popular Belief in the Controversy between Augustine and Julian of Eclanum." *Augustinian Studies* 38 (2007): 175–87.

———. "Exégèse et orthodoxie: Augustin et Pélage sur la grâce." In *L'esegesi dei Padri latini: Dalle origini a Gregorio Magno: XXVIII Incontro di studiosi dell'anchità cristiana, Roma, 6–11 maggio 1999, vol. 1: Oriente, Africa*, Studia Ephemeridis Augustinianum 68, 219–23. Rome: Institutum Patristicum Augustinianum, 2000.

———. "A New Style of Argument in Christian Polemic: Augustine and the Use of Patristic Citations." *Journal of Early Christian Studies* 8 (2000): 559–78.

———. "Sermones." In Fitzgerald, *Augustine through the Ages*, 773–92.

———. "Sociologie de la deviance et orthodoxie. Le cas de la controverse pélagienne sur la grace." In *Orthodoxie, Christianisme, Histoire/Orthodoxy, Christianity, History*, edited by S. Elm, É. Rebillard and A. Romano, Collection de l'École française de Rome 270, 221–40. Rome: École française de Rome, 2000.

Rees, B. R. *The Letters of Pelagius and His Followers*. Rochester, NY: Boydell Press, 1991.

———. *Pelagius: A Reluctant Heretic*. Woodbridge: Boydell Press, 1988.

Refoulé, F. "Datation du premier concile de Carthage contre les Pélagiens et du 'Libellus fidei' de Rufin." *Revue des études augustiniennes* 9 (1963): 41–49.

———. "La distinction 'Royaume de Dieu—Vie éternelle' est-elle pélagienne?" *Recherches de science religieuse* 51 (1963): 247–54.

———. "Julien d'Éclane, théologien et philosophe." *Recherches de science religieuse* 52 (1964): 42–84, 233–47.

Reuter, Hermann. *Augustinische Studien*. Gotha, 1887.

Ribreau, Mickaël. "Augustin hérésiologue dans le Contra Iulianum." *Revue d'études augustiniennes et patristiques* 55 (2009): 189–213.

———. "La constitution du dossier patristique du *Contra Iulianum* d'Augustin." *Augustiniana* 69 (2019): 239–75.

———. "Un dialogue de sourds? Argumentation et modes de pensée dans le *Contra Iulianum* d'Augustin." *Augustiniana* 68 (2018): 59–90.

———. "Des *Virtuoses et la multitude* de J.-M. Salamito à *Pélage et le Pélagianisme* de W. Löhr: Augustine et la controverse pélagienne: Bilan bibliographique et perspectives (2005-2015)." *Revue des études tardo-antiques* 5 (2015–2016): 307–49.

Rivière, Jean. "Hétérodoxie des pélagiens en fait de rédemption?" *Revue d'histoire ecclésiastique* 41 (1946): 5–43.

Rondet, Henri. *Original Sin: The Patristic and Theological Background*. Translated by Cajetan Finegan. Staten Island, NY: Alba House, 1972.

Rordorf, W. "The Lord's Prayer in the Light of Its Liturgical Use in the Early Church." *Studia Liturgica* 14 (1981): 1–19.

Sage, Athanase. "Le péché originel dans la pensée de saint Augustin, de 412 à 430." *Revue des études augustiniennes* 15 (1969): 75–112.

———. "Péché originel. Naissance d'un dogme." *Revue des études augustiniennes* 13 (1967): 211–48.

BIBLIOGRAPHY 357

———. "Praeparatur voluntas a Domino." *Revue des études augustiniennes* 10 (1964): 1–20.

Salamito, Jean-Marie. *Les virtuoses et la multitude. Aspects sociaux de la controverse entre Augustin et les pélagiens.* Collection nomina. Grenoble: Millon, 2005.

Santorelli, P. "Note sulla terminologia retorica in Giuliano d'Eclano." In *Giuliano d'Eclano e l'Hirpinia Christiana: Atti del Convegno 4–6 giugno 2003,* edited by A. V. Nazzaro, 73–86. Naples: Arte tipografica, 2004.

Scheck, Thomas P., trans. *Pelagius: Commentaries on the Thirteen Epistles of Paul with the Libellus fidei.* Ancient Christian Writers 76. New York: The Newman Press, 2022.

Scholl, Lindsey A. "The Pelagian Controversy: A Heresy in Its Intellectual Context." PhD diss., University of California Santa Barbara, 2011.

Shaw, Brent D. *Sacred Violence: African Christians and Sectarian Hatred in the Age of Augustine.* Cambridge: Cambridge University Press, 2011.

Sieben, H. J. "Konzilien in Leben und Lehre des Augustinus von Hippo," *Theologie und Philosophie* 46 (1971): 496–528.

———. *Die Konzilsidee der Alten Kirche.* Paderborn: Schöningh, 1979.

Smith, A. J. "The Latin Sources of the Commentary of Pelagius on the Epistle of St. Paul to the Romans." *Journal of Theological Studies* 19 (1918): 162–230; 20 (1919): 55–65, 127–77.

Solignac, Aimé. "Autour du *De natura* de Pélage." In *Valeurs dans le stoïcisme: De Portique à nos jours,* edited by M. Soetard, 181–92. Villeneuve-d'Ascq: Presses universitaires de Lille, 1993.

Sotinel, Claire. "Paulinus diaconus." In *Augustinus-Lexikon,* edited by Robert Dodaro, Cornelius Mayer, Christof Müller, 4:537–40. Basel: Schwabe, 2012–2018.

Souter, Alexander. "Another New Fragment of Pelagius." *Journal of Theological Studies* 12 (1910–11): 32–35.

———. "The Commentary of Pelagius on the Epistles of Paul: The Problem of its Restoration." In *Proceedings of the British Academy, 1905–1906,* 409–39. London: Oxford University Press, 1907.

———. *The Earliest Latin Commentaries on the Epistles of St. Paul: A Study.* Oxford: Clarendon Press, 1927.

———. *Glossary of Later Latin to 600 A.D.* Oxford: Oxford University Press, 1949.

———. *Pelagius's Expositions of Thirteen Epistles of St. Paul.* 3 vols. Texts and Studies 9. Cambridge: Cambridge University Press, 1922–1931.

Squires, Stuart. "Augustine's Changing Thought on Sinlessness." *Augustinianum* 54 (2014): 447–66.

———. "Jerome's Animosity against Augustine." *Augustiniana* 58 (2008): 181–99.

———. "Jerome on Sinlessness: A *Via Media* between Augustine and Pelagius." *The Heythrop Journal* 57 (2016): 697–709.

———. *The Pelagian Controversy: An Introduction to the Enemies of Grace and the Conspiracy of Lost Souls.* Eugene, OR: Pickwick Publications, 2019.

———. "Reassessing Pelagianism: Augustine, Cassian, and Jerome on the Possibility of a Sinless Life." PhD diss., The Catholic University of America, 2013.

———. "The Reception of Pelagianism in Contemporary Scholarship." *Annales theologici* 35 (2021): 135–52.

Stein, Markus. "Bemerkungen zu Iulianum von Aeclanum." *Jahrbuch für Antike und Christentum* 43 (2000): 122–25.

Studer, Basil. "Augustine and the Pauline Theme of Hope." In *Paul and the Legacies of Paul*, edited by William S. Babcock, 201–21. Dallas: Southern Methodist University Press, 1990.

———. *The Grace of Christ and the Grace of God in Augustine of Hippo: Christocentrism or Theocentrism?* Translated by Matthew J. O'Connell. Collegeville: The Liturgical Press, 1997.

———. "Patristic Argumentation." In *Encyclopedia of Ancient Christianity*, edited by Angelo Di Berardino et al., 1:222–25. Downers Grove, IL: IVP Academic, 2014.

———. *Schola Christiana: die Theologie zwischen Nizäa (325) und Chalzedon (451)*. Paderborn: F. Schöningh, 1998.

Tauer, Johann. "Neue Orientierungen zur Paulusexegese des Pelagius." *Augustinianum* 34 (1994): 313–58.

Teske, Roland J. "Augustine's Appeal to Tradition." In *Tradition & the Rule of Faith in the Early Church: Essays in Honor of Joseph T. Lienhard, SJ*, edited by Ronnie J. Rombs and Alexander Y. Hwang, 153–72. Washington, DC: The Catholic University of America Press, 2010.

TeSelle, Eugene. *Augustine the Theologian*. New York: Herder and Herder, 1970.

———. "The Background: Augustine and the Pelagian Controversy." In Hwang et al., *Grace for Grace: The Debates after Augustine and Pelagius*, 1–13.

———. "Rufinus the Syrian, Caelestius, Pelagius: Explorations in the Pre-History of the Pelagian Controversy." *Augustinian Studies* 3 (1972): 61–95.

Thier, Sebastian. *Kirche bei Pelagius*. Berlin: W. de Gruyter, 1999.

Thonnard, François-Joseph. "Saint Jean Chrysostome et saint Augustin dans la controverse pélagienne." *Revue des études byzantines* 25 (1967): 189–218.

Tilley, Maureen. "Redefining Donatism: Moving Forward." *Augustinian Studies* 42 (2011): 21–32.

Toczko, Rafał. "Heretic as Bad Rhetorician: How Augustine Discredited Pelagius." *Augustinian Studies* 42 (2011): 211–31.

———. "Rome as the Basis of Argument in the So-Called Pelagian Controversy (415–418)." In *Studia Patristica* 70, 649–60. Leuven: Peeters, 2013.

Trapé, Agostino. "Tradux Peccati: A proposito di un libro recente." *Augustinianum* 19 (1979): 531–38.

———. "Verso una riabilitazione del pelagianesimo?" *Augustinianum* 3 (1963): 482–516.

BIBLIOGRAPHY

Trout, Dennis E. *Paulinus of Nola: Life, Letters, and Poems.* Berkeley: University of California Press, 1999.

Ulbrich, H. "Augustins Briefe zur entscheidenden Phase des Pelagianischen Streites (Von den Verhandlungen in Jerusalem und Diospolis im Jahre 415 bis zur Verdammung des Pelagius im Jahre 418)." *Revue des études augustiniennes* 9 (1963): 51–75 and 235–58.

Van Bavel, T. "Inféras—inducas. À propos de Mtth. 6, 13 dans les oeuvres de saint Augustin." *Revue Bénédictine* 69 (1959): 348–51.

Van Egmond, Peter. "The Confession of Faith Ascribed to Caelestius." *Sacris Eruditi* 50 (2011): 317–39.

———. "A Confession without Pretence: Text and Context of Pelagius' Defence of 417 AD." PhD diss., Vrije University, 2013.

———. "*Haec fides est*: Observations on the Textual Tradition of Pelagius's *Libellus fidei*." *Augustiniana* 57 (2007): 345–85.

———. "Pelagius and the Origenist Controversy in Palestine." *Studia Patristica* 70 (2013): 631–47.

Vessey, Mark. "The Forging of Orthodoxy in Latin Christian Literature: A Case Study." *Journal of Early Christian Studies* 4 (1996): 495–513.

———. "*Opus Imperfectum*: Augustine and His Readers, 426–435 A.D." *Vigiliae Christianae* 52 (1998): 264–85.

Villegas Marín, Raúl. "The Best Defence Is a Good Offence: Arnobius the Younger's *Praedestinatus* and the Debates on Predestination in Mid-Fifth-Century Rome." *Nottingham Medieval Studies* 63 (2019): 23–35.

Vinel, J.-A. "L'argument liturgique opposé par saint Augustin aux pélagiens." *Questions liturgiques* 68 (1987): 209–41.

———. "Le rôle de la liturgie dans la réflexion doctrinale de Saint Augustin contre les pélagiens." Louvain-la-Neuve, 1986.

Warfield, B. B. "Introductory Essay on Augustin and the Pelagian Controversy." In *St. Augustine: Anti-Pelagian Writings*, vol. 5 of *A Select Library of the Christian Church: Nicene and Post-Nicene Fathers, First Series*, edited by Philip Schaff, xiii–lxxi. Edinburgh: T&T Clark, 1887.

Weaver, Rebecca H. *Divine Grace and Human Agency: A Study of the Semi-Pelagian Controversy.* Macon, GA: Mercer University Press, 1996.

Weber, Dorothea. "For What is so Monstrous as What the Punic Fellow Says?" In *Augustinus Afer: Saint Augustine: africanité et universalité, Actes du colloque international Alger-Annaba, 1–7 avril 2001*, edited by P.-Y. Fux, J.-M. Roessli and O. Wermelinger, 75–82. Fribourg: Éditions universitaires, 2003.

———. "Klassische Literatur im Dienst theologischer Polemik: Julian von Eclanum, Ad Florum." *Studia Patristica* 38 (2001): 503–9.

———. "Some Literary Aspects of the Debate between Julian of Eclanum and Augustine." *Studia Patristica* 43 (2006): 289–302.

Weiss, Jean-Pierre. "Le semi-pélagianisme se réduit-il à une réaction contre Augustin et l'augustinisme de la première génération?" *Studia Ephemeridis Augustinianum* 24 (1987): 465–81.

Wermelinger, Otto. "Marius Mercator." In *Dictionnaire de spiritualité ascétique et mystique: doctrine et histoire*, edited by Marcel Viller, vol. 10, 610–15. Paris: G. Beauchesne et ses fils, 1980.

———. "Marius Mercator." In *Lexikon für Theologie und Kirche*, edited by Walter Kasper, 3rd ed., vol. 6, 1386–87. Freiburg: Herder, 1997.

———. "Neuere Forschungskontroversen um Augustinus und Pelagius." In *Internationales Symposion über den Stand der Augustinus-Forschung vom 12. bis 16 April 1987 im Schloss Rauischholzhausen der Justus-Liebig-Universität Giessen*, edited by C. Mayer, Cassiciacum 39/1, 189–217. Würzburg: Augustinus Verlag, 1989.

———. "Das Pelagiusdossier in der Tractoria des Zosimus." *Freiburger Zeitschrift für Philosophie und Theologie* 26 (1979): 336–68.

———. *Rom und Pelagius: die theologische Position der römischen Bischofe im pelagianischen Streit in den Jahren 411–431*. Stuttgart: A. Hiersemann, 1975.

———. "Staatliche und Kirchliche Zwangmassnahmen in der Endphase des pelagianischen Streites." In *Agostino d'Ippona "Quaestiones disputatae,"* edited by Francisco Giunta, 75–100. Palermo: Edizioni Augustinus, 1989.

Whitehouse, John. "The Course of the Donatist Schism in Late Roman North Africa." In Miles, *Donatist Schism: Controversy and Contexts*, 13–33.

Wickham, Lionel. "Pelagianism in the East." In *The Making of Orthodoxy: Essays in Honour of Henry Chadwick*, edited by Rowan Williams, 200–213. Cambridge: Cambridge University Press, 1989.

Wilhite, David E. *Ancient African Christianity: An Introduction to a Unique Context and Tradition*. Oxford: Routledge, 2017.

Williams, Rowan. "Baptism and the Arian Controversy." In *Arianism After Arius: Essays on the Development of the Fourth Century Trinitarian Conflicts*, edited by Michel R. Barnes and Daniel H. Williams, 149–80. Edinburgh: T&T Clark, 1993.

Willis, Geoffrey. *St. Augustine and the Donatist Crisis*. London: SPCK, 1951.

Wright, D. F. "The Origins of Infant Baptism—Child Believers' Baptism?" *Scottish Journal of Theology* 40 (1987): 1–23.

Yamada, Nozomu. "Rhetorical, Political, and Ecclesiastical Perspectives of Augustine's and Julian of Eclanum's Theological Response in the Pelagian Controversy." *Scrinium* 14, no.1 (2018): 161–93.

BIBLIOGRAPHY

Yates, Jonathan P. "Augustine's Appropriation of Cyprian the Martyr-Bishop against the Pelagians." In *More than a Memory: The Discourse of Martyrdom and the Construction of Christian Identity in the History of Christianity*, edited by J. Leemans, 119–35. Leuven: Peeters, 2005.

———. "The Use of Rom 2:14–15 in the Christian Latin Tradition ca. 365–ca. 411—Augustine Excepted." *Studia Patristica* 44 (2010): 213–25.

———. "Was there 'Augustinian' concupiscence in pre-Augustinian North Africa?" *Augustiniana* 51 (2001): 39–56.

Young, Frances M. *Biblical Exegesis and the Formation of Christian Culture*. Cambridge: Cambridge University Press, 1997.

Zocca, E. "La *Vita Ambrosii* alla luce dei rapporti fra Paolino, Agostino e Ambrogio." In *Nec timeo mori. Atti del Congresso internazionale di studi ambrosiani nel XVI centenario della morte di sant'Ambrogio. Milano, 4–11 aprile 1997*, edited by M. Rizzi and L. F. Pizzolato, 803–26. Milan: Vita e Pensiero, 1998.

Zumkeller, Adolar. "Bono uiduitatis (De-)." In *Augustinus-Lexikon*, edited by Cornelius Mayer, 1:666–71. Basel: Schwabe, 1986–1994.

———. "Correptione et gratia (De-)." In *Augustinus-Lexikon*, edited by Cornelius Mayer, 2:39–47. Basel: Schwabe, 1996–2002.

———. *Sankt Augustinus Lehrer der Gnade: Schriften gegen die Pelagianer*. Vol. 2. Würzburg: Augustinus-Verlag, 1964.

Index

A

Adam's sin. *See* original sin

Aemilius of Beneventum, 45–46, 277n72

Africa, 2, 4–6, 9, 18, 25, 27, 29–30, 32, 34, 38–39, 48–49, 51, 62, 64, 67–68, 70–77, 87, 115, 128, 134, 137–38, 145, 148, 169, 178–79, 189, 195, 216, 223, 225–29, 233–34, 237, 240–41, 251, 263, 266, 273–74, 287, 295, 300, 304–5, 309n18, 311n28, 315: bishops of, 9, 18–19, 78–79, 161n101, 175, 178–79, 181, 187, 190, 193–95, 214–20, 222n161, 224–32, 234, 236–40, 250–53, 258–59, 267, 269n38, 278, 300, 306n8, 309n18; church of, 7–9, 17n52, 19, 87, 114, 129n172, 177n1, 194, 279n80, 282, 299, 308n17; theology of, 122, 236, 273

Alaric, 1, 47, 71, 76, 137n17, 311n28

Albina, 43, 48, 241–43, 256, 309n18, 311n28

Albinus, 269

almsgiving, 8n25, 165–67

Alypius, 45–46, 51, 138, 190, 232–36, 267, 273–74, 277, 281n84, 288–89

Ambrose, 5–6, 11–13, 54, 62, 77, 87n45, 147, 151, 154–56, 165n113, 171–72, 191–93,

195, 231, 243–47, 249, 254–57, 270, 275–76, 279–83, 292–94

Ambrosiaster, 37, 62, 278n78

Anastasius (pope), 43, 58–60

Annianus of Celeda, 65–66, 199n83

Anicii (gens Anicia), 43, 50–52, 60, 137–40, 232–33

Antiochene theology, 63–64, 67

apatheia, 36

apokatastasis, 287n104

Apringius, 310n24, 310n26

Apronianus, 44, 53, 55

Aquileia, 263–64, 266

Aristotle, 265, 283

Arnobius Iunior, 31n8, 77n11, 116n128, 305n5

Athanasius, 13n41

Atticus of Constantinople, 187–88, 218–19, 287–88, 289

Augustine of Aquileia, 263

Augustine of Hippo, writings of: *Ad catholicos fratres*, 291n123; *Ad Cresconium*, 70n164; *Ad Donatistas post collationem*, 310n26; *Ad Simplicianum*, 39n43; *Breuiculus collationis*, 310n26;

363

Confessiones, 32, 51n94, 85, 134n11, 139–40, 157n87, 186n35, 290; *Contra duas epistulas Pelagianorum*, 13n40, 20n57, 30n1, 65n143, 114n122, 133n7, 172n136, 219–20, 223n164, 225n176, 229–30, 239–41, 251–52, 261, 264n11, 272n53, 274, 277–81, 288, 293n133; *Contra Faustum*, 14n44, 290; *Contra Gaudentium*, 290–91; *Contra Iulianum*, 14, 20n57, 65–66, 91n58, 133n7, 199n83, 220n145, 261, 264n8, 271–72, 281–86, 293, 296–97, 306n7; *Contra Iulianum opus imperfectum*, 20n57, 25–26, 133n7, 196n72, 240n226, 242n240, 261, 263n6, 265–66, 272n52, 281n84, 288–90, 292–94, 296; *Contra litteras Petiliani*, 290; *Contra Priscillianistas*, 158n90; *De anima et eius origine*, 20–21, 123n154; *De baptismo*, 12–13, 16–17, 126n164; *De bono coniugali*, 307, 322; *De bono uiduitatis*, 20n58, 32n12, 51, 138–42, 186n35, 233n199; *De ciuitate Dei*, 1–2, 14n44; *De correptione et gratia*, 295; *De doctrina Christiana*, 2; *De dono perseuerantiae*, 32n12, 134n11, 139n28, 186n35, 295n146; *De Genesi ad litteram*, 2, 91n58; *De gestis Pelagii*, 6n20, 13, 20n57, 31–32, 41n48, 49n84, 73n179, 74n183, 76–77, 79–80, 87, 115n125, 128–29, 133n7, 144–46, 148n53, 159n97, 168n121, 171, 173–74, 177, 180, 188, 195–216, 233n201, 235–36, 242n236, 249, 286–87, 303–6, 308–9, 311–15, 318–19; *De gratia Christi*, 20n57, 31–33, 35n22, 37n33, 45n63, 48n79, 50n88, 57, 62n130, 78–80, 82n26, 91n57, 115n125, 123n150, 133n7, 138n21, 177, 204n98, 219–21, 223–26, 229n185, 231–32, 239–47, 249–57, 266, 268n35, 270–71, 275n61, 303, 306; *De gratia et libero arbitrio*, 295; *De haeresibus*, 2, 83n29; *De libero arbitrio*, 47, 156n86; *De musica*, 265; *De natura et gratia*, 6n16, 13n40, 20n57, 33n14, 35–37, 49, 55, 62n129, 82n26, 133n7, 145–57, 165n113, 167, 172n136, 175, 186, 190–92, 195, 243n241, 245n249, 247n255, 256, 293; *De nuptiis et concupiscentia*, 20n57, 65, 91n58,

121n144, 133n7, 261, 266n24, 269–71, 274–77, 281, 284, 288, 290, 293; *De peccatorum meritis*, 2n3, 13n40, 15n46, 20n57, 32n12, 41n48, 61n128, 79–81, 83–112, 116–29, 131–34, 139–40, 143–44, 146n47, 148, 153–54, 157, 159, 172, 186n35, 205–6, 217n132, 231, 233n199, 249, 256, 268–69, 274–76, 303–10, 313–16, 318–21, 323; *De perfectione iustitiae hominis*, 20n57, 133n7, 144n39, 148n52, 160–67, 192; *De praedestinatione sanctorum*, 295–96; *De sancta uirginitate*, 140n31, 307, 322; *De spiritu et littera*, 20n57, 85, 131–37, 139–41, 186n35; *De Trinitate*, 2; *Enchiridion*, 2; *Enarratio in Ps.* 50, 91n58, 109n106, 318n61; *Epistula* 75, 126n164; *Epistula* 82, 12–13; *Epistula* 98, 12n37; *Epistula* 101, 265n14; *Epistula* 118, 311n29; *Epistula* 122, 311n29; *Epistula* 124, 311n29; *Epistula* 126, 49n82, 148n54; *Epistula* 133, 310; *Epistula* 134, 310; *Epistula* 137, 310n26; *Epistula* 138, 310n26, 321n72; *Epistula* 139, 120, 132–33, 303, 305n4, 308–10, 320–21; *Epistula* 140, 129n171, 132, 310n26, 316n50; *Epistula* 146, 76n5, 211–12, 311n31; *Epistula* 147, 13n41; *Epistula* 148, 13n41; *Epistula* 157, 20n58, 142–45, 159, 165n114, 169, 173, 303–4, 306, 309n18; *Epistula* 166, 91n58, 123, 158–59; *Epistula* 167, 158; *Epistula* 169, 157–58, 181n20; *Epistula* 175, 20n58, 80n19, 179, 188–91, 193n62, 195, 214n122, 216n130, 220n148, 303, 306n8; *Epistula* 176, 20n58, 64n141, 188–91, 195, 216n130; *Epistula* 177, 20n58, 35n26, 49n85, 145n42, 188–93, 195, 214n122, 216n130; *Epistula* 178, 188n46, 193–94; *Epistula* 179, 20n58, 32n12, 35n26, 36n29, 49n83, 139n29, 145n42, 179–80, 186–87, 189, 191n57, 195, 214n122; *Epistula* 186, 20n58, 31n2, 46, 147n48, 195n68, 232–36, 309n18; *Epistula* 187, 233n199; *Epistula* 188, 51, 138, 232–33, 267n27; *Epistula* 190, 240n230, 267; *Epistula* 191, 233n199, 267–68; *Epistula* 192, 233n199, 268; *Epistula* 193, 82n28, 266n26, 268–69;

INDEX

Epistula 194, 193n63, 267–68, 271n46, 295; *Epistula* 200, 266–67, 269; *Epistula* 207, 281n85, 286n100; *Epistula* 214, 295; *Epistula* 215, 17n52, 295; *Epistula* 217, 295n140; *Epistula* 224, 288n111, 320n70; *Epistula* 4*, 196n72, 257, 286; *Epistula* 6*, 219n140, 287, 289; *Epistula* 10*, 288–89; *Epistula* 16*, 271n49; *Epistula* 19*, 145n42, 167n118, 178–80, 185–87, 189n48, 195n66, 309n18; *In epistulam Iohannis ad Parthos tractatus* 4, 91n58; *In Iohannis euangelium tractatus* 38, 91n58; *Retractationes*, 2, 12n36, 132–33, 233n199, 269n40, 282n86, 304–7, 309n18, 314, 320, 321n73; *Sermo* 26, 228n182; *Sermo* 30, 228n182; *Sermo* 131, 227, 236; *Sermo* 150, 228n182; *Sermo* 151, 228n182; *Sermo* 152, 228n182; *Sermo* 153, 228n182; *Sermo* 154, 228n182; *Sermo* 155, 228n182; *Sermo* 156, 228n182; *Sermo* 157, 228n182; *Sermo* 158, 228n182; *Sermo* 159, 228n182; *Sermo* 163, 228n182; *Sermo* 165, 228n182; *Sermo* 174, 91n58, 109n106, 111n111, 318n61; *Sermo* 176, 91n58, 109n106; *Sermo* 183, 91n58, 109n106; *Sermo* 227, 135n12, 140n32; *Sermo* 293, 20n58, 81, 86–87, 91n58, 106–11, 116–17, 129, 134n9, 274n59, 313n39, 317–18, 323; *Sermo* 294, 6n20, 20n58, 81, 86–87, 89n53, 91n58, 96, 106, 109–13, 115–17, 119–21, 126, 128–29, 134n9, 148, 205–6, 231, 256, 269n36, 274n59, 276n67, 313, 317–18, 320–21, 323; *Sermo* 299, 86n42, 88n50, 106–7, 129n171, 313n39, 317–18, 323; *Sermo* 348A, 20n58, 32n12, 85n39, 101n83, 104n90, 158n92, 160n98, 167n117, 178–87, 189, 214n122, 216n130, 309n18; *Sermo* 357, 312
Aurelius of Carthage, 67, 69, 78–79, 85–87, 138n19, 144n38, 171, 189–90, 197–98, 205, 211n114, 213, 216n130, 219n140, 230n188, 267, 287, 305, 308–9, 313–15, 317–18, 320, 323
Avita, 55

B

baptism, 7, 12n36, 14n43, 15, 20, 38, 56, 72, 80–81, 83–84, 86, 88–100, 102, 104–14, 116, 118–22, 125n161, 127–29, 143–44, 149, 158–59, 174, 187n36, 189, 193–95, 201, 206, 217, 222–24, 230–31, 234n207, 248–49, 268–69, 271n45, 274–76, 278, 281n83, 282, 284, 292, 300, 306n7, 319, 321n73
Basil of Caesarea, 6n17, 54, 65–66, 272, 283, 293
Basiliscus, 226–29
believers, infants as, 92–96, 111–12, 116, 119, 269n36
Boniface, 271, 274, 277, 281
Britain, 30
Brown, Peter, 2, 40–41, 47, 52–54, 189, 261–62, 288
Budapest Anonymous, 37, 64, 84n33
Burnaby, John, 302

C

Caecilian, 68
Caelestius, writings of: *Definitiones*, 133n7, 161; *libellus* (411), 80, 83, 85–86, 98, 107n100, 223–24, 226, 306–7, 315, 322; *libellus* (417), 219–21, 223–24, 226, 230, 247, 250
Caesarean Mauretania, 240n230, 267–68
Carthage (411), *iudicium*/trial of, 39, 49–50, 57, 60, 78–80, 85–86, 98n75, 107n100, 109n106, 114, 123, 133n7, 144, 159n97, 173, 188n46, 204, 220, 225n176, 252, 304–9, 312n33, 314–23
Carthage (416), Council of, 18, 178–79, 188–90, 227–28, 234, 306n8
Carthage (418), Council of, 17–18, 177, 237n219, 239–40
Celestine, 233n199, 240n230, 258, 268, 296n150
Charus, 180
Chromatius of Aquileia, 56n112, 174n146, 199n83

Cicero, 265, 283

Cilicia, 58, 288

Claudius, 281, 286

Clement of Rome, 53–54, 66, 219

communion, infant, 93, 217n132, 235n209

concupiscence, 90, 96, 102, 164, 166, 249, 270, 287

Conference (with the Donatists), 67–68, 71, 77n6, 80, 85, 132, 291, 305n4, 310n26, 312, 314–16, 318, 320, 323

Constantine, 39–40, 53n101, 68

Constantinople, 43, 64–65, 187, 218–19, 241n231, 258, 272, 277n72, 287–89, 296–97

Constantius (bishop), 33n13, 221n154

Constantius (general), 265n21

Cornelius (pope), 114

creationism, 105, 123, 158

Crispinus, 69–71

Cyprian, 12–14, 63, 87, 109n105, 112–17, 120–22, 124, 126, 129, 148, 153, 158–59, 171–72, 205–6, 231, 256, 275–76, 278–83, 293–94, 300

Cyril of Alexandria, 187, 196–97, 257, 286–87

D

Dalmon, Laurence, 215, 222, 224

Daniel, 103–4

De diuitiis, 142n34

Delaroche, Bruno, 314–16, 319

Demetrias, 43, 50–51, 137–38

Diocletian, persecution of, 68

Diospolis, Synod of, 5n14, 8–9, 18, 46, 56n112, 65, 79n18, 129, 131, 133n7, 159n97, 167n118, 168n121, 170–75, 177–82, 186–88, 190, 194–99, 203, 206, 208–15, 217, 220, 229n185, 231, 233–36, 242, 247–49, 252–54, 259, 282, 286–87, 300–301

disunity. *See* schism

Donatists/Donatism, 2–4, 7–8, 12–14, 16–18, 30, 67–74, 77n6, 80, 85, 87, 97, 114–15, 126, 128, 132, 175n147, 189, 245, 263n6, 285n97, 290–91, 301, 305n4, 310, 312, 314–16, 318, 320, 323

Donatus, 68, 263

Dulcitius, 291

Dunn, Geoffrey, 225

Dunphy, Walter, 7–8, 54, 57, 59–61, 72–73, 87, 106, 123, 315–16, 318–21

Duval, Yves-Marie, 5

E

eastern churches, 6, 30, 52, 66, 73, 87, 96n69, 109, 115–16, 128, 129n172, 148, 175, 178, 194, 199n83, 205–6, 213, 215, 217n131, 259, 279, 299–300

Egypt, 40, 43–44, 241n231, 257

Elizabeth, 87n45, 104, 154, 191, 243, 246

Eno, Robert, 16–18

Ephesus, 64, 218, 306n8

Ephesus, Council of, 58, 258, 297n151

Epiphanius of Salamis, 43

eternal life, 82–83, 91–96, 99, 109–12, 189, 204, 217, 230, 234–35, 281n83

Eulalius, 271

Eulogius of Caesarea, 172, 186, 189n48, 195–96

Eusebius of Caesarea, 11

Eustochium, 261n130

Evans, Robert, 55, 147

Evodius, 32n12, 157n87, 181n20, 190

excommunication, 19n55, 47, 216–17, 221, 226n177, 240, 251, 306n8

exorcism, 15, 97–98, 249, 268n35, 271n45, 274–76, 278n76

exsufflation, 15, 97, 249, 268n35, 274–76, 278n76

F

fasting, 165–67

Faustus, 290, 292

Firmus, 167n118, 268–69, 271n46

Flavius Marcellinus. *See* Marcellinus

INDEX 367

Florus, 288–89

Frede, H. J., 64

free will/choice, 3n6, 24, 27, 36, 55, 63n135, 101–2, 123, 134, 139, 141, 163, 183, 222, 234, 275, 282, 295–96, 299, 301

G

Galla Placidia, 265n21

Gaudentius (Donatist bishop), 290–92

Gennadius, 50

Gerontius, 47–48

godparent, 96, 98, 111, 116, 119, 269n36

grace, 3, 8, 15, 24, 27, 32–33, 36–37, 39, 45, 56, 63n135, 76, 84–85, 89–90, 99, 101n83, 111, 131–35, 138n21, 139, 141–42, 144, 146, 148–51, 153, 155–57, 161, 163–65, 168n121, 182–84, 187, 189–92, 201, 206–10, 213, 224, 227, 234, 242–48, 254, 267, 275, 277n71, 281–82, 295, 299, 301–2, 311, 321–22

Gratus, 68

Gregory of Elvira, 13n41

Gregory of Nazianzus, 13n41, 54, 66, 231, 282–83, 293

H

Hadrumetum, 295–96

Heraclian, 133n6, 137–38, 318n61

Heros of Arles, 172–73, 179, 186, 188n46, 201n86, 208–11, 214, 220–22, 224–25, 238n223, 250–52, 259

Hilary (associate of Prosper), 295

Hilary of Narbonne, 188n46, 194n65

Hilary of Poitiers, 5–6, 62, 147, 151, 153–54, 156, 171–72, 195, 256, 278, 282–83

Hilary of Syracuse, 25n70, 142, 161, 169, 173, 204

Hippo Diarrhytus, 311n29

Hippo Regius, 76, 80, 86, 120, 132, 142n35, 148n52, 157, 178–81, 211n114, 267, 269, 286, 288, 295, 308n15, 310–12, 314–18, 322–23

Honorius (emperor), 67, 70, 137n17, 177, 239–41, 263, 265–66, 271, 305n4

I

imitation (as mechanism for the transmission of sin), 88–90, 143

Innocent (pope), 18–19, 35n26, 45, 48, 138n21, 170n128, 172, 177, 179, 188–91, 193–95, 216–18, 220–21, 225, 227–36, 241n235, 243–44, 248–54, 259, 265, 267, 272, 278, 281n83, 294n138, 300, 306, 322

Innocent (priest), 179–80, 187n39

Irenaeus, 282–83

Italy, 7, 25, 43–45, 47, 70, 73, 78, 137n17, 232, 258, 263, 265–66, 271, 273–74, 281, 286, 288, 292, 294, 296–97, 309n20

J

James (friend of Timasius), 36n29, 49, 145–49

Jerome, 1, 6, 11–13, 34n17, 40–41, 43–44, 49–53, 57, 59, 61–62, 65, 81n24, 105–6, 116n126, 120, 122–26, 129, 138, 147–48, 151, 153, 156, 158–59, 167–68, 171–73, 178–81, 185–87, 195n66, 196–97, 199n83, 206, 214–16, 242, 256, 259, 269n38, 282

Jerusalem, 241n231, 246

Jerusalem (415), *conuentum* of, 159, 168, 170, 186n32, 207–208, 214

Job, 103–4, 153

John Cassian, 26n75

John Chrysostom, 5–7, 43–46, 50, 62–63, 65–66, 147, 151, 156, 172n136, 263, 271–72, 277n72, 282–83, 293

John of Jerusalem, 35n26, 43–44, 64, 139n29, 168–71, 186–87, 189n48, 191n57, 195–96, 207–10, 214, 216n130, 221, 259

Jovinian, 31n4, 34n17, 42n49, 124–26, 159, 222n156, 319n67

Jovinus of Ascalon, 56n112, 174n146, 199n83

Julian of Eclanum: *Ad Florum*, 25–26, 133n7, 265–66, 272n52, 288–90, 293–94, 296; *Ad Turbantium*, 65–66, 133n7, 272, 274, 281–82, 286, 288, 290

Juliana, 43, 50–51, 137–40, 232–33, 267n27

Julius (bishop), 194–96, 216n130

Justus, 286–87

K

kingdom of God/heaven, 79, 83–84, 91–96, 99, 109, 142–43, 204, 224, 230, 248, 275–76, 287

Koopmans, J. H., 316–17

L

Lactantius, 5–6, 62–63, 147, 151–52, 172n136

Lamberigts, Mathijs, 222

Lazarus of Aix, 172–73, 179–80, 186, 188n46, 201n86, 208–11, 214, 220–22, 224–25, 238n223, 250–52, 259

Liber de fide, 59–60, 64n138, 84n32, 105, 307n11

liturgy/liturgical praxis, 6n18, 10, 14–16, 96, 100–101, 103n87, 105n95, 110–11, 128, 135, 137, 140, 149, 163, 184–85, 268n35, 276, 278n75, 302

Löhr, Winrich, 41, 146

Lord's Prayer, 15, 32n12, 85, 101–6, 114n122, 125n161, 127–29, 136–37, 141–42, 149–51, 156, 162–64, 166–67, 174, 183–86, 190, 192–93, 206, 278, 282, 287, 292, 300

M

Majorinus, 68, 263

Mani, Manichaeism, 26, 47, 65–66, 70, 222n156, 262, 271–76, 280–82, 290, 292

Manichaeism. *See* Mani

Marcella, 40, 43

Marcellinus (imperial official), 2, 7, 67, 71–73, 80–81, 83, 85–88, 114, 117–18, 123, 128, 132–34, 159, 205, 304–5, 307–10, 312–13, 315–16, 318, 320–23

Marcellinus (Carthaginian subdeacon), 227, 229, 236, 238n222, 240n226

Marcellus of Ancyra, 11

mare clausum, 226n178, 232n196, 236, 305n4

Marius Mercator, 31, 35n25, 55n108, 57–65, 79n18, 107n101, 179n4, 187, 218–21, 229n185, 240–41, 257–58, 265–66, 268–69, 288, 304–6

Matteoli, Sara, 37

Maximian, 69

Mediterranean Sea, 2, 76, 194n65

Melania the Elder, 40, 44–45, 47, 49–50, 52–54, 60n123, 66

Melania the Younger, 43–45, 47–49, 241–43, 256, 309n18, 311n28

Memor(ius), 264

Milevis (416), Council of, 64n141, 179, 188–90, 194n65, 217, 227–28, 234

N

Nestorius, 63, 65, 258, 289n116, 296–97

Noah, 103–4

O

obtestatio, 229, 237–38

Olybrius, 138n22

Olympius, 283

Optatus (Spanish bishop), 267

Origen/Origenism, 36–37, 43–44, 48–49, 52, 54–56, 59, 61n126, 63–64, 66, 157–58, 168, 170, 172n136, 215, 287n104, 290n117

origin of the soul, 81–82, 105–6, 123, 158, 267, 278n76

original sin (Adam's sin/transmission of sin), 2–3, 15, 22, 27, 32, 34, 36–39, 50, 55, 57–61, 63, 66, 79–84, 88–91, 96–97, 99, 105–6, 109–13, 116–27, 133n7, 143, 156,

158, 174, 191, 204n98, 220, 223, 230–31, 234–35, 240n226, 242, 247–50, 254, 264, 267n29, 269–71, 273–76, 278, 282, 284, 287, 299, 321n73

Orosius, 31n2, 138n21, 142n35, 145n42, 157–61, 167–73, 175, 178–79, 181, 186n32, 187n38, 191n57, 199n83, 208–9, 214, 259, 304n3, 306n8

Ostia, 311n28

Our Father. *See* Lord's Prayer

P

Palatinus, 180–81, 185

Palestine, 23n63, 25, 40, 43–44, 48–49, 59, 64, 76, 138n21, 142n35, 145n42, 158–61, 167, 170–72, 180, 187, 199n83, 216n130, 218–19, 221, 241, 257, 300, 312, 323

Palladius, 44–45

Pammachius, 43, 49–50, 57

Parmenian, 68

Passerio, 186

Pater Noster. See Lord's Prayer

patristic argumentation, 11, 126, 129n172, 131, 281

Paula, 40, 216n130

Paulinus of Milan, 72, 77–81, 83–84, 88n49, 123, 159n97, 220, 223, 226, 229–31, 240n226, 248, 250–51, 256n276, 259, 294n137, 305, 308n17, 314–15, 322

Paulinus of Nola, 32–33, 37, 43, 45–47, 54, 221n154, 232–34, 236

Pelagius, writings of: *chartula*, 180, 186, 195–96, 204n98, 212; *De natura*, 5–6, 33, 35–37, 41n48, 47, 49, 55, 62, 87n45, 115n125, 123, 131, 133n7, 145–49, 151, 153n69, 157, 160–61, 169, 172n136, 174–75, 186, 190–91, 195, 218, 243, 256, 300; *Epistula ad amicum*, 196; *Epistula ad Demetriadem*, 35, 51, 138, 232n196, 244n243; *Epistula ad Innocentium*, 221n154, 232, 244, 248; *Expositiones*, 31n8, 33, 35, 37–39, 55, 62, 63–64, 79n16, 82–84, 86, 88n51, 105, 116–19, 127, 133n7, 146, 208, 248, 308n15, 309, 318;

323; *Libellus fidei*, 35, 219n141, 221–22, 225, 244, 248, 264; *Pro libero arbitrio*, 25n71, 35, 62n130, 138n21, 191n55, 204n98, 221n154, 236, 242–44, 248, 255–56

Petilian, 290, 292

Pinianus, 43–45, 47–49, 241–43, 256, 309n18, 311n28

popular belief/piety, 16, 19–20, 92, 109, 116, 254n271, 283–85, 292

Possidius, 69–71, 190, 267

prayer, 10, 15–16, 32n12, 85, 97, 101–3, 106, 117n130, 136–37, 139–40, 149–51, 155, 162–66, 174, 182–86, 189–90, 194, 217, 259

Praylus, 221, 257

Primian, 68–69

Priscillianism, 158

Proba, 50–51, 137

Prosper of Aquitaine, 16n47, 31n2, 239n225, 240n230, 258n283, 295–96

Publicola, 45

Punic, 94–95, 294

R

Ravenna, 70, 167n118, 239–40, 265, 267n27, 269, 271, 273–74, 281n84, 284, 289

rebaptism, 12–13, 17n49

Refoulé, F., 314

Reticius, 283

Rome: aristocrats from, 7, 29, 30–31, 40–44, 51–54, 62, 66, 72, 241; clergy of, 18, 193, 233n199, 239n225; refugees from, 2, 72–73, 76, 78, 114, 125, 128, 317; sack of, 1, 25, 41n46, 51, 76, 78, 128, 137, 311n28

Rufinus of Aquileia, 7, 40, 42–48, 50, 52–63, 66–67, 73–74, 80, 115n125, 123, 167–68, 170, 174n146, 199n83, 264

Rufinus the Syrian, 42, 57–62, 307n11

Rufus of Thessalonica, 65, 272–73, 278n74, 297

S

schism, 7–9, 12n36, 22, 27, 30, 67–68, 71–73, 78, 87, 115n123, 127, 129, 147, 262–63, 289, 291

Semipelagianism, 21, 296n148, 302

Serapion of Thmuis, 65n144, 272n52

Shaw, Brent, 70

Sicily, 25, 48, 49n81, 142, 144n39, 161, 169, 311n28

sinlessness, 2, 8, 15, 36–37, 39, 56, 81, 82, 85, 87n45, 88, 100–104, 106, 127, 133, 142, 144, 146, 149–51, 153–55, 159n96, 161, 164, 169–70, 191–92, 244–46, 282, 287, 321n73

Sixtus (author of the *Sentences*), 6, 45, 53–55, 62, 66, 147, 151, 156, 172n136

Sixtus (5th century pope), 233n199, 267–68, 271n46, 295

Smith, A. J., 62

Synod of the Oak, 44

T

Tall Brothers, 43

Tertullian, 63

Thagaste, 45, 48, 241, 311n28

Theodore of Mopsuestia, 58, 63, 65, 272n52, 288

Theodotus of Antioch, 257

Theophilus of Alexandria, 43

Timasius, 36n29, 43, 48–49, 145–49

Titia, 46

Tractoria, 232n195, 240–41, 248–49, 252, 254n270, 257, 263, 265–67, 294n138, 301

tradition, 5–6, 8–10, 17, 20–22, 24, 29–30, 42, 61–62, 66–67, 73–74, 76, 87, 90, 94–95, 102–3, 105–7, 109, 115, 128, 136, 149, 151, 153n69, 157, 163, 167, 174, 178, 181–82, 185, 193–95, 197, 215, 231n192, 241, 243, 255–57, 259, 264, 275–76, 281, 285, 297, 299–301

traducianism, 105–6

transmission of sin. *See* original sin

Turbantius, 264n8, 271, 289n115

U

uolumen, 229–31, 237–40

Uranius, 47n71

Urbanus of Sicca, 32n12, 104n90, 157n87, 183

unity (ecclesial), 5, 7–10, 18–22, 27, 29–30, 67–68, 73–75, 87, 115n123, 129n172, 131, 175, 178, 188, 215–16, 259–60, 262, 282, 296–97, 299–302

Utica, 311n29

V

Valentine (abbot), 295

Valerius (of Ravenna), 266–67, 269–71, 274, 276–77, 281

Vessey, Mark, 11

Vincent of Lerins, 282n91

Vindemialis, 269

Visigoths, 1, 76

Vitalis, 295n140

Volusianus (prefect of Rome), 265n21

W

Wermelinger, Otto, 264

Z

Zechariah, 87n45, 104, 154, 191, 243, 246

Zosimus (pope), 19, 53, 177, 218–34, 236–41, 247–54, 259–60, 263, 265–67, 271–72, 277, 281n83, 284, 294n138, 300–301

JOHN CHRYSOSTOM,
THEOLOGIAN OF THE EUCHARIST
by Kenneth J. Howell

THE POWER OF PATRISTIC PREACHING:
The Word in Our Flesh
by Andrew Hofer, OP. Foreword by Paul Blowers

BEDE THE THEOLOGIAN:
History, Rhetoric, and Spirituality
by John P. Bequette

CROSS AND CREATION:
A Theological Introduction to Origen of Alexandria
by Mark E. Therrien